ULMS 151 Organisations and Management

Custom Publication

University of Liverpool

ULMS 151 Organisations and Management

Custom Publication

Compiled For

Gary Brown and Claire Hookham Williams

University of Liverpool

palgrave
macmillan

First published 2013 by
PALGRAVE MACMILLAN

Palgrave Macmillan in the UK is an imprint of Macmillan Publishers Limited,
registered in England, company number 785998, of Houndmills, Basingstoke,
Hampshire RG21 6XS.

Palgrave Macmillan in the US is a division of St Martin's Press LLC,
175 Fifth Avenue, New York, NY 10010.

Palgrave Macmillan is the global academic imprint of the above companies
and has companies and representatives throughout the world.

Palgrave® and Macmillan® are registered trademarks in the United States,
the United Kingdom, Europe and other countries.

ISBN 978–1–137–30044–7

This book is printed on paper suitable for recycling and made from fully
managed and sustained forest sources. Logging, pulping and manufacturing
processes are expected to conform to the environmental regulations of the
country of origin.

A catalogue record for this book is available from the British Library.

A catalog record for this book is available from the Library of Congress.

Printed and bound in Great Britain by
CPI Antony Rowe, Chippenham and Eastbourne

Contents

List of Figures   vii
List of Tables   ix
Acknowledgements   xi
Introduction   xiii

1   Using your reading in your essays   1
    Godfrey – How to use your reading in your essays

    Evolution of Management 1 – Scientific Management
2   Work routines   51
    Mike Noon and Paul Blyton – The Realities of Work

    Evolution of Management 2 – Bureaucracy
3   Studying work and organizations   87
    John Bratton, Peter Sawchuk, Carolyn Forshaw, Militza Callinan,
    Martin Corbett – Work and Organizational Behaviour

4   Organizational design   129
    John Bratton, Peter Sawchuk, Carolyn Forshaw, Militza Callinan,
    Martin Corbett – Work and Organizational Behaviour

    Evolution of Management 3 – Human Relations
5   Managing the human factor   171
    Paul Thompson and David McHugh – Work Organisations

    Individuals, Groups and Teams
6   Personality and identity   189
    John Bratton, Peter Sawchuk, Carolyn Forshaw, Militza Callinan,
    Martin Corbett – Work and Organizational Behaviour

7   Work groups and teams   227
    John Bratton, Peter Sawchuk, Carolyn Forshaw, Militza Callinan,
    Martin Corbett – Work and Organizational Behaviour

McDonaldisation

8   The social nature of work   271
    John Bratton, Peter Sawchuk, Carolyn Forshaw, Militza Callinan,
    Martin Corbett – Work and Organizational Behaviour

    Enterprise/Entrepreneurship 1 – Changing Nature of Work/Employment

9   The changing context of work   315
    Mike Noon and Paul Blyton – The Realities of Work

    Enterprise/Entrepreneurship 2 – Importance of Changing Nature of
    Organisations/Morgan's Metaphors

10 Managing the Entrepreneurial Organization   345
    Paul Burns – Corporate Entrepreneurship

    Management/Surveillance/Corporate Cultural Control – Call Centres

11 Control and resistance   371
    Paul Thompson and David McHugh – Work Organisations

Index   397

List of Figures

1.1	Time management for using your reading in your essay	43
2.1	Work categorisation framework and trends in skill change	79
2.2	Work categorisation framework and paradigms of work organisation	81
3.1	Contemporary theories of work organizations	106
3.2	An open system	110
4.1	An example of a simple organizational structure	134
4.2	A tall organization structure versus a flat (team-based) structure	136
4.3	The strategy-structure thesis	140
4.4	Determinants of organizational structure and end-results. DOL, division of labour: ROI, return on investment	146
4.5	Types of organizational restructuring	147
4.6	Five basic elements of an organizational structure	149
4.7	Engineering company with a functional design	151
4.8	An auto company with a product design	152
4.9	Divisional organizational structure based on strategic business units	153
4.10	An engineering company with a matrix design	154
6.1	Perceived characteristics of behaviours that are seen as reflecting an individual's personality	192
6.2	Two hypothetical personality profiles using Cattell's 16PF test	195
6.3	Eysensk's major personality dimensions	196
6.4	Freud's conception of the personality structure: 'the Freudian iceberg'	199
6.5	Bandura's model of reciprocal determinism	204
6.6	Holland's individual–occupation hexagonal model	213
6.7	A model of proactive personality and individual job performance	214
6.8	Measurement approaches used to assess personality	217
7.1	Classification of work teams	231
7.2	A model of group dynamics	233
7.3	The incremental effects of group size on relationships	235
7.4	Five phases of group development	237
7.5	A conceptual framework for examining intragroup conflict	243
7.6	Cohesiveness, norms and group performance	246

9.7	An example of the cards used in Asch's experiment in group conformity	247
7.8	Oldham and Hackman's job characteristics model	254
9.9	The three dimensions of group work: technical, governance and social	255
8.1	The panopticon building	284
8.2	A craft union response to Taylorism	288
8.3	Development of work organization and employment relationships	296
8.4	The notion of the work–life balance	301
10.1	Work effectiveness through change	349
10.2	The change cube	353
10.3	Freedom vs control	356
10.4	Organizational structure and management style	359
10.5	Organizational structure, management style and the concept of cycling	360
10.6	Risk classification	361
11.1	Mapping misbehaviour	390

List of Tables

1.1	Stages in using the Svensson and Wood article	41
1.2	Stages in using the Carr article	41
2.1	The key critics of Braverman's thesis	63
4.1	The re-engineered and virtual organization	155
6.1	The Big Five model of personality trait structure and the associated lower-order traits	197
6.2	Psychoanalytic defence mechanisms	201
6.3	Holland's typology of personality and congruent work environments, and occupations	213
7.1	Task-related and emotion-related behaviours in groups	242
7.2	Symptoms of groupthink	248
8.1	The nature of traditional work and knowledge work	293
9.1	Changes in employment in UK manufacturing and services, 1971–2005 (thousands)	329
9.2	Change in numbers of males and females in employment in Britain (thousands), 1959–2005	330
9.3	Incidence and composition of part-time employment in OECD countries,[a] 1990–2004	332
9.4	Unemployment rates in 25 industrial countries, selected years 1994–2005 (rate as proportion of civilian labour force)	335
9.5	Temporary employment in the UK, 1992–2004	338

Sources

This custom publication has been compiled for use in the University of Liverpool. The chapters included are reproduced from the following works:

Chapter 1 from Godfrey: How to use Your Reading in Your Essays © Jeanne Godfrey 2009

Chapter 2 from Noon and Blyton: The Realities of Work © Mike Noon and Paul Blyton 1997, 2002, 2006

Chapter 3 from Bratton, Sawchuk, Forshaw, Callinan and Corbett: Work and Organizational Behaviour 2nd Edition © John Bratton 2010

Chapter 4 from Bratton, Sawchuk, Forshaw, Callinan and Corbett: Work and Organizational Behaviour 2nd Edition © John Bratton 2010

Chapter 5 from Thompson and McHugh: Work Organizations 4th Edition © Paul Thompson and David McHugh 1990, 2002, 2005, 2009

Chapter 6 from Bratton, Sawchuk, Forshaw, Callinan and Corbett: Work and Organizational Behaviour 2nd Edition © John Bratton 2010

Chapter 7 from Bratton, Sawchuk, Forshaw, Callinan and Corbett: Work and Organizational Behaviour 2nd Edition © John Bratton 2010

Chapter 8 from Bratton, Sawchuk, Forshaw, Callinan and Corbett: Work and Organizational Behaviour 2nd Edition © John Bratton 2010

Chapter 9 from Noon and Blyton: The Realities of Work © Mike Noon and Paul Blyton 1997, 2002, 2006

Chapter 10 from Burns: Corporate Entrepreneurship 2nd Edition © Paul Burns 2005, 2008

Chapter 11 from Thompson and McHugh: Work Organizations 4th Edition © Paul Thompson and David McHugh 1990, 2002, 2005, 2009

Every effort has been made to trace all copyright holders, but if any have been inadvertently overlooked the publishers will be pleased to make the necessary arrangements at the first opportunity.

Introduction

As Module Leaders, it is often difficult to find a 'one text fits all' textbook, as we aim to include lots of different examples and personal research into the module content. Usually one textbook includes some of the learning we want to impart, however there are always noticeable gaps! In order to counteract this, we decided to amalgamate a series of textbooks for you, so we could select relevant chapters and capture them in one concise textbook.

This Custom Text was written with you, the ULMS 151 student, in mind and we aim to capture the central aims of the module:

- To provide a comprehensive foundation to the study of management theory and its application in practice.
- To consider the conceptual frameworks relevant to the behaviour of individuals and groups in organisations, and the issues which are raised in their management.
- To provide a critical understanding of the nature of organisations and management in different historical, social, economic and cultural contexts.
- To provide an understanding of the changing nature of organisations, in theory and practice, in traditional organisational settings and within new organisational forms.

We hope that upon using the content of this book, the lectures, tutorials and completion of this module you will have had the opportunity to acquire the following key skills:

- To identify relevant characteristics of organisations in terms of structure, functions, technology and work patterns.
- Consider the nature of differences between individuals and the implications this has in organisations.
- To outline and evaluate theoretical approaches to motivation, job satisfaction and work design.
- To distinguish between management and leadership functions in organisations.
- To examine the role and functions of groups and teams in organisations.

- To organise and conduct research into organisations and management for written assignments, projects, dissertations and seminar presentations.

We hope you will find this Custom Text useful, engaging, informative and supportive of your studies throughout this module.

We look forward to teaching you!

Dr Gary Brown
Dr Claire Hookham Williams
May, 2012

CHAPTER 1
Using your reading in your essays

1.1   How do you decide what to read?

It seems obvious that for a good essay you need good sources but what exactly *is* a 'good' source? When looking for sources, don't be tempted to just type your essay title straight into a general search engine in the hope that something useful will come up. Knowing what types of sources are suitable for university work and spending some time thinking about what information you need, will save you a great deal of time and will result in a much better piece of work. This section gives you the key steps and information you need for finding the best sources for your essay.

Five key steps for deciding what to read

Step 1   Think: what question do you want to answer?
Do some thinking before you start searching for sources. Check that you really understand the title of your essay. For example, does the title ask you to develop an argument, give your opinion, give examples, or some of these things together? Does it ask for definitions, information on a process, advantages and disadvantages, or for different views on an issue? Rewrite the title in your own words as this will really help you to understand it.

Step 2   Think: what ideas of your own do you already have?
You will probably already have done some reading and discussion on the essay topic during your course, so think about what you have read that is relevant to the essay title and what your own thoughts are on the essay question.

Step 3   Think: what *types* of source will you need?
Make notes on any suggested reading and other instructions about sources your tutor has given you and think about what types of sources you will need, to answer your essay title.

For example, which of the following will you need?

- An introductory textbook to give you some initial ideas;
- chapters in more advanced textbooks;
- important major works on the topic;
- original data from experiments or other research;
- recent academic journal articles on new developments or ideas on the topic;
- non-expert or public opinion on an issue.

Step 4   Do a first search

First, you need to decide how good you want your essay to be and how much time and effort you are willing to give to finding the right sources for it. Then use the notes you have made on the types of sources you need, and start searching. Searching for sources is called a 'literature search' and it is the start of your own academic research. As you search, keep checking that your sources are relevant, specific and reliable.

Content and chapter headings of books, and journal article abstracts, can help you to decide whether a source is relevant. Reading the introduction and conclusion of a book chapter or journal article is also a quick way of finding out whether a source will be useful. The reference list at the end of one book or article may provide you with details of further useful sources.

Remember however, that abstracts, summaries and reviews are useful for a first search but are not acceptable as sources for your essay; you will need to read the full article or book section. Similarly, basic introductory and/or college-level books or encyclopaedias may be useful to get some initial ideas but are not good enough as a source for a university-level essay.

It is important at this stage to write down the precise details of each source (name, date, title, publisher etc.) and also where and how you found it, in case you need to find it again at a later stage in your research. You may not think that it is important to do this but you will be surprised how useful this information is – and remember that for academic work, *who* wrote something is as important as what they wrote about.

Step 5   Think, sort and select your sources for detailed reading

When you have done your first search for sources, think again about what you will want to say in your essay and what you think your conclusion will be. This may change as you read more, but by now you should have some idea of how you want to answer the essay title.

You might need to do some general background reading on a topic but most essay titles will ask for something specific. Try not to waste time reading sources which may be on the correct general topic but which are not specific enough.

Select your sources for more detailed reading and ask yourself the following questions about each source.

- What type of source is it and who wrote it?
- Is it relevant and specific to my essay?
- Is it a reliable and academic source?
- Why am I going to read it?

- Will it probably support my conclusion or give an opposing viewpoint?
- Will I probably use it as an important piece of information or only as a minor source?

What is a reliable source?

At university you are expected to make sure that your sources are reliable – that you can trust what they say. This usually means knowing who wrote something and that they are an authority on their topic. Reliable sources are generally those that have a named author as this ensures that readers know who is responsible and accountable for the information given. Anonymous sources are much more likely to be of poor quality and/or contain incorrect information.

Up-to-date information will probably be more reliable than older information, so check when your source was written. You may want to read older sources because they are important texts and to build up your knowledge, but for most topics you will also need current sources. Always check online sources to see when they were last updated and whether any links are active.

A reliable source is also one that gives information which is as accurate and complete as possible, rather than giving only the information which suits a particular purpose (called bias). Business and political organisations, for example, may present information in a biased way. However, bear in mind what 'reliable' means for the type of information you need. If your essay is about public opinion in the media, then newspapers and television programmes would be a reliable source for this particular type of information. Equally, if you are writing about the views of different political organisations, then the leaflets and websites of these organisations would provide reliable information on what these views are, even though such information may not be balanced or reliable in the general sense of the word.

Primary and secondary sources

You should try to find the original (primary) source of information where possible, as something that is reported second or third hand may not be accurate and will be less reliable. If you want data on the results of an experiment, try to read the original report rather than a later article that discusses the experiment and data (this is called a secondary source). Similarly, if you want to write about what an expert has said, read the actual book or article they have written, rather than an article by another author who discusses what the expert has said. In reality, it will not always be possible or necessary to use only primary sources, but be aware that you will usually be expected to read the key primary sources on a topic.

What is an academic source?

For most assignments at university, you will need to use information from sources which are not only reliable but are also regarded as academic. Academic sources are those written by experts (or authorities) on a topic and which have been peer-reviewed. The peer-review process is when the book or article is sent by the publisher to other experts for checking and discussion before being published. Peer-reviewed sources are reliable and are called 'academic' (or 'reputable' or 'authoritative') sources because they have been written by people who have attained a high standard of knowledge and research in their subject. Reliable and academic sources always have a named author or organisation. The academic community relies on knowing who wrote what, so that academics in a particular field of study can question, discuss and work with each other to build knowledge and develop ideas.

Non-academic sources

Below is a list of source types which are not academic and should not normally be used as sources for essays:

- newspapers (including long articles in quality papers such as *The Times* or the *Guardian*);
- magazines (including quality magazines such as *The Economist*, *Newsweek* and *New Scientist*);
- news or TV channel websites (e.g. the *BBC News*);
- trade publications and company websites;
- publications and websites of charities, campaign or pressure groups;
- student theses or essays;
- Wikipedia;
- pamphlets and brochures;
- blogs and wikis.

Checking that your sources are academic

Books and journals on the library shelves and on your reading lists will usually be reliable and academic. However, you may want to find other sources and you will need to make the effort to check that these are also reliable and academic. Books have normally gone through a peer-review process and so are usually reliable. Journals described as an academic journal, a peer-reviewed journal or a scholarly journal will be reliable and academic.

Check your online sources

Take particular care when you are using online sources. Your tutor will suggest suitable places to search online but it is your responsibility to check that your sources are reliable and academic. Wikipedia may be useful for some initial definitions and to give you links to other sources but you should not use it as an actual source in your essay. This is because Wikipedia is a type of encyclopaedia and is therefore only a basic summary and a secondary source. It is also anonymous and is not peer-reviewed and is therefore not reliable and not academic.

Words that should warn you that an online article is probably not academic are: *magazine, digest, news, press release, correspondent, journalist, special report company, classified, personals* and *advertisement.* Don't be fooled into thinking that an online article is reliable and academic just because it is well written and has an author's name, statistics and in-text references. Even words such as *journal, research, volume/ issue number, Society* or *Research Centre* are being increasingly used by unreliable and non-academic sources and websites. You need to check that the article is in fact from a peer-reviewed journal.

Check your online databases

Some online databases contain only peer-reviewed academic journals but some of them (even some which describe themselves as a 'research database') also contain newspapers, magazines and trade publications. Read the description of the database before you go into it; what does it say it contains? You may be able to google a database and get a description of its publications from the 'home' or 'about us' page. Remember – always check whether an article is academically reliable even if you have found it through a database.

Check your web search engines

Search engines such as Google, Wanadoo and Yahoo are not good places to look for academic sources. Google Scholar is useful as it finds only scholarly literature but you still need to be careful, as not all of this literature is peer-reviewed material – it also includes some magazines and student theses.

Where to check a website

If you are not sure about the reliability of an online website, article, database or search engine, try to find its homepage and look under sections such as 'about us', 'contact us', 'editorial board', 'board of directors', 'information for authors', 'submission process', 'sponsors', 'funders' and 'partners'.

These sections will give you information about who runs and supports the site and whether its articles are peer-reviewed.

Practice 1: Would you use these sources?

Read the descriptions below of ten potential sources for five different essay titles. Do you think these sources are 'not reliable', 'reliable but not academic' or 'reliable *and* academic'?

Sources for an essay on government support for people with disabilities
1. An article written in July 2006 in an online magazine called 'Mobility Now'. It has news, information and stories and is a magazine for people with

disabilities. It is published by a leading charity organisation for people with disabilities.

Sources for an essay on youth crime

2. A recent online article on ASBOs written by Jane Smith, Home Correspondent. The URL is the online business section of a national quality newspaper.

Sources for an essay on recent developments in stem cell research

3. An online article on stem cells, published jointly by three authors in 2002. The article has a date, volume and issue number. The article appears on a website called 'Stem Cells'. This seems to be the title of the journal and at the bottom of the page there is a publisher: Beta Res Press. In the 'information for authors' section, the website tells authors how to track the progress of their article as it goes through the peer-review process.

4. Three different online science publications with similar titles, which all look like magazines. They all have news sections, advertisements and jobs sections. They all have issue numbers and two of them also have volume numbers.

    4a. The first one has an 'about us' page which describes how its correspondents get their information by contacting leading scientists, reading scientific journals and websites, and attending conferences.

    4b. The second magazine has the name of an organisation at the top of its website. On its 'about' page it describes the magazine as its journal and states that it is a peer-reviewed general science journal. When you read another page you find that the members of its board of directors are all university academics.

    4c. The third publication has no 'about us' information, so you enter the magazine title on Wikipedia. Wikipedia describes the magazine as 'a well-respected publication despite not being peer-reviewed'.

Sources for an essay on recent developments in animal cloning

5. An article from a printed booklet titled 'Animal Cloning' published in 1999. There is a series of booklets, each with a volume and issue number. Each booklet contains a collection of short articles and newspaper and magazine clippings which give a simple introduction to issues and public debate on a scientific topic.

Sources for an essay on business ethics

6. A well-written report (which starts with an executive summary) on business ethics in companies. The website is run by an organisation called SEB – Social Ethics in Business. On the 'about us' page, the organisation describes itself as part of a network of business organisations that focus on corporate responsibility. Its funders and partners are large national and international business foundations and development agencies.

7. An online article titled 'Business Ethics Guidelines'. The website address is 'Harold Jones International Company'.

8. An online article about McDonald's on a website called 'Centre for Management Research'. There is no 'about us' page but there is a homepage which states that the centre is involved in business research, management consulting and the development of case studies and training materials.

9. An online article on business ethics found on the website of the 'Centre for Business Ethics' of a university. On the centre's homepage it states that the centre helps businesses and the community and offers workshops, conferences and lectures. It also states that the centre publishes its own 'Journal of Ethics'.

10. An online article about a drinks company's activities in India. The article has no author but is well written and says 'for immediate release' at the top of the page. The website is titled as a 'Resource Centre'. The 'home/about' page states that the centre has grown out of networks and discussions by activists, and describes itself as a platform for movements to publicise demands and to put pressure on governments.

(The articles and websites are fictitious but are closely based on real examples.)

1.2 How do you understand and question what you read?

When you sit down to read a book, chapter or article (we can call all of these 'texts') you should usually already know what type of text it is, who wrote it, that it is reliable and academic and that it is relevant and specific to your essay question. You will probably also have some idea of what it is about and why you are going to read it. You may think then that actually reading the text would be quite straightforward. However, one of the most common reasons why students get low marks for their essays is that they have not read carefully enough or not properly understood the main points of the text. To use your sources effectively you need to really understand each text and to read it with some questions in mind. This section gives you steps, examples and practice for doing this.

Three key steps to understanding and questioning what you read

Step 1 Think: what questions will you have in mind as you read?
Before you start reading a text, decide what type of information you are looking for. For example:

- Are you looking for the answers to specific questions (for example, what business ethics is or whether it is important)?
- Are you looking for general information on a point that you don't know much about and that will help you develop your own ideas and argument?
- Are you just looking for a few basic facts or do you need to read in detail so that you can follow the author's argument?
- Are you looking for evidence and examples as support for what you want to argue in your essay?
- Are you looking for points that you will then argue against?

Step 2 Read and think
Read with your questions in mind. If you are only looking for one or two facts, you can just quickly scan the text for this information. Usually however, you will want to read in more detail.

It may be better *not* to write anything down at this stage. Read the first section of the text (or all of a short text) and just try to understand:

- what the main point of the text is;
- which parts of the text are main points, which are more minor points and which parts of the text are examples of points made;
- which parts of the text are facts or description and which are the author's opinion.

Try to identify what the author is trying to do. For example, are they giving information, putting forward an idea or theory, arguing and trying to persuade you of something, or a combination of these things?

Then try to explain to yourself what the main point of the text is, in your own words.

Step 3   Read and ask questions

Read the text again and this time, question, evaluate and locate what the author says, using the prompts below (you can do this either in your head or on paper).

Questioning what the author says
- What assumptions does the author make?
- Do you think these assumptions are correct?
- Are the stages of the argument clear and logical?
- Does the conclusion follow from the evidence given?

Evaluating what the author says
- Are you persuaded by what the author says? Why/why not?
- If someone asked your opinion of the author's viewpoint, what would you say?
- How will you use what the author says in *your* argument?

Locating the author in the subject area
- What is the author's position on the issue?
- How does the author's argument and position fit in with what you already know?
- How is the author's argument different from or similar to those of other experts on this subject?
- Does the author's argument belong to a particular school of thought (e.g. behaviourism, Marxism, feminism)?

Opinion, critical analysis and argument

Students often think (or are told) that they should not give their opinions in an essay. It is true that you should not just give your personal opinion about something based only on your feelings. However, you *are* expected to give your opinion on an issue or essay question, provided that you have arrived at this opinion through clear reasoning. Your reasons should be supported by evidence and you should come to a conclusion which is persuasive because it follows logically from your reasoning and evidence. This sequence is called an argument. 'Arguing' in academic study does not mean that you have to argue *against* something; an argument in the academic sense means a logical, structured and evidenced response to an issue or question.

As part of your argument, you will need to state whether you agree or disagree with the sources you discuss and you won't be able to do this unless you have questioned, evaluated and located them, as shown above. This thought process is called *critical thinking* or *critical analysis*. As with the word *argument*, *critical thinking* in the academic sense does not mean that you can only say negative things about a text; indeed, you might want to be very positive about something you read. Critically analysing a text just means that you have asked yourself questions about what it says and formed your own views on it, based on clear reasoning rather than just your personal experience or opinion.

Looking at an example of questioning, evaluating and locating a text

Below are three short sections from a long article which a student read for his business ethics essay. Read the extracts to give you some idea of the authors' arguments and then look at the informal notes, which show the student's thoughts when he questioned, evaluated and located the whole article.

A Model of Business Ethics

If one searches the literature, it appears that in the thirty years that business ethics has been a discipline in its own right a model of business ethics has not been proffered. This paper attempts to address this gap in the literature by proposing a model of business ethics that the authors hope will stimulate debate. . . . This model is one that is predicated on the tenets of developed countries operating within a capitalist paradigm.

. . .

Socially responsible managers do the right thing because it is the right thing to do. It is the correct action to take and an action that society expects. Executives should 'act ethically not out of fear of being caught when doing wrong. Rather, they should embrace ethical behaviour in business because of the freedom, self-confirmation, and success that it brings' (Thomas et al., 2004, p. 64).

. . . it is important to see business ethics as a highly dynamic and continuous process without an end. A process, however, that is predicated on the interrelationship between business and society where each one is interdependent and responsible together for the outcomes. Hoffman and Moore (1982) suggest that the pre-eminence of business ethics is because of a perceived failing, by the general community, of business to act for the general good of the society. They, therefore, suggest that the mutual obligations of business to the community and the community to business need to be restated.

(Extracts from: Svensson, G. and Wood, G. (2008) 'A Model of Business Ethics'. *Journal of Business Ethics*, 77, pp. 303–22.)

The student's thoughts on the text

Questioning

The authors look at businesses operating in a developed world, capitalist context. Presumably there are lots of businesses outside this type of context – how do they behave? Svensson and Wood also seem to assume that individuals and society always expect businesses to behave well, and that people trust businesses – I don't think they do. They also assume that there are socially responsible managers who want to do what is right – this might not be a correct assumption and they don't give any examples as evidence of this.

Evaluating

It's a good persuasive argument – seems to be well researched and expert. The article is very clear and well-structured and has detailed points. Their conclusion is supported by evidence, although this is mainly by reference to other authors – I will need to read a couple of these primary sources for myself.

Svensson and Wood argue strongly and clearly that business and society influence each other and are dependent on each other and have a responsibility to each other to behave ethically. However, they seem to ignore the fact that not everyone thinks we should trust businesses or that organisations should be responsible to society and their argument seems to be based on some unproven assumptions. Also, Svensson and Wood leave out some other simple models of business ethics I've read about and they don't use real business examples for some of their points – they only make references to primary sources which have examples.

Still, I think that this article is solid enough to use as one of my main sources as evidence for what I think my conclusion will probably be, which is that business ethics is important both to businesses and to society.

Locating

The article puts forward a theoretical model which they say has not been done before and that it is therefore doing something new, filling a gap in theory. They probably expect other academics to argue or disagree with their model of business ethics.

Their argument fits in with what I think. Svensson and Wood agree with other articles I have read by Esty, Collins, Shaw and Barry and these are all on the opposite side to Freidman, Wolf and Carr. I think that this article is an important one on the issue because it is very recent and seems to bring together in a detailed and persuasive way what a lot of the other articles from the last 10 years have said.

Practice 2: How would you question, evaluate and locate this article?

Below are sections from another article (a 1968 article by Albert Carr) which the student used for his business ethics essay. Read the sections and then briefly question, evaluate and locate them. You should be able to do this without any specific business knowledge.

Is business bluffing ethical?
We can learn a good deal about the nature of business by comparing it with poker. Poker's own brand of ethics is different from the ethical ideals of civilized human relationships as the game calls for distrust of the other fellow. . . .

That most businessmen are not indifferent to ethics in their private lives, everyone will agree. My point is that in their office lives they cease to be private citizens; they become game players who must be guided by a somewhat different set of ethical standards. . . .

The illusion that business can afford to be guided by ethics as conceived in private life is often fostered by speeches and articles containing such phrases as, 'It pays to be ethical,' or, 'Sound ethics is good for business.'

Actually this is not an ethical position at all; it is a self-serving calculation in disguise. The speaker is really saying that in the long run a company can make more money if it does not antagonize competitors, suppliers, employees, and customers by squeezing them too hard. He is saying that oversharp policies reduce ultimate gains. This is true, but it has nothing to do with ethics.

To be a winner, a man must play to win. This does not mean that he must be ruthless, cruel, harsh, or treacherous. On the contrary, the better his reputation for integrity, honesty, and decency, the better his chances of victory will be in the long run. But from time to time every businessman, like every poker player, is offered a choice between certain loss or bluffing within the legal rules of the game. If he is not resigned to losing, if he wants to rise in his company and industry, then in such a crisis he will bluff – and bluff hard.

Whatever the form of the bluff, it is an integral part of the game, and the executive who does not master its techniques is not likely to accumulate much money or power.

(Adapted extracts from: Carr, A. Z. (1968) 'Is business bluffing ethical?' *Harvard Business Review*, 46 (1), pp. 143–53.)

1.3 What should you write down?

Why bother making notes?

Writing good essays involves a continuous process of thinking, reading and writing, and making notes is an important part in this cycle. The mental and physical process of making notes helps you to understand, think and reflect on what you have read. Making notes also helps you to formulate thoughts and ideas, to make connections in your mind with other pieces of knowledge, and to remember information.

Importantly, the writing process of making notes also helps you to start using your own words, which is essential for when you come to writing your essay. Making notes helps you to develop thinking that is less dependent on the text and helps you to control how you use your sources rather than letting your sources control your essay.

For all these reasons, students who make notes on their reading usually get better marks than those who go straight from reading a text to essay writing. However, for your notes to be really effective, they need to be clear, meaningful and of real use to you in the essay writing stage. This section gives you some steps, examples and practice to help you write effective notes.

Three key steps for making notes

Step 1   Write down the reference details

You should already have written down details such as the author, title and date of each source (called the reference or bibliographic details) when you found them. For books this should include the publishing company and where it was published. These days we are all used to getting bits of information from the media and websites without always knowing or needing to know where the information came from. However, for academic writing and work, knowing exactly who wrote something and where the text can be found is vital, as people actually own the knowledge or ideas they have written about.

Write down the bibliographic information accurately and be particularly careful not to change capital letters or punctuation in the titles of books or articles. At this stage you don't need to worry about the order of the information, just make sure you record it fully and accurately.

You should also write down where and how you found your sources. This will save you time if you need to go back to check a source and will help you find new sources in the future. You can simply write down these details in a notebook or save the information electronically.

Below is an example of the student's research record (also called a research log) for the article by Albert Carr. The student found the article by using an e-database on 20 November 2008.

Reference details:

Albert Z. Carr. 1968. 'Is business bluffing ethical?' Harvard Business Review. Vol. 46 Issue 1, pages 143–153.

Research details:

HBR is a peer-reviewed acad. journal. Got ref. from list at back of Crane and Matten 2007.

Found it on 20/11/08 in Infolinx → Business Source Complete → Business Resources → Titles → HBR.

Step 2   Make notes on your reading

People make notes in different ways and you may like to use diagrams, flow charts, bullet points or index cards. You may want to make notes on only parts of the text, on one particular aspect of the text or on the whole text, depending on why you are reading it.

Whatever method you use to take notes, you should always:

- Write down the reference details, page numbers (particularly for quotations) and the date on which you make your notes.
- Read carefully and make accurate notes – don't accidentally change the meaning of the text.
- Make clear in your notes which ideas are major points, which are only examples of these major points and which are more minor points of information.
- Make sure your notes are not too brief *or* too detailed.

    If your notes are too brief, the meaning will be unclear and you won't understand them in a month's or year's time. If your notes are too detailed then it probably means you are copying too much – note taking does not mean copying whole sections from the text.
- Try to use some of your own words and abbreviations.

    You may be worried about changing the meaning of the text accidentally, of 'moving away' from the text, or you may feel that you can't put things into your own words as well as the original. However, if you are reading thoughtfully and with understanding rather than just copying, you will naturally start using some of your own words. It is important that you start doing this, and your confidence will increase with practice.
- Have a system which allows you to clearly see in your notes where you have used:

    exact words from the text (quotations);

most of the same words from the text (close paraphrase);

your *own* words to describe ideas in the text (paraphrase);

your own ideas or comments.

You must record these differences carefully so that when you use your notes to write your essay, you do not accidentally claim words or ideas from your sources as your own. Clearly recording your *own* thoughts will also help you to make full use of them and so get credit for them in your work.

Step 3   Write a short reflection from your notes

When you have finished making your notes, use them (and your critical analysis) to write a short reflection. Your reflection can be informal and take any form that you find helpful. However, it is a good idea to write in your own words and in full sentences and to use quotation marks for exact phrases from the original text. Your reflection should include a short summary of what you have learnt. If the text has a diagram or table, try to summarise what it shows in one sentence. Your reflection should also include your thoughts from your questioning, evaluation and location of the text.

Writing a short reflection from your notes will consolidate your reading, thinking, questioning and note making and will maximise the effectiveness of the whole process. It will help you to restate information and ideas from your sources in your own words and will enable you to further develop your own ideas. It will help you to relate what you have read to what you already know and will put you in a position where you can see how and where you want to use your sources in your essay.

Looking at an example of some notes

Below are the student's notes from the sections of the Svensson and Wood article on page 10.

	Svensson, G. and Wood, G. (2008) 'A Model of Business Ethics'. *Journal of Business Ethics*, 77, pp. 303–322 Notes written on 1/3/2009
p. 310 true? no model?	In 30 yrs of BE as a subject, no model of BE – S + W want to fill this gap in BE theory, for debate.
p. 310 does it? – don't think so.	'Socially responsible managers do the right thing because it is the right thing to do'. Soc. expects the correct action. (CP)
p. 319 (conclusion)	Mangs. should want to be ethical because it brings success and freedom. (S + W citing Thomas et al. 2004)

| p. 319 main point | BE– '. . . dynamic and continuous process . . .' – 'interrelationship between businesses and society . . .' – each responsible for the other. |
| good point re. importance of BE | BE becoming impt. because people feel that buss. do <u>not</u> behave ethically ∴ the 'mutual obligations need to be restated' (from Hoffman and Moore 1982). |

Comments on the notes
- The student's notes are brief but contain enough detail to be meaningful. If the first line of the notes had been *In 30 yrs no model – S + W want to fill this gap,* this would have been too brief and when reading these notes at a later stage the student would have been asking himself: '30 years of what?' 'A model of what?' 'What type of gap do they want to fill?'
- Notice how the student has a clear system for recording which parts of his notes are quotation, close paraphrase or paraphrase and which are his own thoughts. First, he has used the margin for page numbers and for his own comments and ideas. Secondly, he has put phrases and key words taken from the text in quotation marks and has been careful to write down quotes accurately, using three dots to indicate when a quotation is not a whole sentence. He has also noted the details of when Svensson and Wood have quoted other authors (Thomas et al. and then Hoffman and Moore). Finally, he has used the letters CP (close paraphrase) to remind himself when he has used *mostly* the same words as the text. This is important, as he will need to put these ideas much more into his own words if he wants to use them in his essay.
- You can see that in making notes the student has naturally started the process of using his own words and phrases.

Looking at an example of a short reflection

Below is a short reflection on the Svensson and Wood article, which the student wrote after reading and critically analysing the text and then making and re-reading his notes. You will notice that by now he is using mostly his own words and style of expression.

The authors propose and describe their own model of business ethics which centres around a 'dynamic and continuous process' between business and society. They argue persuasively that business and society influence each other, are dependent on each other and have a responsibility to each other. Importantly, they stress that the ethical standards of society are also those of business and that therefore business ethics is important.

Their model assumes that individuals and society always expect businesses to behave well and that we should be able to trust businesses. Svensson and Wood also assume that good managers exist who are socially responsible. I think that these assumptions may be true some of the time but are ove-simplistic.

However, their model is well-researched and comprehensive and is supported by a great deal of other research in the field and their idea of an 'interrelationship between business and society' accords with Esty, Collins and Shaw and Barry. I agree with them that the way businesses behave does affect society and vice versa and I will use Svensson and Wood as a key source to support my argument that business ethics are important.

Practice 3: Make notes and write a reflection

Before you can come up with your own system for making clear and meaningful notes, you need to be aware of how you normally *do* take notes. To do this, read and make notes on the extracts from the article by Carr on page 12 (or use a short text of your own choice if you prefer). Read your notes a week later and compare them with the original text. Check for the following:

- Is the meaning clear in your notes?
- Can you distinguish between major and minor points?
- Have you copied down the exact words from the text; have you used a mixture of your own and the author's words; or have you used your own words? Is it clear which is which?
- If anything is unclear, how could you improve the way you take notes so that you really would be able to use them accurately and effectively in an essay?

After you have reviewed and improved your notes, use both your notes and critical reading of the text to write a short reflection. You can compare your notes with the student notes on page 48 although, as stated, there is no one correct way of taking notes.

1.4 Why and how should you quote?

Why use quotations?

Quotations are *exact* phrases or sentences taken from your reading. Below is a section from a student's business ethics essay which includes a quotation (given in blue with an in-essay reference in red).

> Many companies list only the quality, naturalness and sustainability of their products as their underlying ethical message. One example of a company statement which also includes the human dimension is the following: 'we will operate our business with a strong commitment to the well being of our fellow humans and the preservation of the planet' (Body Shop International, Policy on donations, May 2006, p. 1).

Most of the time you should use your reading in your essay by reinterpreting it in your own words. Only use exact words or phrases from a text for something which you think is particularly interesting or well expressed. Quotations can be a powerful tool in writing a good essay but only if you use them sparingly and for the right reasons.

Reasons to quote
Use quotations to:

- give a definition;
- state a fact or idea that the author has expressed in a unique and powerful way;
- establish or summarise an author's argument or position;
- provide an interesting and important start or end to your essay.

Reasons *not* to quote
Don't quote someone just because:

- you think that putting quotations in your essay will make it look academic and will impress your tutor;
- some of the articles you have read used lots of quotations so you think your essay should too;
- you have written half of your essay and haven't used any quotations yet so you think you should put some in;
- you haven't given enough time to reading critically and taking notes, so it seems much easier to cut and paste some quotations into your essay rather than putting things into your own words.

How many quotations should you use?
A mistake students often make is to use too many quotations. The important thing is to think about *why* you are quoting, not how much. An essay may not have *any*

quotations (or very few) but may still be a powerful and successful piece of work because the student has expressed her sources effectively using her own words. Indeed, using too many quotations (for more than a quarter of your essay, for example) is a type of plagiarism, even if you have put in all the correct in-essay references and quotation marks. This is because you can't really claim that your essay is your own work if it is made up mainly of quotations from other people. The number of quotations you decide to use will also depend on your subject area and your essay title; the business ethics essay, for example, has about 6 per cent of its word count as quotation.

Looking at examples of using quotations effectively

Below are three extracts from a student's business ethics essay which contain quotations (given in blue, with in-essay reference features in red). Read the extracts and think about why the student decided to quote from his reading.

1. Shaw and Barry (2007) define business ethics as 'the study of what constitutes right and wrong (or good and bad) human conduct in a business context' (p. 25). Another definition describes business ethics as the 'principles and standards that guide behaviour in the world of business' (Ferrell and Fraedrich et al., 2002, p. 6).
2. Others such as Wolf share this view, and Prindl and Prodham (1994) suggest that 'Finance as practised in the professions and in industry is seen as a value-neutral positive discipline promoting efficiency without regard to the social consequences which follow from its products' (p. 3).
3. Secondly, an even stronger argument for the view that good ethics in business do in fact exist, is that given by Collins (1994) and other prominent experts on the subject. This is that 'good ethics is synonymous with good management' (p. 2). (*et al.* = and the other authors.)

Comments on the quotations
The student decided to quote in extract 1 to give examples of different academic definitions of business ethics. In extract 2 he decided to quote to demonstrate his point that some academics and business people feel that business should not concern itself with ethics. The student also felt that this particular sentence from Prindl and Prodham was an important and well-expressed statement.

In extract 3 the student used the quotation to support the main point of his essay, that business ethics is central to business. He also felt that the statement was a very strong and clear summary by Collins of this idea.

Note that in all three extracts, the student has introduced the quotation clearly so that the reader understands why it has been used. In other parts of his essay, the student quoted two individual words, *bluffing* and *dysfunctional*, because he felt that these were key words used by the authors in a unique way.

Four key steps for using quotations properly

Step 1
Being able to use quotations effectively starts from when you select and read with questions in mind, critically evaluate, take meaningful notes and reflect on how you will use your reading in your essay. If you follow this process, you should be able to make good choices in what to quote.

Step 2
Before you put a quotation into your essay, ask yourself *why* you are putting it in. Is it special enough? Is it really relevant to your point? Would it not be better to put it into your own words?

Step 3
When you have written the first draft of your essay, separate out each quotation with its surrounding sentences. Read the quotation and its surrounding sentences slowly and carefully. Have you introduced the quotation clearly? Does it clearly support your point?

Step 4
Once you are sure that your quotation is worth putting in, check that you have quoted accurately, that you have used quotation marks *and* an in-essay reference and that you have used the correct grammar and punctuation before, during and after the quotation.

Four common mistakes students make with the content of quotations

The four most common and serious mistakes students make are:

- using a quotation that is not special enough and where they should therefore have used their own words. This includes common facts or knowledge, which don't usually need to be quoted;
- using a quotation that does not directly support the student's point;
- not introducing or showing clearly why a quotation has been used;
- using a reporting verb (e.g. *states, shows, suggests, points out, claims*) which is not correct for the context and function of the quotation.

Practice 4: Would you use these quotations?

Below are some quotations from student essays on bioscience topics. Read them and identify which of the above mistakes the students have made.

1. Kzanty (2004) states that 'Organs such as the heart, liver, small bowel, pancreas and lungs are used for transplants' (p. 11).

2. Logan (1999) states that 'The second world war ended in 1945' (p. 111).
3. The main benefit or organ transplant is that it saves lives. As stated by Smith (2005), 'heart transplantation can save lives, but the procedure carries serious risks and complications and a high mortality rate' (p. 12).
4. Improvements in transplantation have made it possible for animal organs to be used. This is beneficial, as patients are not forced to wait for transplants. As stated by Kline (2005): 'advances in genetic techniques mean that there is less chance of animal organs being rejected by the human immune system' (p. 53).
5. Transplantation carries the risk of being attacked by the immune system and the patient is therefore at risk of organ failure. As stated by Smith (2005): 'Everyone reported common side effects which included diarrhoea, edemas, fatigue and ulcers' (p. 5).

Three common mistakes students make with in-essay references for quotations

The three most common and serious mistakes students make when referencing quotations are:

- Forgetting that you must use quotation marks **and** an in-essay reference.

Some students make the mistake of using quotation marks but do not give an in-essay reference, because they think that the quotation marks and a reference in the bibliography at the end of the essay are enough. Other students make the mistake of giving a quotation with an in-essay reference but no quotation marks, because they think that the in-essay reference is enough.

The rules of writing at university are that if you use another person's words, you must always indicate this with quotation marks *and* an in-essay reference, as well as a reference in the bibliography. If you give an in-essay reference without quotations marks, it is always assumed that you are expressing an idea from a source but *in your own words*. Therefore, quoting without using quotation marks is plagiarism (claiming someone else's words or ideas as your own) even if you have given an in-essay reference. The only time you do not use quotation marks is for long quotations of more than three sentences; for these quotations indentation is used to show that you are using someone else's words.

Look again at the essay extract below and notice how the student introduces the quotation, gives an in-essay reference (including the page number) *and* uses quotation marks.

Another definition describes business ethics as the 'principles and standards that guide behaviour in the world of business' (Ferrell and Fraedrich et al., 2002, p. 6).

- Giving an in-essay reference for a primary source when you have only read the secondary source.

You must make clear in your essay which book or article you have actually read. In the correct example below, the student has used the phrase *cited in* to show that he did not read the Hoffman and Moore article itself but read their quotation in the article by Svensson and Wood. It would be poor scholarship and a misrepresentation of what you have read to give only the reference for Hoffman and Moore.

Hoffman and Moore (1982) suggest that the public feels that businesses fail to behave in a socially acceptable manner and that '. . . the mutual obligations of business to the community and the community to business need to be restated' (Hoffman and Moore, 1982, cited in Svensson and Wood, 2008).

- Putting brackets in the wrong place.

Look again at the extract from the business ethics essay below. Notice that for the first quotation the student uses Shaw and Barry as part of his introductory sentence, so he only puts brackets around the year of publication and for the page number. For the second quotation, however, the student does not use the authors Ferrell and Fraedrich et al. as part of his sentence, so both the names and year of publication are in brackets at the end of the quotation.

Shaw and Barry (2007) define business ethics as 'the study of what constitutes right and wrong (or good and bad) human conduct in a business context' (p. 25). Another definition describes business ethics as the 'principles and standards that guide behaviour in the world of business' (Ferrell and Fraedrich et al., 2002, p. 6).

Practice 5: Are these quotations referenced properly?

Below are four incorrect versions of the first part of the essay extract above. Look at these altered versions and identify what the mistakes are in the way these quotations have been referenced.

1. Business ethics is the study of what constitutes right and wrong (or good and bad) human conduct in a business context.
2. Shaw and Barry (2007) define business ethics as the study of what constitutes right and wrong (or good and bad) human conduct in a business context (p. 25).
3. Business ethics is 'the study of what constitutes right and wrong (or good and bad) human conduct in a business context'.
4. (Shaw and Barry, 2007) define business ethics as 'the study of what constitutes right and wrong (or good and bad) human conduct in a business context'.

Four common mistakes students make with grammar and punctuation in quotations

The most common mistakes students make with the grammar and punctuation of quotations are:

- Changing some of the words in the quotation.

    You cannot change *any* words in a quotation. If you want to miss out part of the quotation use three dots (called 'ellipsis') to indicate that you have left out some words. If you need to add a word of your own to make the quotation fit with its surrounding sentence or to clarify meaning, use a square bracket to show that you have added something which was not in the original text, for example: Emille (2002) states that 'They [the public] only hear what they want to hear' (p. 10).

- Putting in an extra 'he/she/it/they' or topic word before a quotation.

    If you use the author's name as part of your sentence you do not need to also use 'he/she/it/they/their' in the introductory sentence. Equally, if you use the topic word (e.g. 'business ethics') in your introductory sentence, you should not repeat it in the quotation.

- Changing the first letter of a quotation from lower case (e.g. *we*) to upper case (e.g. *We*).

    If your quotation is not the start of a sentence in the original, do not change the first letter to a capital letter in your quotation – keep everything exactly as it is in the original text.

- Putting punctuation marks in the wrong place at the end of a quotation.

    Don't worry too much about making small mistakes with the punctuation of quotations but do try to develop correct use over time. Keep question marks and other punctuation from the original text *inside* the quotation marks. The exception to this is the full-stop; for the author/year in-essay reference style you should put the full-stop at the very end, after the page number brackets.

Practice 6: Is the grammar and punctuation of these quotations correct?

Below is one of the extracts from the business ethics essay followed by four incorrect versions. Identify the mistakes in each incorrect version. The answer section includes a correct version of this extract using a numeric referencing system.

Correct extract
Secondly, an even stronger argument for the view that good ethics in business do in fact exist, is that given by Collins (1994) and by other prominent

experts on the subject. This is that 'good ethics is synonymous with good management' (p. 2).

Incorrect versions

1. Secondly, an even stronger argument for the view that good ethics in business do in fact exist, is that given by Collins (1994) and by other prominent experts on the subject. This is that 'good business ethics is synonymous with good management' (p. 2).
2. Secondly, an even stronger argument for the view that good ethics in business do in fact exist, is that given by Collins (1994) and by other prominent experts on the subject. This is that 'good ethics is good management' (p. 2).
3. Secondly, an even stronger argument for the view that good ethics in business do in fact exist, is that given by Collins (1994) and by other prominent experts on the subject. This is that good ethics 'good ethics is synonymous with good management' (p. 2).
4. Secondly, an even stronger argument for the view that good ethics in business do in fact exist, is that given by Collins (1994) and by other prominent experts on the subject. This is that 'good ethics is synonymous with good management.' (p. 2).

1.5 Why and how should you use your own words?

Paraphrasing is when you express ideas and information from your sources in your own way, using your own words. The ability to paraphrase well is central to university study and writing, and is also an ability which employers look for in graduates. This section gives you essential points on paraphrasing, takes you through some examples of good and poor paraphrasing and gives you a short practice exercise to help you acquire this complex skill.

Why paraphrase?

Restating what you have read, in your own way, is one of the most fundamental aspects of all academic writing because it allows you to:

- go through a mental process which helps you to understand and think about what you read in a more independent way;
- express the information and ideas from sources in your own style of thinking and writing so that you can integrate them smoothly into your own argument and essay;
- restate information and ideas from your sources in a way that best supports your own argument;
- show your tutor that you have understood what you have read and that you have used your reading to develop your knowledge and ideas;
- express information and ideas from complicated texts more clearly and simply;
- restate information and ideas from your sources which are not special enough to quote.

Looking at examples of good paraphrasing

Below are two extracts from one of the books the student read for his business ethics essay. Each extract is followed by the section in this essay where he introduces his own point and then paraphrases the source (in blue). Read and compare the source extracts with the essay extracts.

Source extract 1

There has also been an outpouring of books, magazine, journal and newspaper articles on the subject, as well as web pages, blogs, and other electronic publications – amazon.com currently stocks more than 2,000 books related to business ethics and corporate responsibility, whilst a google search on 'business ethics' returns more than 4 million hits at the time of writing. . . . One annual UK survey, for instance, estimates the country's 'ethical market' (i.e. consumer spending on ethical products and services) to be worth something like €40bn annually.

(Extract from: Crane, A. and Matten, D. (2007)
Business Ethics, p. 14.)

Essay extract 1

The subject of business ethics has become increasingly important over the past few decades and now appears to be a prevalent factor in consumer choice. . . . The UK ethical market is valued at over 40 billion euros per year and there are currently over 2,000 books and 4 million web entries related to business ethics (Crane and Matten, 2007).

Source extract 2

. . . there is indeed considerable overlap between ethics and the law. In fact, the law is essentially and institutionalisation or codification of ethics into specific social rules, regulations, and proscriptions. Nevertheless, the two are not equivalent. . . . The law might be said to be a definition of the minimum acceptable standards of behaviour. However, many morally contestable issues, whether in business or elsewhere, are not explicitly covered by the law. . . . In one sense then, business ethics can be said to begin where the law ends. Business ethics is primarily concerned with those issues not covered by the law, or where there is no definite consensus on whether something is right or wrong.

(Extract from: Crane, A. and Matten, D. (2007)
Business Ethics, pp. 5 and 7.)

Essay extract 2

When describing what business ethics is, it is essential to clarify that it is not synonymous with the law or with morals in general. Although the law overlaps with ethics, it usually only regulates the lowest level of acceptable behaviour (Crane and Matten, 2007). In fact, business ethics is mainly concerned with issues and areas of business conduct which are not specifically covered by the law and which are therefore vulnerable to exploitation and to what is viewed as immoral behaviour, even though it may be legal (ibid.).

(*ibid.* means that this source is exactly the same as the one previously referred to.)

Comments on the paraphrases

Notice how the student has not just replaced individual words in his paraphrases. His paraphrases are a complete rewriting of the source, based on his independent understanding, and written from his notes in his own style so that they make sense to him. His paraphrases are less complex than the original and he has changed the order of the information.

In essay extract 2, the student has emphasised the fact that ethics is not the same thing as the law. He has emphasised this difference because in this part of his essay he is defining and describing what business ethics is and so wants to point out the differences between ethics, the law and morals.

Notice that both paraphrases are shorter than the original. A paraphrase may be as long and as detailed as the original text but may also be shorter because you have condensed the points and used simpler language. The paraphrase in essay extract 1 is shorter than the original extract because the student has used this paraphrase in his essay introduction as only a brief example of the importance of business ethics. Paraphrase 2 is also shorter than the original extract because although the student has included all the points from the original text, he has used simpler language and condensed the ideas in his own way.

Five key points to remember when you are paraphrasing

1.   Check that your paraphrase clearly supports the point *you* are making
Don't let your paraphrases take control of your essay. Decide what point you want to make and then check that your paraphrase is relevant and that it supports your point. You would normally only paraphrase short sections from a source as support for your own thoughts and ideas. Check that you have expressed the information and used reporting verbs (e.g. *show*, *suggest*, *claim*) in such a way as to give the emphasis which best supports your argument.

2.   Write your paraphrase from your notes and reflection, not straight from the original text
If you have approached your reading in a similar way to that suggested in Sections 1.1, 1.2 and 1.3, you will already be more than halfway to writing good paraphrases. Your paraphrase should be your own understanding and rewriting of short sections of a source, not a translation straight from the text.

3.   Use your own words and writing style
When you paraphrase you must use your own words as far as possible – around 90% of the wording should be your own. The rules of academic writing do not allow you to change only a few words, and even changing about half of the words from the original text still counts as plagiarism. You must either change nothing and use the source as a quotation, or rewrite the source as a paraphrase, using over 90% of your own words. The word order and pattern of the sentences should also be your own as far as possible. Finding your own words will be much easier if you have gone through the process of taking good notes and writing a reflection on your reading.

- Keeping words from the original text

There will be some words or short phrases you can't change; in the example paraphrases these words are *business ethics, ethical market, law* and *behaviour*. You do not need to put quotation marks around such commonly used words. However, if you are keeping a word from the source which the author has used in a unique or special way, or if the word is a new term which the author has invented, you should use it as a one-word quotation and put quotation marks around it. Always check that you have not accidentally used the same words or sentence patterns as the original text unless absolutely necessary.

You should also try to rephrase statistics. For example, *one fifth* can also be expressed as *20%*, and *more than double* can be expressed as *over twice as many/much*. It may not always be possible or make sense to rephrase numbers and statistics but you should do this if you can.

In order to paraphrase, you will need to know an adequate number of words commonly used in academic writing and be able to use them in a precise way. We will look at this vocabulary in Part B.

4.   Always use an in-essay reference

Using in-essay references with your paraphrases is essential, not optional. You must *always* give in-essay references when paraphrasing because the ideas and information you have restated are not yours, even though you have used your own words.

One of the most common types of accidental plagiarism is when students paraphrase but do not give an in-essay reference, because they think that using their own words means that they do not need to reference. However, paraphrasing without giving an in-essay reference is plagiarism, because if something is not referenced, it is assumed to be both your own words *and* your own idea.

Giving in-essay references is also an important way of getting marks. Your in-essay references will show your tutor that you have done some reading and that you have understood it. In-essay references also show your tutor (and yourself) how the authors you have read have helped to develop your own ideas. Finally, using in-essay references shows that you know where your own essay is located in your subject area.

5.   Use reference reminder phrases

Giving an in-essay reference at the start of your paraphrase will often not be enough. In essay extracts 1 and 2 above, the student gives an in-essay reference at the end of the first sentence of each paraphrase. This is adequate for paraphrase 1 because it is only one sentence long. For paraphrase 2 however, the student also puts *ibid.* at the end of the second sentence to make clear that the idea in the second sentence also comes from Crane and Matten rather than himself.

Below is an example of another section from the business ethics essay, where the student paraphrases from Carr. The student has used the reference reminder phrase *he suggests that* to make clear that the ideas in the second sentence are still those of Carr.

Carr (1968) uses the analogy of a poker game to argue that a successful businessman needs to play by the rules of business in which 'bluffing' is an acceptable form of behaviour and that these rules are distinct from personal or social values. He suggests that even if a manager claims that good ethical conduct is also good for business, s/he is not really making a choice to be ethical but is merely using ethical conduct as a profitable business strategy.

If you don't use reference reminder phrases, it may become unclear in your essay which of your sentences express your own ideas and which ones express the ideas of other authors. This lack of clarity could lead you to accidentally plagiarise because, as stated above, it is always assumed in academic writing that anything which is not referenced is your own comment or idea.

How much paraphrasing should you do in an essay?

The amount you paraphrase in an essay will depend on how many sources you use and this will depend on your essay title and subject matter. If you are conducting your own experiment or research, you may not be using many sources and therefore may not be paraphrasing. However, most types of undergraduate essay and writing will consist of many short paraphrases from different sources. If you look at some academic journal articles in your subject you will see that some of them consist of a total of up to 50% paraphrase (from lots of different sources and therefore with lots of different in-essay references). The business ethics essay has about 60% of its word count as paraphrase. Note that this essay is still original to the student because of which sources he has decided to use and how he has used them.

Four common mistakes students make when paraphrasing

- Not showing clearly where a paraphrase begins and ends.
  Student essays often do not show clearly enough which sentences are their own words and ideas and which sentences are paraphrases of sources. For example, if you only give one in-essay reference in brackets at the end of a long paragraph, it probably won't be clear which sentences in that paragraph are paraphrase and which sentences are your own ideas. As discussed in the key points above, you must use both in-essay references and reference reminder phrases.
- Not making enough changes from the original source.
  Students sometimes use just a few of their own words to 'sew together' unchanged sentences or phrases from a source or from several different sources. Even if you give the relevant in-essay references, this type of 'sewing' is plagiarism because the words and style of most of the sentences are not your own.
- Changing individual words but keeping the same sentence pattern as the original.
  This might happen if you don't take notes and reflect on your reading but just try to 'translate' word by word from the text straight into your essay. Even if you change all the words, your paraphrase will still have the same style and pattern as the original text and this is still therefore a type of plagiarism.

- Accidently changing the meaning of the original text.

This might happen if you have not read and understood the text carefully enough or thought critically about it, or have not made clear notes. Make sure you understand from the text what is fact and what is opinion, and pay particular attention to small but important words such as *no*, *not* or *not as* and comparatives such as *faster*. For example, saying that smoking cannabis is *not as* damaging as smoking cigarettes is very different from saying that smoking cannabis is not damaging.

Looking at some examples of poor paraphrasing

Below is a short extract from a journal article which looks at whether mobile phones are a health risk.

The extract is followed by three unacceptable paraphrases which all try to use the article to support the view that mobile phones do not damage health. Read the extract and then the unacceptable paraphrases. Finally, read the comments and example of a good paraphrase of the article extract.

Source extract

So far there is no clear evidence from health studies of a relation between mobile phone use and mortality or morbidity. Indeed, tantalising findings in humans include a speeding up of reaction time during exposure, particularly during behavioural tasks calling for attention and electrical brain activity changes during cognitive processes. It is not clear, however, whether these findings have any positive implications for health.

(Adapted from: Maier, M., Blakemore, C. and Koivisto, M. (2000)
'The health hazards of mobile phones'. *British Medical Journal*, 320 (7245), pp. 1288–1289.)

Unacceptable paraphrases
1. Maier et al. (2000) show that there is no clear evidence from health studies of a relation between mobile phone use and mortality or morbidity. They state that in fact, tantalising findings in humans include a speeding up of reaction time during exposure, particularly during behavioural tasks calling for attention and changes in brain electricity during cognitive processes. It is not clear, however, whether these findings have any positive implications for health.
2. Some studies point to interesting results which suggest that while using a phone, the user has quicker reaction times to some behavioural tasks (Maier et al., 2000). In fact, there are interesting findings in humans that show a speeding up of reaction time during exposure, particularly during behavioural tasks calling for attention and changes in brain electricity during cognitive processes. It is unclear whether these findings have any positive implications for health.
3. Maier et al. (2000) show that up to now there is not any strong proof from studies on disease, of a link between the use of mobile phones and death or disease. In fact, interesting results in humans include a faster time of reaction during

use, especially while doing practical tasks that need concentration and brain electricity change during the thought process. It is unclear whether these results imply any health benefits (ibid.)

(*Maier et al.* means 'Maier and other authors'.)

Comments on the unacceptable paraphrases

Paraphrase 1

The student has correctly used an in-essay reference and the reference reminder phrase *They state that.* However, the only changes she has made from the source are to put in these references, take off the first two words and reword the phrase 'electrical brain activity changes'. Everything else is copied word for word from the source without any use of quotation marks. This is plagiarism.

Paraphrase 2

The student has used an in-essay reference and she has also made some significant changes in wording. However, there are two problems with this paraphrase. The first is that there are still several long phrases which are unchanged from the original source (underlined below). This could be seen as plagiarism. Secondly, there is no reference reminder phrase and so the reader is not sure whether the information in the second sentence comes from Maier et al. or from the student. By the time the reader gets to the third sentence, it could easily be assumed that the point expressed in this sentence is that of the student and this could therefore be seen as plagiarism. Indeed, this paraphrase counts as plagiarised on two counts: lack of referencing, and copied phrases from the original source.

> Some studies point to interesting results which suggest that while using a phone, the user has quicker reaction times to some behavioural tasks (Maier et al., 2000). In fact, there are interesting <u>findings in humans</u> that show <u>a speeding up of reaction time during exposure, particularly during behavioural tasks calling for attention</u> and changes in brain electricity <u>during cognitive processes</u>. It is unclear <u>whether these findings have implications for health.</u>

Paraphrase 3

The student has used nearly all her own words and has used two in-essay references. However, she has merely translated the original, word by word, as she goes along. The student has been too dependent on her source and instead of making and using notes, has gone straight from reading the article to writing her paraphrase. The result is a paraphrase that has exactly the same 'pattern' as the original. This does not show a clear understanding of the original or control of her source and is a type of plagiarism.

An example of a good paraphrase of the extract

Studies point to interesting results which suggest that mobile phone users experience quicker reaction times to tasks which require both changes in electrical brain activity and concentration (Maier et al., 2000). Although it has not been shown that these effects represent actual benefits to health, there has equally been no data from any disease studies to suggest that mobile phones actually damage health in any way (ibid.).

Practice 7: What do you think of these paraphrases?

Below is a short extract from a different article on the issue of mobile phones and health risks. Underneath the extract are four unacceptable paraphrases. Read the extract and paraphrases and identify what is wrong with each paraphrase. (The example of a good paraphrase in the answer section is given using both the author/year and the numeric referencing system.)

Source extract

Mobile phones provide an interesting example of a source risk to health which may be largely non-existent but which cannot be totally dismissed. Such risks, when possibly serious and with long-term consequences, are typically dealt with by appeal to the so-called precautionary principle but, of course, precaution comes at a price.

(Cox, D. R. (2003) 'Communication of risk: health hazards from mobile phones'. *Journal of the Royal Statistical Society: Series A (Statistics in Society)*, 166 (2), pp. 214–246.)

Unacceptable paraphrases

1. Advising caution in the use of mobile phones is an example of a typical approach to the fear of a possible health risk which may be of a serious nature. Such an approach may have negative consequences, but is taken because although there may in fact be no health risk, this has not yet been proven.
2. Cox (2003) suggests that advising caution in the use of mobile phones is an example of a typical approach to the fear of a possible health risk which may be of a serious nature. Such an approach may have negative consequences, but is taken because although there may in fact be no health risk, this has not yet been proven.
3. Advising caution in the use of mobile phones is an example of a typical approach to the fear of a possible health risk which may be of a serious nature. Such an approach may have negative consequences, but is taken because although there may in fact be no health risk, this has not yet been proven (Cox, 2003).
4. Mobile phones provide an interesting example of a source risk to health which may be largely non-existent but which cannot be totally dismissed (Cox, 2003). So far there is no clear evidence from health studies of a relation between mobile phone use and mortality or morbidity.

1.6 Why and how should you summarise?

A summary is when you express the main points from a source in your own way, using your own words. Both paraphrasing and summarising require you to use your own words and in-essay references. The difference between paraphrasing and summarising is that a paraphrase expresses *all* the information contained in a short, specific part of a text, whereas a summary gives only the *main* points from a much larger section or from a whole text. Summarising is a complex skill and one that you will need both at university and in your future career. This section gives you key points and steps for summarising, looks at common problems and gives examples of good and poor summarising.

Why summarise?

Summarising is a key element in writing essays and other types of assignment, and is important for the same reasons as those given for paraphrasing at the beginning of section 1.5 on page 25.

A summary can be an even more powerful writing tool than a paraphrase, however, because it allows you to show that you have understood the key point of a text and that you can express this clearly in your own way. Summarising therefore allows you great control over how you use your sources.

There are two main reasons for giving a summary in your essay:

- to give evidence and support for your own argument;
- to give an overview of different sources and authors who support a particular position.

  An overview of sources (sometimes called a 'literature review') is common near the beginning of an essay although you can give a brief overview of the literature at any stage in your essay when you are setting the scene for a point in your argument. Giving a summary of the position of key authors shows that you understand where they are located in the subject, i.e. which authors hold similar positions to those of yourself and of each other and which authors hold different viewpoints.

How long should a summary be?
The length and level of detail of your summary will depend on what you want it to do in your essay. A summary which includes all the main points of a text may be up to a third as long as the original text. Often however, you will want to give a very

brief summary of only a few sentences or even just one phrase to express the key point of a text.

Looking at some examples of good summaries

Below are two separate extracts from the student's business ethics essay. Read each extract and think about why and how the student has briefly summarised his sources in the essay (the summaries are in blue). Then read the comments on each extract.

Essay extract 1

Opponents of the concept of ethics in business include those who claim that making a profit is the only responsibility a business has to society (Friedman, 1970, cited in Fisher and Lovell, 2003). Others such as Wolf (2008) share this view and Prindl and Prodham (1994) suggest that 'Finance as practised in the professions and in industry is seen as a value-neutral positive discipline promoting efficiency without regard to the social consequences which follow from its products' (p. 3). Carr (1968) uses the analogy of a poker game to argue that a successful businessman needs to play by the rules of business, in which 'bluffing' is an acceptable form of behaviour, and that these rules are distinct from personal or social values.

Essay extract 2

Secondly, an even stronger argument for the view that good ethics in business do in fact exist, is that given by Collins (1994) and other prominent experts on the subject. This is that 'good ethics is synonymous with good management' (p. 2). Collins states that if managers only concern themselves with profit, they will in fact become 'dysfunctional'. This is because any business is made up of people: employees, customers and other stakeholders. He states that if businesses do not operate with a degree of trust, co-operation and consideration, they will be putting constraints on profitability. This idea of the interdependence of any business organisation is also supported by Shaw and Barry (2007), Green (1994), Fritzsche (2005) and Svensson and Wood (2008).

Comments on the extracts

In essay extract 1, the student summarises the view of Friedman in one sentence and then summarises the position of Wolf in only three words by stating that Wolf shares the same view. The student then uses a key quotation as a type of summary to state the position of Prindl and Prodham. The extract ends with a one-sentence summary of Carr's position. The essay extract gives an effective overview of key authors who oppose the concept of business ethics.

In essay extract 2, the student first establishes his own point by using a key quotation, which also acts as a summary of Collins' position. He then explains Collins' view in a bit more detail by giving a two-sentence summary. In the final sentence of the extract the student summarises the main point of six other authors in a phrase of only nine words: 'This idea of the interdependence of any business organisation . . .'. By doing this, the student shows that he understands that all of these texts have interdependence as their key point and that therefore these authors all hold a similar position on the issue.

Five key points to remember when you are summarising

- Express only the main point or points in the text.
- Give an objective and balanced summary of the key points and do not include your own opinion or comments.
- As with paraphrasing, your summary should be your own expression, style and words as far as possible. It is not acceptable to change only a few words of the original text or to sew together key sentences copied from the text (unless you use them as quotations).
- As with paraphrasing, you must always give in-essay references with your summary because the ideas and information you have restated are not yours, even though the way you have expressed them is. Summarising without giving an in-essay reference is a form of plagiarism.
- If your summary is more than one sentence long, check whether you need to use reference reminder phrases to make clear that the later sentences are still points from your source.

Five key steps for writing good summaries

Step 1   Identify how the source text is organised
Writing a good summary starts with your reading. Make sure that you understand how the text is structured. Read the title, sub-headings, introduction and conclusion of the text to help you identify the key points. Identify which parts of the text are main points and which are examples of these points or more minor points.

Step 2   Understand, make clear notes and critically reflect on your reading
If you have approached your reading in a similar way to the steps given in Sections 1.1, 1.2 and 1.3, you will already be more than halfway to writing a good summary. If you have written a critical reflection on what you have read, you will probably have written a short summary as part of it.

Step 3   Summarise what the text is about in one or two sentences
A really useful exercise is to start by using your notes to write a very short summary consisting of only one or two sentences. Doing this helps you to clarify in your

mind what the main point of the text is. You can then write a longer, more detailed summary that includes all the main points if you need to.

Step 4 Think about why and how you want to use the summary
Before you put your summary into your essay, ask yourself how it fits into your essay plan and argument. Make sure you use your summary to clearly support your own point.

Step 5 Check that you have used your own words and style, in-essay references and reference reminder phrases
As with paraphrasing, check that you have written your summary using your own words as far as possible and that you have used adequate in-essay referencing.

Six common mistakes students make when summarising

- accidently changing the meaning of the original text;
- giving too much detail and putting in minor points, examples or definitions from the text, rather than just the main points;
- adding their own opinion or comments;
- not making enough changes in words and style from the original source;
- not making clear where the summary begins and ends (i.e. not using clear in-essay references and reference reminder phrases);
- giving the primary source as the in-essay reference when they have only read a secondary source.

Practice 8: What is wrong with these summaries?

It is not possible in this book to give you a whole article or book to summarise. So, below is a short text written by J. Robinson in which she describes an article by Côté and Morgan.

Read the short text and make your own notes. Use your notes to write first a one-sentence summary of the text then a longer summary consisting of three or four sentences. (You may also like to use your notes to write a reflection – an example reflection is given in the answer section.)

After you have written your own summary, read the five unacceptable summaries and identify which common mistakes the students have made. Finally, read the comments on each summary.

A study on links between emotion regulation, job satisfaction and intentions to quit

Emotion regulation is the conscious and unconscious efforts people make to increase, maintain or decrease their emotions and is manifested by changes in facial expression and by changes in vocal and body signals. People often regulate their emotions at work. An example of emotion suppression is when a worker tries to hide anger they might be feeling towards a colleague or manager. Emotion amplification on the other hand, is when one pretends to be happier than one actually is. For example, an insurance or telephone salesperson may amplify their display of positive emotion to customers in order to increase their level of sales and quality of service.

Côté and Morgan (2002) conducted a study which looked at the relationship between emotion regulation, job satisfaction and intention to quit one's job. They collected two sets of data from 111 workers. The participants gave informed consent and were asked to complete two questionnaires on how they felt they had regulated their emotions at work and their feelings about their job. There was a time interval of four weeks between the two questionnaires to allow enough time for changes in emotion regulation and also to have a short enough period within which to retain the participants.

Côté and Morgan showed from their data that the amplification of pleasant emotions happened more frequently than the suppression of unpleasant emotions. Importantly, they also found a strong correlation between emotion regulation and job satisfaction and intention to quit. They demonstrated that, as they predicted, the suppression of unpleasant emotions leads to a decrease in job satisfaction and therefore an increase in intention to quit. Their findings also suggest that an increase in the amplification of pleasant emotions will increase job satisfaction, because it increases positive social interaction and more positive responses from colleagues and customers.

Although their experiment showed that emotion regulation affects job satisfaction, there was no strong evidence to suggest an opposite correlation, i.e. that job satisfaction and intention to quit influence emotional regulation.

Reference List
Côté, S. and Morgan, L. M. (2002) 'A longitudinal analysis of the association between emotion regulation, job satisfaction, and intentions to quit'. *Journal of Organizational Behaviour*, 23, pp. 947–962.

Text written by J. Robinson, 2008.

Unacceptable summaries

1. Emotion regulation is the conscious and unconscious efforts people make to increase, maintain or decrease their emotions. Côté and Morgan (2002) have conducted a study which looked at the relationship between emotion regulation, job satisfaction and intention to quit one's job. Côté and Morgan showed from their data that the amplification of pleasant emotions happened more frequently than the suppression of unpleasant emotions. Importantly, they also found a strong correlation between emotion regulation and job satisfaction and intention to quit.

2. A study has shown a strong link between emotion regulation and job satisfaction and intention to quit (Côté and Morgan, 2002, cited in Robinson, 2008). An example of emotion regulation is when someone attempts to hide

the anger they feel towards their boss or when they pretend to be happier than they really are during a work meeting or when dealing with customers. Côté and Morgan tested 111 workers by asking them to complete two questionnaires at an interval of four weeks. They found that workers exaggerate positive emotions more than they hide negative feelings. The findings also showed that suppressing negative emotions leads to a decrease in job satisfaction and that amplifying positive emotions leads to more positive interaction at work and therefore more job satisfaction.

3. Robinson (2008) describes a study conducted by Côté and Morgan, in which they obtained data on emotion regulation from 111 workers. The findings suggest that workers exaggerate positive emotions more than they hide negative feelings and that there is strong evidence that how you feel about your job influences how you regulate your emotions at work.

4. A study has shown a strong link between emotion regulation and job satisfaction and intention to quit (Côté and Morgan, 2002, cited in Robinson, 2008) and that workers exaggerate positive emotions more than they hide negative feelings. This might be because workers are worried that if they show their negative feelings, they might not get promoted, or worse, that they may lose their job. The findings also showed that suppressing negative emotions leads to a decrease in job satisfaction and that amplifying positive emotions leads to more positive interaction at work and therefore more job satisfaction.

Comments on the unacceptable summaries

1. This summary consists of four key sentences copied word for word from the original text. This is therefore plagiarism. In addition to this, the student has only given an in-essay reference for Côté and Morgan, which implies that they have read the primary Côté and Morgan article, when in fact they have only read the Robinson text. This is a misrepresentation of what the student has read and of Côté and Morgan.

2. The first and the last two sentences of this summary are good, with a correct in-essay reference. However, in the middle of the summary the student has included different examples of what emotion regulation is and also details of the method of the study, neither of which should be in a summary.

3. This summary starts with a correct in-essay reference but it does not state the key point of the text. In addition to this, the last point in the summary is not correct – the study showed that emotion regulation can influence how you feel about your job but there was *no* evidence that job satisfaction affects emotion regulation.

4. This summary starts well, with a clear statement of the key point and a correct in-essay reference. However, the second sentence is the student's own idea of why workers might hide negative feelings, and this should not be part of the summary. Any comments or opinion by the student on the results of the Côté and Morgan study should come after the summary rather than mixed up within it.

An example of an acceptable one-sentence summary

A study has shown a strong link between regulating emotions at work and job satisfaction and intentions to quit (Côté and Morgan, 2002, cited in Robinson, 2008).

An example of an acceptable three-sentence summary

A study has shown a strong link between emotion regulation and job satisfaction and intention to quit (Côté and Morgan, 2002, cited in Robinson, 2008). The findings also demonstrated that workers exaggerate positive emotions more than they hide negative feelings. Côté and Morgan also found that suppressing negative emotions leads to less job satisfaction and that amplifying positive emotions leads to better social interaction at work and therefore more job satisfaction (ibid.).

1.7 Putting it all together in your essay

This final section reviews the process of using sources and looks at how to integrate quotation, paraphrase and summary into an essay paragraph. It also gives you some final comments and advice on plagiarism and a practice exercise to help you become more aware of how you integrate sources into your own writing.

Throughout we have used extracts from the business ethics essay as examples of how to use sources, and below is another colour-coded extract from the essay as a final example.

Clearly then, businesses are not isolated from society. Svensson and Wood (2008) show that the two are in fact mutually dependent and that both are responsible for the consequences and effects of the other as part of a constant two-way process. Their model importantly demonstrates that the ethical standards of society are also those of business. Carr's argument that business ethics are different and separate from the ethics of other social contexts does not seem to hold true.	← Student point ← Summary of source as support Conclusion of student point, using a summary ← of another source

Five key points to remember

- It is essential that you become really familiar with what you read so that you have a clear and independent understanding of it.
- Everyone approaches writing differently and there is not one correct way to write an essay. It is important that you care about your writing and that you feel it is your own individual piece of work. Even if you use lots of sources, it will be original because of *how* you have used them to answer the essay question.
- Get the best marks possible for your work by always giving in-essay references.
- An effective use of quotation, paraphrase and summary will enable you to control your sources and make them work for you in your essay.
- Confidence in quoting, paraphrasing and summarising will only come with practice.

Table 1.1 Stages in using the Svensson and Wood article

Stage 1   The article by Svensson and Wood.
. . . it is important to see business ethics as a highly dymanic and continuous process without an end. A process, however, that is predicated on the interrelationship between business and society where each one is interdependent and responsible together for the outcomes.

(Extract from: Svensson, G. and Wood, G. (2008) 'A Model of Business Ethics'. Journal of Business Ethics, 77, pp. 303–322.)

Stage 2   Student critical analysis.
Svensson and Wood argue strongly and clearly that business and society influence each other and are dependent on each other and have a responsibility to each other to behave ethically. . . . I think that this article is solid enough to use as one of my main sources as evidence for what I think my conclusion will probably be.

Stage 3   Student notes.
BE – ' . . . dynamic and continuous process . . .' – 'interrelationship between business and society . . .' – each responsible for the other.

Stage 4   Student reflection.
The authors propose and describe their own model of business ethics which centres around a 'dynamic and continuous process' between business and society. They argue persuasively that business and society influence each other, are dependent on each other and have a responsibility to each other.

Stage 5   Paraphrase in the business ethics essay.
Clearly then, businesses are not isolated from society. Svensson and Wood (2008) show that the two are in fact mutually dependent and that both are responsible for the consequences and effects of the other, as part of a constant two-way process. Their model importantly demonstrates that the ethical standards of society are also those of business.

Table 1.2 Stages in using the Carr article

Stage 1	Article extract.
Stage 2	Critical analysis.
Stage 3	Notes.
Stage 5	Paraphrase in essay.

Reviewing the whole process from reading your sources to writing your essay

To remind you of how the whole process works, Table 1.1 gives you each stage of using a short section of the Svensson and Wood article, with the relevant page numbers so that you can go back and review the stages in full. Note that at each stage the student increasingly interprets his source in his own way. Table 1.2 lists the relevant page numbers for using the Carr article.

Time management for each stage of the process
Figure 1.1 is a diagram which summarises each stage, from reading to essay, and which gives you an approximate minimum time you would need if you were

searching online and using four journal articles. The precise time needed will be different for each individual and will depend on many different factors. However, one reason students get poor marks for their essays is that they have not given enough time to each part of the process, so you may find some rough time guidelines useful.

A final word on plagiarism

Common causes of purposeful or accidental plagiarism are:

- not giving enough time to reading and understanding texts;
- not taking notes or writing a reflection;
- not understanding what counts as plagiarism in writing;
- lack of ability or confidence in restating something in your own words;
- not wanting to highlight the fact that you have used lots of sources;
- not giving clear in-essay referencing.

This chapter has taken you through key steps and practice exercises which address each of these issues. These sections have, hopefully, helped you to understand what plagiarism is and given you the knowledge and confidence to use your sources properly and effectively. Plagiarising will not do anything to help you learn and will not help you gain the skills you need for a good career. Even if your goal at university is only to get good marks, plagiarising is still a waste of time because plagiarised work is almost always of poor quality. It is easier and more enjoyable to do the work needed to produce a good essay yourself.

Building your own house

You might find it helpful to think of the essay writing process in terms of designing and building a house (the house is your essay and the materials and fittings are your sources).

The first thing you would need to do is to be clear about the purpose of the house; why you were building it and what requirements you wanted it to meet. Even if you had been given the basic design and requirements of the house (the essay title), you would still need to think about exactly how to meet the specifications of the design.

The materials for building the house (your sources) would need to be well researched, reliable and right for the job. The different materials and fittings you would use would mainly be ones that someone else had produced but the house would be original to you because of your design features, the materials and fittings you had decided to use, and how you had decided to use them. You would also keep receipts and manufacturer's details (a research log) in case of any problems and for use on future building projects.

When you had finished your house and were showing people round (anyone who reads your essay) they would be interested in who had designed and made various fittings such as the windows or kitchen units. You would, hopefully, be proud

Thinking; thoughts and ideas on the essay title.	Thinking	Reading, question-ing, evalu-ating and locating the texts.	Thinking	Re-reading and making clear and meaningful notes.	Thinking	Writing a critical reflection on each text from your notes.	Thinking	Deciding why and how you want to use the texts to support your argument.	Thinking	Para-phrasing, summaris-ing and quoting the texts in your draft essay.	Thinking	Checking that your sources precisely support your points and that you have used adequate rewriting and in-essay refer-encing.
Finding and selecting four rele-vant texts. Recording research details.												
2 hours		4 hours		4 hours		4 hours		1 hour		2 hours		1 hour

Figure 1.1   Time management for using your reading in your essay

43

to answer their questions honestly. No-one would expect you to have made the kitchen units or windows yourself (and it would be obvious to anyone with any building experience that you had not done so). What would be important would be to show your intelligence and skill in finding and selecting materials, understanding how they worked and using them effectively in your own way to build your own house.

Practice 9: What do you think of the way these students have used this source in their essay?

Below are three paragraphs from three separate essays addressing the title: *In what ways might personality affect job satisfaction?*

All three students have used the text by J. Robinson on page 36–37. Read the three paragraphs and use the Robinson text to decide what the problem is in each case, then read the comments on each paragraph.

Finally, look at the example of a good paragraph, on page 45–46, in which the student has used their notes and reflection on the text as a basis for integrating the source information into their essay.

Unacceptable essay paragraphs

1. There does seem to be a link between personality and job satisfaction, although there are different views on how strong this link is. One interesting study on emotion regulation has demonstrated that there is a strong link between how we regulate our emotions at work and how satisfied we are with our jobs (Côté and Morgan, 2002, cited in Robinson, 2008). Their data showed that the amplification of pleasant emotions happened more frequently than the suppression of unpleasant emotions. Importantly, they also found a strong correlation between emotion regulation and job satisfaction and intention to quit. These findings would suggest that if you are good at regulating your emotions and particularly if you are able to be (or at least pretend to be) positive, you are likely to have a higher level of job satisfaction than someone who cannot or does not want to amplify positive emotions. Although emotion regulation is not synonymous with personality, it seems likely that personality type is linked to emotion regulation and therefore to job satisfaction.

2. There does seem to be a link between personality and job satisfaction, although there are different views on how strong this link is. A study has shown that there is a strong link between how we regulate our emotions at work and how satisfied we are with our jobs. Workers exaggerate positive emotions more than they hide negative feelings. In addition, suppressing negative emotions leads to less job satisfaction and amplifying positive emotions leads to better social interaction at work and therefore more job satisfaction. If you are good at regulating your emotions and particularly if you are able to be (or at least pretend to be) positive, you are likely to have a higher level of job

satisfaction than someone who cannot or does not want to amplify positive emotions. Although emotion regulation is not synonymous with personality, it seems likely that personality type is linked to emotion regulation and therefore to job satisfaction (Côté and Morgan, 2002, cited in Robinson, 2008).

3. Côté and Morgan claim that there is a strong link between emotion regulation and job satisfaction and intention to quit (Côté and Morgan, 2002, cited in Robinson, 2008). The findings showed that workers exaggerate positive emotions more than they hide negative feelings. Côté and Morgan also found that suppressing negative emotions leads to less job satisfaction and that amplifying positive emotions leads to better social interaction at work and therefore more job satisfaction.

Comments on the unacceptable essay paragraphs

1. This paragraph starts well, with the student introducing her own point that there is a link between personality and job satisfaction. She then starts to paraphrase the Robinson article and gives a correct in-essay reference. However, the third and fourth sentences are copied word for word from the Robinson text without any quotation marks; this is therefore plagiarism. The paragraph ends well with the student's own comments.
2. The student starts well by introducing her own point. She continues by summarising the Robinson text in her own words, which is good. However, she does not give any in-essay references or reference reminder phrases; this is plagiarism. After her summary she continues with her own comments on the implications of the study. Finally, she gives an in-essay reference in brackets at the end of the paragraph. This is inadequate referencing, as the reader would have no idea where the divisions were between the student's own points and her summary of the source.
3. This paragraph contains only the summary of the Robinson text. There are in-essay references but there is no introduction or conclusion by the student and we therefore have no idea of what point the student is trying to make. This is a case of the sources controlling the essay – the student has merely found sources she thinks might be relevant and put them in, without introducing them or thinking about what point she wants them to support in her essay.

Example of an acceptable essay paragraph using the Robinson text

There does seem to be a link between personality and job satisfaction, although there are different views on how strong this link is. One interesting study on emotion regulation has demonstrated that there is a strong link between how we regulate our emotions at work and how satisfied we are with our jobs (Côté and Morgan, 2002, cited in Robinson, 2008). The findings showed that workers exaggerate positive emotions more than they hide negative feelings. Côté and

← Student point

← Summary of source used as evidence and support

Morgan also found that suppressing negative emotions leads to less job satisfaction and that amplifying positive emotions leads to better social interaction at work and therefore more job satisfaction. These findings would suggest that if you are good at regulating your emotions and particularly that if you are able to be (or at least pretend to be) positive, you are likely to have a higher level of job satisfaction than someone who cannot or does not want to amplify positive emotions. The fact that if you suppress negative emotions, you will have less job satisfaction, suggests that if you are someone who can express negative feelings in a constructive way at work in order to find a solution to the problem, you will probably have more job satisfaction than someone who hides negative emotions without trying to resolve them. Although emotion regulation is not synonymous with personality, it seems likely that personality type is linked to emotion regulation and therefore to job satisfaction.

← Student's ideas on the implications of the findings

← Conclusion of student's point

Appendix 1

Glossary

Abstract a summary (usually of about 100 words) of an article, report or book, which includes the main argument or problem, the procedures, results and conclusion. Abstracts are always written by the authors of the source and are normally used by readers to decide whether they want to read the whole text.

Academic/scholarly journal a journal which contains reliable, peer-reviewed articles of good quality.

Academic source a book, article or other type of text which has been peer-reviewed and/or is written by experts in the subject.

Argument a sequence of reasons to support a particular theory or point of view.

Bibliographic details the full details of a source, given at the end of a written text.

Citation information on who wrote something, given within the piece of writing. *Citation* is also sometimes used to mean a quotation.

Close paraphrase when most of the words of the original source are used with only small changes. Close paraphrase should only be used when taking notes.

Critical analysis/thought the process of identifying the argument of a text and then questioning and evaluating it to decide whether it is based on correct assumptions, logical reasoning and sound evidence.

Digest a brief summary of one source or a compilation of summaries of many different sources on a particular topic. It can be written by the authors themselves or by a third party.

Draft a rough version of an essay or other piece of written work, which is changed and improved to produce the finished piece.

et al. abbreviation of the latin *et alii* meaning 'and others'. Used for in-essay referencing when a source has more than two authors.

Evaluation, to evaluate to reflect on and assess the information and argument of something.

Extract a section of text.

ibid.   from the latin *ibidem* meaning 'in the same place'. Used as an in-essay reference to indicate that the source is exactly the same as the one previously given.

i.e.   from the latin *id est*, meaning 'that is'. In writing, *i.e.* is used to mean 'that is to say' or 'in other words'. Be careful not to confuse *i.e.* with *e.g.* With *i.e.* you must restate the complete idea or complete set of items. With *e.g.* you only give one or two examples of the set.

Literature review   summarising and comparing the key authors and sources on a particular topic or issue.

Literature search   the process of looking for, finding and selecting relevant material and sources.

Paraphrase, to paraphrase   re-expressing all the information and ideas from a section of text in your own words and style.

Peer-review   the system by which articles are checked for quality and accuracy by relevant academic experts before being published.

Plagiarism, to plagiarise   presenting someone else's ideas, information, wording or style (or any combination of these) as your own, even if it is only a single sentence. Plagiarism also includes claiming that work done jointly with other students is solely your own work (this is called 'collusion'). Plagiarism can occur accidentally due to poor writing and referencing, or on purpose to gain a particular advantage or benefit.

Primary source   the first, original source of information or ideas, for example the original report written by the person who conducted an experiment or the original article or book written by an author.

Quotation, to quote   a phrase, sentence or section of a source given in your writing, word for word, without any changes in wording from the original text.

Research   any type of organised search, study, investigation or work that is done in order to develop ideas and knowledge.

Scan   to look at or read something quickly in order to identify key points or to assess whether something is relevant for more detailed reading.

School of thought   a way of thinking, set of beliefs, or accepted theory or approach, e.g. behaviourism, socialism, Marxism, feminism.

Secondary source   a source which writes about, discusses or uses a previously written primary source.

Text   a word used to describe any type of written document when focusing on the content rather than the type of document.

Appendix 2

Answers to practice execises

1.1 How do you decide what to read?

Practice 1

1. Reliable information for general issues on disability but may be biased. Not an academic source.
2. Not reliable and not an academic source.
3. Reliable and an academic source but 2002 is quite old for such a topic, which decreases the reliability of the information.
4. a. Reliable for some ideas on issues but may be biased and inaccurate. Not an academic source.
   b. Reliable and an academic source.
   c. Quite reliable but not an academic source.
5. Reliable for introducing main issues but not an academic source. Also the booklet is quite old for this topic and this further decreases how reliable the source is for information on animal cloning.
6. Probably reliable as information from businesses but not an academic source. You would also need to check when the website was updated.
7. Not reliable and not an academic source.
8. Reliable as information from businesses but not an academic source.

9. Reliable for general discussion and ideas but not peer-reviewed and therefore not academically reliable. You should find and use articles from the centre's 'Journal of Ethics' for academic sources.
10. Not reliable and will be biased, as it seems to be written by a pressure group. Not an academic source.

1.2 How do you understand and question what you read?

Practice 2

Questioning

Carr assumes that businessmen are ethical in their private lives – this may not be true. He also assumes that all businesses operate in the same way, that they all have ethical standards separate from private ones and that you always have to choose between losing and lying. This may not be true – there may be other options or other types of business models.

Evaluating

His style is quite persuasive – I instinctively feel he is partly right – but he is very cynical and over-simplifies. He gives no evidence for his views and doesn't try to be objective or look at opposing evidence. His argument isn't very well ordered as it is continuous opinion rather than a developed argument. I agree with Carr that some people feel they do need to lie in business but not that this is always the case or that business ethics are totally separate from social norms – particularly now-adays? I will use Carr as a key source to show an expert who opposes the idea of business ethics and I will then criticise his argument by giving opposing evidence from Svensson and Wood.

Locating

Carr's article seems to have been radical and important at the time (1968) because a lot of other texts still refer to it. In terms of business ethics he is definitely in the 'no' camp. His article is very dated now and things have moved on since then – now there is more legislation on regulation of corporate behaviour, corporate transparency and accountability and more emphasis on ethics and sustainability.

1.3 What should you write down?

Practice 3

Example notes

	Carr, A. Z. (1968) 'Is business bluffing ethical?' *Harvard Business Review*, 46 (1), pp. 143–153.
	Notes written on 16/2/2009
p. 145 main point.	Ethics of bus. are like the rules of poker (distrust) – diff. from 'civilised human relationships'.
p. 145 (bottom) Not true?	Most busmn. are ethical in private lives, but at work they stop being 'private citizens' + follow the *different*. ethical rules of bus.
p. 148	The image that bus. gives of using ethics from private life e.g.'"Sound ethics is good for business"' is only a self-serving + profit making deception, not a true ethical position.
p.153 (Conclusion) Not true now/all (lying)	'To be a winner, a man must play to win'. Busmn will sometimes have to choose betwn. losing and 'bluffing'

businesses? – other choices?	like poker. To succeed he will have to 'bluff hard'.
2nd main point	'Bluffing' is 'integral' to business.

NB 'Sound ethics is good for business' is a quotation by Carr in the original text. The student has made this clear in his notes by using double and then also single quotation marks to show that Carr is quoting someone else.

1.4 Why and how should you quote?
Practice 4
1. This quotation is not special in what it says or how it is expressed. The student should have given this information in their own words as far as possible, for example: *Kzanty (2004) states that organs such as the lungs, pancreas and heart are used in transplantation.*
2. This information is common fact and knowledge so can be given in the essay without attribution to the author.
3. The quotation partially contradicts the student's point that transplants save lives.
4. The quotation is about the student's first point (improvements in transplantation techniques using animal organs), not about the point that is immediately in front of the quotation, that patients do not have to wait for transplants.
5. The quotation is not introduced clearly – it does not explain which trial or study is referred to or who 'everyone' is.

Practice 5
1. There are no quotation marks and no in-essay reference. This is plagiarism.
2. There is an in-essay reference but no quotation marks. This is plagiarism.
3. There are quotation marks but no in-essay reference. This might be seen as plagiarism.
4. There are quotation marks and an in-essay reference, but the authors' names should not be in brackets and the page number is missing. The page number must be included for quotations if you use the author/year system of referencing.

Practice 6
1. The student has added the word 'business' to the original wording. She should either take this word out or put it in square brackets, e.g. [business].
2. The student has taken out the words 'synonymous with' from the original text. She should use ... to show this, for example: *This is that 'good ethics is ... good management' (p. 2).*
3. The topic words 'good ethics' are used twice, once in the introductory sentence and again in the quotation. They should be used in one or the other but not both, for example: *This is that good ethical behaviour 'is synonymous with good management' (p. 2),* or *This is that 'good ethics is synonymous with good management' (p. 2).*
4. The full-stop at the end of the quotation is inside the quotation marks. It should come outside the quotation marks after the page number brackets, for example: *This is that 'good ethics is synonymous with good management' (p. 2).*

Correct version of the extract using a numeric system of referencing
Secondly, an even stronger argument for the view that good ethics in business do in fact exist, is that given by Collins and by other prominent experts on the subject. This is that 'good ethics is synonymous with good management' (1).

Works Cited
1. J. W. Collins. 'Is business ethics an oxymoron?' *Business Horizons* 1994; 37 (5): 1–8.

1.5 Why and how should you use your own words?

Practice 7

1. The paraphrase itself is good as it is written in the student's own words. However, there are no in-essay references and so this counts as plagiarism.
2. The paraphrase is rewritten in the student's own words and has an initial in-essay reference. However, there is no reference reminder phrase in the second sentence and so it is not clear whether this sentence is an idea from the student or from the source. This could be seen as plagiarism.
3. There is only one in-essay reference, given at the end of the paragraph. It is therefore not clear whether the first sentence is the student's idea or an idea from the source – this could be seen as plagiarism. It is much better to integrate a reference into the first sentence of a paraphrase and then to use reference reminder phrases.
4. This paraphrase consists of one sentence copied from Cox and a second sentence copied from the Maier, Blakemore and Koivisto text. The sentences have been stitched together without the use of quotation marks and without adequate referencing. This is plagiarism.

Example of an acceptable paraphrase of the Cox extract

Using the author/year style of in-essay referencing:

> Cox (2003) suggests that advising caution in the use of mobile phones is an example of a typical approach to the fear of a possible health risk which may be of a serious nature. He states that such an approach may have negative consequences, but is taken because although there may in fact be no health risk, this has not yet been proven.

Using the numeric style of in-essay referencing:

> Cox (1) suggests that advising caution in the use of mobile phones is an example of a typical approach to the fear of a possible health risk which may be of a serious nature. He states that such an approach may have negative consequences, but is taken because although there may in fact be no health risk, this has not yet been proven.

> Works cited
> 1. D. R. Cox, 'Communication of risk: health hazards from mobile phones'. *Journal of the Royal Statistical Society: Series A (Statistics in Society)* 2003; 166 (2): 214–246.

1.6 Why and how should you summarise?

Practice 8

Example of a good personal reflection on the Robinson text

Robinson states that Côté and Morgan's study shows a strong link between regulating emotions at work and job satisfaction and intentions to quit.

Robinson doesn't go into great detail about the Côté and Morgan study, so I would need to read the original text to really do a critical analysis of it and find out whether the experiment has any flaws. However, just from reading Robinson's summary of the study, it seems to me to be an important experiment – the only one I have found so far on emotion regulation. I think that the idea of regulating emotions at work and the effects this has on how someone feels about their job is very interesting.

Thinking about the essay title, I think that Côté and Morgan's findings imply that if you have a personality that is good at regulating your emotions and particularly that if you are able to be (or at least pretend to be) positive, then you are likely to have a higher level of job satisfaction than someone who can't or doesn't want to amplify positive emotions.

The findings also show that if you suppress negative emotions, you will have less job satisfaction. I think that this shows that if you are someone who can express negative feelings in a constructive way at work in order to find a solution to the problem, then you will probably have more job satisfaction than someone who just always hides negative emotions without trying to do anything about them.

Practice 9   (See pages 36–37)

CHAPTER 2
Work routines

KEY CONCEPTS

Taylorism	flexible specialisation
Fordism	polarisation of skills
deskilling	compensatory theory of skill
labour process	automating and informating
upskilling	range of work
human capital	discretion in work
offshoring	work organisation paradigms

CHAPTER AIM

To explain the dominant forms of work organisation and explore competing theories of skill change.

LEARNING OUTCOMES

After reading and understanding the material in this chapter you will be able to:

1. Describe the main features of Taylorism and assess their relevance to contemporary work.

2. Describe the methods and application of Fordism.

3. Explain the theory behind the deskilling thesis.

4. Outline and evaluate the main criticisms of the deskilling thesis.

5. Explain the theory behind the upskilling thesis.

6. Outline and evaluate the main criticisms of the upskilling thesis.

7. Describe alternative approaches to examining skill change.

8. Use the work categorisation framework to analyse jobs.

9. Explain the relationship between skill change and work organisation paradigms.

Introduction

This chapter addresses a puzzle that has occupied the minds of researchers and theorists for decades: whether the fundamental shifts that have been occurring in the overall nature of work are causing people to experience either deskilling and degrading, or upskilling and enrichment, in their working lives. We have previously noted some of the structural changes occurring in patterns of employment, but here we assess the impact of these broader employment dynamics by focusing on the nature of work tasks.

To explore these issues, the first examines two dominant traditions in work organisation – Taylorism and Fordism – using contemporary examples to illustrate the central principles of each. Each of which examines a different perspective on how work is changing: the deskilling thesis, the upskillin\g antithesis, and the attempts to synthesise these contrasting approaches.

Learning outcome 1: Describe the main features of Taylorism and assess their relevance to contemporary work

Dominant traditions of work organisation – Taylorism and Fordism

Routine work in the service sector – burgers and Taylor

Imagine the scene: you are visiting a city for the first time. It is lunchtime and you are feeling hungry, you do not have much money to spend on food, and you only have 30 minutes before your train leaves. As you look along the busy, unfamiliar street you recognise a sign in the distance: a large yellow letter 'M'. A sense of relief overwhelms you as you head for that emporium of American pulp cuisine, McDonald's. Any uncertainty and anxiety has been replaced by the predictability of the McDonald's experience: no matter where you are, you will get the standard-tasting burger, covered with the same relish, lodged in the same bun, served in the same packaging for consumption in the familiar decor of the restaurant.

Consistency is McDonald's strong selling point – if you are one of the company's 50 million daily customers, you will know exactly what you are going to get when you order your Big Mac and large fries, in any one of McDonald's 30,000 outlets in 119 countries. Of course, to guarantee such a standardised product, the work processes as well as the food have all been standardised. So leaving aside the issue of the product itself, how can we characterise and understand work at organisations like McDonald's?

If we use a metaphor, we can describe McDonald's as a well-maintained machine in almost every aspect of its operations, from the customer interface to the centralised planning and financial control (Morgan, 1986). Employees at McDonald's (or 'crew members' as they are called) are treated as components of this machine. Each receives simple training to perform a number of tasks which require little judgement and leave limited room for discretion. Crew members are given precise instructions on what to say, what to do and how to do it. They are the necessary 'living' labour joining the precisely timed computer-controlled equipment that cooks the burgers, fries the potatoes, dispenses the drinks, heats the pies, records the order and calculates the customer's change.

> Much of the food prepared at McDonald's arrives at the restaurant pre-formed, pre-cut, pre-sliced and pre-prepared, often by non-human technologies. This serves to drastically limit what employees need to do .... McDonald's has developed a variety of machines to control its employees. When a worker must decide when a glass is full and the soft-drink dispenser needs to be shut off, there is always the risk that the worker may be distracted and allow the glass to overflow. Thus a sensor has been developed that automatically shuts off the soft-drink dispenser when the glass is full.
>
> (Ritzer, 1993: 105–6)

This logic of automation is extended to all the processes, with the consequence that the employees push buttons, respond to bleeps and buzzers and repeat stock phrases to customers like subjects in a bizarre Pavlovian experiment. The dehumanising effects can often be seen in the glazed expressions of the young people who serve. But the most poignant, if not ironic, aspects of all this is that one of the world's most successful multinational corporations at the beginning of the twenty-first century relies on labour management techniques that were developed at the beginning of the twentieth century. Indeed, the pioneer of 'scientific management', F. W. Taylor, would have certainly recognised and endorsed the principles of rationality upon which McDonald's is organised.

Exercise 2.1

What do you think?

Managers at the global fast food chain, McDonald's, recognised that they might have gone too far in adopting the sort of standardisation associated with Taylorism. The crew members (the employees) in all McDonald's restaurants had been obliged to greet and say goodbye to all customers in the same manner, according to a set script. However, McDonald's research revealed that customers disliked this, and as a result the crew can now speak to customers however they want – within accepted boundaries of politeness, of course. The managers of McDonald's describe this as empowerment.

1. Are McDonald's right to move away from this aspect of standardisation? Why, or why not?
2. Is the abandonment of standardised scripts really 'empowerment' for the crew members?
3. Should other aspects of McDonald's be less standardised?
4. What are the advantages and disadvantages of standardisation?

F. W. Taylor's guiding principles

The ideas of Taylor have been well documented elsewhere (see for example Kelly, 1982; Littler, 1982; Rose, 1988) so it is necessary here only to reiterate the central principles, to see how closely aligned the contemporary work processes at McDonald's are to concepts that were originally published in 1911. Efficiency was Taylor's guiding obsession. His own work experience as an engineer led him to believe there was an optimum way of performing any job: the 'one best way'. It was the task of management to discover this through the application of rigorous scientific testing, which involved breaking all activities down into their smallest components, and systematically analysing each step. No activity was too complex or too mundane to be subjected to this scientific analysis, argued Taylor (see Excerpt 2.1).

Excerpt 2.1

Applying scientific management
Taylor illustrates his theory with the example of managing pig-iron handling and shovelling.

> Probably the most important element in the science of shoveling is this: There must be some shovel load at which a first-class shoveler will do his biggest day's work. What is that load? ... Under scientific management the answer to this question is not a matter of anyone's opinion; it is a question for accurate, careful, scientific investigation. Under the old system you would call in a first-rate shoveler and say, 'See here, Pat, how much ought you to take on at one shovel load?' And if a couple of fellows agreed, you would say that's about the right load and let it go at that. But under scientific management absolutely every element in the work of every man in your establishment, sooner or later, becomes the subject of exact, precise, scientific investigation and knowledge to replace the old, 'I believe so,' and 'I guess so.' Every motion, every small fact becomes the subject of careful, scientific investigation.
>
> (Taylor, 1911: 51–2)

> Now one of the very first requirements for a man who is fit to handle pig iron as a regular occupation is that he shall be so stupid and so phlegmatic that he more nearly resembles in his mental make-up the ox than any other type. The man who is mentally alert and intelligent is for this reason entirely unsuited to what would, for him, be the grinding monotony of work of this character. Therefore the workman who is best suited to handling pig iron is unable to understand the real science of doing this class of work. He is so stupid that the word 'percentage' has no meaning to him, and he must consequently be trained by a man more intelligent than himself into the habit of working in accordance with the laws of this science before he can be successful.
>
> (Taylor, 1911: 59)

Having discovered the 'one best way' of performing a task, management's responsibility was to allocate tasks to employees, attempting to fit the right person to each job. The employee should have the requisite skills, acquired through systematic training, to complete the task at hand, and no more than those required by the job.

Emerging from Taylor's principles of organising the work process is a distinctive managerial ideology in which four themes dominate.

- *Division of labour*: this involves the separation of manual work (the doing) from mental work (the thinking). By removing from the employee any discretion over the organisation and execution of work, managers are able to secure control over the method and pace of working. As we shall see, this can have important consequences for determining the skill definition of a work activity.
- *Planning*: managers play an important role in planning each activity to ensure that it is in line with business objectives. In pursuit of these objectives, employees are to be used dispassionately, along with capital equipment and raw materials, in the search for greater efficiency, productivity and profitability. As a consequence, rigorous selection and training of people (to inculcate required behaviours) becomes a critical management function.
- *Surveillance*: based on the assumption that people cannot be trusted to perform their jobs diligently, there needs to be control through close supervision and monitoring of all work activities. Hierarchies of authority are constructed giving legitimacy to surveillance, and simultaneously constructing a 'division of management' (Littler, 1982: 53).
- *Performance related pay*: Taylor's deeply entrenched belief was that people were essentially instrumental, and so money could be used as a powerful motivator providing it was linked directly to the productivity of the individual: a linkage achieved by piece-rate payment systems.

While the logic of Taylorism is impeccable, the conditions of work it produces are often dehumanising and bleak: a set of highly segmented work activities, with no opportunity for employees to use their discretion, and a system of close supervision to monitor their work performance. However, the practice of Taylorism has not necessarily followed the theory as closely as its original protagonist would have wished, leading some commentators (notably Edwards, 1979; Palmer, 1975) to argue that Taylor's influence has been overstated because the practical impact of his ideas were limited – not least because of the collective resistance exerted by employees through trade unions.

It is certainly the case that in Taylor's own lifetime the diffusion of the principles of scientific management was modest. Many managers remained unconvinced about the possibility of planning and measuring activities sufficiently accurately to enable the 'science' to work. There were also competing ideas about the nature of job design from the human relations movement (starting with the famous Hawthorne experiments in the 1920s) which brought out the importance of the social factors at work, thus challenging the rational-economic assumptions underlying Taylor's theory of work design (for a full analysis see Schein, 1965).

Notwithstanding these reservations, Taylor's ideas *have made* (and continue to make) a crucial impact on the thinking about job design and the division of labour. Indeed, as Littler (1982) argues, we must be cautious of assuming a linear progression of management theory where each set of ideas neatly supersedes the previous ones. The persistence of Taylorist principles in contemporary organisations is testimony to the resilience of Taylorism (for example, see the discussions by Bain, Watson, Mulvey, Taylor and Gall, 2002; Jones, 2000; Nyland, 1995). Of particular importance is the way that service sector organisations like McDonald's can use features of 'classic' Taylorism in a similar way to manufacturing industry. Indeed, we might ponder whether shovelling chips into a cardboard carton is the twenty-first century equivalent of shovelling pig iron into a furnace which Taylor studied a century earlier.

The pervasiveness of a Tayloristic division of labour in the expanding service sector was noted by Ritzer (1993). He contends that McDonald's represents the archetypal rational organisation in search of four goals: efficiency, calculability, predictability and control. McDonald's is a contemporary symbol of a relentless process of rationalisation, where the employee is simply treated as a factor of production. Ritzer's thesis (rather pessimistically) is that both theoretically and empirically this constitutes a general process of 'McDonaldisation' which extends beyond work into the culture of society (Ritzer, 1998). His conclusion suggests that there is an inevitable tendency towards a dehumanisation of work – a theme that echoes the work of the deskilling theorists, whose ideas are explored after considering a second key actor in the design of jobs in the twentieth century.

Exercise 2.2

What do you think?
Taylor was obsessed with finding the ultimate solution to the problem of organising work. He believed that by analysing and measuring work activities it was possible to find the optimum method of performing every task. In effect, he was suggesting that by careful, scientific, logical analysis, using his guiding principles, managers can find the best way of managing.

1. What is your opinion about Taylor's theory? What are your reasons for agreeing or disagreeing with him?
2. Why do some organisations follow his methods, whilst others reject them?
3. Consider your own work experiences. Would you describe the work as Tayloristic? If not, does it have elements that reflect Taylor's principles of work organisation?
4. Are some jobs impossible to Taylorise?

Routine work on the assembly line – chickens and Ford

If asked to visualise an assembly line, many people would probably have an image of a car plant, with a steady procession of partly finished vehicles passing groups of workers (or robots) who are rapidly attaching windscreens, wheels, trim and so on. This has been the pervasive image of assembly line work, not least because its innovative form was originally developed and exploited by the Ford Motor Company – an issue that we return to below.

First, though, imagine a different contemporary work setting. You are in a massive room dominated by the sound of humming and churning machinery, while intermittently the voices of the all-women workforce can be heard. The room is cool and the air laden with the smell of blood. Overhead, weaving around the factory is a conveyor from which hooks are suspended; hanging from each hook is the carcass of a dead bird. It is a chicken factory, comprising a variety of 'assembly lines' that convert live birds into the cellophane-wrapped, ready-for-roasting meat displayed in supermarket freezers.

The work is Tayloristic in the sense that it is segmented into simple, repetitive operations. For example, 'packing' involves four distinct tasks each performed by different employees: inserting the giblets and tucking the legs in, bagging the chicken, weighing it, and securing the top of the bag. But not only are these and similar tasks around the factory simple and repetitive, the pace of the work is also relentless. This is vividly portrayed by an employee performing 'inspection' in such a chicken factory, interviewed for a television programme, *Dangerous Lives*:

> *Employee*: The line was coming round with about four and a half thousand birds an hour and you used to have to check the chickens for livers, hearts or anything, by putting your hand in the backside of a chicken, feeling around and then bringing anything out, dropping it in the bin, and then going on to the next. Used to be, sort of, every other chicken.
> *Interviewer*: You were doing two chickens at a time?
> *Employee*: Yes, both hands in chickens together. You hadn't got time to wipe your nose or do anything really.
> *Interviewer*: Did that line ever stop?
> *Employee*: Only if they had a breakdown, you know, a pin went in the line, or there was a breakdown or anything.
> *Interviewer*: So you were doing over 2000 chickens an hour?
> *Employee*: Yes.
> *Interviewer*: 14,000 chickens a day?
> *Employee*: Yes.
> *Interviewer*: What did you think about that?
> *Employee*: Hard work. Real hard work!

Similar experiences of unremitting 'hard work' have been found by researchers studying the harsh realities of factory life in different industries, for example, Pollert (1981) in the tobacco industry, Westwood (1984) in hosiery, Cavendish (1982) in motor components, Beynon (1973) and Linhart (1981) in cars, and Delbridge (1998) in auto components and consumer electronics. The experiences of employees are explored in closer detail, but for now, the emphasis is on the work organisation principles which give rise to the assembly line.

Henry Ford's methods

The name most commonly associated with the development of the assembly line is that of Henry Ford, whose unique contribution was in adapting Taylorist principles to a factory setting geared to the mass production of standardised products. Ford established a production method benchmark against which assembly line work has since been assessed, and the term 'Fordist' has come to be used to describe the combination of linear work sequencing, the interdependence of tasks, a moving assembly line, the use and refinement of dedicated machinery and specialised machine tools (for a detailed discussion, see Meyer, 1981). It has been argued that Fordism is therefore distinguishable from Taylorism in that it constitutes a form of work organisation designed for efficient mass production (Wood, 1989).

The success of Ford, however, can only be fully understood if seen as part of a system of industrial organisation that also sought to create, perpetuate and satisfy mass consumption. The development of mass markets provided the demand for large numbers of rapidly produced standardised products, epitomised by the output at the Highland Park factory which rose from 13,941 Model-T Fords in 1909 to 585,400 by 1916 (Williams, Haslam and Williams, 1992: 550). This volume of mass production was only possible because of the development of capital equipment capable of producing on a large scale and the creation of an efficient electricity supply to drive the machinery. In other words, mass production, mass consumption, technological innovation and segmented work organisation were ingredients in Ford's recipe for success. Consequently, as Littler (1985) has argued, Fordism came to predominate as the preferred form of organising work for mass production. It was adopted by Ford's main competitor in the United States, General Motors, and then by Ford's European rivals – Austin, Morris and Citroen. Fordism also transferred to other, newer industries such as electrical engineering and chemicals.

A widely accepted view is that Fordism is synonymous with mass production, rigidity and standardisation, and that the impact of the ideas pioneered by Ford has been widespread. However, there are some voices of dissent. Notable among these are Williams and colleagues (1987 and 1992), who contend that Fordism has become a stereotype, distorted over time by British and US academics who are keen to attribute failing industrial performance to the persistence of an outdated form of production. In a detailed analysis of Ford's production operations at Highland Park (1909–19), Williams, Haslam and Williams (1992) reveal a picture of greater flexibility and less standardisation of the product than most texts on the subject would suggest. Overall, however, such findings do little to dispel the picture of an authoritarian work regime with closely monitored, machine-paced, short-cycle and unremitting tasks.

As the chicken factory example illustrates, Fordist principles persist in contemporary work settings, and these are not restricted to factory work. It can be argued that the assembly line has been transposed into other work settings (see Excerpt 2.2).

McDonald's might be interpreted as displaying Fordist elements in terms of its mass production of standardised products for mass consumption. Similarly, the supermarket in general, and checkout operations in particular, epitomise a Fordist approach to retailing: the customer's items pass along the conveyor and are swept across the barcode reader by an operator who performs a monotonous series of repetitive actions. The flow-line, the dedicated machinery and the segmented work tasks are evidence of Fordist principles of work organisation. Thus the chicken, as an object for consumption, is typically reared through (Ford-like) battery farming, slaughtered and processed in a Fordist factory, and sold through a Fordist retail outlet (the supermarket) or even consumed as chicken pieces in a Fordist restaurant.

Excerpt 2.2

The white-collar assembly line?
Researchers undertaking an extensive study of call centres in Scotland have come to the conclusion that although not all call centres are identical, the majority of them can justifiably be seen as 'white-collar factories' because employees are subjected to Tayloristic management techniques and the type of routinised, repetitive work normally associated with the assembly line (Taylor and Bain, 1999; Taylor, Hyman, Mulvey and Bain, 2002). The following is a quote from their study:

> The typical call centre operator is young, female and works in a large, open plan office or fabricated building .... Although, probably full-time, she is increasingly likely to be a part-time permanent employee, working complex shift patterns which correspond to the peaks of customer demand. Promotion prospects and career advancement are limited so that the attraction of better pay and conditions in another call centre may prove irresistible. In all probability, work consists of an uninterrupted and endless sequence of similar conversations with customers she never meets. She has to concentrate hard on what is being said, jump from page to page on a screen, making sure that the details entered are accurate and that she has said the right things in a pleasant manner. The conversation ends and as she tidies up the loose ends there is another voice in her headset. The pressure is intense because she knows her work is being measured, her speech monitored, and it often leaves her mentally, physically and emotionally exhausted .... There is no question that the integration of telephone and computer technologies, which defines the call centre, has produced new developments in the Taylorisation of white-collar work.
>
> (Taylor and Bain, 1999: 115)

An alternative perspective is taken by Korczynski, Shire, Frenkel and Tam (1996) in their detailed analysis of three call centres (two in Australia and one in Japan). They argue that while the customer service representatives have routine aspects to their work, it is misleading to equate their jobs with the sort of routine work typically found in factories. This is because service work relies on the extensive use of social skills when dealing with customers, which can provide a source of creativity for employees. In short, they are cautious not to equate service work with routinisation or deskilling, yet also suggest that there is little evidence of substantial upskilling taking place, even though there were some opportunities for it to occur in their case study companies.

To sum up

The significance of Taylor, Ford and mass production for the way work has been organised is profound. These principles and methods changed the work process by introducing greater amounts of rigidity and regulation, which in turn had important consequences for the skill content of jobs. In particular, this raises the question of whether work, in general, is becoming less or more skilled. The evaluation of the different attempts to answer this question begins with the deskilling thesis.

Learning outcome 3: Explain the theory behind the deskilling thesis

Thesis – the deskilling of work

The year 1974 saw the publication of one of the most influential books concerned with the study of work: Harry Braverman's *Labor and Monopoly Capital*. Braverman's thesis is that an inevitable tendency towards the degradation and deskilling of work takes place as capitalists search for profits in increasingly competitive economic environments. His contribution to the study of work must not be underestimated. Although his thesis has since been subjected to a great deal of criticism, it played a fundamental role in injecting adrenaline into the lethargic 1970s body of industrial sociology, and it continues to have an impact on how work is analysed. Indeed the book was republished in 1998, which is evidence of its abiding relevance. The discussion below explains the central argument of this 'deskilling thesis' and identifies the main criticisms.

Harry Braverman's argument

At the risk of over-simplifying, Braverman's argument runs as follows. Managers perpetually seek to control the process by which a workforce's labour power (its ability to work) is directed towards the production of commodities (goods and services) that can be sold for a profit. The control of this labour process is essential because profit is accumulated through two stages: first, through the extraction of the surplus value of labour (the price of a commodity greater than the costs incurred in its production); and second, through the realisation of that value when the commodities are actually sold. These two stages are frequently referred to as 'valorisation'. In other words, managers are seeking to control the way work is organised, the pace of work and the duration of work, because these affect profitability. Thus, control of labour is the link between the purchase of labour power and valorisation. In Braverman's analysis the managerial obsession with labour control is the key to an understanding of capitalism, and leads managers to seek ways of reducing the discretion exercised by the workforce in performing their jobs. In order to exert their own control over the workforce and limit the control and influence of employees, managers are seen to pursue a general strategy of deskilling which, according to Braverman, can be identified in two forms: organisational and technological.

Organisational deskilling

Organisational deskilling is embedded in the Tayloristic principle of the separation of the conception and execution of work. The conceptual tasks (the more challenging and interesting parts of the job, such as planning, diagnosing problems and developing new working methods) are transferred to technical and managerial staff, while the execution of the work (often the mundane, less challenging part of the job) remains in the hands of shopfloor workers. Theoretically, this process allows managers both to limit the discretion of the shopfloor workers and to secure a monopoly over technical knowledge about the work, which can then be used to exercise greater direct control over the activities of the workforce.

> A necessary consequence of the separation of conception and execution is that the labor process is now divided between separate sites and separate bodies of workers. In one location, the physical processes of production are executed. In another are concentrated the design, planning, calculation and record-keeping... The physical processes of production are now carried out more or less blindly, not only by the workers who perform them, but often by lower ranks of supervisory employees as well. The production units operate like a hand, watched, corrected, and controlled by a distant brain.
>
> (Braverman, 1974: 124–5)

Technological deskilling

Technological deskilling occurs when automation is used to transfer discretion and autonomy from the shopfloor to the office (from blue-collar to white-collar workers) and to eliminate the need for some direct labour. Braverman focuses on the example of the operation of machines by numerical control (NC) – the latest technology at the time he was writing and before the invention of the microchip – which allowed the planning and programming of the machines to be undertaken away from the shopfloor by technical staff, who prepared punched paper tapes that contained the information for the machine to run automatically. Prior to NC, the machinists would use their own judgement and discretion to set and operate the machines, but they were subsequently left only with the relatively simple tasks of loading and switching the machines. In other words, a technological development (NC) allowed the separation of task conception from task execution. Numerical control has more recently been superseded by computer numerical control (CNC), which works on the same principle of separation of programming and operation, but is controlled through a microprocessor. This sort of new technology does not *inevitably* lead to a deskilling of work, but Braverman argues that managers selectively use automation to this end, in order to secure their central objective of exerting control over labour.

> In reality, machinery embraces a host of possibilities, many of which are systematically thwarted, rather than developed, by capital. An automatic system of machinery opens up the possibility of the true control over a highly productive factory by a relatively small corps of workers, providing these workers attain the level of mastery over the machinery offered by engineering knowledge, and providing they then share out among themselves the routines of the operation, from the most technically advanced to the most routine .... [But such a possibility] is frustrated by the capitalist effort to reconstitute and even deepen the division of labor in all its worst aspects, despite the fact that this division of labor becomes more archaic with every passing day .... The 'progress' of capitalism seems only to deepen the gulf between workers and machine and to subordinate the worker ever more decisively to the yoke of the machine ....The chief advantage of the industrial assembly-line is the control it affords over the pace of labor, and as such it is supremely useful to owners and managers whose interests are at loggerheads with those of their workers.
>
> (Braverman, 1974: 230–2)

There have been plenty of writers willing to comment on Braverman's work. McLoughlin and Clark (1994) divide these into 'sympathisers' and 'agnostics' (see Table 2.1). If you want to explore the issues in more detail, a good starting point is Thompson (1989) followed by the chapters in the edited collection by Knights and Willmott (1990). There is also a thorough and persuasive defence of the value of Braverman's thesis by Tinker (2002), who particularly takes to task the more recent postmodern criticisms of Braverman's analysis of the labour process (for instance, O'Doherty and Willmott, 2001). The main criticisms of and revisions to Braverman's thesis, but before reading this, attempt Exercise 2.3.

Exercise 2.3

What do you think?
Interview someone who has been employed in the same organisation for about ten years and ask them about the changes they have experienced. The interview need not be long, but you should structure it in such a way to ensure that you find out about the type of changes introduced and the effect they have had on work.

You must then use this information to assess whether this helps to substantiate or refute Braverman's deskilling thesis, and produce a written or verbal report. Remember there were two components to Braverman's argument, organisational deskilling and technological deskilling, so your interview should be designed in such a way as to elicit information on both these aspects of change. Your report should make explicit reference to these.

Table 2.1 The key critics of Braverman's thesis

Sympathisers	Agnostics
Accept the general approach but offer some refinement.	Acknowledge some value in the approach, but consider it inadequate.
Friedman, 1977a, b, 1990	Littler, 1982
Burawoy, 1979	Wood, 1982
Edwards, 1979	Littler and Salaman, 1982
Zimbalist, 1979	Knights, Willmott and Collinson, 1985
Armstrong, 1988	Knights and Willmott, 1986, 1990
Rose, 1988	Watson, 1986
Thompson, 1989	

Source: based on McLoughlin and Clark (1994).

Learning outcome 4: Outline and evaluate the main criticisms of the deskilling thesis

Six common criticisms of the deskilling thesis

Criticism 1: The deskilling thesis ignores alternative management strategies

Friedman (1977a, 1977b, 1990) argues that it is false to assume a single trend towards deskilling, since this fails to acknowledge the occasions when it is in the interest of managers to leave some discretion in the hands of employees. He calls this a strategy of 'responsible autonomy', and contrasts it with the 'direct control' which Braverman described. Friedman had in mind job enrichment and quality circles, but a contemporary expression of responsible autonomy is the notion of 'empowerment', whereby individual employees are expected to take responsibility for their own actions and initiate improvements in the way they work for the benefit of the organisation as a whole. Under responsible autonomy, employees are not deskilled but management continue to control the labour process. Thus, the argument here is that there is a wider choice in the mechanisms employed by management for the accumulation of capital than Braverman suggests.

Criticism 2: The deskilling thesis overstates management's objective of controlling labour

The control of the labour process is not an end in itself, but a means to achieve profit. To concentrate solely on labour control objectives ignores the importance of valorisation.

> It is not simply the *extraction* of surplus value in the labour process which is problematic for capital, but the *realisation* of that surplus through the sale of commodities in markets .... In other words we need to consider the *full circuit* of industrial capital as the starting point for analyses of changes in the division of labour: purchase of labour power; extraction of surplus value within the labour process; realisation of surplus value within product markets. There is no sound theoretical reason for privileging one moment in this circuit – the labour-capital relation within the labour process – if our objective is to account for changes (or variations) in the division of labour.
>
> (Kelly, 1985: 32, emphasis in original)

Moreover, the assumption that labour issues (rather than, for example, product development, marketing or investment) are the central concern of management during strategy formation is highly questionable (Purcell, 1989, 1995). Thus, as Littler and Salaman (1982: 257) contend, the process of capital accumulation acts beyond the labour process:

> The firm is primarily a capital fund with a legal corporate personality, linked to a production process .... While the production process results in a flow of income to the firm, this does not preclude alternative sources playing a major role or even a predominant one e.g. currency speculation, cumulative acquisition and asset stripping, commodity speculation, and credit manipulation of various kinds.

Child (1972, 1984, 1985) has highlighted the importance of political manoeuvring by managers in an organisation who, as key decision makers, are making 'strategic choices' that reflect their own values and vested interests. Thus, the argument here is that the internal politics of the organisation have a greater impact on deciding how the work is organised and the skill requirements than Braverman implies. The logic of capitalist accumulation may remain the over-arching tendency, but this can be mitigated by managers at all levels who are defending their vested interests.

As a consequence, the criticism is that Braverman's thesis underestimates the diversity and complexity of management objectives. The assumption that there is a single shared objective by management – that of labour control – ignores the plurality of interests within management, and the diverse and sometimes competing objectives (Batstone, Gourley, Levie and Moore, 1987; Buchanan and Boddy, 1983; Buchanan, 1986; Child, 1985). For example, in research into technological change in the UK provincial newspaper industry undertaken by one of the authors (Noon, 1994), it was found that when managers were questioned about the objectives for introducing new technology, they stressed different reasons which seemed to reflect their own functional responsibilities. In other words, the objective of increased control over labour was not the primary focus for most managers. Instead, they said technological change provided new opportunities in terms of product quality, product development, production control, efficiency and flexibility, together with a reduction in labour cost. This suggests that while labour control objectives may be relevant, they must be placed within the context of broader business objectives. As Armstrong (1989 and 1995) argues, the pervasive influence of management accountants at board level in UK companies tends to lead to more strategic thinking based on financial concerns rather than human resource matters.

Criticism 3: The deskilling thesis treats labour as passive

Employees have not been totally compliant, and have resisted change towards deskilling through both trade union collective action and individual action. Indeed, Edwards (1979) argues that management has sought more sophisticated forms of control as a direct response to (and as a way to suppress) worker resistance. He argues there has been a shifting reliance from the 'simple control' typified by the methods of direct supervision that Taylor advocated, to the 'technical control' of the mechanised assembly line (and more recent developments in computer technology) and the 'bureaucratic control' of workplace rules, procedures and a regulated internal labour market.

Criticism 4: The deskilling thesis understates the degree of consent and accommodation by employees

The work of Burawoy (1979) stands as an important counterpoint to Braverman in that it explores the extent to which the workforce *consents* to its own subordination. In part, this contrasts also with the previous criticism because it suggests that, rather than challenging management control of the labour process, the workforce may develop an informal culture that offers alternative definitions of the work situation and provides the opportunity for meaningful activity. The labour process is thereby redefined as a type of game through which the employees can derive satisfaction (for example, by beating the clock, outwitting the supervisor or manipulating the machinery). These games act as powerful means of social regulation (self-control) among the work groups, and obscure the exploitative nature of the labour process. In so doing, they unwittingly provide alternative additional sources of control for management. Such a brief summary hardly does justice to the subtleties of Burawoy's work.

Criticism 5: The deskilling thesis ignores gender

Beechey (1982) has argued that several problems emerge from the gender-blind nature of Braverman's argument. First, he fails to appreciate the importance of women's distinct role as domestic labourers because of his 'conceptual isolation of the family from the labour process and of both the family and the labour process from an analysis of the capitalist mode of production as a whole' (Beechey, 1982: 71). Second, his discussion of the pre-industrial family can be criticised for romanticising the past and ignoring the existence of patriarchal structures. Third, his concept of skill fails to explore gender dimensions; where it was noted that the social construction of skill is particularly important in creating 'gendered jobs', resulting in the under-valuation of women's labour power and skills.

Criticism 6: The deskilling thesis overlooks skill transfer possibilities

The failure of Braverman to recognise that deskilling in one area of work may be compensated by upskilling in another is most forcefully argued by Penn (1983, 1990), whose ideas are examined in some detail later. However, it might be argued that this constitutes one of the most unfair criticisms of Braverman. As Armstrong (1988) points out, Braverman explicitly recognised that change would occur unevenly across industries, and that in some instances new skills and technical specialities might be temporarily created within the workforce.

A defence of Braverman's thesis

A persuasive defence of Braverman comes from Armstrong (1988), who argues that:

> any sensitive reading of his work should reveal that Braverman actually regarded the deskilling tendencies of technical change as a system-wide dynamic or 'law of motion' in capitalist economies which could, temporarily and locally, be interrupted or reversed by a variety of factors, many of which have been rediscovered by his critics as supposed refutations.
>
> (Armstrong, 1988: 157)

This is an important point because, like all meta-theory, Braverman's thesis will never be able to explain all contingencies, yet this does not necessarily mean its analytical thrust is worthless. Indeed, as Armstrong suggests, many of the 'critics' are in practice offering revisions and amendments to the theory, rather than rejecting it.

Another defender of Braverman, Spencer (2000), suggests that the constant revisions and modifications to Braverman's original ideas by subsequent labour process theorists (academic commentators and researchers) show they have lost sight of the subversive intent of Braverman's original text, and have become obsessed with the social relations of the workplace, rather than the broader critique of capitalism. In short, Spencer laments the way that Braverman's ideas have been brought into the mainstream, and now run the risk of aiding rather than tormenting capitalism.

Braverman has also been defended against the attacks from academics of a post-modern leaning by Tinker (2002), who suggests that such attacks are deficient for a host of reasons, which he elaborates in detail. One of his main arguments is that the political aims and impact of Braverman's work are under-appreciated (not least the wide reading of the text by non-academics), and that postmodernist analysis:

> is blind to the social and historical specificity of Braverman's political task; exposing 'skill upgrading via education' as an ideology that obfuscates economic decline, recession and deindustrialization.
>
> (Tinker, 2002: 251)

He is also scathing about the philosophical position of postmodernists, which leaves them resorting to philosophies of indecision, and able to offer only frivolous, condescending and politically timorous advice to working people (ibid: 273). In contrast, for Tinker, the abiding value of Braverman's analysis is that 'It debunks academic dogmas of management, popular nostrums about skill upgrading via education, and the tacit promises to restore a "golden past" (ibid: 274).

While some commentators (for example, Lewis, 1995) remain unconvinced by defenders of Braverman, a re-reading of the original text reveals that Braverman had a less deterministic approach than is frequently attributed to him. Therefore, the deskilling thesis needs to be seen as an overall tendency, rather than a universal law applying in all cases.

> Braverman does *not* propound a universal law of deskilling. What he *does* claim is that there exists a general tendency for deskilling to occur in capitalist economies which will become actual where products and processes make this possible and where its effects are not masked by initiatives aimed at changing technology for other reasons.
>
> (Armstrong, 1988: 147, emphasis in original)

If Braverman's thesis is to be countered, it should be challenged on comparable terms: rather than a tendency towards deskilling, there is an opposite trend towards upskilling occurring within capitalist economies. It is to this antithesis that the discussion now turns.

Antithesis – the upskilling of work

Whereas the deskilling thesis drew from Marxist economic theory and the crisis of capitalism in industrial societies, the upskilling thesis tends to be based on the economics of human capital theory concerning a supposed new stage of capitalism: the post-industrial society. Human capital theorists (Becker, 1964; Fuchs, 1968) suggest that increasingly, firms are investing in their workforce through greater training provision, thus shifting the emphasis to 'human capital' as a central means of accumulating profit. It is held that rapid advances in technology require a more educated, better-trained workforce in order to cope with the increasing complexity of work tasks (Kerr, Dunlop, Harbison and Myers, 1960; Blauner, 1964). In turn, this is linked to an ever-reducing demand for manual/physical labour as Western capitalist economies undergo a structural shift away from manufacturing towards service sector activities (Fuchs, 1968).

This shift in the economic base of advanced industrial societies is considered by commentators such as Daniel Bell to signal a fundamental transformation to the post-industrial society, in which theoretical knowledge becomes 'the axis around which new technology, economic growth and the stratification of society will be organized' (Bell, 1973: 112). In other words, the upskilling thesis suggests that the general tendency is towards more complex work requiring higher levels of skill. As a consequence, the shift in the pattern of work organisation will not be towards degradation (as Braverman suggested) but to an enrichment of work. Excerpt 2.3 provides survey evidence of general upskilling in the UK, while Excerpt 2.4 reveals some findings from European surveys.

Excerpt 2.3

Upskilling in the UK (1986–2001)
Felstead, Gallie and Green (2002) undertook an analysis of various UK skills surveys in order to identify the changes in skill that have been occurring between 1986 and 2001. Although they conclude that there is a general pattern of increasing skills, they also note that this is accompanied by a marked decline in task discretion. Below are some of their key findings.

Qualifications
- A significant rise in employers' requirements for qualifications.
- A higher proportion of degree-level jobs (10 per cent in 1986 to 17 per cent in 2001).

Training
- Fewer jobs have required a cumulative training time of under three months: 66 per cent in 1986 falling to 61 per cent in 2001.

- Fewer jobs require under one month 'to learn to do well': 27 per cent in 1986 compared with 20 per cent in 2001.
- More jobs require employees to learn new things on the job: this requirement applied to 76 per cent of jobs in 1992 and 81 per cent in 2001.

Generic skills
(These are literacy, physical skills, number skills, technical know-how, higher-level communication, horizontal communication, client communication, planning, problem solving and checking.)

- A rise in the generic skill requirements of most jobs.
- A rise in nine out of ten of the measures of generic skills; the exception is the use of physical skills which has not changed.

Task discretion
- A marked decline in the control employees can exercise over their jobs. In 1986 52 per cent of employees reported they had a great deal of choice over the way they do their job, whereas in 2001 this proportion had fallen to 39 per cent. The proportions reporting a great deal of influence over what tasks are done fell from 42 percent in 1992 to 30 per cent in 2001.
- A decline occurred for both men and women.
- A particularly sharp decline was experienced by 'professional' workers.
- A marked decline was experienced by workers in the following sectors: education, public administration, finance, and real estate/business services.

Source: summarised from Felstead, Gallie and Green (2002: 10).

The upskilling thesis found expression in the concept of 'flexible specialisation' propounded by Piore and Sabel (1984). They argue that the crisis of accumulation under capitalism is leading to an important shift away from Fordism towards more craft-based, flexible, innovation-led and customer-focused work organisation. Thus, just as the move from traditional craft production to mass production constituted 'the first industrial divide', the move from mass production to flexible specialisation is described by Piore and Sabel as 'the second industrial divide'.

The new emphasis lies on flexible production systems which can meet the demands for customised products in increasingly diversified markets. In particular, developments in microelectronic technology allow for more flexibility in the use of capital equipment: machinery no longer needs to be dedicated to specific tasks but can be reprogrammed to perform a variety of tasks. Traditional production methods typically involve long set-up times for the machinery, which mean large production runs are necessary to recover the cost; short production runs for small batches are an inefficient use of the equipment. In contrast, computerised machinery requires shorter set-up times, enabling greater diversity of (small batch) production without incurring the inefficiencies. In other words, economies of *scale* are now complimented by economies of *scope*. This is important because customers are supposedly becoming increasingly discerning and want a greater variety of goods which allow them to express their individual identity (Sabel, 1982). Therefore, economies of scope become a necessity in a dynamic, competitive market. Computerised production and information-processing capabilities provide the technological infrastructure, and allegedly bring with them a demand for upskilled rather than deskilled labour.

Coupled with this are changes in work organisation that mean employees are expected to work in different ways. Principal among these is teamworking, which is seen as a move away from the individualised, segmented work processes to flexible teams of employees who are multiskilled and take greater responsibility for their work through increased task discretion (control over the work methods, time and quality). It is argued that working in this fashion requires employees to develop and use a wide range of skills. In particular this has been associated with various supposedly post-Fordist production techniques in manufacturing, such as lean production (Womack, Jones and Roos, 1991) and business process re-engineering (Hammer and Champy, 1993).

Excerpt 2.4

Skill change in Europe

Gallie (2005) assessed the impact of skill change in 15 EU countries by analysing the results of two surveys of employees – one conducted in 1996, the other in 2001. Skill change was measured by asking people whether or not their jobs have become more skilled, evaluating the amount of training received, and assessing the extent to which employees considered they had control over their work (the first two are measures of complexity, the third is a measure of discretion).

Among Gallie's findings are the following:

- The dominant trend is upskilling.
- The pace of upskilling slowed down after the mid-1990s.
- Women are less likely than men to have experienced increases in skill.
- The decline in the pace of upskilling has affected women and men in similar ways.
- The reduction in the pace of upskilling is evident in 12 of the 15 countries in Europe surveyed.
- The decline in the pace of upskilling is statistically significant only in Finland, Germany, Great Britain, Greece, Ireland, the Netherlands and Spain.

One particular aspect of skill that showed clear evidence of decline was job control (the measure of discretion). Employees were asked questions about whether they have a say in what happens in their jobs. Gallie found the following:

- There is a significant decline in job control between the two periods.
- Women were typically in jobs with lower opportunities for control than men in both 1996 and 2001, but the decline in job control was similar for both sexes.

- Job control scores declined in nine of the 15 countries, although the trend reached statistical significance in only seven countries: Belgium, France, Great Britain, Italy, the Netherlands, Spain and Sweden.
- Only in Denmark was there evidence of an increase in control over jobs.

Source: summarised from Gallie (2005).

Learning outcome 6: Outline and evaluate the main criticisms of the upskilling thesis

Five criticisms of the upskilling thesis

Criticism 1: The upskilling thesis falsely assumes that the growth of the service sector will create skilled jobs

The growth of the service sector and the associated importance of a customer orientation can give the impression that all white-collar workers are now engaged with handling customer interactions and that the traditional routinised factory work associated with manufacturing has given way to more varied, expressive forms of work involving customer interaction. It is certainly the case that customer-facing work involves the use of skills that require the management of emotions, but much of the new service work is as monotonous and dull as work on an assembly line.

Korczynski (2004) analysed the work of back-office staff in an insurance company and two banks in Australia. He found that work tended to be routinised with little scope for discretion in how the tasks were performed (particularly in the case of the insurance company). This was reinforced through performance-monitoring systems which set targets (for example, processing a set number of applications per day) and measured work quality. There was no customer interaction, staff were not required to have (or learn) customer-oriented skills, and on a day-to-day basis they referred to customers in an impersonal way. Echoing the findings of earlier case studies (Crompton and Jones, 1984; Sturdy, 1992), the conclusion that Korczynski drew is that back-office work in financial services resembles the formalised, routinised and regulated processes consistent with a traditional bureaucratic forms of work organisation. This makes back-office, service work very similar to Fordist production work.

Front-line service work – where the majority of the working day involves dealing with customers either face-to-face or over the phone – tends to be organised in ways that are slightly less rigid, because of the variation in customer interaction requiring social skills and elements of emotional labour. Even so, front-line service employees are typically faced with a huge amount of routine and repetitive activity. (See Excerpt 2.2 for two perspectives on call centre workers.) Korczynski (2002) uses the term 'customer-oriented bureaucracy' to suggest that the essential features of bureaucracy are present (the rules and procedures that constitute the formalised rationality of work organisation) but that the customer is cared for in the process.

The concept of the customer-oriented bureaucracy captures the requirement for the organisation to be both formally rational, to respond to competitive pressures to appeal to customers' wishes for efficiency, and to be formally irrational, to enchant, responding to the customers' desire for pleasure, particularly through the perpetuation of the enchanting myth of customer sovereignty.

(Korczynski, 2002: 64)

This means that employees have to work within clearly defined rules and follow procedures and protocols, while ensuring that customers feel satisfied about the service they are receiving and gain the impression that they are in control (the myth of customer sovereignty). This can require employees to use a range of skills to manage their own emotions and those of the customers.

Criticism 2: The upskilling thesis overstates the extent to which advanced technology requires higher skill levels from employees

The upskilling thesis is as vulnerable as its deskilling counterpart to the criticism that there are numerous managerial objectives which reflect vested interests and political manoeuvring, so the design of work will be based on these just as much as 'technical' decisions about skill requirements. In the 1980s, research revealed that managers can choose to implement technology in different ways that have variable skill consequences for employees. For example, in their study of United Biscuits, Buchanan and Boddy (1983) show that even within one company there can be a mixture of skill changes associated with the introduction of advanced technology which makes any generalisation of upskilling or deskilling difficult to substantiate. Similarly, Sorge, Hartman, Warner and Nicholas (1983) reveal how CNC technology was used by British managers to deskill shopfloor workers and turn them into mere machine minders, while in Germany the same technology was implemented in such a way as to integrate the (skilled) programming into the work of the operators, thereby enhancing their skill. Of additional relevance here is Zuboff's (1988) dual impact theory of technology.

Criticism 3: The upskilling thesis overstates the extent of change

Generally, theorists who support the upskilling thesis, and those who support flexible specialisation in particular, assume that a radical break with Fordism is taking place. However, this understates the resilience of mass production for mass markets. For example, the almost insatiable demand for consumer electronics over the past two decades typically has been met by the supply of goods manufactured using production systems that are labour intensive and low skilled (see for example Delbridge, Turnbull and Wilkinson, 1992; Sewell and Wilkinson, 1992a). Similarly, the flexible specialisation thesis overstates the extent to which small batch production will create upskilled and multiskilled workers. As Pollert (1991) and Smith (1989) point out, small batch production can and has adopted low-skilled, short-cycle assembly line techniques. Hence, the criticism here is that the upskilling thesis relies on a false dichotomy between mass and craft production (see for example Hyman, 1991; Williams, Cutler, Williams and Haslam, 1987; Wood, 1989).

Criticism 4: The upskilling thesis overstates the skill-enhancing impact of new working methods

Employees have not experienced an enhancement of their skills through teamworking to the extent that the upskilling thesis suggests. In an analysis of survey data covering the period from 1996 to 2001, Gallie, Felstead and Green (2004) found that teamworking in the UK was on the increase, but this was accompanied by a decline in task discretion (measured by asking people how much influence they had over how hard they worked, what tasks they did, how they did the tasks and quality standards). This means that although an increasing proportion of the workforce is working in teams, these are not the semi-autonomous teams envisaged by the upskilling thesis.

A survey of ten European countries (Benders, Huijen and Pekruhl, 2001) revealed that forms of team or group working existed in 24 per cent of the workplaces, but in the majority of these only a minority of core employees were covered, or else the groups only had a very restricted range of decision-making rights, mainly concerning the regulation of day-to-day tasks, such as scheduling the work and improving the work processes. Issues such as controlling absence or organising job rotation were least likely to be delegated, and in only 4 per cent of organisations were the majority of core workers in what might be described as semi-autonomous teams. There was also notable variation between countries, with organisations in Sweden and the Netherlands being the most likely both to have work groups and for such groups to possess real decision-making authority. Italy and Ireland were the countries with organisations least likely to have adopted group working. The authors of this European survey purposely used the term 'group working' rather than 'teamworking' because they argue it more accurately captures the range of forms or working arrangements, only some of which require upskilling.

Other studies confirm that the term 'teamworking' can incorporate a variety of meanings (Procter and Mueller, 2000), and in the case of service sector work, it has been shown that 'team' often signifies nothing more than a group of workers who share one supervisor (Frenkel, Korczynski, Shire and Tam, 1999), and as such, teamworking cannot be equated with upskilling.

Case studies can be particularly useful in revealing how changes such as increased flexibility and teamworking do not result in enhancing skills so much as increase the volume of work at the same skill level. For example, commenting on the impact of multiskilling in a case study of a bank, Grimshaw, Beynon, Rubery and Ward (2002: 105) note that 'multi-skilling was introduced with limited employee discretion over how to vary and control and the timing and division of tasks .... Expansion in the range of job content was associated with increased pressure and a strong loss of autonomy.' Equally, in their case study of a telecommunications call centre these authors found that teamworking did not involve multiskilling or job rotation, but was a form of teambuilding based on social activities during work time, representing an attempt by managers to break the monotony of the routinised work of employees.

Criticism 5: The upskilling thesis needs to be put into a global perspective

With the rise of the multinational organisation it is no longer sufficient to consider change simply in a national context. For example, a shift in the manufacture of consumer electronics from Western Europe to South-East Asia removes the demand for low-skilled work in one country, only to increase its demand in another. As a result, it becomes problematic to try to interpret a fall in the demand for low-skilled labour in one national context as a sign of general upskilling. Equally it may indicate a global redistribution of demand for skills, reflecting the mobility of capital in the search for lower labour costs and the pursuit of greater profitability.

A good illustration of this point is the tendency for large organisations in advanced capitalist economies to outsource parts of their customer services and back-office data processing to countries where labour is considerably cheaper. Typically Australian companies are outsourcing to India and Indonesia, UK companies to India, US companies to the Philippines and Costa Rica, and French companies to Morocco. This process, known as 'offshoring', means that when customers make an inquiry to their bank, insurance company, phone company or rail network they are likely to find themselves talking to an employee in a call centre in India or elsewhere. Service sector organisations can now use information and communication technology (allowing real-time interaction with customers) to relocate parts of their operation anywhere that can provide an equivalent but cheaper service. In addition to voice services, paper-based operations (such as customer complaints, application forms, financial transactions and so forth) can take place in remote locations without it affecting the quality of service. This global shift in the location of customer service work means that skill increase in one location may be matched with a decline in other locations, as organisations find new means of sustaining and accumulating profit – and of course this is not at all surprising to supporters of the deskilling thesis.

Excerpt 2.5

Cyber coolies in India?
A research institute funded by the Indian government has produced a damning report on the working conditions inside call centres. It has labelled the educated, intelligent graduates who work there as 'cyber coolies', and claims that they are wasting their talents on undertaking mindless, repetitive work for Western organisations.

According to *The Observer* newspaper, the study claims that the call centre workers

> are employed under constant surveillance, in an atmosphere similar to that in 'nineteenth century prisons or Roman slave ships'. Despite the relatively high salaries, and modern working environments, the study concludes that 'most of these youngsters are in fact burning out their formative years as cyber coolies' doing low-end jobs.
>
> The true monotony of the work is disguised by 'camouflaging work as fun' – introducing cafes, popcorn booths and ping-pong tables into the offices. Meanwhile, quotas for calls or emails successfully attended to are often fixed at such a high level 'that the agent has to burn out to fulfil it', the report claims.

With employees working through the night to cater for clients in different time zones, the work requires staff 'to live as Indian by day and Westerner after sun-down' and takes a 'heavy toll' on agents' physical and mental health, the study states. But more importantly, call centre work 'leads to a wastage of human resources and de-skilling of workers' which will have a high impact on Indian industry in the long-term.

Source: *Observer* (2005) 'Painful truth of the call centre cyber coolies', 30 October.

Exercise 2.4

What do you think?
Consider criticism number 5 of the upskilling thesis and read Excerpt 2.5.

1. What might be the limitations to the offshoring process that might mean some skilled jobs in the service sector cannot be transferred to places like India?
2. To what extent is technology playing a role in the offshoring process?
3. Have the so-called 'cyber coolies' been upskilled or deskilled by the offshoring? Explain your reasoning.
4. Who are the winners and losers in the case of offshoring to India?

To sum up

The upskilling thesis is as ambitious as the deskilling thesis in attempting to arrive at a theoretical framework that reflects a general tendency of skill change in one direction. However, in both cases the unidirectional argument needs to be qual-ified, as the various criticisms have shown. Indeed, the question of whether the dynamics of skill change can be simplified in such a way is highly problematic. A more robust theoretical approach might be to hypothesise multidirectional change within different sectors, industries, occupations and tasks. Three approaches which address such a synthesis.

Learning outcome 7: Describe alternative approaches to examining skill change

Syntheses – polarisation, compensation and the dual impact of automating and informating

There have been various attempts to synthesise the perspectives of deskilling and upskilling by arguing that both are occurring, with some people being upskilled while others are deskilled. This section reviews three different approaches to explain how and why this might occur: polarisation, compensation and the dual impact of technology. There is some commonality between the three approaches, and they should not be seen as competing theories but rather as complimentary explanations of the effects of upskilling and deskilling.

The polarisation of skills

The polarisation of skills perspective argues that different segments of the workforce will be affected in different ways. For instance, higher occupational groups such as professionals and managers might see their skill levels increase, while those lower in the occupational hierarchy, such as operatives, might experience a diminution in skill. Similarly, those workers on permanent, full-time contracts might be upskilled while their co-workers on part-time or fixed term contracts (and other nonstandard arrangements) might find they are given fewer opportunities to increase their skill levels. Polarisation approaches might also argue that the differences could be linked to structural features, such as the sector or industry, or argue that other contingencies, such as whether or not employees can exert influence through trade unions, will affect the likelihood of being upskilled or deskilled.

Research in the Netherlands (see Excerpt 6.6) and the United States reveals the differential impact of technological and organisational change on the work of different employees. Milkman's (1997) case study of the General Motors' plant in Linden, New Jersey depicts a complex picture of work transformation, but reveals how skilled workers were given opportunities to acquire new skills and retrain, while their semi-skilled counterparts on the production line were denied such opportunities. The consequence is upskilling for one group and deskilling for the other, hence a polarisation effect is occurring.

Excerpt 2.6

Skill polarisation in the Netherlands
As part of a research programme examining the effects of automation on job content, de Witte and Steijn (2000) analysed the responses of 1022 Dutch employees to a questionnaire survey. The respondents were asked to report on the extent of autonomy in their work, the complexity of their job (both measures being used to assess the skill level of their jobs) and the extent of automation. They were also asked a range of background questions. Their research reveals a wide range of findings, but those of most relevance to us are the following:

- There is a general trend in upskilling associated with increasing automation.
- Professionals and white-collar workers experience the most upskilling.
- The upskilling is most evident among professionals.
- Blue-collar workers are least likely to experience upskilling.
- Some blue-collar workers experience substantial deskilling.

To explain the deskilling amongst blue-collar workers, de Witte and Steijn suggest that internal differentiation is occurring. This term means that automation leads to an increase in the complexity of the job but not the autonomy of the job. This internal differentiation is less likely to occur amongst the professional and white-collar workers – in other words, automation brings both an increase in complexity and an increase in autonomy for the employee.

The compensatory theory of skill

The argument put forward by proponents of the compensatory theory (Penn and Scattergood, 1985; Penn, 1990; Penn, Gasteen, Scattergood and Sewel, 1994) is that the general theories of both upskilling and deskilling are inadequate to explain the complexity of skill change, and that empirically derived middle-range theory offers a better way forward. The proposition is that technological change generates *both* deskilling and upskilling, with empirical expression in two forms. First, the effects are international: 'the shift of routine manufacturing from advanced, core economies to less developed, peripheral economies, and the increasing internationalisation of the capital goods (machinery) industry' (Penn, 1990: 25). Second, the effects differ between and within occupations: some groups are advantaged by having a more skilled and central role, while others find themselves deskilled and marginalised. More specifically:

> technological changes tend to deskill *direct productive roles* but put an increased premium on a range of *ancillary skilled tasks* that are associated with the installation, maintenance and programming of automated machinery. This is because modern machinery incorporating micro-electronics tends to simplify many production skills but renders maintenance work far more complex .... [However] within maintenance work itself ... there is a far greater need for new electronic based maintenance skills than for traditional mechanical maintenance skills.
>
> (Penn, 1990: 25, emphasis in original)

There is a somewhat technologically-determinist undertone to part of this argument: the suggestion that microelectronics have tendencies to impact on certain jobs, independent of the actions and choices of those who design, commission or purchase the technology. Nevertheless, the general thrust of the argument is of interest since it highlights the importance of acknowledging a broader picture of skill change across occupational groups, industries and national contexts.

Automating and informating – the dual impact on skill change

The important role of advanced technology in reconfiguring skills is explored in detail by Zuboff (1988). She argues that a distinction must be drawn between the processes of *automating* and *informating*, since they have impacted upon skills in different ways. The process of automating work operations involves the replacement of living labour with technology, thus it is characterised by a deskilling of work and a reassertion of management control over the work process. Increasingly, however, technological developments also provide an opportunity to generate detailed information about the work operations themselves which, if systematically gathered and analysed, increases the visibility of the productive and administrative work undertaken in an organisation. In other words, technology is informating the work process, and the data requires interpretation through the use of cognitive ability. This constitutes an upskilling of work and provides 'a deeper level of transparency to activities that had been either partially or completely opaque' (Zuboff, 1988: 9).

Taken together, the processes of automating and informating lead to a reduction in action-centred skills (doing) but an increase in intellective skills (analysing). At the same time:

> these dual capacities of information technology are not opposites; they are hierarchically integrated. Informating derives from and builds upon automation. Automation is a necessary but not sufficient condition for informating.
>
> (Zuboff, 1988: 11)

Moreover, Zuboff argues that although automating displaces human presence, it is not yet clear what the full effects of informating are. While managers can choose either to exploit or to ignore the informating process, her own case study evidence suggests that the tendency has been for managers to stress the automating process and ignore the informating potential. This is not surprising because the informating capacities of advanced technology force managers to rethink traditional structures, work organisation and forms of control.

> The shifting grounds of knowledge invite managers to recognize the emergent demands for intellective skills and develop a learning environment in which such skills can develop. That very recognition contains a threat to managerial authority, which depends in part upon control over the organization's knowledge base.... Managers who must prove and defend their own legitimacy do not easily share knowledge or engage in inquiry. Workers who feel the requirements of subordination are not enthusiastic learners .... Techniques of control that are meant to safeguard authority create suspicion and animosity, which is particularly dysfunctional when an organization needs to apply its human energies to inventing an alternative form of work organization better suited to the new technological context.
>
> (Zuboff, 1988: 391–2)

The analysis presented by Zuboff is detailed, so this summary cannot really do justice to the subtlety of her argument. Nevertheless, it illustrates how both the deskilling and upskilling theses are inadequate as single explanations of skill change, because while the former concentrates on the process of automating, the latter is focused on the process of informating. As a result, the dual impact of advanced technology is overlooked by both approaches.

To sum up

It is notable that the syntheses above are based more firmly on empirical research than either the deskilling or upskilling thesis, and readily address the complexity of skill change. All three syntheses identify the possibility of deskilling and upskilling occurring simultaneously, and therefore they reject the notion of an overall general tendency in one direction only. In moving away from general theorising to context-specific understanding of skill change, they can more easily accommodate the diversity of empirical evidence, and they converge in concluding that the overall picture is one of *differing experiences* of skill change.

Learning outcome 8: Use the work categorisation framework to analyse jobs

Discussion – towards a conceptual framework

The possible trends in work transformation represented by the various approaches explored above can be depicted by developing a simple framework. As with any conceptual schema that seeks to simplify the complexities embedded in work organisation, this is necessarily limited in its explanatory powers, but it does allow us to theorise some analytical distinctions. The framework draws from Fox (1974), Friedmann (1961) and Littler (1982) by proposing that work can be described as varying along two dimensions:

- *The range of work.* Work can vary according to the range of tasks that the employee performs. At one extreme, an employee will perform a very narrow range of tasks, while at the other extreme the employee will be expected to perform a wide range of different tasks.
- *The discretion in work.* This refers to the extent to which employees have the ability to exercise choice over how the work is performed, deciding such aspects as the pace, quality, quantity and scheduling of work. At one extreme there will be very little opportunity for employees to use their discretion in this way, while at the other extreme the work will require employees constantly to use discretion in completing the tasks.

By combining these two dimensions as in Figure 2.1, it is possible to visualise the way jobs may vary and to plot four ideal-type cases:

1. *Specialist work*: high discretion over a narrow range of work.
2. *Specialised work*: a narrow range of prescribed tasks.
3. *Generalised work*: a wide range of prescribed tasks.
4. *Generalist work*: high discretion over a wide range of work.

The best way of illustrating this typology is to look at a single work setting and assess how different jobs within that setting can be placed in one of these four

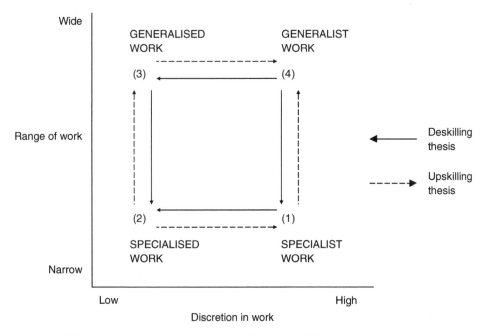

Figure 2.1   Work categorisation framework and trends in skill change

categories. For example, in a hospital the paramedics and nurses are undertaking generalised work, the doctors perform generalist work, the porters do specialised work and the surgeons are responsible for specialist work. To take another example, consider a nightclub. The manager is doing generalist work, the DJ is doing specialist work, the bar staff are doing generalised work and the bouncers are doing specialised work. This type of categorisation can be undertaken for any workplace. Of course not all jobs will fit neatly into one category, but that is always a limitation of such frameworks. However, if a job does not fit neatly into a category it may well indicate that the work is undergoing a transition – the sort of skill change that we discussed above and elaborate below.

Exercise 2.5

What do you think?
Think of a workplace with which you are familiar, list the main jobs and attempt to categorise them using the work categorisation framework. Remember, this framework cannot tell us about the importance of the work. It does not indicate the value of the work, but it helps us to classify the nature of the work.

Now take several of these jobs and speculate how they could change along the two dimensions (range and discretion) in line with the two theses. You will need to think about the specific tasks required by the jobs.

Learning outcome 9: Explain the relationship between skill change and work organisation paradigms

Mapping the skill changes

In addition to classifying the nature of jobs, the work categorisation framework can be used to show the trends proposed by the skill change theses:

- The deskilling thesis is based on the premise that there is a general trend towards low-discretion jobs comprising a narrow range of tasks. This manifests itself in the form of a degradation of work along the 'discretion' dimension. In other words, discretion is removed from generalist work (making it more generalised) or from specialist work (making it more specialised). Similarly the deskilling thesis suggests a simplification of work along the 'range' dimension, so the work would entail a narrower range of tasks. This would turn generalised work into specialised work, and generalist work initially into specialist work, and then into specialised work through the degradation process. These trends are represented by the solid arrows in Figure 2.1.
- The upskilling thesis identifies an opposite trend towards high-discretion jobs comprising a wide range of tasks. There is an enrichment of work along the 'discretion' dimension: by increasing the extent of discretion, specialised work becomes increasingly specialist and generalised work becomes increasingly generalist. In addition, the upskilling thesis suggests that multi-tasking is becoming a feature of all work, so there are changes along the 'range' dimension. Specialised work is becoming more generalised and specialist work is becoming more generalist. The broken arrows in Figure 2.1 show these trends.
- Those researchers who reject a general tendency of either deskilling or upskilling would argue that a mixed pattern emerges. This means that change could occur along any of the paths represented by the arrows, and such changes are likely to vary greatly both between and within countries, sectors, industries, occupations, workplaces and workgroups.

Conclusion – mapping skill change onto work organisation paradigms

Finally, we can return to the issue of work organisation with which we began the chapter. We argued that Taylorist and Fordist methods have had a dominant influence on work organisation, so how do these relate to the different theories of skill change? In Figure 2.2, the work categorisation framework is drawn again, but this time we have mapped onto it the dominant forms of work organisation that can be associated with each work category. The term 'paradigm' – which means a distinctive pattern or approach – can be used to describe these forms of work organisation. In other words, it is possible to refer to, for example, the Fordist paradigm or the post-Fordist paradigm. So what do these terms mean, and how do they relate to the theories of skill change?

The word 'Fordism' appears in all the paradigms. This is no accident because the Fordist paradigm is considered by most commentators to have had a massive impact on how work was organised during the twentieth century. That is why we discussed it so much at the beginning of this chapter. As a result of this dominance, other paradigms of work organisation can be defined in relation to Fordism. Therefore:

- *Post-Fordism:* means 'after Fordism' and refers to types of work organisation that do not rely on the principles of Taylor or the methods of Ford.
- *Neo-Fordism:* means 'new Fordism' and refers to types of work organisation that have *adopted* many of the basic methods of Ford, but have *adapted* them – particularly through more flexible working practices – to fit contemporary circumstances.
- *Ante-Fordism:* means 'before Fordism' and refers to types of work organisation that are based on methods of craft-based skills, often associated with the independent, self-employed artisan.

The deskilling and upskilling theses both accept that the dominance of craft/artisan production in the nineteenth century gave way to Fordism, which dominated the majority of the twentieth century, but they offer contrasting interpretations of how work organisation is now changing. The upskilling thesis suggests that a dramatic change has taken place in advanced capitalist economies during the final quarter of the twentieth century. It is suggested that this constitutes a 'paradigm shift' to

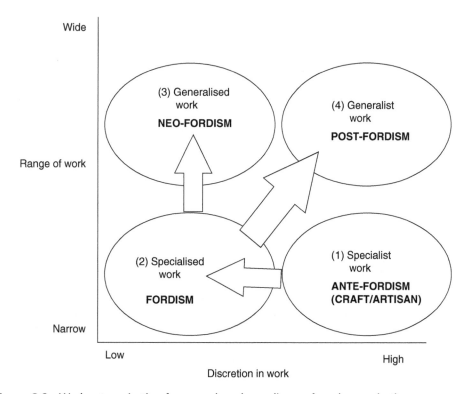

Figure 2.2 Work categorisation framework and paradigms of work organisation

post-Fordism based on new concepts of work organisation (incorporating multi-skilled workers, self-managed teams, networked organisations and teleworking), an increasingly dominant service-based economy, and frequently characterised as the post-industrial society in which knowledge workers dominate.

In contrast, the deskilling thesis suggests that the Fordism paradigm is continually being renewed as the dominant mode of work organisation under capitalism, so there has been no paradigm shift. The consequent effect is to perpetuate specialised work comprising a narrow range of low-discretion tasks. A variant of this deskilling approach comes from commentators who suggest that Fordism has evolved into neo Fordism (see for example Harvey, 1989). This perspective contends that by introducing multi-tasking, new management techniques (such as just-in-time, lean production and business process re-engineering) and increasingly automated and internationalised production processes, Fordism enters a new era of capitalism. Thus, proponents of this view (for example Aglietta, 1979) stress the importance of recognising continuity with the past, rather than characterising change as a quantum leap into a new dimension of capitalism. From this perspective, new forms of work organisation continue to replicate traditional divisions of labour and produce essentially dispiriting and alienating experiences for employees, who cope with these in the best way that they can, and who sometimes join together for collective support to make their voices heard.

References

Aglietta, M. (1979) *A Theory of Capitalist Regulation*, London: New Left Books.

Armstrong, P. (1988) 'Labour and monopoly capital', in R. Hyman and W. Streeck (eds), *New Technology and Industrial Relations*, Oxford: Blackwell: 143–59.

Armstrong, P. (1989) 'Management, labour process and agency', *Work, Employment and Society*, 3 (3): 307–22.

Armstrong, P. (1995) 'Accountancy and HRM', in J. Storey (ed.), HRM: *A Critical Text*, London: Routledge: 142–63.

Bain, P., Watson, A., Mulvey, G., Taylor, P. and Gall, G. (2002) 'Taylorism, targets and the pursuit of quality by call centre management', *New Technology, Work and Employment*, 17 (3): 170–85.

Batstone, E., Gourlay, S., Levie, H. and Moore, R. (1987) *New Technology and the Process of Labour Regulation*, Oxford: Clarendon.

Becker, G. (1964) *Human Capital*, New York: National Bureau of Economic Research.

Beechey, V. (1982) 'The sexual division of labour and the labour process: a critical assessment of Braverman', in S. Wood (ed.), *The Degradation of Work?*, London: Hutchinson: 54–73.

Bell, D. (1973) *The Coming of Post-Industrial Society*, New York: Basic Books.

Benders, J., Huijen, F. and Pekruhl, U. (2001) 'Measuring group work: findings and lesions from a European survey', *New Technology, Work and Employment*, 16 (3):204–17.

Beynon, H. (1973) *Working for Ford*, Harmondsworth: Penguin.

Blauner, R. (1964) *Alienation and Freedom*, Chicago: University of Chicago Press.

Braverman, H. (1974) *Labor and Monopoly Capital*, New York: Monthly Review Press.

Buchanan, D. A. (1986) 'Management objectives in technical change', in D. Knights and H. Willnott (eds), *Managing the Labour Process*, Aldershot: Gower: 67–84.

Buchanan, D. and Boddy, D. (1983) *Organisations in the Computer Age: Technological Imperatives and Strategic Choice*, Aldershot: Gower.

Burawoy, M. (1979) *Manufacturing Consent*, Chicago: University of Chicago Press.

Cavendish, R. (1982) *Women on the Line*, London: Routledge.

Child, J. (1985) 'Managerial strategies, new technology and the labour process', in D. Knights, H. Willmott and D. Collinson (eds), *Job Redesign*, Aldershot: Gower: 107–41.

Crompton, R. and Jones, G. (1984) *White Collar Proletariat*, London: Macmillan.

De Witte, M. and Steijn, B. (2000) 'Automation, job content and underemployment', *Work, Employment and Society*, 14 (2): 245–64.

Delbridge, R., Turnbull, P. and Wilkinson, B. (1992) 'Pushing back the frontiers: management control and work intensification under JIT/TQM factory regimes', *New Technology*, Work and Employment, 7 (2): 97–106.

Edwards, R. (1979) *Contested Terrain: The Transformation of the Workplace in the Twentieth Century*, London: Heinemann.

Felstead, A., Gallie, D. and Green, F. (2002) *Work Skills in Britain, 1986–2001*, London: Department for Education and Skills.

Felstead, A., Gallie, D. and Green, F. (2004) 'Job complexity and task discretion', in C. Warhurst, I. Grugulis and E. Keep (eds), *The Skills That Matter*, Basingstoke: Palgrave: 148–69.

Fox, A. (1974) *Beyond Contract*, London: Faber and Faber.

Frenkel, S. J., Korczynski, M., Shire, K. A. and Tam, M. (1999) *On the Front Line: Organization of Work in the Information Economy*, New York: Cornell UniversityPress.

Friedman, A. (1977a) *Industry and Labour: Class Struggle at Work and Monopoly Capitalism*, London: Macmillan.

Friedman, A. (1977b) 'Responsible autonomy versus direct control over the labour process', *Capital and Class*, 1 (Spring): 43–57.

Friedman, A. (1990) 'Managerial activities, techniques and technology: towards a complex theory of the labour process', in D. Knights and H. Willmott (eds), *Labour Process Theory*, London: Macmillan: 177–208.

Friedmann, G. (1961) *The Anatomy of Work*, London: Heinemann.

Fuchs, V. (1968) *The Service Economy*, New York: Basic Books.

Gallie, D. (2005) 'Work pressures in Europe 1996–2001: trends and determinants', *British Journal of Industrial Relations*, 43 (3): 351–75.

Gallie, D., Felstead, A. and Green, F. (2004) 'Changing patterns of task discretion in Britain', Work, *Employment and Society*, 18 (2): 243–66.

Grimshaw, D., Beynon, H., Rubery, J. and Ward, K. (2002) 'The restructuring ofcareer paths in large service sector organizations: delayering, upskilling and polarisation', *Sociological Review*, 50 (1): 89–116.

Hammer, M. and Champy, J. (1993) *Reengineering the Corporation: A Manifesto for Business Revolution*. New York: Harper Business.

Harvey, D. (1989) *The Condition of Postmodernity*, Oxford: Blackwell.

Hyman, R. (1991) 'Plus ça change? The theory of production and the production of theory', in A. Pollert (ed.), *Farewell to Flexibility?* Oxford: Blackwell: 259–83.

Kelly, J. (1982) *Scientific Management, Job Redesign and Work Performance*, London: Academic Press.

Kerr, C., Dunlop, J. T., Harbison, F. H. and Myers, C. A. (1960) *Industrialism and Industrial Man*, London: Heinemann.

Knights, D. and Willmott, H. (eds) (1990) *Labour Process Theory*, London: Macmillan.

Korczynski, M. (2002) *Human Resource Management in Service Work*, Basingstoke: Palgrave.

Korczynski, M. (2004) 'Back-office service work: bureaucracy challenged?', *Work, Employment and Society*, 18 (1): 97–114.

Korczynski, M., Shire, K., Frenkel, S. and Tam, M. (1996) 'Front line work in the "new model service firm": Australian and Japanese comparisons', *Human Resource Management Journal*, 6 (2): 72–87.

Lewis, A. (1995) 'The deskilling thesis revisited: on Peter Armstrong's defence of Braverman', *Sociological Review*, 43 (3): 478–500.

Littler, C. R. (1982) *The Development of the Labour Process in Capitalist Societies*, Aldershot: Gower.

Littler, C. R. (1985) 'Taylorism, Fordism and job design' in D. Knights, H. Willmott and D. Collinson (eds), *Job Redesign*, Aldershot: Gower: 10–29.

Littler, C. R. and Salaman, G. (1982) 'Bravermania and beyond: recent theories ofthe labour process', *Sociology*, 16 (2): 251–69.

McLoughlin, I. and Clark, J. (1994) *Technological Change at Work*, 2nd edn, Milton Keynes: Open University Press.

Meyer, S. (1981) *The Five–Dollar Day: Labor Management and Social Control in the Ford Motor Co., 1908–21*, Albany, NY: SUNY Press.

Milkman, R. (1997) *Farewell to the Factory: Auto Workers in the Late Twentieth Century*, Berkeley: University of California Press.

Morgan, G. (1986) *Images of Organization*, London: Sage.

O'Doherty, D. and H. Willmott (2001) 'Debating labour process theory: the issue ofsubjectivity and the relevance of poststructuralism', *Sociology* 35: 457–76.

Palmer, B. (1975) 'Class, conception and conflict', *Review of Radical Political Economics*, 7 (2): 31–49.

Penn, R. (1983) 'Theories of skill and class structure', *Sociological Review*, 31 (1): 22–38.

Penn, R. (1990) *Class, Power and Technology*, Cambridge: Polity Press.

Penn, R. and Scattergood, H. (1985) 'Deskilling or enskilling? An empirical investigation of recent theories of the labour process', *British Journal of Sociology*, 36 (4): 611–30.

Penn, R., Gasteen, A., Scattergood, H. and Sewel, J. (1994) 'Technical change and the division of labour in Rochdale and Aberdeen', in R. Penn, M. Rose and J.Rubery (eds), *Skill and Occupational Change*, Oxford: Oxford University Press: 130–56.

Piore, M. J. and Sabel, C. F. (1984) *The Second Industrial Divide*, New York: Basic Books.

Pollert, A. (1981) *Girls, Wives, Factory Lives*, London: Macmillan.

Pollert, A. (ed.) (1991) *Farewell to Flexibility?*, Oxford: Blackwell.

Procter, S. and Mueller, F (eds) (2000) *Teamworking*, Basingstoke: Macmillan.

Purcell, J. (1989) 'The impact of corporate strategy on human resource management', in J. Storey (ed.), *New Perspectives on Human Resource Management*, London: Routledge: 67–91.

Purcell, J. (1995) 'Corporate strategy and its link with human resource management strategy', in J. Storey (ed.), *Human Resource Management: A Critical Text London*: Routledge: 63–86.

Ritzer, G. (1993) *The McDonaldization of Society*, Thousand Oaks, Calif.: Pine ForgePress.

Ritzer, G. (1998) *The McDonaldization Thesis*, London: Sage.

Rose, M. (1988) *Industrial Behaviour*, 2nd edn, Harmondsworth: Penguin.

Sabel, C. F. (1982) *Work and Politics: The Division of Labour in Industry*, Cambridge: Cambridge University Press.

Schein, E. H. (1965) *Organizational Psychology*, Englewood Cliff, NJ: Prentice-Hall.

Sewell, G and Wilkinson, B. (1992a) 'Empowerment or emasculation? Shop floor surveillance in a total quality organisation', in P. Blyton and P. Turnbull (eds), *Reassessing Human Resource Management*, London: Sage: 97–115.

Smith, C. (1989) 'Flexible specialisation, automation and mass production', *Work, Employment and Society*, 3 (2): 203–22.

Sorge, A., Hartman, G., Warner, M. and Nicholas, I. (1983) *Microelectronics and Manpower in Manufacturing Applications of Computer Numerical Control in Great Britain and West Germany*, Aldershot: Gower.

Spencer, D. (2000) 'Braverman and the contribution of labour process analysis tothe critique of capitalist production: twenty-five years on', *Work, Employment and Society*, 14 (2): 223–43.

Sturdy, A. (1992) 'Clerical consent', in A. Sturdy, D. Knights and H. Willmott (eds), *Skill and Consent*, London: Routledge.

Taylor, F. W. (1911) *The Principles of Scientific Management*, New York: Harper.

Taylor, P. and Bain, P. (1999) '"An assembly line in the head": work and employee relations in the call centre', *Industrial Relations Journal*, 30 (2): 101–17.

Taylor, P., Hyman, J., Mulvey, G. and Bain, P. (2002) 'Work organisation, control and the experience of work in call centres', *Work, Employment and Society*, 16 (1): 133–50.

Thompson, P. (1989) *The Nature of Work*, 2nd edn, London: Macmillan.

Tinker, T. (2002) 'Spectres of Marx and Braverman in the twilight of postmodernistlabour process research', Work, *Employment and Society*, 16 (2): 251–81.

Westwood, S. (1984) *All Day Every Day*, London: Pluto.

Williams, C. L. (1992). 'The glass escalator: hidden advantages for men in the"female" professions', *Social Problems*, 39: 253–66.

Williams, K., Cutler, T., Williams, J. and Haslam, C. (1987) 'The end of mass production?', *Economy and Society*, 16 (3): 405–39.

Williams, K., Haslam, C. and Williams, J. (1992) 'Ford versus "Fordism": the beginning of mass production?' *Work, Employment and Society*, 6 (4): 517–55.

Womack, J. P., Jones, D. T. and Roos, D. (1990) *The Machine that Changed the World*, New York: Rawson Macmillan.

Wood, S. (ed.) (1989) *The Transformation of Work?* London: Unwin Hyman.

Zuboff, S. (1988) *In the Age of the Smart Machine*, Oxford: Heinemann.

CHAPTER 3

Studying work and organizations

CHAPTER OUTLINE

- Introduction
- Classical approaches to studying work
- Contemporary theories of work organizations
- The value of theory about contemporary organizational behaviour
- Summary and end-of-chapter features
- Chapter case study 1: Butting out smoking in Russia
- Chapter case study 2: Research at Aeroprecision AB

CHAPTER OBJECTIVES

After completing this chapter, you should be able to:

- explain the classical approaches to studying work through the ideas of Marx, Durkheim and Weber
- explain contemporary theories of work organizations and the importance of theory to understanding work and behaviour in the workplace

---

Introduction

This chapter examines classical and contemporary approaches to studying work and work organizations. We begin by considering the classical social theories about paid work through the ideas of Marx, Weber and Durkheim. These can be described as classical partly because they had their roots in European industrialization and culture – from about 1800 through to the early 1900s – and also because, in their response to industrial capitalism, the early social theorists set out a series of themes, concepts, assumptions, problems and ideas that continue to exercise an enormous influence over contemporary organizational theory. As others have pointed out, both the perspectives of analysis that are clearly set out in the works of the classical theorists, and the characteristic focuses of those traditions, continue to dominate study of the sociology of work.[1–3]

Over the last three decades not only have organizations fundamentally changed how they organize work, but new approaches and concepts have also been developed for studying work organizations. In the 1970s, the orthodox consensus on organization theory focused on 'functionalism', which emphasized consensus and coherence rather than asymmetrical power relations and conflict.[4] The key concept is that of the organization as a 'system' that functions effectively if it achieves explicit goals, which are formally defined through 'rational' decision making. Alternative theoretical approaches have since challenged the supremacy of functionalism.

A multitude of contemporary theories of formal organizations exist, so we cannot hope to do justice to the complexities of such a wide-ranging debate. We therefore seek here to highlight the major distinguishing themes related to work and organizations. Drawing on the work of Keith Grint,[5] we review 12 competing theoretical perspectives or 'conversations' in organization theory: the technical, human relations, neo-human relations, systems thinking, contingency, cultures, learning, control, feminist, social action, political and postmodernist perspectives.

Classical approaches to studying work

Marx, Durkheim and Weber each analysed the new work forms, but also placed their analysis within a wider discourse on modern society and social change. While Karl Marx focused on social fragmentation, conflict and social change, Emile Durkheim concerned himself with social fragmentation and the nature of order, and Max Weber developed his theory of rationality and bureaucracy.

Karl Marx (1818–83)

Marx believed that industrialization was a necessary stage for the eventual triumph of human potential, but that the mainspring of this social formation was capitalism, and not industrialism as such. It is only capitalism that carries within it the seeds of its own destruction. For Marx, the human species is different from all other animal species, not because of its consciousness, but because it alone produces its own means of subsistence.

Marx's argument is that what distinguishes humans from other animals is that our labour creates something in reality that previously existed only in our imagination:

> We presuppose labour in a form that stamps it as exclusively human ... But what distinguishes the worst architect from the best bees is this, that the architect raises his structure in imagination before he erects it in reality. At the end of every labour process we get a result that existed in the *imagination* of the labourer at its commencement. He not only effects a change of form in the material on which he works, but he also realizes a purpose. (ref 6, p. 178, emphasis added)

Plate 1 Karl Marx
Source: Marxists Internet Archive.

Marx calls this process whereby humans create external objects from their internal thoughts objectification. This labour does not just transform raw materials or nature; it also transforms humans, including human nature, people's needs and their consciousness. We can begin to understand Marx's concept of objectification by thinking of the creative activity of an artist. The artist's labour is a representation of the imagination of the artist: 'the art work is an objectification of the artist'.[7] In addition, through the labour process, the artist's ideas of the object change, or the experience, may prompt a new vision or creativity that needs objectification. Labour, for Marx, provides the means through which humans can realize their true human powers and potential. By transforming raw materials, we transform ourselves, and we also transform society. Thus, according to Marx, the transformation of the individual through work and the transformation of society are inseparable.

objectification: Karl Marx's term to describe the action of human labour on resources to produce a commodity, which under the control of the capitalist remains divorced from and opposed to the direct producer

Marx's discussion of work under capitalism focuses on the nature of employment relationships. Under capitalism, the aim is to buy labour at sufficiently low rates to make a profit. Marx is careful to distinguish between 'labour' and 'labour power'. Human labour is the actual physical or mental activity incorporated in the body of the worker. Labour power, on the other hand, refers to the *potential* of labour to add use value to raw materials or commodities. This labour power is bought by the capitalist at a value less than the value it creates. In purchasing the worker's potential or capacity to labour and add use values to materials, at a wage level less than the value created by the worker's labour, the capitalist is able to make a profit.

We can begin to appreciate the significance of Marx's use of the term 'labour power' when we think of it as a promise: it is therefore indeterminate, and there may be a gap between the potential or promise of labour and the actual labour. This distinction between 'labour' and 'labour power' allowed Marx to locate the precise mechanism that creates profit in capitalist societies. It also gives rise to the creation of two classes that are potentially, if not always in practice, in conflict with each other.

Capitalism involves the work relationship between the buyers and sellers of labour power. Marx's concept of surplus value is rooted in this social relationship. Surplus value is the value remaining when the worker's daily costs of subsistence have been subtracted from the value that she or he produces for the capitalist. As such, it is unpaid and 'goes to the heart of the exploitation of the worker'.[8]

surplus value: the portion of the working day during which workers produce value that is appropriated by the capitalist

In the workplace, the primacy of profit and conflict relationships gives rise to three broad necessary features of activity and change. Each of these involves substantial shifts in the work performed. Most significant is the need for the capitalist to centralize the labour power that is purchased, and to discipline the interior of the factory, by organizing space, time and the behaviour of workers whose commitment is unreliable. The aim is to close or minimize the gap between potential labour power and actual labour power. For Marx, the accumulation of profit is inevitably and irrevocably mediated by managerial control strategies. It is the inevitable outcome of capitalism: 'The directing motive, the end and aim of capitalist production, is to extract the greatest possible amount of surplus-value, and consequently to exploit labour-power to the fullest possible extent' (ref. 6, p. 331).

The second broad plane of activity changing the nature of work is the division of labour. To increase control and surplus value for the capitalist, extensive division of labour takes place within the factory. According to Marx, 'Division of labour within the workshop implies the undisputed authority of the capitalist over men that are but parts of a mechanism that belong to him' (ref. 6, p. 356). As an example, Marx described the manufacture of horse carriages. In pre-capitalist production, the manufacture of carriages involved the simple cooperation of various trades: coach construction, ironwork, upholstery and wheelwright work. Each of these trades was regulated by guilds in order to maintain their specialization and control over these operations. In capitalist production, simple cooperation gives way to what Marx described as 'complex cooperation', as individual trades lose their specialized skills, and workers perform operations that are disconnected and isolated from one another, and carried out alongside each other. According to Marx and his colleague Engels, this mode of production also creates a hierarchy of managers and supervisors:

division of labour: the allocation of work tasks to various groups or categories of employee

> Modern industry has converted the little workshop of the patriarchal master into the great factory of the industrial capitalist. Masses of labourers, crowded into the factory, are organized like soldiers. As privates of the industrial army they are placed under the command of a perfect hierarchy of officers [managers] and sergeants [supervisors]. (ref. 9, p. 227)

Marx examined the impact of technological change on employment relationships. He argued that machinery is used by the capitalist to increase surplus labour by cheapening labour, to deskill workers and thus make it easier to recruit, control and discipline workers. Machinery, he argued, led to the progressive reduction of skills:

> On the automatic plan skilled labour gets progressively superseded. The effect of improvements in machinery [results] in substituting one description of human labour for another, the less skilled for the more skilled, juvenile for adult, female for male, [and] causes a fresh disturbance in the rate of wages. (ref. 6, p. 443)

Machinery allows the capitalist to transfer the knowledge and skill in production from the worker to reliable agents of capital – that is, managers. Marx described the process like this: 'Intelligence in production expands in one direction, because it vanishes in many others. What is lost by the detail labourers, is concentrated in the capital that employs them' (ref. 6, p. 361). Machinery also increases the capitalist's control over workers' work activities. In what Marx referred to as the despotism of the factory, machinery sets the pace of work and embodies powerful mechanisms of control: 'the technical subordination of the workman to the uniform motion of the instruments of labour [machinery] ... gave rise to a barrack discipline'. He continued: 'To devise and administer a successful code of factory discipline, suited to the necessities of factory diligence, was the Herculean enterprise, the noble achievement of Arkwright!' (ref. 6, pp. 423–4).

These characteristics of work in industrial capitalism have two major consequences: the alienation of the workers, and conflict resulting ultimately in social change. Whereas objectification embodies the worker's creativity, work under capitalism is devoid of the producer's own potential creativity and sensuousness. Because workers' labour is not their own, it no longer transforms them. Hence, the unique quality of human beings – their ability to control the forces of nature and produce their own means of existence, to realize their full creative capacity through work – is stultified by capitalism.

alienation: a feeling of powerlessness and estrangement from other people and from oneself

Drawing on the 1807 work by Georg Hegel, *The Phenomenology of Mind*, Marx developed the theory of alienation. In essence, alienation ruptures the fundamental connection that human beings have to the self-defining aspect of their labouring activity.[8] Marx broke down the formulation of alienation into four conceptually discrete but related spheres. First, workers are alienated (or separated) from the product of their labour. The product – its design, quality, quantity and how it is marketed and disposed of – is not determined by those whose labour is responsible for its manufacture.

Second, workers are alienated from productive activity. Marx emphasized the tendency for machinery to deskill work:

> Owing to the extensive use of machinery and to division of labour, the work of the proletarians has lost all individual character, and, consequently, all charm for the workman. He becomes an appendage of the machine, and it is only the most simple, most monotonous, and most easily acquired knack, that is required of him. (ref. 9, p. 227)

Thus, work offers no intrinsic satisfaction. Workers only work for the money; workers only work because they have to. Marx called this the 'cash nexus'. Accordingly, work takes on an instrumental meaning: it is regarded simply as a means to an end.

The third type of alienation discussed by Marx is alienation from the human species. Marx contended that self-estrangement develops because of the 'cash nexus'. In order to be clear on Marx's meaning, we need to know that Marx believed that people were essentially creative and that individuals expressed creativity through their work. Work, according to Marx, is the medium for self-expression and self-development. It is through work that people should be able to shape themselves and their communities in accordance with their own needs, interests and values. Under alienating conditions, however, work becomes not a social activity that personifies life, but simply a means for physical survival: people become detached from their true selves.

The fourth type of alienation discussed by Marx is alienation from fellow human beings and from the community. This results when the sole purpose of life is competition and all social relations are transformed into economic relations. Workers and managers are alienated from each other. This economic relationship – between those who are controlled and the controllers – is an antagonistic one. And this asymmetry of social relationships in the workplace creates the foundation for a class structure that necessitates sharp differences in power, income and life chances.

Marx's analysis of the social organization of work underscores the fact that people express themselves through their work, and in so far as their labour is merely a commodity to be paid for with a wage, they are alienated. Although Marx did not explicitly focus on the analysis of emotion in the workplace, he did acknowledge that the way in which industrial work was organized and managed did provoke in workers feelings of numbness, anger and resentment. Alienation is characteristic of a certain kind of organization of work – industrial capitalism – that is predicated on a set of socioeconomic conditions. In short, then, capitalism destroys the pleasure associated with labour, the distinctively human capacity to shape and reshape the world.

The second major consequence of work in capitalism, that relations between capitalists and workers are in constant conflict, is the engine of social change. Impelled by its internal **contradictions**, the reverberation of work under capitalism helps the development of class consciousness among the workers or proletariat. The defining features of work – deskilling, intensification of work, constant pressure to lower the wages allocated to labour – encourage the development of class conflict. Marx and Engels explain the logic whereby capitalism develops and then destroys itself. In their search for profits, capitalists closely control and discipline workers.[9]

contradictions: contradictions are said to occur within social systems when the various principles that underlie these social arrangements conflict with each other

class consciousness: Karl Marx's term for awareness of a common identity based on a person's position in the means of production

class conflict: a term for the struggle between the capitalist class and the working class

Capitalism creates new contradictions, such as the concentration of workers into factories. As workers are concentrated under one roof, they become aware of their common exploitation and circumstances. As a result, over time, workers begin to resist capitalist controls, initially as individuals, and then collectively as groups. Gradually, the workers become organized, through trade unions, and increasingly they become more combative and engage the ruling class in wider social struggles, which Marx believed would culminate in replacing the rule of the bourgeoisie and ridding society of capitalism: 'What the bourgeoisie therefore produces above all, is its own gravediggers. Its fall and the victory of the proletariat are equally inevitable.'[9] Thus, those selling their labour power, the workers, are exposed to such exploitation and degradation that they begin to oppose capitalists, in order to replace the system.

bourgeoisie (or capitalist class):   Karl Marx's term for the class comprising those who own and control the means of production

proletariat (or working class):   Karl Marx's term for those who must sell their labour because they have no other means of earning a livelihood

Marx provides a sophisticated theory of capitalism, with the working class as the embodiment of good, but his concentration on the extraction of surplus value in the labour process inhibits him from considering managerial and government strategies that serve to develop consent and cooperation. The capitalist mode of production is not characterized solely by the conflict between employer and labour: it is also marked by competition between organizations and economies. To put it another way, profits are realized by gaining a competitive advantage, and the need to gain workers' cooperation undermines the contradictory laws that promote constant conflict and crises. Thus, Marx systematically underestimates the possibility that management may need to organize on the basis of consent as well as coercion.

The reconceptualization of management as necessarily engaged in consent building also suggests that Marx's zero-sum theory of power is insufficient. Critics argue that although the interests of labour and capital do not coincide, the assumption that they are irreconcilably and utterly antagonistic is misleading. Therefore, the inadequacy of Marx's account lies at the level of analysis. Marx emphasized the irreconcilable interests of social classes at the societal level, and this obscures the very real way in which, in the workplace, the interests of employers and employees may be very closely intertwined.

Despite the strong criticisms of Marx's analysis of work on capitalism, his impact on the sociology of work is immense. His illumination of the politics of work and organizations – the relationship between work and the distribution of interests and power in the society outside the workplace, and the relationships of power and managerial strategies inside the workplace – still informs contemporary analyses of work and employment relations, as we shall see later in this chapter.

weblink

Go to the following websites for more information on Marx: http://plato.stanford.edu/entries/marx; www.anu.edu.au/polsci/marx/classics/manifesto.html; www.marxists.org

Emile Durkheim (1858–1917)

Emile Durkheim's contribution to our understanding of work is essentially derived from his book *The Division of Labor in Society*,[10] and its discussion of the relationship between individuals and society, and the conditions for social cohesion. Durkheim was preoccupied with the issue of social solidarity and unity during a time when France was subject to the profound revolutionary changes that created modern society. The popular belief of the time was that the collapse of social life was imminent, in response to the expansion of the division of labour, ever-increasing industrialization and urbanization, and the declining significance of traditional moral beliefs. This was described as the transition from *Gemeinschaft* or 'community' forms of society, to *Gesellschaft* or 'social' forms, representing mere 'associations' where social solidarity was disintegrating. Durkheim suggested that such fears were not just exaggerated, but actually wrong. His thesis held that heightened feelings of group solidarity and order were being reconstructed in a different form. Durkheim's position was that the interdependence resulting from the progressive differentiation and specialization of labour gave rise to a new form of social solidarity, which is the bond that unites individuals when there is no normative consensus.

social solidarity: the state of having shared beliefs and values among members of a social group, along with intense and frequent interaction among group members

urbanization: the process by which an increasing proportion of a population lives in cities rather than in rural areas

Durkheim's prime question was, if pre-industrial societies were held together by shared understandings, ideas, norms and values, what holds a complex industrial society together? He believed that the increasing division of labour has enormous implications for the structure of society. In pre-industrial society, social solidarity is derived from people's similarities and the rather suffocating effects of uniformity of experience and thought. Such societies are held together through the collective consciousness at the direct expense of individuality: 'individual personality is absorbed into the collective personality', as Durkheim put it (ref. 10, p. 85). He called this form of social unity mechanical solidarity. In contrast, the increasing division of labour causes a diminution of collective consciousness, and 'this leaves much more room for the free play of our imitative' (ref. 10, p. 85).

mechanical solidarity: a term to describe the social cohesion that exists in pre-industrial societies, in which there is a minimal division of labour and people feel united by shared values and common social bonds

Complex industrial societies, with new work forms based on functional specialization, are held together by relations of exchange and people's reciprocal need for the services of many others. This symmetry of life Durkheim called organic solidarity. He believed that in societies whose solidarity is organic, individuals are linked increasingly to each other rather than to society as a whole. The totality of the nature of these social links compels individuals to remain in contact with one another, which in turn binds them to one another and to society. Thus, each of us becomes aware of our dependence on others and of the new cultural norms that shape and restrain our actions.

organic solidarity: a term for the social cohesion that exists in industrial (and perhaps post-industrial) societies, in which people perform very specialized tasks and feel united by their mutual dependence

Plate 2   Emile Durkheim
Source: Wikipedia.

For Durkheim, only the division of labour could furnish social solidarity and ethical individualism: 'Since the division of labour becomes the source of social solidarity, it becomes, at the same time, the foundation of moral order' (ref. 10, p. 333). In summary, he argued that there was no necessary correlation between increased division of labour and decreasing solidarity. On the contrary, it was a source not of disorder and conflict, but of order and social solidarity. The nature of moral solidarity in industrial society has not disappeared, but changed.

Of course, Durkheim was not oblivious to the reality of industrialization in Western Europe, which might have been argued to show the opposite. Not least, there were intense class conflicts and widespread labour strikes in France, often led by radical workers known as revolutionary syndicalists, in unions organized in the *Confédération Générale du Travail*. Durkheim explained the existence of instability and social fragmentation by analysing what he called 'abnormal' forms of the division of labour. These abnormal forms occur when the development of the division of labour is obstructed and distorted by various factors. He identified these as the anomie division of labour, the forced division of labour and the mismanagement of operations.

The first abnormal effects can arise because of the 'anomie' condition of the division of labour. The word anomie comes from the Greek *anomia*, meaning 'without law'. For Durkheim, anomie results from a condition in which social norms and/or moral norms are confused or simply absent. Generally, Durkheim believed that anomie results from widespread business failure, or when there is rapid and uneven economic development that has expanded ahead of the necessary developments in social regulation. In such circumstances, he suggests, breaches occur in the social solidarity existing between specialized occupations, causing tensions in social relationships and eroding social cohesion.

anomie: a state condition in which social control becomes ineffective as a result of the loss of shared values and a sense of purpose in society

Durkheim also considered anomie as another 'pathology' of industrialization, but believed that such deviant behaviour could be 'cured' through the proper level of regulation. He argued that occupational associations centred within civil society are the most effective means of regulating anomie in modern society. Such collective institutions provide moral authority, which dominates the life of their members. They are also a method by which individualistic egotism can be subordinated harmoniously to the general interest.

Durkheim explained the importance of occupational groups like this: 'wherever a group is formed, a moral discipline is also formed.' He continued:

> A group is not only a moral authority regulating the life of its members, but also a source of life *sui generis*. From it there arises warmth that quickens or gives fresh life to each individual, which makes him disposed to empathise, causing selfishness to melt away. (ref. 10, p. 111)

Durkheim also warned that the mere construction of consensually grounded goals without any associated provision of opportunities to achieve such goals would extend the form of social 'pathology' under which anomie prevailed.

The second factor causing abnormal development, according to Durkheim, is the 'forced division of labour' (ref. 10, p. 310). He emphasized that the division of labour is frequently not 'spontaneous' because of class and inherited privilege that operate to limit life chances. Durkheim, then, is considered to be a supporter of meritocracy. The normal division of labour would occur if social inequalities mirrored what Durkheim took to be personal inequalities:

> The division of labour only produces solidarity if it is spontaneous, and to the degree that it is spontaneous. But spontaneity must mean not simply the absence of any deliberate, formal type of violence, but of anything that may hamper, even indirectly, the free unfolding of the social force each individual contains within himself ... In short, labour only divides up spontaneously if society is constituted in such a way that social inequalities express precisely natural inequalities. (ref. 10, pp. 313–14)

Thus, Durkheim's 'normal' division of labour is a 'perfect meritocracy' produced by the eradication of personal inheritance.[1,5] For the division of labour to engender solidarity, society must allocate functions based on ability, not class or hereditary tendencies, so that 'The sole cause then determining how labour is divided up is the diversity of abilities' (ref. 10, p. 313).

The third factor responsible for an 'abnormal' development of the division of labour is mismanagement of functions in society. Durkheim believed that when functions are faltering or are badly coordinated with one another, individuals are unaware of their mutual dependence, and this lessens social solidarity. Thus, if work is insufficient, as a result of mismanagement and organization, Durkheim argues that solidarity 'is itself naturally not only less than perfect, but may even be more or less completely missing' (ref. 10, p. 326).

In addition, if class-based social inequalities are imposed on groups, this not only forces the division of labour, but also undermines social linkages. It means that individuals are mismatched to their functions, and that linkages between individuals are disrupted, and this creates inequitable forms of exchange. In the absence of restraint from a centralized authority (either the state or the government), there is disequilibrium, which leads to instability and conflict. For Durkheim, most of the pathologies of the new industrial order were attributed to the prevalence of anomie.

In sum, while Marx's critique was directed at capitalism, Durkheim's critique was aimed not at the essence of capitalism, but at industrialism. Whereas Marx is against the fragmentation of work and for the reintegration of skills, Durkheim is for the expansion of specialization in line with individuals' 'natural' abilities. Although the concepts of alienation and anomie lead to significantly different analysis and political results, and are different too in their assumptions about human nature, the two concepts have been compared by sociologists. For Marx, alienation results from certain kinds of social control; on the other hand, according to Durkheim, anomie results from the absence of social control. While Marx's solution to the crisis of capitalism is dependent on the state or government, Durkheim argued that centralized government was too far removed from the everyday experience of people to play this role. He believed that mediating organizations would form the primary mode of social organization. For Durkheim, the crisis of modern society is a moral one, caused by a lack of social unity. The solution is therefore achieved by socially regulated institutions coupled with an ever-widening division of labour. He believed this would facilitate the development of individual potential and create a future Utopia. The process of social change was to be evolutionary, not revolutionary.

In this chapter, we cannot provide a thorough critique of Durkheim's theory of the relationship between the increasing differentiation and specialization of labour, and transformative social change. However, we must critically assess some of his assumptions, for example those about 'natural' inequalities. He regarded men as more intelligent than women, and industrial workers as more intelligent than farmers. Durkheim also assumed that the gender-based domestic division of labour was a good example of the social harmony generated when social inequalities were allowed to mirror 'natural' inequalities. His assumptions about gender relations provoked the beginnings of a critique of patriarchy.[5]

---

weblink

Go to the following website for more information on Durkheim: www.epistemelinks.com/Main/Philosophers.aspx?PhilCode=Durk

---

Max Weber (1864–1920)

Max Weber's work is broad and wide-ranging, and has been much misrepresented. It is often assumed to be a dialogue with the ghost of Marx, but that does not do justice to it. Weber wrote on a wide range of topics including art, architecture and music; he examined the role of ideology in social change; and he explored the emergence and nature of modernity. His contribution to the study of work and work organizations has been extensive. The main contributions he made are: first, his theory concerning the rise of capitalism; second, his arguments concerning rationality, the nature of bureaucracy and authority; third, his theory of social class and inequality; and fourth, his methodology and theory of knowledge.

The rise of capitalism and rationalization

Weber's interpretation of the rise of capitalism in the West is presented in his best-known work, *The Protestant Ethic and the 'Spirit' of Capitalism* (written in 1905),[11] which links the rise of modern capitalism to Protestant (or, more precisely, Calvinist) religious beliefs and practices. Briefly, he argued that a new attitude to work and the pursuit of wealth was linked to the rise of Calvinism. In this attitude, work became a means of demonstrating godliness, and Weber saw this cultural shift as being associated with the rise of 'rational' capitalism itself.

According to Weber, while Catholics believed they could secure their place in heaven through (among other things) 'good works' on behalf of the poor or by performing acts of faith on earth, Calvinism developed a set of beliefs around the concept of predestination, which broke the hold of tradition. It was believed by followers of Calvin that it was already decided by God ('predestined') whether they would go to

Plate 3   Max Weber
Source: Wikipedia.

heaven (as one of the 'elect') or hell after their death. They had no means of knowing their ultimate destination, and also no means of altering it. This uncertainty led Calvinists to search for signs from God, since naturally they were anxious to be among the elect. Wealth was taken as a manifestation that they were one of God's elect, and this encouraged followers of Calvin to apply themselves rationally to acquiring wealth. They did this through their ascetic lifestyles and hard work.

The distinctive features of 'rational capitalism' that Weber identified – limits on consumption, especially luxury consumption, and a tendency to reinvest profits in order to systematically accumulate more wealth – had a clear similarity to the Calvinist lifestyle. Although Weber did not believe that Calvinism was the cause of the rise of industrial capitalism, he did believe that capitalism in part grew from Calvinism. Contrary to Marx, Weber argued that the development of rational capitalism could not be explained through wholly material and structural forces; the rise of modern Western society was embedded in the process of rationalization.

Rationalization

Central to Weber's analysis of the rise of capitalism and new organizational forms is this concept of rationalization. But what did he mean by this term? Weber's use of **rationality** is complex and multifaceted. He used the term to describe the overall historical process 'by which nature, society and individual action are increasingly mastered by an orientation to planning, technical procedure and rational action' (ref. 8, p. 218). For Weber, all societies exhibit rationality, in that all people can explain the basis of their behaviour, but only in the West does a particular type of rationality, based on capitalization, bureaucracy and calculation, become dominant.

The essence of the concept consisted of three facets: secularization, calculability and rational action.

rationality: the process by which traditional methods of social organization, characterized by informality and spontaneity, are gradually replaced by efficiently
administered formal rules and procedures – bureaucracy

Rationality means the decline of magical interpretations and explanations of the world. Scientific models of nature and human behaviour are good examples of this type of rationalization, which involves calculating maximum results at minimum cost. It means the replacement of 'traditional' action by 'rational' action. Ration-alization depends on two types of activity: strategies of human action, and modi-fication of the means and ends of action in the pursuit of goals. Rather than doing things for emotional reasons, people do things because they calculate that the ben-efits will outweigh the cost, or because they assess the action as being the most efficient way to achieve their goals. Human actions are also guided by the use of rational decision making in pursuit of unlimited profit. Rules are obeyed because they appear to be built upon rational principles and common sense. In the business sphere, for example, technical and managerial rules are obeyed because they result in efficiency and profits.

Rationalization is different from rationality. Rationalization, the principal process of modernity, refers to the overall process by which reality is increasingly mastered by calculation and rational action, while rationality refers to the capacity of human action to be subject to calculation about means and ends.

Four types of rationality have been identified in Weber's work: practical, theoreti-cal, formal and substantive:

- *Practical rationality* assumes that there are no external mystical causes affecting the outcome of human actions, and sees reality in terms of what is given.
- *Theoretical or technical rationality* involves a cognitive effort to master the world through causality, logical deduction and induction. This type of rationality allows individuals to understand the 'meaning of life' by means of abstract con-cepts and conceptual reasoning.
- *Formal rationality* refers to the accurate calculation procedures that go into deci-sions, to ensure consistency of outcome and efficiency in attaining goals.
- *Substantive rationality* refers to the degree to which human action is guided or shaped by a value system, regardless of the outcome of the action. Accordingly, 'Where formal rationality involves a practical orientation of action regarding out-comes, substantive rationality involves an orientation to values' (ref. 8, p. 222).

Although these four different rationalization processes can complement each other, they can also conflict. For example, the pursuit of efficiency and produc-tivity by calculating the 'best' means to achieve a given end (formal rational-ity) sometimes conflicts with ethical behaviour (substantive rationality). When examined through a substantive lens, formal rationality is often irrational. In his book, *The McDonaldization of Society*,[12] George Ritzer makes a strong case that for-mal rationality, embodied in standardized fast-food products, undermines values of social responsibility and individualism in the pursuit of efficiency. In the early twenty-first century, rationalization shapes the subjective experiences of peoples as they understand and evaluate climate change and global warming in terms of non-sustainable growth, profit maximization and corporate social responsibility.

corporate social responsibility: an organization's moral obligation to its stakeholders

Bureaucracy

According to Weber, bureaucratization is an inescapable development of modern society. Weber's analysis of the development of capitalism was similar to that of Marx, in that he believed that the rise of capitalism had been marked by the centralization of production, by increased specialization and mechanization, by the progressive loss by workers of the means of production, and by an increase in the function and growth of management. With centralized production, all human activity gives way to a more systematic, rational and extensive use of resources, including labour, which is facilitated by calculable techniques such as accounting. Weber's contention was that 'Where capitalist acquisition is rationally pursued, the corresponding action is oriented towards the calculation of capital. In other words, such action takes place within a planned utilization of material or personal output' (ref. 11, p. 359).

bureaucratization: a tendency towards a formal organization with a hierarchy of authority, a clear division of labour and an emphasis on written rules

According to Weber, bureaucracies are goal-oriented organizations, administered by qualified specialists, and designed according to rational principles in order to efficiently attain the stated goals. He saw the development of bureaucracy as involving the exorcism of emotional or 'irrational' personal elements such as hate, love or sentiment. In his *Economy and Society*, written in 1921, Weber explained that 'Bureaucracy ... is fully developed in the private economy only in the most advanced institutions of capitalism' (ref. 13, p. 956). He also noted that as the complexity of modern society increases, bureaucracies grow. He defined the bureaucratic 'ideal type' by these characteristics: business is continually conducted, there are stipulated rules, individual spheres of competence are structured in a hierarchy, offices (that is, positions at work) are not owned, selection and promotion is through proven ability, and rewards are commensurate with people's qualifications, ability and performance.

Two core ideas underscore Weber's concept of bureaucracy: formal rationality and formalized decision making. Formal rationality operates on the principles of expert knowledge and calculability, whereas formalized decision making operates on the basis of set procedures. This means that decisions can be judged as correct or otherwise by reference to a body of rules.

formalization: the degree to which organizations standardize behaviour through rules, procedures, formal training and related mechanisms

It would, however, be a misrepresentation of Weber to assume that he was an avid supporter of bureaucracy. Weber was not unaware of the dysfunctions of any over-formalized work form. Bureaucracy removes workers from the decision-making process. It consists of rational and established rules, and restricts individual activity. As a result, it can resemble an 'iron cage and it can mean that organizational behaviour becomes less and less regulated by ethical principles, as these are replaced by technical means and ends' (ref. 8, p. 297). Weber's argument is that because bureaucratic work forms remove workers, including white-collar and managerial staff, from ownership of the means of production, there is a loss of democracy in the workplace, and a panoply of managerial control measures are then necessary to keep the workers in line.[13]

Types of authority

All systems of work require a minimum of 'voluntary compliance' and some mechanism of coordination and control over the activity. This compliance, which is defined as 'an interest in obedience' (ref. 13, p. 212) of the subordinate controlled (such as a worker) to the dominant controller (such as a manager), is based on the ulterior motives of the subordinate, which are governed by custom and a material calculation of advantage, as well as her or his perception of the employment relationship.

Weber's analysis of authority relations provides another insight into the changing structure of work systems. Weber used the terms 'domination' and 'authority' interchangeably in *Economy and Society*. Both derive from the German term *Herrschaft*, which points to leadership, and his theory of domination does have direct relevance to theories of organizational leadership. However, Weber did make a distinction between power and domination. He defined **power** as the ability to impose one's will on others in a given situation, even when the others resist. Domination, or authority, is the right of a controller to issue commands to others and expect them to be obeyed. Underscoring Weber's study of authority is his concern for 'legitimacy'. Essentially, he was interested in knowing on what basis subordinates actively acknowledge the validity of authority figures in an established order, and give obedience to them, and on what basis men and women claim authority over others.

power: a term defined in multiple ways, involving cultural values, authority, influence and coercion as well as control over the distribution of symbolic and material resources. At its broadest, power is defined as a social system that imparts patterned meaning

Subordinates and the controlled obey dominant controllers by custom and for material advantage and reward, but a belief in legitimacy is also a prerequisite. Weber pointed out that each authority system varies 'According to the kind of legitimacy which is claimed, the type of obedience, the kind of administrative staff developed to guarantee it, and the mode of exercising authority' (ref. 13, p. 213). He then went on to propose three types of legitimate authority: traditional, rational-legal and charismatic. All types of authority, however, require a managerial system characterized by efficiency and continuity.

Traditional authority is based on the sanctity of tradition and the legitimacy of those exercising authority under such regimes. It is usually acquired through inheritance: this, for example, is the kind of authority held by kings and queens in

Plate 4 Rational-legal authority is derived from the rationality of the authority. For example, car drivers usually obey police officers imposing traffic laws (like this one in Paris) because their actions appear to make sense, not because police officers have some inherited authority or are charismatic

Source: Nick Tutton.

monarchies. Compliance rests on a framework of obligations that binds followers to leaders by personal loyalties.

Rational-legal authority is derived from the rationality of the authority. For example, car drivers usually obey traffic laws because they appear to make sense, and not because police officers have some inherited authority or are charismatic.

Charismatic authority refers to an attribute or exceptional quality possessed by an individual. In charismatic domination, the leader's claim to legitimacy originates from his or her followers' belief that the leader is to be obeyed because of his or her extraordinary attributes or powers of inspiration and communication.

Weber's typology of authority is important in understanding why individuals behave as they do in the workplace. He was one of the earliest social theorists who saw domination as being characteristic of the relationship between leaders and followers, rather than an attribute of the leader alone.

Social class, inequality and types of class struggle

Authority is equated to possessing power, and difference in the degree of power is one factor that gives rise to differentiated social classes. Weber's description of social class was similar to Marx's, in that he defined a social class by property ownership and by market relations. He stated that:

> a class is a number of people having in common a specific causal component of their life chances. This component is represented exclusively by economic interests in the possession of goods and opportunities for income, under the conditions of the commodity or labour markets. (ref. 13, p. 927)

However, whereas Marx had proposed that individuals carry forward their class interests by virtue of dominant economic forces, Weber argued that the 'mere differentiation of property classes is not "dynamic", that is, it need not result in class struggles and revolutions' (ref. 13, p. 303). He argued instead that the complex and multidimensional nature of social stratification in modern society necessarily inhibits the acquisition of the degree of class consciousness that is necessary for a revolution to occur.

In this argument, people who experience inequality and who have a degree of political consciousness are much more likely to form into rational associations (such as trade unions and social democratic political parties) that would thrust them to the forefront of political activity, than they are to start a revolution. Under these conditions, there are no class interests as such, only the 'average interests' of individuals in similar economic situations, and therefore the class struggle and revolution predicted by Marx are extremely unlikely to happen. Instead, the nature of class conflict changes in a modern society in two fundamental ways. First, there is a shift from direct confrontation between the owners of capital and workers to mediated pay disputes, and second, conflicts between social classes are resolved through the courts and legal means.

Weber's methodology

Between 1902 and 1903, Weber wrote two papers that were central to shaping his views about the nature of doing research in the social sciences, and which continue to influence contemporary inquiry into work and behaviour in the workplace. Let us look at two concepts he developed: ideal types and *Verstehen*.

The ideal type is one of Weber's best-known contributions to contemporary organizational theory. At its most basic level, an ideal type is a theoretical abstraction constructed by a social scientist, who draws out important characteristics and simultaneously suppresses less important characteristics. It can be viewed as a measuring rod or yardstick whose function is to compare empirical reality with preconceived notions of a reality. Weber put it like this: 'It functions in formulating terminology, classifications, and hypotheses, in working out concrete causal explanation of individual events' (ref. 13, p. 21). As a methodological construction, ideal types are neither ideal nor typical. That is, they are not ideal in any evaluative sense, nor are they typical because they do not represent any norm. They merely approximate reality. To put it differently, ideal types are heuristic devices (teaching aids) that are used to study slices of reality and enable us to compare empirical forms. Organizational theorists refer for example to an 'ideal type of bureaucracy' or 'ideal flexibility'.

ideal type: an abstract model that describes the recurring characteristics of some phenomenon

empiricism: an approach to the study of social reality that suggests that only knowledge gained through experience and the senses is acceptable

The second concept, *Verstehen*, we introduced when we discussed research methods. Weber believed that social scientists must look at the actions of individuals and examine the meanings attached to these behaviours. His approach to understanding human behaviour suggests that observational language is never theoretically independent of the way in which the observer sees a phenomenon and the questions he or she asks about the action. As a consequence, an individual researcher's interpretation of human activity is an inherent aspect of knowledge about organizational behaviour. Weber's 'interpretative' methodology is based on *Verstehen*, meaning 'human understanding'. Human subjects, in contrast to the objects studied in the natural sciences, always rely on their 'understanding' of each other's behaviour and on the 'meanings' they assign to what they and others do.

Verstehen: a method of understanding human behaviour by situating it in the context of an individual's or actor's meaning

This interpretive approach to studying reality is best illustrated by distinguishing between someone walking in a park as a pleasurable leisure experience, and someone walking in a park in an aimless way to kill time because he or she is unemployed and bored. The outer behaviour is exactly the same, but the inner state of the two people is different. It is difficult for a researcher to understand and explain the fundamental distinction between the inner states of the employed and unemployed (in this case) just by observing their outer states, or behaviour. We need an interpretive understanding in order to give a convincing analysis of what is seen.

Weber's theories have been challenged. For instance, it is argued that the earliest examples of rational capitalism are not restricted to Calvinist or even Protestant nations. Some Calvinist countries, such as Scotland, failed to 'take off' as capitalist industrialized nations, and some Catholic nations, such as Belgium, were among the market leaders.

As our review of the theories of work moves from the classical sociological theories of the 'big three' – Marx, Durkheim and Weber – to contemporary perspectives on work organizations, we will be better equipped to see how these classical theories continue to inform contemporary theories of work, organizational design and managerial behaviour.

weblink

Go to this website for more information on Weber: www.marxists.org/reference/archive/weber

stop reflect

Can you think of any workplace studies that have based their findings on data gathered through observing people in the workplace? How should the interpretative method affect your evaluation of the studies?

Contemporary theories of work organizations

Organizational studies constitute a discipline in itself, with a plethora of alternative theoretical perspectives. In recent years, different theoretical approaches to studying work and organizations have forced organizational theorists to re-examine and be more reflexive about organizational 'knowledge'. With these changes, as Clegg and Hardy put it, 'Gone is the certainty about what organizations are; gone, too, is the certainty about how they should be studied' (ref. 4, p. 3). In this chapter, we cannot hope to do justice to the complexities of the bewildering variety of perspectives, and we shall therefore seek to highlight what Clegg and Hardy call the major 'conversations' in organizational studies.

How we represent these conversations always involves a choice concerning what theories we wish to represent and how we represent them. To help, we have drawn a schema of organizational theories. The competing theories are plotted along two interlocking axes: the horizontal critical–managerial axis, and the vertical positivist–interpretivist axis (Figure 3.1).

The *critical–managerial axis* represents the political left–right continuum. At one extreme, the managerial pole positions those perspectives which are essentially

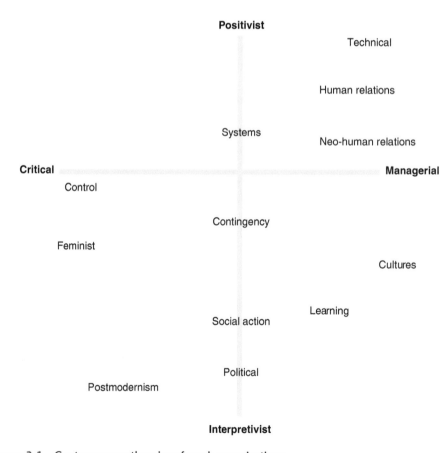

Figure 3.1   Contemporary theories of work organizations

concerned with issues of organizational efficiency and performance. Thus, researchers adopting this approach have tended to develop theoretical frameworks and generate empirical data aimed at understanding organizational structures, work arrangements and social processes that can improve labour productivity and organizational effectiveness, or can help solve people-related 'problems' in the workplace. This particular framework is often viewed as mainstream thinking in organizational behaviour texts. At the other extreme, the critical pole, lie critical explanations of work and organizational behaviour that have traditionally been concerned with issues of exploitation and the alienating effects of dividing and routinizing paid work. Researchers adopting this perspective tend to conceptualize organizational structures and management behaviour as control mechanisms that function to fulfil economic imperatives.

The *positivist–interpretivist axis* affirms the importance of epistemological considerations when conducting research: what is (or should be) regarded as acceptable knowledge in organizational behaviour theory. The axis distinguishes between the doctrines of 'positivism' and 'interpretivism'. The positivist epistemological position is generally taken to involve the application of natural science research methods to the study of work organizations. It puts emphasis on the scientific and technical way in which organizational activities can be studied and assessed (using goals, efficiency ratios, rational decision making, productivity measures and so on). In contrast, the interpretivist position maintains that human behaviour is not fully controllable, and therefore a research strategy for organizational behaviour must respect the differences between people and inanimate objects. For interpretivists, the role of the social scientist is to grasp the subjective meaning of behaviour or social action. Researchers focus on the indeterminate and contingent nature of social reality, the unintended consequences of human action and the influence of interpretation.

Where these 12 conversations or theories are plotted on the 'map' is clearly a matter of interpretation and subject to dispute; here the map's function is to act as a heuristic device.

Technical

The 'technical' approach to studying work organizations is most closely associated with the work of Frederick Winslow Taylor (1865–1915). Taylor, an engineer at an American steel mill, experimented with work arrangements to improve labour productivity. Taylor's work configuration rests upon the principle of the technical and social divisions of mental and manual labour. The technical division of labour generally refers to how a complex task is broken down into component parts. Adam Smith's classic observations on pin manufacturing[14] give us one of the first discussions of this in relation to potential increases in labour productivity.

The social division of labour refers to issues of which individuals occupy specific positions in the technical division of labour, how, why and for how long. In addition, scientific management, or Taylorism (as it became known), involved the following five principles: maximum job fragmentation, the separation of planning and doing, the separation of direct and indirect labour, minimum skill requirements and minimum material handling. These five job design principles gave to management 'the collective concept of control' (ref. 15, p. 97).

scientific management: this involves systematically partitioning work into its smallest elements and standardizing tasks to achieve maximum efficiency

Other important theorists contributing to this organization studies genre were Henry Gantt (1861–1919), a protégé of Taylor, who designed the Gantt chart, a straight-line chart to display and measure planned and completed work as time elapsed, Frank Gilbreth (1868–1924), who helped to improve labour productivity through the pioneering use of time and motion techniques, and Henry Ford (1863–1947), who perfected the application of the principles of scientific management to assembly-line production, an approach others would later call 'Fordism'. For most of the twentieth century, the essential principles of Taylorism and Fordism represented a 'common-sense' management strategy in North America and Western Europe.[16–18]

weblink

Go to the following websites for more information on Taylorism and Fordism: http://kapitalism101.wordpress.com/frederick-taylor-the-biggest-bastard-ever; www.nationmaster.com/encyclopedia/Taylorism; www.nosweat.org.uk; www.nationmaster.com/encyclopedia/Fordism

Human relations

Disenchantment with the technical approach to work and organizational design led to the development of the human relations school of thought. Data gathered at the Hawthorne plant of the Western Electric Companies – subsequently known as the Hawthorne studies – suggested a positive association between labour productivity and management style. The phenomenon can be explained like this: 'The determinants of working behaviour are sought in the structure and culture of the group, which is spontaneously formed by the interaction of individuals working together' (ref. 19, p. 99).

human relations: a school of management thought that emphasizes the importance of social processes in the organization

Elton Mayo is most closely associated with the Hawthorne studies. Another pioneering management theorist, Mary Parker Follett, is associated with the early human relations management movement. She contended that traditional authority as an act of subordination was offensive to an individual's emotions, and therefore could not serve as a good foundation for cooperative relations in the workplace. Instead, Follett proposed an authority function, whereby the individual has authority over her or his own job area.[15]

The Hawthorne studies have been criticized at both the technical and the political level. Technically, it has been contended that the researchers used a 'rudimentary' research design and that their analysis of the data was faulty. At a political level, charges of managerial bias, insularity from wider socioeconomic factors, a neglect of workers' organization (that is, trade unions) and organizational conflict were effectively levelled against the researchers. The critique included the charge that human relations theorists conceptualized the 'normal' state of the work organization in 'romantic' and harmonious terms, and neglected workplace conflict because of their pro-management bias.[20,21]

Despite the criticisms, the Hawthorne studies provided the impetus for a new 'common-sense' management strategy sometimes known as 'neo-human relations', which revisited Mayo's work. The human relations school focused on a paternalistic style of management, emphasizing workers' social needs as the key to harmonious relations and better performance, albeit narrowly conceived. Prominent contributors to human relations theory were Abraham Maslow (1908–70), with his idea of 'self-actualization' needs, and Douglas McGregor (1906–64), with his Theory X and Theory Y approach to work motivation. These contributions to organizational studies promoted five principles of 'good' work design: closure, whereby the scope of the job includes all the tasks to complete a product or process; task variety, whereby the worker learns a wider range of skills to increase job flexibility; self-regulation, allowing workers to assume responsibility for scheduling their work and quality control; social interaction to allow cooperation and reflectivity; and continuous work-based learning.[22]

---

stop reflect

What contemporary jobs tend to incorporate neo-human relations principles into job design, and what kind of jobs seem to be imbued with neo-Taylorism?

Systems theory

Systems theory has played, and continues to play, an influential part in attempts to analyse and explain work organizations. Systems theory involves providing holistic explanations for social phenomena, with a tendency to 'treat societies or social wholes as having characteristics similar to those of organic matter or organisms'.[23] It shows the relationships and interactions between elements, and these in turn are claimed to explain the behaviour of the whole. The notion of 'system' is associated with 'functionalism' and the work of Talcott Parsons (1902–79). Parsons used a systems model that was designed to demonstrate how formal organizations carry out a necessary set of functions to ensure survival.[24] The Parsonian model was also adopted by Dunlop to explain rule-bound behaviour among all major actors within the industrial relations system: unions, management and government.[25] Peter Senge's elaboration of systems thinking provides insight into 'personal mastery', team learning and 'shared vision.[26] A systems perspective is also used to examine the multidimensional and changing nature of the work context.[27]

Figure 3.2 shows a systems model, with a set of interrelated and interdependent parts configured in a manner that produces a unified whole. That is, any working system takes inputs, transforms them and produces some output. Systems may be classified as either 'closed' or 'open' to their environment. Work organizations are said to be open systems in that they acquire inputs from the environment (such as materials, energy, people and finance), transform them into services or products, and discharge outputs in the form of services, products and sometimes pollutants to the external environment.

open systems: organizations that take their sustenance from the environment, and in turn affect that environment through their output

The open-system model emphasizes that management action is not separate from the world but is connected to the wider context. That is, 'The existing internal structure, strategy, and success of an organization is heavily influenced by environmental forces in which it operates and with which it interacts and competes' (ref. 28, p. 209). However, it is too simple to regard the influence of context as only a one-way flow. Systems thinking is closely linked to the Weberian notion of the paradox of consequences in organizational life. A systems approach can illustrate how managerial behaviour and actions designed to advance a goal or solve a problem have unintended consequences that undermine or exacerbate the problem.[5]

stop reflect

Can you think of an example from your own work experience of the paradox of consequences? What did management do, and what was the unintended outcome(s)?

This kind of systems or functionalist thinking highlights the apparent functions of different work organizations. But the system has its critics. Detractors emphasize that systems analysis reifies organizations: in other words, it treats a concept as if it were a real thing. To assert that organizations make decisions implies that organizations have an existence beyond their human members, but it can be argued that this is not so: organizations are merely legal constructs. So when we talk of

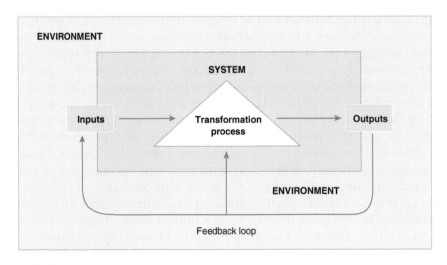

Figure 3.2   An open system

organizations 'making decisions', we really mean that some or all of the dominant controllers of an organization make the decisions.

Second, systems theory suggests a greater degree of stability and order in organizations than might actually exist across time. Third, systems theories tend to downplay the significance of historical developments to explain contemporary organizational phenomena. And finally, the essential thrust of functionalism or systems analysis is towards consensus. It is inherently deterministic: it 'is not only technocratic in its denial of conflicting ideologies and material interests but also deterministic in its pursuit of the correct prediction of behaviour through an analysis of organizational rules' (ref. 5, pp. 132–3).

Contingency theory

Contingency theory focuses on the three-way relationship between structure, contingency and outcomes, and has proved to be one of the most influential of all organizational theories. Contingency, as it applies to work organizations, means that the effectiveness of a particular strategy, structure or managerial style depends on the presence or absence of other factors or forces. Accordingly, there are no absolutely 'one best' strategies, structures or styles. Instead, whether an action is 'best' must be gauged relative to the context, the circumstances or the other factors.

The most noted contingency research was conducted over 40 years ago.[29–32] Joan Woodward, for example, found that there was no best way of organizing production, but that a particular organizational design and managerial style of behaviour was most appropriate for each technological situation (for example, worker-oriented production as found in car assembly compared with process production as found in a chemical plant). She reported that organizations differed not only in the general character of their structure and technology, but also in such detailed respects as managerial behaviour, methods of intermanagement communication, and interactions. In some organizations studied, 'it was not always easy to distinguish between those who gave and those who took orders' (ref. 30, p. 27).

The British writers Burns and Stalker suggested that organizational structures and managerial behaviours differed according to a range of environments differentiated by their degree of predictability and stability. Management styles would tend to be different in what they called 'mechanistic' or 'organic' systems. The American researchers Lawrence and Lorsch developed contingency analysis, by showing the importance of establishing integrative mechanisms to counter the centrifugal forces that differentiate and fragment managers and non-managers alike.

For dominant controllers of work organizations, the appeal of a contingency perspective is in part because the 'if–then' formula represents an explicit fracture with the simpler 'one best way' approach, while offering persuasive normative guidelines for what organizational leaders should do to sustain organizational performance. Where the contingency approach is most vulnerable to criticism is in its construction of independent variables, and this is why it is positioned close to the determinist line. The various studies argue that although some degree of contingency exists, in so far as controllers can choose between different forms of organizational structure, only those who choose the most 'appropriate' structure are likely to be successful. Others have noted the role of 'environmental determinism', and the removal of contingency by specifying the external conditions under which success can be determined: 'environments are not only given determinate power ... but they are literally reified through the language of environments acting on passive organizations' (ref. 33, p. 63).

Culture theory

The notion of applying 'cultural' thinking to organizational studies is derived from Durkheimian concerns for organizational solidarity through ideological consensus, and from Max Weber's pronouncements in *The Protestant Ethic* on the connections between a distinctive 'cultural phenomenon' and Western capitalist modernity. Organizational culture refers to artefacts, the shared beliefs and values and core assumptions that exist in an organization. Typically, the approach tends to be normative: that is, it is intended to explain not so much what the contemporary culture of an organization is, but what it should be. Thus, it may well persuade managers to act as if the preferred cultural attributes already existed, so the acting out of a cultural myth becomes the organizational reality.[34] A less manipulative approach to the significance of organizational cultures is provided by Gareth Morgan.[35] According to Morgan, culture is shared property and has a language and symbolism that can be decoded.

Morgan believes that how we define, understand and conceptualize organizations depends on our images or mental models of the essential shape, artefacts and features of organizations. He has argued that most definitions and theories of work organizations can be associated with a particular organizational metaphor. The most common metaphors view organizations as cultures, organisms, an iron cage, machines, networks or learning systems. These metaphors are embedded in various theories of organizational behaviour.

Charles Handy has suggested that 'role cultures', which are typically found in large bureaucracies, exude rationality, specialization, routines and rule following.[36] Generally speaking, he suggests that the larger an organization, the more expensive its technology, and the more routine its environment, the more likely it will be to adopt a role culture.

The cultural perspective converges with popular human resource management models, which highlight the importance of 'contextual relations' and organizational 'climate' to generate employee commitment.[37,38] Although the use of metaphor has entered popular culture, we need to be aware of the common error of treating metaphors as literal descriptions of social reality (for early literature on this, see ref. 39).

Learning theories

The learning organization and 'workplace learning' are two popular, and relatively new, metaphors in organizational studies. A learning organization is one that 'facilitates the learning of all its members and continually transforms itself'.[34] Proponents of management and workplace learning equate the learning organization with organizational economic success.[40] Typically, the learning organization approach is interpretive, because it is more closely related to the concept of organizational culture than to something tangible. The focus in a learning organization is on creating an environment that fosters learning through strategies that promote a 'growth-oriented workplace'.[22,41,42] A learning organization is normally understood as one that is 'good' at learning because of the types of activity it employs. Learning organizations are understood as places where individuals can be 'creative' and where people 'learn how to learn together'.

organizational learning:	the knowledge management process in which organizations acquire, share and use knowledge to succeed

---

weblink

Go to the following website for more information on organizational learning: www.fieldbook.com

---

Critical insight

Learning organizations and organizational learning
For a critical review and evaluation of the literature on learning organizations and organizational learning, see Chapter 4 of *Workplace Learning: A Critical Introduction*, by John Bratton, Jean Helms Mills and Peter Sawchuk.[22] A review of this literature is also given by Thomas Garavan in his article 'The learning organization: a review and evaluation'.[42]

Social action theory

The most influential contributions to social action theory were those of Silverman.[43] He provided a powerful critique of the reification embodied in systems thinking, and advocated a view of organizations as the product of individuals pursuing their own ends with the available means. He argued that social reality did not just happen, but had to be made to happen. The implication of this was that, through social interaction, people could modify and possibly even transform social meanings, and therefore any explanation of human activity had to take into account the meanings that those involved assigned to their actions. For example, whether a failure to obey a manager's instruction is a sign of worker insubordination or militancy, or caused by the beginnings of deafness, depends not on what managers or researchers observe to happen, but on what the worker involved means by her or his behaviour. This approach drew from Weber's work on the methodology and theory of knowledge action.

The social action approach involves examining six interrelated areas:

- the nature of the role system and pattern of interaction that has developed in the organization

- the nature of involvement of 'ideal-typical' actors and the characteristic hierarchy of ends they pursue
- the actors' present definitions of their situation within the organization, and their expectations of the likely behaviour of others
- the typical actions of different actors, and the meaning they attach to their actions
- the nature and source of the intended and unintended consequences of action
- any changes in the involvement and ends of the actors and in the role system.[44]

This method of analysing workplace behaviour is influenced by the work of George Herbert Mead (1863–1931) and symbolic interactionism. The approach assumes that human beings act towards things on the basis of subject meanings, and these meanings are the product of social interaction in human society. Organizational study, therefore, involves notions of 'symbolic meaning' and 'sense making' so that individuals can make sense of what they do. Critics have stressed that the micro-level approach of symbolic interactionism does not give sufficient attention to the 'big picture' and the inherent conflict of interest between the key actors representing capital and labour.

Political theory

The political approach to understanding work organizations characterizes the workplace as a purposive miniature society, with politics pervading all managerial work. By politics we mean the power relationships between managers and relevant others, and in turn the capacity of an individual manager to influence others who are in a state of dependence. It refers to those social processes which are not part of a manager's formal role, but which influence (perhaps not directly) the distribution of resources for the purpose of promoting personal objectives.

OB in focus

Developing organizational learning in the UK National Health Service

Learning has been identified as a central concern for a modernized British National Health Service (NHS). Continuing professional development has an important role to play in improving learning, but there is also a need to pay more attention to collective (organizational) learning. Such learning is concerned with the way organizations build and organize knowledge.

The recent emphasis within the NHS has been on the codification of individual and collective knowledge – for example, in guidelines and National Service Frameworks. This needs to be balanced by more personalized knowledge management strategies, especially when dealing with innovative services that rely on tacit knowledge to solve problems. Having robust systems for storing and communicating knowledge is only one part of the challenge. It is also important to consider how such knowledge gets used, and how routines become established in organizations to structure the way in which knowledge is deployed.

In many organizations, these routines favour the adaptive use of knowledge, which helps organizations to achieve incremental improvements in existing practice. However, the development of organizational learning in the NHS needs to move beyond adaptive (single-loop) learning, to foster skills in generative (double-loop) learning and meta-learning. Such learning leads to a redefinition of the organization's goals, norms, policies, procedures or even structures. However, moving the NHS in this direction will require attention to the cultural values and structural mechanisms that facilitate organizational learning.

Source: Sandra M. Nutley and Huw T. O. Davies.

Politics in organizations is simply a fact of life. However, as others have observed, the political quality of the management practice is 'denied' or 'trivialized' in many studies of work organizations. And although individual managers might privately question the moral value and integrity of their actions, 'Caught in the maelstrom of capitalist organization, managers are pressured to emulate and reward all kinds of manipulative and destructive behaviours' (ref. 46, p. 39). This perspective on studying organizations offers an approach that examines individual managers as 'knowledgeable human agents' functioning within a dynamic arena where both organizational resources and outcomes can be substantially shaped by their actions. It also reinforces the theoretical and practical importance attached to building alliances and networks of cooperative relationships among organizational members. These negotiating processes shape, and in turn are shaped by, organizational dynamics.

An early study of management adopting a political perspective was undertaken by Dalton in 1959.[47] Building on work by Fox,[48] Graeme Salaman pronounced the political approach most clearly. Power relations that reflect the social inequality prevailing in the wider society determine the structure of work organizations. Organizations are not independent bodies but are embedded into a wider (again political) environment. Furthermore, notions of identity and the part played by organizational life in the construction of both individual and group identity are important.

The political perspective has also drawn attention to the role of strategic choice in shaping organizational structures and management behaviour.[49–52] The strategic choice approach emphasizes the importance of the political power of dominant coalitions and ideological commitments in explaining variations in managerial policies and behaviour, and ultimately explaining variations in managerial effectiveness and organizational outcomes. The political perspective has been criticized for failing to offer little or no explanation of the asymmetrical nature of power, which is the essence of the 'radical' control perspective on management.

Control theories

At the critical pole of the managerial–critical continuum lie the 'control' theories. Much of this work has its roots in Marx's analysis of capitalism. This approach to work and management has come to be associated with the seminal work of

Harry Braverman.[16] Organizational theorists approaching the study of work and organizations from this perspective stress the inherent source of tension in organizations arising from technological rationality.[20,53–58] A related focus is the labour process approach, which conceptualizes organizational managers as controlling agents who serve the economic imperatives imposed by capitalist market relations. Managerial control is thus *the* central focus of management activity. According to this perspective, organizational structures and employment strategies are instruments and techniques to control the labour process in order to secure high levels of labour productivity and corresponding levels of profitability.

labour process: the process whereby labour is applied to materials and technology to produce goods and services that can be sold in the market as commodities. The term is typically applied to the distinctive labour processes of capitalism in which owners/managers design, control and monitor work tasks so as to maximize the extraction of surplus value from the labour activity of workers

The control perspective views work organizations as hierarchical structures in which workers are deskilled by scientific management techniques and new technology. Managerial behaviour is characterized primarily as control relations: 'organizations are structures of inequality and control'.[17] Such an approach recognizes the existence of inconsistent organizational designs and management practices, and these paradoxical tendencies provide the source of further management strategies that attempt to eradicate the tensions caused by them. The most important of these paradoxes is considered to be the simultaneous desire for control over workers, and cooperation and commitment from them.

The control perspective has also attracted much criticism from both critical and mainstream management theorists. For example, critiques of the deskilling and control thesis draw attention to moderating factors such as markets, worker resistance and batch size.[59–61]

Feminist theory

Until relatively recently, studying the workplace using a 'feminist' approach had not been a major topic of inquiry. The organizational discourse is still, in the main, a masculine endeavour to illuminate organizational behaviour. For radical feminists, science is not sexless: on the contrary, 'the attributes of science are the attributes of males' (ref. 62, p. 207). Research about work organizations tends to be both androcentric (focused on males) and ethnocentric (focused on the white Anglo-Saxon culture). One interpretation is that it has focused on the management agenda, and up to now this has consisted largely of 'important' white men in one field (academia) talking to, reflecting on and writing about 'important' white men in another field (organizations).[63]

Theoretically, one of the most important consequences of gender analysis in organizational studies is its power to question research findings that segregate organizational behaviour from the larger structure of social and historical life. Accordingly, much of the recent work most directly related to the feminist approach requires us to look at the interface between social context and work. It is argued that this shapes and reshapes the employment relationship. We need to

Work and Society: Benign control and precarious work

Sociologist Derek Layder argues that interpersonal control in its many forms is the 'bedrock' on which all social institutions (including work organizations) rest. Central to his argument is a distinction between benign and more problematic and exploitative forms of control. Layder (2004) suggests that we are accustomed to thinking about control in negative ways. The typical image of control portrays a stronger person dominating a weaker person. In Layder's view, this negative image of control is only part of the larger domain of control – and we have failed to conceptualize fully the more benign forms of control that lie at the heart of everyday interactions. As he puts it:

> *The common thread in all control is that it is aimed at securing the compliance of the target ... Benignity in control is reflected in its attempt to take the interests of others at least partly into account. By contrast, in domination the interests of the more powerful person are overriding. Also benign control is inherently partial and open-ended ... the control remains benign only as long as a broadly equal reciprocity is maintained, where each party has an opportunity to 'have their say' and 'get their way'. (p. 60)*

Layder's comments on the informal face-to-face interactions that form the basis of all social life offer us a useful vantage point on the social nature of work. In fact, we could use his continuum (benign control at one end and domination at the other end) to think about and describe the nature of control in any given work organization. Especially worthwhile would be exercises that enabled managers and employees to participate in discussions about the qualities that distinguish benign informal social control from domination. Such exercises are valuable not just for their contribution to team building, trust and a sense of security among workers, but also because they prepare employees to participate in the processes of collaborative problem solving that are essential to effective organizations.

It is important, however, to place the idea of benign control in a larger context. Layder is right to stress that academic interpretations of control have focused on its negative forms and features and that, consequently, a theoretical account of benign control has not received sufficient attention. But there is perhaps good reason for this: if we look at work from a historical and comparative perspective, we find no shortage of examples of workers whose working lives have been characterized by coercion and domination.

The history of the employment contract is itself very telling. Mac Neil (2002) notes that the employment contract has roots in the master–servant relationship. Although there is evidence that, throughout the twentieth century, Western industrialized nations have moved away from the idea of a master–servant relationship towards a workplace where benign control has triumphed over coercion and domination, there is also, sadly, evidence of the opposite. Kalleberg (2009) reminds us of the immense variability of employment relations, even in the developed world. Some employment relations are characterized by respect, security reasonable pay and other indications of quality. Yet among large segments of the workforce, there is a trend towards 'precarious work' and an overall reduction in the quality of working life. (Kalleberg cites as a cause of this trend employer efforts to 'obtain greater flexibility to meet growing competition' (p. 12).)

What are the implications of the trend towards precarious work for the forms of social control identified by Layder? As work becomes more precarious, will the balance between benign and more problematic forms of control be tilted towards the problematic end of the continuum? Will historical forms of employment relations reappear, causing workers to once again occupy 'the subservient status of the servant' (Mac Neil, 2002, p. 174)? These questions are best answered by focusing on particular cases.

stop!   Consider the following definition: '"precarious work" ... [is] employment that is uncertain, unpredictable, and risky from the point of view of the worker' (Kalleberg, p. 2). Now, reflect on the following questions:

- What kinds of organization are likely to generate precarious work for their employees?
- Are some workers more likely than others to experience the negative effects of precarious work?
- Will the workers subjected to precarious work inevitably experience problematic forms of social control?
- What can be done to reduce the likelihood that problematic control will trump benign control in organizations employing large numbers of precarious workers?

Sources and further information:

Kalleberg, A. (2009) 'Precarious work, insecure workers: employment relations in transition', *American Sociological Review*, 74, pp. 1–22.
Layder, D. (2004) *Emotion in Social Life: The Lost Heart of Society*, London: Sage.
Mac Neil, M. (2002). 'Governing employment', pp. 171–87 in M. Mac Neil, N. Sargent and P. Swan (eds), *Law, Regulation and Governance*, Dons Mills, ON: Oxford University Press.

Note: This feature was written by David MacLennan, Assistant Professor at Thompson Rivers University, BC, Canada.

look at gender divisions in the labour market, patriarchal power, issues of sexuality and inequality in society and at work, and the interface between home and work (the 'dual-role' syndrome). More importantly, however, incorporating gender development into the study of organizational studies will represent the life experience of both men and women in a more comprehensive and inclusive way.

Postmodernism

A new focus for organization theory is postmodernism. While traditional writings on organization theory tend to view work organizations as fine examples of human rationality, postmodernists such as Michel Foucault regard organizations as more akin to defensive reactions against inherently destabilizing forces.[5,64] The postmodernist perspective has its roots in the French intellectual tradition of post-structuralism, an approach to knowledge that puts the consideration of 'reflexivity' and how language is used at the centre of the study of all aspects of human activity. Thus, postmodern perspectives question attempts to 'know' or 'discover' the genuine order of things (what is known as representation). Researchers must possess the ability to be critical of their own intellectual assumptions (that is, exercise reflexivity).

postmodernism: the sociological approach that attempts to explain social life in modern
                  societies that are characterized by post-industrialization, consumerism
                  and global communications

This approach plays down the notion of a disinterested observer, and instead stresses the way in which people's notion of who and what they are – their agency, in other words – is shaped by the discourses that surround them. This is known as decentering the subject. Postmodernists also believe that researchers are materially involved in constructing the world they observe through language (by writing about it). Thus, where modernists perceive history as a grand narrative of human activity, rationality and progress, postmodernists reject the grand narrative and the notion of progressive intent. Clegg and Hardy frame the postmodern approach this way: 'They are histories, not history. Any pattern that is constituted can only be a series of assumptions framed in and by a historical context' (ref. 4, p. 2).

Michel Foucault's relevance to organizational theory lies in several related spheres.[65,66] First, he argues that contemporary management controls human behaviour neither by consensus nor by coercion, but rather by systems of surveillance and human relations management techniques. Second, he suggests that although an organization is 'constructed by power', its members do not 'have' power. Power is not the property of any individual or group. While modernists see the direction of power flowing downwards against subordinates, and its essence as negative, Foucault argues that power should be configured as a relationship between subjects. It has 'capillary' qualities that enable it to be exercised *within* the social body, rather than *above* it' (ref. 67, p. 39). Third, with the ever-increasing expansion of electronic surveillance in the workplace, Foucault offers his own image of an 'iron cage' in the form of the extended panopticon – hidden surveillance.

Postmodernism is a useful way to study work organizations. In particular, the notion of power as a 'web' within which managers and non-managers are held has much to offer. However, some critics, for example Martin Parker, have described postmodern epistemology as a reactionary intellectual trend, which amounts to a 'fatal distraction' from engagement in a rigorous analysis of organizational changes located within late modernity.[68]

The value of theory about contemporary organizational behaviour

In this chapter, we have reviewed the main themes and arguments of both classical and contemporary theories of work. As we explained, the classical theories are derived from the works of Karl Marx, Emile Durkheim and Max Weber, and are an intellectual response to the transformation of society caused by industrial capitalism. A legitimate question for students of organizational behaviour is, 'Why bother studying sociological classics – three "dead white men"?' We believe that an understanding of the classical accounts of work is important because, as others have also argued, the epistemological, theoretical and methodological difficulties that were identified and debated by Marx, Durkheim and Weber remain central to the conduct of contemporary research on organizational behaviour.[2,69-73] Those of us who study contemporary work organizations are informed by the 'canonical' writers and constantly return to them for ideas and inspiration.

In terms of understanding what goes on in the workplace, theory cannot be separated from management practice. It is used both to defend existing management practices and to validate new ways of organizing work, or *doing*. The nature of the employment relationship is clearly an issue of central importance to understanding human behaviour in work organizations. The classical sociologists developed a body of work that, directly or by inference, provides an account of the relations between employers and employees.

For Marx, conflict is structured into the employment relationship and is, for most of the time, asymmetrical. That is, the power of the employer or agent (manager) typically exceeds that of the workers. Durkheim's work influenced how theorists have studied organizations, and he reminds us that there are multiple ways in which society imposes itself upon us and shapes our behaviour.

A number of Weber's concepts also continue to have much relevance in the early twenty-first century. For example, his concept of charismatic domination is prominent in contemporary leadership theories. In addition, Weber's concepts of bureaucracy and rationalization have been applied to the fast-food sector, and have exposed the irrationality associated with the paradigm of McDonaldization. Weber's interpretive method, and in particular the researcher's capacity to assign different meanings to shared reality, gives a postmodern ring to his theory.

Finally, classical theories enter the contemporary debates on work organization and management practices by reinforcing the message that understanding the nature of the employment relationship necessarily involves considering organizational culture, societal values and norms as well as national institutions. It is through these that individuals acquire a self-identity and the mental, physical and social skills that shape their behaviour both outside and inside the work organization.

Summary

- The three founders of the sociology of work all continue to have their contemporary adherents and detractors.

- Marx's fascination with class, conflict and the labour process formed the basis for the most popular new approach throughout much of industrial sociology, from the late 1960s to the 1980s. It spawned a complete school of thought in the labour process tradition, but its limitations became more evident as the approach attempted to explain all manner of social phenomena directly through the prism of class.

- Durkheim's moral concerns continue to pervade the market economy, and make predictions about human actions that are based on amoral, economically rational behaviour less than convincing. Perhaps where Durkheim has been most vigorously criticized has been in relation to the allegedly cohering effects of an extended division of labour. The mainstream of managerial theories does not support Durkheim on this point: dependency does not generate mutual solidarity.

- Weber's theories of rationalization and bureaucracy have never been far from the minds of those analysing the trend towards larger and larger organizations, and the recent movement towards more flexible work organization patterns. Again, however, Weber's over-rationalized approach underestimated the significance of destabilizing and sectional forces within work organizations.

- This chapter has reviewed 12 theoretical approaches or conversations on organizational studies: the technical, human relations, neo-human relations, systems thinking, contingency, cultures, learning, control, feminist, social action, political and postmodernist approaches. It has adopted a particular form of differentiating between the various theories through an organizational grid based on two axes: managerial–critical and determinist–interpretative. This is a heuristic way of structuring the various possibilities.

Key concepts

alienation   91
androcentrism   116
anomie   96
ideal type   104
labour power   90
paradox of consequences   110
rationality   99–100
strategic choice   115

Key vocab checklist for ESL students

- Alienation
- Anomie
- Bourgeoisie
- Class conflict
- Class consciousness
- Contingency theory
- Contradiction, contradict
- Corporate social responsibility
- Division of labour
- Empiricism, empirical
- Formalization, formal, formalize
- Human relations
- Ideal type
- Input
- Labour process
- Mechanical solidarity
- Objectification, objectify
- Open systems
- Organic solidarity
- Organizational learning
- Output
- Postmodernism
- Power
- Proletariat

- Rationalization, rationality, rational, rationalize
- Scientific management
- Social solidarity
- Surplus value
- Survey
- Urbanization
- *Verstehen*

Review questions

1. To what extent has the decline of Communism undermined the utility of Marx's ideas?
2. Why was Weber so pessimistic about work when Durkheim and Marx were so optimistic?
3. Do we need theory to explain the way organizations work?
4. What is the relevance of Weber's concept of *Verstehen* for organizational behaviour researchers?
5. What is meant by open systems, contingency theory and social action theory? Why is it important to understand each of them?
6. What is meant by the suggestion that theory cannot be separated from management practice?

Research questions

1. Form a study group of three to five people. Having read a review of the classical socio-logical theorists and contemporary approaches to studying work and organizations, is the role of the academics in organizational behaviour to unmask inequality in organizational life or to be detached? Is it possible for organizational behaviour researchers to be value-free and objective in their research? If a researcher adopted a feminist perspective, how would this guide his or her research?
2. Obtain a copy of Stephen Ackroyd and others' (2006) *The Oxford Handbook of Work and Organization* and read pages 2–8. To what extent are this textbook – *Work and Organizational Behaviour* – and the topics selected for study a product of its times? If you had to do some organizational behaviour research, what would your topic be and what factors would influence your choice?
3. Retrieve and read Christine Coupland and others' (2008) article, 'Saying it with feeling: analyzing speakable emotions' (see Further reading, below). What does the term 'con-structionism' mean? How does Marx's analysis of capitalist employer–employee relations help us to understand that how people talk about emotional experiences in the workplace is bound up in relations of power?

Further reading

Bratton, J., Denham, D. and Deutschmann, L. (2009) *Capitalism and Classical Sociological Theory*, Toronto: University of Toronto Press.

Coupland, C., Brown, A. D., Daniels, K. and Humphreys, M. (2008) 'Saying it with feeling: analyzing speakable emotions', *Human Relations*, 61(3), pp. 327–53.

Heracleous, L. and Jacob, C. D. (2008) 'Understanding organizations through embodied metaphors', *Organization Studies*, **29**(1), pp. 45–78.

Jaffee, D. (2001) *Organization Theory: Tension and Change*, Boston, MA: McGraw-Hill, Chapters 1 and 2.

Manning, P. K. (2008) 'Goffman on organizations', *Organization Studies*, **29**(5), pp. 677–99.

Parker, M. (2000) 'The sociology of organizations and the organization of sociology: some reflections on the making of a division of labour', *Sociological Review*, **4**(1), pp. 124–46.

Reed, M. (1999) 'Organizational theorizing: a historically contested terrain', pp. 25–50 in S. R. Clegg and C. Hardy (eds), *Studying Organization: Theory and Method*, London: Sage.

Rowlinson, M. (2004) 'Challenging the foundations of organization theory', *Work, Employment and Society*, **18**(3), pp. 607–20.

Swingewood, A. (2000) *A Short History of Sociological Thought*, New York: St Martin's Press, Chapters 2, 3 and 4.

Tsoukas, H. (1992) 'Postmodernism, reflexive rationalism and organizational studies: a reply to Martin Parker', *Organizational Studies*, **13**(4), pp. 643–9.

Chapter case study 1

Butting out smoking in Russia

Setting

With the collapse of the Soviet Union, the privatization of Russia's tobacco industry began. In the new Russia, tobacco advertising is unavoidable. Smoking is promoted on half of all billboards in Moscow and on three-quarters of the plastic bags in the country. As a result of tobacco companies promoting smoking as part of a 'Western lifestyle' and striving to capitalize on the public's new disposable income, smoking rates have doubled. Russia is now the fourth heaviest smoking country in the world, with one in four boys under the age of 10 and 60 per cent of men over the age of 15 classified as smokers. While most of the Western world is experiencing a decrease in smoking rates, the number of Russian smokers continues to climb.

The government has proposed legislation banning smoking in workplaces and other public places, such as on aircraft, trains and municipal transport as well as in schools, hospitals, cultural institutions and government buildings. The legislation also requires specially designated smoking areas to be set up, and for restaurants and cafes to set up no-smoking areas. The changes will affect not only Russian companies, but also international firms looking to invest in the expanding privatization of the economy. The emerging middle class has produced a potential market of 150 million consumers that lures companies from all over the world hoping to tap into the vast natural resources, advanced technology and skilled workers that Russia has to offer.

The problem

Kendles & Smith is a global British pharmaceutical, medical devices and consumer packaged goods manufacturer, with 150 subsidiary companies operating in over 32 countries. It recently opened a new operation in Moscow as part of a strategy to make its mark on the new prosperous Russian economy.

The management at Kendles & Smith were versed in Russian history and understood that worker attitudes and behaviours had been shaped by 70 years of Communist dictatorship, a centrally planned economic system, and government bureaucracy that had ruled the people's lives. Like most international firms, management at Kendles & Smith found Russian workers to be cooperative and compliant, but not risk takers. Many of the supervisors hired from the local labour pool lacked confidence and drive. Although they followed corporate policies strictly, the employees in turn expected the new company to take care of them and their families.

With the UK having one of the lowest smoking rates in Europe, the management at Kendles & Smith were surprised at the number of the employees who were smokers – almost 65 per cent. As a company with a focus on health products, one of its first goals was to develop a voluntary tobacco reduction programme, including counselling and nicotine cessation aids, to improve the health of its new staff. Unfortunately, only a small group of workers took advantage of the programme in its first year, and the majority of these were supervisors.

The next step was to implement a smoking ban in the Russian operations. Although it was made clear to all employees that the company president wanted to see the worksites smoke-free, regardless of the government's legislation, only the supervisors were to be given an opportunity to express their positions on the matter. Jonathan Williams, one of the UK managers assigned to the Moscow operation, was given the task of doing the research. There were over 100 supervisors, and Jonathan was given only a short time-frame within which to present his findings. Although Jonathan was free to speak to the supervisors, the company president stressed that he really just wanted to know whether or not the majority of the supervisors favoured the ban.

As Jonathan had not conducted workplace research before, he felt overwhelmed when he began reading about the various methods that could be used. He wanted the rich qualitative information that in-person interviews could give, but he thought that taking a more quantitative approach, such as using a questionnaire, would provide the anonymity that the supervisors might need to be honest with their answers.

Tasks

As Jonathan, ask yourself the following questions:

1. What would be the disadvantages of using a questionnaire in this case?
2. What might be missed by gathering only the supervisors' opinions?
3. What qualities do the Russian workers exhibit that could influence the research results? Why?

Further reading

Allan, G. and Skinner, C. (eds) (1991) *Handbook for Research Students in the Social Sciences*, London: Falmer Press.

Bryman, J. (ed.) (1988) *Doing Research in Organizations*, London: Routledge.

Elenkov, D. (1998) 'Can American management concepts work in Russia?', *California Management Review*, **40**(4), pp. 133–56.

Oppenheim, A. N. (1992) *Questionnaire Design, Interviewing and Attitude Measurement*, London: Pinter.

Visit http://pre.ethics.gc.ca/eng/policy-politique/tcps-eptc/readtcps-lireeptc for an example of a research ethics policy.

Note

This case study was written by Lori Rilkoff, MSc, CHRP, Senior Human Resources Manager at the City of Kamloops, and lecturer in HRM at Thompson Rivers University, BC, Canada. Data on smoking in Russia were taken from http://news.bbc.co.uk/2/hi/health/7209551.stm; www.scientific blogging.com/news_releases/russian_women_exercise_post_soviet_free_will_by_smoking_ a_lot_more

Chapter case study 2

Research at Aeroprecision AB

Visit www.palgrave.com/business/brattinob2e to view this case study

Web-based assignment

How are we to make sense of the competing assortment of theoretical approaches to organizational behaviour? We address this question here with reference to the classical accounts of sociology and contemporary approaches to studying formal organizations. Our collective experience in teaching and researching aspects of organizational behaviour has made it clear that the contemporary student of organizational behaviour cannot understand the discipline without an appreciation of the works of Marx, Weber and Durkheim. In their own way, each addressed the following two fundamental questions:

- What is the source of societal and organizational conflict?
- What is the relationship between consciousness (the 'self' or 'inside') and society or social structure (the 'outside')?

On an individual basis, or working in a small group, visit the following websites and write a brief summary of how Marx, Weber and Durkheim have fundamentally shaped the modern debate about work and organizations:

- http://plato.stanford.edu/entries/marx
- www.epistemelinks.com/Main/Philosophers.aspx?PhilCode=Durk
- www.marxists.org/reference/archive/weber

OB in film

The film *Roger & Me* (1989), directed by Michael Moore, is a documentary about the closure of General Motors' car plant at Flint, Michigan, which resulted in the loss of 30,000 jobs. The film provides insight into corporate restructuring and US deindustrialization, and details the attempts of the film maker to conduct a face-to-face interview with General Motors Chief Executive Officer Roger Smith. The film also raises questions about values, politics and the practical considerations of doing organizational behaviour research.

Values reflect the personal beliefs of a researcher. Gaining access to organizations, particularly to top managers, is a political process. Access is usually mediated by gatekeepers concerned not only about what the organization can gain from the research, but also about the researcher's motives.

Watch the documentary, and consider these questions:

- Can organizational behaviour researchers be value-free and objective in their research?
- Who are the gatekeepers in *Roger & Me?* How can gatekeepers influence how the inquiry will take place?

Practical considerations refer to issues about how to carry out organizational behaviour research: for example, choices of research design or method need to be dovetailed with specific research questions.

- What alternative methods could a researcher use to investigate the closure of General Motors' factory at Flint?

References

1. Salaman, G. (1981) *Class and the Corporation*, London: Fontana.
2. Turner, B. S. (1999) *Classical Sociology*, London: Sage.
3. Hurst, C. (2005) *Living Theory*, Boston, MA: Pearson.

4. Clegg, S. and Hardy, C. (1999) *Studying Organization: Theory and Method*, Thousand Oaks, CA: Sage.

5. Grint, K. (1998) *The Sociology of Work* (2nd edn), Cambridge: Polity Press.

6. Marx, K. (1867/1970) *Capital: A Critique of Political Economy*, Volume 1, London: Lawrence & Wishart.

7. Ritzer, G. and Goodman, D. J. (2004) *Classical Social Theory* (4th edn), New York: McGraw-Hill.

8. Morrison, K. (1995) *Marx, Durkheim, Weber*, London: Sage.

9. Marx, K. and Engels, F. (1848/1967) *The Communist Manifesto*, London: Penguin.

10. Durkheim, E. (1893/1997) *The Division of Labor in Society*, New York: Free Press.

11. Weber, M. (1905/2002) *The Protestant Ethic and the 'Spirit' of Capitalism*, London: Penguin.

12. Ritzer, G. (2000) *The McDonaldization of Society*, Thousand Oaks, CA: Pine Forge Press.

13. Weber, M. (1922/1968) *Economy and Society*, New York: Bedminster.

14. Smith, A. (1776/1982) *The Wealth of Nations*, Harmondsworth: Penguin.

15. George, C. S. (1972) *The History of Management Thought* (2nd edn), Englewood Cliffs, NJ: Prentice-Hall.

16. Braverman, H. (1974) *Labor and Monopoly Capitalism: The Degradation of Work in the Twentieth Century*, New York: Monthly Review Press.

17. Littler, C. R. and Salaman, G. (1984) *Class at Work: The Design, Allocation and Control of Jobs*, London: Batsford.

18. Thompson, P. and McHugh, D. (2006) *Work Organizations: A Critical Introduction* (4th edn), Basingstoke: Palgrave.

19. Mouzelis, N. (1967) *Organization and Bureaucracy*, London: Routledge & Kegan Paul.

20. Clegg, S. and Dunkerley, D. (1980) *Organization, Class and Control*, London: Routledge & Kegan Paul.

21. Thompson, P. (1989) *The Nature of Work* (2nd edn), London: Macmillan.

22. Bratton, J., Helms Mills, J. and Sawchuk, P. (2004) *Workplace Learning: A Critical Introduction*, Toronto: Garamond.

23. Cohen, P. S. (1968) *Modern Social Theory*, London: Heinemann.

24. Parsons, T. (1960) *Structure and Process in Modern Societies*, Chicago: Free Press.

25. Dunlop, J. T. (1958) *Industrial Relations System*, New York: Holt.

26. Senge, P. (1990) *The Fifth Discipline*, New York: Doubleday.

27. Scott, R. W. (2003) *Organizations: Rational, Natural, and Open Systems*, Upper Saddle River, NJ: Prentice-Hall.

28. Jaffee, D. (2001) *Organization Theory: Tension and Change*, Boston, MA: McGraw-Hill.

29. Woodward, J. (1958) *Management and Technology*. Problems of Progress in Industry No. 5, London: HMSO.

30. Woodward, J. (1965) *Industrial Organizations: Theory and Practice*, London: Oxford University Press.

31. Burns, T. and Stalker, G. M. (1961) *The Management of Innovation*, London: Tavistock.

32. Lawrence, P. R. and Lorsch, J. W. (1967) *Organisation and Environment: Managing Differentiation and Integration*, Cambridge, MA: Harvard University Press.

33. Thompson, P. and McHugh, D. (2009) *Work Organizations: A Critical Introduction* (4th edn), Basingstoke: Palgrave.

34. Lopez, J. (2003) *Society and its Metaphors: Language, Social Theory and Social Structure*, London: Continuum.

35. Morgan, G. (1997) *Images of Organization* (2nd edn), Thousand Oaks, CA: Sage.

36. Handy, C. (1985) *Understanding Organizations*, London: Penguin.

37. Rigney, F. (2001) *The Metaphorical Society: An Invitation to Social Theory*, Lanham, MD: Rowman & Littlefield.

38. Crow, G. (2005) *The Art of Sociological Argument*, Basingstoke: Palgrave.

39. Etzioni, A. (1988) *The Moral Dimension*, New York: Free Press.

40. Pedler, M., Boydell, T. and Burgoyne, J. (1988) *The Learning Company Project Report*, Sheffield: Employment Department.

41. Fenwick,T. (1998) 'Questioning the concept of the learning organization', pp. 140–52 in S. Scott, B. Spencer and A.Thomas (eds), *Learning for Life*, Toronto: Thompson Educational.

42. Garavan, T. (1997) 'The learning organization: a review and evaluation', *Learning Organization*, **4**(1), pp. 18–29.
43. Silverman, D. (1970) *The Theory of Organizations*, London: Heinemann.
44. Brown, R. K. (1992) *Understanding Industrial Organizations*, London: Routledge.
45. Nutley, S. M. and Davies, H. T. O. (2001) 'Developing organizational learning in the NHS', *Medical Education*, **35**(1), Wiley-Blackwell, p. 35.
46. Alvesson, M. and Willmott, H. (1996) *Making Sense of Management: A Critical Introduction*, London: Sage.
47. Dalton, M. (1959) *Men Who Manage*, New York: McGraw-Hill.
48. Fox, A. (1971) *The Sociology of Work in Industry*, London: Collier Macmillan.
49. Child, J. (1972) 'Organizational structure, environment and performance: the role of strategic choice', *Sociology*, **6**(1), pp. 331–50.
50. Pettigrew, A. (1973) *The Politics of Organizational Decision-Making*, London: Tavistock.
51. Kotter, J. P. (1979) *Power in Management*, New York: Amocom.
52. Kochan, T. E., Katz, H. and McKersie, R. (1986) *The Transformation of American Industrial Relations*, New York: Basic Books.
53. Alvesson, M. (1987) *Organization Theory: Technocratic Consciousness*, Berlin: De Gruyter.
54. Alvesson, M. and Willmott, H. (eds) (1992) *Critical Management Studies*, London: Sage.
55. Habermas, J. (1970) *Towards a Rational Society*, London: Heinemann.
56. Habermas, J. (1971) *Knowledge and Human Interests*, London: Heinemann
57. Marcuse, H. (1964) *One Dimensional Man*, Boston, MA: Beacon.
58. Marcuse, H. (1969) *An Essay on Liberation*, Boston, MA: Beacon.
59. Kelly, J. (1985) 'Management's redesign of work: labour process, labour markets and product markets', in D. Knights, H. Willmott and D. Collinson (eds), *Job Redesign: Critical Perspectives on the Labour Process*, Aldershot: Gower.
60. Wood, S. (ed.) (1982) *The Transformation of Work?*, London: Unwin Hyman.
61. Bratton, J. (1992) *Japanization at Work*, Basingstoke: Macmillan.
62. Sydie, R. A. (1994) *Natural Women, Cultured Men*, Vancouver: UBC Press.
63. Townley, B. (1994) *Reframing Human Resource Management: Power, Ethics and the Subject of Work*, London: Sage.
64. Hassard, J. and Parker, M. (eds) (1993) *Postmodernism and Organizations*, London: Sage.
65. Foucault, M. (1977) *Discipline and Punish: The Birth of the Prison*, New York: Pantheon.
66. Foucault, M. (1979) *The History of Sexuality*, Harmondsworth: Penguin.
67. Sheridan, A. (1980) *Michel Foucault: The Will to Power*, London: Tavistock.
68. Parker, M. (1993) 'Life after Jean-Francois', pp. 204–12 in J. Hassard and M. Parker (eds), *Postmodernism and Organizations*, London: Sage.
69. Ray, L. J. (1999) *Theorizing Classical Sociology*, Buckingham: Open University Press.
70. Craib, I. (1997) *Classical Social Theory*, Oxford: Oxford University Press.
71. Delaney, T. (2004) *Classical Social Theory: Investigation and Application*, Upper Saddle River, NJ: Pearson/Prentice-Hall.
72. Smart, B. (2003) *Economy, Culture and Society*, Buckingham: Open University Press.
73. Goodwin, G. A. and Scimecca, J. A. (2006) *Classical Social Theory*, Belmont, CA: Thomson.

CHAPTER 4
Organizational design

CHAPTER OUTLINE

- Introduction
- Organizational structure and design
- Dimensions of structure
- Typologies of organizational structure
- Determinants of organizational structure: making strategic choices
- Organizational restructuring: a conceptual framework
- Traditional designs of organizational structure: bureaucracy
- Emerging organizational designs: post-bureaucracy?
- Gender, sexuality and organizational design
- Summary and end-of-chapter features
- Chapter case study 1: Strategy and design in Australia's tourist industry
- Chapter case study 2: ABC's just-in-time supply chain

CHAPTER OBJECTIVES

After studying this chapter, you should be able to:

- identify and define the foundation concepts of organizational structure and design
- understand the meaning and significance of complexity, formalization and cetralization
- explain the relationships between strategy, size, technology and capitalist development, and the different forms of organizational design
- describe the difference between classical and modern thinking about organizational design

- describe some of the emerging contemporary forms of organizational design and identify the potential impact on workplace behaviour
- explain and illustrate the basis of criticism of managerial thinking about organizational design with reference to power, gender and sexuality

Introduction

In his influential book *Beyond Reengineering*,[1] Michael Hammer cited the Ford Motor Company as an exemplar of how a few American corporations had restructured and transformed 'beyond recognition' their old ways of doing things in order to meet the challenges of global competition. In February 2009, Ford chairman and CEO Bill Ford and other CEOs from General Motors and Chrysler were publicly explaining to the US Senate banking committee why they needed US$17 billion of emergency financial infusion to prevent bankruptcy. And in March 2009, US President Barack Obama rejected General Motors' and Chrysler's restructuring plans that had been submitted in February, while demanding the resignation of General Motors' CEO, Rick Wagoner, as part of the government's offer to help General Motors to accelerate and deepen their restructuring plans (see OB in focus, below).

In the same period, corporate bail-outs and the restructuring of European companies such as Fiat SpA, Renault SA, Volvo and Opel were reported. These restructuring initiatives were not unique to the manufacturing sector. Accelerated by dysfunctional financial markets and deteriorating global trade, venerable financial firms such as American International Group, Fannie Mae, Freddie Mac, Citigroup, Bank of America, Northern Rock, Bradford and Bingley, Royal Bank of Scotland and HBOS have been bailed out, restructured or nationalized.

Organizational restructuring entails a significant decrease in the resources that it allocates to process activities or product markets in which it has previously engaged, or a reallocation of resources to new geographical locations.[2] A plethora of studies have analysed such a 'downsizing' as part of a process of 'outsourcing' many functions originally assigned to permanent employees. Restructuring has been wrapped in the mantra of flexibility, lean and mean and competitiveness.[3–12] These studies emphasize that 'corporate anorexia' can fundamentally change how work is performed as well as reshape employment relations. Thus, the study of organizational structure and design is essential for a deeper understanding of workplace behaviour. What exactly are senior managers 'restructuring'? What determines organizational design? What is the right relationship between the centre of a company and its periphery? How does the psychological contract between the worker and the employer change after restructuring? And how does organizational design and redesign modify behaviour?

The answer to these questions is the focus of this chapter. We begin by explaining the meaning and nature of organizational structure and design. To help with our analysis of different organizational forms, we offer a conceptual framework of the various types of organizational reconfiguring. We then move on to examine some traditional **formal organizational** designs: functional, product/service, divisional and matrix. New organizational designs that have allegedly supplanted the traditional forms are also examined. We conclude this chapter with a discussion on the links between gender, sexuality and organizational design.

formal organization: a highly structured group formed for the purpose of completing certain tasks or achieving specific goals

---

stop reflect

Think about an organization where you have worked or studied. Can you identify a set of characteristics that help to describe its structure?

OB in focus

OB in focus: Corporate restructuring and the car industry

Since the start of the recession, downsizing has become the management trend around the world, and corporate restructuring has become key to survival. In just one week in November 2008, Britain's BT, Canada's Nortel and German-owned DHL were just three of many firms announcing massive job cuts. In addition to having to trim down the number of employees, businesses are having to rethink the organization of their headquarters. Many are struggling with the problem of maintaining the right relationship between the centre and the periphery. In the 1970s, large multinationals created large headquarters. In the 1990s, the fashion changed to modest, simple centres. In the twenty-first century, headquarters were beginning to expand again – but the recession will probably force organizations to revert to minimalism.

The car industry has been hit especially hard by the recent economic downturn. Three of the largest US car manufacturers – General Motors (GM), Chrysler and Ford – have been forced to make significant changes to how they operate, while the government has had to step in to help out. All three organizations were in the midst of implementing vast restructuring and cost-cutting strategies when they were knocked back again by tightening credit and rising oil prices. The revelation that GM was in danger of running out of cash concentrated executive minds. Although not quite as desperate, Ford was in a similar position, while Cerberus Capital Management (which owned 80 per cent of Chrysler) sought to offload the car maker to another firm. So the struggling car manufacturers were left with just two options: either the US government would have to come to the rescue, or the biggest car companies in America would have to seek bankruptcy protection.

Chrysler did in the end file for bankruptcy (despite evidence that customers would be likely to abandon the products of a car manufacturer that took this step). The US government bailed out GM, and President Obama expressed his hope that the company would emerge 'leaner and meaner' as a result of its financial woes. In some ways, it seems that the Obama administration's automotive task force holds the fate of the US car industry and its future structure in its hands.

Sources: Anonymous (2008) 'Centres of attention', *The Economist*, November 13; Anonymous (2008) 'Follow the money', *The Economist*, October 18, p. 72; Anonymous (2008) 'On the edge', *The Economist*, November 15, 2008, p. 75; Keenan, G. (2009) 'Losses force GM to question its future', *Globe and Mail*, February 27, p. B1; http://news.bbc.co.uk/1/hi/business/8065760.stm.

Organizational structure and design

Organizations are created to produce goods or services and to pursue dominant goals that individuals acting alone cannot achieve. According to Peter Drucker, the purpose of the work organization 'is to get the work done'.[13] However, organizational structure is not easy to define because it is not a physical reality, but rather a conceptual one. Let us begin to explain the concept in this way. To accomplish its strategic goals, an organization typically has to do two things: divide the work to be done among its members, and then coordinate the work. organizational structure refers to the formal division of work and the formal configuration of relationships that coordinate and control organizational activities. The organizational design is the planning and implementation of a structural configuration of roles and modes of operation. Arguably, theories of organizational structure are a product of modernity, because they are largely based on Weber's notions of rationality and bureaucratic specialization.

organizational structure: the formal reporting relationships, groups, departments and systems of the organization

organizational design: the process of creating and modifying organizational structures

Thus, work is divided horizontally into distinct tasks that need to be done, either into jobs, subunits or departments. This horizontal division of labour is associated with specialization on the part of the workforce. The vertical division of labour is concerned with apportioning authority for planning, decision making, monitoring and controlling: who will tell whom what to do? For example, in a small restaurant, the horizontal divisions might be divided into three main work activities: preparing the food, service and running the bar. A vertical division of labour would describe the coordinating and directing work of the head chef, the restaurant supervisor and the head bar tender, all of whom report to the restaurant manager.

This small business has a simple structure. However, the structure could become more complex as more people were hired and as coordination and control became more difficult. As business expanded and management became more complicated, the manager might not have enough time to deal with the accounts and hiring and training of new staff. To solve these problems, the restaurant manager might hire an accountant and a human resource manager, which would increase the vertical division of labour. The growth of an organization might therefore lead to a greater degree of specialization of its workforce.

Alternatively, the restaurant manager might create work teams and allow the team members to coordinate their work activities and hire and train their members.

Plate 1 In a small restaurant, the horizontal divisions might be divided into three main work activities: preparing the food, service and running the bar. A vertical division of labour would describe the coordinating and directing work of the head chef, the restaurant supervisor and the head bar tender, all of whom report to the restaurant manager

This limited 'empowerment' of the workers would then free up time for the head chef, the restaurant supervisor and the head bar tender to handle the accounts for their departments.

Specialization occurs when people focus their effort on a particular skill, task, customer or territorial area. Our simple example of the restaurant illustrates two important points: managers have choices over how to divide labour, and different organizational configurations impact on people's work experience. (For instance, if teams were introduced, additional tasks would have to be learnt and the pace of work might intensify.)

specialization: the allocation of work tasks to categories of employee or groups. Also known as division of labour

An organization chart graphically shows the various parts as boxes, and the coordination and control by lines that connect the boxes. This system is used in Figure 4.1 to demonstrate the simple structure of the restaurant just described, and is used in the sample organization charts that follow. Organizational design refers to the process of creating a structure that best fits a strategy, technology and environment. For example, Ford Motor Company has created a structure on a product basis, with separate divisions for specific models. So why do managers redesign structures? Management designs new structures in order to reduce costs, to respond to changing customer buying patterns or business boundaries, to reset priorities, to shift people and align capabilities, to shift perceptions of service among users, or to 'shake things up'.[14]

organization chart: a diagram showing the grouping of activities and people within a formal organization to achieve the goals of the organization efficiently

Why is organizational structure important? From a managerial perspective, structure may make the task of managing employees more complex, bringing into play the questions of efficiency and consistency that are likely to arise more often when different groups report directly to departmental managers, rather than to a single owner or manager in an organization employing relatively few people. Structure therefore defines lines of responsibility and authority. In terms of organizational performance, a 'good' structure is not a panacea, but it is very important, argues management guru Peter Drucker: 'Good organizational structure does not by itself produce good performance ... But a poor organization structure makes good performance impossible, no matter how good the individual managers may be' (ref. 15, p. 4). The structure of an organization also affects the ability of workers to learn, to be creative, to innovate and to participate in decision making.[16,17]

From a worker's perspective, different structural configurations affect not only productivity and economic results, defined by the marketplace, but also job satisfaction, commitment, motivation and perceptions about expectations and obligations.

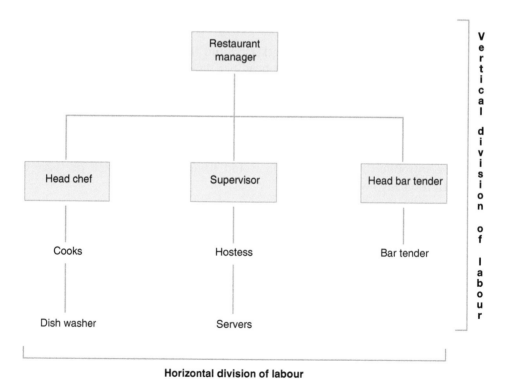

Figure 4.1   An example of a simple organizational structure

Redesigning organizational structure will therefore affect the intangible 'psychological contract' of each individual worker.

The concept of the psychological contract has an important implication for those redesigning organizational structures. Each individual employee will have different perceptions of his or her psychological contract, even when the structure within which he or she works is identical. Therefore, there will be no universal notion of mutual expectations and obligations.[18] Changes in the organization's structure also affect employee relations and organizational governance. All this serves to remind us that organizational success and failure depend on the behaviour of people, who work within the formal structure and who mould and imprint their personality into their work activities.

So far, we have given what could be described as the orthodox or mainstream position, in which organizational structure is rationally designed by managers to meet dominant organizational goals in as efficient a way as possible within the constraints they perceive. However, a critical approach to studying organizational behaviour examines the informal aspects of structure, which consist in part of unofficial working arrangements, social networking cabals and the internal politicking of people. Conceptually, it is argued that these two aspects of organizational structure – the formal and the informal – are dialectically related, in that they are influenced by each other, and activities in one encourage activities in the other.[19,20] For example, a team-based organizational structure designed by senior management to increase flexibility may invite unofficial strategies among line managers who choose to resist being relocated. An organizational structure reflects internal power relationships.[21,22]

informal structure: a term used to describe the aspect of organizational life in which participants' day-to-day activities and interactions ignore, bypass or do not correspond with the official rules and procedures of the bureaucracy

networking: cultivating social relationships with others to accomplish one's goals

organizational politics: behaviours that others perceive as self-serving tactics for personal gain at the expense of other people and possibly the organization

Dimensions of structure

A variety of dimensions can be used to conceptualize organizational structure. There is a disagreement among theorists over what makes up the term 'structure', but a relatively recent way of thinking about organizations and structure is as 'discursive metaphors'. Advocates of this approach suggest that organizations are 'texts', created through discourses, which have symbolic meaning for managers and workers. These meanings are open to multiple readings even when particular meanings become sufficiently privileged and concrete. Here, we take a more orthodox approach to examine how researchers have analysed structure, before discussing how it affects organizational behaviour.[23] While we acknowledge the elastic definitions and various labels attached to organizational phenomena, here we examine three aspects: complexity, formalization and centralization.

Complexity

complexity is the degree of differentiation in the organization. Complexity measures the degree of division of tasks, levels of hierarchy and geographical locations of work units in the organization. The more tasks are divided among individuals, the more the organization is *horizontally complex*. The most visible evidence in the organization of horizontal complexity is specialization and departmentalization.

complexity: the intricate departmental and interpersonal relationships that exist within a work organization

Specialization refers to the particular grouping of activities performed by an employee. Division of labour – for example, accounting activities – creates groups of specialists (in this case, accountants). The way these specialists are grouped is referred to as departmentalization. As the vertical chain of command lengthens, more formal authority layers are inserted between top management and front-line workers. In such circumstances, the organization becomes more *vertically complex*. Therefore, vertical complexity refers to the depth of the organization's hierarchy: the number of levels between senior management and the workers. Organizations with the same number of workers need not have the same degree of vertical complexity. Organizations can be 'flat', with few layers of hierarchy, or 'tall', with many levels of management between the top CEO and front-line employees (Figure 4.2).

During the last decade, organizations have moved towards flatter configurations by eliminating whole levels of middle managers and generally 'doing more with less'. This form of restructuring, commonly called 'downsizing', increases the span of control for the managers who remain. The span of control defines the number of subordinates that a single manager or administrator can supervise effectively. If this span is narrow, managers have few subordinates reporting to them. If it is wide, managers are

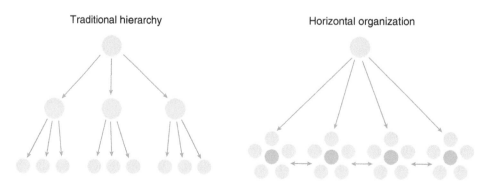

Traditional hierarchy   Horizontal organization

Figure 4.2   A tall organization structure versus a flat (team-based) structure

responsible for many subordinates. The larger the span, the less potential there is for control by direct supervision. When work tasks are routine, the control of subordinates through technology and output performance substitutes for direct supervision. At lower operational levels, it is not unusual to have spans of control of up to 20 individuals. In the managerial ranks, work is less routine, and spans of control tend to be smaller. Thus, the complexity of the task often dictates the span of control.

span of control: the number of people directly reporting to the next level in the organizational hierarchy

Vertical complexity can also affect managerial behaviour by impacting on other factors such as communication networks and manager–worker dynamics. For example, a wide span of control makes it more difficult for a manager to hold face-to-face meetings.

An organization can perform the same work activities in geographically separate locations, a fact emphasized by globalization. The existence of multiple workplaces increases complexity. *Spatial complexity* refers to the degree to which the organization's operations and core workforce are geographically dispersed. As spatial complexity increases, managers face coordination, control and communication challenges relating to their subordinates.[24]

weblink

Go to www.shell.com for an example of team-based organizational design

Formalization

Formalization is the second core dimension of organizational structure, and describes the degree of standardization of work and jobs in the organization. It refers to the extent to which work is defined and controlled by rules. The more rules there are about what is to be done, when it is to be done and how it should be done, the more an organization is formalized. Where formalization is low, employees are given freedom to exercise discretion in their work. The degree of formalization can vary widely within and among organizations.

formalization: the degree to which organizations standardize behaviour through rules, procedures, formal training and related mechanisms

The extent of formalization typically varies with the nature of the work performed and the size of the organization.[25] The most complex and creative paid work is amenable to low degrees of formalization. Formalization also tends to be inversely related to the hierarchical level in the organization. Individuals lower in the organization are engaged in activities that are relatively simple and repetitive, and therefore these people are most likely to work in a highly formalized environment. Although formalization regulates workers' behaviour, it can also impose constraints on managers and subordinates. In a unionized workplace, for instance, contract rules negotiated by union and management can constrain managers' ability to mobilize the skills, creativity, commitment and values of their subordinates.[26]

Centralization

Centralization, the third core dimension of organizational structure, refers to the degree to which decision making is concentrated at a single point in the organization. In essence, it addresses the question, who makes the decisions in the organization? A decentralized organization is one in which senior managers solicit input from members when making key decisions. The more input members provide or the more autonomy they are given to make decisions, the more decentralized the organization.

centralization: the degree to which formal decision authority is held by a small group of people, typically those at the top of the organizational hierarchy

The degree of centralization affects workers' ability to make decisions, levels of motivation and the manager–subordinate interface. An ongoing challenge for managers is to balance the degree of centralization necessary to achieve control on the one hand, and to gain commitment through participation and work-related learning on the other.

Typologies of organizational structure

The three core dimensions of formal organizational structure – complexity, formalization and centralization – can be combined into a number of different types or models. Two popular descriptive models have received much attention: the mechanistic model and the organic model.[27]

The mechanistic organization has been characterized as a machine. It has high complexity, high formalization and high centralization. A mechanistic organization resembles a bureaucracy. It is characterized by highly specialized tasks that tend to be rigidly defined, a hierarchical authority and control structure, and communications that primarily take the form of edicts and decisions issued by managers to subordinates. Communication typically flows vertically from the top down.

mechanistic organization: an organizational structure with a narrow span of control and high degrees of formalization and centralization

Organic organization are the antithesis of mechanistic organizations. They are characterized by being low in complexity, formality and centralization. An organic organization is said to be flexible and informally coordinated, and managers use participative decision-making behaviours. Communication is both horizontal (across different departments) and vertical (down and up the hierarchy), depending on where the information resides.

organic organization: an organizational structure with a wide span of control, little formalization and decentralized decision making

stop reflect

Can you identify organizations that have organic features and organizations that display mechanistic features?

Determinants of organizational structure: making strategic choices

The underlying rationale for mechanistic and organic organizations is, according to conventional organizational theory, explained by the choice of competitive strategy. The mechanistic organization strives for competitive advantage by maximizing efficiency and productivity, whereas an organic organization's competitive strategy is based on maximum adaptability and flexibility. Thus, structural characteristics concern contextual factors within the organization and affect the management process. So far, although we have examined a number of core organizational design concepts, we have not provided much insight into why organizational structures vary so much, or into the forces behind corporate restructuring. The purpose of this section is to discuss theories of organizational design in terms of their relevance for understanding current restructuring endeavours.

competitive advantage: the ability of a work organization to add more value for its customers and shareholders than its rivals, and thus gain a position of advantage in the marketplace

Early management theorists put forward universalistic organizational structure theories: that is, the 'one size fits all' principle applied to organizations. Over the last 30 years, organizational analysts have modified the classical approach by suggesting that organizational structure is contingent (or depends) on a variety of variables or contextual factors. The contingency approach to organizational design takes the view that there is no 'one best' universal structure, and emphasizes the need for flexibility. The significant contingency variables are strategy, size, technology and environment.

weblink

Visit http://www.12manage.com/methods_contingency_theory.html and http://changingminds.org/disciplines/leadership/theories/contingency_theory.htm for more information on contingency theory

Strategy and structure

Strategy can be viewed as a pattern of activity over time to achieve performance goals. The classical position that 'structure follows strategy' assumes that managers choose the structure they have: 'A new strategy required a new or at least refashioned structure' (ref. 28, p. 15). This hypothesis is represented in Figure 4.3.

For example, if top management chooses to compete through product and service innovation and high quality – a differentiation strategy – then managers need to adopt an organic or horizontal organizational structure. A cost leadership strategy, on the other hand, requires products or services to be standardized with minimum costs. A mechanistic, functional structure with more formalization and centralization is most appropriate with this strategy, so that managers can closely control quality and costs.

Figure 4.3 The strategy-structure thesis

A counter-thesis sees strategy as related less directly to organizational design. In this view, 'strategy follows structure'.[29] The design of the organization is the context in which top managers form the business strategy. Thus, the existing organizational configuration affects top managers' perceptions of internal strengths, weaknesses, threats and opportunities (SWOT) outside the organization, and helps shape a strategy.

Empirical research offers support for both views of strategy affecting the design of an organization; this is illustrated in Figure 4.3 by a two-headed arrow between structure and strategy. This recognizes that the link between strategy and structure is affected by other contingency factors, such as size, technology and environment.

In her book *No Logo*, globalization critic Naomi Klein provides a more controversial account of the link between corporate strategy – a focus on 'branding' and the relocation of manufacturing capacity from the core capitalist economy to the periphery, where wage levels are low – and multifaceted structures spanning national frontiers:

> The astronomical growth in the wealth and cultural influence of multinational corporations over the last fifteen years can arguably be traced back to a single, seemingly innocuous idea developed by management theorists in the mid-1980s, that successful corporations must primarily produce brands, as opposed to products ... The very process of producing – running one's own factories, being responsible for the tens of thousands of full-time, permanent employees – began to look less like the route to success and more like a clunky liability.
>
> At around this time a new kind of corporation began to rival the traditional all-American manufacturers for market share; these were the Nikes and Microsoft, and later, the Tommy Hilfigers and Intels ... What these companies produced primarily were not things, they said, but images of their brands. Their real work lay not in manufacturing but in marketing. This formula, needless to say, has proved enormously profitable, and its success has companies competing in a race towards weightlessness: whoever owns the least, has the fewest employees on the payroll and produces the most powerful images, as opposed to products, wins the race. (ref. 30, p. 4)

Of course, as globalization theorists have observed, the notion of 'weightlessness' is only feasible because of the developments in transportation, namely containerization and the Internet.

weblink

Visit www.corpwatch.org, a US-based organization that monitors and critiques global capitalism through education and social action

Size and structure

Most studies define organizational size as the total number of employees, and researchers suggest that larger organizations have different structures from smaller organizations. As organizations increase in size, they tend to develop more written rules and procedures, and division of labour becomes more specialized. A number of theorists have argued that size is an important factor affecting organizational design.[31-33] It seems credible that there is a positive relationship between size and the degree of formalization, specialization and centralization.

Critics of the size imperative have countered that neither formalization nor complexity can be inferred from organizational size. An equally valid alternative interpretation of early empirical data is that size is the result, not the cause, of structure.[34] The key point here is that there are obvious structural differences between large and small organizations, but a statistically significant relationship between size and structural dimensions does not imply causation. For example, technology influences structure, which in turn determines size.

Technology and structure

Technological change is quintessentially a defining feature of the 'knowledge economy', and is also another important contingency variable explaining organizational structure. Researchers have adopted either a restrictive or an expansive definition of technology, and the early research on technology suggests a positive relationship between type of technology and organizational structure.[35,36]

The 'technology–structure' thesis has sought to analyse technology as an independent explanatory variable. The British academic Joan Woodward, for example, classified production technology into three main categories for analysis: unit production (as in a tailor's shop), mass production (as in an automotive plant), and continuous process production (like that of a pulp mill). Perrow classified four types of technology: routine, engineering, craft and non-routine. Routine technologies have few exceptions and easy-to-analyse problems (for example, pulp and paper mills or chemical plants belong to this category). Engineering technologies have a large number of exceptions, but can be managed in a systematic manner (as with the construction of bridges). Craft technologies deal with relatively difficult problems with a limited set of exceptions (such as in hand-crafted furniture making). Non-routine technologies are characterized by many exceptions and difficult-to-analyse problems (as with research and development).

The research found evidence of different types of technology being associated with different organizational designs. Non-routine technology, for instance, is positively associated with high complexity. So as the work becomes more customized, the span of control narrows. Studies also suggest that routine technology is positively related to formalization. Routine technologies allow leaders to implement rules and regulations because the work is well understood by their followers. It has been proposed that routine technology might lead to centralized decision making and control systems if formalization is low. Within this theoretical framework, it is suggested that technology mediates mechanical and integrated forms of management control, which are incorporated into the technology itself. Thus, employee performance is subject to control by technology rather than by direct human supervision.

Joan Woodward died in 1971, but her thesis that technology is a crucial contingency influenced the American sociologist Howard Aldrich. For Aldrich in 2002, as for Woodward, the technology in use in the organization had high priority in accounting for the degree of organizational structure.[37] Both structure and technology are multidimensional concepts, and it is not realistic to relate technology to structure in any simple manner. In addition, all the technological paradigms have their strengths and weaknesses. Conceptualizing technology by degrees of 'routineness' leads to a generalizable conclusion that technology will shape structure in terms of size, complexity and formalization. The strategic choice discourse also suggests that it is managerial behaviour at critical points in the process of organizational change – possibly in negotiation with trade unions – that is critical in reshaping managerial processes and outcomes, including organizational structure.

Environment and structure

The **environment** is everything outside the organization's boundary. The case for the environmental imperative argues that organizations are embedded in society, and therefore a multitude of economic, political, social and legal factors will affect organizational design decisions. The attack on the World Trade Center on September 11, 2001 and the global economic recession that began in 2008–09 are two catastrophes outside organizations that resulted in major restructuring within many airlines and banks.

environment: refers to the broad economic, political, legal and social forces that are present in the minds of the organization's members and may influence their decision making and constrain their strategic choices, such as the national business system

An early study by Burns and Stalker in 1966 proposed an environment–structure thesis.[27] In essence, their study of UK firms distinguished five different kinds of environment, ranging from 'stable' to 'least predictable', and two divergent patterns of managerial behaviour and organizational structure – the organic and the mechanistic configurations. They suggested that both types of structural regime represented a 'rational' form of organization that could be created and sustained according to the external conditions facing the organization. For instance, uncertainty in the environment might cause top managers to restructure in order to be more responsive to the changing marketplace.

stop reflect

Can you think of any developments in the UK or Europe that have changed organizational design?

An organization's environment can also range from *munificent* to *hostile*. Organizations located in a hostile environment face more competition, an adversarial union–management relationship and resource scarcity.

These four distinct dimensions of environments shape structure. The more dynamic the environment, the more 'organic' the structure, and the more complex the environment, the more 'decentralized' the structure.[38] The explosive growth of e-commerce, for example, has created a dynamic complex environment for much of the retail book and clothing industry, and is therefore spawning highly flexible network structures. Despite the criticisms of contingency theory, it has provided insights into understanding complex situational variables that help to shape organizational structure.

Globalization and organizational restructuring

Our aim in this chapter is to offer a multidimensional understanding of organizational structure and restructuring. Existing organizational behaviour texts tend to be more narrowly focused, and give limited, if any, coverage to the causation and consequences of global capitalism.

As a field of study, the term globalization is controversial, as are its alleged effects. Clearly, a detailed study of globalization is beyond the scope of this chapter, but to ground the arguments on organizational structure we need to at least acknowledge the interplay of continuity, restructuring and the diversity of experiences of globalization.

globalization: when an organization extends its activities to other parts of the world, actively participates in other markets, and competes against organizations located in other countries

---

Work and Society: Fordism for doctors?

For those who study occupational change, the professions represent an interesting case. 'Professional' occupations span a broad range of areas – from established occupations such as doctor or lawyer, to so-called 'semi-professional' occupations such as teacher or social worker. What makes the professions unique is that they appear to have resisted many of the trends that have changed the face of work in the twentieth century. Although specialized, the professional worker is not alienated. He or she enjoys considerable discretion over how work is done, the settings in which it is done, and the ways in which it is evaluated. Traditionally, professional workers have maintained control over their work processes, despite efforts by managers and consumers to challenge that control.

The world of professional work has undergone significant change in the last two decades. Professional au-thority has been contested, and there have been efforts to subordinate professional authority to managerial authority. Some of the more dramatic instances of this kind of challenge have occurred in Britain's National Health Service (NHS). Referring to specific moments in this process of reform, David Hunter (1994), a Professor at the Nuffield Institute for Health, offers the following analysis:

Much of the impetus beyond the 1989 reform proposals ... can be seen as an attempt to secure a shift in the balance of power between doctors and managers in favour of

---

the latter. They seek to achieve such a shift in the context of advocating improved efficiency in the use of resources and in the provision of services. Much of the management problem in the NHS has centered on the notion of under-management in respect of the medical side of the service. Getting a grip on the freedom enjoyed by clinicians and holding them to account for expenditure they incur is seen as the last unmanaged frontier in the NHS. (p. 6)

As Hunter suggests, the rationale behind this attempt to limit the professional power of doctors was effi-ciency. But what is the larger historical context of this managerial initiative? Richard Sennett argues that the rationale for reform of this kind can be traced back to Henry Ford's views on how work should be organized. In Sennett's view, 'Fordism' entails a particular perspective on the division of labour: 'each worker does one task, measured as precisely as possible by time-and-motion studies; output is measured in terms of targets that are ... entirely quantitative' (Sennett, 2008, p. 47). Sennett goes on to suggest how Fordism has shaped reforms in the NHS: 'Fordism monitors the time doctors and nurses spend with each patient; a medical treatment system based on dealing with auto parts, it tends to treat cancerous livers or broken backs rather than patients in the round' (p. 47).

How effective has this approach been to managing the clinical world of health-care? Hunter maintains that while the power of doctors was constrained in some ways, doctors continued to exert considerable influence over how health and disease should be understood, and consequently on how the work of producing health and preventing illness should be organized. Moreover, as Sennett notes, 'doctors create paper fictions' to circumvent the practice guidelines imposed by managers in the NHS: 'Doctors in the NHS often assign a patient a disease in order to justify the time spent exploring a puzzling body' (p. 49).

The challenge of how to organize and manage professional work remains a central issue in the field of organizational design. We have yet to answer the question of what might constitute the optimal balance between professional and managerial power. Perhaps the best way to approach this question is to attempt to envision a situation where shared power enhances productivity and quality in the provision of healthcare.

stop! Taking the doctor as an example, where would you position the threshold beyond which too much managerial power might erode productivity and decrease the quality of patient care? Provide some concrete examples to illustrate how a sharing of power between professionals (including allied professionals, such as nurses) and managers will enhance the overall effectiveness of the NHS and national health systems more generally.

Can you identify the major source of managerial authority in a system like that of the USA where private corporations play a key role in the delivery of healthcare?

Consider how these issues may apply to other professions, such as law and teaching.

144

Sources and further information

Freidson, E. (1998) *Professionalism Reborn*, Chicago: University of Chicago Press.

Hunter, D. (1994) 'From tribalism to corporatism: the managerial challenge to medical dominance', pp. 1–22 in J. Gabe, D. Kelleher and G. Williams (eds), Challenging *Medicine*, London: Routledge.

Sennett, R. (2008) *The Craftsman*, New Haven, CT: Yale University Press.

Note: This feature was written by David MacLennan, Assistant Professor at Thompson Rivers University, BC, Canada.

For some, globalization involves the spread of transplanetary connections between people.[39] For others, globalization primarily revolves around two main phenomena. First is the emergence of a capitalist global economy based on a sophisticated system of production, finance, transportation and communication driven by transnational corporations (TNCs). Second is the notion of global culture, which focuses on the spread of particular patterns of consumption and the ideology of consumerism at the global level.[40]

The more radical globalization literature helps us to locate the main driver of organizational design and restructuring in the dialectical development of global capitalism. This argument is based on the theory that organizational restructuring occurs because of systematic contradictions.[41] This approach, which has occupied an immense space in Marxist literature, searches for inherent tendencies in the global capitalist system that create tension and bring about their own conflicts, until such a system can no longer maintain itself without far-reaching structural adjustments. Thus, every phase of capitalist expansion is characterized by the particular model through which business organizations 'make their profits'. In Marxist literature, this is referred to as 'accumulation'.

To apply accumulation theory to the various restructuring initiatives shown in Figure 4.5, below, profit maximization was achieved in the first half of the twentieth century through the use of bureaucracies modelled on Fordist-style production and employment relations. The whole point about bureaucratic Fordism as a profitable undertaking is that it achieves economies of scale: the system produces standardized products at relatively low unit costs.

However, the downside to Taylorism and Fordism is that the success of the operation depends on an expanding market for the same standard product, and mass production cannot readily adjust to changing consumer tastes. The offer to consumers of 'Any colour of car provided it's black' is less compelling when the market is saturated with black cars and competitors are offering a choice of colours. It is perhaps not surprising that, in order to maintain profitability, an early response of employers to the catalogue of problems associated with bureaucratic Fordism was to decentralize and transplant assembly-line systems from core capitalist countries (such as Germany) to the periphery (for example, to Mexico), where wage levels were very low. The systematic contradiction of Fordism and corporate imperatives created divisionalized structures, including strategic business units, as manufacturing was relocated to the newly industrialized economies (NIEs) of South-East Asia, Brazil and Mexico.

In recent years, market changes compelled further restructuring and 'downsizing' towards 'horizontal' or 'lean' organizations. As two US management theorists write, 'American companies were weighted down with cumbersome organizational charts and many layers of management' (ref. 42, p. xiii). Critical accounts of organizational restructuring also describe the associated changes in social relations: nonstandard or precarious employment, and a new 'international division of labour' in which a small number of NIEs participate in the global dispersal of manufacturing by TNCs.

> **weblink**
>
> Visit https://www.cia.gov/library/publications/the-world-factbook for more information on the relative size, by revenue, of TNCs

Feminist scholars have highlighted the exploitative and patriarchal nature of the new international division of labour. The critics of global capitalism argue that, as the dominance of the capitalist global system spreads and deepens, it simultaneously sows the seeds of organizational restructuring by providing resources, forms of organizational capacity and the ideological rationale.[40]

Figure 4.4 is an adaptation of Figure and offers a synthesis of current thinking. It suggests that organizational structure is influenced by business strategy, size, technology, environment and the economics of global capitalism. It is also influenced by internal situational variables, such as culture, managerial and worker behaviour, and the strategic choices available to dominant organizational decision makers. The end results include increased profits for corporations and a new international division of labour.

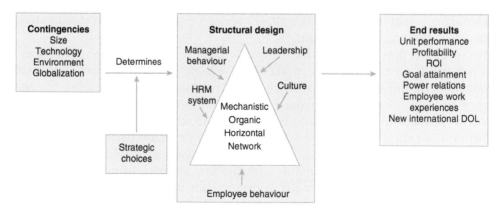

Figure 4.4 Determinants of organizational structure and end-results. DOL, division of labour: ROI, return on investment

Organizational restructuring: a conceptual framework

Much discussion on organizational structure in standard organizational behaviour textbooks tends to be historically blind, economically shallow, culturally illiterate and politically naive. Although organizational structure and redesign are widely assumed to influence behaviour in the workplace, most treatment of the subject gives scant attention to the complex interplay of organizational structure, management strategies and changes in global capitalist development. To help the analysis of the interplay of different dimensions that appear to have been critical in recent organizational restructuring, we have drawn upon the work of Mabey and his colleagues[43] and constructed a conceptual framework using four interconnected dimensions. Each of these is shown in Figure 4.5.

On the bottom horizontal axis is the dimension of capitalist global development over the last century, from national economies to a global scale. On the right vertical axis is the dimension of competitive strategy, covering the spectrum from low cost to differentiation. On the left vertical axis is the dimension of formalization, showing the contrast between high/directive and low/autonomous, and on the horizontal axis at the top of the figure is the dimension relating to decision making, which contrasts centralized and decentralized modes.

At the risk of oversimplification, some alternative structural designs are shown for illustrative purposes. In the first half of the twentieth century, at the lower left of Figure 4.5, the bureaucratic form is located to suggest a low-cost, mass-production competitive strategy, a high degree of formalization and

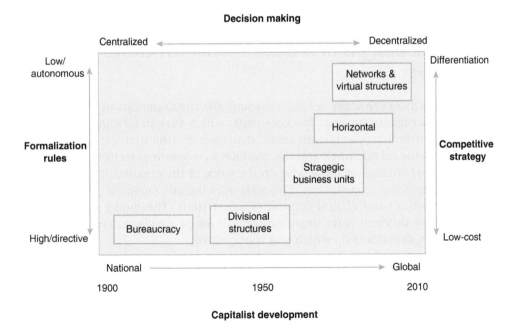

Figure 4.5 Types of organizational restructuring
Source: Adapted from Mabey, Salaman and Storey (1998),[43] p. 235.

direction, and a centralized decision-making mode. Ascending and moving to the right in the figure, from about the 1960s, we see the development of divisional-ized configurations, to the development of strategic business units and then net-works and virtual organizations.

In addition to the changes in conventional structural boundaries, organizations have recently undertaken other types of restructuring involving new commercial relationships. Manufacturing companies have outsourced the production of some parts – note the influence of just-in-time systems – and services (such as payroll, training and benefits handling), and in the public sector so-called non-core activi-ties (such as laundry, catering and cleaning) have been privatized.

This framework is useful in illustrating the different organizational forms and design options facing top managers, when considered in relation to the core dimensions of formal organizational structure and in relation to each other. The argument is that if we are to understand contemporary workplaces and explain what is happening in them, we need to locate restructuring initiatives in a mul-tidimensional framework that includes capitalist global development. While we believe that the actions of TNCs and the international division of labour are inti-mately interconnected with organizational design and restructuring, the inclusion in the framework of capitalist global development does not suggest any inevita-ble linear progression.[39,43] We must remember that millions of people still work in 'sweatshops' and bureaucratic organizations in core economies and NIEs, and these traditional modes of organizing work exist alongside 'new' horizontal and process-based forms and 'frame-breaking' network-based organizations.

The next two sections review the traditional and contemporary types of organiza-tional structure shown in Figure 4.5.

Traditional designs of organizational structure: bureaucracy

In Henry Mintzberg's *Structure in Fives: Designing Effective Organizations*,[44] he suggests that any work organization has five core parts, which vary in size and importance (Figure 4.6). Three line roles include senior management (the strategic apex), middle management (the middle line), and the production (operating, technical) core. The production core consists of those who do the work of the organization, making its products or servicing its customers. Two staff roles include technical support (tech-nological structure) and clerical support (support staff). The model suggests that, given these five different parts, organizations can adopt a wide variety of structural configurations, depending on which part is in control.

At its simplest, work organizations must perform four essential functions to sur-vive and grow in a capitalist economy:

1. A product or a service must be developed that has value.
2. The product must be manufactured or the service rendered by employees who rely on paid work as their only or major source of income.
3. The product or service must be marketed and made available to those who are to use it.

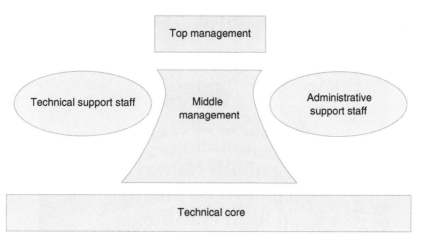

Figure 4.6   Five basic elements of an organizational structure

4. Financial resources are needed in order to develop, create and distribute the product or service provided.

These 'task' functions are the basic activities of the organization, and are undertaken within each of Mintzberg's five basic elements: developing (support), manufacturing the product or providing the service (technostructure and operating core), marketing the product and service (support), and financing the organization (strategic apex and support).

The process of developing, manufacturing the product or providing the service, and marketing it in a capitalist economy also results in a number of organizational imperatives (an imperative being something that dictates something) that centre on issues of control. For those who sit at the strategic apex and for middle-line managers, producing for a market creates pressures to control costs and control uncertainties. Organizations that compete in the marketplace typically face two types of competitive pressure: pressure for cost reductions and pressure to be responsive to changing customer tastes.

Responding to pressures for cost reductions means that managers must try to minimize unit costs by, for example, producing a standardized product and achieving economies of scale. On the other hand, responding to pressures to be responsive to customers requires that managers differentiate the firm's product offering in an effort to accommodate differences in consumers' tastes and preferences. These two types of competitive pressure are even more intense in the global marketplace.[45]

Additionally, the indeterminacy of employees' job performance creates pressures to render individual behaviour predictable and manageable. The control imperatives inherent in capitalist production and employee relations create a need for other managerial behaviour that is supportive of the operating functions of the organization, including human resource management (HRM), industrial relations and public relations. Together, the pressures arising from 'task' functions and 'control' functions shape formal organizational structure as a hierarchy, where decision making is top-down, with subunits or departments, and with managers hired to control employee behaviour.

Plate 2 Government organizations are typically bureaucratic. They have numerous rules and procedures that white-collar workers must follow, and concentrate decision making with high-ranking bureaucrats. This photo shows part of the parliament building in Wellington, New Zealand

Source: iStockphoto.

In the industrial technology era, the organizational dynamics just described caused managers to adopt one of four common structural configurations. They could structure the organization by:

- function
- product/service
- division
- function and product, a matrix.

No formulas exist to guide the choices for organizational structure. Each structure has advantages and disadvantages. The guiding principle is that although there is no one right organizational structure, the right structure for top managers is the one that offers the most advantages and the fewest limitations, or, to put it another way, the one that 'makes their profits'.

Several newer contemporary forms of organizational design have evolved over the last two decades, and are well established in the organizational discourse. These new designs focus on processes or work teams, or the electronic connection of widely dispersed locations and people to form an extended 'virtual' organization. Understanding the strengths and limitations of each structural design helps us to understand what informs design choices, as well as the interplay between different structural configurations and organizational behaviour.

A functional configuration is one in which managers and subordinates are grouped around certain important and continuing functions. For example, in an engineering company, all design engineers and planners might be grouped together in one department, and all marketing specialists grouped together in another department (Figure 4.7). In a functionally designed organization, the functional department managers hold most of the authority and power. Key advantages of functional organizations include the development of technical expertise and economies of scale: it is the classic bureaucratic structure. Disadvantages can include the encouragement of narrow perspectives in functional groups, alienation and demotivation, and poor coordination of interdepartmental activities.

functional configuration: an organizational structure that organizes employees around specific knowledge or other resources

A *product or service design* arrangement is one in which managers and subordinates are grouped together by the product or service they deliver to the customer.

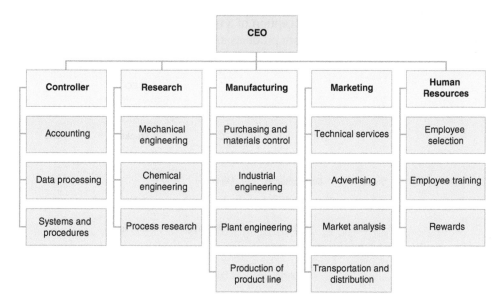

Figure 4.7   Engineering company with a functional design

For example, at Volvo Motors there is a car division, a truck division and so on (as schematized in Figure 4.8). Another example is a hospital where a medical team and support workers are grouped together in different departments or units dealing with particular treatments, such as maternity, orthopaedic surgery and emergencies.

The advantages of product or service structures include increased coordination of functional departments, improvements in decision making, and the location of accountability for production and profit. Disadvantages of product or service structures can include a loss of economies of scale, the duplication of scarce resources and the discouragement of cooperation between divisions.

A divisional structure arrangement uses decentralization as its basic approach. The decentralized divisions can group employees together in one of three ways: by the products or services on which they work, by the sets of customers they serve, or by the geographical locations in which they operate. In the 1980s, these divisional structures developed into strategic business unit, often with 20 levels of management between the corporate CEO and front-line employees in the business units.

divisional structure: an organizational structure that groups employees around geographical areas, clients or outputs

strategic business unit: a term to describe corporate development that divides the corporation's operations into strategic business units, which allows comparisons between each strategic business unit. According to advocates, corporate managers are better able to determine whether they need to change the mix of businesses in their portfolio

The Body Shop uses a divisional structure based on its major operating regions around the world. The company's products are sold in different markets in different parts of the globe. This is based on the premise that marketing The Body Shop's products in Canada is different from marketing skin and hair products in the UK or the Asian region.

Figure 4.9 shows one possible conception of a multidivisional corporation with strategic business units, built around core products and core competencies. Organizations

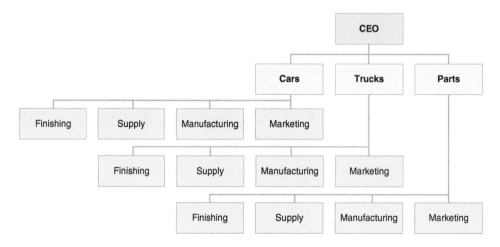

Figure 4.8   An auto company with a product design

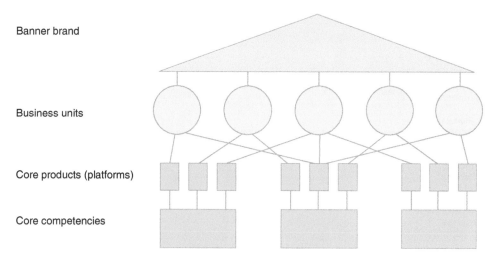

Banner brand

Business units

Core products (platforms)

Core competencies

Figure 4.9 Divisional organizational structure based on strategic business units
Source: Hamel and Prahalad (1994),[24] p. 279.

often evolve from a functional design to a divisional arrangement. As the external environment changes and becomes more complex and uncertain, management might find that it must diversify its operations to remain competitive.[24,45,46] Divisional organizational design emphasizes autonomy in divisional managers' decision making.

There are several advantages associated with a divisional configuration. It improves decision making by allowing many decisions to be delegated to divisional managers, who are generally more knowledgeable about the local markets. Divisional managers are more accountable for their decisions. In many divisional organizations, units are 'profit centres', and divisional managers are evaluated on the overall performance of their unit.

The disadvantages of a divisional structure come partly from its decentralized activities. Economies of scale are lost because many task functions of the organization, such as marketing, and control functions, such as accounting and HRM, are duplicated in each division. Specialists in one division may not be able or willing to share information with similar specialists in other divisions. Thus, the autonomy given to each division to pursue its own performance goals becomes an obstacle to achieving overall corporate goals. As a consequence, warn Hamel and Prahalad in *Competing for the Future*, 'corporate' strategy is little more than 'an amalgamation of individual business unit plans' and managerial strategic behaviour tends to be parochial, focusing only on existing business units (ref. 24, p. 309). From a worker's perspective, the outcome can be catastrophic: relocating to another geographical location means job loss as the firm's products or services are relocated to typically low-wage economies or outsourced and, in the case of public corporations, privatized.

weblink

Go to www.starbucks.com/aboutus/international.asp to examine Starbucks' matrix structure, which combines functional and product divisions, with employees reporting to two heads

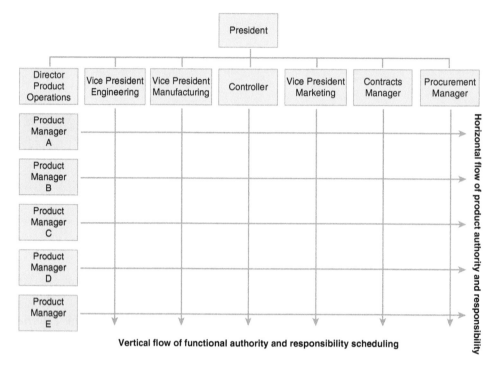

Figure 4.10   An engineering company with a matrix design

In the **matrix structure**, both functional specialities and product or service orientation are maintained, and there are functional managers and product managers. Functional managers are responsible for the selection, training and development of technically competent workers in their functional area. Product managers, on the other hand, are responsible for coordinating the activities of workers from different functional areas who are working on the same product or service to customers. In a matrix design, employees report to two managers rather than to one (Figure 4.10).

matrix structure: a type of departmentalization that overlays a divisionalized structure (typically a project team) with a functional structure

Emerging organizational designs: post-bureaucracy?

Since the 1980s, faced with accelerated changes in global capitalism, the limitations of bureaucracy and new technologies, such as the Internet, new post-bureaucratic forms of organization have emerged in the management literature: the flexible firm,[47] the cellular configuration,[48,49] the adhocracy configuration,[38] the postmodern organization,[50] the individualized corporation,[51] the re-engineered corporation,[52] and the virtual[53] and the networked[54] organization. All the post-bureaucratic forms of organization are conceived as substituting a hierarchical model of structure and implementing a more flexible work regime that gives workers limited empowerment.[55] A centre-piece of employment relations in the post-bureaucratic organization is a 'new pay' paradigm linking individual or group performance to rewards.[56,57] Three leading-edge post-bureaucratic configurations, which we examine here, are shown in Figure 4.5, above: horizontal, virtual and network.

The horizontal or 'lean' structure is the division of work into teams or 'cells' that are responsible for completing a whole process. A team-based organization uses decentralization to move decisions to the work teams, and gives limited autonomy to those teams to decide about product and service design, process design, quality and customer service. Typically, work-based regimes are accompanied by other management techniques such as just-in-time and total quality management.

horizontal or 'lean' structure: an integrated system of manufacturing, originally developed by Toyota in Japan. The emphasis is on flexibility and team work

Business process re-engineering

One design methodology with a process emphasis in a horizontal structure is business process re-engineering (BPR). According to the re-engineering guru James Champy, BPR is 'about changing our managerial work, the way we think about, organize, inspire, deploy, enable, measure, and reward the value-adding operational work. It is about changing management itself' (ref. 26, p. 3).

Structurally, the typical pyramid-shaped industrial model is stood on its head, management structures are leaner or 'delayered', and decision making is pushed down to the 'front line' to meet the contemporary demands for quality, flexibility, low cost and entrepreneurial autonomy. Some writers have described these anti-hierarchical characteristics in organizational design as a shift from 'modernist' to 'postmodernist' organizational forms and employee relations practices.[52]

business process re-engineering: a radical change of business processes by applying information technology to integrate operations, and maximizing their value-added content

The re-engineered organization allegedly has a number of common characteristics (Table 4.1). Central to these organizational forms is the 'reconceptualization' of

Table 4.1 The re-engineered and virtual organization

Characteristic	Bureaucratic model	Re-engineered model
Market	Domestic	Global
Competitive advantage	Cost	Speed and quality
Resources	Capital	Information
Quality	What is affordable	No compromise
Focal point	Profit	Customer
Structural design	Hierarchical	Flattened
Control	Centralized	Decentralized
Leadership	Autocratic	Shared
Labour	Homogeneous	Culturally diverse
Organization of work	Specialized and individual	Flexible and in teams
Communications	Vertical	Horizantal

core employees, from being considered to be a variable cost to being represented as a valuable asset; capable of serving the customer without the need for a directive style of organizational leadership.[58] With the ascendancy of 'customer democracy', employees are encouraged not only to exercise initiative, but also to display emotional labour in creating value for customers. According to BPR proponent Hammer, 'Loyalty and hard work are by themselves quaint relics ... organizations must now urge employees to put loyalty to the customer ... because that is the only way the company will survive' (ref. 1, pp. 158–9). Unlike earlier movements in organizational design, re-engineering is market driven – the 'dictatorship of the customariat' – and, by focusing on the social interaction between the buyer and seller of services, rather than the relationship between employer and employee, BPR emphasizes emotional labour as a key aspect of competitiveness.

emotional labour: the effort, planning and control needed to express organizationally desired emotions during interpersonal transactions

Re-engineering has been criticized largely by academics.[58–63] It is argued, for example, that the 'leaner' organization actually gives more power to a few: 'Removing some of the middle layers of organizations is not the same as altering the basic power structure ... By cutting out intermediary levels [of management] ... the power resources of those at the top can be increased' (ref. 60, p. 192).

> **weblink**
>
> Visit www.wbs.ac.uk/faculty/research, the website at the University of Warwick, for information on publications on BPR. Alternatively, visit www.accenture.com and search for 'business process engineering'

Virtual organizations

In the age of the Internet, it is not unsurprising that the 'virtual' organization has captured the attention of organizational analysts. The virtual organization is a temporary or permanent arrangement of otherwise independent companies or individuals, with a lead firm, to produce a product or service by sharing costs and core competencies. This ever-changing constellation of organizations is connected not through formal rules, but rather through virtual networks. A core competency is a knowledge and expertise base that resides in the organization.[24] The Internet, the World Wide Web and information technology connect members of the network wherever they are in the world. Typically, data are electronically transferred around the virtual network and separate competency sets work on the data either sequentially or in parallel.[64] Several factors have driven organizations to adopt network-based modes of organizing: an increased requirement for flexibility and global learning, reducing market uncertainty, managing joint production, a high-tech base and the perceived need to manage cultural diversity.[65]

'virtual' organization: an organization composed of people who are connected by video-teleconferences, the Internet and computer-aided design systems, and who may rarely, if ever, meet face to face

core competency: the underlying core characteristics of an organization's workforce that result in effective performance and give a competitive advantage to the firm

Corporate global network connections have forerunners in the eighteenth and nineteenth centuries, but they have figured as a pervasive, major aspect of organizational life in the twenty-first century.[39] A network organization is a constellation of several independent organizations or communities of people, usually linked on a large project basis, such as aerospace alliances between specialist engineering firms. The firms or groups in the network have a more formal and long-term commercial relationship than in the virtual organization.[66] Hierarchy is sacrificed in order to speed decision making, and vertical integration is supplanted by horizontal integration across group boundaries. Each group in the network focuses on a set of competencies. This structure enables each community of people to be flexible and responsive to changes.[64]

network structure: a set of strategic alliances that an organization creates with suppliers, distributors and manufacturers to produce and market a product. Members of the network work together on a long-term basis to find new ways to improve efficiency and increase the quality of their products

Networks, argues Castells, have had a transformational effect on structures.[67] Examples of network structures exist at Amazon.com, Cisco Systems, Dell Computers and Mozilla Corporation. Perhaps the best-known company using a network structure is Amazon.com, a virtual bookstore with no inventory, online ordering and electronic links to its customers. Cisco Systems, another exemplar, produces 80 per cent of the world's Internet hardware using a global network of employees and suppliers using web-based technology. In a recent book, Clay Shirky argues that Internet technologies make it increasingly easy to create constellations of networked project groups (see the Critical Insight 'Business without Organizations', below).[68]

A virtual or network structure has neither a corporate head office nor an organizational chart. Mitchell Baker, the CEO of Mozilla Corporation, developer of the Firefox web browser, for example, describes her role not as head of the organization but as 'the coordinator and motivator of a group effort'.[69] Bartlett and Ghoshal describe an integrated global network structure with, for example, a firm in France receiving flows of components from across the globe.[70] The concept of an integrated networked structure emphasizes the shift from inflexible to permeable structures and processes, accompanied by significant flows of components, resources, information and people. Unilever is an example of a networked company that has pursued a transnational strategy, with 17 different and largely decentralized detergent plants in Europe alone.

The network structure offers employers access to wider markets, lower production costs, and the potential to respond quickly to new product and service developments and markets. The weakness of the network arrangement is that associates have little direct control over the functions done by other members of the network. The number of independent members in the network creates a high-dependency relationship between each company within the network. This requires new behaviours and a high trust in network members. Managers and knowledge workers need to radically modify their behaviours as strategic planning, for example, is no longer an independent activity, but a process needing coordination, information sharing and global learning.[70]

Although the networked organization may have been the favoured paradigm of the 1990s, the global economic recession of 2008/09 has caused firms to reassess the efficacy of the networked model. As *The Economist* reported, management wisdom had for two decades been to make companies as lean as possible, expanding just-in-time supplier networks around the globe and outsourcing all but core competencies, lubricated by cheap credit. In September 2008, the abrupt closure of the overnight commercial paper market to lubricate the system meant that most companies need to accumulate cash to meet such basic obligations as paying their employees. Thus, 'ultra-lean supply chains no longer look like a brilliant idea when you have to find cash to keep a supplier afloat that cannot get even basic trade credit' (ref. 71, p. 17). A case perhaps of 'just-in-time' being substituted for a 'just-in-case' network.

More sceptical analysts have found the 'dark side' of networks. A characteristic signature of networks is the exploitation of the less powerful by the more powerful members. Buttressing this assertion is evidence that employees experience 'uncertainty, ambiguity and frustration' in their attempts to enact their professional roles within this organizational form.[72] Countering the academic hype around 'post-bureaucratic' organizations is a recent study by Pulignano and Stewart. Analysing primarily qualitative data from global automotive companies, they persuasively argue that new employment arrangements have, paradoxically, revitalized Weber's typology of bureaucracy. According to the researchers, new employee performance-related incentives have generated behavioural rules that reinforce bureaucratic control at Fiat, VW and Renault: 'Thus, intriguingly, the use of bureaucratic control emerges as the main element of labour control in this type of workplace' (ref. 56, p. 104). Arguably, the binary bureaucratic/post-bureaucratic view of organizational design is a somewhat misleading analytical paradigm. In reality, new organizational structures are likely to be hybrids, new forms coexisting alongside some old enduring elements of bureaucracy.[73]

Critical insight

Business without organizations

The Internet and social networking sites are bringing people together like never before. Websites such as Facebook and Bebo make it extraordinarily easy to meet like-minded people, join groups and exchange ideas. What impact might this be having on business? Clay Shirky, author of the recent book Here Comes Everybody: The Power of Organizing Without Organizations,68 argues that these new technologies could revolutionize the way in which businesses operate. But how? The story of rival web browsers Microsoft Internet Explorer and Mozilla Firefox provides an excellent example.

In the early 1990s, Internet Explorer appeared to have an unassailable lead in the web browser market, with an estimated market share of around 95 per cent in

2002. Microsoft's supremacy seemed assured when rival company AOL abandoned its own Netscape browser, leaving Internet Explorer with a near-monopoly. What happened next is a lesson in the growing power of informal networks and their increasing ability to take on big business. Former Netscape employees grouped together under the title The Mozilla Foundation and, using a small investment from AOL, began work on a new web browser. But The Mozilla Foundation was (and still is) no ordinary company: it is a non-profit-making organization, made up of not only staff, but also a network of volunteers and contributors – essentially, a community of Mozilla enthusiasts whose efforts are organized and coordinated electronically using the open-source model. In the words of Mozilla's CEO, Mitchell Baker, 'we build software, but we also build communities of people who build software and share a particular vision for what the future of the Internet should look like'.

This open-source model has enabled Mozilla to draw on a vast array of talent and creativity without having to become a huge, unwieldy corporation – and in this way, it gains competitive advantage over more traditional business set-ups. Any given individual might only contribute one idea to the development of the browser – their output could be very limited, but their input to the project could be crucial. Mozilla can harness the skills of such individuals without having to employ them full time – meaning that it can avoid becoming a vast, bureaucratic and hierarchical organization.

The success of Mozilla's model speaks for itself: Firefox's market share has increased to around 20 per cent since its foundation, and it now has over 100 million users worldwide – an incredible achievement and a very speedy growth rate, particularly given that it was pitting itself against the fearsome might of an established Microsoft product.

Consider the following question: Do you think that traditional corporations are the solution to our problems or are the problem? How can Facebook and Twitter transform organizational structure and design?

Source: Based on an article by Ken Hunt (2009), 'The chaos theory of organization', *Report on Business*, March, pp. 16–18. Further research: Shirky, C. (2008) *Here Comes Everybody: The Power of Organizing Without Organizations*, New York: Penguin.[68]

Implications for organizational behaviour

The downsizing and restructuring to create 'lean and mean' high-performance workplaces hit employees across the globe with cataclysmic force in the global economic recession that emerged in 2008–09. By definition, downsizing and restructuring include both high and poor performers. Employees are therefore usually correct in predicting job losses, extensive changes in the way they perform their work, work intensification, skill changes and changes in employee relations.

It is well documented that relocating operations to an NIE or outsourcing and privatizing a service in a public sector organization can have major employment implications. Downsizing has a chilling effect on the psychological climate, much as high levels of unemployment depress wage rates. Well-documented empirical research shows that, for the survivors of corporate restructuring, there can be detrimental effects on work motivation and commitment building, as well as fundamentally redefining the contours of employment relations.[43] The trauma of downsizing has predictable negative effects on the psychological well-being of individuals. 'Survivors typically are less loyal and less willing to provide service to customers and support for fellow employees,' opines Denise Rousseau (ref. 74, p. 212). The effects of the global recession and downsizing on the psychological climate also include negative perceptions about corporate leaders and decreased trust in management on the part of the survivors and the public generally.[75]

Gender, sexuality and organizational design

Alongside management debates on organizational structures, there is a body of critical literature that focuses on relationships between gender, sexuality and organizational design. The term 'sexuality' refers to sexual characters and sexual behaviour in the workplace. Sexuality pervades organizations through pornographic pin-ups, innuendo, gossip and sexist joking. While it serves to affirm men's sense of shared masculinity, sexuality can, in a male-dominated workplace, serve to make women feel uncomfortable. Leaving the organization is often seen as the only alternative.[76,77]

Studies of the gendering of organizations emphasize that gender and sexuality make an overwhelming difference to organizational reality.[78–82] The studies draw attention to the double problem of women entering work organizations: discrimination and gender harassment. The first part of the problem is entering occupations and professions that have traditionally been occupied by men (for example, manual trades and white-collar professions).[83] The notion that 'gendered occupations', that is, ones that associate job requirements with the perceived qualities of a particular sex, has generated debate in organizational studies over the extent to which organizations and their hierarchical structures can be considered as gendered. The second part of the problem is that, once in the organization, many women face gender harassment, making it difficult for women to move into positions of authority. This is often referred to as a 'glass ceiling' – invisible, informal barriers to promotion to higher positions of authority in the organizational hierarchy.

Legislation making direct gender discrimination and harassment unlawful means that it is more common for male and even some female subordinates to hinder in indirect ways the promotion of women. Indirect gender harassment may be an identifiable element of an organization's culture. Gender analysis questions research findings and analysis that segregate studies of organizational behaviour from those of gender divisions in the labour market, patriarchal power, issues of workplace inequality and 'dual-role' work–family issues.[84] More importantly, however, including the 'gender and sexuality paradigm' in the study of the organizational structure and restructuring has pushed the boundaries of organizational behaviour by examining the people who are deemed to be the 'recipients' of organizational design.

As sociologist Judy Wajcman observes in her insightful study, the individual and the modern bureaucracy are not gender-neutral. Indeed, more controversially perhaps, she presents a powerful argument for gender-inclusive organizational theories if we accept her main premise that 'gender is woven into the very fabric of bureaucratic hierarchy and authority relations' (ref. 84, p. 47).

OB and Globalization

Gender equality in times of economic transition: women workers in Russia

The late twentieth century brought significant changes to world of work in Eastern Europe and the former Soviet Union. The fall of Communist state governments was accompanied by a massive restructuring of national and local economies, and of the social lives of the workers who populated these institutions. While old-order policies and practices were pushed aside in favour of open markets, social and cultural attitudes about gender endured, often extending into the offices and boardrooms of organizations navigating this massive capitalist shift.

By the late 1990s, the new Russian economy was starting to look up, buoyed by successes in high-tech and natural resource sectors. Russian women, in particular, made strides in the new economy, creating successful businesses catering to the burgeoning Russian consumer culture. Two decades after this transition, scholars and journalists are turning a critical eye to how gendered experiences of work in post-Soviet Russia continue to be affected by enduring cultural attitudes about women in Russian society.

According to Russian *Vogue* magazine editor Alyona Doletskaya, although career opportunities for women in Russia have changed significantly over the past few decades, women workers continue to overpopulate sectors such as fashion, service and public relations (Weir, 2005). Furthermore, women's salaries are substantially lower than those of their male counterparts. Weir writes, 'A recent survey of living standards … suggested that of the poorest 15 percent of Russians, 68 percent are women. Many of the poor are well-educated women who find their skills unrewarded in the new economic order.'

The contemporary experiences of Russian women in the workforce can be linked to the Soviet era, when women were often relegated to undesirable, low-wage work, a pattern that reflected state support for, and reproduction of, wider cultural attitudes about gender roles. Today, although the transition to a free market economy has resulted in access to new types of work for Russian women workers, enduring cultural attitudes about gender roles continue to affect women's abilities to participate fully in the new Russian economy. This period of economic, political and social transition in Russia provides us with an opportunity to consider how cultural attitudes about gender can span major systemic changes, influencing local people's experience of such transitions. It also raises questions about how, over time, the new economic and political orders in Russia will affect local constructions of gender.

stop!   Using gender as an example, consider the often-entwined relationships between cultural beliefs and economic and governance systems. How do local attitudes about gender influence government and economic policy and practice? How do governments and economies influence local constructions of gender?

What kinds of societal attitude and practice related to gender extend into workplaces where you live? Who should be responsible for regulating gender roles and gender equity in the workplace?

How should 'gender equality' be defined? Are there different organizational approaches to achieving equity?

In times of political and economic upheaval, support for social conservatism can surge. How might this claim be used to explain – or dispute – the experiences of Russian women workers described above?

Sources and further information

Ashwin, S. (2005) *Adapting to Russia's New Labour Market: Gender and Employment Strategy*, New York: Routledge.

Brainerd, E. (1998) 'Winners and losers in Russia's economic transition', *American Economic Review*, **88**(5), pp. 94–115.

McGregor, C. (2003) 'Getting beyond the glass ceiling', *Moscow Times*, February 10. Available at: www.clumba.com/news.asp?ob_no=2927 (accessed October 2, 2009).

Weir, F. (2005) 'For Moscow's businesswomen, a powerful new role', *Christian Science Monitor*. Available at: www.csmonitor.com/2005/0308/p07s01-woeu.html; www.usatoday.com/news/world/2005-03-07-russsia-women_x.htm (accessed October 2, 2009).

Note: This feature was written by Gretchen Fox, PhD, Anthropologist, Timberline Natural Resource Group, Canada.

Chapter summary

- We have attempted to cover a wide range of complex issues in this chapter. Organizational structure refers to the formal division of work or labour, and the formal pattern of relationships that coordinate and control organizational activities, whereas organizational design refers to the process of creating a structure that best fits a strategy, technology and environment.

- The three core dimensions of formal organizational structure – complexity, formalization and centralization – can be combined into different types or models. Three descriptive models were examined: mechanistic, bureaucratic and organic. The mechanistic organization has been likened to a machine. It is characterized by highly specialized tasks that tend to be rigidly defined, a hierarchical authority and control structure, and communications that primarily take the form of edicts and decisions issued by managers to subordinates. Communication typically flows vertically from the top down. Thus, it has high complexity, high formalization and high centralization. A mechanistic organization resembles a bureaucracy. A bureaucratic organization is a rational and systematic division of work. Within it, rules and techniques of control are precisely defined. A bureaucratic design allows for large-scale accomplishments. The disadvantages associated with bureaucracy include suppression of initiative through overcontrol.

- Organic organizations are the antithesis of mechanistic organizations. They are characterized by being low in complexity, formality and centralization. A post-bureaucratic organizational structure, such as team-based structures and those produced by BPR, is organic and highly adaptable. However, the binary bureaucratic/post-bureaucratic view of organizational design may be a somewhat misleading analytical device.

- The contingency view of formal organizational design focuses on strategy, size, technology and environment. A change in business strategy may require changing the manufacturing process and the organizational design, for example moving from a functional to a team-based organizational structure. Large organizations will tend to be more centralized and have more rules and techniques of control. Organizations with complex non-routine technologies will tend to have more complex organizational arrangements. Organizations with routine technologies will tend to use written rules and procedures to control people's behaviour, and decision making will be more centralized than in establishments using non-routine technologies.

- An organization's external environment can range from 'stable' to' dynamic' and from 'hostile' to 'munificent'. Distinct external environments help to explain divergent patterns of managerial behaviour and organizational structure. For example, organic configurations are better suited to dynamic and hostile environments so that organizational members can adapt more quickly to changes.

- The external context has a significant impact on managerial and employee behaviour. The external domain influences the formal structure and functioning of a work organization, and in turn the organization's leaders influence the wider society. The linkage between external contexts and the search for competitive advantage through employee performance and managerial activities is complex. We have therefore emphasized that organizational behaviour studies must be able to deal with the new complexities and nuances. Caught up in the drama of severe economic recession, there is a need for a multidimensional approach to the study of organizational behaviour.

- The analysis offered here provides a guide to how formal organizational structure helps to shape the behaviour of managers and employees. The contingency elements identified – strategy, size, technology, environment, culture and HRM systems – are not separate, but are integrated and linked in complex ways. It is within this integrated framework that interpretations of competing resources, conversations and interests take place, and influence people's behaviour in many ways.

Key concepts

bureaucracy   148–49
horizontal   136
mechanistic   138
network structure   157
organic   138
technological change   141
virtual organization   156

Vocab checklist for ESL students

- Artefacts
- Business process re-engineering
- Capitalist, capitalism, capitalize
- Centralization, centralize, central
- Competitive advantage
- Complexity, complex
- Core competency
- Divisional structure
- Emotional labour
- Environment, environmental
- Formal organization
- Formalization
- Functional configuration
- Globalization, globalist, globalize, global
- Horizontal structure
- Information structure
- Lean structure
- Matrix structure
- Mechanism organization

- Networking, network
- Network structure
- Organic organization
- Organization chart
- Organizational design
- Organizational politics
- Organizational structure
- Span of control
- Specialization, special, specialize
- Strategic business unit
- Virtual organization

Chapter review questions

1. Compare and contrast a 'mechanistic' and a 're-engineered' organization. What is it like to be a manager making decisions in these two types of organization? What employees' behaviours are likely to be rewarded? What type of competitive strategy is each best suited to?

2. Why is there no 'one best way' to design an organization's structure?

3. What is the link between organizational structure and technology?

4. Why do organizations in fast-change and unstable environments have different structures from those in stable environments?

5. Review the 'new' forms of organizational design described in this chapter. Discuss the designs that you and other students finding appealing and challenging. Explain your reasons.

6. Does Internet web-based technology have the potential to demolish bureaucracy?

Chapter research questions

1. Read the Critical Insight 'Business without Organizations', above. Form a study group. Thinking about how you use Facebook and Twitter, sketch out how new social networking sites (a) provide an opportunity to change the form of organizational structure and design, (b) can create new services or products, and (c) can enhance the delivery of your orgnizational behaviour course and other courses in your university programme.

2. Obtain a copy of *The Oxford Handbook of Work and Organization* (see Further Reading). 'Post-bureaucracy?', discuss why the authors believe that emerging post-bureaucratic forms operate more as a means of *legitimating* change and innovation than as a concrete indicator of changing forms of work organization.

3. Read the article by Jonathan Morris et al. (2008), listed in Further Reading. What empirical evidence do the researchers provide of a shift towards new governance post-bureaucratic forms of work organization?

Further reading

Acker, J. (2008) 'Helpful men and feminist support: more than double strangeness', *Gender, Work and Organizations*, 15(3), pp. 288–93.

Alvesson, M. and Thompson, P. (2006) 'Post-bureaucracy?', pp. 485–507 in S. Ackroyd, R. Batt, P. Thompson and P. Tolbert, (eds), *The Oxford Handbook of Work and Organization*, York New: Oxford University Press.

Armstrong-Stassen, M. and Schlosser, F. (2008) 'Taking a positive approach to organizational downsizing', *Canadian Journal of Administrative Science*, 25, pp. 93–106.

Bakan, J. (2004) *The Corporation*, London: Penguin.

Currie, G., Finn, R. and Martin, G. (2008) 'Accounting for the "dark side" of new organizational forms: the case of healthcare professionals', *Human Relations, 61*(4), pp. 539–64.

Du Gay, P. (2000) *In Praise of Bureaucracy*. London: Sage.

Fulop, L., Hayward, H., and Lilley, S. (2009) 'Managing structure', pp. 195–237 in S. Linstead, L. Fulop and S. Lilley (eds), *Management and Organization: A Critical Text* (2nd edn), Basingstoke: Palgrave.

Grey, C. (2005) *A Very Short, Fairly Interesting and Reasonably Cheap Book about Studying Organizations*, London: Sage.

Hammer, M. (1997) *Beyond Reengineering*, New York: Harper Business.

Lazonick, W. (2006) 'Corporate restructuring', pp. 577–601 in S. Ackroyd, R. Batt, P. Thompson and P. S. Tolbert (eds), *The Oxford Handbook of Work and Organization*, Oxford: Oxford University Press.

Morris, J., Hassard, J. and McCann, L. (2008) 'The resilience of institutionalized capitalism: managing managers under "shareholder capitalism" and "managerial capitalism"', *Human Relations, 61*(5), pp. 687–710.

Pulignano, V. and Stewart, P. (2006) 'Bureaucracy transcended? New patterns of employment regulation and labour control in the international automotive industry', *New Technology, Work and Employment, 21*(2), pp. 90–106.

Tyler, M. and Wilkinson, A. (2007) 'The tyranny of corporate slenderness: "corporate anorexia" as a metaphor for our age', *Work, Employment and Society, 21*(3), pp. 537–49.

Chapter case study 1

Strategy and design in Australia's tourism industry

Setting

Tourism is a strong contributor to Australia's economy, with over a half million people employed in the sector, and tourism spending reaching over $85 billion a year. The country promotes its beautiful landscapes, Aboriginal art and culture, coastal lifestyles and the outback as main attractions for visitors.

Australia's top five international tourism markets are New Zealand, the UK, Japan, the USA and China. Visitor numbers from the emerging markets of China and India have grown strongly, while the numbers of Japanese and Korean tourists have declined in the last few years. China is now Australia's fifth largest international tourism market, bringing it into second place with New Zealand, and this is set to grow over the next decade.

However, Australia's share of global tourism continues to drop, with a decrease of 14 per cent between 1995 and 2008. Since its peak in 2001, it has also declined as a proportion of Australia's gross domestic product. The Australian tourism industry continues to struggle from the effects of a series of crises, starting with a pilot strike in 1989 and the worldwide economic outfalls of the Iraq War and the SARS outbreak in more recent years. Skilled staff shortages are also contributing to the industry's troubles, with an estimated 42,000 employees needed by 2015.

The problem

Established in the early 1990s, Outback Inc. is an adventure-based tour company located in Sydney, Australia. The company offers a variety of services, including guided tours, accommodation and meals, to those wishing to visit remote and regional areas of Australia. Outback's comprehensive packages of services appeal to travellers from all over the world, particularly visitors from Japan, who typically make up over 80 per cent of their client base. However, despite increased marketing efforts aimed at the general Asian market, the company has seen a decrease in bookings from its traditionally reliable Japanese sector. Outback has yet to attract new clients from China or other Asian countries experiencing more favourable economic conditions.

Although Outback grew from a small, family-owned business in the early 1990s to a moderately sized company with sales of several million dollars a year, it still retains its original functional organizational structure. Outback's managers, typically members of the company's founding family, head up the various departments, which are structured around traditional functions such as marketing, finance and human resources. Although the company does have its own website, management has been hesitant to move away from using standard travel agencies for their client booking purposes.

As with most organizations in the hospitality field, the Outback management uses a traditional leadership style, with decisions made at the top levels of management and communicated downwards. The majority of Outback's employees are young, highly motivated and eager for learning opportunities, but the company struggles to retain them, facing a turnover rate higher than even what is expected in an industry with a notorious turnover culture.

Management recently made the decision to hire a consultant whom they hoped could make some recommendations to help attract new clients and stop the flow of employees walking out of the door.

Tasks

As a consultant hired by the Outback management, prepare a short presentation addressing the following questions:

1. Would you recommend a change in the company's functional structural arrangement? If yes, which of the other three common structural configurations (product/service, division, matrix) would you recommend? Why?

2. How does your recommended structure fit with a strategy that could help with Outback's goal to attract new clients?

3. Would you characterize Outback as a mechanistic organization? How might this contribute to a high turnover of its staff?

Essential reading

Navickas, V. (2007) 'The reasons and consequences of changes in organizational structures of tourism companies', *Economics and Management*, pp. 809–13.

Ogaard, T., Marnburg, E. and Larsen, S. (2008) 'Perceptions of organizational structure in the hospitality industry: consequences for commitment, job satisfaction and perceived performance', *Tourism Management*, 29(4), pp. 661–71.

Tribe, J. (1997) *Corporate Strategy for Tourism*, London: International Thomson Business Press.

For more information on Australia's tourism industry and the challenges it faces, go to www.tourism.australia.com/home.asp

Note

This is a fictional case study. It was written by Lori Rilkoff, MSc, CHRP, Senior Human Resources Manager at the City of Kamloops, and lecturer in HRM at Thompson Rivers University, BC, Canada.

Chapter case study 1

ABC's just-in-time supply chain

Visit www.palgrave.com/business/brattonob2e to view this case study.

Web-based assignment

This chapter discusses the different types of organizational design, and the interconnectedness between structure and restructuring, and organizational behaviour. Organizations can adopt a large number of structures to match their strategy, size, technology and profit-making imperative. Restructuring affects job design and individual workers' perception of the employer and work motivation.

This web-based assignment requires you to explore the web to find a site that displays an organizational chart, or that discusses a method of managing its structure. For example, enter the website of Dell Computers (www.dell.com), Canadian TV and media company Globalmedia (www.globalmedia.ca) or car manufacturer Saturn (www.saturn.com) for an example of a 'flatter' organizational structure.
Consider these questions:

- What kind of organizational structure does the company have (for example, in terms of decision making, is it centralized or decentralized)?
- In what ways is the organizational structure appropriate for the company?

OB in films

The documentary film *The Corporation* (2003) offers an excellent collection of case studies, anecdotes and true confessions from corporate elites, which reveal structural contradictions and behind-the-scenes tensions. The documentary also features many critical perspectives, including interviews with Noam Chomsky, Michael Moore, Maude Barlow and Naomi Klein.

What examples are given to substantiate the claim that corporations, if left unregulated, behave much like individuals with 'a psychopathic personality', creating destruction? What examples of corporate crime does the film illustrate?

References

1. Hammer, M. (1997) *Beyond Reengineering*, New York: Harper Business.
2. Lazonick, W. (2006) 'Corporate restructuring', pp. 577–601 in S. Ackroyd, R. Batt, P. Thompson and P. S. Tolbert (eds), *The Oxford Handbook of Work & Organization*, Oxford: Oxford University Press.
3. Baumol, J. W., Blinder, S. A. and Wolff, N. E. (2003) *Downsizing in America*, New York: Russell Sage Foundation Press.
4. Delbridge, R. (1998) *Life on the Line in Contemporary Manufacturing*, Oxford: Oxford University Press.
5. Gowing, M. K., Kraft, J. D. and Campbell Quick, J. (eds) (1997) *New Organizational Reality: Downsizing, Restructuring, and Revitalization*, Washington, DC: American Psychological Association.
6. Hales, C. (2002) 'Bureaucracy-lite and continuities in management work', *British Journal of Management*, 13(1), pp. 51–66.
7. Innes, P. and Littler, C. (2004) 'A decade of downsizing: understanding the contours of change in Australia, 1990–99', *Asia Pacific Journal of Human Resources*, 42(2), pp. 229–42.
8. Legge, K. (2000) 'Personal management in the lean organization', pp. 43–69 in S. Bach and K. Sisson (eds), *Personal Management*, Oxford: Blackwell.
9. Littler, C. and Innes, P. (2004) 'The paradox of managerial downsizing', *Organizational Studies*, 25(7), pp. 1159–84.
10. Moody, K. (1997) *Workers in a Lean World*, London: Verso.
11. Womack, J., Jones, D. and Roos, D. (1990) *The Machine that Changed the World*, London: HarperCollins.

12. Tyler, M. and Wilkinson, A. (2007) 'The tyranny of corporate slenderness: "corporate anorexia" as a metaphor for our age', *Work, Employment and Society*, 21(3), pp. 537–49.

13. Drucker, P. F. (1997) 'Toward the new organization', pp. 1–5 in F. Hesselbein, M. Goldsmith and R. Beckhard (eds), *The Organization of the Future*, San Francisco: Jossey-Bass.

14. Gadiesh, O. and Olivet, S. (1997) 'Designing for implementability', pp. 53–78 in F. Hesselbein, M. Goldsmith and R. Beckhard (eds), *The Organization of the Future*, San Francisco: Jossey-Bass.

15. Drucker, P. (1954/1993) *The Practice of Management*, New York: HarperCollins.

16. Galbraith, J. R. (1996) 'Designing the innovative organization', pp. 156–81 in K. Starkey (ed.), *How Organizations Learn*, London: International Thomson Business Press.

17. Bratton, J. (1999) 'Gaps in the workplace learning paradigm: labour flexibility and job design', in Conference Proceeding of Researching Work and Learning, First International Conference, University of Leeds, UK.

18. Herriot, P. (1998) 'The role of human resource management in building a new proposition', pp. 106–16 in P. Sparrow and M. Marchington (eds), *Human Resource Management: A New Agenda*, London: Financial Times Management.

19. Watson, T. (1995) *Sociology of Work and Industry* (3rd edn), London: Routledge.

20. Thompson, P. and McHugh, D. (2006) *Work Organizations: A Critical Introduction* (4th edn), Basingstoke: Palgrave.

21. Clegg, S. and Dunkerley, D. (1980) *Organization, Class and Control*, London: Routledge & Kegan Paul.

22. Hardy, C. and Clegg, S. R. (1999) 'Some dare call it power', pp. 368–87 in S. R. Clegg and C. Hardy (eds), *Studying Organization*, London: Sage.

23. Clegg, S., Hardy, C. and Nord, W. (eds) (1999) *Managing Organizations: Current Issues*, Thousand Oaks, CA: Sage.

24. Hamel, G. and Prahalad, C. K. (1994) *Competing for the Future*, Boston, MA: Harvard Business School Press.

25. Daft, R. (2001) *Organization Theory and Design* (7th edn), Cincinnati, OH: South-Western.

26. Champy, J. (1996) *Reengineering Management*, New York: HarperCollins.

27. Burns, T. and Stalker, G. M. (1966) *The Management of Innovation* (2nd edn), London: Tavistock.

28. Chandler, A. (1962) *Strategy and Structure*, Cambridge, MA: MIT Press.

29. Keats, B. W. and Hitt, M. (1988) 'A causal model of linkages among environmental dimensions, macro organizational characteristics, and performance', *Academy of Management Journal*, September, pp. 570–98.

30. Klein, N. (2000) *No Logo*, London: Flamingo.

31. Blau, P. M. and Schoenherr, R. A. (1971) *The Structure of Organizations*, New York: Basic Books.

32. Pugh, D., Hickson, C, Hining, R. and Turner, C. (1969) 'The context of organization structures', *Administrative Science Quarterly*, **14**, pp. 91–114.

33. Child, J. (1972) 'Organizational structure, environment and performance: the role of strategic choice', *Sociology*, **6**(1), pp. 331–50.

34. Aldrich, H. (1972) 'Technology and organizational structure: a re-examination of the findings of the Aston Group', *Administrative Science Quarterly*, **17**(1), pp. 26–43.

35. Woodward, J. (1965) *Industrial Organizations: Theory and Practice*, London: Oxford University Press.

36. Thompson, J. D. (1967) *Organizations in Action*, New York: McGraw-Hill.

37. Aldrich, H. E. (2002) 'Technology and organizational structure: a reexamination of the findings of the findings of the Aston Group', pp. 344–66 in S. R. Clegg (ed.), *Central Currents in Organization Studies*, London: Sage

38. Mintzberg, H. (1993) *Structure in Fives: Designing Effective Organizations* (7th edn), Englewood Cliffs, NJ: Prentice Hall.

39. Scholte, J. A. (2005) *Globalization: A Critical Introduction*, Basingstoke: Palgrave Macmillan.

40. Sklair, L. (2002) *Globalization: Capitalism and its Alternatives*, Oxford: Oxford University Press.

41. Hoogvelt, A. (2001) *Globalization and the Postcolonial World* (2nd edn), Basingstoke: Palgrave.

42. Orsburn, J. and Moran, L. (2000) *The New Self-Directed Work Teams*, New York: McGraw-Hill.

43. Mabey, C., Salaman, G. and Storey, J. (1998) *Human Resource Management: A Strategic Introduction* (2nd edn), Oxford: Blackwell.

44. Mintzberg, H. (1983) *Structure in Fives: Designing Effective Organizations*, Englewood Cliffs, NJ: Prentice Hall.

45. Hill, C. and Jones, G. (2004) *Strategic Management Theory*, New York: Houghton Mifflin.

46. Jacoby, S. M. (2005) *The Embedded Corporation: Corporate Governance and Employment Relations in Japan and the United States*, Princeton, NJ: Princeton University Press.

47. Atkinson, J. (1984) 'Manpower strategies for flexible organizations', *Personnel Management*, August, pp. 14–25.

48. Bratton, J. A. (1992) *The Japanization of Work*, London: Macmillan.

49. Miles R. E., Snow, C. C., Matthews, J. A. and Coleman, H. J. (1997) 'Organizing in the knowledge area: anticipating the cellular form', *Academy of Management Executive*, **11**(4), pp. 7–20.

50. Hassard, J. and Parker, M. (1993) *Postmodernism and Organizations*, London: Sage.

51. Ghoshal, S. and Bartlett, C. A. (1997) *The Individualized Corporation: A Fundamentally New Approach to Management: Great Companies Are Defined by Purpose, Process, and People*. New York: Harper Business.

52. Hammer, M. and Champy, J. (1993) *Reengineering the Corporation: A Manifesto for Business Revolution*, New York: Harper Business.

53. Goldman, S. L., Nagel, R. N. and Preiss, K. (1995) *Agile Competition and Virtual Organizations: Strategies for Enriching the Customer*, New York: Van Nostrand Reinhold.

54. Powell, W. W. (2003) 'Neither market nor hierarchy: network forms of organization', pp. 315–30 in M. J. Handel (ed.), *The Sociology of Organizations*, Thousand Oaks, CA: Sage.

55. Clarke, T. and Clegg, S. R. (1998) *Changing Paradigms: The Transformation of Management for the 21st Century*, London: Collins.

56. Pulignano, V. and Stewart, P. (2006) 'Bureaucracy transcended? New patterns of employment regulation and labour control in the international automotive industry', *New Technology, Work and Employment*, **21**(2), pp. 90–106.

57. Corby, S., Palmer, S. and Lindop, E. (2009) *Rethinking Reward*, Basingstoke: Palgrave.

58. Willmott, H., (1995) 'The odd couple?: re-engineering business processes: managing human relations', *New/Technology, Work and Employment*, **10**(2), pp. 89–98.

59. Reed, M. I. (1993) 'Organizations and modernity: continuity and discontinuity in organization theory', pp. 163–82 in J. Hassard and M. Parker (eds), *Postmodernism and Organizations*, London: Sage.

60. Thompson, P. (1993) 'Fatal distraction: postmodernism and organizational theory', in. J. Hassard and M. Parker (eds), *Postmodernism and Organizations*, London: Sage.

61. Craig, J. and Yetton, P. (1993) 'Business process redesigns critique of *Process Innovation* by Thomas Davenport as a case study in the literature', *Australian Journal of Management*, **17**(2), pp. 285–306.

62. Oliver, J. (1993) 'Shocking to the core', *Management Today*, August, pp. 18–21.

63. Grint, K. and Willcocks, L. (1995) 'Business process re-engineering in theory and practice: business paradise regained?', *New Technology, Work and Employment*, **10**(2), pp. 99–108.

64. Davidow, W. H. and Malone, M. A. (1992) *The Virtual Corporation: Structuring and Revitalizing the Corporation for the 21st Century*, New York: HarperCollins.

65. Ferlie, E. and Pettigrew, A. (1998) 'Managing through networks', pp. 200–22 in C. Mabey, G. Salaman and J. Storey (eds), *Strategic Human Resource Management: A Reader*, London: Sage.

66. Rocket, J. F. and Short, J. E. (1991) 'The networked organization and the management of interdependence', in M. S. Scott Morton (ed.), *The Corporation of the 1990s: Information Technology and Organizational Transformation*, Oxford: Oxford University Press.

67. Castells, M. (2000) *The Information Age: Economy, Society and Culture*, Volume 1: *The Rise of Network Society* (2nd edn), London: Blackwell.

68. Shirky, C. (2008) *Here Comes Everybody: The Power of Organizing Without Organizations*, New York: Penguin.

69. Baker, M. Quoted in Hunt, K. (2009) 'The chaos theory of organization', *Report on Business*, March, p. 18.

70. Bartlett C. A. and Ghoshal, S. (1989) *Managing Across Borders: The Transnational Solution*, London: Random House.

71. Anonymous (2008) 'All you need is cash', *Economist,* November 22, p. 17.
72. Currie, G., Finn, R. and Martin, G. (2008) 'Accounting for the "dark side" of new organizational forms: the case of healthcare professionals', *Human Relations*, **61**(4), pp. 539–64.
73. Dunford, R., Palmer, I., Benveniste, J. and Crawford, J. (2007) 'Coexistence of "old" and "new" organizational practices: transitory phenomenon or enduring feature?', *Asia Pacific Journal of Human Resources*, **45**(1), pp. 24–43.
74. Rousseau, D. M. (1995) *Psychological Contracts in Organizations*, Thousand Oaks, CA: Sage.
75. Clarke, J. and Koonce, R. (1995) 'Engaging organizational survivors', *Training and Development*, **49**(8), pp. 22–30.
76. Mills, A. and Tancred, P. (eds) (1992) *Gendering Organizational Analysis*, Newbury Park, CA: Sage.
77. Hearn, J., Sheppard, D., Tancred-Sheriff, R. and Burrell, G. (eds) (1989) *The Sexuality of Organization*, London: Sage.
78. Dex, S. (1988) 'Gender and the labour market', pp. 281–309 in D. Gallie (ed.), *Employment in Britain*, Oxford: Blackwell.
79. Witz, A. (1986) 'Patriarchy and the labour market: occupational control strategies and the medical division of labour', in D. Knights and H. Willmott (eds), *Gender and the Labour Process*, Aldershot: Gower.
80. Knights, D. and Willmott, H. (eds) (1986) *Gender and the Labour Process*, Aldershot: Gower.
81. Phillips, R. and Phillips, E. (1993) *Women and Work: Inequality in the Canadian Labour Market*, Toronto: Lorimer.
82. Wilson, F. M. (2003) *Organizational Behaviour and Gender*, Farnham: Ashgate.
83. Ledwith, S. and Colgan, F. (eds.) (1996) *Women in Organizations: Challenging Gender Politics*, London: Palgrave Macmillan.
84. Wajcman, J. (1998) *Managing Like a Man: Women and Men in Corporate Management*, Cambridge, MA: Polity Press/Penn State University Press.

CHAPTER 5
Managing the human factor

Before 1912–13, engineering, accounting, and economics were the only bodies of knowledge relevant to systematic management. If consolidations of the 'human factor' were at all involved, they were based on philosophy, ethics and religion. (Shenhav, 1999: 181)

Managers had, by the early part of the twentieth century, already drawn on the expertise of people such as Taylor and other consultants in order to develop systems of controlling the labour process. It was not enough. As Baritz observes in his brilliant account of the historical uses of social science in American industry, 'Increasingly the men who manage and direct industry, find themselves incapable of effectively controlling their organisations' (1960: 3). After the First World War, some major corporations began financing industrial psychology and endowing business schools as part of a process of research and experimentation. That inter-action was eventually to result in the emergence of the *human relations* approach to management. The two approaches have traditionally been seen as opposites. Perrow's somewhat tongue-in-cheek description sums it up: 'From the beginning, the forces of light and darkness have polarised the field of organisational analysis, and the struggle has been protracted and inconclusive' (1973: 2). However, the forces of darkness and light may not be as far apart as they seem. As we shall show, corporate cooperation with social scientists arose from the same source as links with Taylorism: the vulnerability of management to the appeal of planning and science.

The aims of this chapter are to:

- Explore the historical development of human relations ideas and practices, their links to Scientific Management and early corporate life.
- Set out the distinctive characteristics of human relations and the extent to which they derive from the Hawthorne Studies and Mayo's perspectives.
- Examine the (often limited) legacies left for modern management, from work design to corporate culture.
- Demonstrate how human resource management (HRM) emerged from the personnel function and corporate welfare to claim the territory of management of the human factor.

Social science and industry: a courtship

The courtship between social science and industry began with the promise of a dowry in the form of a battery of tests and measurements offered to fit people to jobs. While this does represent a shift from measurement of work to measurement of people, it was not wholly new. This kind of intervention represented a version of Taylor's 'scientific selection of the worker' by other means. In fact the *Bulletin of the Taylor Society* carried articles discussing issues of human personality and arguing that newly recruited workers should be tested for personality, character and temperament. In 1915, an article about one factory noted that:

> 'A system of cards was used, one side of each card contained information about the worker's identity, parents, ethnic origins and previous employment; the other contained a certain amount of medico-psychological information ('anaemic', 'nonchalant') and notes on the individual's degree of motivation and way of life ('father out of work', 'mother agreed to take care of child', etc.). This was followed by his medical record (doctor, optician, dentist) and by basic health advice on the need for rest and fresh air. (Doray, 1988: 188)

This was part of a growing interest shown by engineers in the human factor and employment issues. Professional journals began to run articles such as 'Personality in the Shop Psychology of the Female Employee' (see Shenhav, 1999: 182).

This primitive psychology was openly geared towards manipulation of the 'uncertainties of human nature' (Shenhav, 1999: 174). In this sense, far from being a different academic species, it is arguable that the human relations current was partly prefigured in engineering discourses and derived from a form of Taylorist revisionism. Nor did it challenge Taylorism on its traditional territory of organisation of work. Nevertheless the battle cry of 'neglect of the human factor' did represent a partial critique that was directed against the costs of scientific management in terms of resistance and disenchantment. The simple appeal and apparent applicability of the variety of tests convinced a growing minority of employers. Problems arose when naïve enthusiasm and unrealistic expectations quickly ran up against the crude nature and limited results arising from the techniques. By the mid-1920s, and in changed economic circumstances, the tests had been abandoned by most companies (Baritz, 1960: 71).

Though a similar overlap in topics with scientific management can be observed (see Table 5.1), accounts of the development of British industrial psychology (M. Rose, 1975: 65–87; G. Brown, 1977: 213–28) show it to be more sober, centralised, less consultancy-based and affecting even fewer firms. It took a particular interest – derived from experiences of the Industrial Fatigue Research Board during the war – in monotony. Fatigue was, as we have seen, an issue that also concerned the scientific management movement, linked as it was to the need for the successful measurement of work. Common interests and client relations again meant, as in the US, 'a large proportion of their problems had to be taken over from the scientific managers' (M. Rose, 1975: 86). But despite sharing some common assumptions about efficiency, productivity and work organisation, British researchers established a distance, criticising, for instance, the anti-social and abnormal assumptions underlying

Table 5.1   Contents page of Industrial Psychology, ed. Charles Myers

Chapter

1   Introduction – Charles S. Myers, MD, ScD, FRS

2   Human Factor in Industrial Relations – J. Drever, MA, BSc, DPhil

3   Work and Environment – A. M. Hudson Davies, MA

4   Work and Rest – Rex Knight, MA

5   Ease and Speed of Work – G. H. Miles, DSc, and A. B. B. Eyre

6   Unproductive Working Time – A. Angles, BCom

7   Industrial Accidents – A. Stephenson, BSc

8   The Measurement of Intelligence and Aptitudes – F. M. Earle, MEd, BSc

9   Choosing a Career – Angus Macrae, MA, MB, ChB

10   Square Pegs and Square Holes – Winifred Spielman, BSc

11   Industrial Psychology and Welfare Work – Sheila Bevington, BSc

12   The Economic Aspects of Industrial Psychology – F. W. Lawe, MA, FSS

13   Industrial Psychology and Agriculture – W. R. Dunlop

Source: Myers (1929).

notions of work rate under Taylorism (Myers, 1926: 81). Myers perceptively noted the hostility generated among workers by scientific management through its attack on skills, and the effects of speed-up and time and motion study. He made attacks on the notion of 'one best way', rightly pointing to the greater complexity of behaviour and industrial conditions. This critique was linked to a more sympathetic consideration of the need to convince the trade unions of the validity of social science interventions, and to win more generally the consent of the workforce. The relatively progressive stance of British industrial psychologists is further illustrated by their alliance with a small group of employers centred on the Quaker families such as Rowntree, who shared their enthusiasm for 'scientific planning' and dislike for the harsher aspects of Taylorism. When those companies began to utilise psychologists, however, there was still considerable suspicion and resistance from employees, particularly when it was introduced at the same time as scientific management methods (G. Brown, 1977: 216). The Quaker tapestry firm, Lee's, divided the managerial responsibility for 'psychology' and Taylorist 'mechanics' between the owner's two sons (Johnson and Moore, 1986). Most British employers, however, still preferred to cut costs simply by squeezing wages and exploiting favourable market circumstances.

But industrial psychology was not as isolated a phenomenon as it appeared. In the US particularly it was part of a wider period of experimentation involving human relations and Taylorist management, as employers chose within and between the new techniques. Richard Edwards (1979: 102) gives an interesting example of the Bancroft textile company employing a consultant to introduce welfare work in 1902, and Taylor's follower Gantt to reorganise production in 1905! Welfarism was a significant part of that context. A paternalistic concern for the well-being of employees in return for loyalty and hard work, had a long pedigree in some companies. Company towns were one manifestation, as employers provided houses, schools, stores, sanitation and lighting in order to attract an adequate labour force.

But the rhetoric had shifted from older themes of community and improving the workingman to ones of entitlements and better working conditions (Barley and Kunda, 1992: 372).

Welfare work was also present in conventional circumstances. An increasing number of firms began to employ welfare secretaries whose role ranged from encouraging a 'proper moral atmosphere' to the provision of social and medical facilities. This interest was not philanthropic – 'Capital will not invest in sentiment', as one leading employer put it (quoted in Nelson, 1975: 104). It arose from attempts to grapple with the recruitment and motivation problems deriving from the increasing size of the labour force and a new industrial relations situation shaped by declining loyalty and rising unrest. There was a parallel development in the growth of employment or personnel departments as a means of dealing 'scientifically' with such issues – again showing an overlap with Taylorism. In the US and Britain, professional personnel bodies grew from the seeds of welfare work. But in the latter country, welfarism was strongly connected to the study of fatigue in the laboratory of wartime factories. As in the US, British welfarism was described by one of its leading members as combining 'pity and profit' (quoted in G. Brown, 1977: 185). Lee's issued 'partnership certificates' to employees who had shown a genuine interest in the company. Many workers, particularly the women who were its prime object, saw its motivation as directed primarily towards profit, given the emphasis on improving conditions for the sole purpose of maximising output. After the war, changing economic circumstances saw the decline of welfare initiatives. But in the US, to a greater extent than Britain, there was a broader framework of 'welfare capitalism'. Companies such as General Electric, International Harvester and US Steel continued policies of off-the-job benefits in the form of insurance, healthcare, pensions, social clubs, profit-sharing schemes and other measures (R. Edwards, 1979: 91–7).

The process took many different forms. Take Ford, for example. The company had only limited social provision, but it had social control potential. The 'Sociological Department' had investigators who were empowered to visit homes to check on absentees and monitor an employee's family, values and habits. But this social control mechanism did not exist in the abstract. To act as a counterweight to the assembly line and associated problems of labour turnover and unionisation, Ford had profit-sharing schemes and the famed five-dollar day. The Department could therefore ascertain the 'fitness' of workers for these generous rewards!

In a period in which space was opened up for employers by defeated industrial militancy and repression of socialist organising, welfarism in the US also had close ties to the development of company unions. This was different from the kind of enterprise unions initiated more recently by Japanese employers. The former arose primarily from wartime attempts to institute limited forms of worker representation such as works councils. After the war many large companies, often utilising their new personnel departments, were quick to consolidate this trend by initiating company unions as a focus for formal grievance procedures, thus alleviating the need for independent union representation (Edwards, 1979: 106). There was some success in delaying or undermining unionism, and employers learnt some important lessons on the importance of controlled employee involvement and formal procedures. But, as in Britain, little survived the economic changes associated with the growing depression and sharpening social polarisation. Company unionism and welfarism did not provide an adequate means of pursuing collective interests of workers, while at the same time they became a financial burden for employers without solving any of their fundamental control problems inside the factory.

Hawthorne and beyond

The Hawthorne studies occupy a pivotal place in organisational theory. Begun in the mid-1920s, the research was carried out in the large Hawthorne plant employing 29,000 workers making electrical appliances for Bell as a subsidiary of American Telegraph and Telephone (AT&T). Management regarded themselves as progressive, but this was with regard to a willingness to experiment rather than their general attitudes, for they were strongly anti-union. The significance of Hawthorne does not lie in the results of the research as such, for both its findings and methods are widely regarded as highly questionable (Carey, 1967; Silver, 1987). Rather it reflects two factors. First is the sustained nature of the intervention itself, combining psychologists, sociologists and anthropologists. In this way the courtship between social science and industry became something of a formal engagement. Second, the interpretation of the results became the core of human relations theory and subsequent managerial practices. This was partly due to the propagandising work of Elton Mayo (1946), despite the fact that he did not join the team properly until 1928 and was much more peripheral than those who actually wrote up the detailed research such as Roethlisberger and Dickson (1939/1964) and, to a lesser extent, Whitehead (1938).

Let us retrace these steps briefly. Early experiments centred on varying the lighting for two small test groups of women workers. The purpose was to identify conditions affecting worker performance. Unfortunately no firm conclusions could be drawn, as productivity increased under every level of illumination and even for the control group that was not being subjected to any changes at all! At the time this caused great puzzlement, but it was later theorised that the real change had been the segregation of a small group, which blossomed under special attention and treatment. Thus the 'Hawthorne effect' was born, through which it was recognised that the research intervention itself is an independent variable in its effects on human behaviour. Initially the puzzlement led to a further stage of experiments on groups of women selected for their degree of friendship with one another. Again the emphasis was on manipulation of environmental variables, this time of a greater variety: rest pauses, length of working day, group bonus schemes and so on. Observers, initially placed in a test room, were gradually encouraged to act like supervisors and become more friendly with the group. Until 1929, in almost all cases output rose, with the only consistent factor again the effects of creating a special group with its identity strengthened by the replacement of two 'unco-operative' members. However, worker interest in experiments declined and output fell with the onset of the depression. Furthermore, additional experiments with two other groups to further test the effects of incentives and rest pauses had inconclusive results, both experiments being discontinued amidst some discord.

All this confusion might appear to be grounds for giving up. But a more positive line was taken that a constant factor was the significance of employee attitudes and the influence of supervisory techniques upon them. The successful experiments were those that allowed the individuals to coalesce into a group, though it is difficult to imagine how the special conditions could be transferred.

> Right now I couldn't ask for anything better than I have. I just can't explain what it is but I sure like it in the test room. ... I think we work for the most wonderful man in the Western Electric Company. We have no boss. Mr. ____simply waits on us. ... We have privileges that a lot of the other girls don't have. We are allowed to go down and lie on the couch when we are tired or don't feel good, and the matron was told not to say anything to us. Of course, none of us have done that yet because we always feel pretty good and we have rest periods and can do anything we want to in those ten minutes.
>
> (Roethlisberger and Dickson, 1964: 144)

Attitudes are not simply created by interaction with management. Employee preoccupations arise from a variety of sources, so further means were found of identifying them. Even while the above experiments were going on, the company and researchers had initiated an interviewing programme to explore the relations between employee morale and supervision. 'Counsellors' were trained by researchers to play the role of the observers in the illumination phase. Over a long period of time, a variety of formal and more open-ended techniques of interviewing were utilised as a means of gaining information and of detecting, diverting and redirecting dissatisfactions. The counsellor was told by the company, 'to watch constantly for signs of unrest and to try to assuage the tension of the worker by discussion before the unrest became active' (quoted in Fischer and Sirriani, 1984: 182). Employee complaints were treated as unreliable due to their vagueness (hot, cold, damp, smoky or dusty were apparently inferior to 'the temperature in the room was 67°F'); or because they really revealed some personal, external disturbance. Even when told of grievances, management did not act on them. Aside from letting off steam, the process could also be used to adjust employees to the work situation and screen out effective counsellors as management material.

A final phase of research linked together the concern with employee attitudes and the earlier focus on the group. The famed 'bank wiring room' experiments were based on an existing workgroup carrying out wiring, soldering and inspecting tasks with a supposedly unobtrusive observer present. What was 'discovered' on the face of it was no different from Taylor's observations in the steel industry: the workgroup systematically controlled and restricted output on the basis of their own conception of a fair day's work and enforced group norms on any fellow workers who deviated by overproducing (rate busters) or under-working (chisellers).

> One day an interviewer entered a department unobserved. There was a buzz of conversation and the men seemed to be working at great speed. Suddenly there

was a sharp hissing sound. The conversation died away, and there was a noticeable slowing up in the work pace. The interviewer later discovered from an acquaintance in the department that he had been mistaken for a rate setter. One of the workmen, who acted as a lookout, had stepped on a valve releasing compressed air, a prearranged signal for slowing down.

(Roethlisberger and Dickson, 1964: 386)

The interpretation and reaction were, however, sharply different. Despite the restrictions, cliques and hostilities, a more accommodating picture was endorsed of group identities. Instead of suppressing the group and attempting to individualise its members, human relations is concerned to cultivate its sentiments and switch its loyalties to management. Roethlisberger and Dickson note: 'It is as well to recognise that informal organisation is not "bad", as they are sometimes assumed to be' (1964: 559). As it is fruitless to try and destroy it, management's task is to achieve a greater harmony between the informal and formal organisation. This can be done through controlled participation, effective communication and socially skilled, humane supervision. Referring to the experience of one of the Hawthorne experimental groups, Mayo commented that, 'Before every change of program, the group is consulted. Their comments are listened to and discussed; sometimes their objections are allowed to negative a suggestion. The group undoubtedly develops a sense of participation in the critical determination and becomes something of a social unit' (quoted in Baritz, 1960: 88–9). Here we can see the seeds of every superficial consultation exercise in the managerial toolkit!

As an alternative managerial *tactic* this new way of managing the small group made a lot of sense; indeed a minority of British employers were reaching similar conclusions (G. Brown, 1977: 243). Today, as we shall see later, it is applied in new and more sophisticated ways in current teamwork practices. The problem, however, arises from how Mayo and the human relations tradition theorised their understanding of Hawthorne. They were determined to fashion a general theory of behaviour in organisations. Later management theorists have dubbed a key element of this approach 'social man' (Schein, 1965). For Mayo, this started from a critique of the so-called 'rabble hypothesis' he attributed to economists and management theorists such as Taylor, in which individuals act solely according to rational self-interest. In contrast, 'social man' proceeds from the assumption that the major human need is for social solidarity that can be satisfied through group association. Naturally, this downplays the role of economic incentives. Such associations are seen to create social routines that substitute for logical and individual self-interest. Mayo preferred the term 'non-logical' to 'irrational', but the essential message is clear: workers act according to sentiments and emotions.

Contrary to some accounts, he did not believe that management was by definition and contrast rational, for all individuals were held to be governed by the same abstract instincts and needs. Rather managers and administrators could *become* rational, precisely because they can free themselves from social routines and the accompanying emotional involvement. This is an extremely curious notion, as any analysis of management shows that it has *its own* routines and 'illogicalities'. But it indicates the uncritical attitude of human relations writers towards the economic élites. Interestingly the new theorists of corporate culture manage to maintain the emphasis on emotions, symbolism and 'irrationality' without separating management and workforce in the same way.

It must also be said that the empirical basis for Mayo's assertions in the Hawthorne experience is very shaky. Group solidarity was carefully engineered through the selection and treatment of those workers involved, even to the point of replacing 'unco-operative' workers. Even this did not sustain co-operative activity. Mayo interpreted restriction of output as a combination of group sentiments and lack of trust in management. But there are alternative and simpler explanations: 'Restriction of output by voluntary norms was a rational response by primarily economically-oriented agents to the increasingly likely prospect of unemployment' (Clegg and Dunkerley, 1980: 131). Environmental influences on employee attitudes were recognised, but it was held that the consequences could be dealt with and 'adjusted' inside the enterprise.

The denial of economic factors led to some absurd psychologisms. Mayo used the curious term 'pessimistic reveries' to account for industrial unrest of any kind. Put another way, strikes and other actions that restrict output are obsessive preoccupations and signs of maladjustment, even to the point of identifying industrial unrest with mental breakdown and casting trade union leaders as psychological deviants! Not surprisingly, unions very rarely get mentioned in Mayo's writings. That did not stop later followers. The psychologist McMurry argued that not only were unions unnecessary when management acted fairly, but workers joined unions not to protect their jobs and improve pay but because of unconscious cravings to improve the emotional situation at work (Baritz, 1960: 175). Seemingly, social science had not improved much on the primitive psychology of engineering discourses, which two decades earlier had been describing striking employees as 'explosive workers' with strike-prone personalities and backgrounds of juvenile delinquency (see Shenhav, 1999: 189)!

It would, however, be misleading to view human relations through its excesses. To add to 'social man', a second highly influential level of theorisation emphasised the essentially co-operative nature of the enterprise. In fact the two were linked, as Mayo continually referred to the supposed eager desire of workers for co-operative activity. It is easy to dismiss this kind of analysis, particularly given the capacity of human relations researchers to systematically ignore or reinterpret confl ictual processes. But they *had* identified significant changes in the socio-economic sphere that brought the issue of cooperation to the fore. They pointed to the disparity between the attention paid to technical efficiency and economic functions, and the absence of 'the development of skills and techniques for securing co-operation' (Roethlisberger and Dickson, 1964: 552). The need to improve the latter was especially important because, as Mayo recognised, the balance between technical and social skills had been disrupted as workers' traditional forms of craft socialisation and identity had been undermined by mechanisation and the assembly line.

Emphasis is therefore put on the role of management to use the formal organisation to intervene in the *informal*, so as to create and sustain consent. Only in this context can we understand what appear to be the superficial solutions of human relations practices, with their prescriptions of 'democratic' supervision, good communications, teamwork and socially skilled leadership. Mayo's 'lifelong obsession with social harmony' (M. Rose, 1975: 115) was not based merely on his distorted empirical observations; it was underwritten by an organic model of society in which equilibrium and stability are the natural order of things, while structural divisions and confl icts are pathological. Mayo was worried about the 'extensive maladjustment of our times' as a period of rapid change undermined values and atomised individuals. The task was to recreate a sense of community inside the workplace.

During the same period Chester Barnard, the President of New Jersey Bell Telephone Company, was developing an even heavier emphasis on the basis for human co-operation, which was to have a major impact on later mainstream theorists (Perrow, 1979). Co-operation necessary to the survival of society could be most clearly observed in organisations. Unequal power and resources were irrelevant against the 'fact' that individuals voluntarily entered and submitted themselves to a common goal unachievable without collective effort. Organisations were rational and individuals were not. But this virtual deification of the formal organisation, like Mayo, still reserved the key role for management. The rationality of the 'non-personal' organisation was in practice again located with the executive élite who, as decision-makers, had responsibility for what Peters and Waterman, in praising Barnard, describe as 'managing the values of the organisation' (1982: 26). For co-ordination was still required to make a system, particularly as a sense of common purpose was not always present among the 'lower participants'. Barnard therefore reinforced the emphasis, not just on co-operation, but on the balance of formal and informal. As Perrow points out, this is the most extreme identification with the formal organisation, devoid of any concern about the negative effects of power and domination, or even the stress in human relations on sympathetic supervision and controlled participation.

Consolidating human relations

> Many managers would agree that the effectiveness of their organisations would be at least doubled if they discover how to tap the unrealised potential present in their organisations.
>
> (Douglas McGregor, 1960: 4)

Recognising the significance of co-operative activity was an advance, but it was wrong to transfer the analysis from the workgroup to the organisation as a whole. The fundamental contradiction at the heart of human relations and of Barnard is that co-operation, even of the 'spontaneous' kind, has to be created. Reed refers to an intellectual schizophrenia whereby, 'a theoretical framework is forced to reconcile the contradictions generated by a metaphysic that assumes collective moral consensus as a social given and at the same time advocates the adoption of techniques whereby this may be engineered' (1985: 6). There is a therefore a wide consensus among the critics we have discussed that the significance of the tradition is to be located in its *ideological appeal*. Michael Rose (1975: 124) puts this most succinctly in his memorable comment that Mayoism was the twentieth century's most seductive managerial ideology, in which social scientists and managers fashioned each other in their own image.

There is a great deal of accuracy in the view that one of its major functions was to legitimate the power and authority of both emergent professional 'classes' of managers and industrial consultants. The problem is that such an analysis can slip into giving the impression that human relations was a gigantic, if dangerous, con-trick with no purchase on reality. In part the reverse is true, for it makes sense only as a reaction to and means of shaping new realities. The depth of economic and political crisis meant that 'by the 1930s corporate America felt under siege' (Neimark and Tinker, 1986: 25). Congress had passed corporatist legislation allowing companies greater control over markets and pricing in return for acceptance of codes governing minimum wages and maximum hours, plus guarantees of union membership and collective bargaining rights. In addition, the country was experiencing a huge strike wave of sit-down strikes and factory occupations. Large corporations bitterly resisted the 'New Deal' institutions and the union organising drive. But the more perceptive of them also realised that 'the crisis generated critical problems of social control and legitimation for management' (Boreham, 1980: 25). A second front was opened, drawing extensively on the human relations package of better communication, democratic leadership, co-operation and social integration. This went hand-in-hand with early versions of the managerial revolution thesis, General Motors claiming that the organisation was a community of stakeholders for which management was a trustee.

The success of strikes and union organising drives only consolidated a recognition of the importance of consent and attention to employee attitudes in the more general writings of human relations theorists such as T. N. Whitehead in his *Leadership in a Free Society* (1936). Despite the weakness of the tradition in Britain, Whitehead's book was well received in progressive management circles worried about the changing position of business in a more democratic community. Human relations was able to provide greater legitimation of management authority than Taylor, because it went beyond the narrow confines of 'science' and formal organisation to address issues more in tune with the times. But it would not have made the same impact merely as a body of ideas. It had to help generate new practices.

Though it was still confined to a minority of even the largest employers throughout the 1930s, Bendix, Baritz and other researchers show that an increasing number of firms such as General Electric, General Motors and Proctor and Gamble developed programmes influenced by human relations. The Hawthorne researchers had put considerable emphasis on 'personnel work' in its broadest sense of 'adequate diagnosis and understanding of the actual human situations – both individual and group – within the factory' (Roethlisberger and Dickson, 1964: 591). With this background, greater consideration in many large companies was given to the training of managers and supervisors in the arts of intensive communication, social skills and non-authoritarian leadership that would motivate as well as command. Personnel departments grew further, alongside more use of attitude surveys. General Motors managed to neatly combine them with spying on union activists by employing Pinkerton detectives to carry out the tests! As previously, the war acted as a spur, large companies and the state finding the use of tests an invaluable means of dealing with the problems associated with the sudden employment of thousands of new workers. Despite a sustained attack by more critical academics, the diverse applications and effects of human relations theories had established a bridgehead for the social sciences in industry and, by the 1940s, the movement had gained substantial institutional support (Barley and Kunda, 1992: 374).

The 1950s saw the relationship between social science and industry blossom still further. Th is was facilitated both by the development of OB and related disciplines in business schools that specialised in the human side of the enterprise, and by the training of middle and senior executives in leadership and management development (Barley and Kunda, 1992: 375). The practices or solutions were not necessarily any less superficial than Hawthorne's. Bendix (1956: 326–7) remarks that the National Association of Manufacturer's newfound attachment to 'two-way communication' was based on the assumption that employers relayed *facts* to the workforce to promote co-operation, whereas what workers say is *information* which management can use to 'eliminate misunderstandings'.

Despite the over-emphasis on solving problems through issues of poor interpersonal relations, and the re-rise of harder managerial 'sciences' such as operations research and systems analysis with their associated quantitative and financial techniques, human relations did not disappear. The body of research and to a lesser extent practical intervention moved on to new topics. Some researchers continued to examine leadership styles or search for the qualities of good leadership. Others focused on group processes and dynamics, including the well-known sociotechnical studies of the Tavistock Institute in Britain. Rhetorical claims, however, foundered on a failure to demonstrate an exact and direct relationship between theory and practice. Perrow, for example, has written sceptically of the 'thirty year history of the effort to link morale and leadership to productivity' (1979: 97). In the piece quoted at the beginning of the chapter, Perrow was dismissive of the contributions from 'the forces of light'. From the vantage point of that decade it looked as if studies of the influence of technology and organisational environments, associated with systems theory, had triumphed: 'management should be advised that the attempt to produce change in an organisation through managerial grids, sensitivity training, and even job enrichment and job enlargement is likely to be fairly ineffective for all but a few organisations' (1973: 14).

Competitors and continuities: the rise of human resource management

There were competitors to the new influences. The human relations school gradually became less visible, giving way, even within the territory of managing the human factor, to behavioural psychology. Mayo and others had always provided, in Bendix's words, a vocabulary of motivation. What developed in its wake was a fully-fledged theory of motivation, promoted by figures such as Maslow, McGregor and Herzberg, which had the additional advantage of challenging Taylorism on questions of job design. But Perrow was wrong to believe that a hard structure and systems approach had achieved a durable dominance. The earlier human relations tradition that had lain dormant and often abused for its naïveté suddenly became influential again in the 1980s. Nor was it a question of a particular soft style simply becoming fashionable again. Human relations thinking contained genuine insights within a flawed general framework. The idea that the internal dynamics of the small group could be turned around so that a degree of self-governance could favour management resurfaced in the substantial wave of interest in teamworking from the 1980s onwards (see Buchanan, 2000). At broadly the same time, management theorists and practitioners were also rediscovering the benefits of creating social cohesion and value consensus through organisational 'communities'. The advocates of corporate cultures such as Peters and Waterman (1982) explicitly acknowledged the influence of earlier human relations writers.

Despite such influences, human relations theory as such is still largely regarded as a ghost from a past banquet. When people talk now of managing the human factor, human resource management (HRM) is what comes to mind. We can tell this, in part, as a story about changes in functional structures and practices, though this requires us to retrace a few steps. This chapter has already demonstrated that the origins of personnel work lie in the human relations tradition. As a more specific function was consolidated, the humanistic rhetoric was complemented by practices that reflected the forms of adaptation to 'local' environments. Notable in this were the dominant rule-based and hierarchical systems of bureaucratic control developed in large organisations, and the expanded legal regulation of the employment relationship established as part of the post-war settlement between capital, labour and the state. The outcome expanded the domain and expertise of the personnel function, but created practices that were largely procedural, reactive and low trust.

As part of the general shift in workplace practices and organisational restructuring in the 1980s, these orientations were put into question. The personnel function was recast as HRM, though in this incarnation it was not to be the exclusive property of a narrow functional department (Tichy *et al.*, 1982; Beer *et al.*, 1985). This was a matter not just of territory but of content. HRM always had a dual usage, signifying a new way of describing the field of people management, and a distinctive approach to managing the employment relationship (Mabey, Salaman and Storey, 1998: 1). The emphasis is on the integration of 'personnel' issues within the overall business strategy; with employees becoming a 'resource' equivalent to something like finance, with ownership of HR issues diffused down to other actors, notably line managers. 'Strategic management' is a term continually invoked to refer to the management of employees at all levels, directed towards the creating and sustaining of competitive advantage (P. M. Miller, 1989; Kamoche, 1994).

From the beginning, the various usages have been open to dispute. Some have questioned whether the approach genuinely reflects substantial shifts of policy from the old personnel departments, or is simply 'old wine in new bottles' (M. Armstrong, 1987). Many more have queried whether something radically different was actually being delivered in the practice of managing of the employment relationship. The latter is important, but need not detain us here – our emphasis is on the continuities and changes from human relations to human resource management.

To project itself as something that was not 'simply a new sign tacked on the personnel manager's door' (Thomas, 1988: 3), HRM had to sell itself as a theoretical and normative narrative as well. As one of us has explained in more detail elsewhere (Thompson, 2007), this has centred on the concept of human capital. Though borrowed from the debates about educational performance, the idea of human capital has helped HRM make a business case for the role of the quality and skills of the workforce in competitive advantage. Individual employees had a responsibility invest in the attitudes and expertise that could enhance their usefulness to the firm. Meanwhile, a strategic approach to HRM is said to be marked by investment in the workforce and this would be associated with enhanced skills, training, career structures and skill and knowledge – based reward systems. In turn, this forms the basis for mutual gains and shared interests through the employment relationship. The management of people is thus given a potential seat at the top table. Typical of this approach was Pfeffer's (1994) 'profits through people' message. He examined seven practices that successful organisations needed to have in order to make a difference, including employment security, selective hiring, self-managed teams and decentralized decision – making, high compensation linked to organizational performance, training, minimal status differences and extensive openness in sharing information. Though HRM retains a link with the 'treat people nicely and they will behave better' traditions of human relations, its newfound legitimacy lies in its capacity to escape the association of managing people purely with soft, developmental approaches. The argument is not free-floating. From the middle of the 1980s HRM theorists began to make a more contingent argument that changes in the external environment were making the internal assets of the firm more significant and strategic. More specialised, dynamic markets and technologies required more flexible, better trained labour. The HRM model was cast explicitly in terms of human capital and high involvement (Kaufman, 2003).

The unifying and often derided slogan, was 'people are our most important asset', but beneath the surface lurked two widely observed variants. First, there is a 'hard' version in which HRM is a much more systematic, rational instrument that can support organisational change through effective mobilisation and measurement of human capabilities and performance (Devanna, Fombrun and Tichy, 1984; Huselid, 1995). There is obvious continuity here with more traditional functional practices, but it is the extent to which reward and other forms of performance management are tied in to overall strategy and bottom-line outcomes that is considered to be decisive.

A softer, normative variant can be identified (Kochan, Katz and McKersie, 1986; Guest, 1987), which links HRM primarily to a transformation of employment relationships based on higher levels of employee commitment and involvement. This orientation received a considerable boost with the development of the excellence literature genre, which promoted culture change as a primary managerial resource. In many firms this enabled the HR department to take a leading role in change programmes, as the definer and measurer of value change (Marks *et al.*, 1997). The variants could and should come together through the pathway of high-performance work systems (HPWS). While this can be interpreted as covering all HRM territories (Huselid, 1995), it is more common for it to be associated with a workplace level and issues such as teamwork, quality and continuous improvement (Kochan and

Osterman, 1994). Th is impacts upon the practices of employee relations. As Guest notes, the underlying goal is to get employees to go 'beyond contract' and away from old-style adversarial collectivism, 'thereby reducing the potential for the effort bargain to operate as a potential focus for conflict and grievance' (1998: 239).

While the intent to restructure the employment relationship away from low-trust industrial relations systems is widely approved, the association with an attack on collectivism and trade unions is more controversial. The rise of HRM, with its unitarist philosophy, more individualistic relations between employer and employee, and direct communication between company and workforce, has undoubtedly coincided with some diminution of the significance of collective bargaining and union power (Blyton and Turnbull, 1998: 9). That is not the only controversy. It is certainly possible to produce *models* that integrate different types of practices, of which the 'mutual gains enterprise', which combines strategic, functional and workplace dimensions, is attractive and coherent (Kochan and Osterman, 1994). However, practices on different territories and through hard and soft mechanisms are easier to reconcile rhetorically than in practice (Legge, 1995). While debates focus on conceptual tensions, they are dwarfed by the problem of holding the different facets of the HRM model together in the context of contemporary organisational restructuring. In particular, performance goals such as greater productivity and flexibility in work organisation are proving difficult to reconcile with changes in employment that undermine loyalty, career and stability. In this context, critical commentators argue that hard, cost-driven approaches are predominating over softer, commitment and trust based policies (Blyton and Turnbull, 1992; Storey, 1992, 1995). We will pick up the human capital narrative and examine the debate on the outcomes of HRM policy and practices.

Summary and key points

It is conventional wisdom that Taylorism and human relations are at best opposite ends of a spectrum and worst, deadly enemies. This chapter has shown that they shared many of the same origins and concerns in attempting to apply 'science' to the understanding and control human behaviour, or the 'labour problem' as it was known at the beginning of the twentieth century. There, was, admittedly a difference of territory. Taylorism focused largely on the design of work, human relations on employee adjustment to it. While this is frequently described in mainstream writing as technical and human organisation and the need to integrate the two, it may be more accurately thought of in terms of overlapping or sometimes competing control systems. Whatever its record of patchy practices and inflated theoretical claims about social harmony and the power of leadership and communication, human relations would not exist if it did not bring something distinctive to the table. That distinctiveness is a focus on the informal dimension of organisational life – represented in practices such as teamworking and culture change – which Scientific Management wrongly thought could be excluded or marginalised. This recognition is, in part, retrospective and by the time it came, the human factor franchise had been largely taken up by HRM. We began that discussion with a quote from McGregor, of Theory X and Theory Y fame. Despite being written at the end of the 1950s, its language is identical to that of contemporary HRM. Though he goes on to argue that the major thing holding back the efficient and scientific management of the human factor is the adolescence of the social sciences (1960: 5), we would draw a different conclusion. Influenced by conceptions of human capital, HRM is a more coherent set of ideas and better embedded in managerial practices, but its sustainability is as much about social *life* as the social sciences. While the franchise may have changed hands, it is still proving difficult to produce a durable formula that can transform the conflicting, albeit complex, interests that lie at the heart of the labour process and employment relationship.

Further reading

Once again, Shenhav is good on the links between Taylorism and human relations. Baritz's classic *Servants of Power* is an indispensable account of the way that social science began to be used by management. If you can get hold of it, Browns' *Sabotage* is a British variant that also shows how workers resisted the new trends. When examining human relations and the Hawthorne studies it's good to access the original writings, notably Roesthlisberger and Dickson, but the various editions of Rose are a decent substitute. Perrow sets out the conventional scepticism of the more scientific end of organisation theory. On the move from personnel/industrial relations to HRM, Legge and the articles of Guest are a useful start.

Baritz, L. (1960) *The Servants of Power*, Middletown: Wesleyan University Press.
Brown, G. (1977) *Sabotage*, Nottingham: Spokesman.
Guest, D. E. (1987) 'Human Resource Management and Industrial Relations', *Journal of Management Studies*, 24. 5: 503–21.
Guest, D. E. (1989) 'Personnel and HRM: Can You Tell the Difference?' *Personnel Management*, January: 48–51.
Legge, K. (1995, 2nd edn 2005) *Human Resource Management: The Rhetorics, the Realities*, London: Macmillan.
Perrow, C. (1973) 'The Short and Glorious History of Organisational Theory', *Organisational Dynamics*, Summer, 2–15.
Roethlisberger, F. G. and Dickson, W. J. (1964) *Management and the Worker*, New York: Wiley.
Rose, M. (1975, 1986) *Industrial Behaviour*, Harmondsworth: Penguin.
Shenhav, Y. (1999) *Manufacturing Rationality: The Engineering Foundations of the Managerial Revolution*, Oxford: Oxford University Press.

References

Armstrong, M. (1987) 'Human Resource Management: A Case of the Emperor's New Clothes?' *Personnel Management*, 19. 8: 30–5.
Baritz, L. (1960) *The Servants of Power*, Middletown, CT: Wesleyan University Press.
Barley, S. R. and Kunda, G. (1992) 'Design and Devotion: Surges of Rational and Normative Ideologies of Control in Managerial Discourse', *Administrative Science Quarterly*, 37: 363–99.
Barnard, C. (1938) *The Functions of the Executive*, Cambridge, MA: Harvard University Press.
Beer, M., Spector, B., Lawrence, P., Quin Mills, D. and Walton, R. (1985) *Human Resource Management: A General Manager's Perspective*, Glencoe, IL: Free Press.

Bendix, R. (1956) *Work and Authority in Industry*, New York: Harper & Row.

Blyton, P. and Turnbull, P. (1992) *Reassessing Human Resource Management*, London: Sage.

Blyton, P. and Turnbull, P. (1998) *The Dynamics of Employee Relations* (2nd edn), London: Macmillan.

Boreham, P. (1980) 'The Dialectic of Theory and Control: Capitalist Crisis and the Organisation of Labour', in D. Dunkerley and G. Salaman (eds), *Control and Ideology in Organizations*, Milton Keynes: Open University Press.

Brown, G. (1977) *Sabotage*, Nottingham: Spokesman.

Buchanan, D. (2000) 'An Eager and Enduring Embrace: The Ongoing Rediscovery of Teamworking as a Management Idea', in S. Proctor and F. Mueller (eds), *Teamworking*, London: Macmillan.

Carey, A. (1967) 'The Hawthorne Studies: A Radical Criticism', *American Sociological Review*, 32: 403–16.

Clegg, S. and Dunkerley, D. (1980) *Organisation, Class and Control*, London: Routledge & Kegan Paul.

Devanna, M. A., Fornbrun, C. J. and Tichy, N. M. (1984) 'A Framework for Strategic Human Resource Management', in C. J. Fornbrun, N. M. Tichy and M. A. Devanna (eds), *Strategic Human Resource Management*, New York: Wiley.

Doray, B. (1988) *A Rational Madness: From Taylorism to Fordism*, London: Free Association.

Edwards, R. (1979) *Contested Terrain: The Transformation of the Workplace in the Twentieth Century*, London: Heinemann.

Fischer, F. and Sirriani, C. (eds) (1984) *Critical Studies in Organisation and Bureaucracy*, Philadelphia: Temple University Press.

Guest, D. E. (1987) 'Human Resource Management and Industrial Relations', *Journal of Management Studies*, 24. 5: 503–21.

Huselid, M. (1995) 'The Impact of Human Resource Management Practices on Turnover, Production and Corporate Financial Performance', *Academy of Management Journal*, 38: 635–72.

Johnson, I. and Moore, K. (1986) *The Tapestry Makers: Life and Work at Lee's Tapestry Works*, Birkenhead: Merseyside Docklands Community Project.

Kamoche, K. (1994) 'A Critique and a Proposed Reformulation of Strategic Human Resource Management', *Human Resource Management Journal*, 4. 4: 29–47.

Kaufman, P. (2003) Learning to *Not* Labor: How Working-Class Individuals Construct Middle-Class Identities, *Sociological Quarterly*, 44. 3, June: 481–504.

Kochan, T. and Osterman, P. (1994) *The Mutual Gains Enterprise*, Boston, MA: Harvard Business School Press.

Kochan, T., Katz, H. C. and McKersie, R. B. (1986) *The Transformation of American Industrial Relations*, New York: Basic Books.

Legge, K. (1995) *Human Resource Management: The Rhetorics, the Realities*, London: Macmillan.

Mabey, C., Salaman, G. and Storey, J. (1998) 'Strategic Human Resource Management: The Theory of Practice and the Practice of Theory', in C. Mabey, G. Salaman and J. Storey (eds), *Strategic Human Resource Management*, London: Sage.

Marks, A., Findlay, P., Hine, J., McKinlay, A. and Thompson, P. (1997) 'Handmaid's Tale or Midwives of Change? HR Managers and Organisational Innovation', *Journal of Strategic Change*, 6: 469–80.

Mayo, E. (1946) *Human Problems of an Industrial Civilisation*, New York: Macmillan.

McGregor, D. (1960) *The Human Side of the Enterprise*, New York: Harper & Row.

Miller, P. M. (1989) 'Strategic HRM: What it Is and What it Isn't', *Personnel Management*, February.

Myers, C. S. (1926) *Industrial Psychology in Great Britain*, London: Jonathan Cape.

Myers, C. S. (ed.) (1929) *Industrial Psychology*, London: Thornton Butterworth.

Neimark, M. and Tinker, T. (1986) 'On Rediscovering Marx: Dissolving Agency–Structure in Dialectical Unity', paper presented to the Conference on the Labour Process, Aston-UMIST.

Nelson, D. (1975) *Managers and Workers: Origins of the New Factory System in the United States 1880–1920*, Madison: University of Wisconsin Press.

Perrow, C. (1973) 'The Short and Glorious History of Organisational Theory', *Organisational Dynamics*, Summer: 2–15.

Perrow, C. (1979) *Complex Organizations: A Critical Essay (2nd edn)*, Glenview, IL: Scott Foreman.

Peters, T. J. and Waterman, R. H. (1982) *In Search of Excellence: Lessons from America's Best-Run Companies*, New York: Harper & Row.

Pfeffer, J. (1994) Competitive Advantage through People: Unleashing the Power of the Work Force, Cambridge, MA: Harvard University Press.

Roethlisberger, F. G. and Dickson, W. J. (1939/1964) *Management and the Worker*, Science Editions, New York: Wiley.

Rose, M. (1975, 1986) *Industrial Behaviour*, Harmondsworth: Penguin.

Schein, E. H. (1965) *Organisational Psychology*, Englewood Cliffs, N.J.: Prentice Hall (also 1980, 3rd edn.).

Shenhav, Y. (1999) *Manufacturing Rationality: The Engineering Foundations of the Managerial Revolution*, Oxford: Oxford University Press.

Silver, J. (1987) 'The Ideology of Excellence: Management and Neo-Conservatism', *Studies in Political Economy*, 24, Autumn: 105–29.

Storey, J. (1992) *Developments in the Management of Human Resources*, Oxford: Blackwell.

Thomas, R. J. (1988) 'What is Human Resource Management?' *Work, Employment and Society*, 2. 3: 392–402.

Tichy, N., Fombrun, C. and Devanna, M. A. (1982) 'Strategic Human Resource Management', *Sloan Management Review*: 47–61.

Whitehead, T. N. (1938) *The Industrial Worker*, London: Oxford University Press.

CHAPTER 6
Personality and identity

CHAPTER OUTLINE

- Introduction
- What is personality?
- Trait theories of personality
- The psychodynamic theory of personality
- Sociocultural theories of personality
- Identity and personality
- Applying personality theories in the workplace
- Summary and end-of-chapter features
- Chapter case study 1: Identifying leaders in Nigeria
- Chapter case study 2: Building Anna's self-esteem

CHAPTER OBJECTIVES

After completing this chapter, you should be able to:

- define personality and identity and understand their importance in the workplace
- distinguish between the trait and psychodynamic theories of personality
- understand how cultural and life-long social experience shapes personality
- critically assess how individual identity affects and is affected by the organization
- understand more of the main characteristics of your own personality and identity
- apply the key findings of personality research to the workplace

Introduction

At the morning coffee break, three nurses sat around a table in the hospital's cafeteria. Elizabeth spoke first. 'I'm really disappointed in Alan's behaviour. He became really excitable and loud again during the night shift when I asked him to assist in the emergency ward. He seems to be emotional and excitable whenever we have more than two or three critical cases in the ER. At the interview he came over as so confident and experienced.' And he had a wonderful CV,' Eleanor added.

'Interviews and good reference letters can't tell you about a person's personality and how they will perform under stress,' said charge nurse Judy Finnigan. 'He's not easy to get along with either, especially in the mornings. You ask a question and he jumps down your throat.'

'Yet, you know, he can be totally different outside the ER. He's sociable and pleasant when we go to the pub or when things are quiet on the ward,' replied Elizabeth.

How is Alan able to be such a different person in different situations? Are certain personality types better adapted for certain job types? Should managers try to recruit all employees with similar personalities? How does the personality characteristic influence motivation at work? Why do some people find it difficult to work in a team, while others excel as 'team players'? What personality types make for a 'good' team player?

Behaviour analysts have long been interested in relationships between personality traits and job performance, and whether personality homogeneity (people having similar personalities) facilitates a high-performance workplace. As we shall see in this chapter, many researchers have attempted to understand how both personality and identity are important factors shaping behaviour in the workplace.

> **weblink**
>
> Go to www.queendom.com/tests.html and www.apa.org/science/testing.html for more information on personality testing instruments. In the UK, the British Psychological Society (www.bps.org.uk) assesses employment selection tests

In this chapter, we present psychological and sociological theories that have made significant contributions to our understanding of personality and identity, and some of the ways in which these theories are being applied in the workplace. There are at least 24 academics or groups of researchers who have contributed to theories of personality. Therefore our coverage in this chapter is highly selective, and we can hope to provide only a glimpse of the complexity and scope of the theories. We conclude the chapter with a discussion of the connections between personality and job performance, and personality and social integration, along with a critique of how personality tests are used in the workplace.

What is personality?

The notion of personality permeates popular culture and discussion in the workplace. In Western cultures, the mass media – print, radio, television, films and other communication technologies – endlessly discuss 'cool' or 'nice' personalities. And like Alan in our opening vignette, we sometimes meet people at work who seem to have a personality that does not 'fit' with the job requirements or work group. We all use the term 'personality' quite often, and most people feel they understand it intuitively. But what exactly is personality? Although there is no universally accepted definition, we define personality here as a relatively enduring pattern of thinking, feeling and acting that characterizes a person's response to her or his environment.

There are several aspects of this definition that need further explanation:

- The concept of personality refers to notions of individuality; people differ significantly in the ways in which they routinely think, feel and act.
- Personality refers to an enduring set of characteristics and tendencies of a person. An individual's personality encapsulates her or his way of responding to their world. Personality rests on the observation that people seem to behave somewhat consistently over time and across different life situations. Thus, we would not characterize a person as having a shy personality if that individual tended to be dominantly shy and retiring only some of the time, and on other occasions was frequently observed to be very sociable and outgoing.
- Similarly, we need to be aware that individual behaviour is influenced by social context. Individuals may be shy and retiring in a situation where they perceive the context to be unfavourable (such as meeting new people on the first day of employment), but outgoing when the situation is perceived as favourable. From this perceived consistency comes the notion of 'personality traits' that characterize individuals' customary ways of responding to their environment. Research suggests that stability or consistency becomes greater as we enter adulthood, but even in adulthood, there remains a capacity for meaningful personality change.[1]
- Finally, our definition of personality draws attention to the fact that, in studying personality, we are interested in factors within people that cause them to behave consistently as they do.

The patterns of thinking, feeling and actions that are viewed as reflecting a person's personality typically have three characteristics. First, they are seen as elements of identity that distinguish that individual from other people. Second, the individual's behaviours seem to 'interconnect' in a meaningful fashion, suggesting an inner element that shapes and directs behaviour. Third, the behaviours are viewed as being caused primarily by 'internal' rather than contextual factors.

stop reflect

What do you think of these typical observations of people that give rise to the concept of personality? Do they accurately reflect how you form an opinion of a person's 'personality'?

In studying personality, we need also to look at how social experience structures or shapes personality. People develop a personality by internalizing – or taking in – their social experiences or surroundings. Without social experience, personality cannot develop. Sociological research on the effects of social isolation on feral (meaning 'wild') children points to the crucial role of social experience in forming personality.[2-4] Sociologists suggest that, in the process of interacting with parents, siblings, relatives, teachers and others, people develop an individual identity. We shall examine identity later in this chapter, but we define it here as the core understandings human beings hold about who they are and what is meaningful

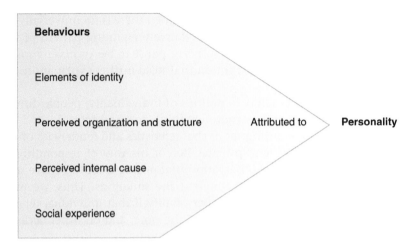

Figure 6.1 Perceived characteristics of behaviours that are seen as reflecting an individual's personality

to them. Figure 6.1 illustrates some perceived characteristics of behaviours that are seen as reflecting an individual's personality.

The trait, psychodynamic and sociocultural perspectives have guided the study of personality. These approaches provide very different conceptions of what personality is and how it functions. No doubt, you will find some of the theories more in accord than others with your own life views. Before we describe and evaluate each of the theories, we need to offer a few words of warning about personality in the workplace:

- As we have already said, there is no 'one best' personality type. Some personality characteristics are useful in certain situations, and organizations need to appreciate the value of diversity. When all employees hold similar personality traits and have similar values, studies suggest that fewer rules are needed to get things done. For many managers, this may seem like a good thing, but in some circumstances this same homogeneity could hinder the organization's ability to adapt to change.[5]
- Although many organizations consider personality to be an important criterion for employment, personality tests are still considered to be a relatively poor instrument for selecting people for key positions, such as management roles.
- The excessive 'classification' of personality types may prevent others from appreciating a person's potential to contribute to an organization.
- If we draw attention to context and social experience, there is less likelihood of exaggerating the effect of personality on individual work-related behaviour. In highly structured situations – such as the armed forces – with clearly defined rules, roles and punishment contingencies, personality will have the least effect on work-related behaviour. In less structured situations – such as a volunteer community organization – personality will have the most effect on organizational behaviour.[6]

In what follows, we examine three approaches to the study of personality: the trait, psychodynamic and sociocultural approaches.

Trait theories of personality

Almost two thousand years ago, the ancient Greeks used the humoral theory to explain individual differences in personality.[7] The body was thought to contain four humours or fluids: black bile, blood, phlegm and yellow bile. The personality of individuals was classified according to the disposition supposedly produced by the predominance of one of these humours in their bodies. Optimistic or sanguine people, who had a preponderance of blood (*sanguis*), were cheerful and passionate. Melancholic people, who had an excess of black bile, had a pessimistic temperament. Phlegmatic individuals, whose body systems contained an excessive proportion of phlegm, were calm and unexcitable. Choleric individuals, on the other hand, had an excess of yellow bile and were bad-tempered and irritable. Although subsequent research discredited the humoral theory, the notion that people can be classified into different personality types has persisted to this day.

If you were to describe the personality of a close friend or relative, you would probably make a number of descriptive statements, for example, 'He is a real extrovert. He likes to be the focus of attention, is abrasive in debate, but is also brilliant and charming. He works hard but he is generous with his time, and he is a truly caring person. He will always try to help if he can.' In other words, you would describe others by referring to the kind of people they are ('extrovert') and to their thoughts ('caring' and 'brilliant'), feelings ('attention'), and actions ('works hard'). Together, these statements describe personality traits, enduring personal characteristics that reveal themselves in a particular pattern of human behaviour in different situations.

The English dictionary contains approximately 18,000 words that could be used to describe personal traits, and obviously it would be impractical, even if it were possible, to describe people in terms of where they fell on some vast scale. Trait theorists therefore attempt to condense various descriptors into a manageable number of core personality traits that people display consistently over time, in order to understand and predict human behaviour.

Gordon Allport (1897–1967) pioneered research on personality traits. He believed that the set of words chosen to describe an individual reflect that person's central traits, personal characteristics that are apparent to others and that shape behaviour in a variety of environments. A central trait is equivalent to the descriptive terms used in a letter of reference (such as 'conscientious' or 'reliable'). Another aspect of what Allport called the 'building blocks' of personality is secondary traits, those which are more specific to certain situations and have less impact on behaviour. An example of a secondary trait is 'dislikes crowds'.[8]

Psychologists have used the statistical tool of factor analysis to identify clusters of specific behaviours that are correlated with one another so highly that they can be viewed as reflecting basic personality traits. Different people fall into these different clusters. For example, you might find that most people who are shy and socially reserved stay away from parties and enjoy solitary activities such as reading. At the other end of the spectrum are people who are talkative and outward-going, like parties and dislike solitary activities such as reading. These behavioural patterns define a dimension that we might label introversion–extroversion. At one end of the dimension are highly introverted behaviours, and at the other end are highly extroverted

Plate 1   Observable traits, such as friendliness, are those traits that are obvious to others

Source: Getty Images.

behaviours. As we describe below, studies have found introversion–extroversion to be a major dimension of personality.

factor analysis: a statistical technique used for a large number of variables to explain the pattern of relationships in the data

In 1965, Raymond Cattell, a British psychologist, built upon Allport's investigations to develop his theory of personality. Cattell used a process of factor analysis to identify clusters of traits that he believed represented a person's central traits. He analysed questionnaire responses from thousands of people, and also obtained ratings from people who knew the participants well, eventually identifying 16 basic behaviour clusters, or factors. These 16 traits he called 'source traits' because they were, in his view, the building blocks upon which personality is built. From his data, Cattell developed a personality test called the 16 Personality Factor Questionnaire (16PF) to measure individual differences on each of the dimensions, and provide personality profiles for individuals and for groups of people. Figure 6.2 compares the personality profiles of a hypothetical individual rated on Cattell's 16PF test.

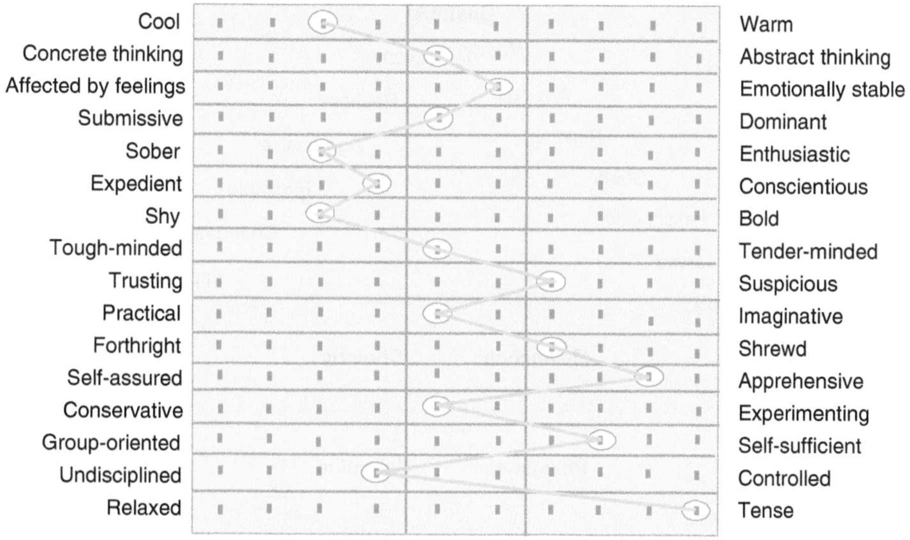

Cool											Warm
Concrete thinking											Abstract thinking
Affected by feelings											Emotionally stable
Submissive											Dominant
Sober											Enthusiastic
Expedient											Conscientious
Shy											Bold
Tough-minded											Tender-minded
Trusting											Suspicious
Practical											Imaginative
Forthright											Shrewd
Self-assured											Apprehensive
Conservative											Experimenting
Group-oriented											Self-sufficient
Undisciplined											Controlled
Relaxed											Tense

Figure 6.2 Two hypothetical personality profiles using Cattell's 16PF test

Eysenck's three-factor model of personality

Hans J. Eysenck (1916–1997), another well-known British psychologist, also used factor analysis to devise his theory of personality. From his research, Eysenck concluded that normal personality can be understood in terms of three basic factors or dimensions: introversion–extroversion, stability–instability and psychoticism.[9] These factors are bipolar dimensions. Introversion is the opposite of extroversion, stability is the opposite of instability (sometimes called neuroticism), and psychoticism is the opposite of self-control.

Introversion refers to a reserved nature and the pursuit of solitary activities. Introverts tend to be shy, thoughtful, risk avoiders, and shun social engagements.

introversion: a personality dimension that characterizes people who are territorial and solitary

Extroversion refers to the opposites of these human characteristics. Extroverts tend to be sociable and spontaneous, thrive on change and be willing to take risks. *Psychoticism* refers to an aggressive, egocentric and antisocial nature. People high on psychoticism display such attributes as aggression, coldness and moodiness, are fraught with guilt and are unstable. People who score low on psychoticism do not show these attributes. Such people tend to be even-tempered and are characterized by emotional stability. Eysenck believed that the most important aspects of a person's personality can be captured by a two-dimensional model (Figure 6.3).

extroversion: a personality dimension that characterizes people who are outgoing, talkative, sociable and assertive

Figure 6.3 illustrates the effects of various combinations of the three dimensions of introversion–extroversion, stability–instability and psychoticism, and relates them to the four personality types described by the Greek physician Galen in the second century AD. We should note that the two basic dimensions intersect at right angles

Figure 6.3 Eysensk's major personality dimensions

Source: Eysenck (1973)[54].

(meaning that they are statistically uncorrelated or independent). Therefore, knowing how extrovert an individual is reveals little about a person's level of emotional stability – she or he could fall anywhere along the stability dimension. The secondary traits shown in the diagram reflect varying combinations of these two primary dimensions. Thus, we can see that the emotionally unstable (neurotic) extrovert is touchy, restless and aggressive. In contrast, the stable extrovert is a carefree, lively individual who tends to seek out leadership roles. The unstable introvert is moody, anxious and rigid, but the stable introvert tends to be calm, even-tempered and reliable.

Eysenck's research produced data to show that test scores measuring these two basic personality dimensions can predict people's key personality patterns, including specific behaviour tendencies or disorders. Leaders, for example, are likely to be in the 'sanguine' quadrant and tend to display outgoing, sociable behaviour. Criminals, on the other hand, are likely to be in the 'choleric' quadrant and tend to display aggressive and impulsive behaviour. Eysenck's trait theory of personality has received considerable support because the three dimensions have been replicated in factor analyses performed by many different researchers.[7]

The five-factor model of personality

As we have seen, trait theorists tend to divide into those who suggest that personality is best captured by measuring a large number of basic traits, such as Gordon Allport and Raymond Cattell, and those who suggest that the basic structure of personality can be captured by grouping 'high-order' dimensions, such as Hans Eysenck. The 'Big Five' model of personality trait structure proposes that personality is organized around only five core dimensions: openness, conscientiousness, extroversion, agreeableness and neuroticism.[10,11] These Big Five personality dimensions, represented by the handy acronym 'OCEAN' (or 'CANOE' if the words are reconfigured), are shown in Table 6.1.

Researchers using the Big Five model hold that when a person is placed at a specific point on each of these five core personality dimensions by means of a test or direct observations of behaviour, the essence of that person's personality is captured. These Big Five personality dimensions may be universal, since they were found to be consistent in a study of women and men in diverse Asian, European and North American cultures.[11–13]

The research also shows evidence that some personality dimensions tend to be more stable than others over time. For example, introversion–extroversion tends to be quite stable from childhood into adulthood and across the adult years. When it comes to stability of behaviour across situations, personality again shows both a degree of stability and some capacity for change. For example, regarding the higher-order trait of 'conscientiousness', an employee might be highly conscientious in one situation (such as handing in class assignments on time to complete a college programme of studies) without being conscientious in another (such as coming to work on time).

stop reflect

Where would you place yourself on the personality scales? What is your reaction to the models? Are personality traits inherited or do they arise from social experience? What are the predictive advantages of the broad general traits and the narrow specific traits?

Table 6.1 The Big Five model of personality trait structure and the associated lower-order traits

Dimensions	Lower-order traits
Openness	Artistically sensitive, intellectual interests, reflective, insightful, curious, imaginative
Conscientiousness	Efficient, reliable, responsible, scrupulous, ethical, persevering, organized, self-disciplined
Extroversion	Talkative, outgoing, candid, adventurous, sociable, assertive, gregarious, energetic
Agreeableness	Good-natured, forgiving, generous, non-critical, warm, gentle, cooperative, trusting, compassionate
Neuroticism	Anxious, self-pitying, nervous, tense, hostile, excitable, emotionally unstable, impulsive

Source: Adapted from Bernstein et al. (2000)[8].

Trait theorists have made an important contribution by focusing attention on the value of identifying, classifying and measuring stable and enduring personality characteristics. But this so-called nomothetic approach to understanding personality has severe limitations. It is argued elsewhere, for example, that researchers need to pay more attention to how traits interact with one another to affect various behaviours if we are to capture the true personality. There is a tendency for researchers to make predictions on the basis of a single measured personality trait without taking into account other personality factors that also might influence the action in question.[1]

nomothetic approach: an approach to explanation in which we seek to identify relationships between variables across many cases

The psychodynamic theory of personality

Many social psychologists and organizational theorists believe that personality emerges from complex processes too dynamic to be captured by factor analysis. The Austrian physician Sigmund Freud (1856–1939) developed the influential psychoanalytic theory of personality, which claims that the dynamic interplay of inner psychological processes determines ways of thinking, feeling and acting. Freud's work introduced such terms as 'ego', 'fixation', 'libido', 'rationalization' and 'repression' into Western popular discourse, as well as having a profound effect on twentieth-century personality research. The significance of psychoanalytic theories of socialization pioneered by Freud has been recognized by sociologists.

When treating patients with the French neurologist Jean Charcot, Freud became convinced that conversion hysteria, a disorder in which physical symptoms such as paralysis and blindness appeared suddenly and with no apparent physical cause, was connected to painful memories, which were often sexual or aggressive in nature, and seemed to have been repressed by the patient. When his patients were able to re-experience these traumatic memories, their physical symptoms often markedly improved or disappeared.

Freud experimented with various techniques, including hypnosis and dream analysis, to unearth the buried contents of the unconscious mind. His research convinced him that personality develops out of each person's struggle to meet her or his basic needs in a world that often frustrates those efforts. Freud suggested that an individual's personality is determined by conscious, preconscious and unconscious brain activity, with the unconscious part of the mind exerting great influence on consciousness and behaviour. He proposed that most psychological events are located in what he termed the subconscious, a vast repository of traumatic events that a person apparently can no longer consciously recall without the use of hypnosis. The conscious mind, which consists of mental events of which people are presently aware, represented just the 'tip of the iceberg' (Figure 6.4).

weblink

Go to www.freud.org.uk, a site dedicated to Sigmund Freud and his work

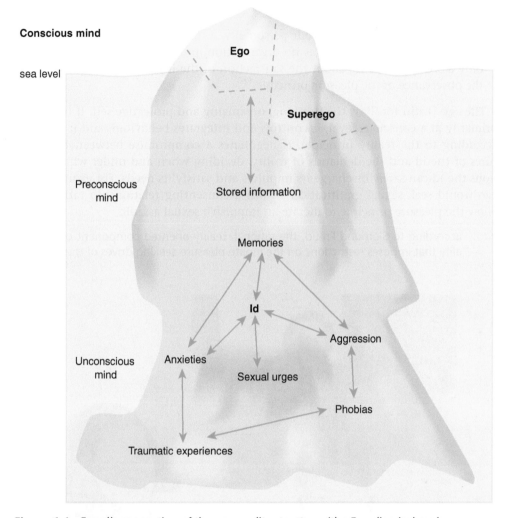

Figure 6.4   Freud's conception of the personality structure: 'the Freudian iceberg'

The structure of personality: id, ego and superego

According to Freud, personality is made up three separate but interacting parts: the id, the ego and the superego. In Figure 6.4, the pointed arrows inside the 'Freudian iceberg' are meant to show the connections and the dynamic nature of the structure of personality. Freud saw the id (the Latin word for 'it') as the unconscious portion of the personality, where the libido, which is the primary source of life instincts, resides. The id is the only structure present at birth, and it functions in a totally irrational manner. The id operates on the pleasure principle, seeking the immediate gratification of impulses produced by two innate drives, sex and aggression.

id: Sigmund Freud's term for the component of personality that includes all of the individual's basic biological drives and needs that demand immediate gratification

For Freud, the id is:

> the dark, inaccessible part of our personality ... It is filled with energy reaching it from the instincts, but it has no organization, produces no collective will, but only a striving to bring about the satisfaction of the instinctual needs subject to the observance of the pleasure principle.[14]

The ego (Latin for 'I') is the thinking, organizing and protective self. It functions primarily at a conscious level, it controls and integrates behaviour, and it operates according to the reality principle. It negotiates a compromise between the pressures of the id and the demands of reality, deciding when and under what conditions the id can safely discharge its impulses and satisfy its needs. For example, the ego would seek sexual gratification within a consenting relationship rather than allow the pleasure principle to dictate an impulsive sexual assault.

ego: according to Sigmund Freud, the rational, reality-oriented component of personality that imposes restrictions on the innate pleasure-seeking drives of the id

Plate 2 Research into the genetic basis of personality suggests that traits such as extroversion may be inherited

Source: Getty Images.

The third component of personality is the superego (Latin meaning 'beyond' or 'above' the ego), which is subdivided into the conscience and the ego ideal, and tells us what we should and should not do. The superego, the moral arm of the personality, determines which actions are permissible and punishes wrongdoing with feelings of guilt. Like the ego, the superego strives to control the instincts of the id, particularly the sexual and aggressive impulses that are condemned by Western society. Whereas the id screams 'I want!', the superego replies, 'Don't you dare! That would be wicked!' For the superego, moralistic principles take precedence over realist ones. Thus, the superego might cause a person to experience intense guilt over sexual deviance.

superego: Sigmund Freud's term for the human conscience, consisting of the moral and ethical aspects of personality

The ego must achieve a compromise between the demands of the id, the constraints of the superego and the demands of reality. This mediating role has earned the ego the title the 'executive of the personality'.[1]

Freud's theory of personality set the scene for a never-ending struggle between the id and the superego for control of the ego. When the ego confronts id drives that threaten to get out of control, anxiety results. Anxiety serves as a signal and motivates the ego to deal with the problem. Freud proposed a number of defence mechanisms to enable people to cope with these conflicts. Examples of defence mechanisms are described in Table 6.2. The principal defence mechanism is repression.

stop reflect

Have you ever found yourself using any of Freud's defence mechanisms? If so, what was the situation?

Table 6.2 Psychoanalytic defence mechanisms

Defence mechanism	Description	Example
Repression	An active defensive process through which anxiety-arousing impulses or memories are pushed into the unconscious mind	A sports celebrity who was sexually abused in childhood develops amnesia for the event
Denial	A person refuses to acknowledge anxiety-arousing aspects of the environment. The denial may involve either the emotions connected with the event or the event itself	A young man who is told he has terminal cancer refuses to consider the possibility that he will not recover
Displacement	An unacceptable or dangerous impulse is repressed, and then directed at a safer substitute target	A female employee who is harassed by her boss experiences no anger at work, but then goes home and abuses her husband and children
Rationalization	A person constructs a false but plausible explanation or excuse for an anxiety-arousing behaviour or event that has already occurred	An employee caught stealing justifies the act by pointing out that the company can afford the loss, and besides, other employees are stealing too

Source: Adapted from Passer et al. (2003)[1].

Freud believed that, in repression, the ego uses some of its energy to prevent anxiety-arousing thoughts, feelings and impulses from entering consciousness. Defence mechanisms operate unconsciously, so people are unusually unaware that they are using self-deception to ward off anxiety.

In Freud's theory, personality develops through seven psychosexual stages: oral, anal, phallic, Oedipus complex, Electra complex, latency and genital – which involve seeking pleasure from specific parts of the body called erogenous zones. A major shortcoming of psychoanalytic theory is that many of its concepts are ambiguous and difficult to define and measure operationally. A second major criticism is that Freud laid too much emphasis on the events of early childhood as determinants of adult personality.

---

weblink

Go to http://pandc.ca for books and theorists on personality and consciousness

---

Sociocultural theories of personality

In this section, we present an introduction to the work of prominent social psychologists and sociologists who, in different ways, are interested in understanding personality from a sociocultural perspective. According to the trait and psychodynamic approaches, personality consists of traits that shape thoughts, feelings and actions. In contrast, those taking a sociocultural approach understand personality to be fundamentally rooted in life experience, communities of practice and relationships. This idiographic approach posits that personality is acquired through learning in an immediate social milieu – the social setting that is directly open to an individual's personal experience. In essence, its central tenet is that personality should not be located within typologies but be understood as a complex social entity, closely related to self-image and identity.

idiographic approach: an approach to explanation in which we seek to explain the relationships among variables within a particular case or event; it contrasts with nomothetic analysis

Sociocultural researchers examine how personality is connected with social experience and the society in which people live: the culture, socialization and social dynamics of social interaction and situations. To illustrate this broad sociocultural perspective, we consider significant *social-cognitive* and *phenomenological* approaches to personality.

The social-cognitive approach, sometimes called the social-learning approach, emphasizes the development of personality through people interacting with a social environment that provides learning experiences. The phenomenological approach to personality suggests that the way people perceive and interpret social experience forms their personalities and influences their thoughts, feelings and actions.

phenomenological approach: a philosophy concerned with how researchers make sense of the world around them, and whose adherents believe that the social researcher must 'get inside people's heads' to understand how they perceive and interpret the world

The social-cognitive approach to personality

The most influential social-cognitive or social-learning theories are those of Julian Rotter and Albert Bandura.[15–17] These theorists have developed an approach that views personality as the sum total of the cognitive habits and behaviours that develop as people learn through experience in their social setting.

social-learning theory: a theory stating that much learning occurs by observing others and then modelling the behaviours that lead to favourable outcomes and avoiding the behaviours that lead to punishing consequences

Julian Rotter (pronounced like 'motor') argued that a person's decision to engage in a behaviour in a given situation is determined by two factors:

- what the person expects to happen following the action
- the value the person places on the outcome, which is called the reinforcement value.

Expectancy is our perception of how likely it is that certain consequences will occur if we engage in a particular behaviour within a specific situation. 'Reinforcement value' is basically how much we desire or dread the outcome that we expect the action to produce. For example, candidates for a particular position may spend a lot of money on new clothes to attend a job interview because past learning leads them to expect that doing so will help secure the job, and they place a high value on having the job.

expectancy theory: a motivation theory based on the idea that work effort is directed toward behaviours that people believe will lead to desired outcomes

Rotter also argued that people learn general ways of thinking about their environment, in particular about how life's rewards and punishments are controlled. Differences in this generalized expectancy concerning the degree of personal control that individuals have in their lives produced Rotter's influential concept of the internal–external locus of control. People with an internal locus of control believe that life outcomes are largely under personal control and depend on their own efforts. In contrast, people with an external locus of control believe that the environment is largely beyond their control, and that their fate has less to do with their own efforts than with the influence of external factors, such as luck.

locus of control: a personality trait referring to the extent to which people believe events are within their control

Research suggests that the locus of control that people develop has important implications for personality in later life. For example, in the workplace, there is evidence that an internal locus of control is positively related to self-esteem and feelings of personal effectiveness, and the internally focused are less likely to experience depression or anxiety, and tend to cope with stress in a more active and problem-focused manner than do externally focused people.[18] One study has shown that because locus of control is fashioned by people's social experience, this aspect of personality can change.[19] In the workplace, for example, experiencing participative decision-making arrangements may cause a shift towards an internal locus of control in managers and non-managers alike.

Figure 6.5 Bandura's model of reciprocal determinism

According to Albert Bandura, neither personal traits nor the social context alone determines personality. Instead, he argues that the environment, the person and the person's behaviour interact in a pattern of two-way causal links to determine personality. In short, personality is determined by what Bandura calls *reciprocal determinism* (Figure 6.5).

weblink

Go to http://sociologyindex.com for major ideas in the sociological study of socialization

One personal variable in this web of influence is particularly important in Bandura's view: **self-efficacy** refers to a person's beliefs about her or his ability to perform the actions needed to achieve desired outcomes. People whose self-efficacy is high have confidence in their ability to do what it takes to overcome obstacles and achieve their goals.

self-efficacy: the beliefs people have about their ability to perform specific situational task(s) successfully

Self-efficacy not only determines whether a person will engage in a particular behaviour, but also determines the extent to which he or she will sustain that behaviour in the face of adversity. For example, if you believe that you are qualified for a job at the BBC, you are likely to apply for an interview. Even if you are turned down for the job, you are apt to apply for an interview at another TV company because you are confident of your abilities. High self-efficacy can facilitate both the frequency and the quality of behaviour–environment interactions, and low self-efficacy can hamper both.[7]

For Bandura, self-efficacy beliefs are always specific to particular situations. Thus, we may have high self-efficacy in some situations and low self-efficacy in others. For example, those who have mastered sophisticated computer software skills do not feel more generally capable in all areas of their life, despite their enhanced computer abilities. Efficacy beliefs are strong predictors of future performance and accomplishment. In short, they become a kind of self-fulfilling prophecy.

stop reflect

Which environmental factors do you feel may be more important for shaping personality? What kinds of personality difference between males and females have you observed? Are these differences genuine or a product of your culture? How do you know?

The phenomenological approach to personality

The most influential phenomenological theories, also known as humanistic theories, of personality are those of Abraham Maslow (1908–1970) and Carl Rogers (1902–1987). These theorists emphasize the positive, fulfilling experiences of life, and argue that the way people perceive and interpret their social experiences forms their personality. Maslow believed that human motivation is based on a hierarchy of needs, and that understanding personality requires an understanding of this hierarchy of needs.[20] According to Maslow, personality is the expression of a basic human tendency towards growth and self-actualization. The innate drive for self-actualization, the realization of a person's true intellectual and emotional potential, is not specific to any particular culture. Maslow considered it as being a fundamental part of human nature: 'Man has a higher and transcendent nature, and this is part of his [sic] essence'.

Like Maslow, Carl Rogers saw personality as the expression of a basic human tendency towards growth and self-actualization.[22] However, unlike Maslow, he did not view personality development in terms of satisfying a hierarchy of needs. Rogers argued that personality development centres on a person's self-concept, the part of social experience that a person identifies as 'I' or 'me'. He believed that people who accurately experience the self – with all its preferences, approval, love, respect and affection – are en route to self-actualization.

The key to forming a psychologically positive personality is to develop a positive self-concept or image of oneself. How does a person do this? According to Rogers, people are happy if they feel that others are happy with them. Similarly, people are unhappy when others are dissatisfied or disappointed with them. People's feelings towards themselves depend significantly on what others think of them. From early childhood, we learn that there exist certain criteria or conditions that must be met before others give us positive regard. Rogers called these criteria 'conditions of worth'. In Rogers's view, rewards and punishment from others are important in personality development because they influence behaviour and shape self-perceptions. In short, personality is formed partly by the actualizing tendency and partly by others' evaluations.[8]

The social-self approach to personality

The traits (nomothetic) approach to understanding personality prevails in organizational behaviour literature, but the sociological concept of the *self* offers an alternative conception of the individual. For sociologists, the processes of socialization, the life-long social experience by which people learn culture and develop their human potential, has great relevance for understanding personality. A century ago in 1902, sociologist Charles Cooley (1864–1929) introduced the phrase the 'looking-glass self' in his book *Human Nature and the Social Order* to mean a conception of self based largely on how we imagine we appear to others, and imagine judgements likely to be made about that appearance.[23]

looking-glass self: Cooley's term for the way in which a person's sense of self is derived from the perceptions of others

Writing almost 30 years before the psychologist Carl Rogers, sociologist George Herbert Mead (1863–1931) expounded the concept of the looking-glass self, and developed a *process-relational theory* to explain how personality is formed through social activity and interaction with other people. Mead's writings have some similarities to those of Maslow and Rogers. Central to Mead's theory of personality is the concept of the 'self', that part of a person's personality composed of self-awareness and self image.[24] Mead believed that people form a personality by internalizing – or taking in – their locale. He rejected the notion that the self is inherited at birth and that personality is formed by biological inner impulses or drives, as argued by Sigmund Freud. According to Mead, the self develops only with social activity and social relationships, and if there is social isolation, as in the case of isolated children, the human body may develop but no self emerges.

After a self is formed, people usually, but not always, manifest it. For example, the novelist Daniel Defoe's character Robinson Crusoe developed a self while he was living in his own culture, and he continued to have a self when he was alone on what he thought was a deserted island. Thus, Crusoe continued to have the ability to take himself as an object.

The self is dialectically related to the human mind. The body, therefore, is not a self but becomes a self only when the mind has developed and engaged in reflexiveness. While Freud concentrated on the denial of the id's drives as the mechanism that generates the self's objective side, Mead drew attention to the source of the 'me' – how we become self-aware – by taking 'the role of the other'. People are interpretative creatures who must make sense of the world they live in. We learn to play different roles in this process. We are at different times children, students, friends, workers, parents and so on, and we do not behave in the same way in every situation. This process of role taking demonstrates that personality is a social product, and that 'group or collective action consists of aligning of individual actions, brought about by individuals' interpreting or taking into account each other's actions'.[25]

Language is an important aspect of socialization and the development of the self. As children learn to understand words and later to use them, they simultaneously learn to categorize their experience and evaluate their own behaviour and that of others. The first words many English or German children say is 'No' or 'Nein'. The use of language is one way individuals emphatically gauge different cultural meanings in disparate social situations and act accordingly. The self is reflexive, in that a person can become the object of her or his thought and actions. Language is central to the development of individual identity, the self. Moreover, 'the dynamics of the self and others are open to complex layers of interpretation and reflexive distancing' (ref. 24, p. 160).

Mead believed that the self has two parts: the 'I' (the unsocialized self) and the 'me' (the socialized self). The 'I' is the spontaneous, incalculable, impulsive, unsocialized and creative aspect of the self. Mead emphasized the 'I' because it is a key source of creativity in the social process, an individual's values are located in the 'I', it holds something that all individuals seek – self-realization – and finally, as society develops, people become increasingly dominated by the 'I' and less by the 'me'.

stop reflect

Make a list of the personality traits you think characterize you. Share your list with others who know you well, and ask what they think. To what extent, if at all, do you think your own personality originates from the interaction between you and your environment? Can you give examples?

> **OB in focus**
>
> **Psychometric Testing: Ensuring the right fit**
>
> In spite of their best efforts, many organizations struggle with consistently finding and hiring successful job candidates. To make better selection decisions, many firms are turning to a less traditional tool: psychometric assessments. Psychometric assessments are scientifically designed to provide a standardized measure of a candidate's general intellectual ability, competencies and personality traits. While there are many different tests available, they can generally be classified into two broad types: ability and personality.
>
> *Ability* is a measure of 'can do'. An ability assessment measures a person's current level of knowledge and her or his capability to acquire further knowledge and skills. It also reveals a candidate's capabilities and learning potential. Examples of assessments that fall in this area include measures of intelligence, verbal ability and mechanical aptitude. Ability assessments are among the best predictors of job performance.
>
> *Personality* is a measure of 'will do'. A personality assessment measures typical behaviour, and discloses what candidates are likely to do on a daily basis. It is designed to measure a person's preference for behaving in certain ways. Personality measures also reveal whether the individual is easy to manage, works hard, offers innovative solutions and works well with others.
>
> Psychometric tests are also used for assessing characteristics that cannot be developed through training but are acquired over long periods of time, such as personality traits or in-depth knowledge of a profession. The use of well-constructed assessments can improve organization fit and address counterproductive behaviours.
>
> Shawn Bakker, a psychologist at Psychometrics Canada
(www.psychometrics.com). Source: Canadian HR Reporter,
March 27, 2006, p. 7.

The 'me' is the social part of the self that is developed as the object of others' attitudes, beliefs and behaviour, including one's own reflections on one's self; it is 'the organized set of attitudes of others which one himself assumes' (ref. 23, p. 197). All social interaction has both parts: individuals initiate action (the 'I' phase of the self), and individuals continue their action based on how others respond to their behaviour (the 'me' phase of the self). Whereas the 'I' is associated with creativity, change and reconstruction of the self, the 'me' has a self-control aspect, in that it serves to stabilize the self. The combining of the 'I' and the 'me' leads to the formation of individual personality.[26] This reflexive process is invariably a social one, in which people form their sense of self in the context of family, peers and the mass media.[27] Thus, a person's personality will change across her or his life course as she or her participates in a community and interacts with different pervasive agents of socialization – family, school, peer group and mass media.

peer group: a group of people who are linked by common interests, equal social position and (usually) similar age

Mead's concept of the 'I' and the 'me' should not be confused with Freud's concept of the id and superego. As others have pointed out, Freud believed that the id and superego were firmly embedded in the biological organism, whereas Mead, on the other hand, rejected any biological element of the self. Furthermore, whereas the id and superego are locked in constant struggle, the 'I' and the 'me' work cooperatively.

Detractors argue that Mead's theory of personality is completely social, neglecting any biological element at all. Moreover, Mead's analysis of personality is rooted in the tradition of symbolic interactionism, a sociological perspective that focuses on the subjective meanings that people create through face-to-face communication in micro-level social settings. This was a perspective that resonated deeply in the North American individualistic culture and early US sociology.[28]

interactionism: what people do when they are in one another's presence, for example in a work group or team

individualism: the extent to which a person values independence and personal uniqueness

Identity and personality

The term 'identity' is derived from the Latin root *idem*, implying sameness and continuity. Its precise meaning is contested, but here we define identity as a complex fusion of the interplay between the inner self and the outer communal culture and social interaction.[29] The identity approach to understanding personality is located within a process-relational view of the subject or individual. According to this perspective, individuals are conceived as having emerging identities that are developed by, and also develop, the institutions and processes of modernity.[30] As children develop, they identify social roles, first within their family and later in the community. They also develop an understanding of status differences, and the ways in which roles interact with class, gender, ethnicity and race to create complex patterns of social behaviour. This process of socialization is therefore affected by whether they are the son or daughter of a neurosurgeon or a hospital porter; whether they grow up in a two-parent or a single-parent household; whether they grow up in London or Londonderry; whether they speak English or Hindi; and whether they worship at a mosque or a synagogue. As a result of socialization, most people acquire a set of attitudes, values, skills and behaviours that enable them to form and sustain relationships with others, work cooperatively with co-workers, avoid deviant behaviour and form a sense of self and identity.

The difference between personality and identity can be understood by answering the question, 'Who am I?' You could respond to this question with a list of personality traits such as 'I am an introvert, thoughtful, and reliable person.' Alternatively, your response could be, 'I am a parent, I work part-time at the Body Shop, and I am a university student.' The second set of responses, unlike the first, makes no reference to personality traits, but portrays a sense of identity on the basis of how we are related to others (for example, partner, mother, employee or student), and as such is deeply contextualized within the multiple social relations within which we are embedded. Identity speaks to social relations, to a fluid process of 'becoming' rather than an end state of 'being'. Identity is not something we are born with: it is structured or shaped by, and also shapes, societal influences. For Peter Berger, identity is defined clearly to be 'socially bestowed, socially sustained and socially transformed' (ref. 31, p. 98; see also ref. 32).

Plate 3 As children develop, they identify social roles, first within their family and later in the community. They also develop an understanding of status differences, and the ways in which roles interact with class, gender, ethnicity and race to create complex patterns of social behaviour

Source: iStockphoto.

The concept of identity is complex and multifaceted. The main sources of identity include social class, gender, disability, sexual orientation and race and ethnicity. Anthony Giddens[33] identifies two types of identity: personal identity and social identity. Personal identity (or self-identity) refers to the ongoing process of self-development through which we construct a unique sense of ourselves and our relationship to the world around us. Identity is constructed through both social relations and discourses around, for example, gender (woman versus man), sexuality (straight versus gay) and race (black versus white). So, for example, ethnocultural factors may define identity. If I am Jewish, my religion may play a larger role in my identity than if I am agnostic, by virtue of the fact that Jewish people have been historically stigmatized. Identity draws upon the work of symbolic interactionists.[34]

personal identity: the ongoing process of self-development through which we construct a unique sense of ourselves and our relationship to the world around us

social identity: the perception of a 'sameness' or 'belongingness' to a human collective with common values, goals or experiences

If self-identity sets people apart as distinct individuals, social identity is the perception of 'sameness' or 'belongingness', the ways in which individuals are the same or members of some human collective – signs that denote who, in a basic sense, that person *is*.[33] Examples of social identities might include occupation, trade unionist, feminist, environmentalist, mother, Asian, disabled, Muslim and so forth. Social identities have a collective dimension and are predicated on a set of common values or goals or experiences. An individual can have multiple identities, some of which

OB and Globalization

Identity and instability in an uncertain economy

When first getting to know someone, it is common practice to ask them what they do for work. Being able to connect a person to a particular profession can help us to identify that person in relation to characteristics we associate with that line of work. For instance, we might imagine that someone working as a librarian might be shy or reserved, while a commodities broker might be assumed to be self-confident and assertive. Although such stereotypes often have little bearing on individuals' actual identities or personalities, we nonetheless persist in the notion that what someone does for work has something to say about who they are as a person. Likewise, many workers identify themselves in terms of the work they do and their social position in the workplace.

For workers in today's uncertain economy, the prospect of being made redundant generates stress not only about lost income, but also about the threat of an unmooring of their personal identities. Psychologists specializing in organizational behaviour note that, for many workers, their sense of self is inseparable from the work they do and the social environment of the workplace. The inability to engage in those familiar practices can leave them feeling ungrounded and even depressed. In a *Financial Times* article (Jacobs, 2008) dealing with redundancy and depression, a former banker explains how an organizational culture that promotes hard work, high achievement and an 'alpha male' approach can position workers for a long fall should they be made redundant:

Some think the world revolves around them, in good times and bad. When things are good they feel like masters of the universe, but when the bubble bursts they take it very hard. It can be devastating.

In such situations, workers can stake their sense of self almost entirely on their work and, more specifically, on their place within the structure of the organization. Being unseated from their position within the organization can be equated to losing the reference point from which they are able to make sense of the world and their place in it. According to London therapist Christine Martin, 'Redundancy demands existential questions alongside the financial worries' (Jacobs, 2008).

Anthropologist Dorothy Holland and her colleagues (Holland et al., 1998) describe identity as a sense of self that is actively and continually constructed, tested and refigured through daily social practices. They explain that these social practices take place in particular cultural realms that provide resources and structures that individuals can draw on to formulate personal identities which reproduce (or resist) those cultural realms. The importance of improvisation, agency and creativity – within defined social worlds – is also central to identity formation.

Using Holland et al.'s approach to identity, we can consider workplace culture in the UK as a cultural realm that provides workers with a set of practices and social relations that they use to position themselves vis-à-vis their work tasks, relationships with colleagues and the world at large. Understanding the links between organizational culture, personal identity formation and economic stability (or instability) can help managers to provide appropriate support services to workers when redundancies are deemed necessary.

stop!   Do you think it is a positive or a negative thing for workers to have identities closely entwined with – even dependent upon – their work? Would such close links between identity and work benefit or hinder the workplace? How might they benefit or hinder other areas of workers' lives?

Sources and further research

Holland, D., Lachicotte, W. Jr., Skinner, D. and Cain, C. (1998) *Identity and Agency in Cultural Worlds*, Cambridge, MA: Harvard University Press.

Jacobs, E. (2008) 'Redundancy and a depression', *Financial Times*, August 19, 2008. Available at: www.ft.com; www.journalisted.com/article?id=763449.

Sheedy, B. (2005) 'All is not lost', *Management Today*, November/December 2005. Available at: www.aim.com.au/DisplayStory.asp?ID=571; www.doningtongroup.com/UserFiles/Media/0905-allisnotlost-SB-AIMmag.pdf.

Note: This feature was written by Gretchen Fox, PhD, Anthropologist, Timberline Natural Resource Group, Canada.

may be more dominant depending on a specific situation. What makes our identity dynamic, rather than static, is our capacity as self-conscious, self-reflexive human beings to constantly construct and reconstruct our identities.

Individuals spend a significant amount of time in work organizations and, unsurprisingly, derive a sense of identity from their occupation or from the organization or a work team within the organization. When a person says, 'I love my work; I am my work,' it connotes a sense of identity and its power to influence proactive behaviours. Each occupation, work group or organization will have a set of shared beliefs, values, norms and demands particular to the group. Organizational goals and processes, such as sustainable products and practices, job design or rewards, can shape the relative value that individuals attach to joining and retaining their membership of groups or organizations. Equally, the termination of the employment relationship can lead to a loss of identity. The advocacy for a 'strong' organizational culture as a motivational strategy in an historical context of high-performance work systems underscores the importance of identity. Cultural control aims to have employees possess direct links to the values and goals of top managers in order to activate the emotion and create an identity that might elevate loyalty and commitment to the organization.

The power of social identity to define an occupation or organization's status relative to others can pose significant challenges to managers. For example, individuals may avoid or disassociate from a low-status organization considered to be managed without due regard to social responsibility, environmental sustainability and ethical practices. Some new theories of motivation, such as self-concept theory and whole-self theory, have linked the psychological treatment of work motivation to the notion of identity or self. Studies suggest that an individual's coherent sense of identity or loss of identity is far more important than most traditional treatments of work motivation acknowledge.[35,36]

Applying personality theories in the workplace

While managers tend to think of diversity in terms of such factors as gender, ethnic origin and disability, the variety of personalities in the workplace is also important. The nomothetic view of personality dominates management literature, partly because it enables management to render individuals 'knowable' and 'quantifiable' by identifying traits through personality testing.[37] Personality attributes determine how people interact with other workers, whether they can work on their own without supervision, whether they are conscientious or just do the minimum to 'get by', how they respond to change, whether they behave ethically or unethically, and much more.[38] For these reasons and others, organizations have developed an array of human resource management techniques to identify personality differences to help them to admit the 'right' people into the organization, and, once staff have been selected, this knowledge will help to identify those with the personality traits said to be required of an effective leader.

John Holland best articulated the view that organizations should consider aligning the requirements of the job and the characteristics of the workplace with personality characteristics.[39] In recent years, the awareness that organizations should focus on the degree of congruence between the individual and her or his work environment has expanded because of the need for workers to change and adapt to new work structures and employment relations. These include team working, individual-oriented performance-related compensation and a 'learning-oriented' organizational culture. Holland's personality–job fit model identifies six personality types – realistic, investigative, social, conventional, enterprising and artistic – each of which has a congruent occupational environment. Holland proposes that high congruence leads to satisfaction and the propensity to remain in that job or career. Table 6.3 defines these personality types and their personality attributes, and gives examples of congruent work environments.

Holland developed a model shaped like a hexagon that shows the relationships among occupational personality types, based on his Vocational Preference Inventory questionnaire, which contains 160 occupational titles. Respondents were asked to indicate which of the occupations they liked or disliked, and their answers were used to construct personality profiles. The closer two fields or orientations are in the hexagon, the more compatible they are. For example, the enterprising and social personality types are adjacent to each other in the hexagon model so, according to Holland's theory, individuals with both enterprising and social personalities have high compatibility (Figure 6.6).

There are three key points we should note about Holland's model:

- Intrinsic differences in personalities exist based on the restrictive Big Five personality model.
- Different types of occupation and work environment are better suited to certain personality types.
- Workers in workplaces and occupations congruent with their personality types should be more satisfied and more likely to remain with the organization than workers in incongruent occupations.

Research appears to strongly support the hexagonal model, but critics have pointed out that the model only incorporates the Big Five personality dimensions, and there are doubts whether the model can be generalized across cultures.[40–42]

With the resurgent interest in recruiting the 'right' people for the 'new' work regimes, and the 'discovery' of the Big Five personality model, research examining the relationships between personality traits and job performance, personality and

Table 6.3 Holland's typology of personality and congruent work environments, and occupations

Personality type	Traits	Workplace characteristics	Congruent occupations
Realistic	Practical, shy, persistent, conforming, stable	Prefers physical activities that require skills and coordination	Mechanical engineer, farmer
Investigative	Analytical, creative, independent, reserved	Work involves thinking and analysing	Mathematician, biologist, systems analyst
Social	Sociable, friendly, outgoing, cooperative	Work involves helping and developing others	Social worker, teacher, counsellor, nurse
Conventional	Dependable, orderly, self-disciplined	Work is unambiguous, rule-regulated, orderly	Accountant, banker, administrator
Enterprising	Confident, ambitious, assertive, energetic	Prefers leading others, verbal activities, result-oriented setting	Lawyer, entrepreneur, salesperson, financial planner/consultant
Artistic	Creative, disorderly, impulsive	Thrives on ambiguous and unstructured activities	Musician, architect, painter, designer

Source: Based on information from Holland (1985)[39] and Greenhaus (1987)[53].

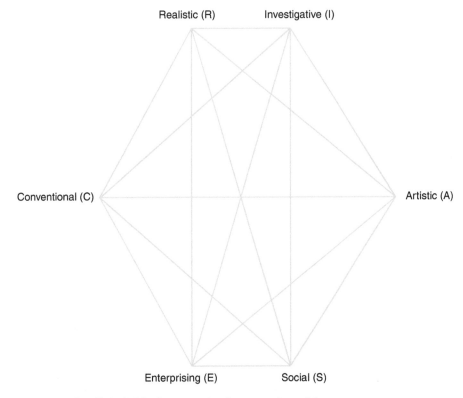

Figure 6.6 Holland's individual–occupation hexagonal model

Source: Holland (1985)[39]. Reproduced by permission of Pearson Education. Inc.

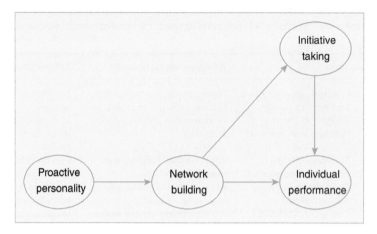

Figure 6.7   A model of proactive personality and individual job performance

social integration, and the efficacy of personality measuring instruments, has flourished. According to the new management parlance on knowledge work, workers are expected to create their own opportunities for innovation and positive change in the organization. Underlying the research on the relationship between personality traits and job performance is a presumption that a proactive personality – defined as a disposition to take action to influence one's environment – promotes job performance.[43] This is achieved by building a network of social relationships within an organization in order to gain access to information, wield influence and effect positive change – a process referred to as social capital. In short, the social capital approach advocates a view that individual power within a work organization is predicated on developing a network of relationships, which in turn enhances job performance (Figure 6.7).

social capital: the value of relationships between people, embedded in network links that facilitate trust and communication vital to overall organizational performance

What do proactive employees do? By definition, employees with a proactive personality are inclined to construct their own environment. Proactive individuals are likely to seek ways to build a network of contacts in the organization that is conducive to their own self-interest. Proactive types, therefore, tend to seek allies and build alliances with other co-workers to support personal initiatives, and actively strive to become friends with people who occupy positions of influence and power. Thompson's quantitative study found a direct positive relationship between a proactive personality, network building and individual performance, suggesting that 'network building may occupy a critical stage in the process by which proactive personality engenders performance'.

Organizational behaviour theorists have long been interested in the connection between personality and innovative behaviours, and between personality and social integration. Henry Moon and his colleagues[44] identified personality and procedural fairness within a work organization as antecedents to proactive behaviour or 'taking charge'. Interestingly, the results show that the antecedents to proactive behaviour are based more on concerns about others than on self-interest. This suggests that getting employees to take charge within the firm may be more about 'we' than it is about 'me'.[44] An important aspect of the current wave of interest in self-managed work teams is the cultural dimension. In addition to changing methods of job performance, work teams demand changes in workers' attitude and behaviour.[45] Accordingly, organizational theorists are devoting increased attention to whether people with similar personalities make up more effective work teams.

The argument is that similar personalities might facilitate social integration among team members, increase the likelihood that co-workers will cooperate with each other, and foster trust between team leaders and members. Employment recruitment practices that create a homogeneous workforce of people with similar personalities and values may appear ideal in a team-based environment. As mentioned above, studies suggest that when employees hold similar personality characteristics, few rules, regulations and formal decision-making processes are needed to get work done. As a consequence, organizational leaders tend to choose people with personality traits similar to their own. The danger in top managers recruiting a workforce with similar personality traits is that homogeneity is a force potentially detrimental to change and long-term organizational survival.[5]

---

stop reflect

If you were recruiting people to join you on an important work project, would you try to hire people with a personality profile similar to your own? If so, why? Can you think of any advantages and disadvantages of this approach?

Work and Society: Why does she behave that way?

Many researchers who study work and personality stress the person–organization relationship. The assumption is that some personalities are a better 'fit' in particular organizational settings. Often, however, the question of person–organization fit is a complex one, and personality traits associated with highly skilled employees can sometimes be problematic.

One such personality trait is narcissism. A recent study suggests those with narcissistic personalities will have little to offer an organization:

> narcissists tend to lack empathy, engage in aggressive behavior and have self-serving motives ... narcissists should be especially unlikely to contribute positively to an organization's social and psychological climate by helping others, being courteous and a good sport, and going above and beyond the call of duty for the greater good. (Judge, et al., 2006, p. 765)

Narcissism would appear to be a personality trait that employers would want to avoid at all costs. However, it is important to realize that personality is only one of several factors that contribute to an individual's behaviour. Consider the following scenario. Sharon Smith had recently been hired by a mid-sized hospital as a specialist nurse practitioner – a new role situated midway between the physician and the traditional nurse. Those employed in more traditional nursing roles at the hospital resented the fact Sharon had taken over some of the more interesting and challenging aspects of their work. Sharon showed little sympathy for their concerns: 'Nurses need to understand that their education does not prepare them to perform these kinds of procedure safely.'

Sharon's interactions with physicians were also problematic. On one occasion, she clashed with Dr William Grant, a senior physician at the hospital. Dr Grant had questioned Sharon's recommendation that a particular patient could benefit from 'lifestyle changes'. Sharon responded without hesitation, 'There is no conclusive diagnosis for this patient, so why not proceed with the treatment the patient believes is best for him?' Later, in a conference with the ward manager, Sharon expressed her anger: 'Dr Grant has no right to question my judgement. In a situation like this, lifestyle changes are a perfectly reasonable course of action.'

Clearly, the idea of personality could prove useful in this context. Recognizing that Sharon exhibited many of the characteristics of a narcissistic personality might help managers make sense of a situation that seems to be getting out of control. However, it is possible to view Sharon's behaviour in a more positive light.

Perhaps Sharon's actions were the function of a conscientious rather than a narcissistic personality. Supporters of this more optimistic view might argue that Sharon was anxious to prove herself as an invaluable member of the healthcare team. But rather than working patiently to secure the trust and respect of her colleagues, she wanted immediate and unqualified validation. With the right 'coaching', however, Sharon could become aware of her personality traits, refine her social skills and make a genuine contribution to the hospital.

It is important to bear in mind that personalities are composed of a complex blend of 'traits' and, with appropriate mentoring, an individual may learn to manage various aspects of his or her personality. Issues of workplace design are also relevant here. When a new occupation is introduced into a well-established, hierarchical division of labour, conflicts are inevitable. Managers need to provide a clear rationale for change well in advance of the actual change. They must also create opportunities for dialogue among different members of the work team as the new occupation is integrated into established work roles and routines.

stop! What do you think? Is Sharon 'programmed' by her personality to be an endless source of conflict at the hospital? Are there steps that could be taken help her become a productive member of a relatively harmonious work team?

What about the role of gender? Is the clash between Sharon and Dr Grant aggravated by the fact that healthcare workplaces have traditionally been dominated by men?

Sources and further information:

Austin, E. and Deary, I. (2002). 'Personality dispositions', pp. 187–211 in R. Sternberg (ed.), *Why Smart People Can Be So Stupid*, New Haven, CT: Yale University Press.

Judge, T., LePine, J. and Rich, B. (2006) 'Loving yourself abundantly: relationship of the narcissistic personality to self- and other perceptions of workplace deviance, leadership and task and contextual performance', *Journal of Applied Psychology*, **91**(4), pp. 762–76.

For more information on the nurse practitioner, see the *Journal for Nurse Practitioners*.

Note: This feature was written by David MacLennan, Assistant Professor at Thompson Rivers University, BC, Canada.

Personality testing

The increased focus given to personality attributes, and how such attributes predict job performance and social integration, has led to increased research on selection methods in general, and personality testing in particular. Recent studies, for example, have explored the predictive validity of the Big Five personality model in relation to job performance through a meta-analysis of 36 studies that related validity measures to personality factors.[46] The empirically based research concluded that 'conscientiousness and emotional stability showed most validity for job performance, and that openness to experience was valid for training proficiency' (ref. 47, p. 239).

If you were a manager and had the task of writing within a week a complete personality description of an applicant you did not know for an important position in your organization, what would you do? Most likely you would seek information in a variety of ways. You might start by interviewing the applicant to elicit information about her strengths and weaknesses, interests and opinions. Based on the theories we have reviewed in this chapter, what questions would you ask? Would you ask questions related to the kinds of trait embodied in the Big Five model? Would you want to know about the person's early childhood experiences? Would you ask how she sees herself with others? Would you be interested in knowing how she responds to problems in various situations? You might ask her to complete a questionnaire that indicates her values, interests and preferences. You might also want to ask other people who know her well and obtain their views of what she is like. Finally, you might decide to ask her to perform job-related tasks and observe how she behaves in a variety of situations. As a manager or potential manager, your answers to these questions would tend to reflect your own view of what is important in describing personality.

The major methods used by organizations to assess personality and predict work behaviour are shown in Figure 6.8. These consist of the interview, inventories, behaviour assessment, personality tests and e-assessment.

The task of devising valid and useful personality measures is anything but simple, and it has taxed the ingenuity of psychologists for nearly a century.[1] To be useful from a managerial perspective, personality tests must conform to the standards of reliability and validity. Reliability refers to the extent to which a technique

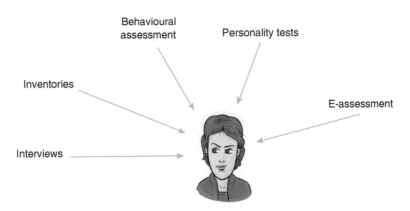

Figure 6.8   Measurement approaches used to assess personality

achieves consistency in what it is claiming to measure over repeated use. For example, a selection test that measures a stable personality trait should yield similar scores when administered to the same individuals at different times (test–retest reliability). In addition, different managers should score and interpret the test in the same way (interjudge reliability). Validity refers to the extent to which a test actually measures what it sets out to measure – in this case, the personality variable. A valid test allows us to predict a person's performance in work that is influenced by the personality variable being measured.

reliability: in sociological research, the extent to which a study or research instrument yields consistent results

validity: in sociological research, the extent to which a study or research instrument accurately measures what it is supposed to measure

The interview is the oldest and most widely used method of personality assessment. For centuries, people have made judgements about others by talking with them and observing them. Structured selection interviews contain specific questions that are administered to every interviewee in order to obtain information about a candidate's thoughts, feelings and other internal states, as well as information about current and past relationships, experiences and behaviour.

Personality inventories, or scales, are used for assessing personality. These are usually self-completed questionnaires that include standard sets of questions, usually in a true/false or rating scale format, which are scored using an agreed-upon scoring key. Their advantages include the ability to collect data from many people at the same time, the fact that all people respond to the same items, and ease of scoring. Their major disadvantage is the possibility that some participants will 'fake' responses by choosing not to answer the items truthfully, in which case their scores will not be valid reflections of the trait being measured.[48]

Human resource practitioners can observe the behaviours they are interested in rather than ask participants about them. In behavioural assessment, psychologists devise an explicit coding system that contains the behavioural categories of interest. Trained human resource recruiters then observe candidates until there is a high level of consensus (interjudge reliability) about how to describe their behaviour.

On of the most widely used personality tests in North America is the Myers–Briggs Type Indicator (MBTI). The test contains 100 questions to participants about how they usually feel or act in certain situations. This personality test then labels participants as introverted or extroverted (I or E), intuitive or sensing (N or S), feeling or thinking (F or T) and perceiving or judging (P or J).

Myers–Briggs Type Indicator (MBTI): a personality test that measures personality traits

Online personality testing is also being used for personnel selection, a technique known as e-assessment. This form of assessment provides managers with the ability to conduct personality tests at any time and any place in the world, with the added advantage of the rapid processing of applicants.[47]

Whether the use of MBTI personality tests in fact accurately predicts future work performance is problematic.[49] It has been argued, for example, that broad traits such as Eysenck's 'Big Two' and the Big Five may be useful instruments for predicting behaviour across a whole range of work situations, much as a wide-beamed floodlight illuminates a large area. However, like a narrowly focused and intense spotlight, an analysis of specific traits such as Cattell's 16PF may be a better instrument in specific situations that call for the behaviours measured by the narrower traits. Personality testing provides organizations with insights into people's thoughts, feelings and behaviour. In other words, it makes aspects of personality quantifiable, and this allows the inner feelings of workers to be transmitted into measurements, about which management decisions can be made.

Critical insight

For many managers, personality tests such as the Myers–Briggs Type Indicator are useful instruments for measuring personality variables and helping to select suitable candidates to join the organization. 'Recruitment and selection', in John Bratton and Jeff Gold's *Human Resource Management: Theory and Practice*,[50] for more information and discussion on psychometric testing. Also obtain a copy of Barbara Townley's *Reframing Human Resource Management: Power, Ethics and the Subject of Work*,[37] and read pages 83–98. What role, if any, does psychometric testing play in making workers known and manageable? Do you think Townley overstates her case? If so, why?

Some critical organizational theorists argue that psychometric testing measures what is effectively a stereotype of an 'ideal' worker or manager. It provides management with new ways of 'knowing' and managing managers and non-managers alike. It also represents a shift in management practices from the coercion of bodies through, for instance, time and motion and other Tayloristic techniques, to the attempted construction of self-regulated minds.[37,51,52] It is argued, for example, that 'The minutiae of the human soul – human interactions, feelings, and thoughts, the psychological relations of the individual to the group – [have] emerged as a new domain for management'. Finally, personality assessment based on limited information can be damaging to the organization. For example, the over-emphasis on traits to identify 'ideal' personality types in which employees 'fit' into the workplace potentially reinforces the notion that workplace problems are embedded only in the personality characteristics of people, rather than being embedded in the organization at large and the inner tensions associated with managing the employment relationship.

Chapter summary

- Personality is the distinctive and relatively enduring pattern of thinking, feeling and acting that characterizes a person's response to her or his environment. In this chapter, we have examined a number of different approaches to personality. Each of these theories offers a view of how personality forms.

- Trait theorists try to identify and measure personality variables. They disagree concerning the number of traits needed to adequately describe personality. Raymond Cattell suggested a 16-factor model to capture personality dimensions, Eysenck offered a two-factor model, and McCrae and Costa suggested the Big Five factor model. Traits have not proved to be highly consistent across situations, and they also vary in consistency over time.

- We went on to examine Freud's psychoanalytic theory, which views personality as an energy system. He divided the personality into three structures: the id, the ego and the superego. According to Freud, the dynamics of personality involve a continuous struggle between the impulses of the id and the counterforces of the ego and superego.

- Sociocultural theorists emphasize the social context, the subjective experiences of the individual, and deal with perceptual and cognitive processes. We examined the theory of Albert Bandura, a leading social-cognitive theorist, who suggests that neither personal traits nor the social context alone determines personality. A key concept is reciprocal determinism, relating to two-way causal relations between personal characteristics, behaviour and the environment.

- Phenomenological theories, also known as humanistic theories, of personality were also examined. Influential humanist theorists such as Abraham Maslow and Carl Rogers emphasize the positive, fulfilling experiences of life, and argue that the way in which people perceive and interpret their social experiences forms their personality. Self-actualization is viewed as an innate positive force that leads people to realize their positive potential, if they are not thwarted by their social context.

- In addition, the chapter examined Mead's theory of personality and his key concept of the self. He argues that people develop a personality by internalizing – or taking in – their immediate environment. He rejected the notion that the self is inherited and that personality is the product of biological inner impulses or drives, as argued by Sigmund Freud. According to Mead, the self develops only with social activity and social relationships.

- The chapter has examined the role that an individual's identity (or identities) plays in determining behaviour in the workplace. Whereas personality is based on a cluster of traits, some of which are believed to be genetic and evident from birth, identity is perceived as socially constructed: it is developed by, and also develops, the institutions and processes of modernity. Identity is fluid and multiple, and emerges through our relationships with others.

- Managers use a variety of instruments and techniques to assess personality. These include the interview, inventories, behaviour assessment, personality tests and e-assessment. We noted also that, to be useful to the organization, personality assessment instruments must conform to standards of reliability and validity.

Key concepts

extroversion   195
factor analysis   194
Freudian iceberg   199
introversion   195
personality   190–92
personality traits   193–94
personality types   195–97
phenomenological approach   202
self-identity   209
social identity   209

Vocab checklist for ESL students

- Ego
- Expectancy theory
- Extrovert, extroverted

- Factor analysis
- Id
- Idiographic
- Individual, individualism
- Interactionism
- Introvert, introverted
- Locus of control
- Looking-glass self
- Nomothetic
- Peer group
- Phenomenology, phenomenological
- Phlegmatic
- Psychodynamic
- Psychometric
- Reliable, reliability
- Sanguine
- Self-efficacy
- Social capital
- Social learning theory
- Superego
- Valid, validity

Chapter review questions

1. What is personality, and why is the concept difficult to define?

2. What is meant by the trait theory of personality? Choose one trait theory, and explain the strengths and weaknesses of this approach to personality assessment.

3. Drawing on your knowledge of Freud's psychoanalytic theory, explain why the ego is sometimes referred to as the 'executive of the personality'. What do you understand by 'defence mechanism', and what relevance has this concept to understanding behaviour in the workplace?

4. Assess critically the importance of understanding the terms 'social self' and 'socialization', and explain how attitudes and values are developed and changed.

5. How are the concepts of personality and identity different?

Chapter research questions

1. Form a diverse study group including, if possible, an international student(s). Discuss the following questions: In what ways has socialization bestowed, sustained and transformed your own sense of identity? What is the relationship between personality, self-identity and social identity? Discuss the power of agents of socialization. Use examples from your work experience or family, or from workplaces you have studied.

2. Read Anthony Giddens' opening chapter, 'The contours of high modernity' in *Modernity and Self-identity*.[30] After reading pages 10–15, how do you think Giddens links modernity to identity? Thinking about your own biography, how important, and why, are lifestyle choices in forming your self-identity?

3. Retrieve a copy of Cameron Anderson and others' (2008) article, 'Personality and organizational culture as determinants of influence' (see Further Reading, below), investigating personality as a determinant of influence in work organizations. How plausible is the evidence that individual effectiveness in initiating change and innovation depends largely on personality?

Further reading

Anderson, C., Spataro, S. and Flynn, F. (2008) 'Personality and organizational culture as determinants of influence', *Journal of Applied Psychology*, **93**(3), pp. 702–10.

Arthur, W., Woehr, D. J. and Graziano, W. (2001) 'Personality testing in employment settings', *Personnel Review*, **30**(6), pp. 657–76.

Bandura, A. (1997) *Self-Efficacy: The Exercise of Control*. New York: Freeman.

Giberson, T. R., Resick, C. and Dickson, M. (2005) 'Embedding leader characteristics: an examination of homogeneity of personality and values in organizations', *Journal of Applied Psychology*, **90**(5), pp. 1002–10.

Institute of Personnel and Development (1997) *Key Facts: Psychological Testing*. London: IPD.

Moon, H., Kamdar, D., Mayer, D. and Takeuchi, R. (2008) 'Me or we? The role of personality and justice as other-centered antecedents to innovative citizenship behaviors within organizations', *Journal of Applied Psychology*, **93**(1), pp. 84–94.

Sternberg, R. (1999) 'Survival of the fit test', *People Management*, **4**(24), pp. 29–31.

Tucker, K. H. (2002) 'Freud, Simmel, and Mead: aesthetics, the unconscious, and the fluid self', pp. 193–227 in *Classical Social Theory*, Oxford: Blackwell.

Wiggins, J. S. (ed.) (1996) *The Five-Factor Model of Personality: Theoretical Perspectives*. New York: Guilford Press.

Chapter case study 1

Identifying leaders in Nigeria

Setting

Nigeria is Africa's most populous country, with over 140 million people. In 2004, the United Nations Development Index, which measures a country's life expectancy, literacy, educational attainment and gross domestic product (GDP) per capita, ranked Nigeria 151 out of 177 countries. Devastating poverty affects 57 per cent of its population, and of the 57.2 million people who make up the labour force, over 10 per cent are unemployed. It struggles to cope with an inadequate infrastructure and under-developed human capital.

Nigeria's economy also has a detrimental over-dependence on a capital-intensive oil sector. At the beginning of the twenty-first century, Nigeria's crude oil production was averaging around 2.2 million barrels per day and providing 20 per cent of GDP, 95 per cent of foreign exchange earnings, and about 65 per cent of government revenues. It is Africa's top oil producer.

In recent years, with a new civilian government taking over from the former military rulers, there have been attempts to diversify the economy. The government has strived to attract foreign investors, citing locally available raw materials and the large national market as opportunities for long-term investments and joint ventures. However, these efforts have been stalled by foreign investors' fears of continued corruption, weak regulations, poor surveillance and inefficiencies.

For those willing to deal with such market impediments, investment advisors recommend that companies thoroughly educate themselves on local conditions and business practices, and establish a local presence. Researchers point out the importance of blending African work principles, such as an emphasis on work group activities and assigning leadership positions based on age (which is associated with experience and wisdom), into the workplace. Instead of front-line supervisors being held responsible for hiring, Nigerian workers expect and respect the involvement of senior managers in the process. Despite this knowledge, contrary foreign management methods still dominate human resource management practices in the multinational companies based in Nigeria. This has resulted in confusion, frustration and malaise among the Nigerian workforce.

The problem

A leading gas company in Europe, German-owned Lebenskraft is one of 200 multinational companies settled in Nigeria. In its over 80-year history, Lebenskraft has developed from a

German regional distributor to an international gas company. As Germany has relatively few natural resources, it must import large quantities of energy, and the company has found ample supplies through its operations in Nigeria, where it first became established nearly a decade ago.

Since its arrival in Nigeria, Lebenskraft's middle- and upper-level positions have been filled by candidates who have been educated and have lived in Germany. As a way of broadening its choice of candidates, Lebenskraft's senior management has decided to consider employees from the Nigerian operations to fill a recent management vacancy.

The company has always used personality testing when assessing individuals for promotional opportunities as part of an overall succession plan. The test they normally use, Review, was developed in Germany and has been previously applied within that country with great success. For this latest management recruitment, it has been suggested that a previously used tailored job benchmark, identifying the desired characteristics for leadership roles, should be used. The test would then be applied to compare the abilities, interests and personality traits of multiple Nigerian candidates to the benchmark to identify the best candidate for the current vacancy.

The company has created the customized benchmark using the characteristics of assessed top performers in their German operations as well as current management input. They hope that by using their Nigerian employees' assessment results, in conjunction with the benchmark, they will successfully fill the management vacancy and perhaps create an effective local succession plan. However, since the personality testing has never been used outside Germany, the company is hesitant to rely on its results. The human resources department in the Nigerian operations has been given the task of making recommendations on the selection process before the local management are asked to proceed.

Tasks

As a member of the human resources department, prepare a short report including answers to the following questions:

1. What advantages do you see in using the testing?
2. What cultural aspects of Nigeria should be considered by the Lebenskraft management team when considering the use of the test's benchmark and in developing the selection process?

Essential reading

Anakwe, U.P. (2002) 'Human resource management practices in Nigeria: challenges and insights', *International Journal of Human Resource Management*, **13**(7), pp. 1042–59.

Cooper, D. and Robertson, I. (1995) 'Selection methods – psychometrics', Chapter 8 in *The Psychology of Personnel Selection*, London: Routledge.

Jackson, T. (2002) 'Reframing human resource management in Africa: a cross-cultural perspective', *International Journal of Human Resource Management*, **13**(7), pp. 998–1018.

Note

This case study was written by Lori Rilkoff, MSc, CHRP, Senior Human Resources Manager at The City of Kamloops, and Lecturer in HRM at Thompson Rivers University BC, Canada

Chapter case study 2

Building Anna's self-esteem

Visit www.palgrave.com/business/brattonob2e to view this case study

Web-based assignment

Form a group of three to five people, and visit the websites of any of the following organizations: Microsoft (www.microsoft.com/uk/graduates), Sainsbury's (www.sainsburys.co.uk), British Airways (www.britishairways.com), and Santander (www.santander.com). What personality attributes are these organizations seeking when they recruit new employees?

Go to www.queendom.com/tests.html and www.psychometricadvantage.co.uk (search for psychometrics) and examine the psychometric tests. Some of these you may take yourself without applying for a job. How accurate, in your view, is your personality profile as revealed by any of the psychometric tests? Do your close friends agree with the assessment? Which kind of psychometric tests do you suppose would be more effective in revealing the more important aspects of your personality? Why? How much weight should organizations give to psychometric test results in employment selection? Explain your reasoning. Write a report detailing your findings.

OB in film

American Beauty (1999) follows the last few days in the life of Lester Burnham, an advertising space salesman with a mid-life crisis. The film is particularly good at showing the multiple factors influencing Lester's behaviour. Some of these reside in his personality and some in the environment. Interestingly, there are many instances when Lester's interaction with events surfaces his personality.

Drawing upon Bandura's model of reciprocal determinism, map Lester's descent into a mid-life crisis in terms of his personality, his environment and his behaviour. How does this analysis of Lester shape your understanding of personality and its role in shaping behaviour?

Note: This feature was written by Professor Jon Billsberry, Senior Research Fellow, Open University Business School, UK.

Bonus OB in Film feature!

Visit www.palgrave.com/business/brattonob2e to see how *The Odd Couple* (1968) can be considered in relation to the subject of leadership.

References

1. Passer, M., Smith, R., Atkinson, M., Mitchell, J. and Muir, D. (2003) *Psychology: Frontiers and Applications*, Toronto: McGraw-Hill Ryerson.
2. Curtiss, S. (1977) *Genie: A Psycholinguistic Study of a Modern-day 'Wild Child'*, New York: Academic Press.
3. Davis, K. (1940) 'Extreme social isolation of a child', *American Journal of Sociology*, **45**(4), pp. 554–65.
4. Rymer, R. (1994) *Genie*, New York: Harper Perennial.
5. Giberson, T. R., Resick, C. and Dickson, M. (2005) 'Embedding leader characteristics: an examination of homogeneity of personality and values in organizations', *Journal of Applied Psychology*, **90**(5), pp. 1002–10.
6. Adler, S. and Weiss, H. (1988) 'Recent developments in the study of personality and organizational behavior', in C. Cooper and I. Robertson (eds), *International Review of Industrial and Organizational Psychology*, New York: Wiley.
7. Carlson, N., Buskist, W., Enzle, M. and Heth, C. (2005) *Psychology* (3rd edn), Toronto: Pearson Education.
8. Bernstein, D. A., Clarke-Stewart, A., Penner, L. Roy, E. and Wickens, C. (2000) *Psychology* (5th edn), New York: Houghton Mifflin.
9. Eysenck, H. J. (1970) *The Structure of Human Personality* (3rd edn), London: Methuen.

10. Goldberg, L. R. (1990) 'An alternative "description of personality": the Big-Five factor structure', *Journal of Personality and Social Psychology*, **59**, pp. 1216–29.
11. McCrae, R. R. and Costa, P. T. (1995) 'Toward a new generation of personality theories: theoretical contexts for the five-factor model', pp. 51–87 in J. S. Wiggins (ed.), *The Five-Factor Model of Personality: Theoretical Perspectives*, New York: Guilford Press.
12. Dalton, M. and Wilson, M. (2000) 'The relationship of the five-factor model of personality to job performance for a group of Middle Eastern expatriate managers', *Journal of Cross-Culture Psychology*, March, pp. 250–8.
13. Paunonen, S. V. (1996) 'The structure of personality in six cultures', *Journal of Cross-Culture Psychology*, May, pp. 339–53.
14. Freud (1933). Quoted in Carlson, N., Buskist, W., Enzle, M. and Heth, C. (2005) *Psychology* (3rd edn), Toronto: Pearson Education, p. 462.
15. Rotter, J. B. (1966) 'Generalized expectations for internal versus external control of reinforcement', *Psychological Monographs*, **80**(1): 1–28.
16. Bandura, A. (1978) 'The self system in reciprocal determinism', *American Psychologist*, **33**, pp. 344–58.
17. Bandura, A. (1997) *Self-Efficacy: The Exercise of Control*, New York: Freeman.
18. Jennings (1990), quoted in Passer, M., Smith, R., Atkinson, M., Mitchell, J. and Muir, D. (2003) *Psychology: Frontiers and Applications*, Toronto: McGraw-Hill Ryerson, p. 565.
19. Frese, M. (1982) 'Occupational socialization and psychological development: an underemphasized research perspective in industrial psychology', *Journal of Occupational Psychology*, **55**, pp. 209–24.
20. Maslow, A. H. (1954) *Motivation and Personality*, New York: Harper.
21. Maslow, A. H. (1964) *Religions, Values, and Peak-Experiences*, New York: Viking.
22. Rogers, C. R. (1961) *On Becoming a Person*, Boston, MA: Houghton Mifflin.
23. Mead, G. H. (1934) *Mind, Self and Society*, Chicago: University of Chicago Press.
24. Ray, L. J. (1999) *Theorizing Classical Sociology*, Buckingham: Open University Press.
25. Blumer, H. (1969), quoted in Tucker, K. H. (2002) *Classical Social Theory*, Oxford: Blackwell, p. 218.
26. Pfuetze, P. (1954). *Self, Society and Existence: Human Nature and Dialogue in the Thoughts of George Herbert Mead and Martin Buber*, New York: Harper.
27. Tucker, K. H. (2002) *Classical Social Theory*, Oxford: Blackwell.
28. Brym, R., Lie, J., Nelson, A., Guppy, N. and McCormick, C. (2003) *Sociology: Your Compass for a New World*, Scarborough, ON: Thomson Wadsworth.
29. Mills, A. and Tancred, P. (eds) (1992) *Gendering Organizational Analysis*, Newbury Park, CA: Sage.
30. Giddens, A. (1991) *Modernity and Self-Identity*, Palo Alto, CA: Stanford University Press.
31. Berger, P. (1966) *Invitation to Sociology*, New York: Anchor Books.
32. Kellner, D. (1992) 'Popular culture and the construction of postmodern identities', pp. 141–77 in S. Lash and J. Friedman (eds), *Modernity and Identity*, Oxford: Blackwell.
33. Giddens, G. (2009) *Sociology* (6th edn), Cambridge: Polity Press.
34. Ravelli, B. and Webber, M. (2010) *Exploring Sociology*, Toronto: Pearson.
35. Fulop, L. and Linstead, S. (2009) 'Motivation and meaning', pp. 411–72 in S. Linstead, L. Fulop and S. Lilley, *Management and Organization: A Critical Text* (2nd edn), Basingstoke: Palgrave.
36. Herriot, P., Hirsh, W. and Reilly, P. (1998) *Trust and Transition: Managing Today's Employment Relationship*, Chichester: Wiley & Sons.
37. Townley, B. (1994) *Reframing Human Resource Management: Power, Ethics and the Subject of Work*, London: Sage.
38. Lee, S. and Klein, H. (2002) 'Relationships between conscientiousness, self-efficacy, self-description, and learning over time', *Journal of Applied Psychology*, **87**(6), pp. 1175–82.
39. Holland, J. L. (1985) *Making Vocational Choices: A Theory of Vocational Personalities and Work Environments* (2nd edn), Englewood Cliffs, NJ: Prentice Hall.
40. Brown, D. (1987) 'The status of Holland's theory of career choice', *Career Development Journal*, September, pp. 13–23.

41. Furnham, A. F. (1997) 'Vocational preference and P-O fit', in J. Arnold (ed.), 'The psychology of careers in organizations', *International Review of Industrial and Organizational Psychology*, **12**, pp. 1–37.
42. Young, R. A. and Chen, C. P. (1999) 'Annual review: practice and research in career counselling and development – 1998', *Career Development Quarterly*, December, p. 98.
43. Thompson, J. A. (2005) 'Proactive personality and job performance: a social perspective', *Journal of Applied Psychology*, **90**(5), pp. 1011–17.
44. Moon, H., Kamdar, D., Mayer, D. and Takeuchi, R. (2008), 'Me or we? The role of personality and justice as other-centered antecedents to innovative citizenship behaviors within organizations', *Journal of Applied Psychology*, **93**(1), pp. 84–94.
45. Procter, S. and Mueller, F. (2000) *Teamworking*, Basingstoke: Palgrave Macmillan.
46. Salgado, J. F. (1997) 'The five factor model of personality and job performance in the European Community', *Journal of Applied Psychology*, **82**, pp. 30–43.
47. Bratton, J. and Gold, J. (2003) *Human Resource Management: Theory and Practice* (3rd edn), Basingstoke: Palgrave.
48. Dalen, L. H., Stanton, N. A. and Roberts, A. D. (2001) 'Faking personality questionnaires in personal selection', *Journal of Management Development*, **20**(8), pp. 729–41.
49. Robertson, I. T., Baron, H., Gibbons, P., Maclver, R. and Nyfield, G. (2000) 'Conscientiousness and managerial performance', *Journal of Occupational and Organizational Psychology*, **73**(2), pp. 171–81.
50. Bratton, J. and Gold, J. (2007) *Human Resource Management: Theory and Practice* (4th edn), Basingstoke: Palgrave.
51. Hollway, W. (1991) *Work Psychology and Organizational Behaviour*, London: Sage.
52. Rose, N. (1990) *Governing the Soul: The Shaping of the Private Self*, London: Routledge.
53. Greenhaus, J. H. (1987) *Career Management*, Chicago: Dryden.
54. Eysenck, H. (1973) *The Inequality of Man*, London: Temple Smith.

CHAPTER 7
Work groups and teams

CHAPTER OUTLINE

- Introduction
- Work groups and work teams
- Group dynamics
- Work teams and management theory
- Work teams: ending bureaucracy and extending employee empowerment?
- Paradox in team-based work systems
- Summary and end-of-chapter features
- Chapter case study 1: Building cars in Brazil
- Chapter case study 2: Teams at Land Rock Alliance Insurance

CHAPTER OBJECTIVES

After completing this chapter, you should be able to:

- distinguish between informal and formal work groups
- explain the current popularity of teams in work organizations
- articulate how group norms and cohesiveness exert influence on individual and group behaviour
- describe and critically evaluate the theories of team development
- explain the pros and cons of using groups to make decisions
- identify the different theoretical perspectives and paradoxes related to work teams

Introduction

Without doubt, everyone will find him- or herself at some point in life to be a member of a group. You have probably already experienced group membership through participating in a sports team, climbing or caving club, jury service, church, political party or study group. In many organizations, people are called upon to work in groups. Work groups influence the behaviour of their members, often enhancing job satisfaction, promoting learning and increasing individual and unit productivity and more effective decision making.

Work groups are not something invented by management consultants. History shows that they have been part of human social development since ancient times. For thousands of years, men and women lived in small hunting and gathering groups, and later they lived in small farming or fishing groups. It is only in the last 200 years, with the advent of industrial capitalism, that small groups have become the exception rather than the rule.[1] The factory system ushered in a minute division of labour and close direct supervision, which substantially improved labour productivity and profits. By the late twentieth century, however, extensive specialization and hierarchical forms of work organization were identified as a 'problem'.

A host of mainstream management literature proselytized the notion that traditional work organization was an obstacle to innovation and competitiveness.[2-4] Team work as a system of paid work is intended to transcend the alleged problems of inflexibility, poor quality, low employee commitment and motivation associated with traditional work structures. Its increased prevalence in Europe and North America is a recognition by employers that competitive advantage comes from so-called lean organizations, the full utilization of their human capital, and a set or 'bundle' of 'soft' human resource management practices that form part of an integrated high-performance workplace (HPW).[5] In the critical literature, team work and HPW initiatives are a means of increasing work intensification, obtaining higher productivity, increasing workplace stress and controlling workers indirectly through a culture of self-control.[5-9]

stop reflect

Before reading on, consider your own experience of group membership. Do people behave differently in groups? You might have experienced working in a study group at college or university. Reflect on your experience, and consider what specific behaviours exhibited during the group sessions were helpful to the group. What specific behaviours exhibited were detrimental to the group? How did the group deal with a member who was constantly late or did not complete his or her assigned work for a group assignment?

If you paused and thought about the questions we asked in the 'Stop and reflect' box above, you should appreciate that understanding groups and teams in work organizations is important for several reasons. Team work has become a significant feature of organizational life. Individuals behave differently when in a work group from how they do when they work independently. Team synergy can potentially transform moribund productivity and improve organizational performance. Finally, understanding group dynamics is seen to be an important aspect of managing (controlling) people more effectively.

This chapter introduces the complex phenomenon of work groups and work teams in organizations. It begins by examining the background, nature and behavioural implications of work groups. We also explore the nature of work groups through the concepts of group norms, cohesiveness and learning. Finally, we go beyond management rhetoric, and present arguments and evidence to suggest that self-managed teams shift the focus away from the hierarchy, and direct and bureaucratic control processes, to a culture of self-control.

control: the collection and analysis of information about all aspect of the work organization and the use of comparisons that are either historical and/or based on benchmarking against another business unit

Work groups and work teams

What are work groups?

The term 'group' can be used to describe a cluster of individuals watching a hockey game or queuing for a bank teller. When studying the behaviour of groups, it is important to distinguish between a mere cluster of individuals and what organizational theorists call a 'psychological group'. This term is used to describe individuals who perceive themselves to be in a group, who have a shared sense of collective identity, and who relate to each other in a meaningful way. We can define a work group as two or more people who are in face-to-face interaction, each aware of their membership in the group, and striving to accomplish assigned work tasks.

work group: two or more employees in face-to-face interaction, each aware of their positive interdependence as they endeavour to achieve mutual work-related goals

The first part of this definition suggests that there must be an opportunity for people to interact socially with each other, that is, to communicate with each other, to behave in each other's presence, and to be affected by the other's behaviour. Over time, group members who regularly interact socially become aware of each other's values, feelings and goals, which then influence their behaviour. Although a work group can theoretically range from two members to an unspecified upper limit, the need to interact limits the size of the group.

The second part of the definition refers to group members' perceptions of the group itself. Members of the group are able to distinguish who is and who is not in the group, and are aware that an action affecting one member is likely to affect all. This part of the definition helps us to exclude mere clusters of people who are simply individuals who happen to be assembled at the same location at a particular time (such as soccer fans, bank customers or airline travellers). These individuals do not consider themselves a part of any identifiable unit, nor do they relate to one another in any meaningful fashion, despite their close proximity.

On the other hand, a soccer team, an airline crew or a project team at the Bank of Scotland would fulfil the criteria for a work group. In a situation of extreme danger – such as the hijacking of an airline – an aggregate of passengers could be transformed into a group. For example, several passengers on US United Airlines Flight 93, which crashed on September 11, 2001, apparently formed a group that stormed the cockpit to prevent the hijackers from carrying out any further terrorist acts.

The third part of the definition implies that group members have common goals, which they work collectively to accomplish. Six individuals drinking coffee in the company rest area at the same time would not necessarily be considered a group. They do not have common goals, nor are they dependent on the outcome of each other's actions. However, six union shop stewards drinking coffee together regularly to discuss health and safety issues or grievances would be considered a work group.

Groups in organizations can be formal or informal. Organizational decision makers create formal work groups to permit collective action on assigned task(s). In this sense, the rationale for creating work groups can be linked to an organization's competitive strategy. A manufacturing strategy that emphasizes flexibility can result in tasks and responsibilities being reassigned from individual employees and supervisors to a group of employees. This process of dividing up the tasks, assigning responsibility and so on, is called job design, and it is through the restructuring of work that formal work groups are created and consciously designed. Managers are interested in ensuring that the behaviour of the formal group is directed toward organizational goals. Not surprisingly, therefore, much of mainstream organizational behaviour research focuses on the dynamics of formal work groups.

job design: the process of assigning tasks to a job, including the interdependency of those tasks with other jobs

In addition to formal work groups, organizations also contain informal work groups. Managers do not specifically establish these work-based groups; they emerge from the social interaction of workers. Although an organization employs people for their intellectual capital, unlike with other forms of capital, the organization gets the whole person. People bring their personal needs to the workplace. Organizational behaviour theorists suggest that informal work groups are formed as an outcome of psychological processes: the perception of a shared social identity and to fulfil social needs for affiliation and supportive relationships. A cluster of employees can become an informal work group when members influence others' behaviour and contribute to needs satisfaction. Informal work groups are important in that they can help shape communication flows in the organization.

informal group: two or more people who form a unifying relationship around personal rather than organizational goals

What are work teams?

The words 'group' and 'team' are often used as substitutes. In the management literature, the word 'team' is more likely to be used in a normative sense as a special type of group with positive traits.[10] Like a soccer team, it has connotations of collaboration, mutual support and shared skill and decision making.[11] The observation and implied criticism that 'He is not a team player' or 'This group is not a team' expresses the difference in meaning between 'group' and 'team' in the management lexicon. A mainstream text defines a team as 'a set of interpersonal interactions structured to achieve established goals' (ref. 1, p. 539), and two popular writers define a team as 'a small number of people with complementary skills who are committed to a common purpose, performance goals, and approach for which they hold themselves mutually accountable' (ref. 2, p. 45).

teams: groups of two or more people who interact and influence each other, are mutually accountable for achieving common objectives, and perceive themselves as a social entity within an organization

Another variant of 'teams' has become part of current managerial rhetoric – the words 'self-managed work team' (SMWT). The SMWT, which suggests a new way of organizing work, is not the same as a 'work group': an SMWT is 'a group of employees who are responsible for managing and performing technical tasks that result in a product or service being delivered to an internal or external customer' (ref. 12, p. xiii). The difference between work groups and SMWTs is explained in terms of the degree of interdependency and accountability. The interdependence among SMWT members is typically high, and the accountability for the work focuses primarily on the team as a whole rather than the individual group member. Another distinguishing feature of SMWTs is their longevity: SMWTs are typically an integral part of a redesigned organizational structure, brought together for long-term performance goals.

self-managed work teams: cross-functional work groups organized around work processes that complete an entire piece of work requiring several interdependent tasks, and that have substantial autonomy over the execution of those tasks

Work teams can be classified according to their position in the organization's hierarchy and their assigned tasks. Figure 7.1 shows three types of work team most commonly found in organizations. Teams that plan and run things are positioned in the top echelon (senior level) of the organization, teams that monitor things occupy the middle levels, and teams that make things occupy the lower levels of the organization. It is important to emphasize, however, that the nature of teams varies considerably among organizations, depending on whether they are engaged in value-added activities in small batches or large batches, or whether they provide financial or other services.

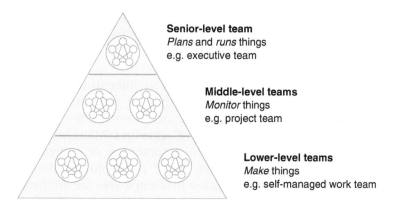

Senior-level team
Plans and *runs* things
e.g. executive team

Middle-level teams
Monitor things
e.g. project team

Lower-level teams
Make things
e.g. self-managed work team

Figure 7.1   Classification of work teams

Plate 1   A self-managed work team allows employees in the core work unit to have sufficient autonomy to manage the work process
Source: Getty Images.

weblink

www.managementhelp.org/grp_skll/slf_drct/slf_drct.htm is an online library devoted to self-managed teams. At http://groups.yahoo.com, people form their own social groups to exchange ideas. Visit the site and see how 'virtual groups' work

The formal definitions of work teams are not so different from the definition of a formal work group, which might explain why both words are used interchangeably in the organizational behaviour literature. However, the conscious use of the word 'team' is not simply a question of semantics. Mainstream management rhetoric is awash with what Bendix called 'a vocabulary of motivation'.[13] In this instance, communication emphasizes the 'team' (with phrases like 'We must all pull together') and the 'family' (suggesting that employees are brothers and sisters and customers are family guests), using these metaphors to obfuscate the power differentials and conflicting interests between management and workers. Whether employees are organized into a 'work group' or a 'work team', the effectiveness of the work configuration will be the outcome of complex group behaviours and processes, which is the focus of the next section.

Group dynamics

Group dynamics is the study of human behaviour in groups.[1] The field studies the nature of groups, group development and the interrelations between individuals and groups. Group dynamics or processes emphasize changes in the pattern of activities, the subjective perceptions of individual group members and their active involvement in group life. Studies on group dynamics by mainstream researchers draw attention to two sets of process that underlie group processes: task-oriented activities and maintenance-oriented activities. Task-oriented activities undertaken by the group are aimed at accomplishing goals or 'getting the job done'. Maintenance-oriented activities, on the other hand, point to the subjective perceptions of group members and their active involvement in keeping acceptable standards of behaviour and a general state of well-being within the group. Conventional wisdom argues that the two processes constantly seek to coexist, and an overemphasis of one realm at the expense of the other leads to discontent and withdrawal. An effective group or team is one that creates a reasonable compromise between both realms.[10,14,15]

group dynamics: the systematic study of human behaviour in groups, including the nature of groups, group development, and the interrelations between individuals and groups, other groups and other elements of formal organizations

Some of the major factors influencing group dynamics are shown in Figure 7.2. The framework does not attempt to offer a theory of group dynamics, nor does it necessarily follow that all elements of the model must, or can, be applied to every

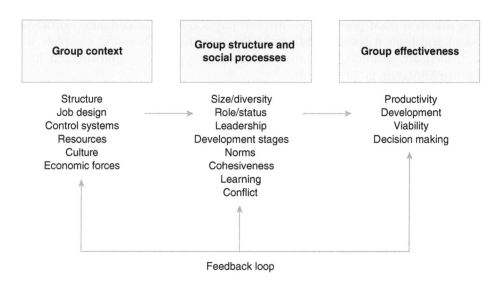

Figure 7.2 A model of group dynamics

work group. We offer it here as a useful heuristic for understanding the complexities of group dynamics. Four major elements are graphically depicted in the model: a context, team structure and processes, group effectiveness, and a feedback loop that links the outcomes back to the other main components. We look at each of the first three elements over the next few pages.

Group context

Although the work group or team is a structure in itself, it is also a subset of a larger structure, the organization. Thus, the work group is constrained to operate within the structure of the organization, and group context refers to organizational and job design, organizational control systems, resources and the external political economy and economic forces.

group context: refers to anything from the specific task a work group is engaged in to the broad environmental forces that are present in the minds of group members and may influence them

The implementation of team-based working requires organizational restructuring, by which we mean changing the core dimensions of the organization: its centralization, complexity and formality. Tasks and responsibilities must be designated within and between teams. Task interdependence, which refers to the level of relationship among members in the work activities, can affect group structure, processes and outcomes. Alternative work configurations are typically followed by alternative control systems. For example, when work groups are introduced, the direct supervisory control of employees is typically replaced by a computer-based control of group performance. The adoption of team work is normally contingent on management installing a system to control the redesigned work process.[6]

Resources are another contextual factor affecting group structure and processes. The amount of resources management is willing to commit to teams is directly related to the organizational context. Specifically, the policies and procedures of the organization must provide for sufficient physical (such as computer software), financial and human resources to enable the team to function and complete the task. Inadequate resources, it is argued, will delay group development and have a negative impact on group outcomes.[3]

Group structure

Work groups and teams have a structure that influences the way in which members relate to and interact with one another, and makes it possible to explain individual behaviour within the group. Have you ever noticed that, when people come together in a new group, some listen while others talk? Such differences between group members serve as a basis for the formation of group structure. As differentiation takes place, social relations are formed between members. The stable pattern of relationships among the differentiated elements in the group is called group structure.

group structure: a stable pattern of social interaction among work group members created by a role structure and group norms

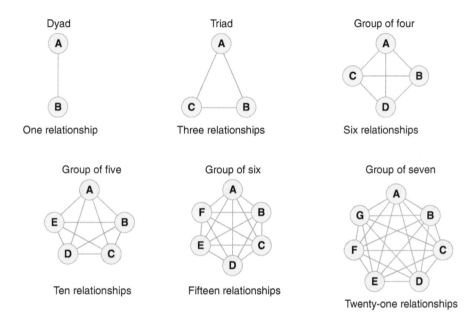

Figure 7.3   The incremental effects of group size on relationships

The group can be differentiated by a number of variables including size, roles, status and leadership. The *size* of the group plays a critical role in how group members interact with one another. The German sociologist Georg Simmel pointed out that increasing the size alters the group's dynamics, since the increased number of relationships results in different interactions.[16] Figure 7.3 shows the incremental impact of group size on relationships. Two individuals form a single relationship; adding a third person results in three relations; a group of seven, however, has 21 relationships. According to Simmel, as groups grow beyond three people, the personal attachments between individuals become looser, and coalitions emerge in which some group members align themselves against other group members. Thus, the more impersonal relationships need additional formal rules and regulations. At the same time, the group's growth allows it to become more stable, because the intensity of the interactions is reduced, and because it becomes better able to withstand the loss of some of its members.

> **weblink**
>
> The notion of diversity and balance in teams is central to Belbin's team role theory. Visit www.belbin.com for more information and www.palgrave.com/business/brattonob2e for an activity on team roles

The *composition* or diversity of work groups is another key variable that influences individual behaviour in a group setting. Work group composition can be diverse in terms of gender, ethnicity, age, hierarchical status, performance levels and educational background. Research suggests that group composition is a predictor of members' creative behaviour and the quality of decision making. Gender and hierarchical status diversity tended to decrease a member's creative behaviour, and this negative effect appeared to be particularly strong for women members in a minority and 'low-power' group situation. The group's composition may also impede the shared exchange, discussion and integration of information, with negative effects on decision quality.[17,18]

All group members are expected to carry out certain functions. The set of expected behaviours associated with a position within the group constitutes the role of the occupant of that position. The role concept helps us understand how a member's behaviour is structured by the prescriptive dictates of the group and/or organization. A team-based culture will influence the roles individuals play within the organization. With HPW forms of organization, a premium is placed on values such as cooperative behaviour with team members, sharing information and expertise with others, and more generally on promoting a social network necessary for effective team performance. Role definition is often used as a diagnostic tool by management consultants to determine causes of poor team performance. Problems of role ambiguity – uncertainty on the group member's part about what exactly he or she is supposed to do – and role conflict – conflicting requests from more than one source – allegedly have far-reaching negative outcomes on group performance.[3] Role ambiguity and role conflict affect the socialization of new employees into existing work groups.[19]

role: a set of behaviours that people are expected to perform because they hold certain positions in a team and organization

role ambiguity: uncertainty about job duties, performance expectations, level of authority and other job conditions

role conflict: conflict that occurs when people face competing demands

Status is the relative ranking that a member holds, and indicates the value of that member as perceived by the group. Status is important because it motivates individuals and has consequences for their behaviour. Almost every work group has either a formal or an informal leader, who can influence communications, decision making, learning and similar processes, thereby playing an important part in group's outcomes.

status: the social ranking of people; the position an individual occupies in society or in a social group or work organization

It is necessary, but not sufficient for team efficacy, to have an organizational design strategy that incorporates adequate resources, effective control systems, role clarity and leadership. To be effective, managers and group members must learn to work in the new work structure. The group processes responsible for group development, norms, cohesiveness and learning are extremely important.

Group social processes

The term group social processes refers to the manner in which various aspects of group behaviour are constructed on a continuing basis, and the behaviour that serves to encourage or discourage group learning and to ameliorate or exacerbate group conflict. Understanding group social processes is important in so far as they are often considered to be key predictors of group effectiveness.

group processes: refers to group member actions, communications and decision making

Group development

Organizational behaviour theorists typically highlight the importance of understanding the developmental stages that a group must pass through: groups are born, they mature and they die. It is suggested that a group must reach the mature stage before it achieves maximum performance. Of course, it is also acknowledged that not all groups pass through all these stages, and some groups can become fixed in the early stage and remain ineffective and inefficient. A good example of the life-cycle metaphor is Tuckman and Jensen's five-stage cycle of group development model: forming, storming, norming, performing and adjourning (Figure 7.4).[20]

In the *forming* stage, individuals are brought together and there tends to be ambiguity about roles and tasks. Group members are polite as they learn about each other and attempt to establish 'ground rules' for accomplishing the assigned task(s). Dependency on the group leader is said to be high at this stage.

In the *storming* stage, individual members become more proactive by taking on specific roles and responsibilities. Members frequently compete for positions in the group, and conflict occurs between individuals, and/or alliances are formed between members. The group leader must be able to facilitate dialogue and handle conflict at this stage.

When group members begin to accept differences of opinion, conform to their roles and cooperate (for instance, sharing information), the group has reached what is called the *norming* stage. As a consensus forms around the group's goals and means of attainment, group cohesion grows.

High productivity is typically achieved at the *performing* stage of group development. A high level of trust in each group member is prevalent at this phase, and

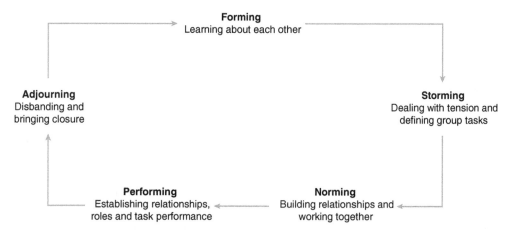

Figure 7.4 Five phases of group development
Source: Tuckman and Jensen (1977)[20].

there is 'consensual validation' in the sense that members are positively valued for their specific attributes and qualities.

A work group does not exist infinitely. The *adjourning* stage refers to individuals leaving the group and being replaced by others, or to the group's disbandment. Social rituals, such as having a party, often accompany group disbandment.

Tuckman and Jensen's model is based on the premise that a group must go through each stage before being able to move on to the next, and every transition holds the potential risk of regression to an earlier stage. Organizational behaviour theorists taking a managerialist perspective have tended to interpret the five-stage model in terms of levels of performance, with group productivity being higher after the second stage. While this assumption may be correct, what makes a work group effective is more complex than this model acknowledges. Although the model has become entrenched in mainstream organizational behaviour texts and in management training, it has more recently been shown 'to be of little or no assistance in getting teams to perform better' (ref. 3, p. 34).

An earlier critique of Tuckman and Jensen's five-stage model found the phenomenon of 'punctuated equilibrium' to be a more useful concept to explain group development.[21] Specifically, a team does not accomplish a great deal up to about the halfway point to completion (this midpoint occurring regardless of the timeframe involved). At the midpoint, there is an acceleration of activity by members to accomplish their assigned work. In essence, the 'punctuated equilibrium' model characterizes work groups as exhibiting long periods of inertia interspersed with shorter bursts of activity, initiated primarily by their members' awareness of the impending completion deadline. This would suggest, therefore, that not all groups develop in a universal linear fashion.

The research on group development has drawn criticism because much of it has tended to be laboratory-based rather than workplace-based research. For example, old favourites like Tuckman and Jensen's model were developed from work with therapy, laboratory or training groups, not 'real teams in real contexts'. Group development models that predict linear sequential phases have particularly been criticized. As Kline graphically points out:

> Imagine the following situation. The cockpit crew of a 747 boards the plane twenty minutes before take-off. You are seated in seat 117B, and as the airplane rushes down runway nine you hope like hell that this team is past the storming stage of group development (ref. 3, p. 5).

Kline argues that there is something, personalities aside, about the aircrew that enables them to fly the aircraft safely, even when they have just met one another. These 'contextual variables', she asserts, are powerful tools for understanding group dynamics and group performance.

Although alternative research suggests that every group does not go through all the development stages, Tuckman and Jensen's model can be a useful heuristic for understanding group dynamics and why some groups fail to perform. A group might be ineffective and inefficient because individuals are pulling in different directions, since the goals of the group have not been agreed. Alternatively, individuals might have a tendency to dismiss or ridicule others' thoughts, ideas and

Plate 2 Organizations send their employees to outdoor corporate training centres where they learn to work as teams
Source: Getty Images.

feelings, which leads to low trust among the group. For all these reasons, effective group functioning and learning might be hindered. The main conclusion drawn from the group development models presented here is that a team-based organizational structure does not imply an effective and efficient organization. Top managers introducing team-based work structures need to attend to the development of group interactions.

Group norms

Have you ever noticed that professors do not normally criticize other professors? Why? The answer is 'norms'. Groups significantly influence their members' behaviour through the operation of norms. Social norms are a set of expected patterns of behaviour that are established and shared by the group's members. Norms inform members on what they ought and ought not to do under certain situations. A group's norms do not occur in a vacuum: they represent the interaction of historical, social and psychological processes. In the workplace, for example, a new employee joining a group will assess the norms for work effort from how most individuals in the group behave. In turn, members of the group observe the extent to which the new member's behaviour matches the group's norms. Norms develop in work groups around work activities (the means and speed), around attitudes and opinions that should be held by group members regarding the workplace, and around communications, concerning appropriate language.

The Hawthorne studies[22] highlighted the importance of **group norms** to management theorists. The researchers identified three important norms: no 'rate-busting' (working too hard), no 'chiselling' (working too little) and no 'squealing' (telling the supervisor anything that could undermine the group). Group members who significantly deviated from these norms were subjected to either ridicule or physical punishment. Groups typically enforce norms that:

group norms: the unwritten rules and expectations that specify or shape appropriate human behaviour in a work group or team

facilitate the group's survival

allow members to express the central values of the group

reduce embarrassing interpersonal problems for group members – for instance, a ban on discussing religion or politics at work.[23]

Norms are communicated to new employees through a process called 'group socialization', whereby the new member learns the group's principal values and how these values are articulated through norms. Emergent group leaders differ from their peers in that they make more attempts to influence the group and play a role in forming team norms.[24]

Group cohesiveness

The term cohesiveness refers to the complex forces that give rise to the perceptions by members of group identity and attractiveness of group membership. The cohesiveness of a group has a major effect on the behaviour of its members, because higher cohesion amplifies the potency of group norms. A series of experiments conducted by Solomon Asch in 1952 and Stanley Milgram in 1963 suggested that group membership can engender conformity, and also that members are likely to follow the directions of group authority figures, even when it means inflicting pain on another individual. These psychological experiments can be used to help explain the brutalizing acts inflicted on prisoners by both male and female US guards at Abu Ghraib prison.[25]

cohesiveness: refers to all the positive and negative forces or social pressures that cause individuals to maintain their membership in specific groups

weblink

For more information on Milgram's classic psychological prison experiment, go to Stanford University's site: www.prisonexp.org

A cohesive group can develop norms that can be a great asset to the organization, for example a norm that prescribes voluntary overtime working when required. Equally, a cohesive group can undermine organizational goals, for example by enforcing conformity to a work effort below what is considered acceptable by managers. Not surprisingly, therefore, sources of group cohesiveness are of considerable interest to mainstream organizational behaviour theorists and managers. For example, a recent study contends that humour can have a positive effect on a variety of group or team processes including group cohesiveness and the management of emotion.[26]

The attractiveness of a group is partly determined by its composition. Members of the group need to get along with each other, which might be difficult if members have very different values, attitudes towards work or interests. Research suggests that behaviour in work groups is shaped by a sex difference in aggressiveness, with male members engaging in more dominating behaviour than female members. Studies have found that, in groups, men talk more frequently, interrupt others and express anger more than women (see ref. 27, especially pp. 181–3). As a result, more men than women are chosen as group leaders. In institutions of learning, the experiences of work groups by women and faculty members from racial and ethnic minorities tend to differ significantly from the experiences of white male group members.[28]

Ensuring diversity in a work group or team is not only an equity matter – a lack of diversity might inhibit some of the benefits of group working. An early study suggests that moderate heterogeneity in a work group balances the requirements of cohesion and productivity.[29] As we will examine in the next section, one notable disadvantage of groups that are *too* cohesive is that their decision-making ability can be impaired by what Janis termed 'groupthink'.[30] He defined this group phenomenon as a psychological drive for consensus at any cost, which suppresses dissent and the evaluation of alternatives in cohesive decision-making groups.

groupthink: the tendency of highly cohesive groups to value consensus at the price of decision quality

---

weblink

For more information on how 'groupthink' can influence decision making, visit www. afirstlook.com; www.abacon.com. Search for 'groupthink'

Group learning

We turn now to another aspect of social interaction within groups and teams: work-based learning. It will be apparent from this review of team theory and practice that expanding workers' skill sets and empowering workers to make prescribed decisions has significant implications for learning in the workplace. Rather than learning a narrow set of skills, the need for flexibility and interchangeability necessitates that workers acquire new knowledge and technical skills to perform the new repertoire of tasks. In addition, the experience of 'lived reality' – decision making, trial and error experimentation – and the social relations associated with teams create their own dynamic environment for enhancing informal work-based learning.

empowerment: a psychological concept in which people experience more self-determination, meaning, competence and impact regarding their role in the organization

If the group or team is going to make its own decisions, control quality and control its own behaviour, members must engage in learning. Adult educators and human resource development theorists have suggested that, in order for a group or team to learn, individual members of the unit must be able to learn: that is, to experiment, reflect on previous action, engage in dialogue, and share and build on their individual knowledge.[31,32] Adopting a culture of learning in the workplace impacts on innovation, employment relations and leadership style.

Group conflict

Work groups do not exist in isolation: they are located within capitalist workplace dynamics and linked by a network of relationships with other groups. Unsurprisingly, with the proliferation of teams in organizations, there is more research on behaviours that serve to ameliorate or exacerbate the effect that group conflict has on their effectiveness. In the critical studies, analysts have highlighted the inevitable tensions between team-based HPW rhetoric and the reality of work intensification and job insecurity.[33] Mainstream research on group conflict is, however, generally limited to investigating how dysfunctional behaviour at individual or group level affects the variance in groups' performance generally. There are many definitions for the term *conflict*. A broad definition describes conflict as 'that behaviour by organization members which is expended in opposition to other members' (ref. 34, p. 411).

Researchers widely recognize that group conflict is comprised of two dimensions: task and emotional conflict.[35] *Task conflict* refers to disputes over group members' tasks or the extent to which members disagree on the utilization of resources or ideas related to group tasks. *Emotional conflict*, which is also known as relational conflict, is more personal and involves personality clashes within groups and incompatibilities among team members, or the extent to which tension or verbal or non-verbal friction characterizes members' interaction within the group. Exemplars of specific types of behaviour associated with task and emotional conflict are shown in Table 7.1.

Psychological studies confirm the notion that individuals' personalities are part of the contributions that group members make to work groups, and, moreover, a mix of these individuals' personalities plays a key role in how intragroup conflict unfolds. It is well documented how many occupations regard team work and support from team members as 'lifelines' in coping with the various demands of work. For example, nurses and air cabin crew are known to rely upon support from fellow

Table 7.1 Task-related and emotion-related behaviours in groups

Task-related behaviours	Emotion-related behaviours
Goal setting	Criticizing
Integrating	Judging
Utilizing resources	Violence
Calculating	Bullying
Compromising	Favouritism
Decision making	Teasing
Evaluating	Sexual harassment

Source: Adapted from Proctor et al. (2009).[90]

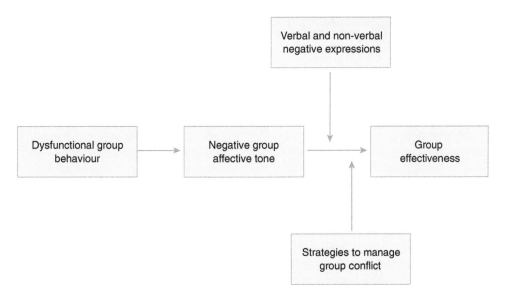

Figure 7.5 A conceptual framework for examining intragroup conflict
Source: Adapted from Cole, Walter and Bruch (2008),[37] p. 946, itself based on Brown et al (2005),[91] p. 793.

co-workers to help them deal with work-related emotion and difficult situations.[36] Studies on the consequences of members' emotions on team performance show that the team members' shared negative emotion, or what is called 'negative affective tone', is inversely related to team performance.[37] A conceptual framework for linking dysfunctional group behaviour and group effectiveness is shown in Figure 7.5.

The proposed sequence of incidents depicted in the model begins with dysfunctional group behaviour causing an increase in what is labelled groups' 'negative affective tone' – groups' collective shared experience of negative emotions. In turn, it is hypothesized that that greater levels of negative group affective tone tend to reduce group effectiveness. It also proposes that 'display rules' capable of adjusting or varying the expression of negative emotions through verbal and non-verbal (for example, facial or body) cues is critical to groups' goal-directed behaviour and effectiveness. A study by Dunlop and Lee found that dysfunctional behaviour predicted 24 per cent of the variance in groups' performance.[38] With this assertion in mind, the model further proposes that emotion management strategies will mediate the effect of negative group affective tone.[37]

Research findings suggest that how well conflict resolution strategies address a group-level balance between task and emotion management is what yields superior group productivity and viability.[39] On the basis of reported results, when work groups withhold displays of negative emotionality, it seems they are better able to control the detrimental performance implications of dysfunctional behaviour.[37]

Intergroup conflict might also occur. One explanation for intergroup conflict is that when a group is successful, members' self-esteem increases, and conversely when group members' self-esteem is threatened, they are more prone to disparage members of other groups.[40-43] Another alternative explanation contends that intergroup conflict is the result of one group's perceiving another group as a threat to its goal attainment.[1,3,44]

Work and Society: Making it work

With the emergence of the idea of 'positive psychology', there has been a pronounced effort to shift research attention away from its traditional focus on abnormal or problematic patterns of human functioning, and towards the study of optimal functioning and human flourishing. This shift in attention away from the problematic and towards the optimal is evident in many fields of study – from organizational behaviour research to studies of marriage. For example, in a pioneering analysis of marriage dynamics, Frank Fincham and his colleagues argue (2007) that the traditional preoccupation with conflict in marriage must be corrected. Their article focuses on 'naturally occurring marital self-repair processes' (p. 282) and seeks to understand the mechanisms that enable some couples to bounce back from conflict while others separate or continue to live together unhappily.

Does this research on marriages have anything to tell us about group dynamics? Obviously, the differences between small work groups and marriages are fundamental, and there is no need to review those differences here. The question is, are there enough similarities between work groups and marriages to derive some insights into group dynamics from recent research on marriages? You be the judge. Consider the following synopsis of the work of Fincham and his colleagues.

Inspired by the move toward positive psychology, Fincham and his co-investigators set out to identify what distinguishes marriages that endure (or 'bounce back' after trouble) from marriages that fall apart. They found that couples who stay together do not necessarily experience conflict-free relationships. What distinguishes these resilient couples from couples who separate are mechanisms that work to defuse conflict, often without the help of external interventions. One might say that spouses in these resilient couples exhibit capacities for 'self-regulation' and the couples themselves are capable of 'self-repair'.

To understand how this works, Fincham and his colleagues suggest we consider how conflicts unfold in time. An initial disagreement or problematic event will often escalate over time as couples become locked into cyclical patterns of 'tit-for-tat' responding. Resilient couples seem to be able to avoid this pattern. They do so by engaging in two kinds of regulation: they regulate both 'the degree to which a negative partner behaviour elicits a correspondingly negative response' and 'the extent to which negative partner behavior produces a change in the overall view of the relationship' (2007, p. 283). With regard to this second kind of regulation, one can imagine a wife (or husband) coming to the realization: this marriage is not worth saving. Spouses in resilient couples seem to be able to avoid these profound and irreversible changes of heart.

The two kinds of regulation associated with resilient couples are clearly relevant to work groups. Work groups experience internal conflict, and people in work groups become locked into cyclical patterns of 'tit-for-tat' responding. As with couples, the likelihood that members of work groups can resolve their conflicts without resorting to external mediation will depend on their capacity to engage in the kinds of regulation identified by Fincham and his colleagues.

Readers may feel comfortable with the analogy between marriages and work group thus far. But consider the proposed explanation of why some couples more than others are able to engage in effective self-regulation. Fincham and his colleagues offer the following list of factors that they believe enhance a couple's capacity for self-regulation and repair:

Without methods for changing negative processes over time, or for changing direction once negative interactions begin, even the best marital skills for dealing with conflict may provide couples with insufficient basis for long-term marital satisfaction. The framework [described in this article has] ... the potential to help us understand the impact [on self-regulatory processes] of forgiveness ... commitment ... valuing sacrifice ... and sanctification. (p. 287)

stop!   Fincham and his colleagues associate this list of qualities – forgiveness, commitment, valuing sacrifice and sanctification – with couples who engage in effective self-regulation. Would these same qualities be associated with the optimal functioning of work groups? How would each of the four qualities contribute to higher levels of self-regulation among work group members?

Given its links to organized religion, the idea of sanctification may seem irrelevant to many work groups. Is there a secular version of sanctification that might be relevant to a broader range of work groups?

Sources and further information

Bakkle, A. and Schaufeli, W. (2008) 'Positive organizational behavior: engaged employees in flourishing organizations', *Journal of Organizational Behavior*, 29, pp. 147–54.
Fincham, F., Stanley, S. and Beach, S. (2007) 'Transformative processes in marriage: an analysis of emerging trends', *Journal of Marriage and the Family*, 69, pp. 275–92.

Note: This feature was written by David MacLennan, Assistant Professor at Thompson Rivers University, BC, Canada.

The traditional managerial perspective tends to hold that conflicts between individuals and groups, and between workers and management, are a bad thing. An alternative perspective, the *interactionist theory*, holds that conflicts in work groups are productive and can increase rather than decrease job performance.[45] The view holds that group leaders should encourage an ongoing 'optimum' level of conflict, which allows the group to be self-critical, creative and viable. But notions of 'win–lose' scenarios complicate estimates of what constitutes an 'optimal level' of conflict. It has been suggested, for instance, that the more the intergroup conflict is defined as a 'win–lose' situation, the more predictable are the effects of the conflict on the social relationships within the group and on relations between work groups.[1]

Group effectiveness

Most group theory examines group effectiveness or outcomes in terms of group performance and group decision making. Since the widespread proliferation of team work, much research has been occupied with investigating the link between work teams and performance. Two aspects of group effectiveness are examined in this section: performance and decision making.

Group performance

Research on group performance has often drawn upon Hackman's normative theory of group effectiveness, where effectiveness consists of (1) productivity, (2) employee development, or the opportunity of the individual team member to learn from her or his experiences within the team as well as from other team members, and (3) team viability, or the degree to which members of the team are able to continue working together in the future.[46] The group literature contends that a combination of high-level cohesion and norms, consistent with organizational objectives, will have a positive effect on team productivity.[47–49] Figure 7.6 illustrates the relationship between group cohesiveness and group performance norms. Improved productivity of employees in SMWTs is said to stem from the fact that the interrelationship between the configuration of job design and employment practices inevitably leads to more intrinsic job satisfaction, higher team member commitment and the mobilization of greater discretionary effort from employees.[50,51]

job satisfaction: a person's attitude regarding his or her job and work content

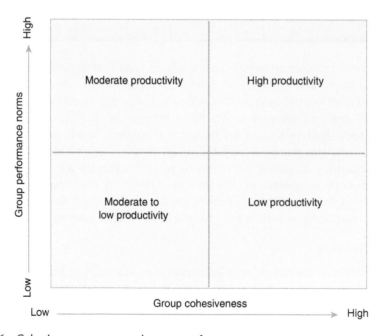

Figure 7.6   Cohesiveness, norms and group performance

Group decision making

In theory, one advantage of cohesive groups is that, by combining member resources, they make better decisions than those made by a single individual. In mathematical logic, this phenomenon of groups, called synergy, suggests that 2 + 2 is greater than 4. The concept is used extensively in mainstream texts to understand group processes and to justify the implementation of work teams. The general assumption is that moderately cohesive work teams (sufficiently diverse to avoid groupthink), together with better communications and 'enlightened' leadership, are best able to encourage the sharing of information and group learning – which results in superior decision-making outcomes. In terms of group decision making, here we examine some important concepts and empirical research on the decision-making performance of groups.

An important concept that might cause groups not to live up to their decision-making potential is *conformity* for people to change their behaviour to fit the norms of a group or team. It may make sense to follow others' behaviour or judgement when you are inexperienced or when the situation is ambiguous, but just how strongly do group norms influence individual behaviour and decision making when the situation is unmistakable?

Research by Solomon Asch and Stanley Milgram provided the answer to this question.[52,53] Asch recruited several groups of students, allegedly to study visual perception. Before the experiment began, he explained to all the students, apart from one student in each group, that the real purpose was to put pressure on the one selected student. Each group of students was asked to estimate the lengths of lines presented on a card. A sample line was shown at the left, and the group was to choose which of the three lines on the right matched it (Figure 7.7). Group members were seated so that the subject answered last. Group pressure did not affect the subjects' perception, but it did affect their behaviour. Initially, as planned, group members made the correct matches (B on Card 2). When, however, Asch's accomplices made incorrect responses, the uninformed subject became uncomfortable, and 76 per cent of the subjects chose to conform by answering incorrectly on at least one trial. The study shows how strong the tendency to conform can be, even when the pressure comes from people we do not know.

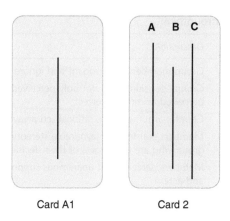

Card A1   Card 2

Figure 7.7 An example of the cards used in Asch's experiment in group conformity

In Milgram's controversial study, a researcher explained to male recruits that they would be participating in an experiment on how physical punishment affects adult learning. The learner, actually an accomplice of Milgram's, was seated in a fake electric chair, with electrodes fastened to the wrist and secured by leather straps. In an adjoining room, the subject, playing the role of educator, was seated in front of a replica 'shock generator' with the capacity to administer an electric 'shock' of between 15 and 315 'volts' to the learner. The educator was directed to read aloud pairs of words, and the learner was asked to recall the second word. Whenever the adult learner failed to answer correctly, the educator was instructed to apply an electric shock. Although the educator heard moans and then screams as the level of voltage increased, none of the subjects questioned the experiment. Milgram's research suggests that people are likely to follow the directions of 'legitimate authority figures', even when it means inflicting pain on another individual. To learn about how this classic experiment by Milgram has been related to contemporary events, see ref. 54.

As previously mentioned, Irving Janis's study illustrates how 'experts' can succumb to group pressure.[30] Interestingly, to illustrate the concept of groupthink, Janis analysed the ill-fated attempt by President Kennedy's administrative team to invade Cuba in 1961. He argues that the executive group advising the US President displayed all the symptoms of groupthink: they were convinced of their invulnerability, and 'self-censorship' prevented members from expressing alternative views even when intelligence information did not align with the group's beliefs. There was, according to Janis, an illusion of unanimity, with silence being interpreted as consent. In other words, the pressures for conformity that can arise in a highly cohesive group can cloud members' judgement and the decision-making process. Table 7.2 outlines some symptoms of groupthink.

Obviously, groupthink results in low-quality decisions. More seriously, it has been implicated in the decision processes that led to NASA's fatal launch of the space shuttle Challenger in 2003, and the US and UK invasion of Iraq in 2003. Prior to the invasion, the US official position was that Iraq illegally possessed weapons of mass destruction in violation of UN Security Council Resolution 1441 and had to be disarmed by force. The decision to embark on the Iraq invasion,

Table 7.2 Symptoms of groupthink

Symptom	Description
Illusion of invulnerability	Group members are arrogant and ignore obvious danger signals
Illusion of morality	Groups decision(s) are not only perceived as sensible, they are also perceived as morally correct
Rationalization	Counter-arguments are rationalized away
Stereotypes of outsiders	Members construct unfavourable stereotypes of those outside the group who are the targets of their decisions
Self-censorship	Members perceive that unanimous support exists for their decisions and action
Mindguard	Individual(s) within the group shield the group from information that goes against its decisions

termed 'Operation Iraqi Freedom' was made by President George W. Bush and a small group of military and intelligence advisers. After investigating the events, which continue to shape the course of twenty-first century history as we write, a US Senate Committee found that the Central Intelligence Agency had dismissed alternative reports, and that the intelligence community as a whole suffered from 'collective group think'.[55] The research by Asch, Milgram and Janis tells us that groups influence the behaviour of their members, altering perceptions of reality and often promoting conformity, which can lead to imperfect and even catastrophic decisions.

The phenomenon of groupthink, therefore, has the potential to undermine the group's ability to appraise alternative choices and make quality decisions. Another phenomenon that has the potential to adversely affect decision making is group polarization. This refers to the tendency of groups to make more extreme decisions than managers and employees working alone. For example, suppose that a board of governors of a college meets to make a decision on the future of a new sports complex for the college. Individual board members might come to the meeting with various degrees of support or opposition to the project. However, by the end of the board meeting, it is highly possible that the board of governors will agree on a more ambitious (that is, a higher financial cost) plan than the average individual had when the board meeting began.

One reason for the more ambitious preference is that individual board members feel less personally responsible for the decision consequences because the entire board of governors makes the decision. Another reason is that board members become comfortable with more extreme positions when they realize that co-members also support the same position. Persuasive arguments favouring the dominant position convince doubtful members and help form a consensus around the most ambitious or extreme option. So persuasion, group support and shifting responsibility explain why groups make more extreme decisions.

OB and Globalization
Power and culture in work team relations

The globalization of work has opened new opportunities for workers from different cultural backgrounds to work closely with each other – both in person and remotely. Diverse work teams can have positive effects on productivity and problem solving by generating a greater number of innovative ideas and approaches (Earley and Gibson, 2002). Many organizations with overseas operations, however, have also encountered challenges in managing multicultural work teams. These challenges are primarily related to team members' different cultural understandings about their role in the team (and within the larger organization) and how the work should be accomplished.

In an insightful study, Mutabazi and Derr (2003) explore the cultural and historical roots of a breakdown in work team relationships at a Franco-Senegalese organization the authors call Socometal, whose work teams were made up of French expatriates and local Senegalese workers. Mutabazi and Derr concluded that inefficiencies and misunderstandings in these multicultural work teams were, to a great extent, connected with the enduring legacy of colonialism. They explain:

> *the problem associated with multiculturalism [on work teams] comes from preexisting attitudes about relations between Africa and the West. This is a deeply-rooted relationship with perceptions distorted by historical consternation. On one side, the West as the dominant partner overemphasizes its own culture, ideals and conceptions of the world ... the resulting tendency is to impose this cultural determination upon the party that is considered inferior ... [and] this characteristic of multiculturalism becomes embedded in the relationship creating a vicious cycle of misunderstanding. (p. 3)*

At Socometal, French managers and work team members did not understand the Senegalese community-based approach to team work, which relies on the circulation of people, goods, services and information through local social and economic networks. Likewise, the Senegalese workers did not understand the approaches of the French expatriate managers and workers, mistaking their focus on top-down decision making and individual competition as an assertion of superiority. The result was the reproduction of colonial power relationships between French and Senegalese workers, and work teams that were 'characterized by indifference toward the values and perspectives of fellow team members ... The professional and personal difficulties that [ensued led] to a breakdown of operations' (Mutabazi and Derr, 2003, p. 4).

This case highlights the centrality of power and culture in organizational behaviour. Gibson and Zellmer-Bruhn (2001) remind us that workplaces are culturally situated, and that relationships within organizations are shaped by culturally and historically embedded power relationships. Misunderstandings about work team relationships and responsibilities can be exacerbated in situations where team members make assumptions about their colleagues' capabilities and motivations based on preconceived notions. The potential of multicultural work teams to excel will remain untapped as long as they are managed according to a single cultural paradigm. Effective management approaches in these situations must address cultural misunderstandings and power imbalances head on, and provide enough flexibility to incorporate multiple approaches to team work and decision making into the organization.

stop! Have you ever worked on a project or a work team with members from different cultural backgrounds? Discuss any culturally based misunderstandings or 'disconnects' that you or your colleagues might have encountered while working on the project. How did you address your differences?

Can you think of any other examples of how historical relationships between nations or cultures could affect organizational behaviour if members of those groups were assigned to the same work team?

Sources and further information

Earley, P. C. and Gibson, C. B. (2002) *Multinational Work Teams: A New Perspective*, Mahwah, NJ: Lawrence Erlbaum Associates.

Gibson, C. B. and Zellmer-Bruhn, M. E. (2001) 'Metaphors and meaning: an intercultural analysis of the concept of teamwork', *Administrative Science Quarterly*, **46**(2), pp. 274–303.

Mutabazi, E. and Derr, C. B. (2003) 'The management of multicultural teams: the experience of Afro-Occidental teams', Research Paper 13, *European Entrepreneurial Learning*. Available at: www.em-lyon.com/%5Cressources%5Cge%5Cdocuments%5Cpublications%5Cwp%5C2003-13.pdf; http://cat.inist.fr/?aModele=afficheN&cpsidt=18098760 (accessed September 22, 2009).

Note: This feature was written by Gretchen Fox, Anthropologist, Timberline Natural Resource Group, Canada.

Research has repeatedly demonstrated that group decision making is not always superior. In reality, groups sometimes do perform better than the average group member but rarely do better than the best member.[56] One explanation is that even relatively homogeneous groups often fail to exchange their members' unique resources. One key assumption underpinning the enthusiasm for group-based decision making is the expectation to benefit from group members' distributed experiences and informational resources. This point is particularly important with regard to group diversity enhancing the quality of group decisions. Increasingly, diversity is an organizational fact of life, and many work groups are diverse in terms of the characteristics of their membership, bringing together members who may differ in gender, ethnicity, age, disability, hierarchical status, educational background and so forth.

Research on diversity in work teams has shown mixed results regarding the effects of group diversity on team decision making. On the one hand, the processing of decision-relevant information may benefit from a wider pool, variety of perspectives and life experiences in more diverse groups. On the other hand, diversity may actually impede the exchange, discussion and integration of decision-relevant information, with consequential negative effects on decision quality.[18] Others suggest that increasing diversity can have both positive and negative effects on group information processing and decision making contingent on 'individuals' beliefs about diversity'.[57] Thus, educating employees in diverse organizations to value diversity can improve the quality of decisions. Furthermore, the positive effects of diversity might be propagated through several structured group processes that are designed to improve the exchange of group members' unique information and the decision quality. These structured group decision-making processes include brainstorming, the nominal group technique and the stepladder technique.

Clearly, group social processes are complex and contentious, and are strongly influenced by the individual characteristics of team members and by dominant gender, race and power patterns. The wealth of research and interest in work teams over the last decade is related to the changing fashion in US and European management theory on how to compete in conditions of globalized capitalism.

weblink

For examples of team working in European and North American companies, visit: www.honda.com; www.sony.com; http://ptcpartners.com/Team/home.htm; www.dti.gov.uk/employment/useful-links/index.html. Search for '2004 employee relations survey'. This site gives a summary of the UK 2004 survey, including a section on work teams

Work teams and management theory

The theoretical interest in work groups or teams draws upon human relations, sociotechnical and Japanese perspectives on organizational design.[5,6,12,58] Pioneering work on human relations by Roethlisberger and Dickson, Mayo, Maslow and McGregor focused top managers' attention on the importance of social relations within work groups.[22,59–61]

The collaborative research by Roethlisberger, an industrial psychologist from Harvard University, and Dickson, a manager at the Western Electric plant, involved studying the job performance of two groups of front-line workers doing identical work but in separate rooms. Each work group's productivity was carefully monitored. One work group – the study group – experienced ergonomic changes including increasing the intensity of the lighting in the workshop. The study group's productivity increased. The other work group – the control group – experienced no changes in lighting. However, to the astonishment of the researchers, its productivity increased also. Even more mystifying to the researchers, when the level of light intensity was lowered for the study group, the results showed that output continued to go up. After repeated experiments over many years, the researchers began to make connections between social interaction and job performance. In 1939, Roethlisberger and Dickson wrote:

> The study of the bank wiremen showed that their behaviour at work could not be understood without considering the informal organization of the group and the relation of this informal organization to the total social organization of the company. The work activities of the group, together with their satisfactions and dissatisfactions, had to be viewed as manifestations of a complex pattern of interrelations. (ref. 59, p. 55–2)

After the Second World War, the work of Maslow and McGregor helped US human relations advocates to clarify their perspective, with its focus on the interrelations between workers and the quality of the employment relationship.

stop reflect

Think about your experience of working in a group. Do Roethlisberger and Dickson's findings resonate with any aspect of your own view on group working? Why?

In Europe, much of the early research on work teams was conducted within the framework of sociotechnical **systems theory**. This theory developed from work in

1951 on autonomous work teams in the British coal-mining industry under the supervision of Trist and Bamforth. These researchers proposed that 'responsible autonomy' should be granted to primary work groups, and that group members should learn more than one role, so that an interchangeability of tasks would be possible within the group. The flexibility would permit the completion of sub-whole units. The studies showed that the labour process in mining could be better understood in terms of two systems: the technical system – including machinery and equipment – and the social system, including the social relations and interactions among the miners.

systems theory: a set of theories based on the assumption that social entities, such as work organizations, can be viewed as if they were self-regulating bodies exploiting resources from their environment (inputs) and transforming the resources (exchanging and processing) to provide goods and services (outputs) in order to survive

Later advocates of the sociotechnical systems approach to organizational design argued that work teams provide a work regime for achieving the 'best match' between technical and social considerations or 'systems'. The term 'best match' is used to describe the relationship between the social and technological systems of the organization, where each is sensitive to the demands of the other.[12]

Attempts to implement the sociotechnical systems approach have included work redesign to 'enrich' jobs. The concept of 'job enrichment' refers to a number of different processes of rotating, enlarging and aggregating tasks. It increases the range of tasks, skills and control that workers have over the way they work, either individually or in teams. Job enrichment theory, also known as job characteristics theory, was given theoretical prominence by the work of Turner and Lawrence, and Hackman and Oldham.[29,62] As a counter to the thinking underlying Taylorism and Fordism, the job enrichment model has been influential in the design of work teams. It suggests a casual relationship between five core job characteristics and the worker's psychological state. If this relationship is positive, it leads in turn to positive outcomes. The five core job characteristics contained in the model are defined as:

job enrichment: employees are given more responsibility for scheduling, coordinating and planning their own work

job rotation: the practice of moving employees from one job to another

job enlargement: increasing the number of tasks employees perform in their jobs

job characteristics model: a job design model that relates the motivational properties of jobs to specific personal and organizational consequences of those properties

1. *skill variety*: the degree to which the job requires a variety of different activities in carrying out the work, requiring the use of a number of the worker's skills and talents
2. *task identity*: the degree to which the job requires completion of a whole and identifiable piece of work

3. *task significance*: the degree to which the job has a substantial impact on the lives or work of other people
4. *autonomy*: the degree to which the job provides substantial freedom, independence and discretion to the worker in scheduling the work and in determining the procedures to be used in carrying it out
5. *feedback*: the degree to which the worker possesses information on the actual results of her or his performance.

stop reflect

What do you think of this job characteristics model? Think about any jobs you have had. Can you use this model to assess the 'quality' of the work you were paid for? What is missing from the model?

The more that a job possesses the five core job characteristics, the greater the motivating potential of the job (Figure 7.8).

The model also recognizes the importance of learning to achieve motivation and outcome goals. Workers' work-related learning is implicitly linked to the existence of the 'moderators' – knowledge and skills, growth need strength and context satisfaction – contained in the model. The presence of moderators is used to explain why jobs that are theoretically high in motivating potential will not automatically generate high levels of motivation and satisfaction for all workers.

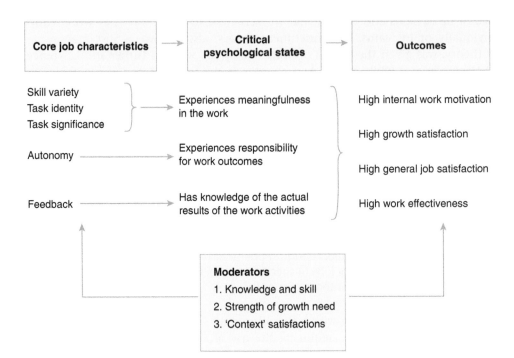

Figure 7.8 Oldham and Hackman's job characteristics model
Source: Oldham and Hackman (1980)[29].

The argument goes that an employee with a low 'growth need' is less likely to experience a positive outcome when her or his work is 'enriched'. Thus, the neo-human relations approach to job design in general, and the job characteristic model in particular, emphasized the fulfilment of social or relatedness needs by recomposing fragmented jobs. In certain circumstances, self-managed teams could provide an alternative to individual job enrichment.

The quality of work and work-related learning in small SMWTs rests on five principles of 'good' job design:

The first principle is *wholeness*: the scope of the job is such that it includes all the tasks to complete a product or process.

The second principle involves individual and group *learning and development*. Opportunities exist to engage in a variety of fulfilling and meaningful tasks, allowing team members to learn a range of skills within a community of practice, and facilitating job flexibility.[63]

The third principle relates to *governance and self-regulation*. With the focus on product differentiation and the rise of knowledge-based economies, the imperatives of work do not permit managers to master all the challenges. As a result, they must allow team and project members to assume responsibility for the pace of work, problem solving and quality control.

The fourth principle involves occupational *wellness and safety*. Work is designed to maintain the safety and wellness of team members and to support a good work–life balance.[64]

Finally, the fifth principle is *social interaction*. The job design permits interaction, cooperation and reflexivity among team members.

Drawing upon the work of Klein and McKinlay et al.,[65] the principles of 'good' job design are achieved by management interventions in the technical, governance and sociocultural dimensions of work (Figure 7.9).

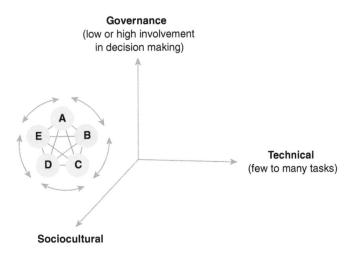

Figure 7.9 The three dimensions of group work: technical, governance and social

The horizontal axis in Figure 7.9 represents the functional or technical tasks that are required to produce the product or service. Group working involves combining a number of tasks on the horizontal axis to increase the cycle times and create more complete and hence more meaningful jobs. The technical dimension is then regarded as the central purpose of work teams, and is concerned with the range of tasks undertaken by members, multiskilling and functional flexibility. The vertical axis represents the governance aspects of the labour process, and shows the extent of workers' autonomy on the job. The third axis, the diagonal, represents the sociocultural aspects of work, one of which is the social interaction that takes place in work groups. The sociocultural dimension is perhaps the most interesting as far as organizational behaviour is concerned, since it represents the behaviour or 'normative' considerations – what ought to happen – to secure effective team performance. This dimension of group work recognizes that employees' compliance and cooperation depend upon the complex interplay of social interactions in the group. It should be noted that, in a five-member team, there are 10 relationships (see Figure 7.3, above).

The SMWT represents an *ideal-type* work regime because it restores the craft paradigm by enlarging tasks on the horizontal axis and by giving members greater autonomy over how the work is accomplished on the vertical axis: a reversal of Taylorism. The movement along the diagonal axis represents the implications of group working in terms of group norms, group cohesion and organizational culture. The three dimensions of work organization in Figure 7.9 help to illustrate the point that top managers make strategic choices regarding how work is designed, and alternative work structures have an impact on social behaviour and organizational culture.

Critical **insight**

Workplace observers agree there is evidence that, in organizations that have been successful in devolving decision making to work groups, there have been benefits for management and workers: a 'win–win' situation. Visit www.jobquality.ca and 'High-performance working' at www.cipd.co.uk. Read also Andy Danford et al. (2008), 'Partnership, high-performance work systems and the quality of working life', *New Technology, Work and Employment*, **23**(3), pp. 151–66. Who are the prime beneficiaries of team-based working? Do SMWTs reduce workplace stress?

Work teams: ending bureaucracy and extending employee empowerment?

Whereas groups as social entities go back thousands of years, management interest in work teams is much more recent. From early experiments in sociotechnical job design techniques in the 1970s, teams became the hallmark of postmodern work organizations in the 1990s. Team work has been popularized by mainstream organizational behaviour theorists and management consultants as a panacea for curing inflexible work systems and allegedly inefficient bureaucratic structures, and for enhancing employee higher-order 'growth' and 'relatedness' needs by job enrichment and empowerment.

Motivated by the prospect of connecting the synergy of work teams with corporate goals, managers have focused on teams to help improve organizational performance. In Sweden, the most celebrated example of work teams was introduced at the new Volvo car plant in Uddevalla in 1987. It was reported that the new assembly line avoided the classic problems associated with Fordism.[66] However, in 1992 Volvo closed its Uddevalla factory. For many organizational behaviour researchers, the Swedish plant had become an icon for a European, human-centred and productive organization, and its closure suggested that Taylorist and neo-Taylorist solutions still dominate management thinking in the automobile industry.[67]

In critical accounts of team work, in which group practices are connected to the class power relations in which they are embedded, there is considerable debate over whether or not these regimes constitute a significant departure from Western-style 'high-autonomy' work teams.[5,68] Some argue that the difference lies in the fact that team work utilizes a control orientation that depends upon 'self-control'. Others persuasively argue that self-managed teams create a culture that enhances management control via self-regulation. This insight into group dynamics focuses on the socialization and organization culture, and on the behaviour deemed necessary to make teams work effectively.[69]

The discussion on different group and team concepts highlights the array of definitions, and the need for commentators to define work groups carefully if comparisons are to be made. As mentioned earlier, the reason that so many organizations have 're-engineered' work processes around teams is that managers are looking for improvements in productivity resulting from the positive synergy associated with teams. Thus, the perceived connections between the way work is designed and organizational performance need to be appreciated to understand the current wave of corporate interest in teams.

In standard accounts of team work, such regimes do not necessarily lead to improved organizational performance. People must learn to work in team-based structures: clearly a lesson from sociotechnical theory, which acknowledges the importance of the dialectic relationship between the technical and social aspects of work. In critical accounts of teams, there is deep scepticism. Work teams do not eradicate the three chronic capitalist antagonisms that centre on issues of managerial control: producing goods and services for a global market, which creates uncertainty and pressure to control costs; designing work structures and employee relations systems that maximize shareholder interests; and managerial top-down control over employee behaviour, in contrast to employee autonomy.

Contrary to the management rhetoric, work teams involve elaborate computer information systems developed to support a control-oriented management philosophy.[12] This observation illustrates the work of critical scholars who tend to be interested in understanding the power relations in team design. For example, one study found that while team members had increased their autonomy in performing their work and additional responsibilities, managers had actually increased their control over value-added activities through a computerized production system. This control-oriented approach can be given the name 'computer-controlled autonomy'.[6]

Another study offered a scathing account of team working in white-collar work, arguing 'that workers experience forms of team organization as being no less coercive than classically understood Taylorism' (ref. 70, pp. 168–9).

Paradox in team-based work systems

How are we to interpret the effects of group membership on employee behaviour? As with the other aspects of organizational behaviour we cover in this text, it depends on the author's approach to the subject. For some, team synergy can be a panacea to bureaucratic ills: 'Teams foster a sense of dignity, self-worth, and a greater commitment to achieving the performance that makes an organization competitive' (ref. 71, p. 10). More critical sociological analysis serves as an antidote to the mainstream assumptions that team work is inherently favourable. The employee commitment implications of team work are not entirely positive. As an empirical reality, working in self-directed teams had no significant effect on employee commitment to the organization, whereas it was associated with higher work-related stress.[72] For others, team work, far from being 'empowering', actually intensifies management control over workers by cultivating a form of self-management through constant peer and self-monitoring.[73] This critical perspective focuses on, among other things, the effect of team ideology and behaviour on the working lives of workers. Whereas the managerialist approach found in most mainstream organizational behaviour texts focuses on the technical and the empowering dimensions of teams and team efficacy, a feature of a critical approach is a focus on the normative dimension of groups and teams, the 'tyranny' arising from team work and paradoxes in team-based work structures.

A paradox involves ambiguity and inconsistency, and both are evident in work group design. A central pillar of team work involves combining a number of tasks on the horizontal axis. This has led many traditional scholars to argue that SMWTs reverse Tayloristic deskilling tendencies by enhancing workers' skills. It is suggested that SMWTs exemplify the re-emergence of the craft model.[74] Critical organizational theorists, however, have challenged the popular logic that SMWTs lead to a more highly skilled workforce. Detractors argue that although they apparently give limited empowerment to workers, they do not necessarily reverse the general 'deskilling' trend, but generate new forms of control that assist management in extracting higher productivity from workers via work intensification as the range of horizontal and vertical tasks expands.[75–80]

Those subscribing to this critique almost invariably draw parallels with Taylorism and Fordism. A number of accounts stress that, with the assistance of micro-technology, re-engineering work into teams is an 'up-dating of Taylor's crusade against custom and practice in which the silicon chip plays an equivalent role in [re-engineering] to that performed by the stop watch in Scientific Management' (ref. 81, p. 96). In other words, it provides a disguised form of intensified managerial control. Others offer more optimistic analyses, in which the outcomes of team working are less deterministic. Whether work teams result in the 'upskilling' or 'deskilling' of workers depends, among other things, on factors such as batch size, managerial choice and negotiation.[6]

Plate 3 Team members can perceive a moral obligation to increase their level of effort on a job, and 'put in a full day' (or more) because of peer group pressure, or 'clan control', thereby unwittingly creating a control culture system
Source: iStockphoto.

Critical organizational theorists have illustrated the paradox in another way. The behavioural dimension of the team work model emphasizes worker empowerment while simultaneously increasing management's control over the labour process. This is achieved using both 'hard' technology (such as computers) and 'social' technology (such as group norms). When decision making is devolved to the team, members begin to think and act like managers, and they internalize company values. In this way, team work influences the attitude and behaviour of the team's members by creating a work culture that reproduces the conditions of employees' own subordination. In other words, team members perceive a moral obligation to increase their level of effort on the job, and 'put in a full day' because of peer group pressure or 'clan control', thereby unwittingly creating a control culture system.[8,9,82–85] Critical studies have found team members' discipline to be more punitive than that of the managers: 'Team members are tougher on fellow workers than management is' (ref. 9, p. 75). A 50-year-old male explained how peer group surveillance influenced the behaviour of the team's members like this:

> I think it's a matter of conscience. A person who under the old system might go away for an hour, now he will think twice: Are they [co-workers] going to think they are carrying me because I've been away? ... Because you are a close-knit community in the [team] system. You get niggly remarks: 'Where have you been all morning?' That sort of thing and it gradually works its way in psychologically. (ref. 6, p. 186)

In their account of team learning processes, Kasl and colleagues unwittingly provide further evidence of the control culture generated by work teams.[86] When one particular work team 'failed', some team members left the company, while others worked on 'disheartened'. Moreover:

> The team became the laughing stock of the whole company and the people who weren't involved in it at all, the people who worked on a different floor, would walk right in and say, 'How's logistics, ha ha ha?' They heard about it, it was like this big disaster. (ref. 86, p. 238)

OB in focus

Few employees have a 'good' job

Despite the hype about improved quality of work arising from the growth of team working, it is reported that 'only 39 per cent of workers think that their job is "good", according to new research from the Chartered Institute of Personnel and Development (CIPD)'. 'Good' roles are defined as 'exciting but not too stressful', according to a new report from the UK institute, *Reflections on Employee Well-Being and the Psychological Contract*.

The research explored how employees felt about their job and their relationships with managers and colleagues. It concluded that employers should make jobs more appealing and interesting to improve commitment from employees. 'Most jobs can be made interesting or even exciting if they are well managed,' Mike Emmott, CIPD employee relations adviser, said. An interesting and exciting job was one with variety and security, and where the role of the employee was clear. Many workers did not believe that their job had these qualities. A fifth of respondents thought that the demands of their job were unrealistic, and the same proportion found their jobs either very or extremely stressful.

Nic Marks, head of well-being research at the New Economics Foundation and co-author of the report, said that interest and excitement were key elements in the psychological contract between employers and employees. 'If employees don't feel their role is exciting, this will be reflected in underperformance and their lack of commitment and satisfaction,' he said.

Source: adapted from Julie Griffiths, 'Only 39 per cent of employees have a "good" job', *People Management Online*, August 9, 2005.

There is another paradox. The managerial literature views team work as organizational synergy unifying people and thus developing members' capacities through dialogue and learning. Critical reflection in workplace learning literature presumes that if team members can just detect their dysfunctional or inefficient practices, they are free to find more creative and efficient ways of doing and thus improve their performance in the workplace. One mainstream assumption is that all members of the work team are equal. Recent empirical research on multiprofessional team work in the health sector, however, contends that, rather than unifying health professions, team work produces unintended divisive effects.[87] It is argued that power relations and the language used by the health professionals both reflect and reproduce structural inequality between surgeons, anaesthetists and nurses within the team. In reality, where team work is characterized by social structures of inequality and clinical power – for example, surgeons and anaesthetists over nurses – critical reflection and dialogue, and thus the mobilization of alternative practices, are suppressed.

The discourse on work teams illustrates competing interpretations. On the one hand, the thinking and prescriptions in mainstream accounts tend to focus on the technical and the 'growth need' dimension of team-based work configurations, as well as the links between group processes and group performance. On the other hand, critical evaluations of team work focus on paradoxes and the effect of team ideology and behaviour on workers. Thus, team work arguably resembles Morgan's 'psychic prison' in the sense that peer pressure and self-surveillance are the norm, and this more accurately resembles reality than the optimistic notion of the learning-empowering, self-managed work team. In his book *Images of Organizations*,[88] Morgan explains that the notion of organizations as psychic prisons is a metaphor that connects the idea that organizations are a psychic phenomenon, in the sense that they are ultimately constructed and sustained by conscious and unconscious processes, with the belief that people can actually become imprisoned or confined by the ideas, thoughts and actions to which these processes give rise.

Chapter summary

- In this chapter, we have examined the background, nature and behavioural implications of work groups. We have suggested that the current wave of interest in work teams, often located within a cluster of other employment practices constituting what is called a 'high-performance workplace', is linked to lean forms of work organizations and the perceived shortcomings of large bureaucratic organizational structures.

- The chapter has emphasized that understanding group processes, such as groupthink, group leadership, informal group learning and intragroup conflict, is imperative for the successful management of the HPW system.

- Management tries to persuade workers of the need to work beyond their contract for the 'common' good and to engage in self-regulatory norms. The SMWT is said to be upskilling and empowering workers.

- However, we have also gone beyond management rhetoric, and presented arguments and evidence to suggest that self-managed teams shift the focus away from the hierarchy, directive and bureaucratic control processes, to a culture of self-control mechanisms.

- The discussion has emphasized that orthodox and critical accounts of team working provide very different views of this form of work organization and employment relations. Both perspectives, however, conceptualize team working as influencing individual behaviour and contributing to improved organizational performance. While both approaches make employee autonomy central to their analyses, each conceptualizes team membership as having a different influence. Additionally, autonomy is theorized as leading to different outcomes (such as growth need versus self-regulation) in each perspective.

Key concepts

group dynamics   247–248
group processes   250
group structure   249
job characteristic model   262
peer pressure   267
psychic prison   268
work group   245
work team   246–247

Vocab checklist for ESL students

- Cohesiveness
- Empowerment, empower
- Formal work group
- Group context
- Group dynamics
- Group norms
- Group processes
- Group structure
- Groupthink
- Increment, incremental
- Informal group
- Job characteristics model
- Job design
- Job enlargement
- Job enrichment
- Job rotation
- Job satisfaction
- Paradox, paradoxical
- Role
- Role ambiguity
- Role conflict
- Role perceptions
- Self-managed work teams
- Systems theory
- Status
- Teams
- Work group

Chapter review questions

1. How useful are group development models for understanding group or team behaviour?

2. What effect, if any, do you expect workforce diversity to have on group processes and outcomes?

3. Explain how the size of the work group might affect group dynamics and performance?

4. 'Self-managed work teams are simply attempts by managers to control individuals at work by mobilizing group processes.' Do you agree or disagree? Discuss.

5. Students often complain about doing group projects. Why? Relate your answer to group processes and the critique of self-managed work teams.

6. What is meant by 'group think', and how important is it in deciding group performance?

Chapter research questions

1. Diversity is an organizational fact of life. In a group, we would like you to examine your own beliefs about diversity and how people stereotype others. Form a study group. (a) Post each term from the following list on separate sheets of paper: Male, Roman Catholic, Asian, Generation Y, Disabled, American, Muslim, Female, Irish, Single mother, Over age 60, West Indian. (b) Circulate the sheets around the group, and write down one stereotype you have heard under each heading. Avoid repeating anything that is already written down. (c) After everyone has finished writing, each group member takes turns to read all the stereotypes under each category. (d) Group members should then discuss (i) their personal reaction, (ii) what they have learned about stereotyping others, and (iii) what managers can do to experience positive effects of diversity.

2. Obtain a copy of Bolton and Houlihan's book *Work Matters: Critical Reflections on Contemporary Work* (see Further Reading). After reading pages 162–79, explain how team working was introduced into a major supermarket chain. How much autonomy did the teams have? How did the leadership style differ between the teams? How was team productivity measured? How did team work help members cope with work-related stress? How might team diversity impact on the team dynamics?

3. Read Rolf van Dick et al.'s article, 'Group diversity and group identification: the moderating role of diversity beliefs' (see Further Reading). Does group diversity positively or negatively affect group decision making? What can managers do to improve the quality of group decision making?

Further reading

Behfar, K., Peterson, R., Mannix, E. and Trochim, W. (2008) 'The critical role of conflict resolution in teams: a closer look at the links between conflict type, conflict management strategies, and team outcomes', *Journal of Applied Psychology*, 93(1), pp. 170–88.

Belbin, R. M. (1993) *Team Roles at Work*, London: Butterworth/Heinemann.

Bolton, S. and Houlihan, M. (eds) (2009) *Work Matters: Critical Reflections on Contemporary Work*, Basingstoke: Palgrave.

Cole, M. S., Walter, F. and Bruch, H. (2008) 'Affective mechanisms linking dysfunctional behavior to performance in work teams: a moderated mediation study', *Journal of Applied Psychology*, 93(5), pp. 945–58.

Cordery, J. (2002) 'Team working', pp. 326–50 in P. Warr (ed.), *Psychology of Work*, London: Penguin.

Danford, A., Richardson, M., Stewart, P., Tailby, S. and Upchurch, M. (2008) 'Partnership, high performance work systems and quality of working life', *New Technology, Work and Employment*, 23(3), pp. 151–66.

Kasl, E., Marsick, V. and Dechant, K. (1997) 'Teams as learners', *Journal of Applied Behavioral Sciences*, 33(2), pp. 227–46.

Kooij-de Bode, H. J. M., Hanneke J. M., van Knippenberg, D. and van Ginkel, W. P. (2008) 'Ethnic diversity and distributed information in group decision making: the importance of information elaboration', *Group Dynamics: Theory, Research and Practice*, 12(4), pp. 307–20.

Proctor, S., Fulop, L., Linstead, S., Mueller, F. and Sewell, G. (2009) 'Managing teams', pp. 539–73 in S. Linstead, L. Fulop and S. Lilley (eds), *Management and Organization: A Critical Text* (2nd edn), Basingstoke: Palgrave.

Russell, N. and Gregory, R. (2005) 'Making the undoable doable: Milgram, the Holocaust, and modern government', *American Review of Public Administration*, **35**(4), pp. 327–49.

Sewell, G. (1998) 'The discipline of teams: the control of team-based industrial work through electronic and peer surveillance', *Administrative Science Quarterly*, **43**, pp. 406–69.

Taggar, S. and Robert Ellis, R. (2007) 'The role of leaders in shaping formal team norms', *Leadership Quarterly*, 18, pp. 105–20.

van Dick, R., van Knippenberg, D., Hagele, S., Guillaume, Y. R. F. and Brodbeck, F. (2008) 'Group diversity and group identification: the moderating role of diversity beliefs', *Human Relations*, **61**(10), pp. 1463–92.

Chapter case study 1

Building cars in Brazil

Setting

Founded in the earlier part of the century, the Cable Motor Company was a traditional, North American automobile manufacturer. They used Fordist management techniques and traditional assembly line production, and worked with a highly unionized workforce. By the mid-1980s, with their sales slumping, the company made the decision to purchase an obsolete automotive assembly plant in Brazil. The company quickly proceeded to upgrade the plant, resulting in a very large, modern, single-storey building of approximately 1.4 million square feet with four major manufacturing centres: stamping, body, paint and final assembly. The plan was to adopt the use of cooperative work teams, which had been used by Swedish car manufacturers such as Saab and Volvo, and to implement the Japanese lean production system originally created by Toyota and later adapted by Mazda.

The company spared no expense in planning for the workforce that would fit the plant's new approach to job design. There were extensive pre-employment screening and selection techniques used to recruit the 1200 people needed for the production run. Unlike the minimalist training normally provided under the Ford system, the company provided intensive classroom time and continuous on-the-job training for employees on the subject of self-managed work teams. Group decision making, integral to team success, was a strong focus.

The company found that the union representing the workers, the National Union of Cable Motor Company Workers, had little influence in the new Brazilian plant. This resulted in a much quicker implementation of the flexible production system. Production shifts of about 100 persons were scheduled with workers performing operations individually and in self-directed two-, three- or four-person teams. Any team member could pull a car off the line to check a quality issue. In such a case, a group walk-around decided if a car needed 'finessing'.

CEO John Miner was impressed with the initial look of the new production system. 'Minimal supervision and a self-directed workforce are what we strive to maintain and encourage,' he remarked. 'We will not get bogged down in traditional thinking, processes or paperwork. All workers are encouraged to be free-thinking and to get creative.'

The problem

The selection of the team leaders was conducted by the senior management group. Maria Lopez, a 30-year-old clerical worker, was moved from the administration office to head up one of the teams. Shortly after, production manager Clive Richards began to notice that Maria's team's production cycle times were increasing. He also noticed conflicts within her group. Clive decided to approach one of Maria's team members, Juan Fernandez, who had formerly worked in a team at another car company's assembly plant in Brazil. 'We can't work with Maria as our team leader,' Juan said. 'The team finds it hard because she is a woman. You have to remove her.'

While Clive struggled to decide what to do with Maria, other problems emerged. Employees were arriving to work late on a consistent basis. City buses, the main source of transportation for the plant workers, ran late if they ran at all. This was beginning to impact the continual on-the-job training as it required workers to arrive at work on time. Other employees were hesitant to do quality checks on their own work, saying that it would create the impression that the supervisors did not trust them.

Clive decided to meet with the CEO to let him know about the increasing issues so that action could be taken before the problems got worse. John was concerned when he heard what was happening at the new plant as he had just returned from a meeting where there were preliminary discussions on opening another in a different Brazilian location. 'I need you to do a presentation for the Board of Directors,' John said to Clive. 'We have to show what we've learned from this experience and how we can move forward.'

Tasks

Prepare a short presentation, incorporating the answers to the following questions:

1. How did Brazilian culture or work ideology contribute to the problems the company experienced with its use of teams?

2. In what alternative way could the team leader have been chosen which may have been more acceptable to the team members?

3. Should the conflicts in Maria's group only be viewed as a negative development?

4. Ask yourself:

5. Why do you think the use of teams could weaken a union's influence or power in the workplace?

Essential reading

Katz, H. C., Lee, W. and Lee, J. (2004) *The New Structure of Labour Relations*, New York: Cornell University Press.

Proctor, S., Fulop, L., Linstead, S., Mueller, F. and Sewell, G. (2009) 'Managing teams', pp. 539–73 in S. Linstead, L. Fulop and S. Lilley (eds), *Management and Organization: A Critical Text* (2nd edn), Basingstoke: Palgrave.

Note

Cable Motor Company is a fictitious company, but the background material for the case is derived from Muller, Rehder and Bannister (1998).[89] Some circumstances of the case organization have been altered. This case study was written by Lori Rilkoff, MSc, CHRP, Senior Human Resources Manager at the City of Kamloops, and lecturer in HRM at Thompson Rivers University, BC, Canada.

Chapter case study 2

Teams at Land Rock Alliance Insurance

Visit www.palgrave.com/business/brattonob2e to view this case study

Web-based assignment

Work groups and teams is one of the most important topics of organizational behaviour, and given that many students have experienced group working and will be called upon to work in groups in organizations, it is important to reflect on how groups influence human behaviour.

For this assignment, we would like you to gain more information on work teams by visiting www.workteams.org and www.berr.gov.uk. In addition, you are asked to explore examples of team working in European and North American companies by visiting the following websites: www.honda.com; www.sony.com; http://ptcpartners.com/Team/home.htm; www.berr.gov.uk.

What main principles can be identified as 'good' job design when applied to work teams? Looking at the companies that have introduced teams, what behaviours or 'norms' are expected of employees? How does the team-based model impact on other aspects of management such as human resource management? Discuss your findings with other students on your course.

OB in film

The film *Twelve Angry Men* (1957) examines the behaviour of 12 members of a jury who have to decide on the innocence or guilt of a young man from a working-class background. At the beginning, 11 jurors are convinced of the youth's guilt and wish to declare him guilty without further discussion. One member of the jury (played by Henry Fonda) has reservations and persuades the other members to review the evidence. After reviewing the evidence, the jury acquits the defendant.

A modern version of this film can be seen in a 2005 episode of the television series *Judge John Deed*, in which Judge Deed (played by Martin Shaw) serves as a member of a jury and persuades the other members to review the evidence in a sexual assault case.

What group concepts do the film or the *Judge John Deed* episode illustrate? What types of power are possessed by the characters played by Henry Fonda and Martin Shaw? What pattern of influencing behaviour is followed by Henry Fonda and Martin Shaw?

References

1. Johnson, D. W. and Johnson, F. P. (2000) *Joining Together: Group Theory and Group Skills* (7th edn), Boston: Allyn & Bacon.
2. Katzenbach, J. R. and Smith, D. (1994) *The Wisdom of Teams*, New York: Harper Business.
3. Kline, T. (1999) *Remaking Teams*, San Francisco: Jossey-Bass.
4. Orsburn, J. and Moran, L. (2000) *The New Self-directed Work Teams*, New York: McGraw-Hill.
5. Procter, S. and Mueller, F. (2000) *Teamworking*, Basingstoke: Palgrave Macmillan.
6. Bratton, J. (1992) *Japanization at Work*, Basingstoke: Macmillan.
7. Thompson, R and Ackroyd, S. (1995) 'All quiet on the workplace front: a critique of recent trends in British industrial sociology', *Sociology*, **29**(4), pp. 615–33.
8. Sewell, G. (1998) 'The discipline of teams: the control of team-based industrial work through electronic and peer surveillance', *Administrative Science Quarterly*, **43**, pp. 406–69.
9. Wells, D. (1993) 'Are strong unions compatible with the new model of human resource management?', *Relations Industrielles/Industrial Relations*, **48**(1), pp. 56–84.
10. Hertog, J. F. and Tolner, T. (1998) 'Groups and teams', pp. 62–71 in M. Poole and M. Watner (eds), *The Handbook of Human Resource Management*, London: International Thomson Business Press.
11. Buchanan, D. (2000) 'An eager and enduring embrace: the ongoing rediscovery of teamworking as a management idea', in S. Procter and F. Mueller (eds), *Teamworking*, London: Macmillan.
12. Yeatts, D. E. and Hyten, C. (1998) *High-performing Self-managed Work Teams*, Thousand Oaks, CA: Sage.
13. Bendix, R. (1956) *Work and Authority in Industry*, New York: Wiley.
14. Crawley, J. (1978) 'The lifestyles of the group', *Small Groups Newsletter*, **2**(1), pp. 26–39.

15. Gil, R., Rico, R., Alcover, C. M. and Barrasa, A. (2005) 'Change-oriented leadership, satisfaction and performance in work groups: effects of team climate and group potency', *Journal of Managerial Psychology*, **20**(3/4), pp. 312–29.

16. Simmel, G. (1908/1950) 'Subordination under a principle', pp. 250–67 in *The Sociology of Georg Simmel* (ed. and trans. K. Wolff), New York: Free Press.

17. Choi, J. N. (2007) 'Group composition and employee creative behaviour in a Korean electronics company: distinct effects of relational demography and group diversity', *Journal of Occupational and Organizational Psychology*, **80**, pp. 213–34.

18. Kooij-de Bode, H. J. M., van Knippenberg, D. and van Ginkel, W. P. (2008) 'Ethnic diversity and distributed information in group decision making: the importance of information elaboration', *Group Dynamics: Theory, Research and Practice*, **12**(4), pp. 307–20.

19. Slaughter, J. E. and Zicker, M. J. (2006) 'A new look at the role of insiders in the newcomer socialization process', *Group & Organization Management*, **31**(2), pp. 264–90.

20. Tuckman, B. and Jensen, M. (1977) 'Stages of small group development revisited', *Group and Organization Management*, **2**, pp. 419–27.

21. Gersick, C. J. (1988) 'Time and transition in workteams: towards a new model of group development', *Academy of Management Journal*, **31**, pp. 47–53.

22. Mayo, E. (1946) *The Human Problems of an Industrial Civilization*, New York: Macmillan.

23. Feldman, D. C. (1984) 'The development and enforcement of group norms', *Academy of Management Review*, 1, pp. 47–53.

24. Taggar, S. and Ellis, R. (2007) 'The role of leaders in shaping formal team norms', *Leadership Quarterly*, **18**, pp. 105–20.

25. Zimbardo, P. (2008) BBC *Hardtalk* interview, April 22, 2008.

26. Romero, E. and Pescosolido, A. (2008) 'Humor and group effectiveness', *Human Relations*, **61**(3), pp. 395–418.

27. Wilson, F. M. (2003) *Organizational Behaviour and Gender*, Farnham: Ashgate.

28. Smith, J. W. and Calasanti, T. (2005) 'The influences of gender, race and ethnicity on workplace experiences of institutions and social isolation: an exploratory study of university faculty', *Sociological Spectrum*, **25**(3), pp. 307–34.

29. Hackman, J. and Oldham, G. (1980) *Work Redesign*, Reading, MA: Addison-Wesley.

30. Janis, I. L. (1972) *Victims of Groupthink*, Boston, MA: Houghton Mifflin.

31. Senge, P. (1990) *The Fifth Discipline*, New York: Doubleday.

32. O'Brien, D. and Buono, C. (1996) 'Building effective learning teams: lessons from the field', *SAM Advanced Management Journal*, **61**(3), pp. 4–11.

33. Jenkins, J. (2008) 'Pressurised partnership: a case of perishable compromise in contested terrain', *New Technology, Work and Employment*, **23**(3), pp. 167–80.

34. Thompson (1960). Cited in Robbins, S. P. (1990) *Organization Theory: Structure, Design, and Applications* (3rd edn), Englewood Cliffs, NJ: Prentice-Hall, p. 411.

35. Varela, O. E., Burke, M. J. and Landis, R. S. (2008) 'A model of emergence and dysfunctional effects of emotional conflicts in groups', *Group Dynamics: Theory, Research and Practice*, **12**(2), pp. 112–26.

36. Bolton, S. (2005) *Emotion Management in the Workplace*, Basingstoke: Palgrave.

37. Cole, M. S., Walter, F. and Bruch, H. (2008) 'Affective mechanisms linking dysfunctional behavior to performance in work teams: a moderated mediation study', *Journal of Applied Psychology*, **93**(5), pp. 945–58.

38. Dunlop, P.D. and Lee, K. (2004) 'Workplace deviance, organizational citizenship behavior, and business unit performance: the bad apples do spoil the whole barrel', *Journal of Organizational Behavior*, **25**, 67–80.

39. Behfar, K., Peterson, R., Mannix, E. and Trochim, W. (2008) 'The critical role of conflict resolution in teams: a closer look at the links between conflict type, conflict management strategies, and team outcomes', *Journal of Applied Psychology*, **93**(1), pp. 170–88.

40. Tajfel, H. (1978) 'Social categorization, social identity, and social comparison', pp. 61–76 in H. Tajfel (ed.), *Differentiation between Social Groups*, London: Academic Press.

41. Tajfel, H. (1981) 'Social stereotypes and social groups', in J. C. Turner and H. Giles (eds), *Intergroup Behaviour*, Oxford: Blackwell.

42. Turner, J. (1987) *Rediscovering the Social Group: A Self-categorization Theory*, New York: Basic Books.

43. Miller, N. and Brewer, M. B. (eds) (1984) *Groups in Contact: The Psychology of Desegregation*, New York: Academic Press.
44. Sherif, M., Harvey, O. J., White, B. J., Hood, W. R. and Sherif, C. W. (1961) *Intergroup Conflict and Cooperation*, Norman, OK: Oklahoma Book Exchange.
45. De Dreu, C. and Van de Vliert, E. (eds) (1997) *Using Conflict in Organizations*, London: Sage.
46. Hackman, H. R. (1986) 'The psychology of self-management in organizations', pp. 89–136 in M. S. Pallack and Perloff, R. O. (eds), *Psychology and Work: Productivity, Change and Employment*, Washington, DC: American Psychological Association.
47. Banker, R. D., Field, J. M., Schroeder, R. G. and Sinha, K. (1996) 'Impact of work teams on manufacturing performance: a longitudinal study', *Academy of Management Journal*, 39(2), pp. 867–90.
48. Cohen, S. G. and Bailey, D. E. (1997) 'What makes team work: group effectiveness research from the shop floor to the executive suite', *Journal of Management*, 23(3), pp. 239–90.
49. Steiner, I. D. (1972) *Group Processes and Productivity*, New York: Academic Press.
50. Horwitz, F. M., Chan feng Heng and Quazi, H. A. (2003) 'Finders, keepers? Attracting, motivating and retaining knowledge workers', *Human Resource Management Journal*, 13(4), pp. 23–44.
51. Stewart, P. and Danford, A. (2008) 'Editorial: Union strategies and worker engagement with new forms of work and employment', *New Technology, Work and Employment*, 23(3), pp. 146–50.
52. Asch, S. E. (1951) 'Effects of group pressure upon modification and distortion of judgements', in H. Guetzkow (ed.), *Groups, Leadership and Men*, New York: Carnegie Press.
53. Milgram, S. (1973) *Obedience and Authority*, London: Tavistock.
54. Russell, N. and Gregory, R. (2005) 'Making the undoable doable: Milgram, the Holocaust, and modern government', *American Review of Public Administration*, 35(4), pp. 327–49.
55. Koring, P. (2004) 'Iraq war based on "flawed" reports', *Globe and Mail*, p. A11.
56. Winquist, J. and Franz, T. (2008) 'Does the stepladder technique improve group decision making? A series of failed replications', *Group Dynamics: Theory, Research and Practice*, 12(4), pp. 255–67.
57. van Dick, R., van Knippenburg, D., Hagele, S., Guillaume, Y. R. F. and Brodbeck, F. (2008) 'Group diversity and group identification: the moderating role of diversity beliefs', *Human Relations*, 61(10), pp. 1463–92.
58. Benders, J. and Van Hootegem, G. (1999) 'Teams and their context: moving team discussion beyond existing dichotomies', *Journal of Management Studies*, 36(5), pp. 609–28.
59. Roethlisberger, F. J. and Dickson, W. J. (1939) *Management and the Worker*, Cambridge, MA: Harvard University Press.
60. Maslow, A. H. (1954) *Motivation and Personality*, New York: Harper.
61. McGregor, D. (1960) *The Human Side of Enterprise*, New York: McGraw-Hill.
62. Turner, A. N. and Lawrence, P. R. (1965) *Industrial Jobs and the Worker*, Boston: Harvard University, Graduate School of Business Administration.
63. Hoeve, A. and Nieuwenhuis, L. (2006) 'Learning routines in innovation processes', *Journal of Workplace Learning*, 18(3), pp. 171–85.
64. Lowe, G. (2000) *The Quality of Work: A People-centred Agenda*, New York: Oxford University Press.
65. Klein, J. (1994) 'Maintaining expertise in multi-skilled teams', *Advances in Interdisciplinary Studies of Work Teams*, 1, pp. 145–65.
66. 'Volvo's radical new assembly plant: "the death of the assembly line"?', *Business Week*, August 28, 1989.
67. Cressey, P. (1993) 'Kalmar and Uddevalla: the demise of Volvo as a European icon', *New Technology, Work and Employment*, 8(2), pp. 88–96.
68. Elger, T. and Smith, C. (eds) (1994) *Global Japanization?*, London: Routledge.
69. Thompson, P. and Wallace, T. (1996) 'Redesigning production through teamworking', *International Journal of Operations and Production Management*, 16(2), pp. 103–18.
70. Baldry, C, Bain, P. and Taylor, P. (1998) '"Bright satanic offices": intensification, control and team Taylorism', pp. 163–83 in P. Thompson and C. Warhurst (eds), *Workplaces of the Future*, Basingstoke: Macmillan.

71. Manz, C. C. and Sims, H. P. Jr. (1993). *Business Without Bosses*, New York: Wiley.

72. Danford, A., Richardson, M., Stewart, P., Tailby, S. and Upchurch, M. (2008) 'Partnership, high performance work systems and quality of working life', *New Technology, Work and Employment*, **23**(3), pp. 151–66.

73. Thompson, P. and McHugh, D. (2006) *Work Organizations: A Critical Introduction* (4th edn), Basingstoke: Palgrave.

74. Piore, M. and Sabel, C. (1984) *The Second Industrial Divide*, New York: Basic Books.

75. Turnbull, P. (1986) 'The Japanisation of British industrial relations at Lucas', *Industrial Relations Journal*, **17**(3), pp. 193–206.

76. Sayer, A. (1986) 'New developments in manufacturing: the just-in-time system', *Capital and Class*, **30**, pp. 43–72.

77. Tomaney, J. (1990) 'The reality of workplace flexibility', *Capital and Class*, **40**, pp. 29–60.

78. Clarke, L. (1997) 'Changing work systems, changing social relations? A Canadian General Motors Plant', *Relations Industrielle/Industrial Relations*, **52**(4), pp. 839–65.

79. Malloch, H. (1997) 'Strategic and HRM aspects of kaizen: a case study', *New Technology, Work and Employment*, **12**(2), pp. 108–22.

80. Willmott, H., (1995) 'The odd couple?: re-engineering business processes: managing human relations', *New/Technology, Work and Employment*, **10**(2), pp. 89–98.

81. Thompson, P. (1989) *The Nature of Work* (2nd edn), London: Macmillan.

82. Burawoy, M. (1979) *Manufacturing Consent*, Chicago: University of Chicago Press.

83. Burawoy, M. (2002) 'What happened to the working class?', pp. 69–76 in K. Leicht (ed.), *The Future of the Market Transition*, New York: JAI Press.

84. Shalla, V. (1997) 'Technology and the deskilling of work: the case of passenger agents at Air Canada', in A. Duffy, D. Glenday and N. Pupo (eds), *Good Jobs, Bad Jobs, No Jobs: The Transformation of Work in the 21st Century*, Toronto: Harcourt.

85. Wood, S. (1986) 'The cooperative labour strategy in the U.S. auto industry', *Economic and Industrial Democracy*, **7**(4), pp. 415–48.

86. Kasl, E., Marsick, V. and Dechant, K. (1997) 'Teams as learners', *Journal of Applied Behavioral Science*, **33**(2), pp. 227–46.

87. Finn, R. (2008) 'The language of teamwork: reproducing professional divisions in the operating theatre', *Human Relations* **61**(1), pp. 103–30.

88. Morgan, G. (1997) *Images of Organization* (2nd edn), Thousand Oaks, CA: Sage.

89. Muller, H. J., Rehder, R. R. and Bannister, G. (1998) 'The Mexican–Japanese–U.S. model for auto assembly in Northern Mexico', *Latin American Business Review*, **2**(1), pp. 47–67.

90. Proctor, S., Fulop, L., Linstead, S., Mueller, F. and Sewell, G. (2009) 'Managing teams', pp. 539–73 in S. Linstead, L. Fulop and S. Lilley (eds), *Management and Organization: A Critical Text* (2nd edn), Basingstoke: Palgrave.

91. Brown, S. P., Westbrook, R. A. and Challagalla, G. (2005) 'Good cope, bad cope: adaptive and maladaptive coping strategies following a critical negative work event', *Journal of Applied Psychology*, **90**, 792–8.

CHAPTER 8
The social nature of work

CHAPTER OUTLINE

- Introduction
- Work and non-work
- The development of work
- Work in organizations: an integration of ideas
- Gender and the sexual division of work
- Work less, live better? Managing the work–life balance
- Summary and end-of-chapter features
- Chapter case study 1: Service with a smile: McJobs in China
- Chapter case study 2: Home-working at Matherdom City Council

CHAPTER OBJECTIVES

After completing this chapter, you should be able to:

- explain the function and meaning of work
- explain the relationship between work and an individual's personal and social identity
- summarise the historical dimensions of work, pre-industry, the factory system, occupational changes, and the emergence of knowledge work in the virtual worksite
- identify some key strategic issues involved in designing work
- discuss the debates around issues of emotional work and work–life balance

Introduction

It is a paradox of life that its recognizable features are often the most difficult to understand. This observation is highly relevant to the topic of this chapter: work.

Benjamin Franklin said that 'in this world nothing can be said to be certain, except death and taxes'. He was wrong. There is another certainty for most of us, and that is work. Whether defined in conventional economic terms as 'paid work' or defined more inclusively as a broad range of activities beyond the boundaries of paid employment, work is an almost inescapable feature of industrialized societies. Decisions about how paid work is organized and performed have created many different and contrasting types of work and employment relationships.

Since the Industrial Revolution, as factories have become more capital intensive, manual labour has undergone a transformation. Most traditional 'trade' or 'craft' jobs based on tacit knowledge have disappeared or have been 'deskilled', lessening control by craft workers. Factory work has increasingly been influenced by the 'scientific management' principle of 'one best way' of organizing particular work tasks. As employment shifted from manufacturing to the service sector, the process of deindustrialization, the principles of scientific management became incorporated into clerical labour and professional work. A trend throughout the twentieth century has been the growing presence of women in virtually all occupations. Another noticeable trend, especially since the 1990s, has been the global growth of flexible labour, a plethora of employment contracts that are part time, fixed term, short term or seasonal and create what has become known as 'precarious' employment.

deindustrialization: a term to describe the decline of the manufacturing sector of the economy

occupation: a category of jobs that involve similar activities at different work sites

The essence of being human is to engage in waged labour, but most people have little influence over how their labour is designed and performed. Organizations can be regarded as the architects of waged work, as it is within organizations that work is structured, jobs are designed and the employment relationship is formed.[1] Paid work for most individuals and families is the primary source of income that determines their standard of living. But it is important for more than economic reasons. Bolton and Houlihan's latest book, *Work Matters*,[2] juxtaposes both the bad and the good aspects of work. Waged work can be arduous, tedious, dirty, unhealthy and at times dangerous, but it can also bring connections and friendship, be a principal source of individuals' self-fulfilment and form part of their social identity. At the society level, how and where work is performed has consequences not only for the individuals who do it, but also for families and for the communities they live in.

Writing about the 'transformation of work' might be described as a cottage industry. Since the late 1970s, many books and research articles have been published, offering optimistic and pessimistic accounts of the effects of globalization and technological change on the nature of work. The optimistic scenario focuses on the liberating effect of information technology. Andre Gorz in 1982 predicted 'the liberation of time and the abolition of work' (ref. 3, p. 1). For more than a decade, Gorz set the trend for polemical 'future of work' books.[5-12] More recently, Jeremy Rifkin has argued that sophisticated 'Information Age' technologies are 'freeing up' the talent of men and women to create social capital in local communities.[4] Similarly, Microsoft's Bill Gates has argued that computers allow us to increase leisure time.[6] Both Rifkin and Gates write very persuasively, and their material has reached a wide audience.

Critical scholarship offers strikingly different accounts of work found in the Information Age rhetoric and captures the realities of lower-skilled work. Such accounts argue that the latest idiom of flexibility creates regimes that lead to the intensification of work, deskilling, tighter managerial control over work activities, and work-based inequalities.[5,7–12] With a particular eye to the gendering of work, it is argued that 'Where the goal of most employers throughout the world is to get the work of one full-time male done for one part-time female at a fraction of the cost, talk of the new liberation from toil can sound offensive' (ref. 5, p. 752). There is a growing consensus that there is currently a shortage of 'decent' work, with 'good' work being the preserve of a privileged minority in the new 'labour aristocracy' found in the professional, high-tech and creative industries loosely defined as 'knowledge workers'.[2]

flexibility: action in response to global competition, including employees performing a number of tasks (functional flexibility), the employment of part-time and contract workers (numerical flexibility), and performance-related pay (reward flexibility)

This chapter has a very bold objective: to explain the nature of work in advanced capitalist societies, and why the design of work is important to understanding behaviour in organizations. This requires us to trace the evolution of work from early capitalism to late modernity. We look at the historical dimension of work in the belief that present problems associated with work are an outcome of the past, and that the problems of the future are embedded in the social relations of work designed in the present. The broader context of work provides an essential background for understanding the connection between work, identity, work and private life, and behavioural decisions in the workplace, and the implications for managing the employment relationship.

Work and non-work

'What kind of work do you do?' is such a classic question that it is repeatedly asked in social conversation. This question is significant because it underscores the fact that paid work – employment – is generally considered to be a central defining feature of our identity. It is also one important means by which we judge others. Adults with paid jobs usually name their occupation by way of an answer, but we can see this question in a wider sense too. It invites us to explore the nature of work in relation to time, space and social structure.

social structure: the stable pattern of social relationships that exist within a particular group or society

Consider this everyday scene in any Western town or city. It is 2 o'clock in the afternoon, and a neighbourhood park is busy with adults and children enjoying themselves. Some are walking quickly through the park, perhaps going back to their office or store after their lunch break. A city employee is pruning roses in one of the flower beds. Near the bandstand, three musicians are playing a saxophone, a clarinet and a violin. Two people are playing tennis. Others are watching young children play. A man sitting on a bench is reading a book, a woman is using a mobile phone, and a teenager is completing a printed form. This scene draws attention to the blurred boundary between work and non-work activity. It gives us an entry point for answering the question, 'What is work?'

If we try to define some of these individual activities as work, the confusion and ambiguity about the meaning of work will become apparent. For example, the people walking back to their offices or to the shops might prune the roses in their gardens at the weekend, but they are unlikely to see the task in the same way as the gardener who is employed to do tasks such as pruning. The three musicians might be playing for amusement, or they might be rehearsing for an evening performance for which they will be paid. An amateur who plays tennis for fun and fitness does not experience or think of the game in the same way as a professional tennis player. Similarly, a parent keeping an eye on a child playing does not experience child-minding in the same way as a professional nanny. The person using the mobile phone might be talking to a friend, but she could be, say, a financial adviser phoning a client. The person filling in the form might be applying for a student grant, or a clerical worker catching up with an overdue job during his lunch hour. We can see from these examples that work cannot be defined simply by the activities that are carried out.

stop reflect

Write down your own definition of 'work'. To help you, consider a chef preparing a meal at a five-star hotel, and the same chef going home and preparing the family meal. Are both activities 'work'?

So what is work, exactly? 'Work' can be contrasted with 'labour'. According to Williams, labour has a 'strong medieval sense of pain and toil' (ref. 13, p. 335), and 'work' can be distinguished from 'occupation', which is derived from a Latin word meaning 'to occupy or to seize' (ref. 14, p. 2). The terms 'work', 'occupation' and 'job' have become interchangeable: work is not just an activity, something one *does*, but something a person *has*.[3] Conventionally, to 'have worked' or to 'have a job' is to use a place (or space) and sell time.

A substantial number of people have an *instrumental* orientation to work. They work for economic rewards in order to do non-work or leisure activity that they 'really enjoy'. For these people, life begins when work ends. Different occupations provide different levels of pay, so those doing them have different life chances and opportunities in terms of health, education, leisure pursuits and quality of life. Among people who 'have work', it is not simply the case that people need to work in order to have enough money to live on. People do paid work to earn money to acquire 'consumer power'. Thus, paid work for many is a means to an end – commodity consumption (buying designer clothes, fast cars, mobile phones and so on) or social consumption (such as drinking, dining out and holidaying). The central differentiating feature between people 'out of work' and those 'in work' is that the latter have much higher levels of consumer power and more choice about their lifestyle.

However, pay is only part of the equation. Research suggests that many people do paid work not primarily for extrinsic rewards (such as pay), but for the intrinsic rewards that work can bring, such as self-esteem, friendship, enjoyment and the social purpose of work. Traditionally, people occupying higher positions in an organization's hierarchy obtain more prestige and self-esteem than those in lower positions, and most people get satisfaction from participating in activities that demonstrably contribute to human well-being.[15,16]

We can begin to understand the complexity of work and its social ramifications by exploring the following definition:

> Work refers to physical and mental activity that is carried out to produce or achieve something of value at a particular place and time; it involves a degree of obligation and explicit or implicit instructions, in return for pay or reward.

This definition draws attention to some central features of work.[17] First, the most obvious purpose of work is an economic one. The notion of 'physical and mental'

Plate 1 Work in the service sector often requires workers to provide more than physical labour. Jobs such as flight attendants, shop assistants and waiting at tables require workers to manage their feelings in order to create a publicly observable facial display: what Hochschild calls 'emotional labour'

Source: Getty Images.

and 'value' suggests that the activities of both a construction worker and a computer systems analyst can be considered as work. The 'mental activity' also includes the commercialization of human feeling, or what is called 'emotional labour'.

Second, work is structured spatiality – how social life is organized geographically – and by time, and people's spatial embedding shapes work and management practices.[18] Throughout most of the twentieth century, work was typically carried out away from home and at set periods of the day or night. Thus 'place and time' locates work within a social context. However, in advanced capitalist economies, there are new expectations of spatial mobility and temporal flexibility.[19,20] The mass timetable of the '8 to 5' factory world, of the '9 to 5' office world and of recreational Sundays has given way to a flexi-place, flexi-time world. The Internet means that the timing of the working day may be shaped by working times in a number of time zones.

Third, work always involves social relations between people: between employer and employee, between co-workers, between management and trade unions, and between suppliers and customers. Social relations in the workplace can be cooperative or conflictual, hierarchical or egalitarian. When a parent cooks dinner for the family, he or she does tasks similar to those performed by a cook employed by a hospital to prepare meals for patients. However, the social relations involved are quite different. Hospital cooks have more in common (in this sense) with factory or office workers than with parents, because their activities are governed by rules and regulations. They accept 'instructions' from the employer or the employer's agent, a manager. Obviously, then, it is not the nature of the activity that determines whether it is considered 'work', but rather the nature of the social relations in which the activity is embedded. Thus, to be 'in work' is to have a definite relationship with some other who has control of the time, place and activity.

Finally, work is remunerated (that is, there is a reward for it). There are two types of reward, extrinsic and intrinsic. The worker provides physical effort and/or mental application, and accepts fatigue and the loss of control over his or her time. In return, the extrinsic work rewards that he or she usually receives consist (primarily) of wages and bonuses. The intrinsic rewards he or she might get from the job include status and recognition from his or her peers.

extrinsic reward: a wide range of external outcomes or rewards to motivate employees

intrinsic reward: inner satisfaction following some action (such as recognition by an employer or co-workers) or intrinsic pleasures derived from an activity (such as playing a musical instrument for pleasure)

Although our definition helps us to identify key features of work, it is too narrow and restrictive. First, not all work, either physical or mental, is remunerated. We cannot assume that there is a simple relationship in which 'work' means a paid employment or occupation, 'real' work that is remunerated. Our definition obscures as much as it reveals. Most people would agree that some activities that are unpaid count as work. This work can be exhilarating or exhausting. Some of it is household-based work – cooking, child rearing, cleaning and so on – and some of it is done voluntarily, for the good of society – for instance, working for the Citizen's Advice Bureau. The activities that are done in the course of this unpaid or 'hidden' work are identical to those in some paid jobs, such as working in a nursery or advising people on their legal rights. Is it fair to exclude it simply because it is not paid?

---

weblink

Go to the following websites for more information on employment trends: in Britain (www.statistics.gov.uk), Canada (www.statcan.ca/start.html and the Canadian Labour Force Development Board www.hrmguide.net/canada/), the European Union (www.eurofound.europa.eu/eiro), the USA (www.bls.gov and www.hreonline.com, South Africa (www.statssa.gov.za) and Brazil (www.ibge.gov.br/english/)

Furthermore, whether an activity is experienced as work or non-work or leisure is dependent on social relations, cultural conditions, social attitudes and how various activities are perceived by others. So, for example, 'an active woman, running a house and bringing up children, is distinguished from a woman who works: that is to say, takes paid employment' (ref. 13, p. 335). Historically, unpaid work is undertaken disproportionately by one-half of the population: women. This concentrates on paid work, and as a consequence we largely omit the critically important area of women's unpaid work in the household, but that is not to suggest that we see it as unimportant.

Second, our definition of paid work says little about how employment opportunities are shaped by gender, ethnicity, age and abilities or disabilities. For example, when women do have access to paid work, they tend to receive less pay than men doing similar work. Women are disproportionately represented in paid work that involves tasks similar to those they carry out in their domestic life – catering, nursing, teaching, clerical and retail employment. Ethnic and racially defined minorities experience chronic disadvantage in paid work because of racism in organizations and in recruitment. The likelihood of participating in paid work varies with age and certain types of work. For example, young people are disproportionately represented in more physically demanding paid work. Disabled adults, especially disabled young adults, experience higher levels of unemployment and under-employment than do those who are able bodied.[21]

Third, paid work can be dangerous and unhealthy, but the hazards are not distributed evenly. Manual workers face more work-related hazards, and have more accidents at work, than do (for example) office workers. It has been argued that this unequal distribution of work-related accidents is not only related to the risks the individuals face, but is also influenced by **values** and economic pressures.

value: a collective idea about what is right or wrong, good or bad, and desirable or undesirable in a particular culture

values: stable, long-lasting beliefs about what is important in a variety of situations

Our approach to understanding the issue of inequality surrounding work involves an analysis of the differential treatment of people based on class, gender and race. We need to look at who does what job, analysing the social and sexual division of labour. We need to consider what sort of occupations there are, and who exercises power or control over the social institutions.

Fourth, our definition obscures an important element of the employment relationship: the *psychological contract*.[22-25] The 'psychological contract' is a metaphor that captures a wide variety of largely unwritten expectations and understandings of the two parties (employer and employee) about their mutual obligations. Denise Rousseau defines it as 'individual beliefs, shaped by the organization, regarding terms of an exchange agreement between individuals and their organization' (ref. 25, p. 9). Most commentators view the concept as a two-way exchange of perceived promises and obligations. The concept has been around since the early 1960s, but in recent years it has become a 'fashionable' framework to support the development of more nuanced understandings of large and small organization employment relationships.[26] We examine this contemporary concept more fully. As we discuss more fully below and throughout, work shapes the employment relationship, the behaviour of all employees, and the relations between men and women inside and outside the workplace, and it has a significant bearing upon personal identity, fulfilment and social life.[27,28]

The development of work

The structure of the labour market and paid work is not static: it reflects patterns of substantial change in the ways in which work is organized in specific industrial sectors. This is the essence of industrialization and a new emerging form of life – modernity. In this section, we trace the emergence of new work forms, starting with the Industrial Revolution (around 1780–1830) in Britain and finishing with a look at employment in what has been called 'post-industrial' work.

Industrial Revolution: the relatively rapid economic transformation that began in Britain in the 1780s. It involved a factory- and technology-driven shift from agriculture and small cottage-based manufacturing to manufacturing industries, and the consequences of that shift for virtually all human activities

stop reflect

Do you think that managers need to manage the employment relationship differently for knowledge workers and for manual industrial workers? Why and how?

We provide this brief historical overview of work because, in our view, it provides a perspective on contemporary work issues and problems, which often result from decisions made in the past. Additionally, when we look at how work forms have developed, it becomes apparent that most 'new' work forms have deep historical roots. Contemporary management gurus might claim to have 'discovered' the importance of informal work-related learning, but such a mode of learning was important in the apprenticeship system of pre-industrial Europe. Similarly, that 'virtual' home-based work reduces the need for office space and costs was well understood by employers in the eighteenth century who operated the 'putting-out' system of home-working discussed below. In effect, these claims of 'new' or 'innovative', when viewed through a historical lens, might be a rediscovery of past practices that had been forgotten or abandoned.

Before we retrace the organization of work in the economy, we need to take a moment to make some general observations and highlight some challenges that this task presents. The history of work emphasizes that work is a social activity, not an individual one. Even those who work alone do so within a socially constructed network of relations among people associated with the pursuit of economic activity. History tends to contradict the suggestion that divisions on the basis of class, gender and race are systematic features created by, and found solely in, industrial capitalism. The social inequality of work, however, long predates the rise of capitalism. The history of industrial capitalism fosters the image of work as a predominantly male activity, separate from, and unrelated to, the home. Again, this is historically atypical: 'home and the place of work have always been, and still are, intimately connected by a seamless web of social interdependence' (ref. 29, p. 46).

the economy: the social institution that ensures the maintenance of society through the production, distribution and consumption of goods and services

> **stop reflect**
>
> To what extent does a 'good' or 'bad' work design depend on which approach we use and which theorist we believe?

Studying work and organizational forms from a historical perspective is a challenge for a number of reasons. By its very nature, such an exercise involves a compression of time periods and of different ways of organizing work. As Eric Hobsbawm wrote, 'The past is a permanent dimension of the human consciousness, an inevitable component of institutions, values and other patterns of human society (ref. 30, p. 10). The problem for social theorists is to avoid presenting the emergence of new work forms as a coherent, orderly and inevitable process of change.

Looking back from the vantage point of the early twenty-first century, it might seem reasonable to talk of the emergence of the factory, or of new forms of management control. But, as others have pointed out, the development of new work forms and social relations took place piecemeal, sporadically and slowly – and frequently they were resisted. Many features of work in the pre-industrial economy (the period before 1780) survived until late into the nineteenth and twentieth centuries, and similarly many twentieth work forms survive in the early twenty-first century. When we outline general trends, this not only compresses wide variations and collapses time periods, but also attaches a coherent pattern to these changes, which they did not show in reality.[31,32]

With this caveat, the rest of this section examines pre-industrial work, the transition to factory forms of work, the significance of concentrated production, the rise of trade unions and the interventions of the state.[30]

Pre-industrial work

In the middle of the eighteenth century, the most striking feature of the economy in Europe was the importance of agriculture as a basic human activity. Manufacturing operated on a small scale, employed labour-intensive methods and used little fixed capital. Agricultural and industrial work was characterized by low productivity. Population growth created an ever-growing class of landless labourers who were compelled to relocate to towns and sell their labour power to survive. The human movement to the new cities was critical for industrial capitalism to develop. As Max Weber explained, 'only where ... workers under the compulsion of the whip of hunger, offer themselves' to employers does capitalism develop.[33]

labour power: the potential gap between a worker's capacity or potential to work and its exercise

Before 1780, the English economy was characterized by regulation. The central government intervened in the economy. The Statute of Artificers of 1563, for example, set the level of wages and conditions of employment, regulated the mobility of labour (as the government did during the Second World War, 1939–45), and protected and promoted, by force if necessary, domestic manufacturing and trade. In the towns, craft guilds regulated all activities related to their trade, including apprenticeship training, wages and prices, and standards of work.

Away from the town-based guilds, the rural-based putting-out system was a feature of the pre-Industrial Revolution manufacturing of woollen garments and many branches of metal working. The putting-out system was a decentralized method of manufacturing that, in the case of producing woollen cloth for example, involved the various processes of combing, spinning and weaving the wool usually being performed by different workers in their cottages. Such a form of work organization had profound consequences for the social organization of work and the nature of workers' reactions to the Industrial Revolution:

putting-out system: a pre-industrial, home-based form of production in which the dispersed productive functions were coordinated by an entrepreneur

> It could not be used in industries requiring bulky plant and power-driven machinery. Neither was it suitable for crafts demanding a high degree of skill or which needed close supervision ... Even when technical conditions were favourable to the use of out-workers, high costs of distribution and losses arising from pilfering and fraud by the workers were serious weaknesses. (ref. 34, p. 102)

Thus, the putting-out system, a pre-modern variant of home-working, contained considerable rigidities and inefficiencies, which were apparent when markets expanded and there was a need for large-scale manufacturing.

Gender-based patterns of work predate industrial capitalism. In the pre-industrial European family, both men and women produced goods for the household and were also engaged in paid work as part of the putting-out system, but depending on local norms and customs, there were 'rather strict ideas about women's work and men's work within the specific community' (ref. 35, p. 55).

Moreover, work was 'a social activity circumscribed by custom and traditions that went deeper than the cash nexus' (ref. 29, p. 52), and work and family life were not regarded as separate spheres.

Factory-based work

The traditional work rhythms and practices of pre-industrial society gave way to the specialization and discipline of the factory system. We can describe the Industrial Revolution as a fundamental change in the structure of the economy, in which the capitalists' pursuit and accumulation of profit guided the mode of organizing work, harnessing technology and determining the social relations of work. The change was characterized by the rise of the factory, a combination of power technology and specialized machines with specialized occupations. The significance of the concentration of workers lay in the potential for extending the division of labour, installing machines, regulating the flow of raw materials, and controlling and moulding workers' behaviour to meet the specific needs of large-scale production.

factory system: a relatively large work unit that concentrated people and machines in one building, enabling the specialization of productive functions and, at the same time, a closer supervision of employees than did the pre-industrial putting-out system. Importantly, the factory system gave rise to the need for a new conception of time and organizational behaviour

Here, the focus is on the division of labour within the factory organized by the owner. The factory offered the opportunity to improve each specialized task through the use of innovative technology, more than was possible with the decentralized putting-out system: 'The very division of labour ... prepared the ground from which mechanical invention could eventually spring,' wrote one historian (ref. 36, p. 145). The factory also enabled a tighter control of the work in process than was possible with the domestic system. With the putting-out system, it was difficult to control the behaviour of cottage-based workers because the employer had 'no way of compelling his [sic] workers to do a given number of hours of labour; the domestic weaver or craftsman was master of his time, starting and stopping when he [sic] desired' (ref. 37, p. 59). The factory system offered new opportunities for controlling the pace and quality of work by the 'discipline of mechanization' – the actual speed of the machine – and by a hierarchy of control over the work in process.

division of labour: the allocation of work tasks to various groups or categories of employee

Historians have debated the role of technology in factory work organization. For example, it is argued that the origins of management within capitalist production lie not in the extended division of labour created by technical developments, but in the desire for social control on the part of capitalists, so that levels of exploitation could be increased.[38] Factories were not the inevitable results of technical change, nor were they the inexorable results of the search for simple efficiency. The architecture of the new factories had much in common with prisons. Jeremy Bentham coined the term 'panopticon' in 1816 to describe a circular building that

Work and Society: Were socialist firms inefficient?

In a study published over two decades ago, Michael Burawoy asked a provocative question: 'Can state socialist firms be as efficient as capitalist firms?' To answer this question, he and a colleague, Janos Lukacs, studied two machine shops – one in the USA (which they called Allied) and one in Hungary (which they called Banki). Their answer may surprise some readers. In the conclusion to their analysis of the two firms, Burawoy and his co-investigator offered the following summary of their key ideas:

We have argued that the technical efficiency at Banki's machine shop was greater than at Allied's. In comparison to Allied, Banki operators work as hard if not harder and produce higher quality work, norms are better adjusted to jobs, pressure for inno- vation is more continuous, planning on the shop floor is more effective, the external labor market is better able to tie rewards to skills and experience, and bureaucratic rules that interfere with production are more limited. (p. 734)

Among the rationales for this study was a belief that existing views of work in socialist societies were dominated by stereotypes. Burawoy and Lukacs hoped that their research would help readers move beyond these stereotypes towards a more accurate picture of work in the two kinds of society. Their article succeeds in unmask- ing some of the myths that have led to false or superficial accounts of the differences between capitalist and socialist ways of organizing work.

This is no small achievement. In the period after the Second World War, the war of ideology (the Cold War) between the West and the USSR made it difficult to engage in objective comparative analysis of different aspects of life in capitalist and socialist societies. Burawoy and Lukacs broke new ground in their efforts to demon- strate how such research ought to be conducted.

Two features of their research stand out as particularly noteworthy. Both Burawoy and Lukacs spent time working at the machine shops they studied. As a result, they offer detailed accounts of what was actually happening on the shop floor. An accu- rate description of what is happening in two different contexts is a necessary element of high-quality comparative research.

But an accurate and detailed description of social reality is not the only strength of this particular research study. Burawoy and Lukacs also devote considerable atten- tion to the question of causal mechanisms. Put differently: not only do they describe *how* the two patterns of work organization vary, but they also develop an explana- tion of *why* the two patterns of work organization vary. For example, a key differ- ence between the two firms was the willingness of workers and local management to innovate. In the socialist firm levels of innovation were relatively high, while in the capitalist firm levels of innovation were relatively low. How do Burawoy and Lukacs explain this counter-intuitive finding?

They argue that, as a division of a large multinational company, the capitalist firm was forced to adhere to strict rules for organizing production imposed by its corpo- rate headquarters. The capitalist firm had to produce a predetermined number of engines of a specified type, and there was no incentive to innovate. For the socialist firm, however, there was an incentive to innovate. There was some pressure to reduce over time the amount workers would be paid for a specified output (to 'tighten' production norms). However, production norms would be relaxed if management introduced 'New machines or new products' (p. 729). The prospect of looser production norms appealed to both management and workers. As a result, there were higher levels of innovation in the socialist firm. This incentive for innovation is evident in other socialist firms as well: 'in the Hungarian steel industry,' Burawoy and Lukacs note, 'managers [could] more than double their income through sponsoring innovations' (p. 729).

One may question the causal analysis offered by Burawoy and Lukacs, and suggest other possible causes of the innovations they observed in the socialist firm. Perhaps, for example, this willingness to innovate reflected local craft traditions that existed before the industrial revolution and before the socialist takeover of Hungary. It would also be instructive to look at one of Toyota's machine shops to understand how the Japanese system supports or fails to support innovation.

stop! This article encourages you to examine your assumptions about the superiority of particular ways of organizing work. Many successful businesses assumed that their success would last for ever. They assumed further that their approach to organizing work was superior to all others. Can you think of once-successful companies whose current difficulties stem in part from complacency with regard to the organization of work? How might successful companies avoid the trap of complacency?

Sources and further information

Burawoy, M. and Lukacs, J. (1985) 'Mythologies of work: a comparison of firms in state socialism and advanced capitalism', *American Sociological Review*, 50(6), pp. 723–37.
Harvard Business Review on Manufacturing Excellence at Toyota, Boston, MA: Harvard Business School Press, 2008.
Ragin, C. (1994) *Constructing Social Research*, Thousand Oaks, CA: Pine Forge Press.

Note: This feature was written by David MacLennan, Assistant Professor at Thompson Rivers University, BC, Canada.

could provide 'hierarchical observation' and 'normalizing judgement' (Figure 8.1). Observing Victorian architecture and Bentham's idea of a panopticon, the twentieth-century philosopher Michel Foucault asked, 'Is it surprising that prison resembles factories, schools, barracks, hospitals, which all resemble prisons?' (ref. 33, p. 30). The suggestion is that the factory, with its specialization and logical flows of processes, provided capitalists with a formal role as managers or coordinators. An alternative interpretation for the new forms of organizing work emphasizes the inadequacy of the family-based putting-out system in the face of expanding markets.[39]

The new factory system transformed the social organization of work. Factories needed a disciplined workforce. In this lay another key development associated with factory-based work – the shaping of workers' behaviour based on new concepts of commitment and time. In the early period of industrialization, changing workers' behaviour had a number of aspects: both entering the factory itself, and

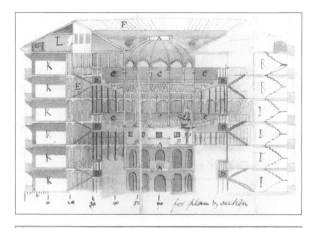

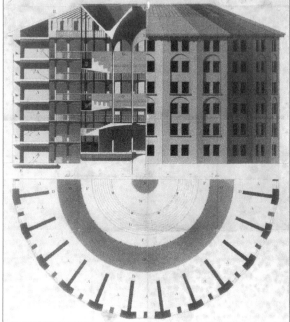

Figure 8.1   The panopticon building

the **work ethic**. Workers, particularly men, were reluctant to enter the factories, with their unaccustomed rules and discipline, because they 'lost their birthright, independence' (ref. 40, p. 51). The majority of workers were women and children, who were more pliant and easier to manage.

work ethic: a set of values that stresses the importance of work to the identity and sense of worth of the individual and encourages an attitude of diligence in the mind of the people

Once in the factory, the employers had to develop 'appropriate' and 'responsible' behaviour that met the needs of the new work regime. This involved the management instilling in workers attitudes of obedience to factory and punctuality. What the employers required was a 'new breed of worker behaviour reacted favourably to the inexorable demands of the pace-machine, factory rationality and the 'tyranny of the clock'. The process took several generations: 'by the division of labour; the supervision of labour; fines; bells and clocks; money incentives; preaching and schooling; the suppression of fairs and sports – new labour habits were formed, and a new time-discipline was imposed' (ref. 41, p. 90). From the preoccupation with workers' work motivation and behaviour, there eventually emerged a specialized branch of management: personnel, or human resource management.

OB in focus
The working week – a matter for the law?

These days, people increasingly expect businesses to be open all hours – yet many companies are having to lay off workers as a result of a downturn in the global economy. As a result, staff are under increasing pressure to deliver more and work harder. Does the law need to intervene?

The European Union Working Time Directive states that working hours should not exceed 48 hours per week, which is causing problems in the UK, as the National Health Service struggles to comply with this rule and reduce doctors' working hours without compromising on care (1). Across the Channel in France, the much-vaunted 35 hour working week, introduced in 2000, has effectively been abolished under a new law passed in 2008 allowing companies to 'strike individual deals with unions on working hours and overtime'(2). Canada is grappling with similar issues as it considers whether middle managers (who are currently 'not covered by labour standards legislation'(3)) should be offered protection.

What do *you* think? What role should the law, and trade unions, play in determining working conditions? Should these laws apply equally to all job types? Are there any cases where 'long hours come with the territory?'(3).

Sources: (1) 'Doctors warn over working rules', BBC news online, May 27, 2009. (2) 'MPs scrap France's 35-hour week', BBC news online, July 24, 2008. (3) Gate, V. (2005) 'Worn-out middle managers may get protection: Labour Code review could expand reach', *Globe and Mail*, January 3, p. B1.

Taylorism and Fordism

In this section, we turn to what others call 'classical' work organization – Taylorism and Fordism. They are considered classical partly because they represent the earliest contributions to modern management theory, but they are also classical because they identify ideas and issues that keep occurring in contemporary organizational behaviour and management literature, although writers now tend to use a different

regulations
whose
etting
eral

Plate 2   The First World War (1914-18) saw large numbers of women finding employment in the munitions and engineering factories
Source: Nick Hedges.

vocabulary.[42] We will now consider each of these influential classical approaches to work organization.

Taylorism

The American Frederick W. Taylor (1856–1915) pioneered the scientific management approach to work organization, hence the term Taylorism. Taylor developed his ideas on work organization while working as superintendent at the Midvale Steel Company in Pennsylvania, USA. Taylorism represents both a set of management practices and a system of ideological assumptions.[27] The autonomy (freedom from control) of craft workers was potentially a threat to managerial control. For the craft worker, the exercise of control over work practices was closely linked to his personality, as this description of 'craft pride', taken from the trade journal *Machinery* in 1915, suggests:

Taylorism: a process of determining the division of work into its smallest possible skill elements, and how the process of completing each task can be standardized to achieve maximum efficiency. Also referred to as scientific management

[The craftsman] is engaged in tasks where the capacity for original thought is exercised: he has refined and critical perceptions of the things pertaining to his craft. His work creates a feeling of self-reliance ... he lives a full and satisfying life. (ref. 43, p. 97)

As a first-line manager, Taylor not surprisingly viewed the position of skilled shop-floor workers differently. He was appalled by what he regarded as inefficient working practices and the tendency of his subordinates not to put in a full day's work, what Taylor called 'natural soldiering'. He believed that workers who did manual work were motivated solely by money – the image of the 'greedy robot' – and were too stupid to develop the most efficient way of performing a task – the 'one best way'. The role of management was to analyse 'scientifically' all the tasks to be undertaken, and then to design jobs to eliminate time and motion waste.

Taylor's approach to work organization and employment relations was based on the following five principles:

- maximum job fragmentation
- separate planning and doing
- separate 'direct' and 'indirect' labour
- a minimization of skill requirements
- a minimization of handling component parts and material.

The centrepiece of scientific management is the separation of tasks into their simplest constituent elements – 'routinization of work' (the first principle). Most manual workers were viewed as sinful and stupid, and therefore all decision-making functions had to be removed from their hands (the second principle). All preparation and servicing tasks should be taken away from the skilled worker (direct labour), and, drawing on Charles Babbage's principle, performed by unskilled and cheaper labour (indirect labour, in the third principle). Minimizing the skill requirements to perform a task would reduce the worker's control over work activities or the labour process (the fourth principle). Finally, management should ensure that the layout of the machines on the factory floor minimized the movement of people and materials to shorten the time taken (the fifth principle).

While the logic of work fragmentation and routinization is simple and compelling, the principles of Taylorism reflect the class antagonism that is found in employment relations. When Taylor's principles were applied to work organization, they led to the intensification of work: to 'speeding up', 'deskilling' and new techniques to control workers, as shown in Figure 8.2. And since gender, as we have discussed, is both a system of classification and a structure of power relations, it should not surprise us that Taylorism contributed to the shift in the gender composition of engineering firms. As millions of men were recruited into the armed forces for the

First World War (1914–18), job fragmentation and the production of standardized items such as rifles, guns and munitions enabled women 'dilutees' to be employed in what had previously been skilled jobs reserved exclusively for men.[43]

> **stop reflect**
>
> Can you think of jobs in the retail and service sector that would support the charge that work systems in the modern workplace continue to be affected by neo-Taylorism?

Some writers argue that Taylorism was a relatively short-lived phenomenon, which died in the economic depression of the 1930s.[44] However, others have argued that this view underestimates the spread and influence of Taylor's principles: 'the popular notion that Taylorism has been "superseded" by later schools of "human relations", that it "failed" … represents a woeful misreading of the actual dynamics of the development of management' (ref. 45, p. 56). Similarly, others have made a persuasive case that, 'In general the direct and indirect influence of Taylorism on factory jobs has been extensive, so that in Britain job design and technology design have become imbued with neo-Taylorism' (ref. 10, p. 73).

Fordism

Henry Ford (1863–1947) applied the major principles of scientific management in his car plant, as well as installing specialized machines and adding a crucial innovation to Taylorism: the flow-line principle of assembly work. This kind of work organization has come to be called Fordism. The moving assembly line had a major impact on employment relations. It exerted greater control over how workers

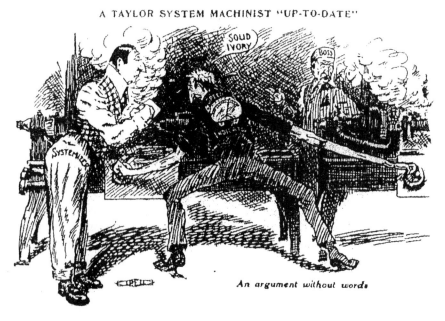

Figure 8.2   A craft union response to Taylorism

performed their tasks, and it involved the intensification of work and labour productivity through ever-greater job fragmentation and short task-cycle times. In 1922, Henry Ford stated his approach to managing shop-floor workers: 'The idea is that man ... must have every second necessary but not a single unnecessary second' (ref. 46, p. 33).

Fordism: a term used to describe mass production using assembly-line technology that allowed for greater division of labour and time and motion management, techniques pioneered by the American car manufacturer Henry Ford in the early twentieth century

The speed of work on the assembly line is determined by the technology itself rather than by a series of written instructions. Management's control of the work process was also enhanced by a detailed time and motion study inaugurated by Taylor. Work study engineers attempted to discover the shortest possible task-cycle time. Recording job times meant that managers could monitor more closely their subordinates' effort levels and performance. Task measurement therefore acted as the basis of a new structure of control.

Fordism is also characterized by two other essential features. The first was the introduction of an interlinking system of conveyor lines that fed components to different work stations to be worked on, and the second was the standardization of commodities to gain economies of scale. Thus, Fordism established the long-term principle of the mass production of standardized commodities at a reduced cost.

Ford's production system was, however, not without its problems. Workers found the repetitive work boring and unchallenging, and their job dissatisfaction was expressed in high rates of absenteeism and turnover. In 1913, for example, the turnover of Ford workers was more than 50,000. The management techniques developed by Ford in response to these employment problems serve further to differentiate Fordism from Taylorism. Henry Ford introduced the 'five dollar day' – double the pay and shorter hours for those who qualified. Benefits depended on a factory worker's lifestyle being deemed satisfactory, which included abstaining from alcohol. Ford's style of paternalism attempted to inculcate new social habits, as well as new labour habits, that would facilitate job performance.

Taylorism and Fordism became the predominant approaches to job design in vehicle and electrical engineering – the large-batch production industries – in the USA and Britain.[10,46]

Post-Fordism

As a strategy of organizing work and people, Taylorism and Fordism had their limitations. First, work simplification led to boredom and dissatisfaction, and tended to encourage adversarial relations and conflict, including frequent work stoppages. Second, Taylor-style work involves control and coordination costs. As specialization increases, so do indirect labour costs as more production planners, supervisors and quality control inspectors are employed. The economies associated with the division of labour tend to be offset by the diseconomies of management control costs.

Third, Taylorism and Fordism affect what might be called 'cooperation costs'. As management's control over the quantity and quality of workers' performance increases, workers experience increased frustration and dissatisfaction, which leads to a withdrawal of their commitment to the organization. The relationship between controller and controlled can deteriorate so much that it results in a further increase in management control. The principles of Taylorism and Fordism thus reveal a basic paradox, 'that the tighter the control of labour power, the more control is needed' (ref. 10, pp. 36–7). The adverse reactions to the extreme division of labour led to the development of new approaches to work organization that attempted to address these problems.

The 'human relations' movement attempted to address the limitations of Taylorism and Fordism by shifting attention to the perceived psychological and social needs of workers. The movement grew out of the Hawthorne experiments conducted by Elton Mayo in the 1920s. Mayo set up an experiment in the relay assembly room at the Hawthorne Works in Chicago, USA, which was designed to test the effects on productivity of variations in working conditions (lighting, temperature and ventilation). The Hawthorne research team found no clear relationship between any of these factors and productivity. However, the study led the researchers to develop concepts that might explain the factors affecting worker motivation. They concluded that more than just economic incentives and the work environment motivated workers: recognition and social cohesion were important too.

The message for management was also quite clear: rather than depending on management controls and financial incentives, it needed to influence the work group by cultivating a culture that met the social needs of workers. The human relations movement advocated various techniques such as worker participation and non-authoritarian supervisors, which would, it was thought, promote a climate of good (neo)-human relations in which the quantity and quality needs of management could be met. This largely forgotten history, which examined concepts such as atmosphere, informal structures and organizational climate, reminds us that twenty-first-century culturalist scholarship is not a completely new development in the thinking about organizations.[47]

Criticisms of the human relations approach charged managerial bias and the fact that its advocates tended to play down the basic economic conflict of interest between the employer and employee. Critics pointed out that when the techniques were tested, it became apparent that workers did not inevitably respond as predicted. The human relations approach also neglects wider socioeconomic factors (see ref. 12 for an excellent critical analysis of this approach to work). Despite these criticisms, however, the human relations approach to job design began to have some impact on management practices in the post-Second World War environment of full employment.

In the 1970s, new approaches to work design stressed the principles of closure, whereby the scope of the job is such that it includes all the tasks to complete a product or process, and task variety, whereby the worker acquires a range of different skills so that job flexibility is possible and the worker can personally monitor the quantity and quality of the work. This thinking spawned new techniques such as 'job enrichment', which gave the worker a wider range of tasks to perform and some discretion over how those tasks were done. For example, in the context of a fast-food outlet, an employee's job would, instead of being limited to grilling burgers, be enlarged to grilling the burgers, preparing the salad, ordering the produce from the wholesaler and inspecting the quality of the food on delivery.

Some theorists have been critical of these new work designs. An influential study argues that although job enrichment techniques may increase job satisfaction and commitment, the key focus remains managerial control. Although post-Fordism work design strategies gave individuals or work groups a wider measure of discretion over their work, or 'responsible autonomy', the strategy is a 'tool of self-discipline' and a means of maintaining or even intensifying managerial control.

With the growth of call centres over the past decade, critical research has drawn attention to 'new' forms of Taylorism. It is alleged that sophisticated electronic eavesdropping on salesperson–client conversations, and peer group scrutiny, have created 'electronic sweatshops' or a form of 'electronic Taylorism'.[12,48-50]

Work teams and high-performance workplaces

The favoured work configuration over the last two decades has been team working. The focus on work teams has grown out of, drawn upon and sometimes reacted against Taylorism and Fordism.[42] The centrepiece of team working is functional

> **weblink**
>
> Go to the 2004 Workplace Employee Relations Survey website www.berr.gov.uk for more information on trends in work organization

flexibility, with members undertaking a wide range of tasks with a high degree of autonomy.

In the 1980s, Japanese work and employment practices were held up as a model for the struggling UK and North American manufacturing sectors.[51-55] The Japanese model has been a 'contested concept' in its description, interpretation and explanation.[56] Pioneering interpretations of the model identify three notable elements: flexibility, quality control and minimum waste.

Flexibility is achieved by arranging machinery in a group – what is known as 'cellular technology' – and by employing a multiskilled workforce. Thus, the work organization is the opposite of that of 'Taylorism': a generalized, skilled machinist with flexible job boundaries is a substitute for the specialized machinist operating one machine in one particular workstation. Higher-quality standards are achieved by making quality every worker's responsibility. Minimum waste, the third element of the Japanese model, is achieved by just-in-time techniques. As the name suggests, this is a hand-to-mouth mode of manufacture that aims to produce no more than the necessary components, in the necessary quantities, of the necessary quality and at the necessary time. Team working has a cultural and social dimension. The practices aim to generate social cohesion and a 'moral commitment' to common organizational goals.

The managerial mantra of the 1990s was flexibility, although various terms were used to describe these fashions in work organization: flexible specialization or 'flexspec', 'lean production', 're-engineering' and 'high-performance work systems' are well established in the literature. In the late 1990s, Japan experienced slow economic growth, and thereafter the US model of work organization was again held up as the exemplar. The new debate focused on whether the high-performance workplace, comprising a combination of work and employment variables or 'bundles' of 'best' practices, can deliver comparative advantage.

Post-industrial work

The 'Information Revolution', which we date from 1980 with the development of the silicon chip, marks, as does the Industrial Revolution 200 years earlier, a fundamental transformation of human activity. One theme running through this chapter has been the continuities as well as the discontinuities across time. There is no doubt that, for many people, paid work has changed profoundly during the Information Age, but these changes must be set in a historical context if we are to appreciate their significance and relevance.

Critical insight

As you study organizational behaviour, you should look at less orthodox material – expanding voices – as well as the established experts in the field. Leslie Salzinger's book *Genders in Production* is an example of the kinds of other voice it is useful to consider.[57] Through case studies of employment and management in four different transnational factories, the author provides a sophisticated analysis of gender relations in the workplace. She explains the variability and flexibility of concepts of femininity and masculinity, and the fact that they are context-dependent behaviours.

As Salzinger asserts, in a globalized world the creation of 'cheap labour' is central to the economic process. However, although the young women at the factories she studied are generally perceived to be intrinsically 'cheap, docile, and dextrous', she comments that 'Panoptimex, like all effective arenas of production, makes not only TVs but workers.'

Obtain a copy of Salzinger's book, 'Producing women – femininity on the line'. What does Salzinger mean when she states that Panoptimex makes not only TVs but also workers?

Knowledge work

The emergence of knowledge work – intellectual capital – and the 'knowledge worker' – employees who carry knowledge as a powerful resource which they, rather than the organization, own – is closely associated with the contemporary, sophisticated, Internet-based information technologies. Defining the notion of knowledge work and knowledge worker has proven problematic. Following Horwitz et al., however, we can say that knowledge work is characterized as 'ambiguity intensive', and a knowledge worker is an individual with the ability to communicate and apply professional knowledge, as well as manage other employees (see ref. 58, p. 31).

knowledge work: paid work that is of an intellectual nature, non-repetitive and result-oriented, engages scientific and/or artistic knowledge, and demands continuous learning and creativity

The nature of knowledge work is said to be fundamentally different from what we have traditionally associated with the 'machine age' and mass production, and hence it requires a different order of employment relations. It should not be confused with routine clerical work. It requires knowledge workers to learn a broad range of skills and knowledge, often with a focus around problems or customers, and to work in small groups or project teams to co-create new insights. It is also said to require a different employment relationship, with a psychological contract that has implications for employee commitment and career trajectory.

These differences in the nature of traditional work and knowledge work are spelled out in Table 8.1. In the Information Age, when an organization's wealth and ability to compete may exist 'principally in the heads of its employees' and human competitiveness can effectively 'walk out the gates' every day, it is not surprising that organizations are concerned with 'better' human resource practices and 'knowledge management' (ref. 59, p. 48). Information technology, new employment contracts and knowledge work have changed the 'spatiality' of work: some people do paid work at home, and others undertake more short-term work assignments as organizations reduce their 'core' employees and contract work out.[19] Critical accounts of contemporary work in advanced capitalist economies offer a counterweight to the bullish management perspectives on the knowledge economy and provide data showing that the International Labour Organization's definition of 'decent work' remains elusive only for the privileged minority.[60,61] As European studies attest, there are too many businesses taking the 'low road' and striving for competitive advantage on the basis of a low-skill and low-pay workplace.[2]

Table 8.1 The nature of traditional work and knowledge work

	Traditional work	Knowledge work
Skill/knowledge sets	Narrow and often functional	Specialized and deep, but often with diffuse peripheral focuses
Locus of work	Around individuals	In groups and projects
Focus of work	Tasks, objectives, performance	Customers, problems, issues
Skill obsolescence	Gradual	Rapid
Activity/feedback cycles	Primary and of an immediate nature	Lengthy from a business perspective
Performance measures	Task deliverables Little (as planned), but regular and dependable	Process effectiveness Potentially great, but often erratic
Career formation	Internal to the organization through training, development, rules and prescriptive career schemes	External to the organization, through years of education and socialization
Employee's loyalty	To organization and his or her career systems	To professions, networks and peers
Impact on company success	Many small contributions that support the master plan	A few major contributions of strategic and long-term importance

Source: adapted from Despres and Hiltrop (1995)[102] and Boud and Garrick (1999)[59].

Emotional work

With the growth of routinized service work, with its demands of customer sovereignty – such as fast food, tourism, hotels and call centres – new kinds of social relationship and aspects of the self have developed and come under scrutiny. As the service sector has grown in importance, there has, not surprisingly, been a growing interest in the embodied attributes and dispositions that are stereotypically feminine, such as patience, deference to the customer and a pleasant demeanour, associated with what sociologists call 'emotional labour'. Much has been written in recent years on how emotion is an important part of the effort–wage exchange, that workplaces in general have 'emotions',[62,63] and that 'strong' cultures strive to engender emotional energy, affection and even love for the organization.

Although the sociological analysis of workplace emotions is an expanding field of research, the classical sociological canons of Marx, Durkheim and Weber do contain important ideas about emotions. For instance, alienation engendered feelings of anger, and sentimentality was eliminated in bureaucracies gripped in the 'iron cage' of rationality. Modern critical scholarship emphasizes the servility of routine interactive workers within the service interface.[64]

It was the pioneering work of Arlie Hochschild that drew attention to the significance of social interaction as a crucial element of service provision. She considered emotional labour as part of the employment contract when 'the emotional style of offering the service is part of the service itself'.[65] Although servers in restaurants have always been trained to 'serve with a smile', there has been growing recognition that emotional labour is far more significant for a larger proportion than this of service employees, as management theorists emphasize 'customer service' as a vital aspect of business competitiveness. Emotional labour exists when workers are required, as part of the wage–effort bargain, to show emotions with the specific aim of causing customers or clients to feel and respond in a particular way. They might do this by verbal means – 'Good morning, sir/madam' – or non-verbal means, for example by smiling. Thus, the recent interest in emotional labour is focused on mobilizing emotions into the 'service' of the organization as an added dimension of the 'self' that the organization can appropriate, as has traditionally occurred with physical and mental labour.[66]

It is important to understand that emotional labour, like physical and intellectual labour, is bought by the employer for a wage. It requires a specific set of attributes and behaviours, and it can be a potential source of stress and alienation. Emotional labour 'carries the potential for individuals to become self-estranged – detached from their own "real" feelings – which in turn might threaten their sense of their own identity' (ref. 15, p. 193). The embodied attributes and skills associated with emotional labour compromise a particular type of working-class masculine identity. Manual labour has traditionally been a key source of identity, self-esteem and power for many working-class men. Emotional labour, however, is antithetical to muscular masculine identity. A study by Nixon in 2009 suggests that unskilled unemployed male workers were psychologically mismatched to the demands of customer sovereignty.[67] He found that those men who had been employed in service jobs did not last long: 'I've got no patience with people basically. I can't put a smiley face on, that's not my sort of thing,' said one 24-year-old unskilled manual worker. Others said they disliked the pressure to 'chase customers', and found work at call centres involved 'Too much talking' (ref. 67, pp. 314–15). The seismic shifts associated with the 'new economy' appear to have eliminated not only particular types of jobs, but also a type of masculine identity.

Our brief history of work organization suggests that when an economy enjoys economic success, its work and management practices will often be regarded as a model by slower-growing economies.[68] Consistent with this prediction, European organizations adopted US management ideas for most of the twentieth century, and adopted the 'Japanese model' in the 1980s, including team working. The 2004 Workplace and Employee Relations Survey (WERS) provides data on how these work practices are applied in UK workplaces.

Much of the literature on 'new' forms of work simplifies the analysis to a polar comparison between 'traditional' Fordism and new 'post-Fordism' work team characteristics. But although it looks elegant to draw up lists of opposite characteristics, this is not a good reflection of reality.[69,70] We can today still witness old 'boring' work forms existing alongside new 'decent' work configurations. Work in post-industrial capitalism is still routinized in both the manufacturing and the service sectors. In this brave new world of work, task variety is low, skill requirements are low, security and dignity are low, and managerial control, reminiscent of Frederick Taylor's philosophy of a century ago, remains rule bound. All this suggests that the nature of work remains largely unchanged for millions of workers, that the design of work is not a smooth transition from one model to another, and that contemporary work regimes are most likely to resemble a hybrid configuration, with elements from the old work design and parts of the new.

Work in organizations: an integration of ideas

In discussing post-Fordism, we emphasized competing claims over whether new forms of work lead to an enrichment of work or the degradation of work. Managerial optimists argue that new work structures empower employees, and celebrate the claim that managerial behaviour has shifted its focus from 'control' to 'commitment'.[71] Critical analysts contend that some new work regimes are 'electronic sweatshops', and are basically a euphemism for work intensification. To capture the new realities of the modern workplace, critics often use the term 'McWorld' or 'McDonaldization', meaning that a vast amount of work experience, especially for young people, women and workers of colour, involves menial tasks, part-time contracts, close monitoring of performance and entrenched job insecurity (for a good critical review of this trend, see refs 50 and 72–75).

McDonaldization (also known as 'McWork' or 'McJobs'):	a term used to symbolize the new realities of corporate-driven globalization that engulf young people in the twenty-first century, including simple work patterns, electronic controls, low pay and part-time and temporary employment

In Figure 8.3, we draw together the developments in work and employment practices over the last 200 years, by highlighting four paradigms or distinctive approaches: craft/artisan, Taylorism/Fordism, neo-Fordism and post-Fordism. Work is shown to vary along two dimensions: the *variety of work* – the extent to which employees have an opportunity to do a range of tasks using their various skills and knowledge – and the *autonomy in work* – the degree of initiative that employees can exercise over how their immediate work is performed.

Here, *craft/artisan* means the types of work organization that are based on craft-based skills and often associated with a narrow range of specialized tasks, a high

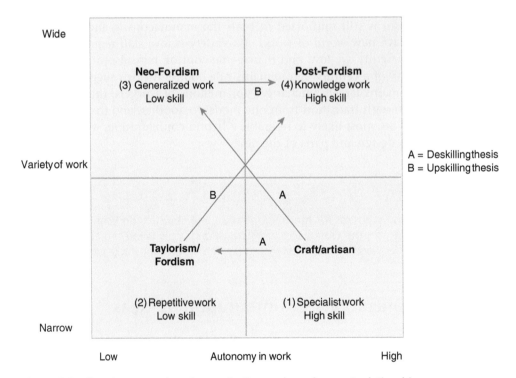

Figure 8.3 Development of work organization and employment relationships

296

level of skill and a high degree of autonomy. Taylorism/Fordism means the adoption of basic scientific management principles and the assembly-line methods pioneered by Henry Ford, and neo-Fordism refers to a work configuration that has modified the core principles of Fordism through flexible working practices to fit contemporary operations. In contrast to the craft/artisan paradigm, the Taylorism/Fordism and neo-Fordism paradigms are often associated with a narrow variety of tasks, a low level of skill and a low degree of autonomy in work. Post-Fordism refers to organizations that do not rely on the principles of Taylorism or Fordism, and is often associated with 'high-performance work systems', with self-management and with a high degree of autonomy in work.

neo-Fordism/post-Fordism: the development from mass production assembly lines to more flexible manufacturing processes

As others have mentioned, the strength of this conceptual model is as a heuristic device – a teaching aid – to help us summarise the complex development of work organization and employment relations. The research on the trends in work design suggests that Taylorism and Fordism have dominated the managerial approaches to work organization.

In addition to the four broad classifications of work organization, the model shows two trends proposed by the proponents of the 'deskilling' and 'upskilling' theses. The deskilling thesis maintains that, in Western capitalist economies, there is a general trend in paid work towards a narrow variety of tasks and low autonomy; the arrows marked 'A' represent this trend in the diagram. The upskilling thesis suggests an opposite trend towards a wide variety of tasks and high autonomy in work; the arrows marked 'B' represents this trend. It is important to understand that different regimes of work organization affect the nature of the employment relationship, whether or not this is explicitly acknowledged in the writings of organizational theorists. For example, if work is reorganized to deskill or upskill employees, this will change the degree of interdependency, and typically the power dynamics, between the employer and employee.

To sum up, some of the more recent empirically based literature offers a context-sensitive understanding of the development of work, and rejects a general tendency towards either deskilling or upskilling. The 'context-sensitive' view makes the point that new work structures do not have uniform outcomes, but are likely to be 'mixed' and contingent on a number of variables, such as business strategy, the nature of new technology, the degree of employee involvement in decision making, union involvement in the change process, and the extent to which 'bundles' of employment practices support the new work regime. In sum, the identification of potential benefits and costs for workers from new work configurations provides a more complex picture, one that strongly supports the hypothesis that changes in the nature of work can strengthen or threaten the 'psychological contract'.

hypotheses: statements making empirically testable declarations that certain variables and their corresponding measure are related in a specific way proposed by theory

hypothesis: in search studies, a tentative statement of the relationship between two or more concepts or variables

Gender and the sexual division of work

Figure 8.3 does not, however, show how gender ideologies shape work or the sexual division of work. To understand contemporary issues of gender – by which we mean the processes of gender roles, inequalities in society and women's subordination and exploitation – we need to look at the historical developments of gender–work patterns.

Gender-based patterns of work and gender inequality were universal in early industrial capitalism. In 1838, over 70 per cent of factory textile workers were adult women and children. Family labour, with women and their children working together, was a feature of employment relations in the new factory system. The factory owner did not accept direct responsibility for the conditions of employment or supervision of the workforce, but subcontracted these people-management functions to an intermediary. Factory owners negotiated with the heads of families for the whole family unit. There is evidence that the worst conditions of employment under industrial capitalism existed in these circumstances. Child labour began at the age of 4 in some cases in order to oblige parents, but most child workers started between the ages of 7 and 10. An adult man entered the new textile factories with his family, and the 'fact that discipline was imposed on the children largely by their own parents made the harshness of the new disciplines socially tolerable' (ref. 76, p. 202).

After 1850, with the exception of waged work in domestic service and textiles, industrial capitalism tended to create a clear distinction between the paid work opportunities of women (particularly married women) and of men. With the spread of the factory system, the need for cheap labour power provided opportunities for working-class women to do wage work in areas unrelated to their former work in the home. Large-scale food-processing factories – for example, bakeries – were female dominated in the late nineteenth century. In working-class families, women often remained in the labour market to support the family income. When middle-class women married, they were primarily expected to withdraw from paid employment to take care of the house and children. Reinforcing the belief that work and family life were two separate spheres – the stereotypes of men as strong and competitive and women as frail and nurturing – began to emerge: 'images that depicted men as naturally suited to the highly competitive nineteenth-century workplace and women as too delicate for the world of commerce' (ref. 77, p. 21).

Gender-based patterns of work changed when war broke out in Europe in 1914. The First World War was the first 'mass' war in the sense that it required the mobilization of massive quantities of products and people. Whereas Napoleon waged war against Prussia in 1806 using no more than 1500 rounds of artillery shells, in 1917 the French munitions industry had to produce 200,000 shells a day: 'Mass war required mass production' (ref. 78, p. 45). It also made it necessary to rethink the social organization of work. As Britain mobilized 12.5 per cent of its able-bodied men for the armed forces, the government encouraged women to enter the munitions and engineering factories, and this led to a revolution in waged work for women outside the household. It resulted in several occupations turning permanently into female preserves, including offices, hotels, shops, cinemas and to a lesser extent transport. In other occupations, such as engineering, men were reabsorbed in 1919 and women went back to pre-war patterns of paid or unpaid work.

Did industrial capitalism segregate the home from work, and allocate women to the former and men to the latter? Gender-based patterns of work and family-located sites of work are forms that predate capitalism: they are not the results of social changes induced by capitalism. Women's work tended to be concentrated around six human activities that predate capitalism: to bear children, to feed them and other members of the family, to clothe the family, to care for the young and old when sick, to educate children, and to take care of the home.[35,79] Explanations for why some work was men's and some was women's are almost as various as the patterns of wages that have existed. In the pre-Industrial Revolution period, there is some evidence that women did a much greater variety of jobs, but even then gender influenced the allocation and reward of work. A disproportionate number of women undertook the most menial, poorly paid and domestically related jobs.

Evidence about work-related gender relations before the nineteenth century is sparse. Contemporary accounts emphasize that the gender division of work is socially constructed, and that work tended to be labelled female or male on the basis of socially changeable expectations about how to view, judge and treat the two sexes. Part of the long historical process of gender inequality at work can be explained by the activities of the pre-industrial craft guilds and the trade unions. The town-based craft guilds, the forerunners of trade unions, tended to be exclusively male oriented, with severe restrictions on women's membership. In the context of competitive pressure to reduce labour costs and the economic effect of female workers in terms of depressing wages, male-dominated trade unions worked hard to maintain or restore wage levels and traditional employment privileges.[80]

trade union: an organization whose purpose is to represent the collective interest of workers

weblink

Go to the following websites for more information on the history of trade unions and current statistics on trade union organization: www.tuc.org.uk; www.icftu.org; www.cosatu.org.za

Trade union bargaining strategies developed gender-based occupational segregation. One function of trade unionism, according to one union leader, was 'to bring about a condition ... where wives and daughters would be in their proper sphere at home, instead of being dragged into competition for livelihood against the great and strong men of the world' (ref. 81, p. 185). Prior to 1858, women participated in medicine quite widely, but thereafter, as in other traditional professions, the work became a male preserve. With the exception of midwifery and nursing, a combination of government legislation and male tactics excluded middle-class women from all medical practices.[82] Feminist critiques of the sociology of work have demonstrated in important ways the manner in which both the theory and practice of work and work behaviour have excluded women as subjects, as well as their experiences and voices.[83]

Married women were systematically removed from waged work after the initial phase of the Industrial Revolution. The new factory system proved beneficial to working-class women, particularly unmarried women, providing waged work outside the grossly exploitative decentralized putting-out system. Throughout the nineteenth century and well into the twentieth century, men managed to effectively exclude working-class and middle-class women from participating in many trade and professional occupations, by retaining old 'skills' or monopolizing new ones, using their professional privilege and power, using strategies of closure and demarcation, and encouraging the concepts of 'skill' and 'profession' to be seen as male property.[84]

In the twenty-first century, although the realities of workplaces have changed, ideas about them have lagged far behind.[85] Many Europeans and North Americans still believe in the 'traditional' male breadwinner/female home-keeper model, even though household lives and financial imperatives no longer reflect it. In Germany, for example, the traditional sense of family roles remains strong, and women who do paid work can be called *Rabenmutter*, meaning a raven mother. Commenting on German social values in 2006, Reiner Klingholz, head of the Berlin Institute for Population and Development, said, 'These old-fashioned ideas about the sexes aren't really part of mainstream German thought any more, but it's still embedded in the neurons of our brains that women have to stay home and take care of the children' (quoted in ref. 86).

---

weblink

Go to the following websites for more information and statistics on women employed in advanced capitalist societies: http://europa.eu/index_en.htm; www.statistics.gov.uk; www.iegd.org

---

Work less, live better? Managing the work–life balance

The interplay between working life, the family and the community, often expressed as 'work–life balance', is a 'hot' topic of debate and research that is receiving increasing attention from policy makers and managers.[87–89] The main message of the debate is that a balance between work and life is desirable, and that too much work has negative effects on private life – in effect, a more sophisticated version of the popular proverb 'All work and no play makes Jack a dull boy.' In spite of the spate of literature, for Warhurst and his colleagues, the current debate on work–life balance remains problematic both empirically and conceptually.[90] Empirical research does indeed reveal a significant degree of interest in many organizations, but data show a mismatch between the work–life balance discourse and the reality in most workplaces.

work–life balance: the interplay between working life, the family and the community, in terms of both time and space

discourse: a way of talking about and conceptualizing an issue, presented through concepts, ideas and vocabulary that recur in texts

This gap is illustrated by the findings from WERS 2006. The European Union Social Charter of 1961 obliged Member States to ensure 'reasonable and weekly working hours', yet research indicates that British workers work the longest hours in the EU-15 Member States.[91] Not surprising, therefore, the UK labour market has been characterized as the 'long hours culture'.[92] Setting a limit on the number of hours an employee must work in a working day and week most directly affects the work–life balance.

The boundary between work and private life is influenced by flexible working arrangements, such as 'home-working'. UK survey data show that the incidence of 'home-working' increased 12 per cent between 1998 and 2004. Women were more likely than men to have access to home-working arrangements, yet home-working was slightly more prevalent in workplaces where women were not in the majority.[93] There are a number of possible causes for this, including inadequate child care provision, non-standard or precarious employment and perhaps, in more recent years, a 'flight to work' in a period of economic uncertainty.

The concept at the centre of the work–life balance debate is problematic. The notion of work–life balance has been defined as 'the relationship between the institutional and cultural times and spaces of work and non-work in societies where income is predominantly generated and distributed through labour markets' (ref. 94, p. 56). Warhurst et al. argue that the concept of work–life *balance* is based on a traditional, large-scale workplace model which presumes that paid work and life constitute two distinct spheres, separated by time and space (Figure 8.4).[90] This orthodox binary interpretation adopts a particular interpretation of labour under capitalism, viewing paid work as an encroachment on people's 'real' private life, particularly family life, and seeing it as something that therefore has to be contained. As the examples and case studies included throughout, work can be boring and alienating – a 'blank patch' between morning and evening – unhealthy and at times dangerous. Yet work brings fulfilment and friendship, and people can potentially derive joy from it.[2] Work brings structure to people's lives, dignity and satisfaction, and is an important source of identity.

Warhurst's et al. premise is that the work–life interface is not best articulated as one of 'balance' because 'interpenetration' occurs between the two spheres.[90] This interpenetration between work and life is most obvious in contemporary home-working, which, through information and communication technology, allows

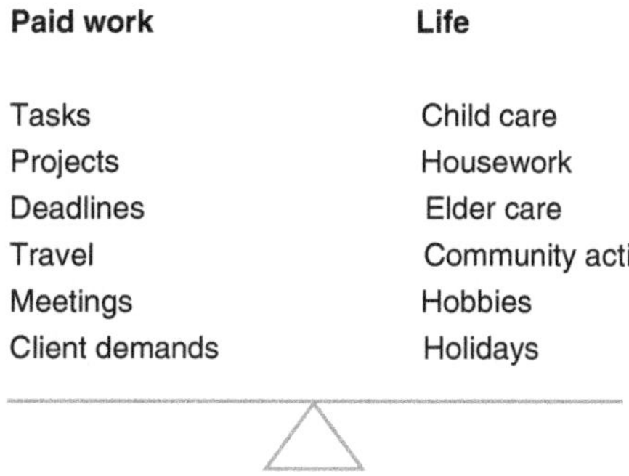

Paid work	Life
Tasks	Child care
Projects	Housework
Deadlines	Elder care
Travel	Community activities
Meetings	Hobbies
Client demands	Holidays

Figure 8.4   The notion of the work–life balance

Plate 3   The interpenetration between work and life is most obvious in contemporary home-working, which allows professionals to engage in paid work and domestic activities in the same physical space, and perhaps even on occasion at the same time
Source: Getty Images.

professionals to engage in paid work and domestic activities in the same physical space and maybe at the same time. Thus, the concept of work–life balance, with its suggestions of a binary opposition between 'work' and 'life', does not indicate how the complex interplay of personal choice and constraints, competing interests and power relations, shapes the relationship between work and life.

People are what Anthony Giddens[95] has called 'knowledgeable agents' – that is, they construct perceptions of work and life – and through their agency they produce social practices, which can be translated into what Warhurst et al.[90] call 'work–life patterns'. These social patterns and practices that human beings construct relate to work, family activities, maintaining friendships and the pursuit of leisure activities. Naturally, depending on the individual's context, the way in which work–life patterns are experienced can vary markedly between individuals. The advocates of the work–life pattern approach identify four implications for researchers and discerning managers:

1. The focus of praxis proposes an analysis of actual work practices and the impact these have on work–life patterns. For example, if work is takes place in a fixed and unmovable location (for example, assembly-line work), work–life patterns are likely to exhibit a clear delineation between work and life.
2. Employment analysts and practitioners need to understand the structural constraints (economic, social and cultural resources) that fashion work–life patterns. For example, economic capital can buy additional time for work (for example, hiring a nanny) or life (for example, only part-time paid work); cultural (for example, education) and social (for example, extended family) resources also affect job opportunities and work–life choices and opportunities.
3. Lifestyles – values, beliefs and work-related perceptions – influence individual practices and work–life patterns. Max Weber first proposed a connection between lifestyle (religion and asceticism) and work–life patterns.[96] The lifestyle of artists, musicians or theatre actors, for example, might promote a fusing or 'amalgamation' of a work–life pattern. Thus, creative artists are more likely to regard 'work as life, and life as work' (ref. 90, p. 14). Neither is the notion of a fusing of a work–life pattern restricted to artistic labour. As Michelle Gillies, a recently unemployed professional who had been a promotion manager and producer in the Canadian broadcasting sector, said, 'My job was me. I spent 10 years so closely linked to what I did there that there were no lines separating the two' (quoted in ref. 97). Examples of work–life amalgamation illustrate that experience of work and life cannot be understood using a simple model that separates the two spheres and sets them into opposition.
4. Work–life patterns are constructed following a range of logics, depending on the context. Whereas work centres on exchanges between effort and pay, life embraces a multitude of logics, such as unconditional love for family, the reciprocity of friendships and self-gratification through conspicuous consumption. These logics of work and life coexist, allowing individuals 'a fairly frictionless *alternation* between the two distinct spheres' (ref. 90, p. 15).

Work–life patterns are continually (re)constructed as employees' work and life cycles change. Examples of such changes might include:

• the shift from independent single person to mid-life with family dependants and so on
• a change in perceived economic insecurity
• government incentives and regulations to help individuals achieve work–life goals.[98]

Complex and problematic though the idea of work–life 'balance' may be, employers' strategies in this area can have important benefits for the organization.

For example, work–life policies and practices might be important for attracting and motivating professionals and innovative behaviours[99,100] – and conversely, failure to introduce such policies and practices can have a detrimental effect. Many law firms in North America, for example, retain 'a dominant male hierarchy and a suspicion of women who crave a balance between work and family', and the industry is losing talented professionals as a result. As one anonymous lawyer attests, 'A lot of male lawyers … were extremely unhappy about losing these really high-calibre people'.[101]

However, the idea of achieving a work–life 'balance' still seems remote for millions of low-income families. As we have seen, the work–life pattern approach is more complex than the notion of 'balance' between two separable spheres, and it is a perspective that has important implications for how work and people are managed in the workplace. We move on to examine how developments in work have been conceptualized and theorized.

---

weblink

Go to the following website for more information on the European Union Working Time Developments:www.eurofound.europa.eu/eiro/studies/tn0804029s/tn0804029s. htm. Information is also available for preceding years, and can be accessed at www. eurofound.europa.eu/eiro/comparative_index.htm

---

OB and Globalization

A family affair – cross-cultural adjustment to overseas work

The rapid growth of multinational organizations has been accompanied by an increase in the number of expatriate workers – people who work for a foreign branch of a parent company based in their home country. Sometimes, expatriate workers leave their families in the home country while they travel abroad for work. At other times, the parent company encourages workers' families to accompany them overseas.

Studies have shown that the rate of failure for overseas placements is high, with many workers returning home before the end of their overseas assignment. One of the top reasons given for this failure is the inability of workers' families to adjust to life in the host country. The failure of overseas work assignments can be personally stressful and defeating for the workers, can cost the parent company money, and can result in damage to business relationships with the host country. A 2008 *New York Times* article (Mohn, 2008) describes the interconnected challenges to work and family life that can accompany overseas work assignments:

The initial excitement of an exotic new posting can turn to culture shock, loneliness, identity loss and depression, and it is often the employee's spouse and children – without the familiar routine of work – who are most affected.

When an employee's family does not adapt well to an overseas work assignment, familial happiness is not the only thing at stake. According to workforce mobility expert Brenda Fender, overseas postings can fail when employees' families are unhappy, resulting in substantial financial losses to companies (Mohn, 2008). This outcome is far from inevitable. Increasingly, organizations relying on expatriate workers to manage overseas operations are recognizing the relationship between organizational success and the ability of workers' families to adjust to life abroad, and they are developing strategies to support both business success and family happiness.

Caligiuri et al. (1998) emphasize the importance of organizations providing cross-cultural support, such as language training, to help expatriate workers and their families achieve social and cultural adjustment in the host country. When expatriate families felt that their cultural and social adjustment was supported by the organization, they were more likely to support the family member working for the organization, which in turn resulted in success for the worker and for the organization.

stop! Imagine that you or a family member is posted to a job overseas. What types of cross-cultural support or information might be important for your adjustment to your new environment?

As an employee posted overseas, how might your sense of 'work–life balance' be affected by the experiences of other members of your family? What is the role of workers' families in organizational culture?

Sources and further information

Caligiuri, P. M., Hyland M. M., Bross A. S. and Joshi, A. (1998) 'Testing a theoretical model for examining the relationship between family adjustment and expatriates' work adjustment', *Journal of Applied Psychology*, 83(4), pp. 598–614.

Expat Finder Blog. Available at: www.expatfinder.com/blog.

Mohn, T. (2008) 'The dislocated Americans', *New York Times*, December 1, 2008. Available at: www.nytimes.com/2008/12/02/business/worldbusiness/02expat.html.

Sharples, J. (2005) 'Regrets and resentment over relocation', *Daily Telegraph*, January 19, 2005. Available at: http://www.telegraph.co.uk/expat/4194833/Regrets-and-resentment-over-relocation.html.

Note: This feature was written by Gretchen Fox, PhD, Anthropologist, Timberline Natural Resource Group, Canada.

Chapter summary

- One of the major themes running through the study of paid work has been the continuities as well as the discontinuities across time. There is no doubt that changes occur all the time, but these must be adequately contextualized if we are to appreciate their relevance. Thus, we can only really talk about a rise in instrumental orientations to work if we know what previously existed.

- Trying to summarise the experience of work over several millennia is a difficult task. There is so much material to cover that no text of conventional size would be able to deal adequately with the complexities. However, this chapter has been written on the assumption that some knowledge is preferable to complete ignorance, especially if, to understand the present, we have to situate it against the past. The chapter has tended to highlight gender issues in the workplace to balance out the conventional preference for male history.

- The complexity of the experience of work defies any simple assumptions about the significance of work. However, we can perhaps salvage from the past a conclusion that illuminates the significance of the social. Work, like other institutions, is inherently and irreducibly constructed, interpreted and organized through social actions and social discourse.

- We explained how, with the growth of routinized service work, new kinds of social relations and aspects of the self have developed and come under scrutiny. As the service workforce has grown in importance, we noted the growing interest in 'emotional work', pioneered by Arlie Hochschild.

- The persistence of gender ideologies on work, discrimination and the sexual division of paid work have been discussed, as has the persistent belief in the 'traditional' male breadwinner/female home-keeper model, particularly in periods of economic recession.

- We have explored the concept of work–life balance and why this orthodox binary view is based on traditional large-scale work and life patterns separated by time and space. As such, paid work is regarded as an activity that is an encroachment on people's private life. A more complex approach is represented by the notion of work–life patterns, which sees the activity of labour itself as an important source of identity and satisfaction.

Key concepts

cellular technology   291
control   286–87
division of labour   281
emotional labour   294
factory system   281
gender-based patterns of work   298–300
Industrial Revolution   278
knowledge work   292
labour power   280
McJobs   296
putting-out system   280
trade unions   299
work   274–75
work–life balance   300
work–life patterns   303–304

Vocab checklist for ESL students

- Artisan
- Control
- Corporation, corporate
- Deindustrialization
- Deskilling
- Discourse
- Division of labour

- Emotional work
- Extrinsic reward
- Factory system
- Flexibility, flexible
- Fordism
- Hypotheses
- Hypothesis
- Industrial Revolution
- Intrinsic reward
- Knowledge work
- Labour power
- Neo-Fordism
- Occupation, occupy
- Post-Fordism
- Post-industrial
- Pre-industrial
- Putting-out system
- Quality of working life
- Social structure
- Taylorism
- Trade union
- Upskilling
- Values, valuable
- Work ethic

Chapter review questions

1. What is work?
2. What were the advantages and disadvantages of the putting-out system?
3. Why were men reluctant to enter the new factories during the Industrial Revolution?
4. Why were male trade unionists so hostile to women entering traditional occupations?
5. Explain the importance of 'control' in a factory system.
6. How does knowledge work different from traditional work?
7. How does emotional labour differ from traditional paid work?
8. What is the difference between work–life balance and work–life patterns? Why is it considered important for managers to understand these concepts?

Chapter research questions

1. Form a study group of three to five people. Look at Figure 8.3, which draws together the development of paid work and employment relations. As a group, discuss how each major job/organization design influences the job of a manager. What intrinsic rewards do employees obtain when working under (a) craft, and (b) post-Fordism? What are the advantages/disadvantages of home-working for (a) the employer, and (b) the employee? Why, if at all, is it important to manage work–life patterns?
2. Obtain a copy of Chris Warhurst's et al.'s (2008) *Work Less, Live More?*[90] 'On the edge of the time bind: time and market culture'. How does the 'market culture' affect the modern family? How can the 'logic of work' crowd out 'life logics', and why is this important in understanding the debate on work–life patterns?

3. Retrieve and read Carol Emslie and Kate Hunt's (2009) article, '"Live to work" or "work to Live"? A qualitative study of gender and work–life balance among men and women in mid-life' (see Further Reading, below). Why should managers understand the work–life interface through a gender lens? How does the author explain how individual choices about work–life patterns are constrained by their socioeconomic resources and cultural norms?

Further reading

Bolton, S. and Boyd, C. (2003) 'Trolley dolly or skilled emotion manager? Moving on from Hochschild's managed heart', *Work, Employment and Society*, **17**(2), pp. 289–308.

Bolton, S. C. and Houlihan M. (2009) *Work Matters*, Basingstoke: Palgrave Macmillan.

Edgell, S. (2006) *The Sociology of Work*, London: Sage.

Emslie, C. and Hunt, K. (2009) '"Live to work" or "work to live"? A qualitative study of gender and work–life balance among men and women in mid-life', *Gender, Work and Organization*, 16(1), pp. 151–72.

Frenkel, S. J. (2006) 'Service workers in search of decent work', pp. 356–75 in S. Ackroyd, R. Batt, P. Thompson and P. Tolbert (eds), *The Oxford Handbook of Work and Organization*, New York: Oxford University Press.

Hardill, L. and Green, A. (2003) 'Remote working – altering the spatial contours of work and home in the new economy', *New Technology Work and Employment*, **18**(3), pp. 212–22.

Kelan, E. (2008) 'Gender, risk and employment insecurity: the masculine breadwinner subtext', *Human Relations*, **61**(9), pp. 1171–202.

Kvande, E. (2009) 'Work–life balance for fathers in globalized knowledge work. Some insights from the Norwegian context', *Gender, Work and Organization*, **16**(1), pp. 58–72.

Lewchuk, W., Clarke, M. and de Wolff, A. (2008) 'Working without commitments: precarious employment and health', *Work, Employment and Society*, **22**(3), pp. 387–406.

McCormick, K. (2007) 'Sociologists and "the Japanese model": a passing enthusiasm?', *Work, Employment and Society*, **21**(4), pp. 751–71.

McIvor, A. (2001) *A History of Work in Britain, 1880–1950*, Basingstoke: Palgrave Macmillan.

McKinlay, A. and Smith, C. (2009) *Creative Labour*, Basingstoke: Palgrave Macmillan.

Noon, M. and Blyton, P. (2009) *The Realities of Work*, Basingstoke: Palgrave Macmillan.

Salzinger, L. (2003) *Genders in Production*, Berkley, CA: University of California Press.

Warhurst, C., Eikhof, D. R. and Haunschild, A. (2008) *Work Less, Live More?*, Basingstoke: Palgrave.

Chapter case study 1

Service with a smile: McJobs in China

Setting

Although McDonald's is well known for its Fordist method of food production, China has had experience using an assembly-line approach to feed many people for over two centuries. As early as the nineteenth century, Chinese public dining halls had perfected breaking down the cooking process into basic procedures performed by a separate team of workers.

McDonald's brought its own brand of food production and management to China in 1990 when it opened its first restaurant in a city called Shenzhen. In 1992, the world's largest McDonald's was opened in Beijing, serving 40,000 customers on that first day. McDonald's now operates 1000 restaurants in more than 190 Chinese cities, with further expansion plans well underway.

More than 70 per cent of McDonald's restaurants worldwide are owned and operated independently by local men and women. In recent years, McDonald's future growth strategy has focused on China's smaller urban areas, known as second- and third-tier cities. McDonald's is not alone as many multinational and domestic companies are now looking to expand outside the traditional economic bases in the larger Chinese centres. McDonald's faces particularly stiff competition from KFC, a fellow American fast-food restaurant chain, which dominates the Chinese market.

While Chinese fast food operators do not deal with the high turnover rates seen in American cities (sometimes as high as 300 per cent for non-managerial employees), the rapid expansion by multiple companies has resulted in competition for quality workers and rising wage costs in the new tighter labour markets.

Problem

Hai Yan is one of the new owners of a McDonald's franchise in an area several hours outside Beijing. As with other franchisees, Hai relied on the McDonald's corporation to assist him with recruiting and training his new employees to bring them in line with the company's expectations.

Peter Bepple, a new Human Resources Manager assigned to the region, flew in from New York to help. Peter had never worked in China before and was looking forward to getting the new franchises up and running. He had been briefed on the recruiting issues and was told that although the Chinese were hard workers who respected management authority and leadership, they also expected their managers to build supportive relationships with them.

Upon his arrival in Hai's area, Peter immediately set up recruitment advertising on the company website, interviewed applicants on the phone, and made arrangements for selected candidates to come into Hai's restaurant for 3 days of work. Accompanied by a McDonald's employee, each candidate tried various roles from waiter to assistant manager in the restaurant. To Hai's dismay, 80 per cent of the candidates were not offered permanent employment. He became concerned that he would not find enough suitable workers to serve customers on his restaurant's opening day. Hai decided to approach Peter to find out why so many of the candidates had not been successful during the recruitment process.

Peter was sympathetic but explained to Hai that he had observed each failed candidate's reactions to the customers and was not impressed. 'The main challenge is to maintain a positive attitude and provide good service,' Peter told Hai. 'The most important characteristic is the willingness to communicate with others and that is best reflected with a smile. Those candidates simply did not smile enough.'

Hai was taken aback by the comment. 'Here in China customers are suspicious of workers who smile on the job,' he said to Peter.

Peter was surprised by this, but decided to check with his counterparts in other McDonald's locations in China to see if this was actually the case. They confirmed what Hai had said. 'Customers in China expect employees to be serious about their work,' he was told. 'The customers are more concerned about the efficiency, reliability and cleanliness of the restaurant than if the worker smiles at them.'

Before returning to New York, Peter's head office called and asked him to prepare a report on what he had learned on his first overseas assignment.

Tasks

Prepare a short report, incorporating answers to the following questions:

1. How important is it for the McDonald's customer service strategy to insist on having its employees provide 'service with a smile'?
2. What possible effects will forcing smiles have on the Chinese workers?
3. How could Peter have better prepared himself for working in China?
4. To what extent do you think the success of the US-based McDonald's corporation influences local Chinese companies to adopt its management practices, despite the cultural differences?

Essential reading

Deery, S. (2005) 'Customer service work, emotional labour and performance', Chapter 13 in S. Bach (ed.), *Managing Human Resources: Personnel Management in Transition*, Oxford: Blackwell.

Earnhardt, M. (2009) 'The successful expatriate leader in China', *Graziado Business Report*, 12(1). Available at: http://gbr.pepperdine.edu/091/expatriatesinchina.html.

Mujtaba, B. and Patel, B. (2007) 'McDonald's success strategy and global expansion through customer and brand loyalty', *Journal of Business Case Studies*, 3(3), pp. 55–66.

Watson, J. (2006) *Golden Arches East: McDonald's in East Asia*, Stanford: Stanford University Press.

Note

This case study was written by Lori Rilkoff, MSc, CHRP, Senior Human Resources Manager at the City of Kamloops, and lecturer in HRM at Thompson Rivers University, BC, Canada.

Chapter case study 2

Home-working in Matherdom City Council

Visit www.palgrave.com/business/brattonob2e to view this case study.

Web-based assignment

Central to the advance of organizational behaviour as a field of critical inquiry is an openness to expanding our understanding of both work and the 'workplace'. We believe it is important to understand that work expands beyond the boundaries of 'paid work', and importantly, the place where work is performed extends beyond the formal organization. The notion of work–life pattern has increasing relevance to workers, particularly to women, in the early twenty-first century.

On an individual basis, or working in a small group, visit the following websites and write a brief report of the research and practical issues associated with (a) home-working, and (b) work–life balance: www.berr.gov.uk; www.tca.org.uk; www.theworkfoundation.com/difference/e4wlb.aspx.

OB in film

The film *Modern Times* (1936) features Charlie Chaplin in a scathing portrayal of North American assembly-line work. The first 15 minutes of the film humorously illustrate the meaning of Taylorism and the stress associated with working on an assembly line. The film led Charlie Chaplin to be banned from the USA and some of the actors to be investigated by the Federal Bureau of Investigation.

Watch the first 15 minutes of the film. What does the film tell us about Taylorism? How would you rate Chaplin's job in terms of 'job enrichment' techniques?

References

1. Rubery, J. (2006) 'Labour markets and flexibility', pp. 31–51 in S. Ackroyd, R. Batt, P. Thompson and P. Tolbert (eds), *The Oxford Handbook of Work and Organization*, New York: Oxford University Press.
2. Bolton, S. C. and Houlihan, M. (eds) *Work Matters*, Basingstoke: Palgrave.

3. Gorz, A. (1982) *Farewell to the Working Class*, London: Pluto.
4. Rifkin, J. (1996) *The End of Work*, New York: Tarcher/Putnam.
5. Pahl, R. E. (ed.) (1988) *On Work*, Oxford: Blackwell.
6. Gates, W., with Myhrvold, N. and Rinearson, P. (1996) *The Road Ahead*, New York: Penguin.
7. Wood, S. (ed.) (1982) *The Transformation of Work?*, London: Unwin Hyman.
8. Zuboff, S. (1988) *In the Age of the Smart Machine*, New York: Basic Books.
9. Hearn, J., Sheppard, D., Tancred-Sheriff, P. and Rand Burrell, G. (eds) (1989) *The Sexuality of Organization*, London: Sage.
10. Littler, C. R. and Salaman, G. (1984) *Class at Work: The Design, Allocation and Control of Jobs*, London: Batsford.
11. Mills, A. and Tancred, P. (eds) (1992) *Gendering Organizational Analysis*, Newbury Park, CA: Sage.
12. Thompson, P. (1989) *The Nature of Work* (2nd edn), London: Macmillan.
13. Williams, R. (1983) *Keywords*, New York: Oxford University Press.
14. Christiansen, C. H. and Townsend, E. A. (2004) *Introduction to Occupation: The Art and Science of Living*, Upper Saddle River, NJ: Prentice Hall.
15. Noon, M. and Blyton, P. (2002) *The Realities of Work*, Basingstoke: Palgrave Macmillan.
16. Rinehart, J. W. (2006) *The Tyranny of Work: Alienation and the Labour Process* (4th edn), Scarborough, ON: Nelson Thomson.
17. Thomas, K. (1999) 'Introduction', pp. xiii–xxiii in K. Thomas (ed.), *The Oxford Book of Work*, Oxford: Oxford University Press.
18. Herod, A., Rainnie, A. and McGrath-Champ, S. (2007) 'Working space: why incorporating the geographical is central to theorizing work and employment practices', *Work, Employment and Society*, **21**(2), pp. 247–64.
19. Hardill, L. and Green, A. (2003) 'Remote working – altering the spatial contours of work and home in the new economy', *New Technology, Work and Employment*, **18**(3), pp. 212–22.
20. Coyle-Shapiro, J. A.-M., Shore, L., Taylor, M. S. and Tetrick, L. (2005) *The Employment Relationship*, Oxford: Oxford University Press.
21. Barnes, C. (1996) 'What next? Disability, the 1995 Disability Discrimination Act and the Campaign for Disabled Peoples' Rights', National Bureau for Disabled Students Annual Conference, March 2, Leeds, UK.
22. Guest, D. E. and Conway, N. (2002) 'Communicating the psychological contract: an employer perspective', *Human Resource Management Journal*, **12**(2), pp. 22–38.
23. Herriot, P. (1998) 'The role of human resource management in building a new proposition', pp. 106–16 in P. Sparrow and M. Marchington (eds), *Human Resource Management: A New Agenda*, London: Financial Times Management.
24. Kramer, R. M. and Tyler, T. R. (1996) *Trust in Organizations: Frontiers of Theory and Research*, Newbury Park, CA: Sage.
25. Rousseau, D. M. (1995) *Psychological Contracts in Organisations: Understanding Written and Unwritten Agreements*, Thousand Oaks, CA: Sage.
26. Atkinson, C. (2008) 'An exploration of small firm psychological contracts', *Work, Employment and Society*, **22**(3), pp. 447–65.
27. Sveiby, K. E. (1997) *The New Organizational Wealth: Managing and Measuring Organizational Wealth*, San Francisco, CA: Berrett-Koehler.
28. Hodson, R. and Sullivan, T. A. (2002) *The Social Organization of Work* (3rd edn), Belmont, CA: Wadsworth/Thomson Learning.
29. Grint, K. (1998) *The Sociology of Work* (2nd edn), Cambridge: Polity Press.
30. Hobsbawm, E. (1997) *On History*, London: Weidenfeld & Nicolson.
31. Littler, C. R. (1982) *The Development of the Labour Process in Capitalist Societies*, London: Heinemann.
32. Salaman, G. (1981) *Class and the Corporation*, London: Fontana.
33. Weber, M. (1927/2003) *General Economic History*, New York: Dover Publications.
34. Clarkson, L. A. (1971) *The Pre-Industrial Economy of England, 1500–1750*, London: Batsford.
35. Alvesson, M. and Due Billing, Y (1997) *Understanding Gender in Organizations*, London: Sage.
36. Dobb, M. (1963) *Studies in the Development of Capitalism*, London: Routledge.
37. Landes, D. S. (1969) *The Unbound Prometheus*, Cambridge: Cambridge University Press.

38. Marglin, S. (1982) 'What do bosses do?: the origins and functions of hierarchy in capitalist production', in A. Giddens and D. Held (eds), *Classes, Power and Conflict*, Basingstoke: Macmillan.

39. Kelly, J. (1985) 'Management's redesign of work: labour process, labour markets and product markets', in D. Knights, H. Willmott and D. Collinson (eds), *Job Redesign: Critical Perspectives on the Labour Process*, Aldershot: Gower.

40. Hobsbawm, E. (1968) *Industry and Empire*, London: Weidenfeld & Nicolson.

41. Thompson, E. P. (1967) 'Time, work and discipline, and industrial capitalism,' *Past and Present*, **38**, pp. 56–97.

42. Grey, C. (2005) *A Very Short, Fairly Interesting and Reasonably Cheap Book about Studying Organizations*, London: Sage.

43. Hinton, J. (1973) *The First Shop Stewards Movement*, London: Allen & Unwin.

44. Rose, M. (1988) *Industrial Behaviour*, London: Penguin.

45. Braverman, H. (1974) *Labor and Monopoly Capitalism: The Degradation of Work in the Twentieth Century*, New York: Monthly Review Press.

46. Beynon, H. (1984) *Working for Ford*, Harmondsworth: Penguin.

47. Parker, M. (2000) *Organizational Culture and Identity*, London: Sage.

48. Friedman, A. (1977) *Industry and Labour: Class Struggle at Work and Monopoly Capitalism*, London: Macmillan.

49. Callaghan, G. and Thompson, P. (2001) 'Edwards revisited: technical control and worker agency in callcentres', *Economic and Industrial Democracy*, **22**, pp. 13–37.

50. Sewell, G. (1998) 'The discipline of teams: the control of team-based industrial work through electronic and peer surveillance', *Administrative Science Quarterly*, **43**, pp. 406–69.

51. Bratton, J. (1992) *Japanization at Work*, Basingstoke: Macmillan.

52. Elger, T. and Smith, C. (eds) (1994) *Global Japanization?*, London: Routledge.

53. Thompson, P. and McHugh, D. (2006) *Work Organizations: A Critical Introduction* (4th edn), Basingstoke: Palgrave.

54. Womack, J., Jones, D. and Roos, D. (1990) *The Machine that Changed the World*, New York: Rawson Associates.

55. Oliver, N. and Wilkinson, B. (1992) *The Japanization of British Industry*, Oxford: Blackwell.

56. McCormick, K. (2007) 'Sociologists and "the Japanese model": a passing enthusiasm?', *Work, Employment and Society*, **21**(4), pp. 751–71.

57. Salzinger, L. (2003) *Genders in Production*, Berkeley: University of California Press.

58. Horwitz, F. M., Chan Feng Heng and Quazi, H. A. (2003) 'Finders, keepers? Attracting, motivating and retaining knowledge workers', *Human Resource Management Journal*, **13**(4), pp. 23–44.

59. Boud, D. and Garrick, J. (eds) (1999) *Understanding Learning at Work*, London: Routledge.

60. Ackroyd, S., Batt, R., Thompson, P. and Tolbert, P. (2005) *The Oxford Handbook of Work and Organization*, Oxford: Oxford University Press.

61. Baldry, C., Bain, P., Taylor, P. et al. (2007) *The Meaning of Work in the New Economy*, Basingstoke: Palgrave.

62. Bolton, S. C. (2005) *Emotion Management in the Workplace*, Basingstoke: Palgrave.

63. Fineman, S. (2003) *Understanding Emotion at Work*, London: Sage.

64. Warhurst, C. and Nickson, D. (2007), 'A new labour aristocracy? Aesthetic labour and routine interactive service', *Work, Employment and Society*, **21**(4), pp. 785–98.

65. Hochschild, A. (2003) *The Second Shift*, New York: Penguin.

66. Linstead, S., Fulop, L. and Lilley, S. (2009) *Management and Organization: A Critical Text* (2nd edn), Basingstoke: Palgrave.

67. Nixon, D. (2009) '"I can't put a smiley face on": working-class masculinity, emotional labour and service work in the "new economy"', *Gender, Work and Organization*, **16**(3), pp. 300–22.

68. Jacoby, S. M. (2005) *The Embedded Corporation: Corporate Governance and Employment Relations in Japan and the United States*, Princeton, NJ: Princeton University Press.

69. Jaffee, D. (2001) *Organization Theory: Tension and Change*, Boston, MA: McGraw-Hill.

70. Vallas, S. (1999) 'Re-thinking post-Fordism: the meaning of workplace flexibility', *Sociological Theory*, **17**(1), pp. 68–85.
71. Walton, R. (1985) 'From control to commitment in the workplace', *Harvard Business Review*, March/April, pp. 77–84.
72. Hyman, R. and Mason, B. (1995) *Managing Employee Involvement and Participation*, London: Sage.
73. Reiter, E. (1992) *Making Fast Food: From the Frying Pan into the Fryer*, Montreal: McGill-Queen's University Press.
74. Ritzer, G. (2000) *The McDonaldization of Society*, Thousand Oaks, CA: Pine Forge Press.
75. Leidner, R. (1993) *Fast Food, Fast Talk: Service Work and the Routinization of Everyday Life*, Berkeley, CA: University of California Press.
76. Mathias, P. (1969) *The First Industrial Nation*, London: Methuen.
77. Reskin, B. and Padavic, I. (1994) *Women and Men at Work*, Thousand Oaks, CA: Sage.
78. Hobsbawm, E. (1994) *Age of Extremes*, London: Abacus.
79. Berg, M. (1988) 'Women's work, mechanization and early industrialization', in R. E. Pahl (ed.), *On Work*, Oxford: Blackwell.
80. Bradley, H. (1986) 'Technological change, management strategies, and the development of gender-based job segregation in the labour process', pp. 54–73 in D. Knights and H. Willmott (eds), *Gender and the Labour Process*, Aldershot: Gower.
81. Turner, H. A. (1962) *Trade Union Growth, Structure and Policy: A Comparative Study of the Cotton Unions*, London: Allen & Unwin.
82. Witz, A. (1986) 'Patriarchy and the labour market: occupational control strategies and the medical division of labour', in D. Knights and H. Willmott (eds), *Gender and the Labour Process*, Aldershot: Gower.
83. Sydie, R. A. (1994) *Natural Women, Cultured Men*, Vancouver: UBC Press.
84. Knights, D. and Willmott, H. (eds) (1986) *Gender and the Labour Process*, Aldershot: Gower.
85. Kimmel, M. (2004) *The Gendered Society* (2nd edn), New York: Oxford University Press.
86. Saunders, D. (2006) 'Politician-mom seeks to change dated German social values', *Globe and Mail*, June 22, p. A3.
87. Greenhaus, J. H. (2008), 'Innovations in the study of the work–family interface: introduction to the Special Section', *Journal of Occupational and Organizational Psychology*, **81**, pp. 343–8.
88. Purcell, J., Purcell, K., and Tailby, S. (2004) 'Temporary work agencies: here today, gone tomorrow?', *British Journal of Industrial Relations*, **42**(4), pp. 705–25.
89. Sturges, J. and Guest, D. (2004) 'Working to live or living to work: work/life balance and organizational commitment amongst graduates', *Human Resources Management Journal*, **14**(4), pp. 5–20.
90. Warhurst, C., Eikhof, D. R. and Haunschild, A. (2008) *Work Less, Live More?*, Basingstoke: Palgrave.
91. European Trade Union Confederation. 'Factsheet: Working Time Directive'. Available at: http://www.etuc.org/a/504 (accessed November 2, 2009).
92. Bonney, N. (2005) 'Overworked Britains?: part-time work and work–life balance', *Work, Employment and Society*, **19**(2), pp. 391–401.
93. Kersley, B., Alpin, C., Forth, J. et al. (2006) *Inside the Workplace: Findings from the 2004 Workplace Employment Relations Survey*, London: Routledge.
94. Felstead, A., Gallie, D. and Green, F. (2002) *Work Skills in Britain: 1986–2001*, London: HMSO.
95. Giddens, A. (1984) *The Constitution of Society*, Cambridge: Polity Press.
96. Weber, M. (1905/2002) *The Protestant Ethic and the 'Spirit' of Capitalism*, London: Penguin.
97. *Globe and Mail*, April 22, 2009, p. C1.
98. Kvande, E. (2009) 'Work–life balance for fathers in globalized knowledge work. Some insights from the Norwegian context', *Gender, Work and Organization*, **16**(1), pp. 58–72.
99. Scholarios, D. and Marks, A. (2004) 'Work–life balance and the software worker', *Human Resource Management Journal*, **14**(2), pp. 54–74.

100. De Cieri, H., Holmes, B., Abbot, J. and Pettit, T. (2002) *Work/Life Balance Strategies: Progress and Problems in Australian Organizations*. Working Paper 58/02. Melbourne: Department of Management, Monash University.
101. Makin, K.(2009) 'Lawyer-moms aim to change law firms' punishing work culture', *Globe and Mail*, April 11, p. 4.
102. Despres, C. and Hiltrop, J-M. (1995) 'Human resource management in the knowledge age: current practice and perspectives on the future', *Employee Relations*, **17**(1), pp. 9–23.

CHAPTER 9
The changing context of work

KEY CONCEPTS

political context

deregulation

privatisation

economic context

globalisation

competitive strategies

industrial structure

workforce composition

part-time employment

self-employment

location of employment

job insecurity

redundancy

unemployment

CHAPTER AIM

To examine how the political and economic contexts of work are changing, and consider the main trends in the composition of the labour force.

LEARNING OUTCOMES

After reading and thinking about the material in this chapter, you will be able to:

1. Identify the main developments in the international political environment that affect the world of work, particularly trade liberalisation and the growth of supranational alliances.

2. Recognise the influence of developments in national political contexts for the nature of work and employment.

3. Develop an understanding of the main changes in the overall economic context, particularly the spread of economic globalisation.

4. Identify the main changes in the industrial structure, particularly the shift from manufacturing to services.

5. Assess the main changes taking place in workforce composition.
6. Consider the changing experience of work in terms of changes in levels of unemployment, redundancies, temporary work and job insecurity.

Introduction

The comment is often made that the world of work has undergone dramatic changes over the past 20 to 30 years. Some commentators have gone so far as to characterise these changes as representing a fundamental shift in the nature of capitalism itself: a shift from 'Fordist' to 'post-Fordist' forms of production, from mass production systems to flexible specialisation, from industrial to post-industrial society, or from modern to post-modern forms of organisation. Such broad characterisations usefully signal the breadth and depth of changes taking place and also the ways in which myriad individual changes can be interpreted as part of much broader trajectories. At the same time, it is important to explore the specific changes themselves because such shorthand categorisations constantly run the danger of obscuring as much as (or more than) they reveal. Not only do they encourage (over) generalisations about the direction in which society is heading, they also (and often more implicitly) embody sweeping assumptions about where it has been.

In this chapter, it is necessary to cover a lot of ground fairly quickly. Its purpose is to present an overview of how the context of work has been and is changing, and in so doing offer a broad landscape within which to locate the more specific experiences of work. Even an overview must be selective, however, since contexts can be defined at several levels – an individual worker is located in a particular work setting, but in turn that workplace is situated within a local economy, which itself is embedded in regional, national and international economic contexts. Further, these economic contexts are interrelated with, and influenced by, political contexts that also operate at each of these levels. Thus, in this chapter it is necessary to note some of the main changes that have been taking place in the political context of work over the past two decades, as well as both broad changes occurring within the economic context, and changing patterns of employment. Many of the issues raised in this chapter feed directly into more specific arguments covered in more detail later. For the moment though, the task is to capture a sense of the breadth of change occurring at the different levels. To this end, the chapter is divided into three main sections:

1. The broad changes occurring in the political context of work over approximately the last two decades are reviewed.
2. A similar examination is made of the central (and often closely related) changes occurring within the economic context, together with some of the main responses to those changes.
3. The major developments occurring in the structure and patterns of employment are explored. To illustrate this discussion we draw on Organisation for Economic Cooperation and Development (OECD) data relating to industrialised countries and on data for single countries where this allows us to explore developments in more detail.

> **Learning outcome 1:** Identify the main developments in the international political environment that affect the world of work, particularly trade liberalisation and the growth of supranational alliances

Changes in the political context

It is impossible to analyse work without giving some consideration to the political context within which it is located. More accurately, work organisations are embedded within a series of political contexts: the international political environment, the national political context and regional and local politics. These are considered briefly below in an attempt to apply some broad brush strokes on the political backcloth against which the realities of work may be examined. The discussion is confined to the aspects of the political context that have impacted upon the workplace.

The international political environment

Of the various international political developments that have been taking place over the recent period that impact upon the world of work, two are particularly notable:

- the gradual extension of trade liberalisation measures
- the creation of supranational alliances in Europe, North America and Asia.

Extension of trade liberalisation

Political intervention over trade is subject to competing pressures as nation states seek to promote trade openness where it enhances economic growth, while at the same time seeking to protect more vulnerable domestic industries and markets. The influence of the latter means that many sectors (most notably agriculture but also various manufacturing activities) continue to maintain considerable tariff barriers (duties or charges on particular classes of goods) which have restricted the development of international trade. Nevertheless, since the founding of the General Agreement on Tariffs and Trade (GATT) in 1946, the overall trend both through GATT negotiations and through regional agreements has been towards a gradually more liberalised trading regime. The signing of the Uruguay Round Agreement of GATT in 1994, for example, committed developed economies to further tariff reductions on imports, though many such tariff barriers remain (Milberg, 1998).

The sector in which trading has become most liberalised is that of financial markets, through the removal of restrictions on international movements of capital (Milberg, 1998: 83). This has acted as a key driver influencing the growth of economic globalisation (see below). Other sectors have also experienced a significant degree of market liberalisation in recent years. Entry into the long-distance telecommunications industry, for example, has been widely liberalised, as has access to local and mobile telecommunications in most industrial countries (OECD, 2000a: 152). Similarly, international air passenger transport has also experienced a degree of market liberalisation in recent years, though market restrictions remain in this, as in many other sectors (see Excerpt 9.1). Where international markets have become noticeably more liberalised is within three major regional groupings of countries in North America, South East Asia, and particularly Europe. We examine these separately below.

Excerpt 9.1

Market liberalisation in the international civil aviation industry

Traditionally, the air transport market has been subject to a high degree of state regulation covering market entry, capacity and prices. State ownership was the norm for the majority of the world's major airlines. These carriers enjoyed national 'flag carrier' status and preferential access to international markets through bilateral agreements between national governments.

Pressure for a relaxation in state regulation has come from a variety of sources, most notably growing political support for 'free market' capitalism within a more liberalised and privatised economic regime (many flag carriers have been privatised in recent years).

Following the deregulation of the US airline industry in the late 1970s, the most significant liberalisation has been in Europe, where a single market for aviation came into being in 1997, with any EU-registered carrier gaining the right to operate services within and between any of the EU member states.

This reduction in state control, particularly over the entry of new carriers, operations, pricing and capacity, has had certain immediate effects, most notably the growth of independent low-cost carriers, many operating from second-tier and regional airports. However, relaxation of state regulation over the passenger airline market remains partial. It remains the case that outside regional agreements such as the European Union, the majority of international routes are operated by the two countries involved, and protected by highly restrictive bilateral air service agreements.

Sources: Blyton, Martinez Lucio, McGurk and Turnbull (2001), OECD (2000a).

The growth of supranational alliances

Just as much of the world's trade takes place within and between the three regional areas of North America, Europe and East Asia, so too the main political steps to create regional free markets have also occurred in these regions, through the formation of the North America Free Trade Agreement (NAFTA), the Association of South East Asian Nations (ASEAN), and the European Union (EU). While NAFTA and ASEAN have remained largely economic alliances, the EU has taken integration considerably further, with an expanding number of member states establishing a widespread political and social agenda, though primarily to support the EU's economic programme.

It is the breadth of this integration in Europe that has made it particularly significant in terms of its impact on work and employment. For example, member states are subject to a growing body of European law which is increasingly impacting upon work organisations by obliging employers (and countries as a whole) to comply with European legislation, even where individual national governments are reluctant. For example, the European Court of Justice (ECJ) has in the past forced the British government to enact additional equal pay provisions to take into account the European legislation covering work of equal value (Rubinstein, 1984).

Likewise, in the mid-1990s, the UK government was required to change the law on employment protection to give part-time workers the same qualifying period as their full-time counterparts in respect of statutory employment rights concerning, for example, redundancy pay and unfair dismissal compensation (Dickens, 1995: 209). More recently, ECJ rulings in 2005 affecting employment in the UK included a decision that the hours that doctors and other healthcare workers spent 'on call' must be included as working time and thus form part of the calculation of hours specified in the Working Time Directive (Tait and Taylor, 2005).

In the process of enshrining European-wide employment rights and better conditions, a key development was the establishment of the European Community Charter of the Fundamental Social Rights of Workers (known as the Social Charter). In 1989 it was accepted by 11 of the then 12 member states (the UK being the exception) as a political proclamation, with no formal legal status. However, it established the direction in which social policy was to develop, and by 1992 the 11 member states acted to begin the process of implementing the Social Charter through the EU institutions by signing a Protocol on Social Policy as part of the Maastricht Treaty (the social chapter). Again the then Conservative government in Britain refused to be a signatory, and it was not until the incoming 1997 Labour government that this opt-out decision was reversed.

The main vehicle for developing the work and employment aspects of the Social Charter has been through the introduction of European directives, on such issues as working time, part-time workers, parental leave, sex discrimination and the rights of employees in European multinationals to works councils (Bach and Sisson, 2000). Once such directives have been issued, they are then implemented via legislative changes at the national levels (see below).

A key political logic behind introducing EU-wide legislation has been to harmonise conditions and rights of employees across national boundaries. This is seen to be particularly important by the more prosperous states such as Germany which might otherwise fall victim to 'social dumping' – a process whereby companies transfer aspects of production to countries within the EU that maintain lower wages, less employment protection and fewer employment rights, thus decreasing the costs and overheads of labour. Such differentials exert considerable pressure on those member states with favourable employment terms and conditions to lower them in order to provide a competitive environment for the companies located there. The logical consequence of such differentials is a spiralling down or 'race to the bottom' on employment protection, with Europe becoming a domain of decreasing employment rights and increasing insecurity and exploitation – a politically and morally undesirable outcome within most member states.

The national political context

The growing significance of international agreements over trade, and the development of supranational political alliances notwithstanding, the national political context continues to represent a major source of influence affecting the world of work and developing patterns of employment. As an economic manager, employer and legislator, the state has a major bearing on the experience of work (Blyton and Turnbull, 2004: 170–213). Indeed, as noted above, even key supranational developments such as the implementation of EU directives are carried out via changes in national legislation (see Bach and Sisson, 2000: 31–3; Gennard and Judge, 2005). Similarly, a central aspect of the move towards greater market liberalisation has been the deregulation of individual national economic sectors. This deregulatory activity has been given a particular impetus by widespread privatisation of former state-owned monopolies. Indeed, in the national political context affecting the nature of work and employment, it is privatisation activity that is among the most prominent national level political developments worldwide over the past generation.

Learning outcome 2: Recognise the influence of developments in national political contexts for the nature of work and employment

Privatisation activity

The 1980s and particularly the 1990s witnessed a substantial growth in privatisation throughout the world, and widespread privatisation activity has continued into the present century. Factors encouraging privatisation have included government desires to raise revenues and avoid new investment costs, and the widespread decline in the power of left-wing parties which in the past have been more in favour of state ownership (Toninelli, 2000).

One estimate is that the overall size of the public enterprise sector in industrial countries halved between the beginning of the 1980s and the end of the 1990s (OECD, 2000a: 154). In 1990, the total proceeds from privatisation were just under US$30,000 million, of which the UK accounted for over 43 per cent. By 1997, however, the total global proceeds from privatisation during that year were over US$153,000 million – an increase of over 500 per cent from the 1990 level (OECD, 1999: 130). In the late 1990s, the most active countries pursuing large-scale privatisation programmes were Australia, France, Germany, Italy, Japan and Spain, and several countries in Latin America, notably Chile and Mexico. Privatisation activity has also become increasingly prominent in Russia and the former Soviet bloc countries in central and eastern Europe, and also to a growing extent in China (Megginson and Netter, 2001; Parker and Kirkpatrick, 2005). Around the world, the main sectors subject to privatisation in the recent period have been manufacturing, telecommunications, financial services, public utilities and transport (OECD, 1999: 135–8).

Labour market deregulation

The UK stood in the vanguard of privatisation activity, and for Conservative governments of the 1980s and 1990s in the UK, privatisation represented a major plank in a broader project of deregulating economic activity. This was particularly marked in relation to the labour market with the objective of allowing employers greater freedom of operation. This policy of labour market deregulation was underpinned by theories of neo-classical economics which hold that economic revival and success is dependent on allowing market forces to operate free from any 'artificial' constraint or government intervention. It was argued that competitiveness had been hampered in the past by high labour costs caused by the restrictions and rigidities imposed on employers by employment protection legislation, and the power and influence of trade unions. On the basis of this reasoning, successive Conservative governments from 1979 onwards embarked on a series of incremental changes that sought to deregulate employment and restrict the influence of trade unions. While some aspects of these policies were reversed or curtailed by the incoming New Labour government elected in 1997 (by for example, the introduction of a national minimum wage and the establishment of rights for trade unions to pursue membership representation cases, as well as the implementation of European directives – see above), many of the broader labour market policies have remained in place.

Deregulating employment – by such means as extending the period that employees had to work before qualifying for employment protection rights, by abolishing wage-setting mechanisms for the least organised groups, and by restricting the operations of trade unions (see Blyton and Turnbull, 2004 for details) – had the effect of shifting the balance away from employment protection towards employment flexibility. This greater flexibility carries a number of consequences for those both in and out of work (see discussion of job insecurity below). However, in identifying the full extent and implications of labour market deregulation in the UK, care needs to be taken, for it is something of a misnomer to talk of UK governments 'deregulating' the relations between capital and labour. Relative to many other economies, the labour market and employment relationships in the UK have never been highly regulated.

In the UK, for example, legislation on such basic employment issues as the maximum hours a worker is permitted to work, or the minimum number of days holiday a person is entitled to, has until recently been notable by its absence. The same holds for the type of employment contracts that an employer can offer – for example, unlike various other countries there is no requirement for employers in the UK to justify the offering of temporary rather than permanent contracts. In this respect, the deregulation of labour markets which took place in the UK in the 1980s and 1990s is all the more significant: it removed and reduced regulations in a context *already characterised* by a low degree of regulation. In a country where labour market regulation is in any event only modest, the further diminution of that basis of regulation has considerable symbolic significance regarding the perceived relations between capital and labour and the lack of any need to protect the latter against the powers of the former.

One of the significant aspects of the UK privatisation for patterns of work and employment is that in the past, an important way that the state regulated employment within and around the public sector was via the practice of Fair Wages resolutions. These were based on the principle that when a private sector firm was awarded a government contract, its employees should be paid at a level commensurate with equivalent work being undertaken by public sector workers. This was part of a broader state approach to acting as a 'good employer', and disseminating its practices more widely. The good employer approach also extended to its encouragement of trade union representation, leading to very high levels of union organisation throughout most of the public sector. However, the shrinking of the public sector through privatisation (a reduction that has only partially been offset by expansion in employment in the health and education sectors in recent years: see Hicks, 2005) coupled with the commercialisation of those activities remaining within the public sector, was accompanied by the abandonment of Fair Wages resolutions. Moreover, the growth in 'competitive tendering' across the public sector in the 1980s and 1990s resulted in most tenders being won on the basis of least cost, with low wage levels being an important means of keeping costs down when tendering. Thus the increase in competitive tendering and the ending of the concept of 'fair wages' acted to remove further 'rigidities' from the labour market concerning wage rates for employees working on government contracts.

Regional and local political environments

As states such as the UK also move to more devolved political arrangements, political activity at regional and local levels becomes more significant. One of the most vivid examples of how sub-national politics can have an impact on work is the extent to which it encourages (or inhibits) capital investment in an area, through such programmes as the creation of local enterprise zones to stimulate economic growth and employment (OECD, 2005b: 107–8). In terms of encouraging capital investment, a UK example from the 1980s of local politics playing a key role relates to the location of the Nissan car company in the north-east of England. In this instance, various parts of the local state (the local authority, the county council and the local development corporation) acted to purchase land in sufficient quantity (over 900 acres) as to attract the car-maker, with the prospect of being able to expand its operations on the site much above its originally stated plans (Crowther and Garrahan, 1988). More recently in the UK and Europe, an important focus of regional policy and development has been the growth of regional airport facilities (and surrounding infrastructures). Much of this growth is closely linked to the rapid expansion in low-cost airline traffic over the past decade (Buyck, 2005).

In the UK the local political context has also proved to be a site where an alternative political agenda can be orchestrated from that prevailing at national level. The elections for a Mayor of London in 2000, for example, created a rallying point for opposition to the national government's policy of privatising the London Underground. Such examples must be treated with caution, however, for while they illustrate the potential importance of local politics in the UK, the influence of the latter remains highly circumscribed, both by the increasing power of Whitehall (Hoggett, 1996) and by the general inability of sub-national political mechanisms such as the Scottish and Welsh Assemblies successfully to challenge the decisions of powerful multinationals. For example, when the Anglo-Dutch steelmaker Corus announced in early 2001 its decision to close substantial parts of its steelmaking and plating facilities in south Wales with the loss of approximately 3000 jobs in Wales (and 6000 in the UK as a whole), this decision could not be modified by the Welsh Assembly, despite the latter's efforts of persuasion and financial incentives (*Financial Times*, 17 January 2001, p. 6; see also Excerpt 9.3 on page 338).

To sum up

The nature of work is influenced by political factors operating at various levels from the international political arena to local political contexts. Many of the political projects being pursued at the different levels are interconnected, including the search for further privatisation, greater labour market deregulation and broader trade liberalisation.

Changes in the economic context

Globalisation and competition

One of the most marked economic developments over the recent period has been the progressive globalisation of economic activity. Just as earlier periods of industrial development witnessed a gradual shift in the extent to which enterprises were oriented towards national rather than local markets, the last quarter-century has seen a marked increase in the cross-national nature of goods and service production. It needs to be recognised that the term 'globalisation' is problematic. Many different meanings have been applied to it, and some commentators have criticised the term for its implication that what is currently occurring is fundamentally different from previous patterns of development rather than an extension of those patterns (see for example Hirst and Thompson, 1996; Kleinknecht and ter Wengel, 1998).

Although the term 'globalisation' has often lacked precision, we concur with the view that there is now compelling evidence that global activity is increasing, that national economies are becoming increasingly integrated into global trading relations, and that large companies increasingly make decisions on a global basis, not least as a result of the trade and capital liberalisation measures that political negotiations have brought about (see above). Futhermore, globalisation reflects the growing number of countries figuring in an increasingly industrialised world, with countries such as Korea, Taiwan, Singapore, Brazil, Mexico and recently Malaysia, Thailand, India and China becoming prominent industrial producers and major international traders.

A workable definition of economic globalisation is 'the integration of spatially separate locations into a single international market' (Blyton, Martinez Lucio, McGurk and Turnbull, 2001: 447). The principal economic dimension to this is simply the reduction in the costs incurred when conducting business on an international basis. This includes, in particular, transport and transaction costs, such as travel time, freight rates and the cost, speed and ease of communication.

Nowhere is the spread of globalisation more clearly illustrated than in the accelerated growth in world trade in recent years. During the 1990s and the early years of the present century, world trade has grown at a considerably faster rate than total output of goods and services. On average, world trade grew by 6.4 per cent per annum during the 1990s (Bank of England, 2000: 234) Throughout that decade, this represented a much higher rate of growth than total output (GDP); indeed in a number of those years (1994/5/7/8) world trade grew at over twice the rate of world GDP. Similarly in the 2000–04 period world trade continued to grow at twice the rate of growth in world GDP (WTO, 2005; see also *National Institute Economic Review*, 2005). Data from the OECD underlines the growing prominence of China in world trade. Between 1991 and 2004 for example, China's trade growth exceeded 20 per cent in seven of those years, and in only two years during that period was trade growth below 10 per cent (OECD, 2005a: 194).

Exercise 9.1

What do you think?
The focus of the discussion here is economic globalisation. However, globalisation also has social, cultural and political dimensions which may be said to reinforce the spread of economic globalisation.

Identify an example of social, cultural and cultural globalisation taking place. (If you wish to develop your knowledge further on these aspects of globalisation, a good starting point is Waters, M. (1995) Globalisation, London: Routledge).

Multinational firms

Within this overall expansion in trade, multinational firms play a very large and increasing role, and as such represent the principal carriers of economic globalisation. Driven by such factors as the differential cost and availability of labour, favourable exchange rates and the importance of being situated within, rather than outside, multicountry free trade areas (such as the European Single Market) the scale of multinational activity has continued to grow (Stopford and Turner, 1985). For example, US multinationals accounted for over four-fifths (83 per cent) of the value of US exports in 1994. A substantial part of this (36 per cent) involved trade between multinational parents and their affiliates, while the remainder (47 per cent) involved trade between multinationals and others (Clausing, 2000: 190).

The overall effect of globalisation, the spread of industrialism, and the increased dominance of multinationals has been to intensify competition in many markets. A growing number of local and domestic markets have become exposed to wider competition, either as a result of international trade or through activities of multinationals producing for the 'host' country market. So much so that a worker in the UK Midlands, for example, could work at the (Japanese owned) Toyota plant, travel to and from work in a British manufactured Ford or Vauxhall car (both US multinationals in the UK), shop at lunchtime in the local (German owned) Aldi supermarket, and travel into Birmingham at the weekend to purchase household goods at the local (Swedish owned) Ikea superstore, before returning home to watch a UK manufactured (in a Japanese owned factory) Sony television, picking up a burger from the local (American owned) McDonald's on the way.

Intensification of competition

Besides the pervasiveness of multinationals, other factors too can be seen to have fuelled the intensification of competition, not least an accelerated diffusion of new technologies, generally resulting in more restricted technological advantage being enjoyed by individual companies for a more limited time. Related to this, technological advances in telecommunications have accelerated the speed with which companies can effectively operate in geographically dispersed markets, thereby undermining any advantage of proximity and exclusivity from which local producers might previously have benefited.

The effects of intensified competition on work and workers can manifest themselves in a variety of ways depending on how employers respond to the competitive pressure. Decisions such as positioning in markets through acquisition, divestment or change in location, which markets to operate in, which products to develop or abandon and which technologies to employ, are all likely to be influenced by the nature and intensity of competition. At the same time, however, in the search for competitive advantage and efficiencies, labour and labour costs frequently play a central role. This is often true not only where labour costs represent a high proportion of total costs, but also where labour costs form a much smaller proportion, but are more open to manipulation (at least in the shorter term) than other, more fixed costs.

In the international air passenger transport industry, for example, labour costs represent only between 25 and 35 per cent of total operating costs (Doganis, 1994: 18); however, many other costs (for example, aircraft and fuel prices) are less open to manipulation, thus making labour one of the few 'variable' elements of cost, at least in the short term. As a result, in the face of deregulation and growing competition in the industry, there has been strong pressure on airline managements to improve competitiveness via cuts in their overall labour costs (Blyton, Martinez Lucio, McGurk and Turnbull, 2001).

There are essentially two contrasting strategies that employers may adopt towards labour in the search for competitive advantage: on the one hand, by increasing the output that labour achieves, or on the other, by reducing its cost. In practice, of course, these two strategies do not represent the sole choice available. Rather, they are located at each end of a continuum of responses, with employers likely to seek improvements in their competitive position by a mixture of responses designed to increase performance and reduce costs. Variation, therefore, is likely to be not between one extreme and the other but rather between the relative priorities given to performance improvement and cost reduction. Yet, it will nevertheless be helpful to delineate the two ends of the continuum in a little more detail, for they indicate how broad economic (and political) strategies have important ramifications for labour.

- One end of the continuum entails seeking competitiveness through improved performance and presupposes the creation of a highly trained and competent workforce, capable of utilising a high level of skill to yield increased levels of output.
- The other end of the continuum, involving a labour strategy based on lowest cost, is likely to entail minimising expenditure on training, resulting in a low-skill, low-productivity, low-cost workforce.

The choice between these strategies (or the relative weight given to each within more complex strategies) is not only an economic choice but also reflects political policies and constraints. An important reason, for example, that employers in Germany have generally pursued a 'high-skill, high-performance' strategy is partly because state policies on training and vocational education have resulted in an extensive training infrastructure, and a comparatively high level of skill development among the labour force. Added to this, alternative strategies such as minimising labour costs by hiring in workers when demand is strong, then firing them when demand drops, are less readily available to German employers, because of statutory restrictions governing redundancy and dismissal. This contrasts with the UK where there is little regulatory constraint on employers' ability to hire and fire. Given this, and the comparatively low development of national training and vocational education provision in the UK, it is evident how political policies in the two countries have influenced markedly different labour strategies (Boyer, 1988; Brunhes, 1989).

It has been widely argued that the UK has been in the vanguard of those countries pursuing a low-cost competitive strategy, with consequences for levels of investment in skills, wage levels (including non-wage labour costs such as sick pay and pension contributions) and the (low value-added) nature of much of the productive activity taking place (for a discussion, see Blyton and Turnbull, 2004). The low wage levels and widespread availability of labour (caused partly by high levels of unemployment for much of the 1980s and 1990s; see below) have been important factors encouraging a high level of foreign direct investment into the UK compared, for example, with other EU countries. Much of this investment has required only low or modest levels of skill development, with many activities (for example, in the motor components sector and consumer durables manufacture) involving assembly operations of one form or another. The paucity of the education and training structure in the UK compared, for example, with many of its western European counterparts, has been well documented (see, for example, Keep and Rainbird, 2005) as has the UK's level of productivity and performance (see Blyton and Turnbull, 2004: 49–55). The broader point for our present discussion, however, is that many of the salient aspects of work – types of jobs available, levels of income, extent of training and skill development, and degree of job security – can only be fully understood within the broader context of overall competitive strategies and the political and economic milieux within which those strategies are formulated and pursued.

Exercise 9.2

What do you think?
Assume that you are a senior human resources manager in an organisation that in the past has competed on the basis of producing high-volume goods to cater for the low-cost end of a consumer market (selling fixed-focus 'point and shoot' cameras).

Because of a change in consumer behaviour to favour higher specification and better quality digital equipment, your company has taken the decision to switch its strategy, get out of the low-cost end of the market, change its brand name, and compete by producing very high specification, and much more high-cost, equipment.

1. In terms of the workforce, what are the main changes that you anticipate will need to be made? List these and rank them in order of importance.
2. Now rank these again in terms of which change you would begin with (followed by second and third in order of priority for introduction), and explain the reasons for your decisions.
3. In addition to meeting the objective of successfully switching production to the higher quality output, what other consequences would you foresee arising from the changes you have listed?

Organising production

Aside from the question of overall strategies aimed at higher performance or lower cost, in other ways too, greater competition and the search for more efficient operations have led to significant changes in how organisations approach the tasks of goods and service production. For example, the twin factors of advances in technological capability and the search for greater efficiency have stimulated the development of more advanced forms of production control, with production processes being 're-engineered' or 're-configured' to improve the sequencing and integration of different stages of productive activity within organisations and the efficiency with which production 'flows' through an organisation with the minimum of bottlenecks. Partly this involves the supply of materials and the timing of manufacturing processes being matched more closely to customer orders, so that goods are produced 'just-in-time' to meet delivery requirements, thereby reducing the amount of capital tied up in stocks of raw materials, work in progress and finished goods. In terms of the possible impact on people's experience of work one effect of just-in-time operations could be an increase in work intensity, or at least a reduced ability to create greater control over work pace by building up 'banks' of part-finished items, which can be drawn upon to ease work pressures at a later point.

Quality

Closely associated with these changes in production processes has been an increased emphasis on output quality, with Japanese manufacturers such as Toyota leading the way in making the management of quality a key component in overall production and competitive strategy. The increased emphasis on quality has manifested itself in a variety of management initiatives such as quality assurance, quality circles and Total Quality Management (TQM) (Deming, 1982; Hill, 1991; Juran, 1979; Oakland, 1989; Strang and Kim, 2005), and has given rise to additional phrases in the management lexicon such as 'continuous improvement', 'zero defects', 'internal customers', 'world best practice' and the more commonplace 'right first time'. Much emphasis has come to be given to assuring quality at the point of production rather than at final inspection, in an attempt not only to ensure a better quality product, but in particular to avoid the cost of reworking defective output. Among the effects of these changes for the experience of work has been an increased emphasis on quality assurance and a requirement for workers to take greater responsibility for inspecting their own work and that of their work colleagues.

To sum up

A major development in the economic context of work is increasing economic globalisation, driven primarily by the expansion of multinational firms. Choices between different competitive strategies impact significantly on the nature of work and employment. Other key changes influencing the experience of work include the increased emphasis on more efficient organisation of production and higher quality output.

Learning outcome 4: Identify the main changes in the industrial structure, particularly the shift from manufacturing to services

Changes in industrial structure and employment

The structure of employment is never static but reflects and delineates patterns of change in particular industries and broader sectors of activity. The pace and some of the contours of change vary from one industrial society to another; nevertheless a number of broad developments are evident, reflected in the changing structure of employment. Measurement of the structure and location of economic activity, the characteristics of the workforce, the nature of employment contracts and patterns of unemployment, redundancy and insecurity indicate the aggregate nature of employment and the ways this is changing over time. A number of measures are interconnected: the simultaneous growth in service sector, female and part-time employment, for example. Also, some of the trends that can be identified are influenced not only by structural shifts in the economy but also by cyclical factors which act to accelerate or inhibit certain longer-term changes at particular periods. At the same time, what is revealing is the robust nature of many of the structural changes. Cyclical effects such as economic recession have in many cases had only a modest influence on several of the aspects of employment change (for example, the growth in part-time working), temporarily slowing some of the trends but rarely causing even a short-term reversal in longer-term developments. This is true even of those aspects of the employment experience, such as redundancy, unemployment and job insecurity, that in the past were closely associated with recession conditions, but in more recent times have seemingly become rather more loosely tied to overall economic conditions (see discussion of job insecurity, and Excerpt 9.4 on page p. 339).

Employment in service and manufacturing industries

Throughout the industrial world, a progressive shift in employment from primary and secondary sectors to the tertiary, service sector has been pronounced (Blyton, 1989: 31–8). In the OECD, almost seven out of ten employees (69 per cent) were working in the service sector in 2004, with Canada, the United States and several European countries registering a level of three-quarters or more of their employees located in services (OECD, 2005c: 17). This contrasts with earlier decades when in 1971, the corresponding proportion of employees working in the service sector in OECD countries was five out of ten, and in 1961 just over four out of ten (Blyton, 1989: 37).

Looking at the UK in more detail, in the period between 1971 and 2005, the number employed in manufacturing in the UK fell by over 4.75 million, or three-fifths (Table 9.1). In the same period, the number employed in services rose by more than 10.5 million, an increase of over 90 per cent. As a consequence, by 2005 almost seven times as many people were employed in the service sector in the UK as worked in manufacturing. When all industries are taken into account (agriculture, forestry and fishing; mining; electricity, gas and water supply, and construction, as well as manufacturing and services) the proportion of total employees engaged in the service sector in the UK stood at over four-fifths (82.2 per cent) by June 2005, up from just over half (52.6 per cent) of the total employees in employment who worked in services in 1971. In contrast, manufacturing employment by 2005 had fallen to less than one in eight (11.8 per cent) of the total in employment.

Within the service sector, employment in some industries has grown far more rapidly than in others in recent years. For example, while employment in the UK real-estate sector grew by 52 per cent between 1995 and 2005, and the numbers employed in education and health rose by 24 per cent and 22 per cent respectively, employment in other sectors registered much smaller increases over that period, including financial services (3.7 per cent increase) and public administration (8.2 per cent increase). Similarly, the continuing decline in employment in production industries in the 1995–2005 period was also unevenly distributed, with the rate of decline in some sectors (for example, clothing manufacture) much more marked than elsewhere (for example, food production and paper manufacture).

Table 9.1 Changes in employment in UK manufacturing and services, 1971–2005 (thousands)

	Manufacturing	Services
1971	7,890	11,388
1981	6,107	13,102
1990	4,756	16,643
2001	3,802	20,524
2005	3,131	21,884
Actual change 1971–2005	−4,759	+10,496
% change 1971–2005	−60.3%	+92.2%

Source: adapted from Employment Gazette (Historical Supplement 4) October 1994 and Labour Market Trends, January 2006.

Learning outcome 5: Assess the main changes taking place in workforce composition

Male and female workers

This increasing predominance of service sector employment has also been reflected in other changes occurring in the nature of the employed workforce, particularly the proportions of male and female, and full and part-time workers in the workforce. The period since the 1970s has witnessed a marked growth in the proportion of the workforce that is female. Several factors are important in accounting for this change, reflecting changes in both the demand for, and supply of, labour. Demand-side factors, however, are dominated by the shift to service sector employment and the increased opportunities for employment among women in service industries. This has been a key factor behind the increase in women's overall share in the workforce over the past generation. As Table 9.2 indicates, in the late 1950s, women comprised just over one-third of the total employed in Britain. By 2005, this proportion stood at almost one-half: of the 25.9 million employees in employment in Britain in September 2005, 12.88 million (49.6 per cent) were women. As the participation rate of women continues to rise, the realisation of a feminised workforce, where a majority of the employees in employment are women, is likely in the

---

Exercise 9.3

What do you think?
The discussion of the growth in female employment has concentrated on labour demand factors, particularly the expansion of the service sector. In addition, however, there are important labour supply factors which help to explain why a greater proportion of women – particularly those with children – are returning to the labour market than previously.

1. List the main factors that you think account for why a higher proportion of women are now returning to the labour market.
2. Rank these factors in order of importance and give reasons for your choice of the most important.

Table 9.2 Change in numbers of males and females in employment in Britain (thousands), 1959–2005

	1959	1979	1999	2005*
Females	7,174	9,435	11,477	12,877
Males	13,817	13,176	10,967	13,072
Total	20,991	22,611	22,444	25,949
Proportion of females in total	34.2%	41.7%	49.0%	49.6%

*September

Sources: Employment Gazette and Labour Market Trends, various dates.

foreseeable future. A workforce where the majority are female is already a reality in several regions in Britain and in various industries, particularly in the service sector.

Part-time employment

Within the overall changes in employment towards a greater proportion of jobs being held by women (the majority in the service sector), there has been a particular growth in the number of people working part-time. Across the OECD as a whole, over one in six employees work part-time. However, among the members of the OECD this proportion varies considerably, with eight countries in 2004 showing a part-time proportion greater than one in five of total employees, while seven other countries recorded a level of less than one in ten employees working part-time (Table 9.3).

Exercise 9.4

What do you think?
Look at the data in the fourth column of Table 9.3 dealing with women's share of total part-time employment. In around half the countries (14) women's share of part-time employment fell between 1990 and 2004. What factors can you think of that might account for this decline?

In the OECD countries as a whole, over seven out of ten part-time jobs are held by women (in the EU countries the proportion is nearer eight out of ten). Overall, around nine out of ten part-time jobs are located in the service sector. (See Naylor, 1994 for a detailed historical examination of the growth of part-time working.)

Self-employment

In addition to the portion of the labour force who are employees, there is also a significant minority who are self-employed. Among industrial countries in the OECD, levels of self-employment are highest where agriculture and small family businesses remain major sectors of activity: for example in Greece, Italy, Korea, Mexico, Portugal and Turkey.

In the UK, self-employment increased substantially (by almost half) during the 1980s, primarily because of the twin forces of, on the one hand, high levels of unemployment and limited job vacancies, and on the other hand, state financial support for those moving from being unemployed to self-employment. In addition, as part of their efforts to cut direct labour costs, many companies from the 1980s onwards abandoned employment contracts in favour of commercial contracts by requiring some of their workers to alter their status from being employees to being self-employed. This occurred, for example, among workers operating outside the main workplace, such as service engineers and milk deliverers, and particularly in the construction sector (see Evans, 1990). Where self-employed individuals are simply selling their skills to an organisation they are sometimes referred to as 'labour only subcontractors', and these comprise a high proportion of the

Table 9.3 Incidence and composition of part-time employment in OECD countries,[a] 1990–2004

	Men		Women		Part-time employment as a proportion of total employment		Women's share in part-time employment	
	1990	2004	1990	2004	1990	2004	1990	2004
Australia	11.3	16.1	38.5	40.8	22.6	27.1	70.8	67.1
Austria	..	3.7	..	29.6	..	15.5	..	86.9
Belgium	4.4	6.3	28.8	34.1	13.5	18.3	79.8	80.6
Canada	9.2	10.9	26.8	27.2	17.0	18.5	69.9	68.8
Czech Republic	..	1.5	..	5.2	..	3.1	..	72.9
Denmark	10.2	11.6	29.7	24.3	19.2	17.5	71.1	64.5
Finland	4.8	7.9	10.6	15.0	7.6	11.3	67.0	63.5
France	4.5	4.8	22.5	23.6	12.2	13.4	78.6	80.6
Germany	2.3	6.3	29.8	37.0	13.4	20.1	89.7	82.8
Greece	4.0	3.1	11.6	10.9	6.7	6.0	60.8	68.6
Hungary	..	2.2	..	5.1	..	3.6	..	67.7
Iceland[b]	7.5	10.2	39.7	31.2	22.2	21.2	81.6	73.1
Ireland	4.4	6.9	21.2	35.1	10.0	18.7	70.3	78.8
Italy	4.0	5.9	18.4	28.8	8.9	14.9	70.5	76.1
Japan	9.5	14.2	33.4	41.7	19.2	25.5	70.5	67.4
Korea	3.1	5.9	6.5	11.9	4.5	8.4	58.7	59.0
Luxemburg	1.6	1.7	19.1	33.3	7.6	14.6	86.6	93.0
Mexico	..	8.1	..	27.6	..	15.1	..	65.1
Netherlands	13.4	15.1	52.5	60.2	28.2	35.0	70.4	76.0
New Zealand	7.9	10.7	34.8	35.4	19.7	22.0	77.4	73.6
Norway	6.9	10.3	39.8	33.2	21.8	21.1	82.7	74.1
Poland	..	7.5	..	17.5	..	12.0	..	65.7
Portugal	3.9	5.8	12.8	14.0	7.6	9.6	70.3	67.0
Spain	1.4	2.6	11.5	17.2	4.6	8.3	79.2	81.0
Sweden	5.3	8.5	24.5	20.8	14.5	14.4	81.1	69.5
Switzerland	6.8	8.1	42.6	45.3	22.1	24.9	82.4	82.1
Turkey	4.9	3.7	18.8	14.8	9.2	6.6	62.6	59.5
United Kingdom	5.3	10.0	39.5	40.4	20.1	24.1	85.1	77.8
United States[c]	8.6	8.1	20.2	18.8	14.1	13.2	68.2	68.3

Notes
a) Part-time employment refers to persons who usually work less than 30 hours per week in their main job.
b) Data in 2004 column is for 2002.
c) Estimates are for wage and salary workers only.
.. not available
Source: adapted from OECD (2005b).

2.5 million enterprises with no employees in existence operating in the UK (Dale and Kerr, 1995: 462).

The growth in self-employment was heralded by UK governments in the 1980s as a mark of success and testimony to an emerging 'enterprise culture'. In practice, however, much of this newly created self-employment involves low remuneration and long hours. In 1993, for example, the full-time self-employed worked, on average, around 7 hours per week more than employees (Butcher and Hart, 1995: 218). Small businesses are also prone to high rates of business failure, and probably attest more to a lack of employment prospects and firms accepting only self-employed status, rather than any significant desire for autonomy within an enterprise culture.

In recent years in the UK, the proportion of the total workforce who are self-employed has fallen slightly (13.1 per cent of the overall workforce were self-employed in 1997, 12.7 per cent in 2005). This reflects the growth in the number of employees being faster during this period than the growth in the number of self-employed.

The location of employment

Size of employing organisation

While it is commonplace to think of a 'typical' employing organisation as one that is fairly or very large, in fact of the 992,000 enterprises with employees operating in Britain in the early 1990s, four out of five employed less than ten people while only 17,000 (1.7 per cent of the total) employed more than 100 employees. Of these, 14,000 were medium-sized (100–499 employees) and just 3000 were large (500 or more employees) (Dale and Kerr, 1995: 462). However, these 3000 largest businesses accounted for over one-third (37 per cent) of total non-government employment. Large-scale enterprises predominate in the energy and water sector, mining and quarrying, chemicals and parts of the financial sector. Small firms on the other hand are particularly numerous in parts of the manufacturing sector (including printing and publishing, furniture and fabricated metal products) as well as in agriculture, construction and most service industries (including business services, entertainment, catering, and vehicle maintenance and repair) (ibid: 463).

In terms of trends in firm size, there is some indication that average firm size is declining and that the proportion of total employees working for smaller firms is gradually increasing. In part, this reflects the shift from manufacturing to service activities (smaller firms being more prevalent in service industries), the closure of many formerly very large establishments (such as steel plants and shipyards) over the past 25 years, and the increase in outsourcing activity by larger firms. Restricted longitudinal data (covering the period 1988 to 1991) collected by the OECD suggests a modest trend throughout the main industrialised countries towards a larger share of employment being concentrated in smaller firms. In the UK between these dates, for example, the share of total employment located in firms with less than 100 workers rose from 47 to 49 per cent (OECD, 1995: 124). Smaller firms also figure prominently in statistics on employment creation. As the OECD (1995: 128) notes, however, 'volatility in employment levels ... appears to be an intrinsic characteristic of small businesses'. In other words, smaller firms figure prominently in statistics of gross job gains and gross job losses (see also Shutt and Whittington, 1987).

Location of work

As employment in production industries, particularly traditional industries such as coal, steel and shipbuilding, has declined, so too has the proportion of total employment located in the main industrial conurbations. There has been a growing tendency to establish and expand service activities and new manufacturing projects on 'greenfield' sites, often in semi-rural areas (Massey 1988: 61; see also Sayer and Walker, 1992). Further, for a significant minority of workers, their work is located in their own homes. One of the areas of growth in homeworking in recent years has been the expansion of teleworking – see Excerpt 9.2; also, Sullivan and Lewis (2001) for a discussion of gender and telework. For a thorough analysis of different forms of working from home, see Felstead, Jewson and Walters (2005a).

Excerpt 9.2

Teleworking doubled in size

According to the Labour Force Survey (LFS) analysed by Ruiz and Walling (2005), by spring 2005 there were just over 2.4 million teleworkers in the UK – that is, workers using both a telephone and a computer to carry out their work, either at home or in different places using home as a base. This total represents a doubling in the proportion of teleworkers in the UK workforce between 1997 and 2005: by 2005 over 8 per cent of the workforce in the UK were teleworkers compared with 4 per cent in 1997.

The LFS tracks two different kinds of teleworker: those working mainly in their own homes, and those working in different places (such as clients' premises, on the train, or in cars) while at the same time using home as a base. In 2005, most teleworkers (1.8 million out of the 2.4 million total) worked in different places using their homes as a base; the remainder (0.6 million) worked mainly in their own homes.

In terms of the characteristics of teleworkers, a majority (62 per cent) were self-employed in 2005. Almost two-thirds (65 per cent) of teleworkers were men, and it is male teleworkers who are particularly likely to telework in different places. Ruiz and Walling's analysis of the LFS also shows that teleworking is more common, and growing at a faster rate, among older workers (50 years and over) than among younger age groups (particularly 16–24 year olds).

In terms of occupation, nine out of ten teleworkers work in managerial, professional, technical and skilled trades occupations. The occupational groups that are most likely to work in their own homes as teleworkers (rather than working in different places) are administrative and secretarial occupations. The rate of teleworking is highest in skilled trades. Among skilled workers, those employed in the building trade are particularly prominent among the teleworking population. The self-employed builder using a computer and telephone to conduct his/her business is a very different picture of a 'typical' teleworker than past stereotypes of white-collar workers being remotely connected to their organisation and using the telephone and computer to undertake tasks at home.

Learning outcome 6: Consider the changing experience of work in terms of changes in levels of unemployment, redundancies, temporary work and job insecurity

Unemployment, redundancy, temporary work and job insecurity

Unemployment

Just as it is difficult to compare unemployment rates between countries because of different definitions of unemployment, so too seeking to draw an accurate comparison of present-day rates of unemployment with those of earlier periods is complicated by the many changes made to the basis on which unemployment statistics are calculated. In the UK since the late 1970s, for example, there have been over 30 such changes (see Blyton and Turnbull, 2004: 75; also Denman and McDonald, 1996: 18; and Department for Education and Employment, 1995a: 398–400).

Despite these difficulties, however, important long-term trends in the rate of unemployment remain evident. The principal one is that levels of unemployment have risen from around 2 per cent in the 1950s and 1960s to a peak of over 11 per cent in the mid-1980s. Even during periods of strong economic growth, unemployment rates have tended to remain higher than the rates prevailing during growth periods a generation ago. Table 9.4 shows a comparative picture among industrial

Table 9.4 Unemployment rates in 25 industrial countries, selected years 1994–2005 (rate as proportion of civilian labour force)

	1994	2004
Australia	9.2	5.4
Austria	3.6	5.0
Belgium	13.1	12.0
Canada	10.4	7.2
Czech Republic	4.4	8.3
Denmark	8.1	5.7
Finland	16.6	8.8
France	12.3	10.1
Germany	8.5	9.9
Greece	9.6	10.2
Hungary	11.0	6.2
Ireland	14.8	4.4
Italy	11.2	8.1
Japan	2.9	4.7
Luxemburg	2.1	2.8
Netherlands	6.9	5.0
New Zealand	8.1	3.9
Norway	5.5	4.5
Poland	14.4	19.0
Portugal	6.8	6.7
Spain	24.2	11.0
Sweden	9.8	6.6
Switzerland	3.7	4.2
United Kingdom	9.6	4.7
United States	6.1	5.5

Source: adapted from OECD (2005c).

countries for the period 1994–2004, which indicates that while unemployment rates fell in many countries between these dates, the levels of unemployment in many countries remained at comparatively high levels.

As well as the variation between countries, unemployment rates vary considerably between different groups. For example, while the OECD average unemployment rate in 2004 was 6.8 per cent, among people under 25 years the average rate was double this figure (13.5 per cent) (OECD, 2005c: 21). In some countries this difference was even more evident. In Italy in 2004, for example, while the general unemployment rate stood at 8.1 per cent, among those under 25 years the unemployment rate was 23.5 per cent. In Poland, a higher general rate of unemployment in 2004 of 19 per cent was again far exceeded by the rate among those under 25 years, among whom the unemployment rate exceeded 40 per cent (ibid).

Alongside this trend of gradually rising unemployment over the past four decades, the proportion of the total workforce that has experienced a period of unemployment in recent years is considerable. The prevailing level of unemployment at any particular time comprises the difference between those coming onto the unemployed register and those leaving it. These unemployment 'flows' are far greater than changes in the unemployment level might suggest. Taking the example of an unexceptional month (we have chosen May 2005 to illustrate the point), the level of registered unemployed in that month was down by 4600 compared with the previous month. This figure, however, is the product of an inflow of new unemployment registrations of almost *40 times* that amount (202,300) during the month, and an outflow of 206,900. In a proportion of cases, the same individuals become unemployed (and re-employed) more than once in any given year, thus figuring several times in the inflow and outflow statistics: studies have shown that between one-third and two-fifths of new registrations are likely to have previously been unemployed during the same year (DfEE, 1995b: 355). What the magnitude of the flows also underlines, however, is the breadth of experience of unemployment within the workforce as a whole. It is also a reflection of a widespread lack of employment security (see also, below).

The level of unemployment does not reflect the total picture of job shortage, however. In addition to those officially counted as unable to find work, there are millions more who have become prematurely (and involuntarily) retired or otherwise dropped out of the labour market because of a perceived lack of prospects of finding work. Changes in the participation rates of men in the labour market indicate the scale of this discouragement effect. The proportions of males of working age who are active in the labour market (in work or registered unemployed) has fallen in several industrial countries over the past two decades, to a point where in the UK for example, approaching one in five males of working age, and not in full-time education, are not active in the labour market – a degree of inactivity which Hutton (1995: 1) identifies as having 'incalculable consequences' for overall well-being and social cohesion in the country.

While men's economic activity rate has declined, women's overall activity rate has increased. As a result, the gap in men's and women's activity rates narrowed from 16 to 10 percentage points between 1992 and 2004 (the male activity rate in 2004 standing at 83 per cent, the female rate at 73 per cent) (Ashton et al, 2004: 30).

Two further points are worth making in regard to unemployment. First, the level of unemployment and the extent to which people have been made unemployed impacts both materially and psychologically not only on those directly affected. In addition, the impact is extended by a general heightening of awareness of job insecurity and the perceived difficulties that can be experienced in gaining employment once unemployed – difficulties clearly expressed in the scale of long-term unemployment. For example, in 2004 almost one-third of those unemployed in OECD countries had been unemployed for at least a year (OECD, 2005b: 258). Furthermore, there is a disproportionate presence of some groups (such as younger and older workers and ethnic minorities) among the long-term unemployed.

The effect on people's attitudes to work and job insecurity of high levels of unemployment still prevailing in several countries, was vividly summed up in the UK in the 1980s by Ron Todd (then chief negotiator at the Ford Motor Company and later general secretary of the T&GWU), who commented that 'we've got 3 million on the dole and another 23 million scared to death' (quoted by Bratton, 1992: 70). The second point is that the rate of flow of individuals onto unemployed registers has been affected by the amount and circumstances under which redundancies have been declared over the recent period. It is to a more detailed consideration of redundancies that we now turn.

Redundancies

Labour Force Surveys in the UK indicate that in between spring 1996 and spring 2005, over 1.5 million redundancies took place. Redundancies are nothing new, of course. What is new in the recent period, however, are the causes of redundancy. In the past, redundancies have been a consequence of economic difficulty, as Cappelli (1995: 577) comments: 'Firms clearly laid off workers because of cyclical downturns or other situations where their business declined, but reductions in other situations were extremely uncommon.' However, increasingly common is the tendency for employers to announce redundancies as a cost-cutting measure even at times when the business and the economic outlook are buoyant. Quoting Cappelli (1995: 577) again, 'workforce reductions are increasingly "strategic or structural in nature" as opposed to a response to short-term economic conditions'. The experience in the UK over the past decade is very similar: firms announce redundancies when they are doing badly and when they are doing well, with the constant shaving of workforce totals being used as a method of cost control. A key reason for this, Cappelli argues, is that outside the organisation – and particularly among shareholders and investment markets – cutting workforce levels has come to be taken as a sign of restructuring, efficiency-saving and likely improvement in profitability. The upshot is that redundancy announcements can improve share prices. Cappelli (1995: 571) quotes one US study, for example (by Worrell, Davidson and Sharma, 1991), which found that stock prices rose on average by about 4 per cent in the days following layoff announcements that were part of general restructurings (see also Excerpt 9.3).

Excerpt 9.3

Redundancies at Corus

On Thursday 1 February 2001, the Anglo-Dutch steelmaker Corus announced 6050 redundancies in the UK – more than a fifth of its UK workforce. This followed 4500 job losses made the previous year by the company, which was formed in 1999 following the merger of British Steel and the Dutch firm Hoogovens.

The job cuts announced in 2001 involved the ending of iron and steel-making at its large Llanwern plant in south Wales, the closing of two finishing plants also in south Wales, and reductions in workforce totals at several other plants elsewhere in the UK.

On the day of the job cuts announcement, the company's share price, which had been falling in the previous period, immediately jumped by almost a tenth (9.7 per cent) in its value, rising from 74.75 pence on the close of business on 31 January to 82 pence at close on 1 February.

Temporary work

There are a number of categories of work that are temporary in nature, in that they are limited in duration. These include jobs that are casual (the work available only on an ad hoc basis) or seasonal, and those which involve fixed-term contracts and temporary work acquired through agencies. This variety of forms that temporary work can take makes cross-national comparisons of trends in temporary work difficult. The general picture, however, appears to be a mixed one. While some countries (including Australia, France, the Netherlands and Spain) recorded increases in the relative size of their temporary workforces in the 1980s and 1990s, others (for example Belgium, Greece, Luxemburg and Portugal) recorded decreases, and still others (for example, Japan, Denmark and Italy) had levels of temporary work that stayed fairly constant (OECD, 2002).

In the UK, temporary workers represented around 6 per cent of the total employed population in 2004 – a decline from the levels prevailing in the late 1990s (Table 9.5).

Of the 1.7 million temporary employees in the UK in 2000, slightly more than half were women (Ashton et al., 2004: 45). The temporary workforce are distributed across a range of industries, though amongst women a significant proportion of temporary workers are located in teaching, childcare and related occupations, and sales.

Table 9.5   Temporary employment in the UK, 1992–2004

	1992	1996	2000	2004
Temporary employees (thousands)	1304	1671	1696	1496
Proportion of total employees (%)	5.9	7.4	7.1	6.1

Source: Labour Market Trends, December 2000 and January 2006.

Job insecurity

Higher average levels of unemployment over the past two decades, the continuing level of redundancies and (in some countries at least) a higher level of temporary working have made job insecurity a more prominent concern to many workers in contemporary workplaces than it was to a majority of their counterparts a generation ago (Burchell et al., 1999). The level of insecurity has also been fuelled by a tendency for more jobs to be offered on the basis of fixed term contracts, rather than as indefinite employment contracts. As Allen and Henry (1996: 66) point out, the growth of subcontracting in the private sector and the move towards contracting out of public services has led to a growth in 'precarious employment', where jobs are secure only for the length of the contract. The effect is the creation of 'an atmosphere of pervasive insecurity' (Allen and Henry, 1996: 67; see also Heery and Salmon, 2000). Heightened levels of corporate merger and acquisition activity have also added to this feeling of job precariousness.

At the same time, it should be noted that many employees continue to spend a significant part of their career with a single employer. In 2000, for example, approaching half (46 per cent) of employees in the UK had at least five years' service with their employer, and over one in ten of these had worked for the same employer for 20 years or more – a figure slightly higher than the proportion (9 per cent) registering at least 20 years' service with their present employer in 1986 and 1991 (ONS, 2001: 88; see also Doogan, 2001). Thus, a significant proportion of those in employment build up long service with a single employer. For others, however, work is a much more precarious affair, with insecurity, redundancy, temporary contracts and unemployment contributing to an overall experience of a fragmented, rather than a unified, working life. This is an experience which Sennett (1998) argues is highly damaging to personal integrity and individual financial solvency, as well as to the degree of societal polarisation between employment-rich and employment-poor households (see Excerpt 9.4).

Excerpt 9.4

The end of career?

In the United States in 1999, the California Management Review (CMR) published a debate over the end of long-term jobs. One of the leading proponents on 'the end of career' thesis, Peter Cappelli (1999), argues that factors such as competitive pressures, volatile markets, more demanding shareholders, the need for flexibility, weaker trade unions, changing skill requirements and technological advances have combined to bring the 'jobs for life' era to an end. His thesis is that a prolonged period of widespread permanent, full-time employment with predictable advancement is over, and is being progressively replaced by shorter-term employment relationships. Richard Sennett (1998: 22) argues a similar point, commenting that the motto of contemporary capitalism is 'no long term'.

The alternative viewpoint in the CMR debate is put by Sanford Jacoby (1999), who argues that this portrayal of contemporary industrial society is not adequately supported by labour market evidence, and is thus an inaccurate one. Jacoby argues that measures such as average job tenure, and more generally the continuing experience of work in many public and private sector industries, indicates that long-term employment relationships remain widespread, and the notion of long-term careers is far from over. This counter-argument agrees that there are changes occurring, both in the overall labour market and within individual organisations, but that currently these do not amount to support for an 'end of career' thesis.

Exercise 9.5

What do you think?

1. Which of the arguments described in Excerpt 9.4 do you find the more convincing? What are your reasons for this?
2. If we take Cappelli's argument to be at least partially correct – or if we assume it will become correct – what do you think are the main implications for employees and those managing them?

To sum up

Developments in the structure of work and employment have significantly changed workforce composition in terms of the size and location of workforces and the distribution of employment between service and manufacturing sectors, the proportion of male and female workers, those working part and full-time, as employees or self-employed. Unemployment, redundancy and the growth of non-permanent contracts have created a heightened sense of insecurity for many employees.

Conclusion

This chapter has illustrated some of the ways in which broader influences and developments impact upon the everyday realities of work. Political policies, from local planning decisions to national strategies on deregulation to the harmonisation of employment conditions across countries, have significantly influenced the context within which work is performed. With the growing integration of many national economies into multinational associations such as the EU, it may be anticipated that the political influences on work will be increasingly evident at the transnational level in years to come – possibly at the expense of both national and local political mechanisms.

This increasing economic and political association between different blocs of countries has also been one of the influences on levels and patterns of competition within individual sectors and markets. The growth in competition in general may be seen to have affected the experience of work in various ways. In particular, this may have been experienced through a more intensive managerial search for both performance improvement and labour cost reduction – objectives which manifest themselves in a variety of managerial strategies concerning the workforce, and which also reflect broader political conditions, such as the degree of statutory regulation of employment and the national provision of education and training. Competitive pressures from rising industrial nations have also been a major factor bringing about fundamental restructuring of most mature industrial societies, with the latter experiencing a decline of many of the sectors on which their industrialism was initially built (such as coal, steel, textiles and shipbuilding) and the growth of other, primarily service sector, industries. This shift has been reflected not only in a decrease in manual and rise in nonmanual jobs, but also in major changes in workforce composition. The prominence of male production workers has given way to an increasingly feminised workforce, and one in which a significant proportion of employees work part-time.

In addition, an important change in the overall context of work over the past generation has been the degree to which work has, for many, become a more precarious activity. Indefinite employment and long service with a single employer have, for many, given way to a more fragmented job history. Higher levels of unemployment, coupled with high redundancy rates and job insecurity, have resulted in a growing proportion of the workforce experiencing paid employment as an intermittent, rather than a regular, activity. One of the issues this raises is whether, as work becomes more fragmented and as the experience of non-work becomes more common, the values associated with work show signs of being in decline. It is to an examination of work values that we now turn.

References

Allen, J. and Henry, N. (1996) 'Fragments of industry and employment', in R. Crompton, D. Gallie and K. Purcell (eds), *Changing Forms of Employment*, London: Routledge: 65–82.

Ashton, J., Clegg, M., Diplock, E., Richie, H. and Willison, R. (2004) *Interim Update of Key Indicators of Women's Position in Britain*, London: Department of Trade and Industry.

Bach, S. and Sisson, K. (2000) 'Personnel management in perspective', in S. Bach and K. Sisson (eds), *Personnel Management*, 3rd edn, Oxford: Blackwell: 3–42.

Bank of England (2000) 'The international environment', *Bank of England Quarterly Bulletin*, August: 233–46.

Blyton, P. (1989) 'Working population and employment', in R. Bean (ed.), *International Labour Statistics*, London: Routledge: 125–43.

Blyton, P. (1994) 'Working hours', in K. Sisson (ed.), *Personnel Management*, 2nd edn, Oxford: Blackwell: 495–526.

Blyton, P. and Turnbull, P. (2004) *The Dynamics of Employee Relations*, 3rd edn, Basingstoke: Macmillan.

Blyton, P., Martinez Lucio, M., McGurk, J. and Turnbull, P. (2001) 'Globalization and trade union strategy: industrial restructuring and human resource management in the international civil aviation industry', *International Journal of Human Resource Management*, 12 (3): 445–63.

Boyer, R. (ed.) (1988) *The Search for Labour Market Flexibility*, Oxford: Clarendon.

Bratton, J. (1992) *Japanization at Work*, London: Macmillan.

Brunhes, B. (1989) 'Labour flexibility in enterprises: a comparison of firms in four European countries', in Organisation for Economic Cooperation and Development (OECD) (ed.), *Labour Market Flexibility: Trends in Enterprises*, Paris: OECD: 11–36.

Burchell, B. J., Day, D., Hudson, M., Lapido, D., Mankelow, R., Nolan, J. P., Reed, H., Wichert, I. C. and Wilkinson, F. (1999) *Job Insecurity and Work Intensification: Flexibility and the Changing Boundaries of Work*, York: Joseph Rowntree Foundation.

Butcher, S. and Hart, D. (1995) 'An analysis of working time 1979–1994', *Employment Gazette*, May: 211–22.

Buyck, C. (2005) 'Wooing Europe's new breed', *Air Transport World*, 42 (9): 32–5.

Cappelli, P. (1995) 'Rethinking employment', *British Journal of Industrial Relations*, 33 (4): 563–602.

Cappelli, P. (1999) 'Career jobs are dead', *California Management Review*, 42: 146–67.

Clausing, K. A. (2000) 'Does multinational activity displace trade?', *Economic Inquiry*, 38 (2): 190–206.

Crowther, S. and Garrahan, P. (1988) 'Corporate power and the local economy', *Industrial Relations Journal*, 19 (1): 51–9.

Dale, I. and Kerr, J. (1995) 'Small and medium sized enterprises: their numbers and importance to employment', *Labour Market Trends*, December: 461–5.

Deming, W. E. (1982) *Quality, Productivity and Competitive Position*, Cambridge, Mass.: MIT Press.

Denman, J. and McDonald, P. (1996) 'Unemployment statistics from 1881 to the present day', *Labour Market Trends*, January: 5–18.

Department for Education and Employment (DfEE) (1995a) 'Changes to the coverage of the monthly count of claimant unemployment', *Labour Market Trends*, November: 398–400.

DfEE (1995b) 'New developments in the pattern of claimant unemployment in the United Kingdom', *Employment Gazette*, September: 351–8.

Dickens, L. (1995) 'UK part-time employees and the law: recent and potential developments', *Gender, Work and Organization*, 2 (4): 207–15.

Doganis, R. (1994) 'The impact of liberalization on European airline strategies and operations', *Journal of Air Transport Management*, 1 (1): 15–25.

Doogan, K. (2001) 'Insecurity and long-term employment', *Work, Employment and Society*, 15 (3): 419–41.

Evans, S. (1990) 'Free labour and economic performance: evidence from theconstruction industry', *Work, Employment and Society*, 4 (2): 239–52.

Felstead, A., Jewson, N. and Walters, S. (2005a) *Changing Places of Work*, Basingstoke: Palgrave.

Gennard, J. and Judge G. (2005) *Employee Relations*, 4th edn, London: CIPD.

Heery, E. and Salmon, J. (eds) (2000) *The Insecure Workforce*, London: Routledge.

Hicks, S. (2005) 'Trends in public sector employment' *Labour Market Trends*, 113 (12): 477–88.

Hill, S. (1991) 'Why quality circles failed but Total Quality Management might succeed', *British Journal of Industrial Relations*, 29 (4): 541–68.

Hirst, P. and Thompson, G. (1996) *Globalization in Question*, London: Polity.

Hoggett, P. (1996) 'New modes of control in the public services', *Public Administration* 74 (1): 9–36.

Hutton, W. (1995) *The State We're In*, London: Cape.

Jacoby, S. M. (1999) 'Are career jobs heading for extinction?' *California Management Review*, 42: 123–45.

Juran, J. M. (1979) *Quality Control Handbook*, New York: McGraw-Hill.

Keep, E. and Rainbird, H. (2005) 'Training', in P. Edwards (ed.), *Industrial Relations: Theory and Practice*, 2nd edn, Oxford: Blackwell: 392–419.

Kleinknecht, A. and ter Wengel, J. (1998) 'The myth of economic globalization', *Cambridge Journal of Economics*, 22 (5): 637–67.

Massey, D. (1988) 'What's happening to UK manufacturing?', in J. Allen and D. Massey (eds), *The Economy in Question*, London: Sage: 45–90.

Megginson, W. L. and Netter, J. M. (2001) 'From state to market: a survey of empirical studies on privatisation', *Journal of Economic Literature*, 39 (2): 321–89.

Milberg, W. S. (1998) 'Globalization and its limits', in R. Kozul-Wright and R. Rowthorn (eds), *Transnational Corporations and the Global Economy*, Basingstoke: Macmillan: 69–94.

National Institute Economic Review (NIER) (2005) 'Economic overview', *National Institute Economic Review*, No. 191: 2–3.

Naylor, K. (1994) 'Part-time working in Great Britain: an historical analysis', *Employment Gazette*, December: 473–84.

Oakland, J. S. (1989) *Total Quality Management*, Oxford: Butterworth-Heinemann.

OECD (1999) 'Privatisation trends', *Financial Market Trends*, no. 72: 129–45.

OECD (2000a) *OECD Economic Outlook*, no. 67, Paris: OECD.

OECD (2002) 'Taking the measure of temporary employment', *OECD Employment Outlook*, Paris: OECD: 129–83

OECD (2005a) *Economic Outlook*, No. 77, Paris: OECD.

OECD (2005b) *Employment Outlook*, Paris: OECD.

OECD (2005c) *OECD in Figures*, 2005 edition, Paris: OECD.

Office for National Statistics (ONS) (2000) *Social Trends 30*, London: The StationeryOffice.

Organisation for Economic Cooperation and Development (OECD) (1995) OECD *Employment Outlook* 1995, Paris: OECD.

Parker, D. and Kirkpatrick, C. (2005) 'Privatisation in developing countries: a review of the evidence and the policy lessons', *Journal of Development Studies*, 41 (4): 513–41.

Rubinstein, M. (1984) *Equal Pay for Work of Equal Value*, London: Macmillan.

Sayer, A. and Walker, R. (1992) T*he New Social Economy: Reworking the Division of Labour*, Oxford: Blackwell.

Sennett, R. (1998) *The Corrosion of Character*, New York: Norton.

Shutt, J. and Whittington, R. (1987) 'Fragmentation strategies and the rise of small units: cases from the north west', *Regional Studies*, 21: 13–23.

Stopford, J. and Turner, L. (1985) *Britain and the Multinationals*, Chichester: Wiley.

Strang, D. and Kim, Y.-M. (2005) 'The diffusion and domestication of managerial innovations: the spread of scientific management, quality circles and TQMbetween the United States and Japan', in S. Ackroyd, R. Batt, P. Thompson and P. S. Tolbert (eds), *The Oxford Handbook of Work and Organization*, Oxford: Oxford University Press: 177–99.

Sullivan, C. and Lewis, S. (2001) 'Home-based telework, gender and the synchronization of work and family: perspectives of teleworkers and their co-residents', Gender, *Work and Organization*, 8 (2): 123–45.

Tait, N. and Taylor, A. (2005) 'On-call hours to count as work for health staff', *Financial Times*, 2 December: 6.

Toninelli, P. A. (ed.) (2000) *The Rise and Fall of State-Owned Enterprise in the Western World*, Cambridge: Cambridge University Press.

Waters, M. (1995) *Globalisation*, London: Routledge.

World Trade Organisation (WTO) (2005) *World Trade in 2004*, New York: WTO.

CHAPTER 10

Managing the Entrepreneurial Organization

CONTENTS

- Barriers to corporate entrepreneurship
- Change
- Managing change
- Freedom and control
- Balance
- Management and structure
- Managing risk
- Summary

LEARNING OUTCOMES

By the end of this chapter you should be able to:

- Describe the barriers to corporate entrepreneurship and explain how they can be overcome;

- Explain how change can be facilitated, resistance reduced and blocks removed;

- Describe the balance between freedom and control needed in an entrepreneurial organization and explain the dimensions on which this can be measured;

- Justify why entrepreneurial firms need loose control but tight accountability, with early warning signs that indicate when risks might materialize;

- Describe how management style and structure must be congruent and explain the dimensions on which this can be measured;

- Use basic risk management techniques such as risk classification and the development of key risk indicators.

Barriers to corporate entrepreneurship

Many traditional management techniques unintentionally discourage corporate entrepreneurship. They dissuade individuals within the organization from behaving entrepreneurially. Examples of this include the way in which some organizations:

- *Focus on efficiency or return on investment*: An entrepreneurial organization is one that is going places, fast. It is probably first into a new market and needs to grow quickly, in order to penetrate the market, persuading customers to buy the product or service before competitors have time to react. It needs to focus on the critical issues that it faces to achieve this, rather than being managed like a mature company – a 'cash cow' – with the simple objective of generating maximum short-term profit through greater efficiency.
- *Plan for the long term and then control against plan*: In a turbulent, changing environment the future is not certain. The entrepreneurial organization needs to have goals and a vision but it also needs to learn from the changing reality as it moves towards its goals, changing the plans as appropriate. Interim milestones need to be set, but progress needs to be re-assessed after each one is reached and benchmarked against reality.
- *Enforce standard procedures, rules and regulations*: This tends to block innovation and lead to missed opportunities. The entrepreneurial organization needs to be flexible, creating rules for specific situations but then being prepared to ditch them when circumstances change. That means having a culture where rules are challenged and only accepted when proved to be for the good of the organization.
- *Avoid risk*: Avoiding risk means missing opportunities. By way of contrast, an entrepreneurial organization will be willing to take measured risks. However, rather than launching headlong into the unknown, it progresses toward its goal in small, spider-like steps, building an understanding of the risks it faces as it progresses. Risks need to be identified, even if they cannot be avoided. Once identified, early warning mechanisms can be put in place so that appropriate action can be taken in good time.
- *Make decisions based on past experience*: In a changing environment the past is not always a good predictor of the future. The entrepreneurial organization takes small steps, testing its assumptions as it goes, learning from the changing reality.
- *Manage functionally*: Functional management disciplines and rigid job descriptions can be a barrier to creativity, which often relies on a holistic approach to problem solving. Entrepreneurial organizations often create multidisciplinary teams to investigate and develop entrepreneurial opportunities.
- *Promote individuals who conform*: This is a certain way to lose innovators. An entrepreneurial organization must be able to accommodate, indeed encourage, those who do not conform. Ideas people and 'doers' need to be encouraged and rewarded.

'To encourage people to innovate more, you have to make it safe for them to fail.'
Michael Dell

There is nothing wrong with these management techniques, in the right environmental context. However they will not encourage the development of an entrepreneurial organization. Approaching the issue in a more systematic way, Morris (1998) believes that barriers to corporate entrepreneurship can be classified into six groups. These are based upon an extensive review of the literature on corporate innovation and entrepreneurship, surveys of medium-sized and large companies and in-depth assessments of three Fortune 500 companies:

1. *Systems*: Inappropriate evaluation and reward systems, excessive and rigid control systems, inflexible budgeting systems, overly rigid and formal planning systems and arbitrary cost allocation systems. Formal systems evolve over a period of time and in most organizations are in place to generate order and conformity in a large complex organization. By way of contrast small, entrepreneurial companies rarely have strong systems. Their strategies evolve and planning becomes contingent, based upon different scenarios. The lesson is clear, if systems are too strong they can act as a disincentive for entrepreneurship.
2. *Structures*: Too many hierarchical levels, top-down management, overly narrow span of control, responsibility without authority, restricted communications and lack of accountability. Hierarchy is anathema to an entrepreneurial organization, instead authority and responsibility are pushed down to the point where they are most effective.
3. *Strategic direction*: No formal strategy for entrepreneurship, no vision from the top, no entrepreneurial role models at the top, no innovation goals, lack of senior management commitment. Visionary leaders with a commitment to make the entire organization entrepreneurial are essential. Equally tangible but achievable goals for product, process and marketing innovation are vital.
4. *Policies and procedures*: Long, complex approval procedures, excessive documentation requirements, unrealistic performance criteria and over-reliance on established rules of thumb. As with systems, small, entrepreneurial firms rarely have sophisticated policies and procedures – and this gives them greater flexibility – but they are needed as the firm grows. The problem is that, as policies and procedures grow in complexity, the lead time to make things happen increases and the temptation 'not to bother' grows. The entrepreneurial organization needs to build some slack and leeway into its procedures so that innovation is encouraged.
5. *People*: Fear of failure, resistance to change, parochial bias, complacency, protection of own sphere of activity, short-term orientation, inappropriate skills and talents. People can be the greatest barrier of all. Changing people – their attitudes and the way they do things – is the biggest challenge facing management. It is never easy. There is a natural tendency to resist change and preserve the status quo, and nobody said generating an entrepreneurial culture was easy.
6. *Culture*: Ill-defined values, lack of consensus over priorities, lack of congruence, values that conflict with those of an entrepreneurial culture. Culture is the cement that binds the entrepreneurial organization together. The stronger it is, the stronger the entrepreneurial architecture. Culture comes from the top but it rests on a set of commonly held values and beliefs. If they are not commonly held, or not seen to be held by top management, there is little chance of success.

You can do three things with these barriers:

- Ignore them – but this only works with the less important barriers;
- Work around them – intrapreneurs are particularly good at this;
- Remove them. An entrepreneurial organization is one that embraces change. Often change is resisted by individuals within it. Unblocking barriers to change can be particularly difficult when it comes down to dealing with individuals – and that comes down to the interpersonal skills of its leader.

Case insight

The English pub may be a uniquely friendly place, home for a diverse range of customers but the UK licensed trade is also known for high staff turnover and the problems of keeping a motivated and loyal workforce. **JD Wetherspoon** is a national chain of some 650 pubs that expanded rapidly since it was founded in the late 1980s by **Tim Martin** – still Chairman of what is now a publicly quoted company. It provides good-quality food and drink at reasonable prices in a modern environment free of music. It also specializes in 'real ales' – cask conditioned beers from England's regional brewers. It is famous for its 'Sorry Ronny' meal deals – a beer and a burger at prices cheaper than McDonald's.

The company has grown largely organically and has only made one acquisition, the Lloyds No 1 chain, purchased from Wolverhampton & Dudley Breweries in 2001. Lloyds No 1 offers a similar formula, but with music and entertainment. Under its new owners sales more than doubled in the space of five years. One of the reasons for this organic growth is Wetherspoon's preference for selecting and fitting out its own sites rather than converting other people's ideas into the Wetherspoon format. Pubs typically have an above-average floor space and are in high customer-density areas, like high streets.

Wetherspoon has won many awards recognizing the excellence of its staff and management. Most JD Wetherspoon staff are hourly paid – called 'associates'. It recognizes that many will not stay for all their working lives but it wants to encourage motivation and loyalty. To do this it uses a range of approaches to create a positive culture including pay and benefits, training and development and involvement in deciding on new ways of doing things.

- *Pay and benefits*: Staff are generally paid more than competitors. Staff receive a bonus, based on the pub's performance. There are incentive schemes, including a monthly competition for customer care. There is a share option scheme for employees.
- *Training and development*: The company is known for the excellence of its training, which is closely linked to the qualifications offered by the British Institute of Innkeeping. Staff are encouraged to identify their development needs and the obtaining of National Vocational Qualifications is actively encouraged. Training leads to promotion. 54% of pub managers started out as associates, 40% of area managers were once pub managers.

→

- *New ideas*: Staff are encouraged to come up with new ideas as to how products or service might be improved and good practice is disseminated throughout the organization. Kitchen staff might come up with menu, food preparation and serving suggestions. They might suggest which meals should be promoted. Many small but frequent changes are made in this way. Every fortnight the company holds a 'big meeting' which includes the chairman, directors, pub managers and some associates. This considers performance and future initiatives.

Change

The skill of managing change is crucial. Any entrepreneurial organization will face change aplenty, often seeming like a succession of crises. As the organization passes through each change, individuals can encounter a roller coaster of human emotion as they find themselves facing a different role with new demands. The classic change/ denial curve used by Kakabadse (1983) is shown in Figure 10.1. This illustrates these changes very well and can offer insights into the attitude of staff at each stage.

- *Phase 1*: The unfamiliarity of individuals with their new roles makes them feel anxious about their contribution and so their effectiveness drops slightly. They need to get used to the new circumstances. Within a short time, having become used to the role using previously successful skills, and finding support to help them, their effectiveness improves and they start to believe that they do not have to change. This is the denial phase.

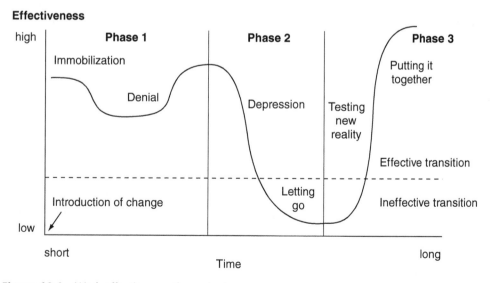

Figure 10.1   Work effectiveness through change

- *Phase 2*: Hard demands are now being made and individuals experience real stress as they realize that they do have to develop new skills to keep up with the job. They need to relearn their role. Although they may eventually learn how to do their new job, a period of anxiety makes them less effective because they can no longer rely on their old skills and they may believe that they can no longer cope. In fact this 'low' indicates that the person is realizing that they have to change and then, at some point, they abandon the past and accept the future. However, this is the most dangerous point in the change cycle as they feel really stressed and may be tempted to give up.
- *Phase 3*: This testing period can be as frustrating as it can be rewarding. Mistakes can recreate the 'low', but, as the newly learnt skills are brought into play effectively, entrepreneurs' performances improve and they achieve a higher level of effectiveness than at the beginning of the stage. They now have a set of new skills alongside their old ones. However, this transition is not inevitable and some people fail to acquire new skills or cannot pull themselves out of the 'low'. The risk is that they may give up. The challenge for the entrepreneurial leader is to lead staff successfully through the three phases again and again and again.

Managing change

As we have seen, the key to a culture of continuous improvement and change is the acquisition of new knowledge – the development of what is called a learning organization. Learning organizations 'combine an ability to manage knowledge with an ability to change continuously so as to prove their effectiveness' (Jackson and Schuler, 2001). As Hamel (2000) observed 'organizational learning and knowledge management are first cousins to continuous improvement'. Corporate entrepreneurship embraces change, encouraging it to the point where it is seen to be the norm and individuals continuously question the status quo.

But as Machiavelli said: 'There is nothing more difficult to handle, more doubtful of success and more dangerous to carry through than initiating change'. Some individuals inevitably resist change – even if it is ultimately in their own interest. They will even resist it to the point of trying to sabotage it. This could be because:

- They think it will have a negative impact on them;
- It affects their social relationships within the organization;
- It means long-standing habits have to be changed;
- The needs for and benefits of change have not been properly communicated;
- Structures, systems, rewards are not aligned with the changes and inhibit them;
- They feel coerced, not in control.

If any, or all, of these reasons for resisting change can be removed the likelihood of resistance will reduce. Change needs to have the full and unequivocal commitment of those at the top of the organization. At the same time change is more likely to be pushed through if any, or all, of these things occur:

- A compelling reason for change can be communicated effectively – staff buy into a shared vision of the future;

- The change aims to achieve clear, tangible results quickly – and achievement can be readily demonstrated;
- Information about the changes and the change effort are generally and freely available;
- Management are all equally committed to the changes – their need and what they are intended to achieve;
- Change is not piecemeal – do as much as possible, as quickly as possible and make a clean break with the past;
- Address the cultural components of change that could endanger the chances of success;
- Staff are consulted on the need for and the process of change.

Change is never easy to manage. Indeed Jim Clemmer (1995) believes that whilst change can be created, it cannot be managed. 'Change can be ignored, resisted, responded to, capitalized upon, *and created*. But it cannot be managed and made to march to some orderly step-by-step process ... Whether we become change victims or victors depends on our readiness for change'. Which means that to some extent you must realize you cannot always predict its course but rather need to 'go with the flow'.

Staff need to 'buy into' the change and be clear about what they have to do to achieve it. They need to be encouraged and rewarded if they act appropriately and reprimanded and penalized if they do not. It is easier to change behaviour than beliefs. Any potential barriers to the changes need to be tackled in advance. Managing change in a successful, growing organization is easier than in one that is contracting because change brings tangible results that reward everyone. And an entrepreneurial organization will be looking to grow. If it does not succeed at first it will readjust and try again. But an entrepreneurial organization can only experience downsizing for just so long. Its architecture is not appropriate to an organization in the decline phase of its life cycle.

Yukl (2002) argues that successfully implementing change involves engaging in two overlapping sets of actions – 'political and organizational' and 'people orientated'. The political and organizational actions involve eight steps:

1. Deciding who might oppose change and doing something about them. You can try to convince sceptics or you can isolate or remove them.
2. Putting change agents into key positions in the organization. Often new people need to be brought into an existing organization if you are going to bring about major change, particularly when it involves shifts in culture. These sorts of changes need to start near the top and with the full approval of the Board of Directors, otherwise they are likely to be frustrated by the prevailing inertia. The big advantage of 'parachuting in' change agents like these at a senior level is that they are likely to get results – one way or another – quickly. And time is important in business. Either they will displace the status quo or they will leave. This sounds rather like using force instead of persuasion and that threat can be important – 'change behaviour or leave' is the ultimate threat to those blocking change. But actually the change agents can employ any or all of the persuasive, political skills at their disposal. It just means you have more people doing it and that means you are more likely to see results more quickly. You only have to

look to see how often a new Managing Director replaces the top management team to realize that this has almost become a standard procedure when major change is to be pushed through in a limited time span.

3. Building political support for the changes with stakeholders such as shareholders, employees, suppliers, and so on, whether inside or outside the organization, so as to ensure that there is a coalition of support for the changes.

4. Using task forces to push through implementation. The composition of the team depends on the nature of the task it faces and the resulting skills required. It should also reflect the composition required for effective team working. Using multidisciplinary staff from different departments or units ensures a holistic approach to problems and helps subsequently to embed the changes within the organization.

5. Making dramatic, symbolic changes early on – such as changing key personnel. This helps emphasize the importance placed on implementing the changes – and what might happen to blockers.

6. If possible, beginning on a small scale and demonstrating success quickly. This helps convince doubters. It also allows you to learn from mistakes, if you make them, without necessarily jeopardizing the project.

7. Remembering to change relevant parts of the organizational structure as you go along. This is covered in greater detail later in this chapter.

8. Monitoring the process of change so as to learn from it and ensure that the changes are successfully embedded. Resistant people can reverse change all too easily if left to their own devices. On the other hand some of the changes may actually prove to be inappropriate – so always learn from mistakes.

People-orientated actions focus on getting staff motivated to undertake the changes. This involves seven steps:

1. Creating a sense of urgency about the need for change. You find that organizations often embark on change as a result of a crisis (see Marks & Spencer case with questions). They often need that to jolt them out of their lethargy.

2. Preparing people for the effects of change by proper briefings. People want to know how big changes will affect them personally – only this makes it real for them.

3. Helping people deal with change through proper training, counselling and so on. If you are asking people to undertake new or different jobs they will need to be trained. Putting this in place in advance gives them assurance that they will be able to cope.

4. Keeping people informed about the changes being made as they progress and the successes being achieved. Celebrate success so as to build confidence and help convince the sceptics.

5. Breaking up the change process into small parts or stages. These provide opportunities to celebrate success as well as evaluate effectiveness.

6. Empowering staff to make the necessary changes themselves. Task forces should have the necessary authority to undertake the tasks asked of them. There is nothing worse than being held accountable for something over which you have no authority.

7. Demonstrating continued commitment to the changes from the highest levels in the organization right until the project is complete. 'Walking the talk' is important, unblocking where necessary – all demonstrate that pushing through the changes is high on the agenda of senior management. Often a project is unsuccessful because management is diverted from it when the changes are only three-quarters complete and there is no final follow-through.

A final perspective on the scale of the task involved in managing change is given to us by Henry Mintzberg (1998). He developed the concept of a 'change cube', shown in Figure 10.2. The cube is three dimensional: strategy/organization, concrete/conceptual and formal/informal. The face of the cube shows strategy/organization. As we have explained, both have to be addressed in making change happen. However strategy can be highly conceptual (abstract) or concrete (tangible). The most conceptual element of strategy is vision, followed by strategic positioning (repositioning, reconfiguring) then programmes (reprogramming, re-engineering), whilst the most concrete are products (redesigned, replaced). Similarly for the organization, culture is the most conceptual, followed by structures (re-organization), then systems (reworking, re-engineering), whilst the most concrete are people (retrained, replaced). Vision and culture are highly abstract. Products and people are highly concrete and can be changed or replaced relatively easily – without affecting any element above them. However if you change vision or culture you will end up having to change everything below. In fact, wherever you intervene in this cube you have to change everything below it. For example, if you change structures, you must change systems and people.

The final dimension is formal/informal. For example, strategic positioning can be a formal process (deliberate) or an informal process (emergent). Similarly, people can change formally (training) or informally (coaching, mentoring). Mintzberg's point is that, to be effective, change in an organization must include the entire cube: strategy and organization, from the most conceptual to the most concrete, informally as well as formally.

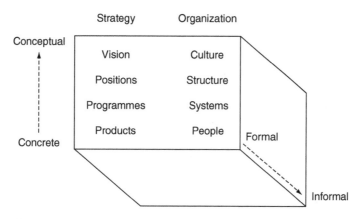

Figure 10.2 The change cube

Source: Adapted from Mintzberg (*op. cit.*).

Toolkit for Managing Change

Exercises to help initiate and manage change can be downloaded free from the US web site *www.esdtoolkit.org*. Written by Rosalyn McKeown with Charles Hopkins, Regina Rizzi and Marrianne Chrystalbridge, they comprise seven exercises with related worksheets:

1. Examining assumptions.
2. Steering around barriers.
3. Inventory of support and resistance.
4. Commitment charting.
5. Creating an action plan.
6. Identifying communication strategies.
7. Recognizing values in action.

Freedom and control

Most organizational control systems are aimed at eliminating risk and uncertainty – something the entrepreneurial firm must tolerate – and promoting efficiency and effectiveness – which can be at the expense of innovation. Innovation requires organizational 'slack' or 'space' – a looseness in resource availability which allows employees to 'borrow' expertise, research, materials, equipment and other resources as they develop new concepts. 3M have slack built into their organization by allowing researchers to spend 15% of their time on their own projects. Garud and Van de Ven (1992) confirm that entrepreneurial activity in a large organization is more likely to continue, despite negative outcomes, when there is slack in resource availability and a high degree of ambiguity about the outcomes. A highly efficient organization has no slack. Everything is tightly controlled, every penny accounted for, all jobs are defined and individuals made to conform. This environment might lead to high degrees of efficiency but it does not encourage entrepreneurship and innovation.

Foster and Kaplan (2001) echo this concern. They advocate a minimalist approach to control: 'Control what you must, not what you can: control when you must, not when you can. If a control procedure is not essential, eliminate it.' They promote the need for 'divergent thinking' to encourage creativity which they say 'requires control through selection and motivation of employees rather than through control of people's actions; ample resources, including time, to achieve results; knowing what to measure and when to measure it; and genuine respect for others' capabilities and potential.'

Morris and Kuratko (2002) say that the core principle in developing entrepreneurial control requires that managers need to 'give up control to gain control'. Rather than tight budgetary controls, they advocate a 'no-surprises' approach – one that 'generates adequate information on a timely basis for all who need to know'. The authors believe that 'open book' management, where there is transparency of information, is important. Control mechanisms should produce indicators or early warning signals of problems before they occur. A by-product of such a system is that it also conveys a sense of trust. Employees are trusted to get on with the job but the outcomes, rather than the processes, are monitored. They envisage the control system becoming 'a vehicle for managing uncertainty, promoting risk tolerance, encouraging focused experimentation, and empowering employees'.

For them giving up control is also about greater accountability and a greater sense of responsibility:

> 'Where there is an elaborate system of control measures, the employee can be secure in the knowledge that, if the control system has been complied with, then his or her accountability is absolved, that his or her responsibility has been fulfilled. He or she need not take any further responsibility for outcomes or the implications of personal behaviour for company performance. However, by giving up control to the employee, there is a much deeper sense of responsibility not only for accomplishing a task or behaving in a certain manner but also for the quality of task performance and the impact it has on the organization ... to give up control is to empower.'

'Open book' management focuses on the outcomes – the bottom line – rather than the processes. It is built around free flows of information and seeks to motivate employees to improve the performance of the organization by thinking outside their narrow job definition and focusing on the consequences of their action. It encourages them to take ownership of and responsibility for their actions. In many ways it is the logical extension of the principles of the learning organization to financial information. But equally it encourages employees to think the way owner-managers would think about their own business. Case (1997) says it is built around six principles:

1. Free access to all financial information that is critical to tracking the firm's performance.
2. A continuous and overt attempt to present this information to employees.
3. Training processes that encourage understanding of this information.
4. Employees learn that part of their job is to improve the financial result in whatever way they can.
5. People are empowered to make decisions in their jobs based on what they know.
6. Employees have a stake in the organization's success or failure.

The leader in an entrepreneurial firm, therefore, faces a crucial dilemma – the amount of freedom given to the management team. Too much, and anarchy or worse might result. Too little, and creativity, initiative and entrepreneurship will be stifled. It is all well and good talking about empowerment, but at what stage does it become licence?

Balance

The answer is a question of 'balance'. Birkinshaw (2003) explains the model used by BP to help guide and control entrepreneurial action. BP's philosophy is that 'successful business performance comes from a dispersed and high level of ownership of, and a commitment to, an agreed-upon objective'. Within BP there are a number of business units. Heads of units have a 'contract' agreed between them and the top executives in the organization. Once agreed they have 'free rein to deliver on their contract in whatever way they see fit, within a set of identified constraints'. BP's model uses four components to help guide and control entrepreneurial action: direction, space or slack, boundaries and support. All four need to be in balance. If they are too tight they constrain the business unit, but if too slack they might result in chaos. This is shown in Figure 10.3.

Direction

This is the company's broad strategy and goals. Heads of units should have considerable scope to develop the strategy for their own unit, in line with BP's general direction, developing new products and markets within these constraints. However, without an overarching sense of values, mission and direction, entrepreneurship becomes a 'random set of initiatives. Although each initiative has its own rationale, when you put them together, the result is a mélange that stakeholders are likely to denounce as incoherent, vague, or chaotic.'

Birkinshaw gives two pieces of advice on getting this balance right:

- Set broad direction and re-evaluate periodically as markets and the environment change.
- Let the company's strategy inform that of the unit and the unit's inform that of the company. A central role for senior executives is to magnify and reinforce those initiatives that most clearly fit the company's goals.

Space or slack

As already explained, space or slack is to do with the degree of looseness in resource availability – monetary budgets, physical space and supervision of time. Companies have a responsibility to their shareholders to see that resources are put to their

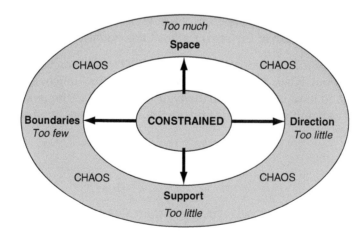

Figure 10.3 Freedom vs control
Source: Adapted from Birkinshaw (op. cit.).

best use and are being used efficiently. However, in a tightly run, highly efficient organization there is no time or other resources to think, experiment and innovate. People do not have the time to work outside their job descriptions. All creative organizations require a degree of space or slack to allow experimentation. New ideas almost always require initial work to refine and adapt them.

To circumvent this problem employees' roles need to be defined by outcome rather than behaviour. As in the case of 3M, slack is built into the system, so that employees can do things that are not formally part of their job. However, if employees are given too much space they run the risk of losing focus on the day-to-day detail of the job and it can be wasteful.

Birkinshaw also gives two pieces of advice on getting this balance right:

- Goal setting should be carefully managed and clear and specific, but individuals should be given freedom in how the goals are to be achieved.
- Individuals should be allowed to learn from their own mistakes.

Boundaries

These are the legal, regulatory and moral limits within which the company operates. They should be tightly defined but adherence should come from the creation of a set of shared values rather than through conforming to a set of rigid rules. Rigid rules without a shared agreement to adhere to them begs for the rules to be circumvented. Not having boundaries courts extreme danger, particularly if breaking them might lead to the failure of the organization.

Birkinshaw again gives two pieces of advice on getting this balance right:

- Identify critical boundaries that, if crossed, threaten the survival of the organization and control them rigorously.
- Manage other boundaries in a non-invasive way through training, induction, codes of conduct and so on.

Support

This refers to the information and knowledge transfer systems and training and development programmes provided by the company to help business unit managers do their job. Systems should encourage knowledge sharing and collaboration. Training and career planning should be top-down. Both should, however, be discretionary. The danger here is that knowledge will not be shared and there will be little collaboration, encouraging the business unit to go its own way and raising the danger of duplication of effort. On the other hand if there is too much support the unit will always be oppressive or 'spoon-fed' and initiative will be stifled.

Birkinshaw gives this final two pieces of advice on getting this balance right:

- Put in place enough support systems to help individuals and ensure they know where to go for help.
- Systems should encourage collaboration.

These elements need to be considered in the whole rather than individually. And balance is the key. Birkinshaw observes that most companies operate in the 'constrained' area in Figure 10.3 – direction defined too tightly, too little space, too tight boundaries and overly complex support structures – rather than the 'chaos' area, so most central management probably needs to 'let go' a little. The point is that management is an art, not a science, and it involves some fine judgements about the individuals you work with – their strengths and weaknesses – as well as their personal characteristics. This brings us back to the idea that *entrepreneurial firms need loose control but tight accountability, with early warning signs should the risks they face materialize.*

One final ingredient is needed to encourage entrepreneurship in this sort of organization – financial and resource support to get the ideas off the ground. The financial support might take the form of internal seed or venture capital that is separate from normal budgets. Different funds might be set up for different purposes, reflecting the stage of development of the idea. They might be administered by a committee or board with well-laid-down procedures for applying for resources – for example the presentation of a brief business plan. 3M support their '15% policy' with funding for equipment and extra help. To get an idea accepted in 3M the researcher must get the personal backing of a member of the main board. At that point an interdisciplinary team is set up to take the idea further.

Case insight

In his article Julian Birkinshaw (op. cit.) raises the interesting question about whether the failure of **Enron** might signal a rethink about the value of corporate entrepreneurship. After all, the company was held up as a model of entrepreneurship, attracting aggressive and creative managers and encouraging internal entrepreneurship to achieve its growth. Whilst hindsight is a wonderful thing that gives everybody 20:20 vision, he concludes that Enron does not merit such a rethink because the company was at the outer boundaries of all four dimensions of BP's model.

Too little direction: In the 1990s the company moved out of the natural gas sector into electricity trading, online trading, weather derivatives and broadband networks. It started out with the goal of being the 'best gas distribution company', this became 'the world's best energy company' and finally 'the world's best company'. Enron's lack of direction became a strength as managers were encouraged to pursue any opportunity that might help in its headlong rush for growth.

Too much space: Enron gave managers enormous freedom to pursue these opportunities. Top management practised a philosophy of 'laissez-faire'. For example one gas trader started an online trading business (EnronOnline) while still working at her original job. It had some 250 people working for it before the President of Enron became aware of its existence.

Too few boundaries: Enron had explicit rules about capital allocation and risk and had a Risk Assessment Control Unit. However, Enron managers regularly broke the rules, for example by setting up new subsidiary companies and financing activities off the balance sheet. Instead of being dismissed for these things, managers were often rewarded. The culture within the organization was one of rule breaking and there was no moral or ethical underpinning.

➤

Too little support: Management at Enron were recruited from top US business schools. After a six-month induction working with different business units, they were largely left to their own devices. The reward system encouraged 'pushy', aggressive people and development start-ups or high growth opportunities. Support was not a function that was rewarded and 'steady performers' did not stay long in the company.

Management and structure

Management is an art not least because the structures of the organization affect how you undertake it – and vice versa. As an entrepreneurial firm moves away from centralized, formal hierarchies to flatter structures with more horizontal communication the need for managers and tight management control lessens. If you are looking for 'dazzling breakthroughs' then autonomy and flexibility are crucial. But if the degree and frequency of entrepreneurship is less, the need for controls will increase. Again, it is all a question of balance.

In this context, Covin and Slevin (1990) argue that entrepreneurial behaviour within an organization is positively correlated with performance when structures are more organic, as shown in Figure 10.4. In reality the dimension of structure from organic to mechanistic is a continuum and ought to correspond to

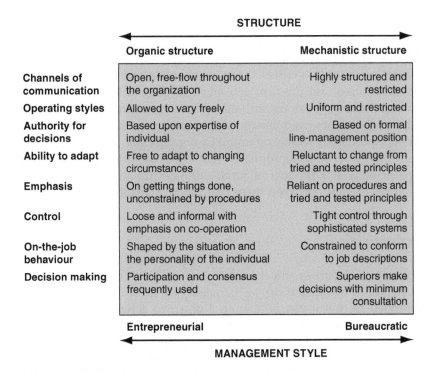

Figure 10.4 Organizational structure and management style
Source: Adapted from Covin and Slevin (op. cit.).

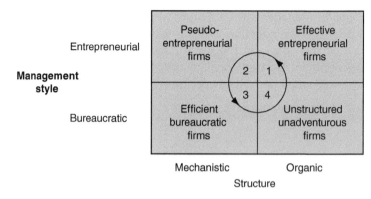

Figure 10.5 Organizational structure, management style and the concept of cycling

the managerial dimension from entrepreneurial to administrative. A mechanistic structure is appropriate for a bureaucratic or administrative style of management because it will result in an efficient albeit bureaucratic organization. However, it will stifle, if not kill, an entrepreneurial style. On the other hand an organic structure facilitates an effective entrepreneurial management style. Organizations are much more problematic when there is an incongruity between structure and style, as shown in Figure 10.5.

Figure 10.5 also demonstrates what the authors call 'cycling', where a successful firm can cycle between quadrants 1 and 3 as it moves from periods of opportunity, innovation and change to periods of consolidation and stability when greater bureaucratic control is needed. This mirrors quite closely the strategy formulation cycle and may give one reason why the transition from growth to consolidation is so often interspersed with a crisis – management style and organizational structures are not synchronized and the firm gets stuck in quadrants 2 and 4. Change, if it is to be successful, must be along both dimensions simultaneously.

As we have already observed, however, it is quite possible to have different units, departments or divisions within an umbrella organization that have the two different, but in their own way, appropriate organizational structures and management styles – particularly as a product or service moves through its life cycle. The only issue is that the interface between them needs to be managed carefully.

Managing risk

Risk is inherent in business and it is at its highest in an entrepreneurial business. Whilst it cannot be avoided, it can be managed – or, more accurately, identified and even quantified so that it can be managed down to acceptable levels. This might improve decision making not least because it encourages discussion about a factor that is inherent in the entrepreneurial organization. It might also help avoid the risks materializing or by putting in place appropriate controls at least provide an early warning of potential problems materializing. If risks can be avoided then less time is spent 'fire-fighting' when they materialize.

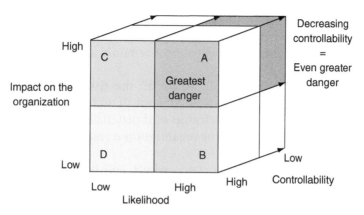

Figure 10.6   Risk classification

The first step is to identify the risks associated with following – or indeed not following – the course of action or strategy being considered. Some risks may be more likely than others whilst some may have a more serious impact on the organization than others. Figure 10.6 shows a useful way of classifying risks along these dimensions. Any risks that have a major impact on the organization are undesirable, but those which are very likely to happen pose the greatest danger (quadrant A). By way of contrast risks with a low impact and a low likelihood of occurrence (quadrant D) pose the least risk. Another dimension to this is controllability. Some risks may be under your control or influence, others might be completely out of your control. Generally, the less you control or influence the risk, the greater the danger it poses. In this way the risk matrix becomes a Rubic cube, with the greatest danger being in the cube with the highest impact, highest likelihood and least controllability.

There are four reactions to risk. You might:

1. *Attempt to eliminate the risk.*   You might withdraw completely from the area of activity that generates the risk – an unlikely course of action initially for an entrepreneurial business, although if the risks continue to be monitored, at some point in the future they may become unacceptable and this may be the best course of action. Generally these will be the risks that pose the greatest danger to the organization – high impact, high probability and least controllable.
2. *Attempt to reduce the risk.*   You might increase internal controls, training or supervision depending on the nature of the risk. Alternatively you might select strategic alternatives that are less risky. Many of these strategies might involve transferring or sharing the risk with others.
3. *Transfer the risk.*   There are many useful techniques that can be used to transfer both internal and external risks; for example insurance, outsourcing, subcontracting and foreign exchange or interest rate hedging. So, companies constantly 'insure' against currency fluctuations – a risk they neither control nor influence – by buying forward in the currency market. If entering a new

market or developing a new product you might find ways of spreading the risk by finding collaborative partners. This might also diminish the resources needed to exploit the opportunity but it will almost certainly also reduce the return that you achieve.

4. *Accept the risk.* You might simply accept all the risks in quadrant D. If you accept the risk completely, all you can attempt to do is plan to manage the risk and put in place early-warning indicators of it materializing, but even this might be uneconomic if the impact on the organization is small.

The riskiest situation in the risk cube is where you have a high likelihood of occurrence, with a high impact in a situation where you have little control. In this situation you might consider any of options 1 to 3, but even if you end up accepting the risk it is vital that you monitor the risk and then take corrective action if it materializes.

Early-warning mechanisms are indicators that alert you before a risk materializes so that you can take remedial action. For major risks it is important to identify parameters or events that indicate an increased propensity for the risk to materialize and to ensure that they are being monitored on a regular basis. A simple example would be bad debts which, in a low-margin business, can have an enormous impact on profitability. If that business is teetering on the edge of bankruptcy it is vital to monitor a *key risk indicator* for this on a regular and frequent basis. Key risk indicators for this might be the ratio of days sales in debtors and the aged listing of debts. To be effective key risk indicators must be easy to monitor as part of the regular activity of the organization, highlight when corrective action is needed and provide guidance on what action is needed. Entrepreneurial firms need to highlight the highest risks they face and monitor the associated key risk indicators for the strategy they are following. Only by doing this can they mitigate against the high risks inherent in what they do.

As we have already noted, corporate entrepreneurship involves a number of other factors that mitigate risk. The fact that decision making is passed down and staff feel empowered should mean that problems can be dealt with quickly by the person or people nearest to them. This improves speed of response but also minimizes information loss. Even if information needs to be passed on within the organization, knowledge transfer should be a strength. Its external orientation, particularly towards the market, should make it sensitive to changes in the environment that might trigger danger. The way the organization approaches strategy and decision making should mean that it is able to change its plans quickly and effortlessly. In other words the architecture of the organization is sensitive to changes that signal danger and can respond quickly once the risk is identified.

'Communicating is one of the most important tools in recovering from mistakes. When you tell someone, be it a designer, a customer, or the CEO of the company, "Look, we've got a problem. Here's how we're going to fix it," you diffuse the fear of the unknown and focus on the solution.'

Michael Dell

Case with questions   M&S

Marks & Spencer (known as M&S) is a famous British retail chain selling clothes, food, household goods and furniture. It has over 450 shops in the UK and some 200 managed under franchise in 30 territories mostly in Europe, the Middle East, Asia and the Far East as well as wholly-owned stores in the Republic of Ireland and Hong Kong. In 2007 it had a turnover of over £7 billion and employed over 70,000 people. M&S's origin was as a chain of 'penny bazaars' (market stalls selling everything for one penny) set up in the late 1800s by a Russian- born Polish-Jewish immigrant, Michael Marks, in Leeds with a £5 loan from Isaac Dewhirst, a wholesaler. Interestingly Dewhirst went into manufacturing and remains the biggest supplier of M&S to this day. Marks opened his first store below his home in Manchester in 1893. He went into partnership with Thomas Spencer (then a Dewhirst cashier) and the first Marks & Spencer store was opened in the prestigious Cross Arcade in Leeds in 1904. After the death of the founders, Simon Marks (son of Michael) took over as Chairman and started to work with his friend Israel Sieff. Together they turned M&S into the iconic British retailer it is today.

The original success was based upon a number of ideas that meant M&S, although never cheapest in the market place, offered high quality but most important of all very good value for money. They did this by adopting the then revolutionary idea of buying directly from manufacturers and placing their own label on goods – originally the St Michael brand (registered in 1928). By the 1950s all goods were sold under this label. By then it was known for selling only British-made goods, entering into long-term partnerships with British manufacturers which required them to commit solely to manufacturing M&S products. It was also known for its policy of accepting the return of unwanted goods, giving a full cash refund if the receipt was shown. Its first overseas store was opened in 1975 and it resisted the lure of television advertising until the mid-1990s.

But it was in the 1990s that M&S started to lose direction and, as can be seen from the financial highlights below, both turnover and profitability started to fall. With the benefit of hindsight, Sir Richard Greenbury's tenure as Chairman (1991–99) saw profit margins pushed to untenable levels, and the loyalty of customers was seriously eroded. A number of things happened. The costs of using British suppliers increased so M&S reduced quality. Meanwhile competitors were sourcing overseas and beating M&S on value for money. M&S's reaction was to switch to overseas suppliers but this undermined a core part of the company's philosophy and appeal. At the same time the company was losing touch with potential younger customers who increasingly saw M&S designs as frumpy and old-fashioned. Alongside this the company steadfastly refused to accept credit cards except for their own store card. In the financial press M&S came to be seen as an aging and famously lethargic and bureaucratic company. They simply failed to see that the high street had changed and competitors were now offering better products at lower prices in more attractive surroundings. The slump took the company by surprise and its share price fell by over two-thirds. The late 1990s saw serious boardroom instability. But how do you encourage a firm with over 100 years of history to re-invent itself and become, again, entrepreneurial? How do you drive through the necessary changes? Answer – you bring in new people... and you start at the top.

→

Year ending March/April	Turnover (£bn)	Profit before tax (£m)	Basic earnings per share (p)
2007	8.6	965	40.4
2006	7.8	746	31.4
2005	7.5	505	29.1
2004	8.3	782	24.1
2003	8.0	678	20.7
2002	8.1	336	5.4
2001	8.1	146	.0
2000	8.2	418	9.0
1999	8.2	546	13.0
1998	8.2	1,155	28.6
1997	7.8	1,102	26.7
1996	7.2	966	23.3

Sir Richard Greenbury retired in 1999 and Luc Vandevelde, a Belgian, took over as both Chairman and Chief Executive. He had previously been Chairman and Chief Executive of Promodès, the French hypermarket chain, where he oversaw a merger with Carrefour, its rival. Roger Holmes was brought in at about the same time and he became Chief Executive later in the year. Drastic action was needed simply to survive. Stores were closed on the Continent and in the USA, and jobs were cut as the company also closed down its Direct catalogue so as to enable it to focus on its core UK retail business. Sourcing was moved overseas, cutting back on UK suppliers, in order to increase margins and make prices more competitive. At the same time the supply chain was modernized, allowing clothes to be brought to market more quickly, bureaucracy was reduced and new talent brought in to drive innovation. Shops opened on Sundays and accepted credit cards.

Clothing fashions were improved by bringing in new people. George Davies, founder of Next, was brought in to produce a young, fashionable collection called Per Una. In the same year Yasmin Yusuf, the brains behind the Warehouse clothing chain, was appointed as creative director. The fashion strategy became one of targeted sub-brands, such as the Limited Collection label, Blue Harbour men's casual wear, the Perfect range of classic pieces and the more expensive Autograph label which has designers such as Betty Jackson, Sonja Nuttall and Anthony Symonds. Fashion sales started to increase. By 2002 the company was gaining market share in areas like lingerie and men's casual wear. New ways of presenting clothes meant the average spend increased as shoppers were encouraged to buy entire outfits rather than just single products. M&S started innovating again with products ranging from seam-free underwear to 'steam cuisine' microwave meals. It opened new convenience food outlets called Simply Food, targeting new markets. Some, within railway stations and motorway service areas, are run by Compass Group, the specialist catering company, under franchise. Vittorio Radice, the brains behind the regeneration of the department store Selfridges was brought in to experiment with stand-alone homeware stores, the first of which was opened in Gateshead in 2004 with the name Lifestore. But not all the initiatives worked and many of the underlying management problems remained.

In 2004, amid rumours of a possible take-over bid, M&S announced that Chairman Luc Vandevelde would be leaving with immediate effect and that the Chief Executive,

→

Roger Holmes would be replaced by Stuart Rose. At the same time Paul Myers, chairman of Guardian Media Group, took over as Chairman. Timing is crucial in business because shortly after this Philip Green, boss of the fashion retailers Arcadia Group, which includes Bhs stores, announced a take-over bid for M&S. Stuart Rose came to M&S with a track record of turning around struggling retailers. Indeed he is credited with turning around Arcadia Group, which is quite a coincidence. He was also a friend of Philip Green. Stuart quickly put together a recovery plan which included selling off the financial services business to HSBC Bank, buying control of the Per Una range, closing the Gateshead Lifestore (Vittorio Radice along with many senior managers subsequently left M&S) and stopping the expansion of the Simply Food outlets (there were about 20 at the time). Philip Green later withdrew his bid after failing to get sufficient backing from shareholders.

Son of a civil servant, Stuart Rose was educated at a Quaker boarding school and started his career in retailing in 1972 after joining M&S as a management trainee. He remained with the company for 17 years, holding a variety of jobs in the textiles and food divisions before being appointed commercial director for M&S's European operation in Paris. In 1989 he joined Burton Group, which included Debenhams, Top Shop and Dorothy Perkins stores. The group later demerged into Arcadia and Debenhams. In 1998 he was appointed chief executive of the Argos catalogue/shop chain. Later as boss of Booker, the cash-and-carry business, he arranged a merger with the frozen food retailer Iceland and became the new group's chief executive. He joined Arcadia in 2000, a company with £250 million of debt, which he turned around and then sold two years later to Philip Green for £855 million – making £25 million for himself. He took over as Chief Executive of M&S in 2004 at the age of 55.

Although always smartly dressed, Stuart Rose is known for his informal management style that circumvents formal structures. If he wants to know something he is quite likely to go directly to the person who should have the answer rather than ask for a management report. He is seen as 'very good at motivating people and giving them clear instructions. He brings the best out in people ... a dedicated networker, always lunching with someone from the City or the media ... He maintains a helicopter position ... [but nevertheless] ... sits in on merchandising reviews, knows how many of which style is sold where, and can reel off financial data about each of his many retail chains at will' (Times Online, 25 January 2007). He is also known for bringing in his own trusted managers to focus on the minutiae – which is precisely what he did, reshuffling and firing many of M&S's top managers. For example, Steve Sharp was brought in as new Marketing Director. He met Stuart Rose at Debenhams where he was Marketing Director. At M&S he introduced the new Your M&S brand, together with the new clothing advertising campaign featuring the celebrated model Twiggy and younger models associated with the Bohemian styles of 2005–6. He was also responsible for the TV advertising campaign for their food range featuring Dervla Kirwan with the tag line 'This is not just food, this is M&S food'. Managerial and directorial changes followed, including the appointment in 2007 of Martha Lane Fox, co-founder of Lastminute.com, as non-executive director to advise on the company's Direct business.

Stuart Rose focused on three things: product, environment and service. Getting the product right was also top of the agenda. Many slow-moving, expensive suppliers were replaced by quick-turnaround specialists, often overseas. Prices were

→

frequently cut whilst quality was maintained. Improving value, style and the amount of new product was important. In clothing the company initially focused on the classic designs it had historically always excelled at – the Classic Collection – but other lines have been expanded, particularly the Per Una range. It rationalized its menswear. For both menswear and womenswear it introduced innovative products such as machine washable suits and seam-free underwear. In food M&S focused on offering high quality, innovative products such as the additive free 'Marks and Spencer Cook!' range. After a pause the Simply Food stores started to expand once more so that by 2007 there were about 200. Getting the environment right meant stores were completely rede-signed with white tiles (black in Foods) replacing carpets and laminate flooring, brighter lighting, new product stands, display styles, mannequins, till points and staff uniforms. By 2007 some 35% of stores had been completely refurbished in this way and many others temporarily updated as part of a massive investment programme costing over £520 million. M&S also moved to improve its service levels by investing in its biggest ever customer service training programme based around the Mary Gober Method – called 'Your M&S – Our Service Style'. Our Service Style is defined as 'We are friendly, helpful, courteous people, who are knowledgeable and enthusiastic about taking care of our customers'. The company also overhauled its pay rates and improved career planning for its 'customer assistants', reducing the number of grades to just four with clear progression. As well as attractive salaries staff are paid a performance bonus, which in 2006 totalled £70 million or an average of £500 per employee. The company also has a saving scheme that allows staff to buy M&S shares at a 20% discount. As the turnaround gathered pace in January 2007 sizable bonuses were triggered – a total of £56 million or an average of £4700 per member – based upon a share price that had tripled in less than three years.

What Stuart Rose did in focusing on product, environment and service was to return to the core M&S value(s) propositions:

- M&S's vision is 'to be the standard against which all others are measured'.
- M&S's mission is 'to make aspirational quality accessible to all'.
- M&S's values are 'quality, value, service, innovation and trust'.

'Our plan remains the same – to drive further growth from our core business through the delivery of better products, service and environment. We are also starting to broaden the business, by stretching the brand into new product areas, expanding space, driving our Direct business and growing our brand internationally.'

Up-to-date information on M&S can be found on their website: www.marksandspencer.com.

Questions
1. What are the lessons you learn from M&S about how to turn around an ailing, bureaucratic firm?
2. What lessons do you learn from Stuart Rose about the role of leader in this situation?
3. How important was it to change senior management at M&S?

Summary

Many traditional management techniques discourage corporate entrepreneurship. These need to be avoided in an entrepreneurial organization. The barriers can be classified into six groups:

1. Systems
2. Structures
3. Strategic direction
4. Policies and procedures
5. People
6. Culture

J D Wetherspoon encourages entrepreneurship through pay and benefits, training and development and by pushing decision making down and encouraging new ideas.

The key to a culture of continuous improvement and change is the acquisition of new knowledge. Nevertheless people resist change even if it is for their own good. To make change happen two overlapping sets of actions must be engaged – 'political and organizational' and 'people-orientated'. The change cube demonstrates the complexity of what is required with all aspects of strategy and organization potentially having to change in the concrete and conceptual dimensions and the formal and informal dimensions.

Marks & Spencer faced a severe crisis before radical changes in top management were made which resulted in a complete reappraisal of their strategies. New strategies, policies and procedures were brought in but, in particular, new people were brought in to effect the change quickly, underlining its importance.

In working through change, organizations experience three phases:

1. Immobilization and denial.
2. Depression and letting go.
3. Testing the new reality and putting it together.

Managers must give up control to gain control. Entrepreneurial firms need loose control but tight accountability. Too much control stifles creativity, innovation and entrepreneurship. However, too little control can lead to chaos. Most firms place too many constraints and controls on managers. Some, like **Enron**, do not have enough. What is needed is 'balance', as in **BP's** model which involves:

- Space or slack – a looseness in resource availability;
- Direction – the broad strategy and goals;
- Support – knowledge transfer and training systems;
- Boundaries – not just rules but underlying morals and ethics.

The concept of space or slack – a looseness in resource availability – is important for entrepreneurship. Some slack is necessary for experimentation and innovation. Internal seed or venture funding is also needed to take ideas further.

Open book management encourages employees to focus on the bottom line and the effects their actions have on the financial performance of the organization.

For change to work the structure of the organization and the style of management must be synchronized. As an entrepreneurial firm moves away from centralized, formal hierarchies to flatter structures with more horizontal communication the need for managers and tight management control lessens. If you are looking for 'dazzling breakthroughs' then autonomy and flexibility are crucial. But if the degree and frequency of entrepreneurship is less, the need for controls will increase. Again, it is all a question of balance.

Many successful firms cycle between organic/entrepreneurial and mechanistic/bureaucratic structure and styles as they grow – mirroring the growth → crisis → consolidation process noted in strategy development.

Risk is an ever-present danger in an entrepreneurial firm. It can be classified in terms of likelihood, impact and controllability. The riskiest situation is where you have a high likelihood of occurrence with a high impact in a situation where you have little control. Once risks are identified it is important to monitor key risk indicators that give early warning signs of the risks materializing. Entrepreneurial firms need to locate the highest risks in the strategies they are following and then monitor the associated key risk indicators.

Essays and discussion topics

1. Discuss why the seven conventional management techniques listed might discourage corporate entrepreneurship. Can you think of other examples that fit with the classifications proposed by Michael Morris?
2. Does your national culture accept failure? Does it encourage success? What are the implications of your views for corporate entrepreneurship?
3. You can never change people. Discuss.
4. Change can be created, but never managed. Discuss.
5. The inter-relationships in Mintzberg's change cube are so complicated that no major change is ever likely to be 100% successful. Discuss.
6. Why has Wetherspoons been so successful?
7. Why does tight control stifle creativity, innovation and entrepreneurship?
8. Why is slack or space so important for creativity, innovation and entrepreneurship?
9. How do you achieve 'balance' between freedom and control? Who makes the judgement?
10. How can you have loose control but tight accountability? Give examples.
11. With freedom comes accountability. Discuss.
12. Freedom without accountability leads to anarchy. Discuss.
13. Is 'open book' management practical?
14. Why do so many managers resist 'open book' management?
15. Why are boundaries important?
16. What moral and ethical boundaries would you place on business?
17. Why are management style and organizational structure interlinked?
18. What is meant by 'cycling'? Why should this also be linked to strategy formulation?
19. If you cannot manage risk, you might as well ignore it. Discuss.
20. Risk is the biggest issue facing corporate entrepreneurship. Discuss.

Exercises and assignments

1. Using an example of a major change of which you have experience, chart how the changes were made, the problems encountered and the solutions put in place. Were the changes successful? Explain.
2. Describe the risks facing an organization of which you have experience (it might be your university). Classify them using the risk cube in Figure 10.6 and indicate what would be the key risk indicators that need monitoring.
3. Research the reasons for Enron's failure and critically evaluate Birkinshaw's contention that it was at the extremes of boundaries of BP's model for entrepreneurial development.
4. Arthur Andersen was once considered to be the most entrepreneurial of accounting firms. Research the reasons for its failure and apply Birkinshaw's model.
5. Download the Toolkit for Managing Change from www.esdtoolkit.org and use the Worksheets to plan around a change situation.

References

Birkinshaw, J. (2003) 'The Paradox of Corporate Entrepreneurship', *Strategy and Business*, 30.

Case, J. (1997) 'Opening the Books', *Harvard Business Review*, 75, March/April.

Clemmer, J. (1995) *Pathways to Performance: A Guide to Transforming Yourself, Your Team and Your Organization*, Toronto: Macmillan Canada.

Covin, D. and Slevin, J. (1990) 'Judging Entrepreneurial Style and Organizational Structure: How to Get Your Act Together', *Sloan Management Review*, 31 (Winter).

Foster, R. and Kaplan, S. (2001) *Creative Destruction: Why Companies that are Built to Last Underperform the Stock Market*, New York: Doubleday/Currency.

Garud, R. and Van de Ven, A. (1992) 'An Empirical Evaluation of the Internal Corporate Venturing Process', *Strategic Management Journal*, 13 (special issue).

Hamel, G. (2000) 'Reinvent your Company', *Fortune*, 12, June.

Jackson, S. and Schuler, R. (2001) 'Turning Knowledge into Business Advantage', in J. Pickford (ed.), *Mastering Management 2.0*, London: Prentice Hall.

Kakabadse, A. (1983) *The Politics of Management*, London: Gower.

Mintzberg, H. (1998) in H. Mintzberg, B. Ahlstrand and J. Lempel, *Strategy Safari*, New York: The Free Press.

Morris, M.H. (1998) *Entrepreneurial Intensity*, Westport: Quorum Books.

Morris, M.H. and Kuratko, D.F. (2002) *Corporate Entrepreneurship*, Fort Worth: Harcourt College Publishers.

Yukl, G. (2002) *Leadership in Organizations*, Upper Saddle River, NJ: Prentice Hall Inc.

CHAPTER 11
Control and resistance

Asked what the secret of successful automotive management was, a senior General Motors executive replied, 'Control. Deal control. Product control. Labour control.' (Quoted in Huczynski, 1993: 185)

The aims of this chapter are to:

- Assert the significance of control against a tendency of mainstream analyses to present it as marginal or of diminishing relevance.
- To elaborate critical perspectives on control, particularly those that derive from labour process theory and its emphasis on a variety of managerial strategies within the contested terrain of the workplace.
- To examine various objections to labour process concepts and to make a qualified defence of them.
- To discuss and evaluate more recent research on control, particularly those that argue for a decisive shift towards surveillance and self-discipline, ultimately pointing to patterns of continuity as well as change.

We can see from the discussion in the previous chapter that practically and theoretically management is intertwined with control. Yet why and how is strongly contested between mainstream and critical approaches. This chapter examines contrasting perspectives on understanding control. It is primarily about conceptualisation rather than current evidence of the *outcomes* of control strategies and techniques.

Mainstream mis/understandings

The treatment of control in mainstream writing is ambiguous at best, marginal at worst. Frameworks that assume goal consensus can often simply ignore or trivialise the issue. When it is discussed explicitly in standard textbooks, the chapters devoted to it are sometimes of a rather bizarre nature in almost omitting any reference to conflicts between groups. The talk is of technical inputs and outputs in a self-adjusting system, performance standards and feedback mechanisms. It is also seen in a unitary way: 'controlled performance' with an assumption of goal-consensus.

Control is reduced to a *monitoring* device, with management's role to check progress, ensure that actions occur as planned, correct any deviation, or reassure us that what we are doing is appropriate (O'Reilly and Chatman, 1996). Some writers (Lawlor, 1976) put an emphasis on people desiring control, for example getting enjoyment from dependence on higher authority. This is the other side of the coin from attributing control to the pathological desires of particular individuals – those that are described as 'control freaks'. Resistance is smuggled in occasionally when discussing the *behavioural* implications as people 'react' to control processes, requiring management to adjust strategies accordingly.

This apparent absence of control from the mainstream is, however, somewhat misleading. The issues are there but they are articulated in different language and concepts. As the influential mainstream writer Pfeffer notes, 'control is at once the essential problem of management and organisation and the implicit focus of much of organisation studies' (1997: 100). The key term here is *implicit*. When control is discussed it is often alongside co-ordination. Any complex division of labour requires mechanisms to set goals, allocate responsibilities and evaluate the effectiveness of performance. Co-ordination is a more neutral term than control and more compatible with an assumption that management is a largely neutral set of techniques and competencies.

Even when texts do have chapters with control in the title, they often pass over quickly into other issues such as job design, organisational structure or leadership. In the first instance, debate is focused on designing structures which facilitate levels of control and co-ordination appropriate to types of work that require different levels of discretion and standardisation. In the second, discussion of leadership styles such as the classic polarity of authoritarian versus democratic is a way of discussing control, but through the language of influence and motivation. So what is described in mainstream writing as technical and human organisation and the need to integrate the two could be alternatively thought of in terms of competing control systems. For example, in their historical survey of American managerial discourse, Barley and Kunda (1992) distinguish between rational (for example, scientific management, systems theories) and normative (for example, human relations, organisational culture) ideologies of control. Rather than one simply displacing another, there are successive and alternate waves paralleling broad cycles of economic expansion and contraction.

We do accept that not all control processes arise from, or are structured by, antagonistic interests. Stock inventories and financial budgeting are necessary and not always conflictual features of any system of work organisation. A written job description may under certain conditions actually allow employees to assert power or control. But most control processes remain difficult to separate from the social relations of work, even when they appear to be neutral. This was the important conclusion of Blau and Schoenherr (1971), who used the concept of *insidious* controls to highlight the way in which management can utilise impersonal and unobtrusive means. Examples include selective recruitment of staff whose sense of professionalism or expertise enables them to work without direct controls; use of resource allocation as a financial discipline; and controls embodied in technology. Thus even those staff who exercise considerable work autonomy, such as those in higher education, have a series of indirect constraints over their actions.

In practice mainstream theory is more uncomfortable with its own marginalisation of control than the above discussion might suggest. The simple indication of that can be seen in the frequency with which the death of Taylorism or bureaucracy is announced. Implicit in these pronouncements is the recognition that control does exist, but the preference that it *shouldn't*. From the human relations writers of the 1950s, with their distinctions between (bad) theory X and (good) theory Y, to the advocates of 1970s-style job enrichment, control has been presented as unnecessary and outdated. Democratic leadership styles and autonomous workgroups have been seen as the basic precondition for job satisfaction and high productivity. Recent formulations have moved the debate further on. It is said that we now live in a world where change is so frequent and expertise so fundamental to the work process that 'command and control' is not merely undesirable, it is actually bad for business. Picking up on themes from the academic literature (Walton, 1985), the editor of a Scottish business journal asserts that:

> The pyramidal, hierarchical school of management is, at long last, being dragged to its knees and kicked to death. Command and control is not an option in what is rapidly becoming an economy founded on knowledge and the skills of those who have it. In such an economy it seems employees will have to be involved in strategic decision-making if organisational goals are to be achieved. (B. Millar, *Scottish Business Insider*, October 1998)

The language of contemporary management theory and practice has therefore been based around two axes: empowerment and commitment. The former suggests that organisations are delegating control to project groups and work teams, so that they become *self*-managing; the latter implies that values rather than rules have become the prime means of co-ordination. As indicated earlier, it is not our intention to examine these claims at this point. We will merely observe that they represent a continued evasion of the relevant issues. Control is either rhetorically abolished or presented in softer, more neutral terms. One of the problems with such approaches is their aspirational nature and the subsequent tendency to conflate prescription and description. Take, for example, the empowerment literature. In an incisive review, Hales (2000: 503) comments that, 'the burgeoning prescriptive or celebratory literature is replete with conceptions of empowerment which display equivocation, tautology and contradiction in equal measure'. He suggests that it is not clear whether power is to be achieved or received, what kind of powers are being enhanced (voice in decisions or choice over actions?), or the extent to which individuals or teams are expected to exercise delegated responsibilities. Such ambiguities tend to be terms – such as 'directed autonomy' – that paper over in words what is likely to be contradictory in practice (Waterman, 1988). Mainstream theory lacks conceptual frameworks that are robust enough to deal with the nature, types and levels of control. For this we have to turn elsewhere.

Critical perspectives: labour process theories of control and resistance

Pfeffer rightly observes that 'the ambivalence about the effects (if not the effectiveness) of social control is in part responsible for the development of a critical perspective on organisations and their control practices' (1997: 135). In contrast to mainstream theorists, radical writers on organisation and management frequently *begin* from an analysis of control relations. Whereas mainstream perspectives treat control and co-ordination together, radical theorists argue that management performs a *dual* function in the enterprise (Carchedi, 1977; R. Edwards, 1979). Managerial practices are a necessary means of *co-ordinating* diverse activities, but they also bear the imprint of conflicting interests in the labour process, a conflict that reflects the unique nature of labour as a commodity. This orientation was reflected in the first radical text to make a major impact as organisation theory, which began by defining the theoretical rationale of organisational analysis: 'For this volume we have proposed as such an object the concept of organisation as control of the labour process' (Clegg and Dunkerley, 1980: 1). This framework derived from Marx's analysis of the capitalist labour process, which was updated and revitalised by Braverman (1974) and a range of other 'labour process' theorists discussed below.

All societies have labour processes, but under capitalism they have specific characteristics. The most significant is what Marx referred to as the transformation of labour power into labour. In other words, when capital purchases labour it has only a potential or capacity to work. To ensure profitable production, capital must organise the conditions under which labour operates to its own advantage. But workers pursue their own interests for job security, higher rewards and satisfying work, developing their own counter-organisation through informal job controls, restriction of output, and the like.

To resolve this problem, and because they are under competitive pressure from other firms to cut costs and raise productivity, employers seek to control the conditions under which work takes place. This argument is often misunderstood. Pfeffer says that Marxist analysis 'asserts that control, not efficiency, is the object of organising arrangements' (1997: 180). While radical approaches would challenge particular conceptions of efficiency, control is not an end in itself, but a means to transform the capacity to work, established by the wage relation, into profitable production. It is a term summarising a set of mechanisms and practices that regulates the labour process (P. K. Edwards, 1990). Richard Edwards (1979: 18) distinguishes three elements in any system of control:

1. direction and specification of work tasks
2. evaluation, monitoring and assessment of performance
3. the apparatus of discipline and reward to elicit co-operation and compliance.

Such elements may, however, be best described as detailed control, in that they are normally connected to immediate work processes, whereas general control refers to management's capacity to subordinate labour to their direction of the production process as a whole. This distinction made by P. K. Edwards (1990) and other writers is of significance in that it allows for recognition of tremendous variations in how detailed control is exercised. Such a model can even allow for employers giving workers significant discretion over tasks, as in semi-autonomous work groups, if it maintains their overall control. Control is also not absolute, but, at least at the immediate level, a contested relationship. Conflict is built into the wage–effort bargain, with even mainstream writers recognising that an employment contract outlining required performance runs up against employees with their own goals and wants. As each 'party' seeks to exert its influence over the formal and informal aspects of the employment relationship, the outcome is a constantly changing 'frontier of control' (Goodrich, 1975) or 'contested terrain' (R. Edwards, 1979).

This latter point illustrates the centrality of resistance to labour process analysis. Richard Edward's research shows how control and resistance exist in dialectical relation. In other words, forms of worker self-organisation and action stimulate management to develop control practices, out of which a systematic pattern might emerge (such 'strategies' are discussed in the next section). Over a period of time, workers learn new ways of resisting those practices, and so on. Labour process accounts became known as a 'control and resistance' model. One of the best illustrations came from the British researchers Edwards and Scullion (1982). Detailed case studies show how workers adapt their behaviour, through actions such as diverse as absence, labour turnover and sabotage to particular modes of control over work organisation or rewards. Equally, they are able to demonstrate how management develop policies and practices on issues such as the provision of overtime as a means of trying to counter powerful shop-floor controls. In another important contribution, Hodson (1995; 2001) examines a range of ethnographic studies to illustrate how forms of resistance, ranging from sabotage to pilferage, develop through openings created by managerial control systems.

What about the role of management? Claims of independent actors carrying out a neutral role are disputed by evidence concerning the top strata of management (Zeitlin, 1974). By their motivation, social background and connections, rewards and shareholdings in corporations, most managers are part of the capitalist class. While a useful corrective, this 'sociological' analysis is not the crucial point. For example, a number of entrepreneurs are from a traditional working-class background. But what matter are the structural location and functions in the organisation. If anything, entrepreneurs from this background tend to identify even more closely with their new role. These roles require management to carry out functions of control and surveillance, exercising hierarchical authority over workers separated from the means of production. While it is not always clear that it is possible to distinguish between a 'neutral' co-ordination and an 'antagonistic' control, managers do act as agents carrying out the 'global functions' of capital, functions which, were delegated as part of the bureaucratisation of production. The idea of agency conjures up rather crude images of conspiracies and empty vessels: 'In the capitalist system, the principal function of management is to exploit labour power to the maximum in order to secure profits for the owners of capital' (Berkeley Thomas, 1993: 61). But the generality 'to the maximum' is meaningless. There are only specific and diverse means through which the requirements of capital are brought about, in which management takes an active rather than predetermined role.

Critical analyses sometimes get tangled up in attempts to designate managers to precise class positions. This theme does not concern us here (though see Johnston, 1986 for a critical account). What is important is that we have available a framework for understanding management practices which provides an alternative to the dominant combination of behavioural and managerial revolution theories. The fact, for example, that executives of a large corporation have the formal status of employees is, as Braverman observes, merely the form given to the domination of capital in modern society:

> Their formal attribute of being part of the same payroll as the production work-
> ers, clerks and porters of the corporation no more robs them of the powers of
> decision and command over the others in the enterprise than does the fact that
> the general, like the private, wears the military uniform, or the pope and the
> cardinal pronounce the same liturgy as the parish priest. (Braverman, 1974: 405)

Instead of the separation of ownership and control, radical writers distinguish between real or economic ownership and agents holding actual possession (De Vroey, 1975; Carchedi, 1977). Managerial agents are governed by the external constraints imposed by the dynamics of competition and capital accumulation, with profitability remaining the crucial criteria through which the successful management work is judged. If anything, this is enhanced by property ownership and related forms of control becoming increasingly depersonalised with the rise of finance, pension funds and other institutional shareholders. Individual enterprises become 'simply units in a structure of intercorporate relations' (J. Scott, 1985: 142), the divi-sion of ownership and possession resulting in greater vulnerability for managers who know they may be removed from office (Holland, 1975). A structural analysis does not imply that the growth of new forms of managerial labour is irrelevant. The heterogeneity of management has increased with the sheer extent and diversity of delegated functions and the competing groups, such as accountants and engineers, who lay claim to them.

Management strategies

Critical perspectives have been conditioned by Braverman's (1974) argument that the twentieth century saw the tightening of managerial control, primarily through the application of Taylorist and scientific management strategies. Detailed evidence is provided of the extension of such methods from simple to complex production and its use in the transformation of clerical labour. When allied to managerial shap-ing of science and technology through mechanisation and automation, work design and organisation continue to embody key Taylorist principles such as task frag-mentation and the separation of conception and execution. Braverman provided an important corrective to the widespread view that Taylorism was a failed system, superseded by more sophisticated behavioural theories to be used for motivational and job design tools (see M. Rose, 1975).

But it is widely recognised that Braverman overestimated the dominance of Taylorist strategies and practices, and underestimated the varied and uneven implementation, influenced by worker hostility, management suspicion and appropriateness to given environments. We tried to reach a balanced assessment. If Taylorism is taken to be part of a broader movement towards 'scientific' management focused on fragmen-tation of tasks and their subjection to increasing job measurement and evaluation, as well as the structuring of work processes so that skills and planning activities are located off the factory and office floors, then particular elements remain a highly significant component of control strategies, though seldom on their own.

Precisely because Braverman confused a particular system of control with management control in general, the question of *strategy* was put firmly on the agenda because of the resulting debate on alternatives. This is not to say that issues of strategy had no place in the existing organisational literature. How Chandler (1962) regarded strategy, defined as long-term planning and resource allocation to carry out goals, as the characteristic feature of the modern multidivisional firm. But control over employees was not systematically dealt with. Strategy has also been increasingly part of the agenda of the business policy and corporate management literature (Steiner and Miner, 1978). Radical perspectives differ from both in avoiding the prescriptive search for the 'best way'; remaining free to analyse what management does, rather than what it should do.

What of the alternative strategies raised in the labour process debate? As we noted earlier, Richard Edward's (1979) model is based on historically successive dominant modes of control, which reflect worker resistance and changing socio-economic conditions. A nineteenth-century system of *simple* or *personal* control by employers exercising direct authority gave way to more complex *structural* forms with the transition from small business, competitive capitalism to corporate monopolies. The first of these forms was *technical* control typified by the use of the assembly line that can pace and direct the labour process. The contradiction for management is that it created a common work experience and basis for unified shop-floor opposition. In contrast, a system of *bureaucratic* control, embedded in the social and organisational structure of the firm rather than in personal authority, offers management a means of re-dividing the workforce and tying it to impersonal rules and regulations. With his co-thinkers among radical economists (R. Edwards, Reich and Gordon, 1975; Gordon, Edwards and Reich, 1982), Edwards has also argued that employers consciously create *segmented* labour markets as a response to economic crises and as a divide-and-rule strategy, particularly using gender and race.

In contrast, Friedman (1977) rightly eschews the notion of stages, preferring to set out ideal types or strategic poles of responsible autonomy and direct control which run parallel throughout the history of capitalism. Each strategy generates its own inflexibilities in areas such as hiring and firing and task specification. The choice of strategy is governed by variations in the stability of labour and product markets, mediated by the interplay of worker resistance and managerial pressure. There is, however, an element of common ground in the belief that there has been a gradual historical tendency towards more consensual, integrative strategies; utilising internal markets, institutionalised rules and in some cases, work humanisation schemes. This is also the view of the other major control theorist, Burawoy (1979). He periodises the development of capitalist work organisation in terms of the transition from *despotic* to *hegemonic* regimes. The former involved relations of dependence and coercion that did not prove viable for capital or labour. Workers sought collective representation and social protection from the state. Capital also had an interest in state regulation of conflict and a minimal social wage that would boost purchasing power. The shift to hegemonic regimes was also based on an internal state in the workplace that provided an 'industrial citizenship', utilising grievance machinery and regulated bargaining which minimised likely resistance and class solidarity.

Subsequent events have not been kind to such models. The 1980s and 1990s have seen organisational restructuring based on downsizing and de-layering, the search for flexibility in work and employment, a move away from collective and joint regulation of the workplace and a growth in job insecurity. It is always possible, of course, to adjust the model, which Burawoy does by defining the new dominant factory regime as one of *hegemonic despotism*. This is not a return to arbitrary tyranny, but the apparently 'rational' power of a capital that is mobile across the globe, over the workforce (1985: 150). However, the problem is not just with specific projections, but linear thinking more generally. New conceptual categories of this nature merely illustrate the fundamental problem of the control theories we have been examining. Alternative strategies have been put on the map, but too often within what has been described as the 'panacea fallacy' (Littler and Salaman, 1982) or 'monism' (Storey, 1985), that is, the idea that capital always seeks and finds definitive and comprehensive modes of control as the solution to its problems. Admittedly, this is somewhat less true of Friedman, who in his own defence argues that responsible autonomy and direct control have in-built contradictions and are 'two directions towards which managers can move, rather than two predefined states between which managers choose' (1987: 3). But there is still a sense of a search for all-embracing categories, which have their parallels in behavioural theory, such as Etzioni's (1961) structures of compliance, or Schein's (1965) linear models of economic, social and complex man.

Nevertheless, the control debate sparked an extensive and useful amount of empirical work influenced by labour process theory. Early case studies tended to focus on reaffirmation of theses of deskilling and tighter controls (Zimbalist, 1979), or critiques of them highlighting mediating factors such as markets and worker resistance (Wood, 1982). Subsequent efforts were concerned to establish trends in their own right. Studies dealing with the introduction of new technology have stressed that deskilling and direct control represents only one of a range of management strategies (Wilkinson, 1986). Child's (1985) research shows even more clearly how ideas of strategy can be used, while recognising variations in goals and environments. He identified a variety of strategies including elimination of direct labour, subcontracting, polyvalence or multi-tasking and job degradation. These were connected to an even wider set of influences, including those of national economic cycles, government policy and the culture of organisations.

Other research applied models to specific industries, but without any claims for universality. A good example is the use by researchers of Richard Edwards' control concepts. Murray and Wickham (1985) studied two Irish electronics factories employing mainly female semi-skilled workers, showing that direction, discipline and evaluation are all carried out according to explicit rules rather than direct controls. Supervisors do not monitor production performance and enforce discipline. This is left to inspectors on the basis of statistical records that can identify the operators responsible. Supervisors, however, are central to processes of evaluating the social character of the 'good worker' in order to facilitate promotion through the internal labour market. The elaborate and artificial hierarchy created at the plants meant that one third of workers had been promoted from the basic assembly grade, thus confirming Edwards's view that employees are given positive material reasons for complying with bureaucratic rules. More recently Callaghan and Thompson

(2001) used the growth of call centres to revisit Edwards, observing the similarities between automated call distribution systems and previous descriptions of technical control in which managerial authority is embedded within supposed objective mechanisms of work distribution and measurement. We return to this issue and study in the final section of the chapter.

A further direction was to focus on specific strategies and processes of control such as recruitment policies (Fevre, 1986; Maguire, 1986; Winstanley, 1986; Callaghan and Thompson, 2002) that were neglected in an exclusive focus on the labour process. The most extensive research was initially carried out on *gender*. Socially-defined notions of femininity as a form of control have been observed in multinationals operating in the third world (Pearson, 1986). Plant management consciously exploits cultures of passivity and subordination by combining an image of the company as a patriarchal family system with the manager as father figure, Western-style beauty competitions and classes (Grossman, 1979). In the West, Grieco and Whipp's overview argues that 'managerial strategies of control make use of and enhance the sexual divisions in society' (1985: 136). Studies of office and factory workers (Glenn and Feldberg, 1979; Pollert, 1981; Westwood, 1984; Bradley, 1986) show that management uses women's marginality to work, arising from the family, to frame its labour control policies.

In reflecting on the above debates, a degree of common ground emerged. Product and labour markets, worker resistance and a range of other external and internal factors are recognised as mediating control strategies and shaping power relations in the frontier of control between capital and labour. The variations in strategy that result are not random, but reflect the fundamental tension we have talked of between management's need to control and discipline, while engaging workers' commitment and co-operation. Strategies therefore contain inherent contradictions (Storey, 1985; Hyman, 1987). These are enhanced by the difficulty of harmonising the different managerial functions, sites of intervention and decision-making, which includes technology, social organisation of labour and relations with the representative bodies of employees. Hyman notes that 'there is no "one best way" of managing these contradictions, only different routes to partial failure' (1987: 30). Management of large organisations is therefore likely to try combinations of control strategies and practices, appropriate to particular environments or sections of the workforce. As one of us has remarked elsewhere:

> The most consistent weakness of existing theory has been to counterpoise one form of control to another....No one has convincingly demonstrated that a particular form of control is necessary or inevitable for capitalism to function successfully. (Thompson, 1989: 151)

Whatever the limitations of the ideas, as Pfeffer notes, 'labour process theorists have been enormously influential in stimulating a discussion of work place control, not from the point of view of organisational efficiency or management but from the point of view of its determinants and its effects on workers' (1997: 184). The above 'consensus' fails to satisfy those within and outside the radical perspective, who are critical of the explanatory power of concepts concerned with management control strategy. For some, the problem with a Marxist-influenced agenda is that, like more orthodox accounts, it wrongly assumes high levels of rationality, this time applied to top management (Bryman, 1984: 401; Grint, 1995: 51). Others go beyond the previously noted criticism of 'panacea fallacies' to object to the treatment of management as omniscient, omnipotent and monolithic. Based on her study of chemical plants, Harris mocks the image of managers who have the attributes of deity and 'papal inerrancy' when dealing with workers, commenting that radical writers assume that senior management 'always know what is in capital's interests and unfailingly order things so that they work together for its greater good' (1987: 70). There are conflicts within management reflecting contending interest groups and the difficulty of carrying out integrative functions. Nor is it always possible to draw a neat dividing line from workers given that managers are also wage labourers subject to controls. The distortions in such analyses are held to derive from a wider determinism and functionalism in which 'managers are regarded as unproblematic agents of capital who dispatch their "global functions" in a rationalistic manner' (Storey, 1985: 195).

Capital's interests are not given and management practices cannot be 'read-off' from them. Assumptions of a 'tight-coupling' underestimate the diversity and complexity of such practices, and the significance for decision-making processes within the enterprise. It is also the case that in addition to the responsibilities that managers have to the control apparatus of the enterprise, they need to control their own personal identities and make sense of their own work in the employing organisation. Managerial work therefore has a 'double control' aspect in which there is a strategic exchange between individuals and organisations (Watson, 1994). The consequence of the above critiques is the belief that too few insights are generated into what 'flesh and blood' managers actually do.

At a general level many of these criticisms would be accepted across a wide spectrum. But some carry it much further: 'current uses of the terms "strategy" and "control" are somewhat misleading guides both to actual management conduct and to the causes of particular outcomes in work organisation and industrial relations' (Rose and Jones, 1985: 82). We can break this down into two issues: do identifiable management strategies exist and are practices centred on controlling workers?

Questioning strategy

Those who argue against the idea of coherent strategies with a fixity of purpose believe that management activities are more likely to be piecemeal, unco-ordinated and fragmented, with at best a striving for logical incrementalism. Management is concerned primarily with 'keeping the show on the road' (Tomlinson, 1982: 128), corresponding with the 'realist' views discussed earlier.

Supportive research was outlined in areas such as work reorganisation schemes (Rose and Jones, 1985) and new technology and skills in engineering (Campbell and Currie, 1987). Any strategic capacity is held to be inevitably undermined by a plethora of sites of decision-making, varied objectives among different management specialists and interest groups, the need to smooth over diverse and contradictory practices, and the requirement of sustaining a consensal accommodation with employee organisations. The result is an unpredictable variety of managerial intentions characterised by a 'plant particularism' (Rose and Jones, 1985: 96), and control structures as merely 'temporary outcomes' (Storey, 1985). Campbell and Currie plump for the idea of 'negotiated preferences' and there is a general orientation towards explanations based on *practices* rather than strategy.

Some of these differences may reflect the sector being researched. For example, engineering is well known for its 'seat-of-the-pants' approach to management, whereas other sectors such as food or chemicals are noted for more strategic methods. Nevertheless, this kind of approach is confirmed by some writers on industrial relations (Purcell and Sissons, 1983), who note the problems created by the absence of management strategies towards their own employees, particularly ones that are integrated into overall business objectives. Instead there is a continued dominance of reactive and opportunistic practices directed towards immediate problem solving (Thurley and Wood, 1983: 209). What *kind* of strategy is said to be absent is not always made explicit. But the basic model used is similar to that popularised by Chandler, which, like many other adaptations to the business sphere, is strongly influenced by military experience and terminology (Shaw, 1990). That is, it posits detailed and co-ordinated plans of campaign in which conscious, long-term planning based on corporate goals is supported by appropriate courses of action and allocation of resources. This can be seen in the business policy debate (Steiner and Miner, 1978; Porter, 1980) in which generations of students are warned of the negative consequences of the absence of corporate strategy, and scholars debate different models of structure, strategy and competitiveness. Similarly, standard models of strategic HRM emphasise the need for coherence and integration both within its component parts and with wider business strategy (Tichy *et al.*, 1982). Indeed, HRM is sometimes seen only to offer something new if it has strategic value (Kamoche, 1994).

The problem with mainstream notions of strategy is that it is all too easy to counter textbook ideal types of coherence and integration with the messy reality of real companies and sectors. The insights of social science have been applied to demonstrate how organisations muddle through rather than plan rationally. The promise of complete knowledge and controllable environments is seen as neither desirable nor feasible in fragmented, turbulent, postmodern times. As a result, in the last decade strategy has gone from buzzword to boo-word. It has been 'problematised' to the point that the concept is no longer fashionable even in strategic management circles (for a useful overview, see Whipp, 1996). Complaining that discourses of strategy are primarily about shoring up the power of senior managers and consultants, Knights and Morgan reject the concept altogether: 'Nothing new is really added by talking the discourse of strategy; on the contrary, a limit is put on our understanding of the special phenomenon because we are forcing action into a particular rationalistic and individualistic framework' (1990: 480).

But conceptions of management strategy in the above frameworks are in themselves problematic. A stereotyped polarity is set up between a conception of objective rationality that implies perfect foresight, choice and follow-through; and a bounded rationality of constrained choice in complex realities. Too often the critics collude in forcing action into a conceptual straitjacket. By adopting a straw man of 'strong' strategy, they have set criteria for strategy so stringently that it becomes impossible to meet them (Child, 1985). While it is wrong to attribute coherent, rational intent to management, it is equally mistaken to assume that strategy has to be seen as always consistent, systematic and without contradiction. Strategies may not always be effectively followed through at the implementation stage, as with the introduction of new technology. They may not constitute a coherent package for the whole operations of a company, perhaps manifesting a disjuncture between job design plans and employee relations. Coherence is an important variable, but it has to be set against the knowledge of inevitable contradictions and the likelihood of 'loose-coupling' between planning and practices. Strategies are likely to be accompanied by bargaining within management and with the workforce, so making the end result uncertain. As Friedman rightly notes, 'Irrationality, inconsistency, lack of system certainly exist and must be allowed for; however, a more useful concept to introduce is failure' (1987: 294). Even where changes are introduced without clear intent, they can establish the preconditions for subsequent strategy (Hyman, 1987: 47).

While managers frequently act on the world with poor information, they can and do act strategically. It is only necessary for researchers to show a degree of intent or planning, and to infer a logic over a period of time from the frequency and pattern of action, or from 'emergent outcomes' (Hales, 1988: 12). Boxall and Purcell make a similar point in a different way: 'It is possible to find strategy in every business because it is embedded in the important choices the managers and staff of the firm make about what to do and how to do it' (2003: 28). The same criteria apply to the activities of workers. Groups such as printers or doctors do not always behave in a fully conscious or coherent manner. But observation reveals a clear pattern of occupational and job controls, and strategies of closure aimed at excluding competitors, often women (Cockburn, 1983; Witz, 1986). The latter point reinforces research on households that shows that strategies emerge from 'bottom-up', day-to-day activities – a weaker, but still legitimate sense of strategy that relies on social scientists observing and analysing predictable patterns (Wallace, 1993).

Of course, the capacity for strategy is not random. Certain external conditions are likely to push management in that direction. Streek (1987) puts forward a persuasive case that economic crisis and rapidly changing market environments have created a 'general strategic problem' whose core element is the need for *flexibility*. However, the very nature of uncertainty and varied conditions in sectors and countries produces different strategic responses. For example, countries such as Germany and Austria with traditions of tripartite state, union and employer bargaining have seen moves towards economic liberalisation and labour flexibility that retain a strong union role and corporatist regulation of wages, labour and product markets. The hostility of all economic actors in Germany to the prospective takeover of telecommunications giant Mannesman by a UK competitor in 1999 was a case in point. Streek's analysis not only builds in an explanation of such variations, but it also provides a framework for understanding the general conditions under which strategies develop. At times of crisis and readjustment, 'the variety of strategies and structures within the collectivity of firms is bound to increase at least until a new standard of "best practice" has been established' (1987: 284). In other words, there is always ebb and flow in intensity and direction of organisational practices, but strategic patterns do emerge and can be observed, particularly in the cauldron of highly internationalised sectors where a small number of giants compete for dominance.

Questioning control over labour

The second strand of critique questions whether the centrality given to control of labour is actually reflective of managerial behaviour. It is argued that we cannot view management strategies and tactics from the vantage point of the labour process, but must consider the role of product and labour markets, and technologies. Control proceeds in a complex cycle from planning to implementation, involving groups such as accountants and industrial engineers. It is also true that labour costs may be only a relatively small proportion of the total, particularly in capital-intensive industries, so the emphasis of managerial controls may be elsewhere. With such factors in mind, some argue that analysis should focus on the 'multiple constituents' of management expertise beyond the confrontation of capital and labour in the control of the workplace (Miller and O'Leary, 1987: 10). Such a critique can be presented in a Marxist form. Accumulation and costs of production are what matter to capital and its agents, not control. If anything, managers are dominated by problems of the *outcomes* of the labour process, including sales, marketing, supply and cash flow. Kelly uses the concept of the full circuit of capital to argue that we must be concerned not only with the *extraction* of surplus value through controlling the labour process, but its *realisation* through the sale of commodities, as well as the prior *purchase* of labour. On these grounds, 'there is no sound reason for privileging any moment in the circuit' (1985: 32).

Morgan and Hooper used a similar framework in their research into the Imperial Tobacco Group in the 1970s to distinguish between three circuits of capital. *Industrial* capital refers to that used in the management and design of the production process itself; *commercial* to the sphere of buying and selling and therefore functions such as marketing and advertising; and *banking* to the process of capital used in lending and borrowing, governed by accountancy and financial controls.

These distinctions are used to argue that critical theories of the labour process have often lost sight of the role of capital and ownership because of the emphasis on management control. The case study shows a series of strategies pursued in tandem, representing the particular circuits. To break out of a static tobacco market, top management prioritised commercial and banking strategies, rather than developing existing labour processes. In particular, companies such as Imperial were drawn into investments in the share and gilts markets. These proved successful, but when the resultant money was invested in production this had disastrous results. Firms are thus conceptualised as 'sites of a complex integration of circuits of capital' (Morgan and Hooper, 1987: 623), which management must integrate and control. This takes us back to the opening quote of the chapter in which the General Motors executive was seeking control in a number of spheres.

During this period of debate, other writers questioned whether control can be regarded as the factor that distinguishes between a dominant management and a subordinate labour. Management has non-control functions and characteristics of employees, while workers exercise job controls and may be involved in the regulation of others (Melling, 1982: 249). At a more theoretical level, Cressey and MacInnes (1980) observe that workers have an interest in the viability of their own units of capital as well as resisting subordination, matching capital's dual relationship with labour as a commodity and as a source of co-operation necessary for profitable production. Some mainstream writers use their own research into the chemical industry (Harris, 1987) and those of chemicals, engineering and biscuits (Buchanan, 1986) to argue that workers basically accept managerial authority, give commitment and effort willingly, and have convergent interests with management, thus negating any preoccupation with control. This is likely to be linked to a rejection of 'zero-sum' conceptions of power in which one side necessarily gains at the expense of the other (Harris, 1987: 77). Even some radical writers believe that capital and management are not necessarily dominant, with unions having considerably more power, even in a recession, than usually acknowledged (Kelly, 1985: 49; Rose and Jones, 1985: 101).

It is certainly true that, as Hyman observes; 'If most orthodox literature on business strategy ignores or marginalises the conflict between capital and labour, most Marxist literature perceives nothing else' (1987: 34). This has a curious parallel with the virtual total emphasis in organisation behaviour on 'man-management'. So the full circuit of capital is a very useful and necessary concept for understanding the capitalist enterprise. Furthermore, change and crisis often arise from disarticulation of the moments of the circuit (Kelly, 1985), as we saw in the Imperial example. Such concepts can be combined with more orthodox accounts of the changing pattern of *corporate control* which plot how large firms seek to solve their competitive problems by reshaping structures and forms of intervention in the market (Fligstein, 1990). Such 'modes of control' have included vertical and horizontal integration, the multidivisional form and, more recently, financial means of integrating diverse portfolios built up through acquisition.

However, these perspectives do not invalidate a specific emphasis on relations of control between capital and labour. This is not just another process equivalent to marketing or financial accounting. The management of workers and work remains at the heart of the enterprise and indeed of economic reproduction as a whole. But such an orientation need have no marginalising effect on the analysis of other social relations. As P. K. Edwards (1990) observes, the problem of 'privileging' one part of the circuit arises only if the analysis assumes that this one part determines what happens in the others.

As we made clear at the start of the chapter, we are not saying that control is normally the *goal* of management, but rather a *means* embodied in strategies and techniques. It is true that management strategies are not always developed with labour's role in mind. But it is ultimately difficult to separate a concern with 'outcomes' such as product quality of financial targets from acting on labour in some way. Strategies towards markets or technologies will often be constrained or mediated by labour policies and the practices of workers (Friedman, 1987). In addition, as Child notes, 'strategies which are unspecific towards the labour process may still have relevance for it' (1985: 110). An example is the introduction of new technology which, much research shows, is frequently used as a means of more general work reorganisation. Finally, irrespective of the detail of arguments about the outcomes of high-performance work systems, it is widely accepted that labour productivity is the most appropriate measure of human resource management of the firm (Boxall and Purcell, 2003: 8). Given the inherently incomplete nature of employment contracts, a strong focus on labour controls – of various types – is an inevitable corollary, particularly in a mainly labour-intensive service economy.

On the issue of the existence of co-operation and common interests, we would wholly concur. In fact we would go further. As one of us has observed: 'Workers do not always need to be overtly controlled. They may effectively "control" themselves' (Thompson, 1989: 153). Participation in routine practices to create interest or increase rewards can generate *consent* to existing structures of control and power, as Burawoy's (1979) famous studies of production 'games' indicate. What is puzzling is why some writers insist on co-operative and consensual processes being counterposed to those of control and conflict. It is increasingly recognised that all have to be theorised as different products of the contradictory relations within the enterprise. Not only do consent and control coexist; 'the mobilisation of consent' through culture strategies forms an increasingly central part of management–employee relations strategies in many sectors.

We also accept that workers exercise controls, but it would be a serious mistake to regard them as *equivalent* to those of management. This would fail to distinguish between *types* of control, particularly between the general and detailed dimensions referred to earlier in the chapter. At the general level of direction of production, managerial dominance is guaranteed by their stewardship of the crucial organisational resources. This is not 'zero-sum' because it cannot be 'added up'. Clearly, however, control of immediate work processes is largely zero-sum, in that if workers control a given item, then management cannot also do so (P. K. Edwards, 1990).

New directions – surveillance and shifting the locus of control

Having gone through successive forms of criticism concerning ideas of control strategy, the more recent period has seen the emphasis move back to new accounts of control. Some of these arise from empirical shifts in work and employment. For example, the growth of front-line service work means that the *customer* may mediate the standard management–worker dyad, providing information on employees, and directing their behaviour or values (Frenkel *et al.*, 1999; Sturdy *et al.*, 2001). The most significant challenge to established labour process frameworks, however, comes from the argument that the locus of control has shifted from external to internal. We have already identified one version of this earlier in the chapter. A move to seeking employee commitment can be seen as a form of *internalised control* that does not rely on external rewards and sanctions, or rule-following. Cultural controls rely primarily on acceptance of values and peer enforcement. In one of the earliest contributions, Ray (1986) argued that control by corporate culture was the last frontier, in that it had enabled organisations to generate sentiment and emotion, simultaneously internalising control and linking personal with corporate identity. It is argued that the expansion of work that has a higher discretionary content and more ambiguity leads management to give less direction and elicit more reciprocated trust through 'info-normative control' (Frenkel *et al.*, 1995).

At this stage we want to concentrate on a parallel argument about a shifting locus, this time with the emphasis on surveillance replacing, or becoming the dominant mechanism of, control. On the surface this does not appear to be consistent with an internalised direction. After all, surveillance is normally associated with collecting and storing information, using it to monitor behaviour and establish discipline (Dandeker, 1990). However, the argument is less about mechanisms than their *effects*. Case studies (Zuboff, 1988; Sewell and Wilkinson, 1992; Sewell, 1998) of high-tech manufacturing make much of the enhanced capacity of management to collect, display and attribute performance data through electronic surveillance. Because stockpiles of labour and parts are eliminated through quality (TQM) and just-in-time (JIT) systems, production arrangements are highly visible. The information is generated from and fed back through teams of employees that appear to have autonomy, but in practice internalise production norms and discipline themselves through systems such as Nissan's 'Neighbour Watch' (Garrahan and Stewart, 1992). Such information is unobtrusive and perceived to be objective, therefore accentuating its legitimacy. Teams may produce self-surveillance independently of an information-driven process. Delegated responsibilities, whether for routine production decisions or, more exceptionally, induction and evaluation of team members, mean that employees have to develop their own disciplinary 'rules', thus collaborating with management to identify and reward the 'good worker' (Barker, 1993; McKinlay and P. Taylor, 1996). Such studies argue that as a consequence of such discipline and the removal of any 'slack' from the production system, 'worker counter-control (in the sense described by Roy and many others) is effectively eliminated...the ultimate goal of management under a TQM/JIT regime must be recognised to be Total Management Control' (Delbridge, Turnbull and Wilkinson, 1992: 105).

The growth of call centres has also boosted new theories of control. Surveillance undoubtedly plays a pivotal role in the way that integrated telephone and computer technologies facilitate the access and retrieval of data in the service interaction between desk-bound employee and external customer. Of particular importance is a sophisticated capacity remotely to record and assess the speed and 'quality' of the work. Not only are performance data made public, but also a proportion of the calls will be monitored remotely and used to reward and discipline employees. As a result, the previously identified 'objectivity' of the statistics is combined with constant, but unseen surveillance. Not only do employees internalise controls, but also the controllers are redundant: 'In call centres the agents are constantly visible and supervisor's power has indeed been "rendered perfect" – via the computer monitoring screen – and therefore its actual use unnecessary' (Fernie and Metcalf, 1997: 29).

In the most developed theorisation of such trends, Sewell (1998) argues that the interaction of 'vertical' electronic surveillance and 'horizontal' peer-group scrutiny has produced a new model of control, countering the optimistic gloss of the empowerment and team literatures, while moving beyond the limits of traditional labour process theory. The implication of Sewell's argument is that such a combination solves the direct control/responsible autonomy dilemma that has historically troubled generations of managers, to say nothing of management theorists.

Surveillance is not a new phenomenon. Many writers have described the early factory in terms of the attempted subordination and surveillance of recalcitrant workers, using the work of historians to illustrate how employers used new systems of rules and control techniques to induce 'appropriate' morals and work habits.

In the most detailed examination of the issues, Dandeker (1990) links surveillance primarily to processes of bureaucratic rationalisation that have developed throughout this century. By 1990, 10 million workers in the US, including many professional and managerial employees, had become subject to electronic performance monitoring (Pfeffer, 1997: 114). Given these trends and recent socio-technical systems, it is difficult to deny that *some* shift towards electronic and self-surveillance has taken place in *some* industries.

Whether this constitutes an overarching development requiring an entirely new conceptualisation is a different matter. Many practices highlighted in the manufacturing case studies were identified by earlier writers making a critique of lean production (Parker and Slaughter, 1988b). Yet they were described as a form of work intensification – 'management by stress' – in other words, more a shift in the effort bargain than the frontier of control. The idea that electronic surveillance is unobtrusive is a strange one. Performance display is characterised by its visibility to management and employees. It can therefore only be unobtrusive if the information it relays is accepted as objective. Yet there is considerable evidence that employees challenge the accuracy of the data, or use them for their own purposes against management (Zuboff, 1988; Bain and P. Taylor, 2000).

Call centres are clearly a new development, but do we need new concepts to explain them? Callaghan and Thompson (2001) argue that Richard Edwards' control framework provides better insights than recent 'electronic sweatshop' perspectives. His three dimensions of a system of control and distinction between stages of direct, technical and bureaucratic control strategies have been fully outlined earlier in the chapter. Call centres predominantly use a system of technical control. In terms of Edwards' first dimension, automated call distribution systems (ACD) enable management to direct the speed, direction and character of the work tasks. Technical control in call centres goes further than assembly lines in assisting companies to operationalise the second dimension – monitoring and evaluating performance. The performance of individuals and teams can be compared within or across sites. In turn that information can be linked to the apparatus of reward and discipline through the formal assessment and review process. One of the weaknesses of Edwards' framework is its linear nature. If this is dispensed with, we can see that his 'next' system – bureaucratic control – is used in call centres to define skills and tasks, and specify behavioural and performance standards. In the Callaghan and Thompson case study, Telebank has 19 core standards of behaviour and a 7-point scale to measure the skills of operators during appraisal, which is used to generate high and low scores. This indicates that many controls in the modern workplace remain external. To take another example, normative rules in strong culture companies may be different from traditional task-based control, but they are still rules. There is still the question of whether such rules are internalised. Management's sources and use of information may have increased, but there is little evidence that they are unobtrusive or regarded by employees as objective and unconnected to visible authority relations. Far from supervisory power being 'rendered perfect', there is evidence that customer service representatives (CSR) strongly dislike the emphasis put on 'the stats' and the disciplinary uses made of them (Bain and P. Taylor, 2000; Callaghan and Thompson, 2001). Employees distinguish between the 'friendly' supervision of coaching to improve skills and the disciplinary use of performance data. As with manufacturing, CSRs challenge the objectivity of the data and turn it against them: 'I check everything, I take it away and check it, I don't just sign it. I go back into the system, you can actually remember a lot of things when you go back in and see the name. I know that people have had arguments with the research section' (CSR quoted in Callaghan and Thompson, 2001: 32). Though individual, technology-paced working and remote surveillance makes resistance difficult, CSRs learn informally to manipulate the codes used to claim relief from work tasks, and become skilled in setting their own pace and variation from the company scripts when talking to customers (P. Taylor and Bain, 1998; S. Taylor, 1998; Callaghan and Thompson, 2001).

None of the above observations seeking to qualify 'shifts of locus' arguments are intended to deny that changes in the nature and frontier of controls have taken place. These have been recently summarised by Thompson and Harley (2007). Many of the conceptual confusions in analysis of workplace controls would be solved if it was recognised that new forms seldom wholly displace old ones. This is what Thompson and Harley refer to as continuity, in combination. Labour process and other perspectives accept that the normative sphere has been an expanding area of managerial practice, without endorsing the view that these have replaced or even marginalised the more traditional mechanisms of bureaucratic rationalisation, work intensification, or some features of scientific management. This can be seen in both the manufacturing and service sectors. With respect to the former, Japanese-style lean production has combined work intensification and multi-tasking under modified traditional methods, described by Adler as 'democratic Taylorism'. At the same time, management focuses more on the normative sphere in order to by-pass trade union representation and secure worker identification with broader organisational norms (Danford, 1998; Delbridge et al., 2000). As for services, to return to the call centre example, surveillance and monitoring is intended to create an 'assembly line in the head' (P. Taylor and Bain, 1998). Through the work is organised in many ways around very traditional methods, to gain competitive advantage from service interactions, companies frequently seek to generate high commitment and shared identity through corporate cultures or teamworking (Thompson, van den Broek and Callaghan, 2004). The outcome is a distinctive form of high-commitment, low-discretion work system (Houlihan, 2002).

More generally, the outcome in modern work settings is increased hybridity of control structures as environments and organisational structures become more complex (Alvesson and Thompson, 2005). Even in knowledge-intensive industries large companies reply on combined and integrated control structures. A good example is provided in Alvesson and Kärreman's case study of a global consulting firm. The company directs much of its control practices towards 'cultural engineering' in order to shape employee identities and identifications. However, to close any gaps and minimise uncertainties, it also creates 'a vast bureaucratic and output measuring apparatus' (2004: 441), including extensive financial controls, standardised work procedures and formal HRM systems for recruitment, promotion and evaluating performance. The lesson drawn is that:

> Socio-ideological control is thus intimately tied to bureaucracy and output control. It is not, as claimed by most of the literature on control…an alternative to

the latter two, useful in situations where complexity and uncertainty make rules for prescribing behaviour and the precise measurement of results impossible. (Alvesson and Kärreman, 2004: 441)

Interestingly, the authors note that the combined and reinforcing nature of these controls does not guarantee their effectiveness. For example, there was 'overwhelming evidence' that time reports from employees were faked. This brings us back to an earlier theme of the chapter: the linkages between managerial controls and worker resistance.

A further reflection on resistance

In this chapter we have shown numerous examples of the persistence of worker resistance, especially to new normative forms of control that focus on worker attitudes and emotions. Though different judgements are, in part, an outcome of how case study and survey evidence about the extent of worker buy-in to managerial norms is interpreted, it is also a dispute about concepts. Categories used to describe and explain resistance have been strongly influenced by the language and experience of industrial relations with its organised collective actors – trade unions, employers and the state. As Thompson and Ackroyd (1995) and Kelly (2005) have argued, the decline of formal organised conflicts such as strikes, alongside falling trade union membership, has too often been treated as synonymous with the decline and disappearance of conflict as such.

While the concept of worker resistance was an attempt to broaden the categories of description, much of the discussion focused on organised non-compliance in large manufacturing workplaces. Something even broader was needed and eventually supplied through Ackroyd and Thompson's (1999) analysis of 'organisation misbehaviour' (see also Ackroyd and Collinson, 2005; Ackroyd, 2008). Originally directed towards a critique of mainstream and radical views that emphasised the dominance of new forms of cultural control and electronic surveillance, it also acts as an integrated 'map' of worker action and agency focused on four resource territories that both management and employees try to 'appropriate': working time, working effort, the product of work and work identities. The term misbehaviour is used ironically to draw attention to what is missed and misunderstood by orthodox accounts that assume conformity of behaviour as the norm, and to signify counter-productive behaviour – anything you do at work that you are not supposed to do.

These traditions largely focus on conflicts around the effort bargain. The mapping of organisation misbehaviour reflects changes in workplace and academic politics by including identity in the multi-dimensional framework, thus rendering 'a whole new realm of workplace practice…visible' (Fleming, 2001: 191). Put another way, the expanded categories helped us to see a new contested terrain where managerial efforts to mobilise employee emotions, commitment and personality through cultural and socio-technical practices potentially clashes with worker identities and interests. The very ambition of some companies to mould employee identity through culture change programmes and mission statements often patently at

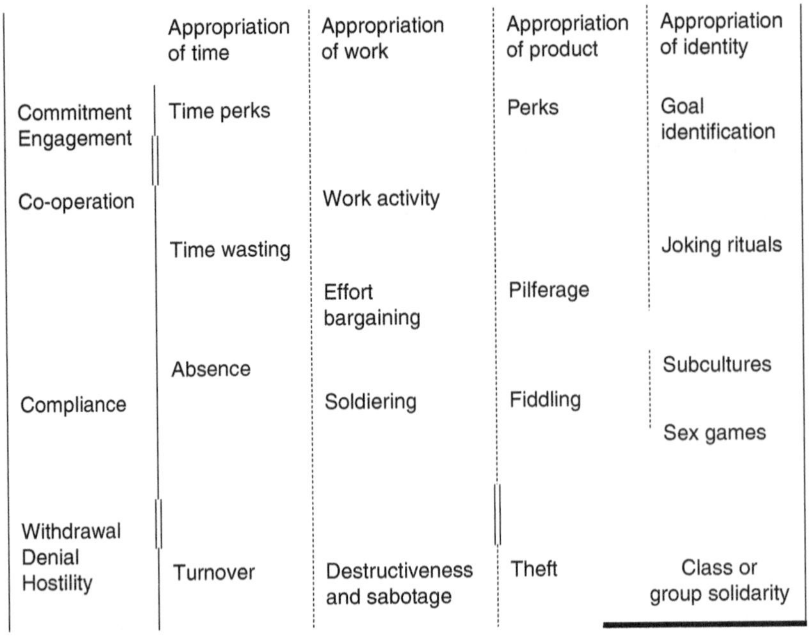

	Appropriation of time	Appropriation of work	Appropriation of product	Appropriation of identity
Commitment Engagement	Time perks		Perks	Goal identification
Co-operation		Work activity		
	Time wasting			Joking rituals
		Effort bargaining	Pilferage	
	Absence			Subcultures
Compliance		Soldiering	Fiddling	
				Sex games
Withdrawal Denial Hostility	Turnover	Destructiveness and sabotage	Theft	Class or group solidarity

Figure 11.1 Mapping misbehaviour

Source: Reproduced with permission from S. Ackroyd and P. Thompson (1999) *Organizational Misbehaviour*, London: Sage.

odds with day-to-day workplace experience renders them vulnerable to employee cynicism that becomes a resource for resistance (Fleming and Spicer, 2002; Fleming, 2005). A good example is provided by Taylor and Bain's (2003) graphic account of how call centre workers use humour, not only as informal dissent, but in one case as part of a campaign for union recognition.

Despite the continuity with the traditions of industrial sociology and opening up of new territories for dissent, some researchers in a labour process tradition (Martinez and Stewart, 1997) have argued that the misbehaviour categories are too individualistic and accept at face value too much from the arguments about the decline of trade unions and collectivism. But Ackroyd and Thompson's intent was to expand the scope of concepts to understand dissenting and non-compliant activities at work, rather than to argue that the conditions for broader forms of collective action and organisation have diminished. When influential Foucauldian arguments about panoptic power are examined.

Summary and key points

In mainstream accounts, neither control nor resistance is treated as a substantial feature of organisational life, but largely as a failure of systems that are otherwise based on creativity, consensus and commitment. By analysing managerial control as a structural imperative of the capitalist labour process given that markets and formal contracts alone cannot deal with the gap between the potential of purchased labour and the desired profitable outcomes of that labour, LPT pushes the issue to centre stage. That perspective is not top down, but is a reciprocal model of control and resistance. Given both the general nature of divergent interests between capital and labour, plus the way that any control system builds up internal contradictions, the conditions for resistance are always present and tend to develop further over time. Nor is it a story solely about constraints on managers. LPT frames its accounts in terms of rival and/or changing strategies of control, Such strategies are seldom coherent in conception or content. But we can observe patterns of labour-control practices that form a significant, though far from sole, feature of the managerial repertoire. Because conditions change and employees learn to evade and exploit existing ways of doing things, control practices are inherently dynamic. In recent debates, considerable emphasis has been put on new forms based on surveillance, cultural engineering and self-discipline. The position taken in this chapter is that, though there has been some shift in the direction of policy, their intended effects – to encourage employees to internalise controls – is far from certain or complete. It is always wise not to confuse the formal capacities of technological and managerial systems with their actual usage and effectiveness. Control systems were never one-dimensional and now, given the diversity of challenges and conditions, their forms are more likely to be combined and hybrid in character. Like control, resistance also sometimes changes its form and content. In the final part of the chapter, we outlined some new ways of understanding such trends, drawing on Ackroyd and Thompson's mapping of organisational misbehaviour. This framework, though only part of the total picture, helps broaden our accounts of resistant and dissenting behaviours, while helping to explain their persistence in a context where others have proclaimed their demise. This is, however, not the end of some of these discussions. We shall return by a different route, to issues of culture.

Further reading

The two Edwards, Richard and Paul, are a good starting point. *Contested Terrain* (R. Edwards, 1979) is probably the most influential book on control and resistance and is a very good read, while the UK-based contribution of P. K. Edwards and Scullion (1982) deserves to be better known. Hyman's (1987) journal article is still the best overview of labour process perspectives on control, an interpretation supported by the fact that it remains one of the most downloaded papers from *Work, Employment and Society* after 20+ years. Of the new Foucauldian-influenced accounts of control and surveillance, Sewell (1998) is deservedly the most influential, though you might also look at the critique by Thompson (2003b). On current debates on resistance, Ackroyd and Thompson's (and associated) various discussions of misbehaviour are a good starting point, and Taylor and Bain (2003) an excellent application to call centres. Hodson (2001) does a similar job, drawing on many of the same ethnographic labour process studies, but ties the discussion into wider issues of dignity at work. Alvesson and Kärreman's (2004) paper is a good example of a contemporary treatment of control that combines a range of concpets and theories discussed in this chapter.

Ackroyd, S. and Thompson, P. (1999) *Organizational Misbehaviour*, London: Sage.

Alvesson, M. and Kärreman, D. (2004) 'Interfaces of Control: Technocratic and Socio-ideological Control in a Global Management Consultancy Firm', *Accounting, Organizations and Society*, 29: 423–44.

Collinson, D. and Ackroyd, P. (2005) 'Resistance, Misbehaviour, Dissent', in S. Ackroyd, R. Batt, P. Thompson and P. Tolbert (eds.), *A Handbook of Work and Organization*, Oxford: Oxford University Press.

Edwards, P. K. (1986) *Conflict at Work: A Materialist Analysis of Workplace Relations*, Oxford: Blackwell.

Edwards, P. K. and Scullion, H. (1982) *The Social Organization of Industrial Conflict: Control and Resistance in the Workplace*, Oxford: Blackwell.

Hodson, R. (2001) *Dignity at Work*, Cambridge: Cambridge University Press.

Hyman, R. (1987) 'Strategy or Structure: Capital, Labour and Control', *Work, Employment and Society*, 1. 1: 25–55.

Sewell, G. (1998) 'The Discipline of Teams: The Control of Team-based Industrial Work through Electronic and Peer Surveillance', *Administrative Science Quarterly*, 43: 406–69.

Taylor, P. and Bain, P. (2003) 'Subterranean Worksick Blues: Humour as Subversion in Two Call Centres', *Organization Studies*, 24. 9: 1487–509.

Thompson, P. (2003) 'Fantasy Island: A Labour Process Critique of the "Age of Surveillance"', *Surveillance and Society*, 1. 2: 138–51.

Thompson, P. and Ackroyd, S. (1995) 'All Quiet on the Workplace Front? A Critique of Recent Trends in British Industrial Sociology', *Sociology*, 29. 4: 1–19.

References

Ackroyd, S. (2008) 'Organisational Conflict', in Cooper, C.L. and Clegg, S.R. (eds), *Handbook of Organisational Behaviour*, London: Sage.

Ackroyd, P. and Collinson, D. (2005) 'Resistance, Misbehaviour, Dissent', in S. Ackroyd, S., R. Batt, R., P. Thompson, and P. Tolbert, P. (eds), *A Handbook of Work and Organization*, Oxford: Oxford University Press.

Ackroyd, S. and Thompson, P. (1999) *Organisational Misbehaviour*, London: Sage.

Adair, J. (1979) *Action-Centred Leadership*, London: Gower.

Alvesson, M. and Kärreman, D. (2004) 'Interfaces of Control. Technocratic and Socio-ideological Control in a Global Management Consultancy Firm', *Accounting, Organization and Society* 29: 423–44.

Alvesson, M. and Thompson, P. (2005) 'Post-Bureaucracy?', in S. Ackroyd, R. Batt, P. Thompson, and P. Tolbert, (eds) *A Handbook of Work and Organization*, Oxford: Oxford University Press.

Bain, P. and Taylor, P. (2000) 'Entrapped by the Electronic Panopticon? Worker Resistance in Call Centres', *New Technology, Work and Employment*, 15. 1: 2–18.

Barker, J. R. (1993) 'Tightening the Iron Cage: Concertive Control in Self-Managing Teams', *Administrative Science Quarterly*, 38: 408–37.

Barley, S. R. and Kunda, G. (1992) 'Design and Devotion: Surges of Rational and Normative Ideologies of Control in Managerial Discourse', *Administrative Science Quarterly*, 37: 363–99.

Berkeley Thomas, A. (1993) *Controversies in Management*, London: Routledge.

Blau, P. M. and Schoenherr, R. A. (1971) *The Structure of Organizations*, New York: Basic Books.

Boxall, P. and Purcell, J. (2003) *Strategy and Human Resource Management*, Basingstoke: Palgrave Macmillan.

Bradley, H. (1986) 'Work, Home and the Restructuring of Jobs', in K. Purcell, S. Wood, A. Watson and S. Allen (eds), *The Changing Experience of Employment, Restructuring and Recession*, London: Macmillan.

Braverman, H. (1974) *Labor and Monopoly Capital: The Degradation of Work in the Twentieth Century*, New York: Monthly Review Press.

Bryman, A. (1984) 'Organisation Studies and the Concept of Rationality', *Journal of Management Studies*, 21: 394–404.

Buchanan, D. (1986) 'Management Objectives in Technical Change', in D. Knights and H. Willmott (eds), *Managing the Labour Process*, Aldershot: Gower.

Burawoy, M. (1979) *Manufacturing Consent: Changes in the Labour Process Under Monopoly Capitalism*, Chicago: University of Chicago Press.

Callaghan, G. and Thompson, P. (2001) 'Edwards Revisited: Technical Control and Worker Agency in Call Centres', *Economic and Industrial Democracy*, 22: 13–37.

Callaghan, G. and Thompson, P. (2002) 'We Recruit Attitude: The Selection and Shaping of Call Centre Labour', *Journal of Management Studies*, 39. 2: 233–254.

Campbell, A. and Currie, B. (1987) 'Skills and Strategies in Design Engineering', paper presented to the Conference on the Labour Process, Aston-UMIST.

Carchedi, G. (1977) *On the Economic Identification of the Middle Classes*, London: Routledge & Kegan Paul.

Chandler, A. (1962) *Strategy and Structure: Chapters in the History of the Industrial Enterprise'* Cambridge, MA: MIT Press.

Child, J. (1985) 'Managerial Strategies, New Technology and the Labour Process', in D. Knights, H. Wilmott and D. Collinson (eds), *Job Redesign: Critical Perspectives on the Labour Process*, London: Gower.

Clegg, S. and Dunkerley, D. (1980) *Organisation, Class and Control*, London: Routledge & Kegan Paul.

Cockburn, C. (1983) *Brothers: Male Dominance and Technological Change*, London: Pluto.

Dandeker, C. (1990) *Surveillance, Power and Modernity: Bureaucracy and Discipline from 1700 to the Present Day*, Cambridge: Polity.

Danford, A. (1998) *Japanese Management Techniques and British Workers*, London: Mansell.

De Vroey, M. (1975) 'The Separation of Ownership and Control in Large Corporations', *Review of Radical Political Economics*, 7. 2: 1–10.

Delbridge, R., Lowe, J. and Oliver, N. (2000) 'Worker Autonomy in Lean Teams: Evidence from the World Automotive Components Industry', in S. Proctor and F. Mueller (eds), *Teamworking*, London: Macmillan.

Delbridge, R., Turnbull, P. and Wilkinson, B. (1992) 'Pushing Back the Frontiers: Management Control and Work Intensification under JIT/TQM Regimes', *New Technology, Work and Employment*, 7: 97–106.

Edwards, P. K. (1990) 'Understanding Conflict in the Labour Process: The Logic and Autonomy of Struggle', in D. Knights and H. Willmott (eds), *Labour Process Theory*, London: Macmillan.

Edwards, P. K. and Scullion, H. (1982) *The Social Organisation of Industrial Conflict: Control and Resistance in the Workplace*, Oxford: Blackwell.

Edwards, R. (1979) *Contested Terrain: The Transformation of the Workplace in the Twentieth Century*, London: Heinemann.

Edwards, R., Reich, M. and Gordon, D. M. (1975) *Labour Market Segmentation*, Lexington, MA: D. C. Heath.

Etzioni, A. (1961) *A Comparative Analysis of Complex Organizations*, New York: Free Press.

Fernie, S. and Metcalf, D. (1997) '(Not) Hanging on the Telephone: Payment Systems in the New Sweatshops', *Centre for Economic Performance*, London: London School of Economics.

Fevre, R. (1986) 'Contract Work in the Recession', in K. Purcell, S. Wood, A. Watson and S. Allen (eds), *The Changing Experience of Employment, Restructuring and Recession*, London: Macmillan.

Fligstein, N. (1990) *The Transformation of Corporate Control*, Cambridge, MA: Harvard University Press.

Fleming, P. (2001) 'Beyond the Panopticon?', *Ephemera*, 1. 2: 190–4.

Fleming, P. (2005) 'Workers Playtime: Boundaries and Cynicism in a "Culture of Fun" Program', *The Journal of Applied Behavioral Science*, 41. 3: 285–303.

Fleming, P. and Spicer, A. (2002) 'Working at a Cynical Distance: Implications for Power, Subjectivity and Resistance', *Organization*, 10: 157–79.

Frenkel, S., Korczynski, M., Donohue, L. and Shire, K. (1995) 'Re-Constituting Work', *Work, Employment and Society*, 9. 4: 773-96.

Frenkel, S., Korczynski, M., Shire, K. and Tam, M. (1999) *On the Front Line: Pattern of Work Organisation in Three Advanced Societies*, Ithaca, NY: Cornell University Press.

Friedman, A. (1977) *Industry and Labour: Class Struggle at Work Monopoly Capitalism*, London: Macmillan.

Friedman, A. (1987) 'The Means of Management Control and Labour Process Theory: A Critical Note on Storey', *Sociology*, 21. 2: 287–94.

Garrahan, P. and Stewart, P. (1992) *The Nissan Enigma: Flexibility at Work in a Local Economy*, London: Mansett.

Glenn, E. K. and Feldberg, R. L. (1979) 'Proletarianising Office Work', in A. Zimbalist (ed.), *Case Studies on the Labour Process*, New York: Monthly Review Press.

Goodrich, C. (1975) *The Frontier of Control*, London: Pluto.

Gordon, D. M., Edwards, R. and Reich, M. (1982) *Segmented Work, Divided Workers*, Cambridge: Cambridge University Press.

Grieco, M. and Whipp, R. (1985) 'Women and Control in the Workplace: Gender and Control in the Workplace', in D. Knights and H. Willmott (eds), *Job Redesign: Critical Perspectives on the Labour Process*, Aldershot: Gower.

Grimshaw, J. (1986) *Feminist Philosophers*, Brighton: Wheatsheaf.

Grint, K. (1995) *Management: A Sociological Introduction*, Oxford: Polity.

Grossman, R. (1979) 'Women's Place in the Integrated Service', *Radical America*, 14. 1: 29–48.

Hales, C. P. (1988) 'Management Processes, Management Divisions of Labour and Managerial Work: Towards a Synthesis', paper presented to the Conference on the Labour Process, Aston-UMIST.

Hales, C. (2000) 'Management and Empowerment Programmes', *Work, Employment and Society*, 14. 3: 501–19.

Harris, R. (1987) *Power and Powerlessness in Industry: An Analysis of the Social Relations of Production*, London: Tavistock.

Hodson, R. (1995) 'Worker Resistance: An Underdeveloped Concept in the Sociology of Work', *Economic and Industrial Democracy*, 16: 79–110.

Hodson, R. (2001) *Dignity at Work*, Cambridge: Cambridge University Press.

Holland, S. (1975) *The Socialist Challenge*, London: Quartet.

Huczynski, A. A. (1993) *Management Gurus*, London: Routledge.

Hyman, R. (1987) 'Strategy or Structure: Capital, Labour and Control', *Work, Employment and Society*, 1. 1: 25–55.

Johnston, L. (1986) *Marxism, Class Analysis and Socialist Pluralism*, London: Allen & Unwin.

Kamoche, K. (1994) 'A Critique and a Proposed Reformulation of Strategic Human Resource Management', *Human Resource Management Journal*, 4. 4: 29–47.

Kelly, J. E. (1985) 'Management's Redesign of Work', in D. Knights, H. Willmott and D. Collinson (eds), *Job Redesign: Critical Perspectives on the Labour Process*, Aldershot: Gower.

Kelly, J. (2005) 'Labour Movements and Mobilization', in S. Ackroyd, R. Batt, P. Thompson and Pamela Tolbert (eds), *The Oxford Handbook of Work and Organization*, Oxford, Oxford University Press.

Lawlor, E. E. (1976) 'Control Systems in Organizations', in H. D. Dunnette (ed.), *Handbook of Industrial and Organisational Psychology*, Chicago: Rand McNally.

Littler, C. R. and Salaman, G. (1982) 'Bravermania and Beyond', *Sociology*, 132: 33–47.

McKinlay, A. and Taylor, P. (1996) 'Power, Surveillance and Resistance: Inside the Factory of the Future', in P. Ackers, C. Smith and P. Smith (eds), *The New Workplace and Trade Unionism*, London: Routledge.

Maguire, M. (1986) 'Recruitment as a Means of Control', in K. Purcell, S. Wood, A. Watson and S. Allen (eds), *The Changing Experience of Employment, Restructuring and Recession*, London: Macmillan.

Martinez, Lucio, M. and Stewart, P. (1997) 'The Paradox of Contemporary Labour Process Theory: The Rediscovery of Labour and the Decline of Collectivism', *Capital and Class*, 62: 49–77.

Melling, J. (1982) 'Men in the Middle or Men on the Margin', in D. Dunkerley and G. Salaman (eds), *The International Yearbook of Organisation Studies 1981*, London: Routledge & Kegan Paul.

Miller, P. and O'Leary, T. (1987) 'The Entrepreneurial Order', paper presented to the Conference on the Labour Process, Aston-UMIST.

Morgan, G. and Hooper, D. (1987) 'Corporate Strategy, Ownership and Control', *Sociology*, 21. 4: 609–27.

Murray, P. and Wickham, J. (1985) 'Women Workers and Bureaucratic Control in Irish Electronic Factories', in H. Newby (ed.), *Restructuring Capital, Reorganisation in Industrial Society*, London: Macmillan.

O'Reilly, C. A. and Chatman, J. A. (1996) 'Culture as Social Control: Corporations, Cults and Commitment', in B. M. Staws and L. L. Cummings (eds), *Research in Organisational Behaviour*, 18: 157–200, Greenwich, Conn.: JAI.

Parker, M. and Slaughter, J. (1988b) *Choosing Sides: Unions and the Team Concept, Labor Notes*, Boston, MA: South End Press.

Pearson, R. (1986) 'Female Workers in the First and Third Worlds: The "Greening" of Women's Labour', in K. Purcell, S. Wood, A. Watson and S. Allen (eds), *The Changing Experience of Employment, Restructuring and Recession*, London: Macmillan.

Pfeffer, J. (1997) *New Directions for Organisational Theory: Problems and Practices*, Oxford: Oxford University Press.

Pollard, S. (1965) *The Genesis of Modern Management*, London: Edward Arnold.

Pollert, A. (1981) *Girls, Wives, Factory Lives*, London: Macmillan.

Porter, M. (1980) *Competitive Strategy*, New York: Free Press.

Purcell, J. and Sissons, K. (1983) 'A Strategy for Management Control in Industrial Relations', in J. Purcell and R. Smith (eds), *The Control of Work*, London: Macmillan.

Ray, C. A. (1986) 'Corporate Culture: the Last Frontier of Control?' *Journal of Management Studies*, 23. 3: 287–97.

Rose, M. (1975, 1986) *Industrial Behaviour*, Harmondsworth: Penguin.

Rose, M. and Jones, B. (1985) 'Managerial Strategy and Trade Union Responses in Work Reorganization Schemes at Establishment Level', in D. Knights, H. Wilmott and D. Collinson (eds), *Job Redesign: Critical Perspectives on the Labour Process*, London: Gower.

Schein, E. H. (1965) *Organisational Psychology*, Englewood Cliffs, N.J.: Prentice Hall (also 1980, 3rd edn.).

Scott, J. (1985) 'Ownership, Management and Strategic Control', in K. Elliot and P. Lawrence (eds), *Introducing Management*, Harmondsworth: Penguin.

Sewell, G. (1998) 'The Discipline of Teams: The Control of Team-Based Industrial Work Through Electronic and Peer Surveillance', *Administrative Science Quarterly*, 43: 406–69.

Sewell, G. and Wilkinson, B. (1992) ' "Someone to Watch over Me": Surveillance, Discipline and the Just-in-Time Labour Process', *Sociology*, 26. 2: 271–89.

Shaw, M. (1990) 'Strategy and Social Process: Military Context and Sociological Analysis', *Sociology*, 24. 3: 465–73.

Steiner, T. and Miner, B. (1978) *Management Policy and Strategy*, West Drayton: Collier-Macmillan.

Storey, J. (1985) 'The Means of Management Control', *Sociology*, 19. 2: 193–211.

Streek, W. (1987) 'The Uncertainties of Management in the Management of Uncertainty: Employers, Labour Relations and Industrial Adjustment in the 1980s', *Work, Employment and Society*, 1. 3: 281–308.

Sturdy, A. and Fineman, S. (2001) 'Struggles for the Control of Affect: Resistance as Politics of Emotion', in Sturdy, I. Grugulis and H. Willmott (eds), *Customer Service: Empowerment and Entrapment*, Basingstoke: Palgrave Macmillan.

Taylor, P. and Bain, P. (1998). 'An Assembly Line in the Head: The Call Centre Labour Process', *Industrial Relations Journal*, 30. 2: 101–17.

Taylor, P. and Bain, P. (2003) 'Subterranean Worksick Blues: Humour as Subversion in Two Call Centres', *Organization Studies*, 24. 9: 1487–1509.

Taylor, S. (1998) 'Emotional Labour and the New Workplace', in P. Thompson and C. Warhurst (eds), *Workplaces of the Future*, London: Macmillan.

Thompson, P. (1989) *The Nature of Work: An Introduction to Debates on the Labour Process*, London: Macmillan.

Thompson, P. (2003b) 'Fantasy Island: A Labour Process Critique of the "Age of Surveillance"', *Surveillance and Society*, 1. 2: 138–51.

Thompson, P. and Ackroyd, S. (1995) 'All Quiet on the Workplace Front: A Critique of Recent Trends in British Industrial Sociology', *Sociology*, 29. 4: 615–33.

Thompson, P. and Harley, B. (2007) 'HRM and the Worker: Labour Process Perspectives', in P. Boxall, J. Purcell and P. Wright (eds), *The Oxford Handbook of Human Resource Management*, Oxford: Oxford University Press.

Thompson, P., van den Broek, D. and Callaghan, G. (2004) 'Teams without Teamwork: Explaining the Call Centre Paradox', *Economic and Industrial Democracy*, 25. 2: 197–218.

Thurley, K. and Wood, S. (1983) *Industrial Relations and Management Strategy*, Cambridge: Cambridge University Press.

Tichy, N., Fombrun, C. and Devanna, M. A. (1982) 'Strategic Human Resource Management', *Sloan Management Review*: 47–61.

Tomlinson, J. (1982) *The Unequal Struggle? British Socialism and the Capitalist Enterprise*, London: Methuen.

Wallace, C. (1993) ' Reflections on the Concept of "Strategy"', in D. Morgan and L. Stanley (eds), *Debates in Sociology*, Manchester: Manchester University Press.

Walton, R. E. (1985) 'Towards a Strategy of Eliciting Employee Commitment Based on Policies of Mutuality', in R. E. Walton and P. R. Lawrence (eds), *Human Resource Management, Trends and Challenges*, Boston, MA: Harvard University School Press.

Waterman, R. H. (1988) *The Renewal Factor*, London: Bantam.

Watson, T. (1994) *In Search of Management: Culture, Chaos and Control in Managerial Work*, London: Routledge.

Westwood, S. (1984) *All Day, Every Day: Factory and Family in the Making of Women's Lives*, London: Pluto.

Whipp, R. (1996) 'Creative Deconstruction: Strategy and Organisations', in S. Clegg, C. Hardy and W. Nord (eds), *Handbook of Organisation Studies*, London: Sage.

Wilkinson, B. (1986) 'Human Resources in Singapore's Second Industrial Revolution', *Industrial Relations Journal*, 17. 2: 99–114.

Witz, A. (1986) 'Patriarchy and the Labour Market: Occupational Controls and the Medical Division of Labour', in D. Knights and H. Willmott (eds), *Managing the Labour Process*, Aldershot: Gower.

Wood, S. (ed.) (1982) *The Degradation of Work: Skill, Deskilling and the Labour Process*, London: Hutchinson.

Zeitlin, M. (1974) 'Corporate Ownership and Control: The Large Corporation and the Capitalist Class', *American Journal of Sociology*, 79. 5: 1073–119.

Zimbalist, A. (ed.) (1979) *Case Studies on the Labour Process*, New York: Monthly Review Press.

Zuboff, S. (1988) *In the Age of the Smart Machine: The Future of Work and Power*, Oxford: Heinemann.

Index

3M, 354
16 Personality Factor Questionnaire (16PF), 194, 219

ability, 207
abstracts
  definition, 46
  for finding sources, 2
academic journals, 4, 46
academic sources, 4
accountability in teams, 231
accountants
  role of accounting controls, 171, 376, 383
accumulation theory, 145
adjourning stage of group development, 238
agency, 375, 389
agriculture, 280
alienation, 91–92
  Marx's theory of, 92
alliances, 115
Amazon.com, 157
androcentrism, 116
anomie, *96*, 96–97
answers to exercises, 47–50
ante-Fordism, 80–82
appraisal, 387
argument, 9–10, 46
assembly line, 57–60
assessment, 218
  online, 218
assumptions, 9
attitudes, 175–178
  surveys, 180
Austria, 382
authority
  charismatic, 103
  rational-legal, 103
  traditional, 102–103
  types of, 102–103

Weber's view of, 102–103
  see also control; power
autonomy
  computer-controlled, 257
  craft workers, 286–287
  of workers, 253, 296
aviation industry, 318

barriers to
  change, 351
  corporate entrepreneurship, 346–348
Bebo, 158
benign control, 117–118
best match, 253
best practice, spread of, 382
bias, 3
bibliographic details, 13–14
Body Shop, 152
bourgeoisie (capitalist class), 93
BP/British Petroleum, 355–356
brainstorming, 251
branding, 140
Braverman, H.
  critics, 63–65
  thesis of deskilling, 60–62
'building a house' analogy, 42–44
bureaucracy, 148–149, 154–155, 373, 388
  bureaucratization, 101
  Weber's concept of, 101–102
business process re-engineering, 155–156, 291

call centres, 59–60, 291, 379, 386, 387
capitalism, 292, 374, 377
  global, 143, 291
  industrial, 91, 279, 280, 298
  Marx's view of, 88–94
  Weber's view of, 98
car industry, corporate restructuring, 131–132

Carr
  article extract, 12
  in business ethics essay, 28–29
  review of process for using the article, 42
case studies
  building self-esteem, 223–224
  equity in the South African police
    service
  home-working, 310
  identifying leaders, 222–223
  just-in-time working, 166–167
  McDonald's in China, 308–309
  organizational research, 122
  team organization, 258
  tourism industry, 165–166
  work teams, 265–266
cash nexus, 92
cellular technology, 291
centralization, 138, 139, 141
change, 182–185
  agent, 351
  cube, 353f
  management, 349–353
  programmes, 183, 389
changing, at a University, case study
  culture theory, 112
charisma
  charismatic authority, 103
Chartered Institute of Personnel and
    Development (CIPD), 260
cheap labour, 292, 298
child labour, 298–299
China
  McDonalds in, case study, 308–309
Cisco Systems, 157
citation
  definition, 46
class (social)
  class conflict, 93, 104
class conflict, 93, 104
class consciousness, 93
class relations, 180, 375, 377, 379
clerical, white-collar employees, 376
closed systems, 109–110
close paraphrase
  definition, 46
  in note making, 16
closure, in work design, 290
cohesiveness, 240–241, 246
collective bargaining, 180, 184, 374, 377,
    382, 387
commitment, 183, 373, 384, 385, 388, 389,
    390
communication(s), 178–179
  flow of, 138
competitive advantage, 139

competitive environment
  intensification, 324–326
  production technologies, 324, 327
  quality, 327–328
  strategies, 325
  see also globalization
competitive tendering, 321–322
complex cooperation, 90–91
complexity, 136–137
  spatial, 137
compliance, 390
  conformity, 389
conditions of worth, 205
conflict
  class conflict, 93, 104
  emotional (relational) conflict, 242
  group conflict, 242–245
  intergroup, 243, 245
  intragroup, 242
  task conflict, 242
conformity of groups, 240, 247
Confédération Générale du Travail, 96
consent, 173, 180, 385
  mobilisation of, 178
consultants, 171, 180, 381
consumption
  mass, 58–59
contemporary theories of, 106–119
  craft/artisan work, 296–297
  development of, 297
contingency theory, 111–112
contract, psychological, 130
contradictions, 93
control, 171, 229, 354–355, 371–373, 388
  benign, 117–118
  bureaucratic, 182, 377, 387, 388
  collective concept of, 107–108
  computer-based, 234
  and consent, 65
  control theories, 115–116
  functions, 292
  locus of, 203, 385
  mainstream perspectives on, 371–373
  and management objectives, 63–64
  management strategies of, 376–380
  managerial, 286–287
  normative, cultural, 372, 385, 387, 388
  personal, pre-bureaucratic, 377
  radical perspectives, 374
  span of, 136
  technical, 377, 379, 387
control strategies
  division of labour, 55, 56
  responsible autonomy, 63
  surveillance, 55, 73
conversion hysteria, 198

cooperation costs, 289–290
core competency, 156
corporate anorexia, 130
corporate social responsibility, 101
cost leadership strategy, 139
craft/artisan work, 296, 296–297
craft guilds, 280, 299–300
Crane and Matten
    extract, 26
    paraphrase of extract, 27
criminals, personality of, 196–197
critical analysis and reflection of, 47–50
    notes on, 48
    research log, 14
critical analysis and thinking, 9–12
critical perspective, 106
cultural, and communication
    in groups/teams, 249–250
culture, 347
    corporate, 178, 385, 388
    organizational, 112
customer democracy, 156
customer-oriented bureaucracy, 70
customer service, 294
customers' tastes and preferences, 149
cycling, 360

databases for finding sources
    reliability, 6
decentralization, 152
decision making, 373, 379, 380
    formalized, 101–102
    in groups, 247–250
deindustrialization, 272
denial, 201
departmentalization, 136
deregulation, 318, 320–322
deskilling, 287, 297
dialectical approaches, 375
differentiation strategy, 139
digest
    definition, 46
disability, 277
discourse, 300
discursive metaphors, 135
displacement, 201
divisional structure, 152–153
division of labour, 90, 281, 289–290
    creating groups of specialists, 136
    Durkheim's analysis of, 94–98
    forced, 96
    horizontal/vertical, 132, 133
    Marxist theory of, 90–91
divisions, women workers, 174
downsizing, 130, 136, 138, 146, 159–160,
    378

draft
    definition of, 46

e-assessment, 218
e-commerce, 143
economy
    competition, 323–328
economy, the, 279
effort bargain, 389
ego, 200
electronic sweatshops, 291, 296
emotional (relational) conflict, 242
emotional labour, 156, 276, 294–295
emotions in organizations, 177–178,
    389
empiricism, 104
employability, 25
employees
    dissatisfaction, 290
    reconceptualization of, 155
employment
    deregulation, 320
    Fair Wages resolutions, 321
    flexibility, 321
    harmonisation of rights, 319
    job insecurity, 339–340
    Marxist conception of, 88–89
    precariousness of, 118, 272
    trends in, 277
employment relationship, 182–185, 375
employment structure
    gender differences, 330–331
    location, 333–334
    manufacturing and services, 329
    part-time, 331
    self-employment, 331–333
    size of organisations, 333
    temporary work, 338
empowerment, 53, 63, 133, 241, 256–258,
    373, 386
engineers
    ideology and practices, 172, 376, 383
environmental determinism, 111–112
environment of the organization,
    142–143
    and structure, 142
equal pay legislation, 318
essays
    key points, 40–41
    review of whole process from reading to
        essay, 41–42
    time needed for reading and using your
        reading, 42, 43
ethics
    ethical individualism, 96
ethnocentrism, 116

European Union
  Social Charter, 301
  Working Time Directive/Developments, 285, 299
evaluating sources, 1–7
examples, good
  essay paragraph using sources, 45–46
  notes, 15–20, 48
  numeric referencing system, 49, 50
  paraphrases, 27, 50
  questioning, evaluating and locating a text, 11, 48
  quotations, 18, 19, 49
  reflection, 16–17, 50
  summaries, 34, 38
expectancy theory of motivation, 203
extra words in sentences, 23
extroversion, 193, 194, 195, 197

Facebook, 158
factor analysis, 193, 194–195
factories
  architecture, 281
  factory system, 228, 281, 283
  historical development of, 273
  panopticon, 281
family, the, 379
family labour, 298–299
feedback, 254
femininity, 292
feminist perspective, 116
fex-spec, 291
first search for sources, 2
flexibility, at work, 382
flexibility of working, 272, 273, 290, 291
flexible specialisation, 68, 71
forced division of labour, 96
Fordism, 58–59, 80–82, 108, 285, 288–289, 295
  for doctors, 143–145
  flow-line principle, 288
  limitations, 145, 289
  neo-Fordism, 296
  post-Fordism, 289–291, 296–297
Ford Motor Company, 130, 133, 174
formalization, 101, 137, 141
formal organization, 130–131
forming stage of group development, 237–238
Foucault, Foucauldian perspectives, 390
France, 94, 96
Freudian iceberg, 199
functional configuration, 151
functionalism, 88, 109, 111
function mismanagement, 97

Gemeinschaft, 94
gender, in organisations
  divisions, women workers, 382
gendering of work, 273, 292, 298–300
  after the Industrial Revolution, 292
  before the Industrial Revolution, 280
  First World War, 286, 288, 298
gender issues
  criticism of Braverman, 65
  employment, 330–331
  groups, 235
  and organizational design, 160–161
  part-time work, 331–333
  skill, 68
  trade unions and, 299
  workplace relations, 291–292
General Motors, 180, 371, 383
Germany, 382
Gesellschaft, 94
glass ceiling, 160
globalization, 73–74, 143, 304–305, 317, 323
  cross-cultural adjustment, 305
  identity and instability, 210–211
  and organizational restructuring, 146
  power and culture in work team relations, 252
  women workers in Russia, 161–162
glossary of key terms, 46–47
Google and Google Scholar as a search engine for sources, 5
governance, 255
group(s), 175–178, 371, 373, 374, 376, 380, 382, 383
  and autonomous working, 373, 374
  cohesiveness, 240–241
  conflict, 242–245
  conformity, 247
  context, 234
  decision making, 247–252
  development, five-stage cycle, 237–238
  dynamics, 233–234
  effectiveness, 234, 245–252
  gender in, 251
  informal, 230
  learning, 241–242
  maintenance-oriented activities, 233
  norms, 239–240, 246
  peer group, 207–208
  performance, 245, 247
  polarization, 249–250
  processes, 236–237
  psychological, 229
  research, criticisms of, 238–239
  resources, 234–235
  size, 235
  socialization, 236

structure, 234–236
  task-oriented activities, 233–234
groupthink, 241, 248–249
  symptoms, 249
guilds, 280, 299–300

Hawthorne studies, 171, 175–179, 108–109,
  239, 290
health and safety issues, 277
hierarchy
  traditional, 136
hierarchy of needs
  motivation and, 205
high-performance working, 256
  workplace (HPW), 228, 236
  work systems (HPWS), 291
high performance work systems (HPWS),
  183, 384
home-working, 279, 301
  case study, 310
horizontal structure, 146, 155
hours/length of work, 285
human capital theory, 67
humanistic theories, 205
human relations, 108–109
human relations movement, 290
  criticisms of, 290
human relations theory, 171, 172, 173, 175,
  177, 372
human resource management (HRM), 171,
  182–185, 381
hypotheses, 297

iceberg
  Freudian, 199
id, 199–200, 206
ideal types, 104, 104–105
identity, 388, 389
  definition, 98
  personal, 209
  and personality, 208–211
  social, 209, 209–210
idiographic approach, 202
individualism
  ethical, 96
industrial capitalism, 91
industrialism, 97
industrial relations systems, 172, 184, 185,
  381, 389
Industrial Revolution, 278, 280–281
industry
  engineering, 381, 384
  financial services, 176
  food/drink, 381
  high-technology, electronics, 378, 386
  iron/steel, 176

inequality, social, 103–104
in-essay referencing
  author/year referencing styles, 19
  reference reminder phrases, 28–29
  when paraphrasing, 28
  common mistakes, 30–31
  practice, 32
  when quoting, 27–29
  common mistakes, 21–22
  practice, 33–36
  when summarising, 34
  common mistakes, 36
  practice, 36–39
informal organisation, practices, 177, 178,
  374
Information Age, 273, 292
Information Revolution, 292
insecurity of employment, 378
instrumentality, 55
integrating your sources into your essay,
  40–46
intellective skills, 77
interaction, social, 255, 256
interactionism, 208
  symbolic, 114
interactionist theory, 245
interests, nature and divergence of, 175, 183,
  372, 374, 380, 384, 385, 389
international comparisons
  part-time working, 331–333
  unemployment, 335–337
Internet, 154, 156
interpretivism, 107
interviews, 218
introversion, 193, 194, 195, 197
inward investment, 322

Japan, 174, 290
Japanese management, methods in Western
  economies, 388
Japanization xxiii
job(s), 274
  characteristics model, 253, 254–255
  design, 230, 255
  enlargement, 253
  enrichment, 253, 291
  rotation, 253
  satisfaction, 246, 260
job insecurity, 339
just-in-time (JIT) production, 327, 386
just-in-time working, 148, 155, 158, 291
  case study, 166–167

knowledge
  knowledge work, 273, 292–293
  management, 350

labour
cheap, 292, 298
division of *see* division of labour
emotional, 156, 276, 294–295
forced division of, 96
horizontal/vertical divisions of, 132, 133,
134
manual, 294
Marxist conception of, 88
power, 88, 280
process, 106
regulation of mobility of, 280
technical and social divisions of, 107–108
v. work, 274
labour markets, 378
labour process
labour power, 61
theory, 60–62
labour process theory
of control, 378, 379, 386, 390, 391
language
and organizational culture
and socialization, 206–207
leadership, 178–181, 372
identifying leaders, case study, 222–223
personality of leaders, 196
styles, 181, 359–360, 372
lean production, 291, 387, 388
lean structure, 146, 155
learning
and development, 255
group learning, 241–242
and motivation, 255
organizational, 112–113
theories, 112–113
literature review, 33
literature search, 1–6
locating a text within the subject, 9, 11
locus of control, 203
looking-glass self, 205

machinery, Marx's views of, 91
magazines as sources, 4
management
managerial labour, 376
managerial work, nature of, 379
objectives, 55, 63–64, 71
scientific, 108
managerial control, 286–287
managerial perspective, 106
managerial revolution theories, 375
managerial revolution thesis, 180
manual labour, 294
marketing, 140
marriage studies, 244–245
Marxist theory, 88–94, 374, 379, 383, 384

masculinity, 292
Maslow's hierarchy of needs
vocabulary of, 232
mass production, 289, 383, 384
matrix structure, 154
McDonaldisation, 56, 296–297
in China, case study, 308–309
mechanical solidarity, 94–95, 95
mechanistic organization, 138, 139
meritocracy, 97
metaphor(s), 112
discursive, 135
minimum wage, 321
misbehaviour, 389, 390
mobile phones and health risks
Cox
article extract, 32
paraphrase, good, 50
paraphrase, poor, 32
Maier, Blakemore and Koivisto
article extract, 30
paraphrase, good, 31
paraphrase, poor, 30–31
monotony in work, 54, 72, 73
motivation, 172, 174
expectancy theory, 203
and hierarchy of needs, 205
and job design, 372, 376
learning and, 254
and satisfaction, 373
Mozilla Foundation, 159
multidivisional structures, 377, 384
multinational corporations, 324
mutual gains, 183
Myers–Briggs Type indicator (MBTI),
218–219
narcissism, 215

National Aeronautics and Space
Administration (NASA), 248
National Health Service (NHS), 143
organizational learning in, 114
nation-state, 317
negative affected tone, 243
neo-Fordism, 80–81, 297
neo-human relations, 109
networking, 158, 214, 135, 242
networks, 157
structure, 157–158
weakness of, 157
neuroticism, 195, 197
newly industrialized economies (NIEs), 146,
159
Nissan, 386
nominal group technique, 251
nomothetic approach, 198, 205–206

non-academic sources, 4
norming stage of group development, 237
norms
    group norms, 239–240, 247
note making
    example of, 15–16
    key points, 14–15
    key steps, 13–15
    practice, 17
    reasons for making notes, 21
    written reflection from notes,
        15, 16–17

objectification, 89
occupation, 272, 274
offshoring, 73–74
one best way, 272
online assessment, 218
online databases and search engines, 5
online sources, 4–6
open-book management, 355
open-source model, 159
open systems, 109–110
organic organization, 138, 139
organic solidarity, 95
organisational behaviour (OB), 181
organisational size, 333
organisation theory, 185, 374
organizational behaviour (OB)
    research, 123–125
    value of theory about, 119–120
organizational design, 130, 132–135
    divisional, 152
    emerging, 154–156, 159
    gender and, 160–162
    post-bureaucracy, 154–160
    sexuality and, 159, 160
    see also organizational structure
organizational politics, 135
organizational research
    case studies, 123–125
organizational see culture, organizational
        structure
    in work team relations, 252
organizational structure, 130, 132–135, 148,
        347, 359–360
    basic elements, 149
    bureaucracy, 148–154
    determinants of, 139
    dimensions of, 135–138
    and environment (of the organization),
        142–143
    formal, 134–135, 136
    informal, 134–135, 136
    size and, 141
    strategy and, 139–140

technology and, 141–142
    typologies of, 138
organization chart, 133–134
original (primary) sources, 3
originality in essays, 40, 42–44
outsourcing, 130, 158, 159
overseas placements, cross-cultural support,
        304–305

panopticon, 281
paradigms, 80–82
paradox
    of consequences, 110
    in team-based work systems, 258–261
paraphrasing
    amount of paraphrasing in an essay, 29
    common mistakes, 29–30
    examples
    good, 27, 50
    poor, 30–31
    key points, 27–29
    practice exercises, 32
    reasons for paraphrasing, 25, 32
participation, of employees, 177, 385
paternalistic organisations, management,
        173
peer group, 207
    pressure, 261
peer-review, 4, 47
performance management, 387
performing stage of group development,
        237–239
personal identity, 209
personality, 172, 189–224
    16 Personality Factor Questionnaire
        (16PF), 194, 219
    and work team membership, 211, 215
    applying theories in the workplace,
        211–219
    behaviours that reflect, 191–192
    Cattell's theory, 194
    of criminals, 196
    definition, 191
    Eysenck's theory, 195–197
    five-factor model, 197–198
    Freud's theory, 198–202
    Holland's typology, 210
    identity and, 208–211
    inventories/scales, 217–218
    and job-fit model, 212
    of leaders, 196
    phenomenological approach, 204
    proactive, 211–212
    psychodynamic theory, 198–202
    social-cognitive approach, 203–204
    social-self approach, 205–208

personality – *continued*
    sociocultural theories, 202–207
    structure of, 199–202
    testing, 217–219
    trait theories, 192–198
personnel function, 171, 174, 180, 182, 183, 185
phenomenological approach to personality, 202, 205
plagiarism
    causes of, 42
    definition, 47
    examples
    in essay paragraph, 44–46
    in paraphrases, 30–31
    in summaries, 37–38
plurality
    of interests, 64, 71
political environment, 317–322
political parties, 104
political theory, 114–115
positive psychology, 244–245
positivism, 107
post-Fordism, 80, 289–291, 296, 297
post-industrial society, 67
post-industrial work, 278, 292
postmodernism, 118–119
    organizational forms, 154
post-structuralism, 118
power, 102, 119
    Foucault's theory of, 119–120
    social theory approaches to
    in work team relations, 252
practice exercises
    critically analysing sources, 12
    note making, 17
    paraphrasing, 32
    questioning, evaluating and locating sources, 12
    quotations
    content, 21
    grammar and punctuation, 24
    referencing, 22–23
    selecting sources, 6–7
    summarising, 36–37
practitioners, 182
pre-industrial work, 280–281
primary sources, 3–4
privatization, 153, 159, 320, 321–322
proactive personality, 211–212
process-relational theory, 206
production
    batch, 68, 71
    JIT, 327
    mass, 58–59, 71
product markets, 377, 382

products, organizational configuration, 151–152
professional occupations, 143
profit, 90, 146
proletariat (working class), 93
psychic prison, 261
psychoanalysis, 198–202
    defence mechanisms, 201–202
psychodynamic theory of personality, 198–202
psychological contract, 278
    changes in work, 135, 297
    key elements, 260
    for knowledge work, 293
psychological groups, 229
psychology
    positive, 244–245
psychology/organisational psychology
    industrial psychology, 172
psychometric testing, 207
psychosexual stages, 202
psychoticism, 195
public sector, 321
punctuated equilibrium, 238
punctuation
    with quotations, 23
    putting it all together, 40–46
putting-out system, 280, 281

quality, 327–328
quality control, 291
quality management
    total quality management (TQM), 386
questioning, evaluating and locating a text, 9–12
questionnaires, personality testing, 217–218
quotations
    amount of quotation in an essay, 19
    common mistakes: content, 20
    grammar and punctuation, 23
    definition, 18, 47
    good examples, 19
    key steps, 20
    practice exercises
    content of quotations, 21
    grammar and punctuation, 24
    referencing quotations, 22–23

racism, 277
rationalisation, 387, 388
rationality, 99–100, 178, 379, 381
    v. rationalization, 99
    types of, 99–100
rationalization, 99–100, 201
    v. rationality, 99

reading
 critical analysis, 9–12
 key steps and strategies for finding and
  selecting sources, 1–3
recession, global, 159
reciprocal determinism, 204
reconceptualization of core employees, 155–156
recruitment and selection, 174, 372, 379, 388
redundancy, 210, 337
reflection, written from notes, 15, 16–17
reflexivity, 118–119
relevance of sources, 1–6
reliability in sociological research, 218
reliability of sources, 3–4
religion, impact of, 98–99
repression, 201–202
 organizational, case studies, 123–125
research log, 14
resilience, 244
resistance, 64
 worker, 377, 378, 389–390
restructuring, organizational, 130
 in the car industry, 131
 conceptual framework, 147–148
 globalization and, 137
 types of, 147–148
review of whole process from reading to
  essay, 40–46
rewards
 extrinsic/intrinsic, 275, 276
reward system, 183, 387
risk
 classification, 360–361
 management, 360–362
Robinson
 summary
  good, 38
  poor, 38
  text, 36
roles in organizations, 237, 241
 role ambiguity, 237
 role conflict, 236
 role culture(s), 112

safety, 255
scholarly journals, 5
schools of thought, 9, 47
scientific management, 108
scripted behaviour, 388
secondary sources, 3–4
self, 205–206
self-actualization, 109, 205
self-concept, 205
self-efficacy, 204
self-esteem
 building, case study, 223–224

self-identity, 209
self-managed work teams (SMWTs), 231,
  246, 255, 258, 261
 as ideal-type work regime, 256
self-realization, 206
self-regulation, 244, 255
sense making, 114
services
 organizational configuration, 140
 outsourcing of, 158, 159
service sector work, 385
sexuality
 and organizational design, 160
size
 of groups, 235
 of organizations, 141
skill
 automating and informating, 76–77
 compensatory theory, 76
 conceptual framework, 78–80
 deskilling, 60–66, 296, 297, 378
 discretion, 55, 68, 69, 78, 174
 polarisation, 75
 range, 78
 upskilling, 67–74, 296, 297, 378
 variety, 253
slack, 356
small firms, 333, 377
social action
 social action theory, 114
social capital, 214
social class
 class conflict, 93, 104
social-cognitive approach, 202, 203–204
social dumping, 319
social function, 96
social identity, 209–210
social interaction, 255, 256
socialisation, 178
socialist firms, 282–283
socialization, 206–208
 group, 236
 language and, 206–207
social learning, 203
social responsibility, corporate, 101
social-self approach to personality, 205–208
social solidarity, 94, 94–95
social structure, 273
sociocultural theories of personality,
  202–208
socio-technical systems, 181
sources
 academic and non-academic, 4–6
 evaluating, 9–12
 finding and selecting, 1–2
 online, 5

sources – *continued*
  primary and secondary, 3–4
  reliability, 3–4
span of control, 136
specialization, 132, 133, 136
stakeholders
standardisation, 52, 53, 58
state, role of, 180–181, 377, 389
status, 235
Statute of Artificers of 1563, 280
steel industry, 338
stepladder technique, 251
storming stage of group development, 238
strategic choice, 64, 391
strategy, 347
  formation of, 182, 377–385
  and organizational structure, 139–141
  strategic business units, 146, 147
  strategic choice, 107
  strategy-structure thesis, 140
stress, 387
  and control, 387
  well-being, 173
  see also leadership
sub-contracting, 378
summaries
  common mistakes, 36
  examples
  good, 34
  poor, 37–38
  key points, 35
  key steps, 35–36
  length, 34
  practice exercises, 36–39
  reasons for summarising, 33
superego, 201, 206
supervisory labour, 177, 178, 179, 387
supranational alliances, 318–319
surplus value, 90
surveillance, 119, 375, 385–389
Svensson and Wood
  article extract, 10–11
  critical analysis of, 11
  notes, 15–16
  reflection of, 16–17
  in review of whole process from reading to writing, 41
sweatshops, 148
  electronic, 291, 296
SWOT (strengths, weaknesses, opportunities and threats) analysis, 140
symbolic-interactionist perspective, 114
systems theory
  socio-technical systems, 387, 389
systems theory, 109–111, 181, 253

tasks
  interdependence, 234
  task conflict, 242
  task functions, 149
  task identity, 253
  task-oriented activities, 233
  task significance, 254
  task variety, 290
Taylorism, 54–56, 108, 173, 181, 184, 286–287, 289, 290, 258, 373, 376, 388
  electronic, 291
  limitations, 145, 289
team building/working, 352
teams, 231
  team organization, case study, 265–266
  team performance, 243
  team work, 228–229
  team working, 291
teamworking, 72, 177–178, 182, 388
  see also group(s)
technical contemporary theories, 107–108
technological change, 141
technology, 156
  automating and informating, 76–77
  classification, 141
  and deskilling, 61
  and organizational structure, 141–142
  role of, 181, 372, 376, 382
  routine/non-routine, 141
  and upskilling, 67–70
teleworking, 334
terrorism, 230,
testing criteria, personality, 216–217
Theory X, 109
Theory Y, 109
time
  liberation of, 272
total quality management, 155
tourism industry, case study, 165–166
trade liberalisation, 317, 322
trade unions, 173, 174, 178, 184, 299, 300, 384, 389, 390
  and gender inequalities, 300
training, 183
  of management, 181
trait theories of personality, 192–198
transnational companies/corporations (TNCs), 145, 148
trust
  low, 182

unemployment, 335–337
Unilever, 157
Unites States
  taken as exemplar for global practices, 291–292

upskilling, 296, 297
urbanization, 94

validity, 218
valorisation, 60–61, 63
values, 174, 179, 276
    surplus, 90
Verstehen, 104, 105
virtual organizations, 156–158
Vocational Preference Inventory, 212
Volvo, 152, 264

wages
    Fair Wages resolutions, 321
    low pay, 325
waste, minimum, 291
weightlessness, 140
wellness, 255
wholeness principle, 255
whole process from reading to essay,
    40–46
Wikipedia, 4
women
    and domestic work, 277
    in paid work, 272, 277, 281
    Russian workers, 161–162
work
    autonomy in, 297
    classical approaches to studying, 88–105
    definition, 275–276
    development of, 278–295
    emotional, 294–295
    fragmentation, 288, 289
    future of, 272
    hazards, 277
    'hidden' 277
    historical perspective, 278–279
    in the home *see* home-working;
        putting-out system
    hours of, 281
    instrumental orientation to, 274
    knowledge work, 292–293
    v. labour, 274
    manual, 277
    nature of, 271
    and non-work, 273–278
    paid, 277
    post-industrial, 278, 292
    pre-industrial, 280–281

    psychological contract, 278
    reasons for doing, 279
    routinization of, 287
    shaping identity, 273
    structured spatiality, 276
    traditional *v.* knowledge, 293
    unpaid, 277
    variety of, 297
    voluntary, 276
work design, 290–291
    job characteristics model,
        253, 254–255
    job enlargement, 253
    job enrichment, 253, 291
    job rotation, 253
    principles of, 107–108
work ethic, 284
work groups, 227–268
    autonomy, 254
    composition, 235–236
    diversity in, 241
    formal, 230
    informal, 230
    psychological groups, 229
working week, length of, 285
work–life balance, 300–304
work organizations, 281
Workplace Employee Relations Survey
    (WERS), 295, 301
workplace learning, 112–113
work systems, high-performance, 291
work teams, 230–233
    best match, 253
    case study, 264–265
    classification, 231–233
    decision making, 251
    discipline in, 261
    diversity in, 241, 251
    employee empowerment, 256–258
    failure, 260
    and management theory, 252–256
    members' personalities, 211, 214
    paradox in work systems, 258–261
    power and culture in, 252
    self-managed (SMWTs), 231, 246, 255,
        256, 258, 261
    senior/middle/lower level, 231
    types of, 231–232
World Wide Web, 156